Multidisciplinary Investigation of Child Maltreatment

Lauren R. Shapiro
Professor
King Graduate School of Urban Studies and Applied
Research at Monroe College

Marie-Helen Maras
Associate Professor
John Jay College of Criminal Justice

JONES & BARTLETT
LEARNING

World Headquarters
Jones & Bartlett Learning
5 Wall Street
Burlington, MA 01803
978-443-5000
info@jblearning.com
www.jblearning.com

Jones & Bartlett Learning books and products are available through most bookstores and online booksellers. To contact Jones & Bartlett Learning directly, call 800-832-0034, fax 978-443-8000, or visit our website, www.jblearning.com.

Production Credits
Executive Publisher: Kimberly Brophy
Executive Editor: William Larkin
Senior Editorial Assistant: Marisa Hines
Production Manager: Tracey McCrea
Marketing Manager: Lindsay White
Art Development Assistant: Shannon Sheehan
Manufacturing and Inventory Control Supervisor: Amy Bacus
Composition: Cenveo Publisher Services
Cover Design: Scott Moden
Rights and Photo Research Coordinator: Ashley Dos Santos
Cover Image: © Angela Waye/Shutterstock
Printing and Binding: Edwards Brothers Malloy
Cover Printing: Edwards Brothers Malloy

Library of Congress Cataloging-in-Publication Data
Shapiro, Lauren R.
 Multidisciplinary Investigation of Child Maltreatment / Lauren R. Shapiro, Marie-Helen Maras.
  pages cm
 Includes bibliographical references and index.
 ISBN 978-1-4496-8698-7 (pbk.)
 1. Child abuse. 2. Child abuse—Investigation. 3. Child welfare. I. Maras, Marie-Helen, 1979- II. Title.
 HV6626.5.S53 2015
 364.15'554—dc23
                          2014042568

6048
Printed in the United States of America
19 18 17 16 15   10 9 8 7 6 5 4 3 2 1

DEDICATION

To my sons, Derek, Blake, and Jeremy,
Always remember...you are my favorite in the whole wide world!

To all the maltreated children, past and present,

"May the sufferer be thoroughly healed, in spirit and in body." [Mi Sheberah]
"Have mercy on us, and fulfill among us what is written in your Scripture: I shall give peace upon
the earth, and you shall lie down with none to make you afraid." [A Prayer for peace]

Kol Haneshamah 2009

In loving memory of George Maras

Την πάσαν ελπίδα μου εις Σε ανατίθημι, Μήτηρ του Θεού, φύλαξόν όλα τα παιδιά υπό την
σκέπην Σου.

CONTENTS

PREFACE

Dr. Lauren R. Shapiro and Dr. Marie-Helen Maras periodically provide training in child and adolescent development, forensic interviewing, and child abuse investigations to the New York City Administration for Child Services. Both authors are trained in criminal justice, with one of the authors also specializing in the field of cognitive and developmental psychology and the other also having expertise in law and investigations. The main problem encountered by the authors when selecting a textbook for the courses they teach is that no single textbook on the market today combines normative development and maltreatment. The authors have had to supplement substantially the textbook they are currently using for their courses with their own notes from their practical experience in the field, numerous academic articles, and examples of real-world cases in order to provide students with the information required to conduct abuse and neglect investigations. Indeed, the available textbooks on the market only partially cover the type of information needed to fully understand maltreatment in American society and how to conduct child abuse investigations. Current books in this area provide a single discipline approach and are limited in their ability to address both normative and abnormal development, as well as criminal justice investigation and prosecution. This book seeks to fill this void in available literature by comprehensively covering normative development of children and adolescents and the signs, symptoms, and consequences of various forms of maltreatment. Furthermore, it provides a complete overview of the ways in which to conduct abuse interviews and investigations and includes a mix of cutting edge research combined with multidisciplinary coverage of knowledge of development in abused and non-abused children and adolescents.

This definitive textbook is written for professionals in criminal justice, law, psychology, social work, medicine, and human services and students in undergraduate and graduate courses in those fields as it provides them with the social science and legal background to appropriately conduct abuse investigations. Specifically, it is an ideal primary text for child abuse and neglect courses and can be a valuable supplemental resource for investigation and victimology courses. Additionally, social science, human service, medical, and legal professionals will be given advanced knowledge and investigation procedures to allow them to assess allegations of neglect and maltreatment appropriate to their field of discipline through analogies, examples, and illustrations.

This book also appeals to a wide range of different groups. Given that this textbook covers the knowledge and investigatory tools currently used in the field, it will be of interest to human service and law enforcement agencies plus social science professionals working with abused children and adolescents. Specifically, this book is intended for:

- instructors teaching a course on child abuse and neglect and related fields;
- students and professionals seeking a career in the field of child abuse;
- law enforcement agents seeking to expand their knowledge of investigations to the field of child abuse;
- legal professionals seeking to understand abuse; and
- child protective service workers who may be required by referrals to conduct abuse investigations.

Anyone interested in learning about the impact of maltreatment on development and child maltreatment investigations will also benefit from this text.

ACKNOWLEDGMENTS

We would like to extend our warm thanks to Sean Connelly, William Larkin, Marisa Hines, Tracey McCrea, Lindsay White, and Ashley Dos Santos at Jones & Bartlett Learning for their direction and assistance during the development and production of this textbook. We would also like to show our appreciation to the following individuals for taking the time to speak with us and to provide us with an understanding of the roles, responsibilities, and perspectives of their fields in relation to child maltreatment: Commissioner Ronald E. Richter, Dr. Linda Cahill, Carol Perlman, Kathy Blount, Anne Paulle, George Chin, Michele Rodney, Steven Ippolito, Miguel Ibarra, Joseph Muroff, Nataki Robinson, Lauren Campgna, and Kimberly Weithers. Gratitude is also extended to colleagues and students who have given insightful suggestions and encouragement during this process, including Dr. Basil Wilson, Dr. Denise Benkel, Stacy Quashie, Jose Hidalgo, and Monica Brisco.

REVIEWERS

On behalf of Jones & Bartlett Learning, we would like to thank the following people for their valuable insight in the review of the text:

Alycia Blackwell, MSW
Adjunct Professor and Field Instructor

Denise Ann Bodman, PhD
Principal Lecturer
Arizona State University

Dr. Kathleen Boland
Ceder Crest College

Roger Bonner, PhD
University of Saint Mary

Peggy Bowen-Hartung, PhD, CTS
Chair of the Department of Psychology and Counseling
Alvernia University

Cori D. Buggeln, MA, AIMS
Community College

Richard Conti
College of Saint Elizabeth

Jean Dawson
Franklin Pierce University

Creaig A. Dunton, PhD
SUNY Plattsburgh

Dr. Steven D. Hurwitz
Professor of Psychology and Criminal Justice

Brooke F. Kovac
Assistant Professor of Criminal Justice

Lisa Landis
University of South Florida

Kenneth M. Larimore, PhD, LISW-S

Nancy J Merritt, BS, MCJ

Gerald T. Moote, Jr., LCSW
University at Buffalo, The State University of New York
School of Social Work

Jenny Mosley, MEd, LPC, OSU/OKC

Mia Ortiz
Bridgewater State University

Patricia J. Riley, MA, MS
University of West Georgia

Dr. Rafael Rojas, Jr.
Southern NH University

James Smith
Troy University

Ronald R. Thrasher, PhD
Oklahoma State University
School of Forensic Sciences

Edward G. Weeks III

Chapter 1

Child Victimology: An Introduction

Victimology concerns the comprehensive study of the crime victim. It examines every facet of the victim's life: the physical characteristics of the victim; the victim's work life, home life, and family; his or her medical and psychological history; and the victim's social habits, friends, and acquaintances. In addition, victimology seeks to determine why a particular victim was chosen by an offender. As such, victimology sheds light on the offender, including his or her personality and motives. Moreover, victimology explores the psychological effects of victimization and addresses the victim's experiences during his or her involvement with the criminal justice system.

Crime Victims

In the last few decades, policy-makers, academics, researchers, and legal professionals have paid increasing attention to victims of crime. Over the years, this increased attention directed toward victims has been accompanied by dramatic changes in policies concerning victims' rights. These changes provide victims with a more prominent role in the criminal justice process than they previously held. This newfound role, however, has evoked a debate among scholars regarding the type and amount of victim participation considered acceptable within criminal justice proceedings.

To determine whether a victim should have standing within criminal court proceedings of a crime, a closer look at the definition of crime is required. Crime can be thought of as an offense that is committed against an individual or the state, which is punishable by law. Of particular interest is the notion of crime as an offense against the state. Because crimes are viewed to be offenses against society, they are punishable by the state. Where does the victim fit into this process? As Ashworth (2002) noted, "Just because a person commits an offense against me, however, that does not privilege my voice above that of the court (acting 'in the general public interest') in the matter of the offender's punishment" (p. 585). Here, Ashworth concedes that victims do not have the right to voice their opinion, with his reasoning being based on social contract theory.

Social contract theory holds that "political structures and the legitimacy of the state derive from an (explicit or implicit) agreement by individual human beings to surrender (some or all of) their private rights in order to secure the protection and stability of an effective social organization or government" (Kemerling, 2002, para. 1). The central premise of this theory was expressed in embryonic form in classical Greek works such as Plato's writings. In particular, this theory has its roots in the Platonic dialogue of *Crito*, where Socrates made a compelling argument as to why Crito must stay in prison and accept the death penalty, rather than flee or go into exile in another Greek city.

While traces of social contract theory can be discerned in the Platonic dialogue, it was not until Thomas Hobbes (1588–1679) that the theory itself became rightly associated with modern moral and political theory. Moreover, it was because of Hobbes's work that it was given its full exposition and defense (Friend, 2004). According to Hobbes, "given that men are naturally self-interested, yet they are rational, they will choose to submit to the authority of a Sovereign in order to be able to live in a civil society, which is conducive to their own interests" (Friend, 2004, p. 4). When the Hobbesian view of social contract theory is applied to criminal court proceedings, the basic idea is as follows: Individuals give up their rights to use self-help (i.e., to pursue justice) to the state in return for the state pursuing some level of security. This notion, put another way, expresses the legal doctrine that "the state may be said to undertake the duty of administering justice and protecting citizens in return for citizens giving up their rights to self-help (except in cases of urgency) in the cause of better social order" (Ashworth, 2002, p. 585). As a consequence of this relationship, the state has an obligation to provide a means of preventing crime and prosecuting the alleged offender (the expected outcome). Prosecution then is considered a matter for the state to handle, and the state carries this burden on behalf of citizens in general. As a result of the nature of this process, victims do not have any special standing within these proceedings. Accordingly, the belief is that victims have no place, per se, within the criminal justice process.

This view is certainly not shared by all. In fact, Nils Christie (1977) has criticized such a position and advocated for the need for victim participation within the criminal justice process. Specifically, Christie (1977) has identified two key features of the legal system: (1) The parties who are involved in the conflict are represented by attorneys and (2) the victim, who is represented by the state, "is so thoroughly represented that she or he for most of the proceedings is pushed completely out of the arena" (p. 3). It is this nonexistent role of the victim that leads Christie to question the effectiveness of a system in which the victims do not play an integral role in their own proceedings. He suggests that returning victims to a role within the criminal justice process is critical if the criminal justice system's response to crime is to be at all effective. Furthermore, he believes that through participation and input, victims will be able to reassert "ownership of the conflict," which had been previously misappropriated from them to the state (Erez, 1999).

Over the last few decades, the "treatment of crime victims by various agents of the criminal justice system" is believed to have considerably improved (Erez, 1994, p. 17). However, this "improved treatment" is not afforded to all victims. Erez's contention may hold true for the victims whom the criminal justice system views as the "ideal" type. The analysis here compares "ideal" and "non-ideal" victims and considers how they experience the criminal justice system. This comparison, along with relative examples, is intended to illustrate how the criminal justice system denies "non-ideal" victims the basic rights of recognition, sympathy, assistance, and support afforded to "ideal" victims.

Ideal Versus Non-ideal Victims

The notion of the "ideal" victim stems from the works of Nils Christie (1986). Consider the following scenario: In the middle of the day, an elderly woman is on her way home after caring for her sick sister when she is hit on the head by a big man, who then snatches her purse. This man uses the money from her purse to buy alcohol or drugs. This scenario illustrates Christie's notion of the ideal victim. According to Christie, the ideal victim is "a person or category of individuals who—when hit by a crime—most readily are given the complete and legitimate status of being a victim" (p. 18). Christie (p. 19, cited in Lambda Legal, 2001, pp. 7-8) extends this notion further by indicating five attributes of victims that are used to distinguish them as "ideal" victims:

1. The ideal victim is weak (e.g., infirm, old, or extremely young).

2. The victim is carrying out a respectable project (e.g., caring for a family member).

3. The victim is somewhere that he or she could not be possibly blamed for being (e.g., in the street during the daytime).

4. The offender is big and bad.

5. The offender is unknown and has no personal relationship to the victim.[1]

In his article "The Ideal Victim," Christie adds a sixth attribute: A "victim has the right combination of power, influence, or sympathy to successfully elicit victim status without threatening (and thus risking opposition from) strong countervailing vested interests" (Dignan, 2005, p. 17).

Under this model, the "non-ideal" victim is considered to lack one or all of these characteristics (Lambda Legal, 2001, p. 8). An example of such a victim is provided by Christie (1986)—namely, a young man whose money is stolen from him after the young man is hit on the head by an acquaintance at a bar. Research has shown that, in contrast to Christie's ideal type, "victims of violence are often young men who hang around bars and become involved in altercations, with other young men, with whom they may already

---

[1] Christie, N. The Ideal Victim, 1986, St. Martin's Press. In Fattah, E. (ed.). *From Crime Policy to Victim Policy.* London, United Kingdom: Macmillan. Reproduced with permission of Palgrave Macmillan.

be acquainted" (Dignan, 2005, p. 20). Such a situation occurs because violence-related victimization patterns are—to some extent—related to certain aspects of an individual's lifestyle, such as frequent visits to clubs or pubs, consumption of alcohol, and so on (Dignan, 2005, p. 20). Victimization theories, such as victim lifestyle theory, attempt to explain why some individuals are more likely than others to become victims of crime (Hindeland, Gottfredson, & Garofalo, 1978). Also, research has shown that "victims are not always simon-pure but recruited in great measure from much the same demographic and geographical populations as offenders, bystanders, and witnesses, and that violent people are likely to become the victims of violence" (Pederson, 2001, cited in Rock, 2002, p. 11).

The non-ideal victim encompasses more than just individuals fitting Christie's (1986) description. Consider corporations as an example. According to Young (2002), "Corporations are not ideal victims. They lack human vulnerability, having no bloodied faces to display, no feelings to be injured, no fears to be allayed, no lifestyles to be undermined" (p. 136). Other non-ideal victims include, but are not limited to, the following: victims with a prior criminal record, victims of human trafficking, victims of paramilitary organizations, and victims of miscarriages of justice. For instance, victims of miscarriages of justice, such as victims of police brutality, have at times been ignored by the criminal justice system. The reasoning for this is that if these individuals are accepted as victims, then society would be acknowledging that there is something wrong with the criminal justice system and/or its agents (Elias, 1986). Similarly, individuals who have "been assaulted or raped in prison, mental hospitals, or other institutions, are also victims of crime" (Herman, 2002, p. 5) and should have equal access to any or all services available. Victims of intimate-partner violence who remain in their relationships with abusers and suffer continuous acts of rape, physical trauma, and psychological abuse should also have access to victims' services, but sometimes they are denied such access because of the common misperception that these individuals are "willing victims."

Experiences of the Criminal Justice System

The ideal victim is someone who is vulnerable, passive, sympathetic, honest, and convincing (Brennan, 2001). Today's ideal victim is one who is characterized as innocent and good—that is, one whose background, personality, and characteristics are "wholesome" (Anttila, 1986; Winter, 2002). Individuals who fall into Christie's (1986) category are given complete and legitimate status as victims. Such ideal victims are viewed and treated positively by the criminal justice system and are provided with all of the proper benefits, such as information, assistance, support, and compensation.

Non-ideal victims, by comparison, experience the criminal justice system in an entirely different manner. When individuals are not characterized as ideal victims, they are not perceived as worthy or deserving of the status of a victim by those in the criminal justice system. They have to work twice as hard to obtain the support, assistance, and benefits that are rightly theirs, and sometimes they are denied these services. Specifically, non-ideal victims, when dealing with the criminal justice system, can be denied justice (by depriving them of their basic rights as a victim, such as the attainment of victim status), treated with indifference and insensitivity (as opposed to sympathy), denied fairness through equal treatment (i.e., equal access to support and assistance), and refused compensation (based on the acknowledgment only of ideal victims). Accordingly, these types of victims have negative experiences of the criminal justice system. Consequently, they have difficulty obtaining the benefits, such as recognition, information, assistance, support, and compensation, that are readily available to ideal victims.

Rights: Denial of Justice

"In order to receive the benefits of victimization (sympathy, assistance, support, and sometimes financial reparation), those who are harmed must be recognized as victims" (Hamill, 2002, p. 49). Depriving victims of the benefits of victimization violates their inherent right to such services. One way this can be accomplished is by denying non-ideal victims their recognition as victims. Within the criminal justice system, the determination of who can be a victim is formulated around the concept of the innocent and deserving victim (Goodey, 2005). Therefore, individuals who are of questionable character are unjustly considered undeserving of the victim status. As a result, they are denied some of the basic principles of justice and are treated as individuals who are to blame for the crimes committed against them.

The importance of character within the criminal justice process can be seen in the following scenario: A prostitute who is beaten senseless by her pimp (or customer) might not be considered a victim. The prostitute was assaulted, so a crime was clearly committed against her. Why, then, is she not considered a victim? The answer to this question is simple: She is denied the status of a victim *because* she is a prostitute. This denial of victim status occurs because of society's view of the victim. Here, an individual's prior conduct or behavior is scrutinized. An individual, such as a prostitute, is judged on the basis of society's perception of that person. In this case, society's disapproval and stigmatization of the prostitute's profession means that she will not be identified as a victim of crime.

Accordingly, the character, clothing, and other features of the victim play a significant role within the criminal justice process and determines whether the individual will receive recognition as a victim. Individuals who are considered by the public to have questionable character or criminal backgrounds include "prisoners, victims of police maltreatment, or 'deviants' such as drug addicts, prostitutes and paedophiles" (Brennan, 2001, p. 6). The result of a victim's denial of recognition can be an adverse effect on the victim. Victims can be denied their inherent right to the basic principles of justice. An example of this can be seen in the film *The Accused* (1988). The movie was based on a real-life gang rape that occurred on March 6, 1983, at Big Dan's Bar in New Bedford, Massachusetts. The victim of the New Bedford gang rape, according to Benedict (1992), was one of the "worst-treated rape victims of the decade" (Horeck, 2000, p. 3). Why was this so?

The rape victim had a past (prior criminal record)—one that was used against her in a court of law. Her questionable character and lifestyle were the main reasons why her attorney agreed to lighter sentences (i.e., charges of reckless endangerment instead of rape) for her attackers. As a result of this lighter sentence, she was not classified as a victim of rape; likewise, her attackers were not labeled as rapists. Why was she denied this right? The perpetrators were not labeled as rapists because during the night in question the victim was drinking, had smoked pot, was dancing provocatively with one of her assailants, and even kissed one of them on the mouth. She did not represent the stereotype of a rape victim—one that is "not only morally and sexually virtuous" but also unprovocative (Larcombe, 2002, p. 131). Basically, she was not an ideal victim. Her "alleged failure to comply with the sexual and behavioral standards of the normative victim" would have discredited her testimony of being a victim of rape (p. 131). The blaming of the victim dates back to the pseudo-Freudian notion that most women have an unconscious desire to be forcibly dominated. As a consequence of this perception, the victim received justice only to the extent that the men who raped her were behind bars. However, instead of being tried and convicted as rapists, they were indicted on a lesser charge. In so doing, the criminal justice system single-handedly robbed the victim of her status as a rape victim and of the chance for the world to know of the wrong committed against her.

Box 1-1 The Evolving Nature of Rape and Sexual Assault

On May 6, 2013, three women who had been missing for nearly a decade and a six-year-old girl were found locked in a house in Cleveland, Ohio. Specifically, Amanda Berry (who was 16 years old when she was kidnapped) was held in captivity by her abductor and abuser, Ariel Castro, for 10 years (Schwirtz, 2013). Amanda Berry gave birth to Castro's child while in captivity and raised her under horrific conditions. Two other women were also held in captivity for 9 and 11 years, respectively: Gina DeJesus, who was the last victim abducted and had been 14 years old at the time of her abduction, and Michelle Knight, who was 21 years old when she was abducted (Gabriel, Kovaleski, Yaccino, & Goode, 2013). The women had been repeatedly raped and beaten, chained to the walls of the cellar, impregnated and forced to miscarry, starved, psychologically and emotionally abused, and denied access to hygiene and medical treatment.

Similar cases abound—for instance, the ordeals of Elizabeth Smart and Jaycee Dugard. On June 5, 2002, 14-year-old Smart was abducted from her bedroom in Salt Lake City, Utah, by Brian David Mitchell. During her 9-month captivity, she was repeatedly raped. In 1991, the 11-year-old Dugard was abducted by convicted sex offender Phillip Craig Garrido (McKinley & Pogash, 2009). She was held in captivity for nearly 18 years, during which she was repeatedly raped by her abductor and forced to bear two daughters, who themselves were raised in captivity (McKinley, 2011). In both Smart's and Dugard's cases, the wives of the assailants were complicit in the abductions and the sexual assaults.

Although these cases involved male rapists and female children, currently the laws describe rape as gender neutral. Accordingly, it can involve victims and perpetrators of any gender. In 2013, in Florida, a prosecutor sought felony charges against an 18-year-old high school senior, Kaitlyn Hunt, who was arrested for two counts of lewd or lascivious battery after having sexual relations with a 14-year-old girl (Harrison, 2013). Hunt refused a plea deal that would require her to register as a sex offender, insisting that the pair were in a same-sex relationship and so the sex was consensual (Slifer, 2013).

Furthermore, an individual's recognition as a victim depends on whether the person is blamed for the offense committed against him or her. For example, if the person's lifestyle is considered undesirable by society, he or she may be perceived as causing the crime rather than being the victim of it. This notion is consistent with the "just world hypothesis" (i.e., people get what they deserve) held by many in society, including those in the criminal justice system (Lerner, 1980). Consider the following scenario: A prostitute takes a client (i.e., john) back to her room. He rapes her, beats her, and steals her money. Society would condemn the prostitute because it would attribute the criminal offense as being the victim's fault. According to the just world hypothesis, society concludes that the prostitute is deserving of the crime against her because she was willing to participate in a criminal activity (i.e., prostitution); and as such, she is not perceived as a "victim" (Hart, 1993, cited in Byrne, KilPatrick, Howley, & Beatty, 1999).

A plethora of such cases exist within the criminal justice system. As clearly indicated by both the literature and the examples cited here, non-ideal victims can be—and have been—denied their basic right of receiving victim status. Moreover, these victims may be denied other rights that should be afforded to them by personnel working in the criminal justice system, including sympathy, support, and assistance. Yet, consistent with the views of the larger society, officers and other members of the criminal justice system tend to offer these benefits only when the victim is perceived to be vulnerable and blame free.

Assistance and Support: Fairness Denied

The basic roles and obligations of the agents of the criminal justice system are to provide victims with the appropriate services and to help them through the process. The Crime Victims' Rights Act of 2004 (18 U.S.C. § 3771)[2] prescribes the rights of crime victims. According to the Office of the United States Attorneys of the Department of Justice (n.d.), these rights are as follows:

- The right to be reasonably protected from the accused.
- The right to reasonable, accurate, and timely notice of any public court proceeding, or any parole proceeding, involving the crime or of any release or escape of the accused.
- The right not to be excluded from any such public court proceeding, unless the court, after receiving clear and convincing evidence, determines that testimony by the victim would be materially altered if the victim heard other testimony at that proceeding.
- The right to be reasonably heard at any public proceeding in the district court involving release, plea, sentencing, or any parole proceeding.
- The reasonable right to confer with the attorney for the government in the case.
- The right to full and timely restitution as provided by law.

---

[2] Reproduced from The Crime Victims' Rights Act of 2004 (18 U.S.C. § 3771).

- The right to proceedings free from unreasonable delay.
- The right to be treated with fairness and with respect for the victim's dignity and privacy.

These rights and services should be available to the victim from the moment the crime is reported to the police and continually offered throughout the entire criminal justice and corrections processes. The services provided include information, assistance, and support.

As previously mentioned, victims have the right to receive information and assistance when a crime is committed against them. However, the reality is not as generous. The literature shows that "victims of rape, domestic violence, and child abuse all too frequently continue to encounter denials of their rights to equal protection and equal justice in the criminal justice system" (De Santis, 2000, p. 1). Generally, the victims who are denied such rights are those who fall into the category of non-ideal victims. In fact, non-ideal victims have sometimes even been denied information concerning the services available to them.

Another part of the services owed to victims is effective handling and investigation of their cases by agents of the criminal justice system. Nevertheless, research has shown that the following occurs: "Officer discrimination against and mistreatment of victims, failures to write reports, half-hearted investigations, failure to collect evidence, prosecutorial refusals to file charges despite sufficient evidence, give-away plea bargains, slap-on-the wrist sentencing," and so on (De Santis, 2000, p. 1). Such dereliction of duty, inappropriate handling of cases, and mistreatment of victims are associated, to some extent, with the alleged bias and prejudice that exist toward non-ideal victims.

Victims of crime have the right to be treated fairly by the criminal justice system. This means that each victim of crime, whether considered deserving or undeserving by its agents, has the right to such services. For example, "battered women who abuse drugs need shelter and support just as much as those who don't" have substance abuse problems (Herman, 2002, p. 5). The effects of such classifications of victims are illustrated in the following excerpt:

> Certain women—for example, those in stable relationships—come under the description of the deserving victim. In comparison, women with independent lifestyles and who were regarded as sexually liberated (for example, . . .[unmarried women who are sexually active with men, either within or outside a steady relationship]) were not, and continue not to be, given the degree of due process and service provisions as victims who comply or fit criminal justice constructions of the deserving victim." (Kennedy, 1992, and Lees, 1997, cited in Goodey[3], 2005, p. 22)

Furthermore, the denial of services, such as assistance and support, can be attributed to the existence of the so-called hierarchy of victims. Within this hierarchy, some victims are

---

[3] Goodey, J. (2000), 'An Overview of Key Themes', in A. Crawford and J. Goodey (eds.), *Integrating a Victim Perspective Within Criminal Justice*, Aldershot: Dartmouth Publishing.

placed above others in terms of their needs. Here, "The idea of innocence and non-complicity in one's own victimization is central to understanding how certain people and certain experiences of criminal victimization are typically excluded from consideration as victims. As a result, the very real needs of certain undesirable victim categories are neglected" (Goodey, 2005, pp. 124–125). This practice raises some alarming questions about the conduct of the criminal justice system. For example, why does it arrange the importance of human worth into a hierarchy? Why should a woman who was sold by her family into prostitution in a foreign country be of less worth than an elderly woman who is attacked in broad daylight and raped? Such a hierarchy should not exist within the criminal justice system. When it is constructed and applied, victims may be denied their right to fairness and equal treatment. All victims should be respected equally. Unfortunately, this is not always the case.

The Child as the Non-ideal Victim

In the past, maltreatment of children has been discounted or children have been blamed (at least in part) for the crimes that were committed against them. This devaluation was due primarily to the fact that prior to the 15th century, childhood was not acknowledged to be a separate time period from adulthood. In the middle ages, life for everyone was harsh and not valued (Empey, Stafford, & Hay, 1999). Children in particular were treated with indifference, as objects to be used or abused for one's own amusement, as evidenced by widespread infanticide (i.e., killing of newborns) and the absence of child protection laws against maltreatment.

The notion that children should be cherished and protected, given time to learn and grow, and treated with respect and love for them to become productive citizens is a relatively modern one (Aries, 1965). Two major contributors to this new conception of childhood were religion and social science research. Early religious thought emphasized that children were by nature sinners and incorrigible; thus, it was deemed their parents' responsibility to prevent them from indulging in evil, including disobedience and rudeness to adults. Physical punishments (e.g., beatings and even death), therefore, were appropriate and encouraged responses to child misbehavior (Empey et al., 1999). However, Locke's idea of "tabula rasa" (i.e., infants are born innocent) changed these notions and encouraged parents instead to provide positive learning situations for their children. Social science research likewise provided evidence that physical and cognitive growth and socioemotional development during infancy, childhood, and adolescence could be severely and negatively impacted by different types of maltreatment, resulting in adults who have severe problems. Several social policies were developed consistent with the "childhood as a special period" viewpoint, including providing formal education even for the poor, making child labor illegal, penalizing maltreatment against children as civil and/or criminal actions punishable by law, and creating a separate criminal justice system to handle crimes by juvenile offenders.

The character of the child victim, then, plays a significant role within the criminal justice process. A case in point is Rolan Adams, who was 15 years old at the time of his murder. Adams was considered an undeserving (i.e., non-ideal) victim because agents of the criminal justice system claimed that he was murdered as the result of a territorial dispute between two rival gangs. For that reason, they suggested that the victim was partly to blame for his murder (Younge, 1999). Does the same hold true for children who have been abused? Child abuse victims are considered innocent, weak, and defenseless. According to Knox (2001), "elderly victims of robberies, burglaries and assaults, children who are sexually abused, victims of medical negligence, come close to the 'ideal victim'" (p. 9). Despite popular belief, sexually abused children are not considered ideal victims by agents of the criminal justice system. In fact, like other non-ideal victims, they have been denied recognition as victims and prevented from exercising their rights in that role.

Usually, child abuse occurs without any witnesses to such conduct, making investigations—specifically, physical and mental examinations and interviews conducted by child protection workers and other members of a multidisciplinary team, such as medical professionals and agents of the criminal justice system—essential to establishing and proving the case. The government is loath to interfere with the family's rights to raise a child, unless there is evidence to support the contention that civil or criminal statutes have been violated, such as in families experiencing intimate-partner violence. Key components in the decision to prosecute an offender are the age and maturity of the victim (i.e., is the case winnable?). Often, the needs of the child victims and their families are not considered, as evidenced by the lack of support provided during criminal justice and/or family court proceedings. Moreover, prosecutors rarely pursue cases when there are no corroborating witnesses or evidence (the absence of which unfortunately is typical), sending the unintentional message to child victims (and perhaps to the members of their support system) that the perpetrator will never be punished. Even when cases are pursued, offenders commonly plead guilty to lesser charges or receive informal sanctions, such as mandatory counseling or probation, instead of incarceration, even for such heinous crimes as sexual offenses.

Scope of Child Abuse and Neglect

Three main sources are used to determine the scope of child abuse and neglect. One source is research conducted on child maltreatment using clinical and nonclinical samples. This data is retrospective in nature and has the typical pitfalls of information that relies on memory. A second source is the National Child Abuse and Neglect Data System (NCANDS) created by the Children's Bureau of the U.S. Department of Health and Human Services. On an annual basis, NCANDS collects data and analyzes statistics on child abuse and neglect from state child protective services (CPS) agencies. The data provided by CPS are based on the child abuse and neglect cases reported to each agency. From these data, NCANDS produces child maltreatment reports, particularly when the offender is a family member of the victim. Given that these reports are based only on data that are voluntarily submitted to the system, they do not accurately depict the scope of child abuse and neglect.

A third source of information on child abuse and neglect is the National Incidence Studies (NIS). According to the Administration for Children and Families of the U.S. Department of Health and Human Services (n.d.), the NIS "is a congressionally mandated, periodic research effort to assess the incidence of child abuse and neglect in the United States." In response to requirements established by the Child Abuse Prevention and Treatment Act of 1974, NIS data collection has been conducted roughly once each decade. The NIS data are designed to estimate the incidence of child maltreatment using both conservative and lax definitions and are considered to be an extension of the NCANDS reports, as they include both cases reported to authorities (police and CPS, among others) and unreported cases.

To date, four studies have been conducted. Specifically, pursuant to Public Law (P.L.) 93–247 (1974), the first study, NIS-1, was conducted between 1979 and 1980 and its results published in 1981. The second study, NIS-2, was conducted between 1986 and 1987, as mandated by P.L. 98–457 (1984); its results were published in 1988. Under the Child Abuse Prevention, Adoption, and Family Services Act of 1988 (P.L. 100–294) and the Child Abuse, Domestic Violence, Adoption and Family Services Act of 1992 (P.L. 102–295), the third study, NIS-3, was conducted between 1993 and 1995. The results of this study were published in 1996. The fourth study, NIS-4, was conducted between 2005 and 2006 pursuant to the Keeping Children and Families Safe Act of 2003 (P.L. 108–36). The results of this study were published in 2010. The principal objectives of NIS-2, NIS-3, and NIS-4 are to provide information on the nature and extent of child abuse in the United States and to measure any changes from earlier studies. The scope of maltreatment as determined through the use of the NIS datasets has varied over the years with subsequent changes in the definitions used, particularly for the harm and endangerment criteria. The need for these modifications is exemplified in the next section.

The Critical Need for Understanding Child Maltreatment and Existing Interventions: A Case Study

Children as young as 2 or 3 can provide testimony against their sexual abusers. On December 6, 2012, a 49-year-old male, John Burbine, was accused in Middlesex County (Massachusetts) of sexually assaulting 13 infants and toddlers ("Prosecutor: Man raped, abused," 2012). Authorities claim that beginning in August 2010, he raped and abused children between the ages of 8 days and 3 years at his wife's daycare business (Andersen, 2013). Burbine faces similar charges in Essex County, where he is accused of raping children, the youngest of whom was 5 years old, when he was providing child care services between May 16, 1990, and January 8, 1994 (Ballou, 2013). Burbine recorded his assaults on children on video. It was later revealed that the Massachusetts State Department of Children and Families had investigated him in 2005 and again in 2009 on suspicion of sexually abusing young boys; however, in neither of these instances were charges brought against Burbine (Ballou, 2013). Moreover, in 1989, Burbine had three convictions involving indecent assault and battery on a child and was classified as a Tier I offender on the sex offender register (Ballou,

2013). Tier I offenders must be registered for 15 years and update their information annually. The Tier levels of the sex offender registry are a form of assessment that seeks to predict the likelihood that a sexual offender will reoffend; those persons in Tier I are believed to have a low risk of reoffending. Marian Burbine, John's wife, was alleged to have known about her husband's prior convictions and the 2005 and 2009 suspicions of sexual assault on young boys. She was charged with recklessly endangering children.

This case and many others like it have drawn society's attention to the need to better understand the causes and consequences of child maltreatment (i.e., child neglect and abuse) and the multifaceted interventions (by, for example, CPS workers, law enforcement officers, and the agents of the criminal and family court) directed at resolving it. The goal of this text is to aid in this process.

Chapter Summary

Victims' experiences within the criminal justice system depend on what type of victim they are—that is, ideal or non-ideal. This distinction is critical in understanding why non-ideal victims' experiences of the criminal justice system are so often negative ones. Non-ideal victims are frequently denied their basic rights as victims. Some are denied their recognition as victims; others are denied basic services and support from agents of the criminal justice system. Whatever the case may be, such individuals are often stigmatized within the criminal justice system and their needs go unmet. As a result, they are denied basic principles of justice such as fairness and equality.

Children are classified as non-ideal victims because they have long been denied recognition as victims and prevented from exercising their rights as victims. Decisions by the agents of the family court and criminal justice system are often taken irrespective of the needs of a child. Sometimes offenders are not prosecuted due to the lack of witnesses and/or corroborating evidence in child sexual abuse cases. When such cases are pursued, child sexual abuse offenders usually plea bargain and receive informal sanctions.

Review Questions

1. What is victimology?
2. What role does the victim have in criminal proceedings?
3. What are the differences between an ideal and non-ideal victim?
4. What are the implications of being considered as a non-ideal victim?
5. Why can a child be considered as a non-ideal victim?

References

The Accused [Film]. (1988). Jonathan Kaplan, director. USA: Paramount Pictures.

Administration for Children and Families of the U.S. Department of Health and Human Services (n.d.). The National Incidence Study (NIS). https://www.childwelfare.gov/ systemwide/statistics /nis.cfm

Andersen, T. (2013, May 1). Accused in sex abuse case faces more charges. *Boston Globe*. http://www
.bostonglobe.com/metro/2013/04/30/john-burbine-facing-more-child-sex-abuse-charges-this-
time-essex-county/pvxGdpq8Nag0R3RovjsUPP/story.html

Anttila, I. (1986). From crime policy to victim policy? In E. Fattah (Ed.), *From crime policy to victim
policy* (pp. 237–245). London, UK: Macmillan.

Aries, P. (1965). *Centuries of childhood: A social history of family life*. New York, NY: Vintage.

Ashworth, A. (2002). Responsibilities, rights, and restorative justice. *British Journal of Criminology*,
42(3), 578–595.

Ballou, B. (2013, May 2). List of charges against sex offender grows. *Boston Globe*. http://www
.bostonglobe.com/metro/2013/05/01/former-daycare-provider-john-burbine-arraigned-
new-child-sex-abuse-changes-essex-county/zWgRj7sMNfWJot9oG2nk3H/story.html

Benedict, H. (1992). *Virgin or vamp: How the press covers sex crimes*. New York, NY: Oxford University Press.

Brennan, C. (2001). The victim personal statement: Who is the victim? http://webjcli.ncl.ac.uk/2001
/issue4/brennan4.html

Byrne, C. A., KilPatrick, D. G., Howley, S. S., & Beatty, D. (1999). Female victims of partner versus
non-partner violence: experiences with the criminal justice system. *Criminal Justice and Behaviour*,
26(3), 257–292.

Christie, N. (1977). Conflicts as Property. *British Journal of Criminology*, *17*(1), 1–15.

Christie, N. (1986). The ideal victim. In E. Fattah (Ed.), *From crime policy to victim policy* (pp. 17–30).
London, UK: Macmillan.

De Santis, M. (2000). Online handbook: Advocating for women in the criminal justice system in cases
of rape, domestic violence and child abuse. Women's Justice Centre. http://www.justicewomen
.com/handbook/intro.html

Dignan, J. (2005). *Understanding victims and restorative justice*. Berkshire, UK: Open University Press.

Elias, R. (1986). Community control, criminal justice and victim services. In E. Fattah (Ed.), *From
crime policy to victim policy* (pp. 290–316). London, UK: Macmillan.

Empey, L. T., Stafford, M. C., & Hay, H. H. (1999). *American delinquency: Its meaning and construction*.
Belmont, CA: Wadsworth.

Erez, E. (1994). Victim participation in sentencing: And the debate goes on . . . *International Review
of Victimology*, *3*(1–2), 17–32.

Erez, E. (1999, July). Who's afraid of the big bad victim? Victim impact statements as victim
empowerment and enhancement of justice. *Criminal Law Review*, 545–556.

Friend, C. (2004). Social contract theory. http://www.iep.utm.edu/s/soc-cont.htm

Gabriel, T., Kovaleski, S. F., Yaccino, S., & Goode, E. (2013, May 8). Cleveland man charged with
rape and kidnapping. *New York Times*. http://www.nytimes.com/2013/05/09/us/cleveland-
kidnapping.html?pagewanted=all

Goodey, J. (2005). *Victims and victimology: Research, policy, and practice*. Harlow, UK: Longman
Criminology Series.

Hamill, H. (2002). Victims of paramilitary punishment attacks in Belfast. In C. Hoyle & R. Young
(Eds.), *New visions of crime victims* (pp. 49–69). Oxford, UK: Hart.

Harrison, C. (2013, May 21). Florida student, 18, arrested for sex with teammate, 14. *New York
Times*. http://www.nytimes.com/2013/05/22/us/florida-18-year-old-arrested-for-encounters-
with-friend-14-gets-online-support.html

Hart, B. (1993). Battered women and the criminal justice system. *American Behavioral Scientist*, *36*(5),
624–638.

Herman, S. (2002). Parallel justice: A matter of conscience. National Centre for Victims of Crime.
http://www.ncvc.org/ncvc/main.aspx?dbName=DocumentViewer&DocumentID=32832

Hindeland, M., Gottfredson, M., & Garofalo, J. (1978). *Victims of personal crime.* Cambridge, MA: Ballinger.

Horeck, T. (2000). "They did worse than nothing": Rape and Spectatorship in The Accused *Canadian Review of American Studies, 30*(1), 1–21.

Kemerling, G. (2002). Philosophy pages: Dictionary. http://www.philosophypages.com/dy/s7.htm

Kennedy, H. (1992). *Eve was framed: Women and British justice.* London, UK: Vintage.

Knox, C. (2001). The "deserving" victims of political violence: "Punishment" attacks in Northern Ireland. *Criminal Justice, 1*(2), 181–199.

Lambda Legal. (2001). Brief of amici curiae of Parents of Murdered Children, Inc. and National Centre for Victims of Crime in support of appellant, Joann Brandon. http://data.lambdalegal.org /pdf/12.pdf

Larcombe, W. (2002). The "ideal" victim v successful rape complaints: Not what you might expect. *Feminist Legal Studies, 10*(2), 131–148.

Lees, S. (1997). *Ruling passions: Sexual violence, reputation and the law.* Buckingham, UK: Open University Press.

Lerner, M. J. (1980). *The Belief in a Just World: A Fundamental Delusion.* New York: Plenum Press.

McKinley, J. (2011, June 2). Couple sentenced to prison in 18 year kidnapping case. *New York Times.* http://www.nytimes.com/2011/06/03/us/03garrido.html?_r=0

McKinley, J., & Pogash, C. (2009, August 27). Kidnapped at 11, woman emerges after 18 years. *New York Times.* http://www.nytimes.com/2009/08/28/us/28abduct.html

Office of the United States Attorneys, Department of Justice. (n.d.). Crime victims' rights ombudsman. http://www.justice.gov/usao/eousa/vr/victims_rights.html

Pederson, W. (2001). Adolescent victims of violence in a welfare state. *British Journal of Criminology, 41*(1), 1–21.

Prosecutor: Man raped, abused 13 infants, children and videotaped attacks. (2012, December 6). *NBC News.* http://usnews.nbcnews.com/_news/2012/12/06/15735891-prosecutor-man-raped-abused-13-infants-children-and-videotaped-attacks?lite

Rock, P. (2002). On becoming a victim. In C. Hoyle & R. Young (Eds.), *New visions of crime victims* (pp. 1–22). Oxford, UK: Hart.

Schwirtz, M. (2013, May 6). Three women, missing for years, found in Cleveland. *New York Times.* http://www.nytimes.com/2013/05/07/us/three-women-gone-for-years-found-in-ohio.html

Slifer, S. (2013, May 24). Kaitlyn Hunt update: Fla. teen charged over same-sex underage relationship rejects plea deal. *CBS News.* http://www.cbsnews.com/8301-504083_162-57586099-504083 /kaitlyn-hunt-update-fla-teen-charged-over-same-sex-underage-relationship-rejects-plea-deal/

Winter, J. (2002). The trial of Rose West: Contesting notions of victimhood. In C. Hoyle & R. Young (Eds.), *New visions of crime victims* (pp. 173–196). Oxford, UK: Hart.

Young, R. (2002). Testing the limits of restorative justice: The case of corporate victims. In Hoyle, C. and Young, R. (eds.). *New visions of crime victims* (pp. 133–172). Oxford, UK: Hart.

Younge, P. (1999, February 13). Why Stephen? *BBC News.* http://news.bbc.co.uk/1/hi/uk/278369.stm

Section I

Normative Infant, Child, and Adolescent Development

In the chapter *Child Victimology: An Introduction*, we introduced the notion of child victimology as a basis for understanding the maltreated child as a non-ideal victim, the problems in prosecuting perpetrators, and the difficulty in obtaining services for victims. This section of the book focuses on various aspects of normal development. The physical, cognitive, social, and emotional developmental processes that contribute to forming a whole person from infancy through adolescence are described. All of these aspects of development interact and influence one another. The goal of this section is to allow professionals to form expectations about normal development that can serve as a framework for understanding the impact maltreatment can have on infants, children, and adolescents (which is described in the next section *The Negative Effects of Maltreatment on Development*). The chapter *Physical and Cognitive Development* describes brain and body growth, improvement in motor skills, play, and sexual development, as well as acquisition and development of language and cognitive processes, which contribute to academic performance. The chapter *Emotional and Social Development* examines both emotional and social processes, as well as individual characteristics present at birth and their roles in relationships that form in infancy and evolve in childhood and adolescence.

Chapter 2

Physical and Cognitive Development

This chapter begins by describing the central aspects of physical development and behavior of infants (from birth up to, but not including, 3 years of age), children (ages 3 to 11 years), and adolescents (ages 12 to 18 years). An examination of the brain and the senses reveals how their development allows the evolving child to interact with and learn about the world. Next, a description of motor skills and play is given, both of which allow the evolving child to explore and interact with the external environment. Information on body growth and changes, the role of routines in health and well-being, and sexual development is then provided. The second half of the chapter focuses on three main areas in cognitive development: language, cognition (attention, knowledge, memory, planning, and problem solving), and academic ability (intelligence, school performance, and literacy). In each section, various developmental delays and their effects on the child are presented.

Physical Development

The Brain and Senses

This section examines development in the brain, describing the structures in this organ and their functions for the body and behavior, and coordination of the senses with perception. Distinct changes in the brain and nervous system—in terms of increases in myelination (fatty sheaths covering nerve axons)—occur as the brain grows and nerves become increasingly more complex and connected. As the human body matures, lateralization of the brain develops along with handedness, and the cortex becomes specialized into motor, somatosensory (auditory, visual), and association areas.

Brain Growth

Changes in the brain during infancy and early childhood stem from the formation of neurons, increased myelination of neurons (coating of nerves with an insulating fatty sheath that increases efficacy of information transfer), and creation of synaptic connections based on personal experiences (called synaptogenesis) in conjunction with programmed cell death to make space for these new structures (approximately 20% to 80% of the surrounding neurons die). The brain's size at birth is only 30% of the adult weight of the brain; this proportion increases to 70% of the adult size by age 2 years and then to 90% by age 6 years. Having an overabundance of neural connections allows children to rapidly develop a variety of motor, cognitive, and social skills for interacting with their world. In childhood and adolescence, synaptic pruning occurs, which reduces the number of underutilized connections (approximately 40%). Around age 9 or 10 years, new synapses are formed, and there is an increase in myelination of speech and motor centers and in the prefrontal cortex. In adolescence, the number of new synapses increases, particularly between reasoning and emotions; this growth spurt is followed by synaptic pruning.

Brain Structures, Lateralization, and Cortical Specialization

The brain is composed of two hemispheres separated by a band of fibers called the corpus callosum, which allows communication between the two sides to coordinate movement and to integrate perception with attention and memory, language, and problem solving. Development in the corpus callosum increases in the first year after birth, peaks in the preschool years, and then continues at a slow, steady pace in middle childhood and adolescence. Some brain functions are controlled exclusively in the left hemisphere, some in the right hemisphere, and the rest in both hemispheres. The motor cortex on the right side of the brain controls the left side of the body; conversely, the left side of the brain controls the right side of the body. The processes of lateralization and dominance, respectively, begin at birth as one hemisphere gains control of a specific set of brain functions; infants then show a stronger preference for one side over the other (e.g., right over left), which in turn affects the development of motor, cognitive, and language skills.

The immature brain (i.e., one that has not lateralized) has plasticity—that is, in the event of injury to the brain, it is able to restructure functions originally associated with a damaged region to another region. It is during the period from birth to preschool age in which the overabundance of synaptic connections leads to redundancy and allows the brain to be reorganized to assume different functions when necessary (e.g., brain injury, stroke). For example, when injuries occur prenatally or within the first six months neonatally, Stiles (2008) and colleagues (Stiles, Reilly, Paul, & Moses, 2005) have reported that children show language and spatial skills delays in development until about age 3.5 years, but that these children's language—but not spatial—abilities are able to rebound to normal levels by age 5 years.

Coinciding with lateralization is the development of hand dominance. Initially, infants and toddlers are ambidextrous (use both hands). Handedness—that is, hemisphere dominance of one side over the other—is established by the end of the second year of life. Most people are right-handed (90%), with language (spoken and written), math, science, logic, detailed perspective, and positive emotions specialized in the left hemisphere, and visual–spatial abilities, reading facial expressions, intuition, artistic and musical skills, overall perspective, and negative emotions in the right hemisphere. The rest (10%) are left-handed or even mixed-handed (i.e., able to use both hands); in these individuals, the reverse hemispheres control these functions or are less specialized. Evidence suggests that these rules are not absolute, as some right-handed people manage language functions in their right hemispheres and some left-handed people control language in their left hemispheres. Research has also shown that unusual lateralization is associated with increased speed and flexibility in cognitive, verbal, and mathematical abilities (Flannery & Liederman, 1995).

Table 2-1 lists each brain structure and its corresponding function. The brain stem, which includes the spinal cord, is responsible for basic functions, such as breathing.

Table 2-1 Brain structures and functions

Brain stem (functions without conscious effort)

Medulla	Controls heartbeat, blood pressure, and breathing
Pons	Coordinates movement; controls sleep–wake cycle
Thalamus	Receives sensory information (except smell) and routes it to higher brain regions; sends information to medulla and cerebellum
Reticular formation	Affects arousal (alertness, consciousness, controlled attention)
Cerebellum	Controls nonverbal learning and memory; coordinates balance, reflexes, and voluntary movement

Limbic system

Amygdala	Perception of emotion; processing of emotional memories; controls aggression
Hypothalamus	Influences moods, motivation, and drives, like hunger and thirst; temperature; sexual behavior; and hormonal process; reward center associated with pleasures (eating, drinking, sex)
Hippocampus	Processes new memories of facts and episodes, spatial images

Cerebral cortex

Sensory cortex	Parietal lobes	Processes sensory (touch, pain, and pressure) and spatial information (body position) ; processes comprehension (e.g., visual and tactile functions)
Motor cortex	Parietal lobes	Controls and monitors body movements
Prefrontal cortex	Frontal lobes	Processes complex thinking (decision making, problem solving, planning) and recall, fine and gross motor activity, speech, and self-control
Visual cortex	Occipital lobes	Processes visual information
Auditory cortex	Temporal lobes	Processes hearing, visual and factual memory, and emotion

Data from Bailey, R. (2014). Anatomy of the brain. Retrieved at http://biology.about.com/od/humananatomybiology/a/anatomybrain.htm; MDhealth.com (2014). Parts of the brain and their functions. Retrieved at http://www.md-health.com/Parts-Of-The-Brain-And-Function.html

The cerebellum allows humans to balance and move. Although the four lobes of the cerebrum or cortex have distinct functions, coordination among them is required for sensation, perception, and activity. As the cerebral cortex becomes specialized in function, these regions replace involuntary reflexes for control over the body.

Figure 2-1 depicts the functional areas of the cerebral cortex. The somatosensory cortex (composed of auditory and visual cortices) demonstrates accelerated gains in the first year. The prefrontal cortex has the longest stage of development, beginning its operation in infancy, increasing and refining its synaptic connections during early and late childhood, and accelerating its growth in adolescence, culminating with the adult level being reached around age 25 years. Adolescents have an increased ability to think abstractly, coordinate and integrate information, and regulate thoughts with emotions, but have difficulty with judgment, restraining their impulses (especially for pleasurable experiences), planning their actions, considering the value of long-term future goals, and regulating their reactions to negative, stressful events.

Lesions or damage to the somatosensory cortex causes impairments in sensory discrimination, inability to recognize objects through touch, and neglect of the nondominant (contralateral) side of the body (e.g., failure to recognize one's own left hand if right-handed). When damage occurs to the visual cortex, a person will have cortical blindness, difficulty tracking objects, and failure to recognize colors and movements. In contrast, when damage occurs to the auditory cortex, the individual will have difficulty understanding language and tone of voice. Damage that occurs to the prefrontal cortex results in impaired moral reasoning and low inhibition.

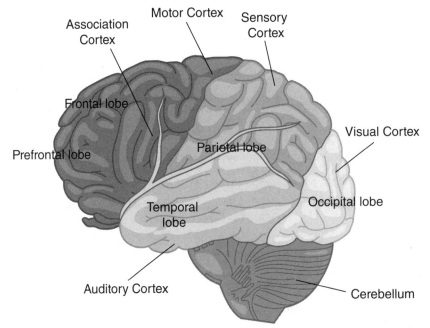

Figure 2-1 Functional areas of the cerebral cortex, lateral view of the left hemisphere

Sensation and Perception

The senses operate at a basic level (sensation), allowing infants to interact with their environment until the brain has developed and is capable of interpreting those sensory signals (perception). The five senses are in different stages of development at birth and, therefore, vary in their ability to abstract information from the environment. Similarly, the infant's brain is in the process of becoming differentiated and specialized, but until it reaches an advanced development stage, information is interpreted at the senses' level (e.g., eyes, ears, nose, mouth, skin). After the brain makes connections with the senses, it attaches meaning to the sensory information so that the infant can understand the world.

Hearing begins to operate in the fetal period four months prior to birth, such that the fetus is capable of hearing the mother's voice. The fetus is able to discriminate different tones and intensities two months before birth and can direct its attention toward sounds one month prior to birth. Both the auditory cortex (which interprets sounds) and the receptor cells in the inner ear are immature at birth. The neonate is able to hear, however, and has a preference for high-pitched human voices at this stage. By one month of age, the infant can make fine distinctions between categories of sounds, such as "pa" and "ba." There is a delay of about 2.5 seconds between a sound occurring and the infant hearing it before turning towards it.

Visual acuity (fineness of details) in infants is very poor, such that what an adult sees at 20 feet appears as it would 400 feet away to the infant, making infants legally blind. The infant can see objects within 8 to 12 inches, with visual acuity eventually reaching the adult level around 12 months of age. Infants are particularly cued to focus on faces, as well as other objects with high contrast, and their ability to differentiate between familiar and unfamiliar faces increases along with their scanning capabilities between 2 and 5 months of age. The ability to perceive depth is acquired between 3 and 6 months of age using two abilities: *accommodation*, in which the brain monitors eye muscles when focusing on objects to determine distance (parallel when far, almost crossing when near), and *retinal disparity*, which provides slightly different perspectives of an object from each eye. Vision operates at the sense level at birth because the visual cortex, which interprets visual signals from the eyes, is underdeveloped in the newborn.

Taste is developed at birth. Similar to adults, infants prefer sweet tastes (demonstrated by them smiling, licking their lips, sucking) over sour (demonstrated by them pursing their lips, wrinkling their noses, blinking) and bitter tastes (demonstrated by them sticking out their tongues and spitting). The mother's milk, like the amniotic fluid, absorbs the flavor of the foods the mother eats, the taste of which is then transmitted to the infant. Smell is also developed in infants at birth, such that they react similarly to adults by turning away from unpleasant odors (e.g., sulfur) and being drawn to smells that are pleasant, including those associated with the caregiver (e.g., clothes).

Touch is the key to survival for human infants. Touch (e.g., cuddle, caress, rock, hold) provides sufficient stimulation for normal development and allows caregivers to keep infants in an alert state, encourage unaroused infants, and help calm over-aroused and crying infants. Infants can and do feel pain in the same way adults do, including pain from circumcision (removal of foreskin on the tip of the penis).

Temperature regulation does not operate correctly for the first four to nine weeks after birth, forcing infants to engage in particular behaviors to compensate—they have a lot of surface area exposed and low insulation. For example, the infant who is hot will lie still to conserve energy and stretch out to allow air flow to cover the body; in the same situation, an adult's blood vessels dilate and move toward the surface of the skin. The infant who is cold will cry, which generates heat and gets the caregiver to respond by picking the child up and sharing body heat, and will reduce body surface by drawing in limbs and curling the body. By comparison, in an adult who is cold, the blood vessels constrict and move deeper, away from the surface of the skin.

Children diagnosed with sensory processing disorder (SPD) have a problem with the way their nervous system processes sensory signals and translates them into motor and behavioral responses (Sensory Processing Disorder Foundation, 2012). Hence, the brain cannot properly interpret the sensory information, resulting in a variety of problems: clumsiness, poor posture, acting out, emotional distress, and academic failure. This disorder can affect one sense or many senses, and responses vary from overacting/need to avoid sensation (e.g., finding clothing tags irritating), or underacting/need to seek sensation (e.g., hard pressing when hugging).

Motor Development

This section describes interaction with the environment through infant states and reflexes, development of motor skills from infancy through adolescence, and growth and physical changes in the body from infancy through puberty.

Interacting with the Environment Using Motor Reflexes and Skills

Infant States.　Infant states can be classified as asleep, awake, and inflexibly focused. Newborns sleep about 16 to 18 hours per day, with sleeping time organized into short nap periods that correspond to their need to eat every few hours (Hanrahan, 2006). The overall amount of sleep required by an individual decreases with age from birth to early childhood, with a long sleep period in the nighttime supplemented by a short nap in the daytime. The two asleep states are (1) *active sleep*, which is characterized by movement and irregular breathing and includes rapid-eye-movement (REM) sleep believed to be necessary for brain development (neurological self-stimulation), and (2) *quiet sleep*, which is non-REM or regular sleep in which there is no movement and shallow breathing. The three awake states are (1) *alert and active*, which enables the infant to focus and interact with the world; (2) *quiet*, which involves the infant sitting still and being content to learn, which is considered to be equivalent to the state of attention in adults; and (3) *drowsy*, in which the child startles easily and the eyes are glassy or semi-closed. The *inflexibly focused* state includes adverse reactions to stimulation (such as fussing, crying) while the infant is in an awake state, as well as having difficulty being soothed by caregiver (being held) or self (e.g., sucking thumb, pacifier).

Reflexes.　Initially, infants use innate reflexes (the inborn set of involuntary motoric reactions), which are controlled by the lower brain stem, as a means for interacting with their

Table 2-2 Neonatal reflexes

Type of reflex	Examples	Length of time
Survival	Blink, gag, cough, sneeze, yawn, righting (when laid on stomach, infant will lift head to free airways)	Do not disappear
Feeding	Sucking (object touches roof of mouth, lips close, sucking in bursts)	2 months
	Swallowing	Does not disappear
	Rooting (when cheek stroked , infant turns towards stimulation)	4 months
Heritage	Moro startle (perceived loss of support or startling causes infant to flail limbs outward and then bring them inward)	2–6 months
	Palmer grasping (fingers and toes wrap around object and grip can support infant's weight)	2–6 months
	Tonic neck (when laid on back, infant will stretch out limbs on same side as direction of face while pulling opposite limbs inward like a fencer)	2–6 months
	Galant (when laid on stomach and stroked back near spine, infant will curve body towards side being stroked	2–6 months
Precursors	Crawling (when placed on stomach, infant will make crawl movements)	2–24 months
	Stepping (while supporting infant's weight with feet on surface, each foot will lift and set back down as though walking)	2–24 months
	Babinksi (when side of foot is stroked, toes fan out and foot turns inward)	2–24 months
	Swimming	2–24 months

Data from Volpe, J. J. (2008). Neurological examination: Normal and abnormal features. In J. J. Volpe (Ed.), *Neurology of the Newborn.* (5th ed.) Philadelphia, Pa: Saunders Elsevier.; Weiss, R.E. (2014). How newborn reflexes help babies survive. Retrieved from http://pregnancy.about.com/od/newborntesting/a/Newborn-Reflexes.htm

world (Table 2-2). These reflexes can be grouped into four types—survival (necessary to protect the body), feeding (to aid in nourishment), heritage (a legacy of our evolutionary past, but not needed today), and precursors (autonomic responses of postural reflexes that will subsequently need to be learned). As the higher centers of the brain (i.e., motor cortex) develop and take over voluntary control for movements, many of these reflexes disappear. For example, a swimming reflex allows the infant to "swim" by moving the arms and legs and holding the breath when submerged in water. However, this reflex disappears between four and six months after birth in conjunction with motor cortex development, resulting in the infant needing to learn how to swim.

Box 2-1 How Do You Know That the Newborn Is Healthy?

Apgar Scale

Every newborn is assessed against the Apgar scale at 1 minute to determine if immediate medical intervention is needed, and again at 5 minutes after birth to determine if progress was made, particularly when initial scores were low. Virginia Apgar (1953), a physician, created this scale, which was subsequently named for her, as a means for evaluating newborns (American Academy of Pediatrics, 2006). Infant health is determined using scores from each of five categories (Activity/muscle tone; Pulse/heart rate; Grimace/reflexes; Appearance/skin color; Respiration/breathing rate) summed together, with total scores ranging from 0 to 10. Scores of 7–10 indicate the healthy range, a score in the range of 4–7 signifies some health issues that may necessitate resuscitation (e.g., <100 beats per minute; shallow breath), and a score of 0–3 indicates a requirement for immediate resuscitation (i.e., no heart beat, no respiration, limp, blue/gray coloring, no response). Any newborn that has a low score (less than 4) will be observed for signs of sudden infant death syndrome (SIDS) and likely have a monitor to detect whether the infant stops breathing (i.e., apnea). Parents are encouraged to place infants on their backs to sleep, rather than on their stomachs, to prevent deep sleep often associated as precursor for apnea.

Brazelton Neonatal Behavioral Assessment Scale

Tests using the Brazelton Neonatal Behavioral Assessment Scale are performed only on newborns and infants up to two months of age who are suspected of having neurologic problems to determine the extent of the damage. The assessment evaluates the central nervous system in terms of maturation and social behavior and can predict potential developmental problems. Four areas of behavior are examined: motor behaviors (i.e., reflexes, coordination, and muscle tone); interactive, adaptive behaviors relating to infant states (i.e., alertness, cuddliness); response to stress (i.e., startle reaction); and physiological control (i.e., the infant's self-regulation or ability to calm down and be consoled when over-aroused).

Developmental delays in cortical development are signified by the continuation of neonatal reflexes past the time when they should dissipate—for example, the Moro (startle) reflex persists in children with cerebral birth injury (i.e., brain damage), asymmetric tonic reflex is present in individuals with cerebral palsy (a disorder affecting tone, movement, and skills related to muscles), and a negative palmar grasp reflex indicates neurologic problems (Moini, 2013; Weiss, 2014).

Motor Skills

As the body matures, changes occur in both *gross* (large muscles, such as the legs and arms) and *fine* (small muscles, such as the hands, fingers, lips, and tongue) motor movements, which follow three principles of growth.

- Cephalocaudal (i.e., head to toe) development allows for control first over the muscles in the neck and head (e.g., lifting the head); then in the shoulders, arms, chest, and abdomen (e.g., rolling over, crawling); and finally in the hips, thighs, legs, and feet (e.g., sitting up, standing, walking), which allows the child to perform increasingly complex movements.

- Proximodistal (i.e., center to extremities) development allows for control of movement in the shoulders (e.g., to direct the torso toward an object), then the arms (e.g., to swipe at objects), then the hands (e.g., to grasp or scoop objects), and finally in the fingers (e.g., to use the thumb and the forefinger to pick up small objects).

- Differentiation (i.e., refinement) allows for control of movement from general to specific motoric reactions (i.e., response to stimulation from the full body to a specific location) and for complex reactions that combine and integrate specific skills. For example, for an infant to proceed from a lying down to a sitting position requires integration of muscles of the arm, which are used as levers; muscles of the abdomen, which lift the upper body; and muscles of the neck, which control the head.

Our genes dictate skill development during certain stages (i.e., toddlers learn to walk around 12 to 14 months of age), whereas our environment influences its timing (e.g., some infants are able to walk by 9 months and others not until 18 months, but despite variations, they all do walk eventually).

Infants and Toddlers. By age 6 months, infants can hold up their heads while sitting, roll over from front to back and from back to front, and push themselves up on their arms. By age 9 months, infants are able to use their legs by holding on and standing. There is evidence that the American Academy of Pediatrics (2013a) recommendation to put infants to sleep on their back is associated with a delayed onset of crawling, which can be remedied by encouraging "tummy time" to allow infants to strengthen their muscles. By 18 to 24 months, toddlers can walk forward alone, walk backward, jump, dance, run, stand on one leg with aid, bend over to pick up something on the floor, and ascend and descend stairs leading with the same foot initially and then alternating feet.

Delays in gross motor ability of infants are indicated when by 9 months they do not have proper flexion; favor one side; cannot roll, sit with support, or bear weight on their legs; and retain certain reflexes. Similarly, signs of development delay include an inability to crawl, right oneself, or sit without supports by age 12 months. Gross motor delays in toddlers are present when they do not have a normal gait for walking (i.e., heel to toe) and drool excessively at 24 months. Preschoolers demonstrate gross motor delays when at 36 months of age they show clumsiness, inability to jump, and problems with using stairs. Fine motor delays in infants are present after 6 months when they keep their hands in a fisted position, after 9 to 10 months when they cannot grasp or bring items to the mouth or midline/center of the body, and by 12 months when they cannot self-feed.

Early Childhood. Gross motor skills are affected by a shift in the child's center of gravity and change in body size, allowing the young child to coordinate upper and lower body movements into fluid actions. Preschoolers develop advanced skills in locomotion (e.g., run, hop, gallop, skip, jump), ball skills (e.g., throw, catch), and coordinated movements, particularly in conjunction with objects (e.g., ride a bike, climb a ladder). Fine motor skills for preschoolers focus on improvements in the care of oneself through patience and practice. The two main types of activities include self-help skills for feeding and dressing and eye–hand coordination required for playing sports and games.

It is important to distinguish between normative developmental progress and delayed or lack of progress in development in early childhood. Young children will show signs of awkwardness in many gross and fine motor activities when first developing these skills. For example, they often lose their balance when performing large motor actions, such as walking, jumping, and skipping. Additionally, they are seemingly incapable of coloring within the lines of predrawn figures (e.g., in coloring books) or restricting their writing to the paper itself, demonstrating difficulty with these fine motor activities. However, delays are indicated when children fail to make progress over time. For example, children should advance through stages of catching in which they initially pull their hands and arms toward their chests out-of-sync with the ball, but then refine this action in line with the ball as they learn to bring their hands together and anticipate the arrival of the ball.

Middle Childhood and Adolescence.   Gross motor skills are affected by improvement in reaction time due to advances in eye–hand coordination. Boys and girls are equal in overall physical capacity, but differ in development of four athletic skills. Boys are more advanced than girls in flexibility, which requires movements to be pliable, as their ligaments and increasing muscle strength makes children contortionists (e.g., hand stands, cartwheels), and in force (i.e., the ability to perform strong motions, such as kicking hard or throwing far). Girls are more advanced than boys in balance, which requires the ability to stand still or walk a narrow beam, and in agility (i.e., quick, accurate movements, as in jump rope and hopscotch). During adolescence, the body increases in size and muscle, with previously developed motor skills becoming fluid and dynamic. Compared to adolescent boys, adolescent girls' gains in gross motor are slow and gradual, probably owing to practice and societal (and parental) expectations for sport accomplishments (Fredricks & Eccles, 2002; Williams, Haywood, & Painter, 1996). Fine motor skills for school-age children involve improvements in manual dexterity—that is, the enhancement of eye–hand coordination, which involves a combination of hands, body, and mind and results in the proximodistal pattern of development in writing and drawing (girls are more advanced than boys).

Boys and girls progress at different rates through the various gross and fine motor skills. However, delays are indicated when these progressions are minimal or simply not achieved. For example, when the ball is pitched during kickball, children should be able to coordinate and anticipate the ball coming within the appropriate distance to their foot, aim, and then kick the ball with strength. The immature responses would include running up and passing it, missing it altogether, and kicking it softly. Another example would be failure to use alternating legs to climb or descend stairs.

Types of Play to Enhance Cortical Development

Six types of play allow practice and development of sensory, physical, social, and cognitive skills as the cortex become differentiated and specialized (Piaget, 1963).

- *Sensory* play allows the child to explore the pleasures of using senses (e.g., ears, eyes, hands). For example, children may mix mashed potatoes with gravy or listen and watch a musical mobile as it turns.
- *Mastery* play helps children learn new motor skills, but requires parents to serve as a safety net to protect them from hazards (especially when their skill level is low and enthusiasm is high). Children may jump over cracks, tie their shoelaces, or make a snack from marshmallows, chocolate pieces, and graham crackers.
- *Rough-and-tumble* play involves mimicking aggression within a play environment (e.g., wrestling, leap frogging over each other). This type of play encourages constructive, interactive gross motor skills while exploring one's social limits. The key to distinguishing between a "victim" of true aggression and a playmate in rough-and-tumble play is that a child in the former case is crying, whereas a child in the latter scenario is smiling. Hence, children learn to ascertain if the others involved are similarly enjoying the game or are instead upset.
- *Cognitive* or *practice* play allows the child to increase cognitive skill through repetitiveness involving intellectually interactive activities (e.g., Scrabble), creating something (e.g., puzzle, story), or playing with words (e.g., jokes, puns, riddles).
- *Symbolic* or *sociodramatic pretend* play allows children to act out everyday and imaginary roles for nonpresent objects (e.g., grocery shopping, princess tea party, pirates).
- *Competitive* play entails the use of games with rules, allowing the child to comply with the larger social world through structured activities (e.g., baseball, board games, Wii/Xbox).

As children become more active around the home, they are at-risk for accidental injuries and falls from furniture, stairs, or playground equipment. This is particularly true for children younger than four years, who do not yet have complete control over their bodies and often misjudge their movements and abilities. During exploration and play, infants and toddlers need constant supervision, as they may choke on almost any object that fits into their mouths, drink poisonous liquids, drown in the toilet or bathtub, be strangled on cords and wires, and get scalded by hot liquids in pots, cups, bathtub, or sink. Parents must child-proof inside (e.g., place objects out of reach) and outside (e.g., install fences and gates around pools) their homes, periodically adjusting these measures consistent with physical changes in the children (e.g., being able to stand or climb), to ensure their safety and welfare.

Risk factors associated with accidents include gender, temperament, and socioeconomic status. Boys are more likely than girls to be injured during play because their play often takes place outside rather than inside the home, they are likely to be active rather than passive, and they are less often supervised (Borse, Gilchrist, Dellinger, Rudd, Ballesteros, & Sleet, 2008). Children who have a "daredevil" temperament, regardless of gender, and those from disadvantaged neighborhoods, who must play within unsafe environmental conditions (e.g., broken glass, abandoned buildings), are also at risk for injury through accidents.

Body Growth and Changes

Children reach a variety of developmental milestones during infancy, childhood, and adolescence. Indeed, three distinct patterns of growth have been identified.

From birth to age 2 years, physical growth completes a rapid, then decelerating, pattern of development. The physical dimensions of infants include large, round heads and eyes, but small mouths and noses, which adults perceive to be "cute." Rapid weight gain occurs such that birth weight is essentially doubled by age 5 months, tripled by 12 months, and quadrupled by 24 months. A similar growth spurt in height occurs, such that birth length increases by 50% in the first year after birth and by 75% in the second year. Consequently, the toddler will continue to have a large head and chest, but the trunk gets broader and the legs get longer while the hands and feet remain small. Infants get 20 baby teeth, which first emerge around six months of age with the two front lower ones and finish with upper molars between 30 and 36 months.

In early and late childhood, growth follows a linear, steady increment pattern (approximately 2 inches in length and 5 pounds in weight per year) to puberty, resulting in body proportions that match head size. The face changes as well, particularly to make room for larger, permanent teeth after the loss of 8 baby teeth starting at approximately age 6 to 8 years, followed by loss of the final 12 between ages 10 and 13 years. In infancy and childhood, boys are somewhat heavier and taller than girls, but girls have slightly more fat and body mass than do boys. Growth spurts in late childhood are triggered by the combination of growth and sex hormones. Girls' growth spurt begins around age 9 or 10 years and ends at about 15 years, making girls taller and heavier than boys at this age. Boys begin their growth spurt around 11 or 12 years and end at 16 or 17 years, at which point they are taller and heavier than girls.

In adolescence, an accelerated pattern of growth cumulates in a sharp decrease as adult body size is reached. Physical changes in early adolescence include growth spurts (i.e., increasing 10 to 11 inches in height), increased muscle strength, and redistribution of body weight (gaining 50 to 75 pounds). Specifically, boys develop a higher lean-muscle-mass-to-height ratio than girls, who in turn accumulate a higher percentage of body fat than boys (Siervogel, Wisemandle, Maynard, Guo, Chumlea, & Towne, 2000). Adolescents appear awkward and disproportionate in their bodies due to accelerated growth in their legs, hands, and feet.

Routines and Pediatric Health Examinations

Children desire predictability, and establishing routines provides them with the emotional security of knowing what to expect every day (which in turn makes the parents' lives easier). Proper sleep and healthy nutrition are the keys to normative physical growth and development. Caregivers must schedule specific times for naps (from infancy through preschool) and bedtime as part of the daily routine. Children who do not get enough sleep may have delayed reaction and attention problems in school, headaches, and health problems (e.g., obesity, diabetes). Newborns sleep up to 18 hours per day, infants require up to 15 hours of sleep per day, toddlers and preschoolers up to 14 hours, school-age children up to 10 hours, and adolescents 8 to 9 hours.

Breastmilk is recommended by the American Academy of Pediatrics (2013b) as the only "food" provided to infants until 6 months of age, followed by the slow introduction of supplements (i.e., one fruit or vegetable every few days) to determine if there is a food allergy for infants aged 6 months to 1 year. Breastmilk is ideally suited for infants given it is digested easily and it provides the infant with antibodies to repel infection. Some research (Centers for Disease Control and Prevention [CDC], 2007; Jackson & Nazar, 2006; Quigley, Kelly, & Sacker, 2007) suggests that breastmilk promotes early immune system development, lowers the incidence of childhood illnesses (e.g., diarrhea, lower respiratory infections, colds, ear infections) and lowers the risk for serious diseases and health problems (e.g., type 2 diabetes, obesity, sudden infant death syndrome). Young children should avoid certain foods that are likely to induce choking (e.g., hot dogs, popcorn, grapes), contain bacteria (e.g., unpasteurized milk and fresh fruit juices), or trigger diseases (e.g., botulism in honey, Salmonella in raw eggs). A healthy diet for children and adolescents, according to the current recommendations of the U.S. Department of Agriculture, includes consumption of 6 ounces of grains (half of which should be whole-grain options), 2.5 cups of vegetables, 1.5 cups of fruit, 5 ounces of protein from meats or beans, and either 2 cups (if age 2 to 8) or 3 cups (if age 9 or older) of milk. Exercise and physical activity (e.g., riding bikes, running, playing sports) for 30 to 45 minutes per day are also recommended.

Well-child examinations screen children by monitoring growth and development changes in height, weight, head size, and chest size; ensuring that the senses are functioning properly; reviewing nutrition and basic needs with caregivers; and determining if the child has physical ailments or non-normative development (e.g., autism). Infants should undergo several physical examinations by their pediatricians during the first year of life; toddlers are examined a few times, and then yearly examinations are recommended for preschoolers through adolescents. Immunizations for typical childhood diseases (e.g., measles, mumps, rubella) are administered to infants and toddlers, with boosters being given in childhood and adolescence.

Despite immunizations, adequate sleep, good nutrition, and healthy physical activity, most children will experience respiratory illnesses (e.g., colds) and stomach infections with accompanying symptoms (e.g., vomit, diarrhea), especially in early childhood. This timing reflects the fact that from early childhood through adolescence, the immune system adapts to the environment and becomes resistant to common infections. Typical, highly contagious childhood illnesses include respiratory syncytial virus (RSV, a respiratory illness that can be deadly to infants), fifth disease (a viral infection causing signs and symptoms of fever, running nose, headache, and bright red cheek rash), hand/foot/mouth disease (a viral illness causing fever, skin rash, and mouth sores in infants and children younger than age 5), croup (a viral infection causing inflammation of the upper airways, leading to a barking cough; infants and children up to age 3 years are particularly vulnerable), scarlet fever (a bacterial infection that causes a rash on the face that spreads to the rest of the body, sore throat, and fever), and impetigo (a bacterial infection that causes blisters and sores on the face, neck, hands, and genitals). All of these diseases can spread quickly in daycare centers.

Children who do not consume a healthy diet may suffer from undernutrition and malnourishment, including the extreme forms of marasmus (a "wasting" disease characterized by the body breaking down fat and muscle to make energy), which is caused by ingesting too few nutrients, and kwashiorkor (a disease characterized by stunted growth, bloated bellies, and thin limbs), which is caused by ingesting too little protein. A reduction in protein, calorie, and/or iron intake is associated with behavioral problems, including listlessness, irritability, and passivity (Lozoff, 2007), as well as learning problems due to hunger interfering with attention, disrupting fine motor coordination, and increasing stress (Bryce, Coitinho, Darnton-Hill, Pelletier, & Pinstrup-Andersen, 2008; Fernald & Grantham-McGregor, 1998). Poor diet results in specific health problems, such as anemia, obesity, or death, but also impairs normative growth and general health, leading to short stature and small body parts and damage to the brain, heart, and liver (Muller & Krawinkel, 2005).

Normative Sexual Development

It is important for parents and professionals to be cognizant of which sexual behaviors exhibited by infants, children, and adolescents are typical for their age and which are not. Adults who discover that youths (either alone, as in masturbation, or together) are engaged in sexual behaviors might wonder whether these actions are part of normative sexual exploration or are a signal that sexual abuse has occurred. Initial responses often include shock or anger, but these reactions should be suppressed while the adult assesses the child and the behavior.

Three components must be considered when evaluating the appropriateness of sexual behaviors:

- Like any behavior, sexuality develops in stages. Parents should ask themselves, "Was the expressed behavior consistent with the child's developmental stage?"
- A child's expression of sexuality will be filtered through the lens of his or her family's beliefs and behaviors (Gil & Johnson, 1993). Some families may have a lax attitude toward privacy, whereas others have a heightened one (e.g., no nudity). Similarly, some families will not expose their children to media containing sexualized content or discuss sex, whereas others will allow sexualized content exposure and/or have open dialogues about sex. Parents should ask themselves, "Was the expressed behavior consistent within our family's restrictions?"
- The context in which sexual behaviors are expressed must be examined, as it will have a bearing on their appropriateness (Kaeser, 2010). For example, there are

public settings in which curiosity and body exploration are natural, such as in the changing room before entering the pool, which often entails full or partial nudity, whereas other environments, such as the playground, do not normally stimulate children's interest and investigation of body parts. Parents should ask themselves, "Was the expressed behavior conditional on or prompted by the environmental cues?"

Stages of Development

Birth to Age 3 years. Infants, toddlers, and two-year-olds are curious about their bodies and will not only explore them, but will also be interested in touching other people's bodies. It is not unusual for children who have been nursed to seek comfort, after being weaned, by reaching down their mothers' clothing to touch their breasts. Boys are able to have penile erections (and have since the fetal period), and it would not be unusual for them to stimulate themselves for pleasure or for them to awaken with an erection. Whenever the child has an opportunity to touch himself, such as during diaper changes or when wearing loose clothing, he will do so. Girls are able to have vaginal lubrication and will also stimulate their vulvas for pleasure by rubbing themselves with their hands or against a soft object (e.g., stuffed animal).

Children will talk about their private areas, using the terms they have been taught. It is advisable that they learn the appropriate names for these body parts, such as breasts, anus, penis, and vagina, so they can use terms commonly understood by the rest of society. They will be curious about the differences between boys and girls, and parents should explain in simple terms the functions that genitals serve (e.g., elimination of body waste, pregnancy, birth). It is recommended that parents teach their children societal norms and anti-abuse measures, such as touching one's own genitals should be done in private, not in public, and that they have control over their body; specifically, parents should indicate that no one else should be touching their privates (outside of normative caregiving routines and pediatric check-ups). Children should not be made to feel ashamed of or guilty about their sexual desires, which are rudimentary (i.e., sensual) at this stage.

Preschoolers (Ages 4 and 5 years). Preschoolers also experience erections and vaginal lubrication and engage in manual stimulation of their genitals for pleasure. Boys and girls at this age still play in mixed groups, although they may express preference for same-sex groups. It would not be unusual for boys and girls to act upon their curiosity by either visually or physically examining other children's bodies or playing games, such as "doctor" or "kissing" or "making babies." They will test their own body functions and want to watch others to see if their bodies function similarly. Preschoolers enjoy being naked and may experimentally insert fingers or small objects into their genital or anal openings, but will cease once this act induces pain. They engage in word play, particularly as related to bodily functions. It is important to reemphasize that their sexuality should be expressed in private, preferably at home, and that unwanted touches by others should be reported to the parents. Additionally, information about the body and its functions should be provided by the parents rather than by other children, strangers, and other adults in their lives.

Preschoolers often are ready to learn more about how babies are made, how they grow in the womb, and what the birth process involves, particularly if they are exposed to women who are visibly pregnant. Parents should provide information at the child's level of understanding and should wait until the child asks about the topic before introducing it.

At this time, preschoolers are confirming their understanding of gender roles by adhering rigidly to stereotypical beliefs of how men and women function in society. Their stubborn refusal to acknowledge that men and women have equal roles in society may be extremely frustrating to parents who try to teach their children an egalitarian approach to gender. In reality, this constraint is simply a limit of preschooler's cognitive ability that will dissipate with age and with multiple exposures to men and women serving in different roles that violate the stereotype (e.g., a male nurse, a female officer, a father cleaning the house, a mother mowing the lawn).

Grade Schoolers (Ages 6 to 8 years). When they reach elementary school age, children show a pronounced preference to be with children of their own gender and engage in "boundary adherence" whenever a child fails to socialize with his or her own sex group exclusively. The purpose of teasing violators is to reduce the risk that children will socialize with those of the opposite sex, which would lead to early sexual behavior. Children are aware of the social stigma and taboos of sex based on exposure to both peers (and similar-age relatives, such as siblings and cousins) and the media. Consequently, they are less likely to discuss sexuality with parents than with peers, particularly when their parents have been hesitant about discussing sex openly with their children. However, it is important that parents provide information about sex regardless of whether the child asks questions. Basic explanations about sexually transmitted infections (STIs) transmitted through oral, anal, and coital sexual activities, which may develop into sexually transmitted diseases (STDs) when symptoms are present (e.g., gonorrhea and AIDS); emotional relationships between adults; and sexual maltreatment by predators should be given. Additionally, children need to learn about puberty and the changes that their bodies will undergo (e.g., breast buds, pubic hair, menstruation) so that they will not be worried when this development occurs.

Grade school children are still curious about how other children's bodies work and may engage in mutual sexual exploration of same-sex peers, but not because of homosexual desires. Children may find acceptable outlets for touching others, such as holding hands, kissing, tickling, or wrestling, and engaging in conversations with peers about sexual behaviors, including dirty jokes. They may play-act what they have learned in movies or books with their peers as a way of exploring their own sexuality with those they trust. Children are able to understand various aspects of sex and intercourse within a relationship, aside from a couple's desire to reproduce. At this point, children have developed advanced self-concepts, including an understanding of and a preference for their own gender roles.

To develop a healthy sexuality, parents should explain to children of this age that some people are attracted to members of the opposite sex, whereas others prefer members of the same sex. It is important to emphasize that all orientations are acceptable. One way to introduce this topic would be to discuss gay marriage laws and their benefits. Another way is to discuss different types of families (e.g., those where the parents are homosexual and those where they are heterosexual), indicating that all of them have value and should be respected. The family's preferences for sex, marriage, and relationships may be provided in simple terms. However, support for the child's natural inclinations, particularly for gender orientation, is recommended.

Preadolescents (Ages 9 to 12 years). Preadolescents are cognizant about themselves as emerging adolescents and often feel confused and anxious about their sexuality, in both their thoughts and their behaviors. They are self-conscious about themselves, questioning whether what they experience sexually is normal, such as their desire to masturbate, and unsure of how to handle their impending puberty. Boys, in particular, may compare their penis sizes and discuss the penis's various functions, such as erection and ejaculation. Preadolescents understand the concept of sexual orientation and may use derogatory sexual remarks as a weapon against others. Parents need to explain that changes, including nocturnal emissions and menstruation, whatever the timing, are normal as the rates of sexual maturation vary (sometimes occurring early and sometimes emerging late).

At this point, preadolescents have developed advanced gender roles as boys or girls, discarding rigid stereotypes that contradict their own self-image (e.g., girls can play basketball). They make and understand sexual jokes and often pretend that they are aware of all aspects of sex. However, parents need to continue to provide open communication about sex with their preadolescents, while respecting their privacy. An important caveat here is that parents have the right to keep their children safe, even if that means monitoring Internet and cell phone use to prevent "sexting" between peers and to prevent adult predators from having access to their children. Parents should explain to their preadolescents that sexual relationships, particularly those involving intercourse, require a mature interchange that they are likely not quite ready to handle cognitively or emotionally. Conversations about abstinence are appropriate between parents and children in this age group, as are discussions about contraception, sexual feelings, pornography, and emotional attachments. Dating at this age may involve a different pairing each week and experimentation in sexual behaviors, include "petting or rubbing and touching each other's bodies, French kissing, and dry humping" (Boyce et al., 2006).

Adolescents (Ages 13 to 17 years). Adolescents have developed an understanding of themselves as sexual beings and at least a reasonable—if not always realistic—knowledge of the impact of sexual expression in their everyday lives. They have been taught by their parents and health teachers how to recognize positive and negative relationships and the consequences of unprotected sexual intercourse (e.g., pregnancy, STIs that may become STDs). Their beliefs about sex are a tenuous balance of their parents' views, values, and opinions and those of society as expressed through the media and peers. Adolescents may be capable of understanding their own sexual orientation, but parents may need to provide terms for what they are feeling, such as heterosexual, gay, lesbian, bisexual, or transgender. The family may wish to discuss (again) their own beliefs regarding sex, marriage, and relationships, while supporting the child's natural sexual orientation.

Toward the end of high school, many adolescents choose to have intimate and loving relationships despite their family's religious proscriptions against such behavior. Parents should make sure that their adolescent's knowledge about sex includes precautions for what to do after unprotected sexual intercourse (e.g., emergency contraception, STI/STD testing, alternatives for an unwanted pregnancy). It is also important to emphasize that the decision to have sexual intercourse should be mutual—that is, involving both partners without pressure or intention to exploit the other. Adolescents should be able to identify uncomfortable sexual situations and learn how to avoid and escape from them safely. Finally, parents should make adolescents aware of how their decision to have sexual intercourse can lead to pregnancy, which may negatively impact their future life options, particularly if the adolescent parents plan to attend college.

Puberty
During puberty, adolescents undergo significant changes in their bodies, which affect their thinking and understanding of themselves as sexual beings.

Physiological Changes in the Reproductive System. At puberty, an increase in hormones triggers the development of primary and secondary sex characteristics, resulting in physical changes in the body over the next two to six years (Susman & Rogol, 2004). Table 2-3 identifies the Tanner stages, which are used to assess puberty in boys and girls (Tanner, 1990). Primary sex characteristics directly involve the reproductive organs. A girl's ovaries produce estrogen, which causes the uterus and vagina to grow and body fat to increase to the requisite levels to prompt the onset of ovulation and menarche (first menstruation, occurring between ages 10½ and 14 years). A boy's testes produce androgens (e.g., testosterone, beginning at ages 9½ to 13½ years), causing them to enlarge as the scrotum reddens and thins (the first physical finding of puberty), followed by growth of the penis (ages 10½ to 14½ years) and spermarche (i.e., first ejaculation/ability to produce sperm cells, occurring between ages 12 and 16 years). Secondary sex characteristics do not involve the reproductive organs. Specifically, the release of sex hormones allows both boys and girls to grow underarm and pubic hair (ages 10 to 15 years for boys; ages 8 to 14 years for girls). Boys develop an Adam's apple, deeper adult male voices, and hair on their faces and chest (ages 12½ to 15½ years), and their bodies become more muscular (ages 13 to 17 years), resulting in leaner bodies and broader shoulders and chests (University of North Carolina at Chapel Hill, 2001). Girls form breast buds (the first external sign of puberty, at ages 8 to 13 years) that develop into breasts (ages 10 to 17 years); subsequently, their hips widen in preparation for child birth.

Timing of Puberty. The body changes due to puberty may occur at about the same time, earlier, or later than the majority of adolescents. Sex differences in timing are natural as girls mature earlier than do boys, showing external signs between ages 10 to 14 years as

Table 2-3 Tanner stages of puberty for boys and girls

Stage	Boys	Girls
1	Testes < 4 mL, long axis < 2.5 cm	Breast at papilla elevation
	Penis, no growth; infrequent erections spontaneously or by masturbation	Vagina, no growth
	Pubic hair: absent	Pubic hair: villus only
2	Testes 4 mL, long axis 2.5–3.2 cm	Breasts: enlarged areolae, palpable buds
	Penis, no or minimal growth	Pigmentation of labia
	Erections frequent, occasional ejaculation (by masturbation); fertile	Clitoral enlargement
	Pubic hair: minimal coarse, pigmented hair at base of penis	Pubic hair: minimal coarse, pigmented hair on labia
3	Testes 12 mL, long axis 3.6 cm	Breast contour elevated, areolae enlarge
	Penis increased length and width	
	Frequent ejaculation (masturbation or wet dreams)	
	Pubic hair: coarse, dark curly hair over pubis	Pubic hair: coarse, dark curly hair over mons pubis
	Gynecomastia (enlarged breast tissue) may occur	Axillary hair
	Voice breaks	
4	Testes length 4.1–4.5 cm	Breast areolae forms secondary mount on breast
	Penis increases length and width	
	Pubic hair: adult quality, not spread to medial thigh with perineum	Pubic hair: adult quality, not spread to medial thigh with perineum
	Axillary hair	
	Voice deepens	Menstruation
5	Testes length > 4.5 cm, 3 cm wide, 3 cm deep	Adult breast contour, areola recesses to general contour
	Penis mature size (average 5–7 inches)	
	Pubic hair: adult distribution spread to medial thigh with perineum	Pubic hair: adult distribution spread to medial thigh with perineum
	Facial hair on sides	
	Gynecomastia disappears	

Data from American College of Obstetricians and Gynecologists (2009). Tanner Staging. Tool Kit for Teen Care, 2nd ed.; Feingold, D. (1992). Pediatric endocrinology (pp. 9.16–9.19) *Atlas of Pediatric Physical Diagnosis* (2nd ed.). Philadelphia: W. B. Saunders.; Moses, S. (2013a). Female Tanner Stage. Family Practice Notebook. (2013a, 2013b); Tanner, J.M. (1990). Sequence, tempo, and individual variation in growth and development of boys and girls aged twelve to sixteen. In R. E. Muuss (Ed.), *Adolescent behavior and society: A book of readings* (pp. 39–56). NY: McGraw-Hill Publishing Co.

opposed to ages 12 to 16 years, respectively (Lee, Appugliese, Kaciroti, Corwyn, Bradley, & Lumeng, 2007, 2010). The well-documented decline in the age at which boys and girls in industrialized countries reach sexual maturity is likely the result of improvement in diet and health (Goldstein, 2011; Herman-Giddens, 2006; University of North Carolina at Chapel Hill, 2001). Researchers have also shown that timing of puberty is related to heredity, such that girls are likely to experience its onset at around the same time as did their mothers (Ersoy, Balkan, Gunay, Onag, & Egemen, 2005).

Timing of puberty may also differ due to ethnicity. Malina, Bouchard, and Bar-Or (2004) have reported that African American girls reached menarche by age 9 years, a year earlier than European American girls. A study by Herman-Giddens, Wang, and Koch (2001) indicated that the average ages of onset for genital growth and pubic hair, respectively, were 9.5 and 11.2 years for African American boys, 10.1 and 12 years for European American boys, and 10.4 and 12.3 years for Mexican American boys.

External signs of puberty exhibited prior to age eight years by girls and prior to age nine years by boys are labeled *precocious puberty*; however, medical intervention is not sought unless breast or pubic hair development occurs prior to age seven years in European American girls and age six years in African American girls or unless secondary sex characteristics occur prior to age nine years in boys (Kaplowitz, 2010). Failing to reach adult height is a serious consequence for these children (i.e., final heights may be less than 5 feet for girls and less than 5 feet 4 inches for boys). Girls who are heavier or have more body fat are likely to experience puberty earlier than their thin or average-weight peers (Lee et al., 2007). Tumors in the central nervous system or abnormalities of ovaries or testes or of hormones could also stimulate early puberty and are the most likely explanations of precocious puberty in boys, whereas no cause is found in most cases for girls.

Absence of increased testicular growth by age 14 years in boys or breast development by age 13½ years in girls is labeled *delayed puberty*. This condition occurs more commonly in boys than in girls. There is a concern for reduced bone density for these children (Itman, Wong, Hunyadi, Ernst, Jans, & Loveland, 2011). Most cases are due to constitutional delay, evidenced by delayed external signs in several family members. Other causes of puberty-onset delays include chronic medical conditions (e.g., diabetes), genetic conditions, organ problems (e.g., pituitary gland, ovaries, testes), and malnutrition. Delays in boys may also be due to exposure to endocrine-disrupting chemicals (e.g., plastics, paints, detergents), which damage cells (Itman et al., 2011), and to being overweight in comparison to their same-age peers (Lee et al., 2010).

Sexually Active Preadolescents and Adolescents

Preadolescents and adolescents in the United States are exposed to explicit, sexualized language, images, and story plots through radio, television shows, advertisements, music, movies, magazines, and the Internet. The media message repeatedly communicated to naïve juveniles is that casual, carefree, premarital and extramarital sexual gratification is normal. Yet, this notion often opposes their own family's and community's proscriptions against sexual encounters outside of marriage, leaving them trying desperately to cope with sexual desires without an adequate understanding of their sexuality or any preparation for dealing with it (Crockett, Raffaelli, & Moilanen, 2003). Moreover, the media conveniently portray positive consequences of promiscuity (i.e., enjoyment, status) while downplaying or simply omitting the physical and emotional realities of sexual encounters, such as pregnancy, STIs/STDs, and regret (Beaver, 2001). An examination of the types of sexual activities engaged in by preadolescents and adolescents sheds light on some ways that they resolve these contradicting messages.

Penile–Vaginal Sexual Intercourse.   Although there is little research involving preadolescents in middle school (e.g., San Francisco Youth Risk Behavior Survey [SFYRBS], 1997), the overall initiation rate of sexual intercourse reported was low, ranging from 4% to 17% and had not varied from 1991 to 1997. A two-year longitudinal investigation (1994–1996) was conducted using predominantly minority (51% African American, 30% Latino American), inner-city New Jersey students. Santelli et al. (2003) found that sexual intercourse was initiated for 13% of adolescents between the beginning and end of the seventh grade and for another 15% between the end of seventh grade and eighth grade. Cross-sectional studies suggest that this rate more accurately reflects the eighth graders' involvement rather than that of the younger adolescents (de Rosa et al., 2010).

Both gender and ethnicity influence rates for initiating sexual intercourse. A higher proportion of boys than girls initiate coital activity, according to surveys administered in Los Angeles (13% versus 5%; de Rosa et al., 2010) and San Francisco (17% versus 9%; SFYRBS, 1997). Moreover, rates for coital activity for predominantly minority students (Latino American, African American) showed a gradual increase from sixth to eighth grades (4% to 19%) in both the national and the Los Angeles studies (Albert, Brown, & Flanigan, 2003; de Rosa et al., 2010). Rates were higher for male than female minority, inner-city adolescents in New York and New Jersey, with 52% to 75% of boys and 20% to 28% of girls indicating that they were sexually active by the end of eighth grade (O'Donnell, O'Donnell, & Stueve, 2001).

Not surprisingly, penile–vaginal intercourse rates for adolescents in high school are higher than those for preadolescents in middle school. Although 13% of adolescents prior to age 15 years indicated they had engaged in coital activity, this proportion rose to 61% by age 17, 70% by age 19 years, and 75% by age 20 years (Abma, Martinez, & Copen, 2010; Chandra, Martinez, Mosher, Abma, & Jones, 2005; Martinez, Chandra, Abma, Jones, & Mosher, 2006; Mosher, Chandra, & Jones, 2005). In the United States, between 2006 and 2008, fewer than half of high school students (about 42%) reported having had penile–vaginal sexual intercourse (Abma et al., 2010), which is actually a decline from the 48% reported in 1989 (Maticka-Tyndale, 2008) and the 54% reported in 1991 (Lindberg, Jones, & Santelli, 2008). A comparison of rates of initial coital activity by Canadian high school students indicated either little variation or a slight decrease over time from 2003 to 2005, revealing that approximately one-third of 15- to 17-year-olds and two-thirds of 18- to 19-year-olds were sexually active (Boyce et al., 2006).

Reports of sex differences in the initiation of sexual intercourse by high school students have been mixed. Some studies have shown no significant differences between boys and girls on surveys administered in the 1990s (Leigh, Morrison, Trocki, & Temple, 1994). In contrast, sex differences have been reported in terms of initiating sexual intercourse in national studies of adolescents aged 12 to 19 years, at least at the younger ages (e.g., SFYBS, 1997). According to Child Trends Databank (2012, Appendix 1) using statistics from 1991 to 2011, a higher proportion of male than female ninth graders were sexually active; by 10th grade, however, the proportions of sexually active male and female adolescents were basically the same. Leigh et al. (1994) also reported gender differences in initiation rates reported by adolescents aged 12 to 17 years in 1990 (see Table 2-4). More recently, Herbenick et al. (2010) indicated that gender differences were not present in adolescents ages 14–15 years (10%) or 16–17 years (30%), although a higher proportion of 18- and 19-year-old girls than boys reported being sexually active (62% versus 53%).

Ethnic group differences in sexual intercourse have also been reported. According to a national survey (Leigh et al., 1994), a higher proportion of African American than Latino American and European American high school students had sexual intercourse (40%, 24%, and 25%, respectively). In a national study from 2006 to 2008, Chandra, Mosher, and Copen (2011) indicated that a higher proportion of African American (55%, 60%) than Latino American (both 48%) and European American (both 42%) girls and boys aged 15–19 years engaged in penile–vaginal sexual intercourse. Although this conclusion is speculative, higher rates of sexual intercourse for African American adolescents may be related to their early pubertal maturation.

Anal Sexual Intercourse. Low rates of anal intercourse have been reported among adolescents, but sexual experimentation seems to be linked to prior coital activity. Overall, 10% to 11% of adolescents ages 15–19 years reported ever engaging in anal sexual intercourse according to surveys from 1991 to 2001 (CDC, 2002; Lindberg et al., 2008), whereas at-risk 15- to 21-year-olds reported anal sex rates of 16% in the last three months (Lescano et al., 2009). Of the adolescents who indicated they had already engaged in penile–vaginal intercourse, 21% reported having anal intercourse, compared to only 1% of virgins (Lindberg et al., 2008; Schuster, Bell, & Kanouse, 1996). Herbenick et al. (2010) reported low rates for boys engaging in anal sex as receiver (1% of 14- to 15-year-olds, 1% of 16- to 17-year-olds, and 4% of 18- to 19-year-olds) and as inserter (3% of 14- to 15-year-olds, 6% of 16- to 17-year-olds, and 6% of 18- to 19-year-olds).

Table 2-4 Proportions of male and female high school students who initiated sexual intercourse

Gender	12-year-olds	13-year-olds	14-year-olds	15-year-olds	16-year-olds	17-year-olds
Boy	5%	6%	24%	29%	48%	67%
Girl	0%	3%	3%	37%	48%	56%

Data from Leigh, B. C., Morrison, D. M., Trocki, K., & Temple, M. T. (1994). Sexual behavior of American adolescents: Results from a U. S. national survey. *Journal of Adolescent Health,15*(2),117–125.

Other Common, Noncoital Sexual Behaviors. In addition to sexual intercourse, preadolescents and adolescents participate in a variety of noncoital sexual behaviors. The most common activity is *erotic fantasy*, which allows adolescents to prepare for potential intimate interactions while learning what arouses them (Katchadourian, 1990). Coles and Stokes (1985) reported that 72% of 13- to 18-year-old adolescents engaged in sexual fantasizing.

Masturbation is another typical private (albeit not exclusively, as it is also done alongside a partner in mutual masturbation) behavior performed by both boys and girls (Coles & Stokes, 1985; Leitenberg, Detzer, & Srebnik, 1993) and is considered to be a safe outlet for sexual exploration (Katchadourian, 1990). Masturbation may be combined with erotic fantasy, sex talk by phone or computer, and watching or reading erotica. Sex toys (e.g., dildos, vibrators) may also be used to stimulate sex organs and assist in reaching orgasm. Herbenick et al. (2010) found that rates of masturbation reported by male adolescents were higher than by female adolescents in the United States (Table 2-5).

For preadolescents and adolescents, intimacy is often expressed by *making out*, which includes kissing, heavy petting (rubbing bodies together with or without clothing), and manual genital stimulation. Of minority adolescents aged 14 to 17 years who were virgins, 86% indicated they had kissed, 47% had rubbed their bodies together, and 16% had engaged in genital touching (Miller, Norton, Curds, Hill, Schvaneveldt, & Young, 1997).

Preadolescents experience these types of interactive noncoital activities at lower rates than do high school adolescents. A U.S. study of 9th to 12th graders showed that of almost 50% self-identifying virgins, 30% of them reported engaging in either heterosexual masturbation of or by a partner (Schuster et al., 1996). According to Boyce et al., there was an increase in Canadian juveniles who reported having engaged in French kissing (i.e., open mouth with tongues inserted) and touching, both above and below the waist, from grades 7 to 11 (Figure 2-2). Gender differences reported initially in grade 7, however, were absent in the older two grades.

Table 2-5 Masturbation rates reported by male and female adolescents ages 14 to 19 in the past year and past month

Gender	14/15-year-olds	16/17-year-olds	18/19-year-olds
Past year			
Boy	62%	75%	81%
Girl	40%	45%	60%
Past month			
Boy	43%	58%	62%
Girl	24%	26%	26%

Data from Herbenick, D. et al. (2010). Sexual behavior in the United States: Results from a national probability sample of men aged 14-94. *Journal of Sexual Medicine, 7,* 255-265.

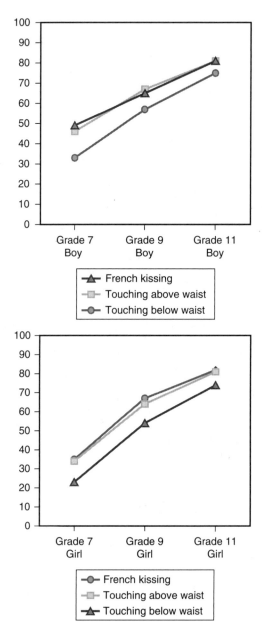

Figure 2-2 Proportion of male and female preadolescents and adolescents engaging in interactive noncoital activities at least once in their lives

Data from Boyce, W., Doherty, M., MacKinnon, D., & Fortin, C. (2003). Canadian youth, sexual health and HIV/AIDS study: Factors influencing knowledge, attitudes and behaviors. Council of Ministers of Education, Canada. Retrieved from http:// www .cmec.ca/publications /aids

Oral sex has become a common means of sexual expression among adolescents. Anecdotal and media articles in newspapers (by Jarrell in *The New York Times*, 2000; by Stepp and by Mundy in *The Washington Post*, 1999 and 2000, respectively) and magazines (by Franks in *Talk*, 2000) alerted the public that middle school students were actively engaging in oral sex by seventh grade, a trend that continued through high school. However, little research has examined oral sex by middle school children or considered whether they initiated it prior to coital activity. De Rosa et al. (2010) reported that 8% of middle school students surveyed at 14 urban, Southern California public schools had oral sex, of whom 5% also had sexual intercourse.

A 1980s survey administered to 13- to 18-year-olds revealed that 20% engaged in oral sex (Coles & Stokes, 1985). An examination of only boys ages 15 to 19 years reported oral sex rates increased slightly from 1988 to 2002 (44% to 51%; Child Trends Databank, 2013; Gates & Sonenstein, 2000). Research has shown that slightly less than half of 15- to 17-year-olds and almost two-thirds of 18- to 19-year-olds have engaged in oral sex (Lindberg et al., 2008). These results suggest that U.S. high school students engage more often in fellatio and cunnilingus than in penile–vaginal intercourse (Halpern-Felsher, Cornell, Kropp, & Tschann, 2005; McKay, 2004). Boyce et al. (2003) reported that Canadian adolescents also engaged in oral sex more often than coital activities according to responses by 9th (30% versus 21%) and 11th graders (52% versus 43%).

Rates of oral sex reported in the 1980s and 1990s for high school–age adolescents who self-identified as virgins ranged from 10% to 24% (Gates & Sonenstein, 2000; Schuster et al., 1996), but were still lower than for nonvirgins, which were about 82% (Newcomer & Udry, 1985). Nonvirgins were also more likely both to give and receive oral sex (69%, 82%) than were virgins (14%, 20%). Sex differences were also reported. Based on its 2006–2010 survey data of 15- to 19-year-olds, Child Trends Databank (2013) reported that 17% of male adolescent virgins and 13% of female adolescent virgins versus 89% of the male nonvirgins and 84% of the female nonvirgins reported having engaged in oral sex. Girls were more likely than boys to report providing oral sex (39% versus 35%), whereas boys were more likely than girls to report receipt of oral sex (47% versus 42%), with this disparate trend found regardless of virginity status (see similar results in Lindberg et al., 2008).

Rates of oral sex between high school students of the same gender have also been examined. Herbenick et al. (2010) reported similar rates of oral sex acts within each age group for girls and boys, although gender differences in experimentation with this activity showed the highest rates were for girls at ages 16–17 years and for boys at ages 18–19 years (Table 2-6). Ethnic differences in the rates for oral sex have also been indicated. According to Child Trends Databank (2013), no differences were found in receiving oral sex, but a lower proportion of African American males and females than European American or Latino American adolescents provided oral sex (Figure 2-3). This effect may be moderated by virginity status and gender. Chandra et al. (2011) reported a higher proportion of European American than African American or Latino American 15- to 19-year-old female

Table 2-6 Rates of oral sex acts by age group

Sexual activity	14- and 15-year-olds	16- and 17-year-olds	18- and 19-year olds
Provide cunnilingus	2%	7%	2%
Receive cunnilingus	1%	5%	4%
Perform fellatio	1%	2%	4%
Receive fellatio	1%	3%	6%

Data from Herbenick, D. et al. (2010). Sexual behavior in the United States: Results from a national probability sample of men aged 14–94. *Journal of Sexual Medicine, 7*, 255–265.

virgins (10%, 5%, and 2%, respectively), but not male virgins (10%, 8%, and 6%, respectively) engaged in oral sex.

Pregnancy.   According to the CDC, the live birth rate in 2010 for U.S. adolescents ages 15 to 19 years was 34.4 per 1000, which represents a decline from 2009 of 12% for 15- to 17-year-olds and 9% for 18- to 19-year-olds, with the latter accounting for two-thirds of all adolescent pregnancies (Hamilton, Martin, & Ventura, 2010, 2011, 2012; Kost & Henshaw, 2012; Kost, Henshaw, & Carlin, 2010). The combination of increased use of birth control, particularly condoms (rates rose from 46% in 1995 to 63% in 2005 and remain stable; Child

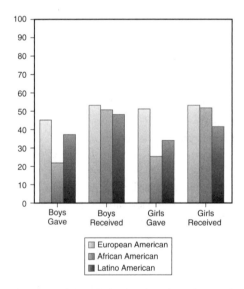

Figure 2-3 Proportion of male and female high school students who gave and received oral sex by ethnicity

Data from Child Trends Databank (2013). Oral sex behaviors among teens. Retrieved from: http://www.childtrends.org /?indicators=oral-sex-behaviors-among-teens

Trends Databank, as cited in Welti, Wildsmith, & Manlove, 2011), and decreased rates of penile–vaginal sexual intercourse is credited for this decline in teenage births (Martinez, Copen, & Abma, 2011; Santelli, Lindberg, Finer, & Singh, 2007). Teenage girls who become pregnant are more likely to give birth (57%) than to abort the fetus (27%) or to miscarry it (14%), even though almost 82% of these pregnancies were unplanned (Hardman, 2012).

Pregnancy rates in 2010 differed by ethnicity, such that 57% of adolescent pregnancy and births were to non-Hispanic African American and Hispanic/Latino American girls, particularly those who were economically disadvantaged (Hamilton et al., 2011). In contrast, the lowest rates of live births were to non-Hispanic European American girls (24%) and to Asian/Pacific Islander girls (11%). As shown in Figure 2-4, the live birth rate has been declining each year and the 2010 rates are the lowest in the decade.

Sexually Transmitted Diseases (STDs). Sexual relations—whether vaginal, anal, or oral—may result in contraction of diseases through the transmission of bacteria (e.g.,

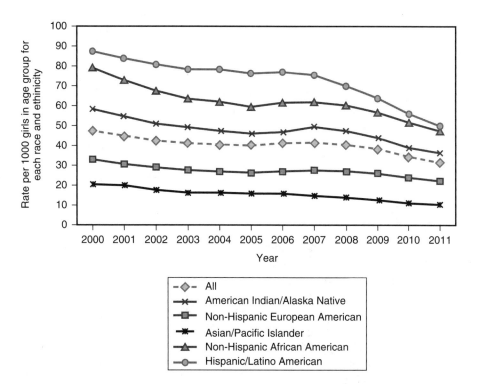

Figure 2-4 Birth rates per 1000 girls aged 15–19 years, by race and Hispanic ethnicity, 2000–2011

Data from Hamilton B. E., Martin J. A., & Ventura S. J. (2011). Births: Preliminary data for 2010. National Vital Statistics Reports, 60(2): Table S-2; Hamilton, B. E., Martin, J. A. & Ventura, S. J. (2012). Births: Preliminary data for 2011. *National Vital Statistics Reports, 61*(5). Table 2.

gonorrhea, syphilis, chlamydia, chancroid) and viruses (e.g., genital warts, herpes, hepatitis B, human immunodeficiency virus [HIV], molluscum contagiosum) in semen, vaginal fluid, or other body fluids. In addition, parasites (e.g., crab lice, scabies, Trichomonas vaginalis) can be transferred through body/body (i.e., fluids) and body/surface contact vis-á-vis bedding, clothing, toilet seats, damp towels, or other means. Antibiotics can cure bacterial, but not viral, infections.

Almost half of STDs diagnosed annually involve adolescents and young adults aged 15 to 24 years, even though they represent only one-fourth of the sexually active population (CDC, 2005). Similar STD rates of approximately 40% were indicated for a group of sexually active girls aged 14 to 19 years (Forhan et al., 2008). STDs are associated with other health problems, such as damage to organs (e.g., heart, kidneys, brain), pelvic inflammatory disease (PID) in women, and epididymis (infection in tissue surrounding testicles) in men. Both PID and epididymis also increase infertility and, if left untreated, may cause death.

Recent evidence has linked human papillomavirus (HPV) transmission during oral sex to throat cancer, with an increased risk of oropharyngeal cancer being incurred by those persons with more than six partners (D'Souza et al., 2007). Risk factors for all STDs include number of sexual partners, gender, type of sexual activity, and use of barrier protection (e.g., condom, "dental dam").

Many adolescents mistakenly believe that oral sex not only allows them to remain "virgins," but also is safer than intercourse in terms of health risks (e.g., STIs/STDs). According to Schuster et al. (1996), 9% of adolescent virgins reported engaging in heterosexual fellatio with ejaculation and 10% engaged in cunnilingus without barrier protection. According to Halpern-Felsher (2008), this common misperception contributes to adolescents' reduced disclosure of STI/STD; rates of disclosure among those who engaged in oral sex only was approximately 2%, compared to 5% for those having only vaginal sex and 13% for those having both vaginal and oral sex.

Cognitive Development

This section focuses on normative cognitive development in infants, children, and adolescents. Cognition refers to our ability to engage in linguistic tasks (communicating through verbal and nonverbal means) and mental efforts (e.g., thinking, knowing, judging, comprehending, planning, problem solving, remembering, storytelling). Thus, cognitive development encompasses growth in one's ability to do all of these tasks, in simple ways initially, and then in more complex ways over time and with experience. The descriptions that follow combine concepts from various cognitive developmental theories (Chomsky, Skinner, information processing, Piaget, Spelke, Vygotsky) that seek to explain the processes children use to function in the world.

Language

Language communicates our needs, desires, and cognitions in complex ways, connecting humans across centuries to accumulated knowledge in socially and culturally appropriate contexts. The interaction view proposes that language is learned through a combination of nativistic and behavioral components (Tomasello, 2006). Consistent with Chomsky's (1968) notions, this perspective proposes that infants are biologically prewired to learn language because they are born with a language acquisition device (LAD). The LAD utilizes a "universal grammar," enabling children inherently to detect sounds and to understand grammar from any spoken language in the world. Support for this capacity is demonstrated by the similar ways in which children acquire language across cultures, their capacity to speak any language (i.e., initially produce sounds from all languages), their production of unique sentences never before heard or spoken, and the types of mistakes they make in applying rules in the language when learning to speak. Although a physical area in the brain corresponding to the LAD has never been found, scientists have identified regions in the brain associated with language—Wernicke's area (which controls written and spoken language comprehension) and Broca's area (which controls speech production)—that work with other cortical regions for producing and hearing language (e.g., parietal lobes for voluntary motor functions for tongue and lips, temporal lobes for listening). Language acquisition is learned in social contexts, with caregivers demonstrating sensitivity toward this process by simplifying the language used, moving close to the child (within 12 inches), and speaking in a high-pitched voice to match communication to the perceptual qualities of the infant (called child-directed speech). The behavioral approach introduced by Skinner (1991, originally 1957), although not considered adequate on its own, does explain that despite the capacity to speak any language, children learn the language they hear spoken in their environment, and their ability to communicate effectively is also environmentally controlled through caregivers' support and involvement within social interactions (Gathercole & Hoff, 2007).

Infants acquire receptive language skills (e.g., the ability to discriminate speech sounds by age four months, involving Wernicke's area) before productive language skills, meaning that they understand the message before they are capable of producing it (approximately 10 to 12 months of age, involving Broca's area). Preverbal communication involves crying (which communicates infant states, such as hunger), cooing and laughing (around 2 to 4 months), gesturing, such as pointing (around 6 months), and babbling (vocalizing sounds used in any language at around 4 to 6 months and becoming specialized to the language spoken in the home at 10 to 12 months). According to Kuhl (2007), until six months of age, infants are capable of learning any language, but thereafter their focus is on learning the language spoken around them. Verbal communication is initiated in one-year-olds with holophrases (i.e., use of one word to mean many things, such as "dada" refers to the child's own father, a man, give me juice, and so on). It progresses in toddlers at 18 months to two-word phrases (e.g., all gone, ma bath), followed at age two years by telegraphic speech (i.e., combines three or more words, but only basic ones without "extras," such as "Where daddy go?"). Language development culminates in the preschool years (three through six years) with multi-word sentences that may or may not be grammatically correct (e.g., "I goed home").

Children's vocabulary increases rapidly between ages one and two years through two main processes: fast mapping and principle of contrast. Fast mapping could occur after a single exposure. It involves the child guessing the name of the object with correction by an older child or adult, or a child pointing to an object with the name provided by an older child or adult (Heibeck & Markman, 1987). Fast mapping includes syntactic bootstrapping, in which children acquire word meanings through syntax (Gleitman, 1990), and semantic bootstrapping, in which children learn how to organize new actions or objects through semantics (Pinker, 1984). When there is a systematic difference between two objects or their interpretations, the child uses the principle of contrast by relying on the known word to figure out the unknown name of an object, without being explicitly told by the adult (Clark, 1987). For example, a child might be asked to bring a pen to the adult, forcing the child to choose between two objects, a pen and pencil, on a table. The child already knows what a pencil is, so the unknown object by default must be a pen.

Toddlers are able to comprehend approximately 50 words by 13 months, but do not demonstrate a vocabulary spurt until they are 18 months, at which time they speak about 50 words (Menyuk, Liebergott, & Schultz, 1995). By age 24 months, they speak and understand about 200 to 300 words (Bloom, Lifter, & Broughton, 1985). Expressive and receptive language grows to about 1000 words by age 36 months and 3000 words by age 48 months (Miller & Paul, 1995; Reed, 2005). Children in the United States accumulate nouns—usually the names of objects—prior to verbs (Woodward, Markman, & Fitzsimmons, 1994).

Parents foster language development in their children in a variety of ways. First, adults speak to infants and young children in child-directed speech (i.e., high-pitched, exaggerated, and simple ways) to increase the likelihood that they will attend to the message because it matches the child's sensory and cognitive abilities (Fernald & Morikawa, 1993). Second, adults provide names for objects, particularly when children point to them (Rowe & Goldin-Meadow, 2009). Third, adults talk to children during the course of their experiences (e.g., grocery shopping, going to the zoo, diaper changes)—before, during, and afterward—and engage children's participation in linguistically meaningful events, such as reading books, singing songs, and playing games. Fourth, adults use expansion, adding details to what children state as part of the conversation (e.g., a child states, "Shoes," and the parent responds, "You have blue shoes"). Finally, adults "recast" what children say, correcting the grammar indirectly within the conversation, as in the parent responding to a child who states, "I goed home," with the sentence, "Yes, you went home" (Karmiloff & Karmiloff-Smith, 2001). Children's systematic errors, such as over-regularization of nouns (e.g., gooses) and verbs (e.g., goed), paradoxically signify an advancement in their language skills, as such errors demonstrate that they understand the grammatical rule as it applies to "regular" words, but mistakenly apply it to irregular words.

Signs of Developmental Delay
Communication disorders affect listening, speaking, and use of language in social communication. Language development problems stem from congenital disabilities or from

neurologic and physical symptoms resulting from childhood illness (e.g., chronic ear infections). An *articulation disorder* (a phonological problem) is diagnosed when children's ability to produce speech sound or phonemes accurately emerges later than is normally developed (e.g., substituting one sound for another). Specifically, the child may be omitting, substituting, distorting, or adding certain sounds at the beginning, middle, or end of the word. This problem can be identified by a speech pathologist, who can also provide the child with therapy to improve intelligibility of the child's speech. *Voice disorder*, either phonation or resonance, refers to problems involving abnormalities in the vocal mechanism and can be resolved through surgery or reconditioning of the voice through therapy. *Fluency disorder* is a problem in which the child repeats sounds (e.g., stuttering) while attempting to find a particular word or idea.

Language impairment problems occur when the development of linguistic skills progresses more slowly than expected, such that the child is using "immature" communication (e.g., telegraphic speech rather than complete sentences). *Expressive language disorder* is diagnosed when the child has learned few vocabulary words and has difficulty using tenses correctly, remembering words, or producing sentences of appropriate length and complexity for their age. *Receptive-expressive language disorder* is diagnosed when both processes are substantially below performance according to nonverbal intelligence measures and the child has difficulty understanding words and sentences.

Cognitive Processes

Cognition involves a variety of processes, including paying attention, knowing, planning, problem solving, decision making, and remembering, that contribute to children's thinking, learning, playing, storytelling, and participating in their world.

Attention

Attention refers to the ability to focus on a particular event, to the exclusion of all others (i.e., selective attention) over a period of time (i.e., sustained attention). Two cognitive functioning processes influence attention: processing efficiency and automaticity. Processing efficiency refers to the speed and accuracy associated with performance; cognitive tasks that are new or complex require a great deal of effort, such that their performance will be slow and inaccurate. Automaticity refers to the ability to perform actions using few cognitive resources or effort (i.e., automatically, without thinking), allowing the person to concentrate on other activities (e.g., walking, riding a bicycle). Attention is interdependent with other cognitive processes—notably, perception and memory. Individual differences in sustaining and focusing attention are a function of genetics and parent–child interactions and will influence the person's cognitive, academic, and social competence (Dilworth-Bart, Khurshid, & Vandell, 2007; Posner, Rothbart, & Sheese, 2007).

Newborns are innately attuned to high-contrast objects (e.g., faces, stripes), whereas young infants show a preference for familiar objects and older infants attend to novel, complex objects as an index of brain development and superior scanning skills. The ability to attend to and process information efficiently and with automaticity increases from early childhood through adolescence (López, Menez, & Hernández-Guzmán, 2005). Preschoolers have short attention spans, such that they can devote approximately 15 minutes of sustained attention to a task. Elementary school children gradually become better at focusing on more than one task at a time, selecting important aspects that must be addressed, splitting their attention when necessary, and ignoring distractions to complete their work. Adolescents have the capacity to pay attention for long periods of time, allowing them to stay focused and to complete complex school assignments.

Attention-deficit disorder (ADD) and *attention-deficit/hyperactivity disorder* (ADHD) are diagnoses given to children and adolescents who have extreme difficulty sustaining attention to information, following instructions, completing tasks due to problems in organization and errors, and controlling their impulsivity and behavior. These children have difficulty functioning at home and in school, requiring behavioral and/or medical interventions. Impulsivity disorders also disrupt effective parenting; that is, parents' difficulty in rearing a hard-to-manage child is the cause—not the result—of poor parenting (Kutscher, 2008).

Knowledge

Our knowledge base is formed in infancy and develops over our lifetime as we learn about our world and participate in activities. Two theories explain how we gain knowledge.

Piaget used the concept of a "schema" to explain the acquisition of knowledge; a schema provides a cognitive framework for categorizing concepts, objects, and experiences as new information is encountered in the environment. For example, when an infant finds or is given a new item (e.g., a block), information about it will be compared to current schemas (e.g., banging schema for toys). If there is a match (e.g., blocks are toys), this new information will be assimilated (i.e., blocks can be banged). New objects (e.g., raw eggs) for which no match is available (e.g., banging schemas for toys) will cause disequilibrium or confusion to occur (e.g., banging eggs breaks them), and the child will need to form a new schema (e.g., patting schema for nontoys) using a process called accommodation (e.g., eggs can be patted) to return to a state of equilibrium (evenness). The aforementioned processes are part of an overall process called adaptation that is employed throughout the lifespan, resulting in the expansion of our knowledge base. In general, older children and adolescents demonstrate broader knowledge bases typically developed over time and through multiple experiences; however, expertise for a domain (e.g., math, science) is not bound by age. Researchers have shown that even young children, when they have an interest in a particular area (e.g., dinosaurs, chess), have learned to organize information in sophisticated ways and thereby become experts (Chi, 1978; Schneider & Bjorklund, 1992).

Information processing theories offer a different view of knowledge acquisition and storage. Such a perspective proposes that declarative ("know that") and procedural ("know how") knowledge is stored in long-term memory (Cohen & Squire, 1980; Tulving, 1972). Semantic long-term memory, which involves conscious thought, stores declarative information about the world (e.g., words and their meanings, general knowledge such as "Albany is the capital of New York" and "lions are animals") gained from a variety of sources, including personal experiences, conversations about others' experiences, informal and formal instruction and training, books, electronic sources, and media. Procedural long-term memory, which is unconscious and automatic, stores procedural information on how to perform actions (e.g., play the piano, ride a bicycle, brush one's hair). Changes in knowledge, according to Klees, Olson, and Wilson (1988, p. 153), may be conceptualized as "accretion (the accumulation of facts), tuning (the gradual modification of old structures to reflect new information) and restructuring (devising new structures to represent new and old information)." As a result, children have access to complex and well-organized knowledge that can be used to reevaluate objects, situations, and relationships between concepts.

Nelson (1986) proposed that general event representations, which are derived from children's own experiences, consist of slots and categories corresponding to the roles actors play, the props used, and the required and optional actions making up the event. Event schemas form the foundation of event knowledge, representing the structure and variability of actions; they are activated when people are in the events and serve as a guide for their behaviors. Specifically, the purposes of event schemas are to help people to anticipate what to do in future event occurrences, to divert cognitive effort for performing other cognitive tasks (e.g., playing, imitating, planning, storytelling) while engaged in the event, and to construct abstract cognitive structures (e.g., semantic categories). By age 14 months, toddlers demonstrate their general knowledge for familiar activities through enactment (Bauer & Mandler, 1990) and even young preschoolers can verbally describe familiar events in scripts (Fivush, 1984) and apply this knowledge to guide recall (Hudson & Nelson, 1983), tell stories and personal narratives (Hudson & Shapiro, 1991; Shapiro & Hudson, 1997), develop plans (Hudson, Shapiro, & Sosa, 1995; Hudson, Sosa, & Shapiro, 1997), and draw inferences (Hudson & Slackman, 1990). The content and format of general event representations, and their verbal counterpart (i.e., the script), become increasingly more complex with age and experience (Nelson & Gruendel, 1986).

Planning and Problem Solving

Planning is a critical component of problem solving. The ability to plan ahead, which begins to emerge in the toddler years and is apparent in two-year-olds, is a necessary preliminary step in accomplishing a goal. Researchers investigating the development of planning have examined obstacle tasks (i.e., based on a desired end state, such that the child creates a solution preventing object completion; Bauer, Schwade, Wewerka, & Delaney, 1999), solution tasks (i.e., obtain a goal, toy, or other item using problem solving; Klahr & Robinson, 1981), and errand tasks (i.e., the child recreates the means to achieve a goal; Hudson & Fivush, 1991). Planning requires memory capacity, verbal ability, and executive functioning, so age-related differences in these capacities will affect the child's success in developing and executing plans (Gredlein, 2007). Even preschoolers can use their event knowledge for advance planning, as well as for developing remedy and prevention plans for problems that may arise (Hudson et al., 1997). As children learn to take an active role and assume responsibility for planning everyday tasks, they will be able to employ these skills to resolve both anticipated and unexpected problems.

Problem-solving solutions take four possible routes: (1) trial-and-error, which involves making multiple attempts until a solution is implemented; (2) algorithms, which involve a step-by-step process that results in solution implementation; (3) heuristics, which involve cognitive shortcuts based on past experiences and knowledge combined with trial-and-error to obtain a solution; and (4) insight, which involves an unexpected and sudden solution, typically after ruminating about the problem. Obstacles to finding or even implementing a solution occur for a variety of reasons. Sometimes we simply do not have enough information or a good plan for understanding the problem and possible solutions. At other times we fall into the trap of fixating on our representation of the problem, perhaps due to previous experiences with it or similar problems, such that we cannot see or consider it any other way. We may also engage in confirmation bias, which prevents us from finding a solution because we are gathering evidence to support only one idea rather than open-mindedly determining how the information bests fits the situation.

Elements of problem solving are present in older infants as they learn causality and means–ends behavioral patterns and apply a simplistic problem-solving strategy of analogy, applying what worked in a previous or similar situation (Chen, Sanchez, & Campbell, 1997). Young children have few experiences, low knowledge, and very concrete ways of thinking that are not conducive to effective problem solving. As they mature, children demonstrate improved problem solving because they have gained perspective-taking abilities and deductive and inductive reasoning; can classify objects; can think logically about more than one aspect of an item (decenter); can reverse operations; and have increased knowledge and experiences that they can use to develop and implement solutions. Adolescents have the potential for solving a wide variety of problems efficiently and effectively—they can think abstractly, hypothetically, and logically, as well as consider and understand different perspectives simultaneously—but they do not always do so, particularly in social contexts.

Memory

Another cognitive process that develops during childhood is memory (the ability to retain information over time). Episodic long-term memory is composed of memories for personal information (e.g., the number of books you own, your pants size) and autobiographic events (i.e., experiences that have shaped who you are as a person). People use memory in different ways:

- Recognition allows us to notice similarities between two or more present items in a task (e.g., responding to a multiple choice exam).
- Recall allows us to retrieve nonpresent information (e.g., writing an essay).
- Reconstruction refers to use of knowledge to interpret and retrieve stored information (e.g., remembering our eighth birthday party).

Psychologists believe that event memory is constructed and reconstructed, meaning that we do not simply record what our senses pick up during our experiences, store it as a reproduction, and retrieve it in its original form. Consequently, event memories can be inaccurate because of errors that occur during encoding, storage, or retrieval of the event, particularly as our perceptions, knowledge, assumptions, expectations, biases, and cues are continually changing. The information process theory describes how information from the environment can be incorporated into the memory system (Atkinson & Shiffrin, 1968; Baddeley & Hitch, 1974).

Three Phases of Memory. The first phase of memory is encoding. That is, information in environment enters sensory memory through the senses (e.g., eyes, ears). If the person is made aware of it (e.g., rotten food smells bad) and/or believes it is important, then this information will receive attention and be stored for a short time. For example, visual information is stored in iconic sensory memory (the location for visually processed stimuli) for 0.5 second, whereas auditory information is stored in echoic sensory memory (the location for auditorily processed stimuli) for up to 3 seconds. Thus, our senses register input from our world (what we see, smell, taste, hear, and touch), which then must be interpreted by the brain as part of perception before it decays. The information that enters storage depends on various factors, such as prior knowledge (which makes it easier to store the new, related information), interest, salience, duration, number of episodes, and amount of stress at time of encoding.

The second phase of memory is storage. Information from sensory memory can be transferred into the limited-capacity working memory, which consists of the central executive and two specialized, separate storage systems that perform operations on verbal and visual information. The central executive has multiple functions: determining which information in the environment will receive attention; assigning priority for some activities over others when multitasking; selecting strategies for problem solving; controlling and coordinating the flow of speech-based and written information into the phonological loop and visual information (i.e., what objects look like, particularly in related to other objects) into the visuospatial sketchpad; and integrating and combining the information from the two storage systems and applying information from long-term memory storage. The phonological store holds spoken words for 1 to 2 seconds, whereas the articulatory control process keeps information active by repetition and converts written words into speech for phonological storage. The visuospatial sketchpad seems to operate in two main ways: to help us travel in our environment without knocking into objects as we move and to display and manipulate visual and spatial information retrieved from long-term memory (Baddeley, 1986, 1997). Information in procedural, semantic, and episodic long-term memory is encoded in various ways—semantically (meaning), visually (picture), and acoustically (sound). This type of memory has potentially unlimited storage available, organized in separate units, for an infinite amount of time.

During the preschool years, children's executive functioning becomes improved, resulting in cognitive flexibility (Diamond, 2006). In particular, preschoolers demonstrate enhanced persistence, increased ability to ignore distractions and switch focus as needed, and better concentration in pursuit of competing tasks.

Table 2-7 Types of mnemonic devices

Device	Description (Example)
Rehearsal	Repeat the information over and over again ("432 432").
Rhymes	Organize the information into a saying that rhymes (e.g., "righty, tighty, lefty, loosey").
Organization	Organize the information into chunks or logical categories (e.g., fruit: pears, apples, bananas).
Acronyms	Form a word or phrase using the first letters or group of letters (e.g., PIES represents "physical, intellectual, emotional, and social changes in pregnancy").
Visualizing	Imagine information (e.g., Peggy has a wooden leg).
Elaboration	Connect the new information to already learned/stored information (e.g., LONGitude runs north and south).
Method of loci	Link a place with the to-be-remembered information (e.g., shopping list of fruits and vegetables: imagining your house with bananas for a door; lettuce for garage; and so on).

Data from Grohol, J. M. (2013). Memory and mnemonic devices. Retrieved from http://psychcentral.com/lib/2010/memory-and-mnemonic-devices/; Congos, D. (2005). 9 types of mnemonics for better memory. Retrieved from http://www.learningassistance.com/2006/january/mnemonics.html

The third phase of memory is retrieval, which leads to our next topic of remembering and forgetting. Remembering and forgetting are inherently linked. A variety of mnemonic devices (Table 2-7) may be used to encode and retrieve information from long-term memory. As children have a poor understanding of their own memory abilities (i.e., metamemory), they rarely use mnemonics spontaneously to encode or retrieve information (Bjorklund & Douglas, 1997). Practice can help us remember information we need to learn. It may be done in a short session through cramming (massed practice) or over several sessions (distributed practice); forgetting is rapid with the first technique and slow with the second one. Using these methods does not guarantee encoding or retrieval. Forgetting information that had been stored in long-term memory may be explained through lack of consolidation, interference, or retrieval failure. That is, you may have problems remembering information because it was not encoded well (i.e., connected to other information in storage). Other problems occur when new information is learned that interferes with information learned in the past (e.g., "deer" versus "dear") or when past information prevents you from learning new information (e.g., driving first in the United States on the right side, and then in England on the left side). Retrieval failures occur when the external (context-dependent) or internal (state-dependent) retrieval cue used to store the information is not present to help us remember.

Academic Ability

Both intrinsic (e.g., intelligence) and extrinsic (e.g., home, school) factors influence academic performance (Dhingra & Manhas, 2009). This section discusses the complex nature of the contributions to achievement made by parents and teachers. The home environment is the first exposure children have to learning about the world around them. Later, children spend a significant portion of their day in school, where they build basic skills with the guidance of their teachers (and peers) in preparation for their entry into and participation in our literate and technology-savvy society.

Intelligence

Intelligence refers to a person's ability to think abstractly (i.e., problem-solving ability). It is not defined the same way by all cultures, however, because members of different societies need different characteristics to survive and flourish. In American society, an intelligent person would need to know how to use technology, whereas an intelligent person who lives in a desert or polar region would need to know how to meet his or her basic needs (i.e., shelter, food, clothing). The ability to adapt to and function in varying situations is also key. If a person was shipwrecked on a deserted island, she or he would benefit from having Mr. Robinson (from the movie *Swiss Family Robinson*) as her/his companion because Mr. Robinson was capable of utilizing almost all of the ship to provide various creature comforts for his family (e.g., beds, sinks). In contrast, if a person was living in a world in which artificially intelligent machines were trying to wipe out humanity, then she/he would want to stand with Sarah Connor (from the movie *The Terminator*), who had gumption and knew what to do to survive in such an environment.

The origins of intelligence were addressed in the work of Binet and Simon (1904, as cited in Sternberg, 2002), who examined children's general intelligence or capacity for several performance tasks required in school (e.g., comprehension, reasoning, judgment, memory). They assessed a child's current mental ability and then compared it to the abilities of other children of the same chronological age to determine whether the child was the same, below, or above those peers. Binet and Simon's goal was noble: They wanted to identify students who needed help and provide them with alternative teaching styles to facilitate learning in school. Unfortunately, there have since been misuses of intelligence testing (a culturally biased assessment whose items are based on knowledge learned by nonminority and middle-class children), including labeling children as stupid, limiting their future employment options, and preventing them from reproducing (Gould, 1996).

Some theorists (e.g., Cattell, 1963; Spearman, 1904) believe that intelligence is a single ability measured by the "g" factor (general underlying intelligence), with perhaps some specific abilities measured by the "s" factor (specific intelligence, such as spatial relations). General ability may be further conceptualized as fluid (novel problem solving, thinking, abstract reasoning) intelligence, which is genetically derived, and crystallized (knowledge, comprehension) intelligence, which is a product of culture and education.

Other theorists (e.g., Gardner, 1993; Sternberg, 1985) believe that intelligence encompasses many abilities—a conceptualization that explains disparities in various domains of the same person (e.g., artistically talented, average in memory). Gardner's (1993) theory of multiple intelligences proposed that there are nine types of intelligence (i.e., naturalist, musical, logical-mathematical, existential, interpersonal, bodily-kinesthetic, linguistic, intrapersonal, and spatial), which are supposedly stored in different areas of the brain and function separately. This would explain why a brain injury may result in impairment of one type of intelligence, but not in other types (Torff & Gardner, 1999). In the real world, most activities do not rely on only a single ability, but instead use multiple abilities (e.g., chess uses logic, spatial reasoning, decision making). Despite critics' concerns about its validity, the theory of multiple intelligences has been accepted and used in education as it is intuitively appealing (e.g., some students learn visually, some learn tactilely).

Although most children have average cognitive abilities, some have below-average abilities. Children who are mentally retarded or intellectually disabled typically score at the extreme low end of the bell curve (i.e., their scores are in the 75th and lower percentiles). Another component of intelligence is adaptive functioning, which refers to the child's ability to function independently conceptually (e.g., reading, writing), socially (e.g., responsibility, rule following), and daily (e.g., feeding, dressing, hygiene). Often with severe forms of mental retardation, other disabilities are present, such as impairment in hearing and vision, seizures, and cerebral palsy (CDC, 2005).

Literacy Skills: Reading, Comprehension, and Writing

The development of reading and comprehension skills begins when parents introduce and read books to their infants and continues when infants and children are exposed to other examples of writing in their world (e.g., magazines, newspapers, billboards). Through shared interactions, the caregiver helps the infant develop a number of emergent literacy skills, such as how to hold a book, how to turn pages to continue the story, how letters are part of words, and how words have meaning, as well as listening and comprehension skills needed to make reading a familiar and enjoyable activity.

The first step in this process is dialogic reading, an active process by which the adult teaches the child about reading by looking at pictures and asking questions about what is happening in the story, while giving the child a chance not just to respond, but also to lead the process of storytelling and meaning making. The second step is pretend reading, in which the child retells the story using the pictures as cues for remembering what is written. Children's experiences with books—including both active involvement and passive listening—facilitate their understanding that the words on the page correspond to the story. The third step occurs when children learn to read words, either incidentally through exposure to print or purposefully through formal instructions. They may first do so by recognizing the letters and their associated sounds (phonological awareness) and by trying to sound out what the words are in the story (phonics approach). Children may also learn the word itself, using a whole-language approach in which common (sight) words are simply memorized and their meaning is recognized within the context of the sentence. Most schools use a balanced reading approach to help children acquire conventional literacy skills that combines both whole-language and phonics approaches.

Exposure to print also stimulates children's interest in writing. Initially toddlers and preschoolers scribble on a piece of paper, sometimes announcing their intentions to write their names, a list, or a story. As writing evolves, it emulates children's knowledge of the written word—for example, the understanding that writing starts at the left and moves to the right sides of the paper, writing starts at the top of the page and moves downward, and writing has meaning.

After children learn how to form letters in the alphabet, which is reliant on fine motor skills, the next step is learning how to spell words, write sentences, and communicate ideas and stories through writing. One of the first words children master in writing is their names. The first author remembers that the ability to write her name was a prerequisite for getting a library card, which she did at age 4. Preschools foster name writing by having children sign in every morning and writing their names on their artwork. Errors in spelling are often phonological reproductions, called "invented spelling," particularly for words that have unusual rules, such as writing "uv" for "of" or writing "sed" for "said."[1]

In elementary school, children learn by rote memory (i.e., to repeat information verbatim, such as dates of famous events or multiplication tables) and the conventional spelling for words is reinforced through spelling tests. Grammatical rules—the same ones that they acquired easily for speaking when infants—are now being learned formally for writing sentences and stories. Composition skills, which involve transforming what the writer knows using planning and organization of ideas, emerge during elementary school and develop further in middle and high schools to aid children's ability to communicate their ideas in a written format.

Technology is available in many homes and schools. Toddlers and preschoolers are introduced to computers and hand-held devices (e.g., smartphones, iPads, Kindles) used initially as entertainment (e.g., games, books) and subsequently for education and communication. Developmental psychologists do not recommend these devices for very young children; such children learn best through play activities (e.g., playing in the sandbox, jump rope, make-believe play). However, use of these devices at older ages serves to stimulate an active role in self-directed learning (e.g., learn about dinosaurs), encourage higher-order cognitive skills needed for complex assignments (e.g., organize objects before using them), provide an alternative way to express interests and abilities beyond what children could do using conventional means (e.g., create songs), empower them to develop skills in new areas (e.g., draw, sing, write), engage in cooperative tasks with peers (e.g., play a game, create a picture), and increase self-esteem through accomplishment. Traditional methods of teaching computers focused on using a keyboard to type assignments, but

---

[1] Like invented spelling, electronic communications, such as instant message (IM) and text messages, use shorthand methods to communicate, such as "u" for "you" and "ty" for "thank you."

have since evolved into technological approaches that enable students to complete various assignments across the curriculum (e.g., writing and performing music; creating artwork, photograph displays, plays, or books; dissecting a frog; giving a PowerPoint presentation). Teachers are taking advantage of their tech-savvy students' desire to stay connected and get immediate feedback by encouraging them to use their phones and other devices in the classroom to complete a variety of tasks, from coordinating group assignments to responding to multiple-choice questions in a game show–type competition.

Two learning disabilities are associated with understanding and using spoken or written language that make it difficult for the child to learn to read or write. These two forms of literacy employ a variety of skills—specifically, attending to printed words, eye movement control, sound recognition, matching sounds to letters, and understanding words (National Institute of Mental Health, 1993). Children are diagnosed with *dyslexia* when they are unable to differentiate sounds in spoken words, making spelling and reading very difficult. They may learn to recognize letters or even words, but they struggle with reading tasks involving understanding of concepts and reading comprehension. Children are diagnosed with *dysgraphia* when they have difficulty with spelling, handwriting, or expressing their ideas in a written form. The task of writing involves coordinating vocabulary, grammar, memory, and hand movements.

Factors Affecting School Performance

Several factors associated with the school environment have been found to influence children's learning: class size, teacher expectations and preparedness, socioeconomic status, ability groupings, and student gender.

Class size is believed to affect student performance. In general, smaller class size should aid learning, particularly in the earlier grades, as teachers can spend more time with students than when class size is large. Class size alone is not sufficient to ensure learning, however; teachers must be prepared, qualified, and enthusiastic for small classroom size to be beneficial. This advantage stems from expectancy effects—teachers who are supportive and encouraging to children will have students with high academic achievement. Real-life examples of such teachers amply demonstrate that their high expectations have actually transformed their students' lives (e.g., Jaime Escalante helped his predominantly Latino American high school students from underprivileged homes to pass the calculus Advanced Placement test).

Poverty often has a negative impact on academic performance, mainly because poor children enter school with cognitive deficits as a result of their parents failing to provide educational stimulation and guidance at home. Consequently, significant differences exist in pre-academic skills of lower- and middle-class children when they enter kindergarten. Without programs like Head Start and Project Follow-through, these children would not be able to catch up or keep up with their economically advantaged peers.

In recognition that students learn at different paces, ability grouping (also called tracking or stratified learning) puts children together who are at the same level of ability/ understanding in an area (e.g., math, reading). Quite reasonably, children at the high end of performance will be challenged and advance rapidly, whereas mixing them in with average and below-average learners has often led gifted children to become bored and frustrated. In contrast, children at the low end can be taught the material at a slow pace, one that matches their current level of understanding. The main criticism of this approach is that tracking stigmatizes low-performing students, resulting in low self-esteem and negative attitudes toward school in general and their school work in particular. Ideally, teachers should closely monitor students' performance to allow students who have demonstrated consistent over-achievement in their current level to be promoted to the next one and those who have shown consistent under-achievement to be regressed to the lower one.

Another factor that affects school performance is gender. Girls have less difficulty than boys succeeding academically overall, particularly in elementary school. The "boy problem" seems to stem from the curriculum, which is geared toward subjects in which girls excel—namely, reading and writing—rather than courses that involve the experiential learning style preferred by boys—such as science labs and physical education. Additionally, biological differences in preferred activity levels for boys and girls may contribute to school performance as part of the "hidden curriculum." That is, schools employ a low activity level strategy, which is preferred by girls, as a means of promoting passive learning and fine motor skills such as writing, thereby allowing girls to excel in this environment. In contrast, a high activity level style (e.g., running and moving around), which tends to be preferred by boys, as a means of promoting active learning and gross motor skills is discouraged, making the school environment difficult for boys.

In contrast, the "girl problem" focuses on the concern that girls do not perform well in math and science, most notably after elementary school. Despite initial assumptions that this problem stemmed from girls' lack of interest and ability in these areas, the evidence points instead to two other explanations. First, girls believe the common misperception that boys are better than they are in these areas. Part of the problem is that girls do not receive encouragement and support from parents and friends to do well in these areas, or are criticized for doing better than boys. Also, teachers call on boys more often than they call on girls, and give boys more attention and feedback than they give girls. Second, girls are anxious about violating this stereotype, preferring not to enter male-dominated fields devoid of role models and mentors to encourage pursuit in these careers. Single-gender classrooms have been introduced as an alternative environment to help meet children's needs within the public school domain.

Chapter Summary

Parents, medical professionals, and other professionals in the field of child protection should have knowledge of proper physical and cognitive development of infants, children, and adolescents. Physical development includes brain growth, senses development, motor development, and body growth. Parent and professionals should also understand abnormal signs and symptoms of child physical development. They should recognize which sexual behaviors exhibited by infants, children, and adolescents are typical for their age and which are not. Studies have shown that preadolescents and adolescents do engage in both coital and noncoital sexual behaviors with their peers; the extent of this normal development in sexuality varies by age. Accordingly, children should learn about sexual intercourse, relationships, and sexually transmitted infections from parents and teachers, rather than from peers.

Parents and professionals should further be aware of what normative cognitive development entails. Cognition includes many processes, such as paying attention, knowing, planning, problem solving, decision making, and remembering. All of these processes contribute to children's thinking, learning, playing, storytelling, and participating in the world. Finally, parents and professionals should be aware of the various factors that affect school performance.

Review Questions

1. Which physical developmental milestones are reached during infancy, childhood, and adolescence?

2. How are accidents the product of changes in children's senses, brain, and motor abilities?

3. Which types of play enhance cortical development?

4. Which concerns should parents have when the timing of puberty occurs before or later than their children's peers?

5. To what extent are preadolescents and adolescents sexually active?

6. Which cognitive development milestones are achieved by infants, children and adolescents?

7. What are communication disorders? Name and provide examples of them.

8. Which factors affect school performance?

References

Abma, J. C., Martinez, G. M., & Copen, C. E. (2010). Teenagers in the United States: Sexual activity, contraceptive use, and childbearing, National Survey of Family Growth 2006–2008. *Vital and Health Statistics*, Series 23, No. 30.

Albert, B., Brown, S. & Flanigan C. (2003). *14 and younger: The sexual behavior of young adolescents* [Summary]. Washington, DC: National Campaign to Prevent Teen Pregnancy.

American Academy of Pediatrics. (2006). The Apgar score. *Pediatrics, 117*, 1444–1447.

American Academy of Pediatrics. (2013a). Back to sleep, tummy to play. http://www.healthychildren .org/English/ages-stages/baby/sleep/Pages/Back-to-Sleep-Tummy-to-Play.aspx

American Academy of Pediatrics. (2013b). Where we stand on breastfeeding. http://www .healthychildren.org/English/ages-stages/baby/breastfeeding/Pages/Where-We-Stand-Breastfeeding.aspx.

American College of Obstetricians and Gynecologists. (2009). Tanner staging: Tool kit for teen care, 2nd ed. http://www.acog.org/~/media/Departments/Adolescent%20Health%20Care/Teen%20 Care%20Tool%20Kit/TannerStaging2.pdf?dmc=1&ts=20130607T1157397655

Apgar, V. (1953). A proposal for a new method of evaluation of the newborn infant. *Current Researches in Anesthesia & Analgesia, 32*, 260–267.

Atkinson, R. C., & Shiffrin, R. M. (1968). Human memory: A proposed system and its control processes. In K. W. Spence & J. T. Spence (Eds.), *The psychology of learning and motivation (Vol. 2*, pp. 89–195). New York, NY: Academic Press.

Baddeley, A. D. (1986). *Working memory*. Oxford, UK: Oxford University Press.

Baddeley, A. D. (1997). *Human memory: Theory and practice*, revised ed. Hove, UK: Psychology Press.

Baddeley, A. D., & Hitch, G. (1974). Working memory. In G. H. Bower (Ed.), *The psychology of learning and motivation: Advances in research and theory (Vol. 8*, pp. 47–89). New York, NY: Academic Press.

Bailey, R. (2014). Anatomy of the brain. http://biology.about.com/od/humananatomybiology/a/anatomybrain.htm

Bauer, P. J., & Mandler, J. M. (1990). Remembering what happened next: Very young children's recall of event sequences. In R. Fivush & J. Hudson (Eds.), *Knowing and remembering in young children* (pp. 9–29). New York, NY: Cambridge University Press.

Bauer, P. J., Schwade, J. A., Wewerka, S. S., & Delaney, K. (1999). Planning ahead: Goal-directed problem solving by two-year-olds. *Developmental Psychology, 35*, 1321–1337.

Beaver, W. (2001). Television influences teen attitudes toward sex In T. L. Roleff (Ed.), *Opposing viewpoints: Teen sexuality* (pp. 29–36). San Diego, CA: Greenhaven Press.

Bjorklund, D. F., & Douglas, R. N. (1997). The development of memory strategies. In N. Cowan (Ed.), *The development of memory in childhood* (pp. 201–246). Hove, UK: Psychology Press.

Bloom, L., Lifter, K., & Broughton, J. (1985). The convergence of early cognition and language in the second year of life: Problems in conceptualization and measurement. In M. Barrett (Ed.), *Children's single-word speech* (pp. 149–180). London, UK: John Wiley & Sons.

Borse, N. N., Gilchrist, J., Dellinger, A. M., Rudd, R. A., Ballesteros, M. F., & Sleet, D. A. (2008). *CDC childhood injury report: Patterns of unintentional injuries among 0- to 19-year olds in the United States, 2000–2006*. Atlanta, GA: Centers for Disease Control and Prevention, National Center for Injury Prevention and Control.

Boyce, W., Doherty, M., MacKinnon, D., & Fortin, C. (2003). *Canadian youth, sexual health and HIV /AIDS study: Factors influencing knowledge, attitudes and behaviors*. Council of Ministers of Education, Canada. http://www.cmec.ca/publications /aids

Boyce, W., Doherty-Poirier, M., MacKinnon, D., Fortin, C., Saab, H., King, M., et al. (2006). Sexual health of Canadian youth: Findings from the Canadian Youth, Sexual Health and HIV/AIDS Study. *Canadian Journal of Human Sexuality, 15*, 59–68.

Bryce, J., Coitinho, D., Darnton-Hill, I., Pelletier, D., & Pinstrup-Andersen, P. (2008). Maternal & Child Undernutrition Study Group. Child undernutrition: Effective action at national level. *Lancet, 371*, 510–526.

Cattell, R. B. (1963). Theory of fluid and crystallized intelligence: A critical experiment. *Journal of Educational Psychology, 54*, 1–22.

Centers for Disease Control and Prevention (CDC). (2002). Trends in sexual risk behaviors among high school students—United States, 1991–2001. *Morbidity and Mortality Weekly Report, 51*, 856–859.

Centers for Disease Control and Prevention (CDC). (2005). *Trends in reportable sexually transmitted diseases in the United States, 2004: National surveillance data for Chlamydia, Gonorrhea, and Syphilis*. Atlanta, GA: Author.

Centers for Disease Control and Prevention (CDC). (2007). Distribution of births, by gestational age—United States. *Morbidity and Mortality Weekly Report, 56*, 344.

Chandra, A., Martinez, G. M., Mosher, W. D., Abma, J. C., & Jones, J. (2005). Fertility, family planning, and reproductive health of U.S. women: Data from the 2002 National Survey of Family Growth. *Vital and Health Statistics*, Series 23, No. 25. http://www.cdc.gov/nchs/data/series/sr_23/sr23_025.pdf

Chandra, A., Mosher, W. D., & Copen, C. (2011). Sexual behavior, sexual attraction, and sexual identity in the United States: Data from the 2006-2008 National Survey of family Growth. *National Health Statistic Reports, 36.* http://www.cdc.gov/nchs/data/nhsr/nhsr036.pdf

Chen, Z., Sanchez, R. P., & Campbell, T. (1997). From beyond to within their grasp: The rudiments of analogical problem solving in 10- and 13-month-olds. *Developmental Psychology, 33*(5), 790-801.

Chi, M. T. H. (1978). Knowledge structures and memory development. In R. S. Siegler (Ed.), *Children's thinking: What develops?* (pp. 73-96). Hillside, NJ: Erlbaum.

Child Trends Databank. (2012). Sexually experienced teens. http://www.childtrends .org/?indicators=sexually-experienced-teens

Child Trends Databank. (2013). Oral sex behaviors among teens. http://www.childtrends .org/?indicators=oral-sex-behaviors-among-teens

Chomsky, N. (1968). *Language and mind.* New York, NY: Harcourt, Brace & World.

Clark, E. (1987). The principle of contrast: A constraint on language acquisition. In B. MacWhinney (Ed.), *Mechanisms of language acquisition* (pp. 1-33). Hillsdale, NJ: Lawrence Erlbaum Associates.

Cohen, N. J., & Squire, L. R. (1980). Preserved learning and retention of pattern analyzing skill in amnesia: Dissociation of knowing how and knowing that. *Science, 210,* 207-209.

Coles, R., & Stokes, G. (1985). *Sex and the American teenager.* New York, NY: Harper and Row.

Congos, D. (2005). 9 types of mnemonics for better memory. http://www.learningassistance .com/2006/january/mnemonics.html

Crockett, L. J., Raffaelli, M., & Moilanen, K. L. (2003). Adolescent sexuality: Behavior and meaning. In G. R. Adams & M. D. Berzonsky (Eds.), *In Blackwell handbook of adolescence* (pp. 371-392). Lincoln, NE: Blackwell.

de Rosa, C. J., Etheir, K. A., Im, D. H., Cumberland, W. G., Afifi, A. A., Kotlerman, J., . . . Kerndt, P. R. (2010). Sexual intercourse and oral sex among public middle school students: Prevalence and correlates. *Perspectives on Sexual and Reproductive Health, 42*(3), 197-205.

Dhingra, R., & Manhas, S. (2009). Academic performance of children a function of interaction with parents and teachers. *Journal of Sociology SSCi, 18,* 59-64.

Diamond, A. (2006). The early development of executive functions. In E. Bialystok & F. I. M Craik (Eds.), *Lifespan cognition: Mechanisms of change* (pp. 70-95). Oxford, UK: Oxford University Press.

Dilworth-Bart, J. E., Khurshid, A., & Vandell, D. L. (2007). Do maternal stress and home environment mediate the relation between early income-to-need and 54-months attentional abilities? *Infant and Child Development, 16*(5), 525-552.

D'Souza, G., Kreimer, A. R., Viscidi, R., Pawlita, M., Fakhry, C., Koch, W. M., . . . Gillison, M. L. (2007). Case-control study of human papillomavirus and oropharyngeal cancer. *New England Journal of Medicine, 356,* 1944-1956.

Ersoy, B., Balkan, C., Gunay, T., Onag, A., & Egemen, A. (2005). The factors affecting the relation between the menarcheal age of mother and daughter. *Child Care Health and Development, 31*(3), 303-308.

Feingold, D. (1992). Pediatric endocrinology. In *Atlas of pediatric physical diagnosis* (2nd ed., pp. 9.16-9.19). Philadelphia, PA: W. B. Saunders.

Fernald, A., & Morikawa, H. (1993). Common themes and cultural variation in Japanese and American mothers' speech to infants. *Child Development, 64,* 637-656.

Fernald, L. C., & Grantham-McGregor, S. (1998). Stress response in school-age children who have been growth retarded since early childhood. *American Journal of Clinical Nutrition, 19,* 19-20.

Fivush, R. (1984). Learning about school: The development of kindergartners' school scripts. *Child Development, 55,* 1697-1709.

Flannery, K. A., & Liederman, J. (1995). Is there really a syndrome involving the co-occurrence of neurodevelopmental disorder, talent, non-right handedness, and immune disorder among children? *Cortex, 31*, 503–515.

Forhan, S. E., Gottlief, S. L., Sternberg, M. R., Xu, F., Datta, D., Berman, S., & Markowitz, L. (2008). *Prevalence of sexually transmitted infections and bacterial vaginosis among female adolescents in the United States: Data from the National Health and Nutrition Examination Survey (NHANES) 2003–2004.* Paper presented at the 2008 National STD Prevention Conference, Chicago, IL.

Franks, L. (2000). The sex lives of your children. *Talk Magazine,* pp. 102–107, 157.

Fredricks, J. A., & Eccles, J. S. (2002). Children's competence and value beliefs from childhood through adolescence: Growth trajectories in two male-sex–typed domains. *Developmental Psychology, 38*(4), 519–533.

Gardner, H. (1993). *Frames of mind: The theory of multiple intelligences.* New York, NY: Basic Books.

Gates, G. J., & Sonenstein, F. L. (2000). Heterosexual genital sexual activity among adolescent males: 1988 and 1995. *Family Planning Perspectives, 32*(6), 295–297, 304.

Gathercole, V. C. M., & Hoff, E. (2007). Input and the acquisition of language: Three questions. In E. Hoff & M. Shatz (Eds.), *Blackwell handbook of language development* (pp. 107–127). Oxford, UK: Blackwell.

Gil, E., & Johnson, T. C. (1993). *Sexualized children: Assessment and treatment of sexualized children and children who molest.* Rockville, MD: Launch Press.

Gleitman, L. (1990). The structural sources of verb meaning. *Language Acquisition, 1*, 3–50.

Goldstein, J. R. (2011). A secular trend toward earlier male sexual maturity: Evidence from shifting ages of male young adult mortality. *PLoS One,6*(8): e14826. doi:10.1371/journal.pone.0014826. Accessed at: http://www.plosone.org/article/info%3Adoi%2F10.1371%2Fjournal.pone.0014826

Gould, J. J. (1996). *The mismeasure of man.* New York, NY: Norton.

Gredlein, J. M. (2007). *The development of planning ability in children: The role of meta-planning, transfer, and individual differences.* Ann Arbor, MI: ProQuest Information and Learning.

Grohol, J. M. (2013). Memory and mnemonic devices. http://psychcentral.com/lib/2010/memory-and-mnemonic-devices/

Halpern-Felsher, B. (2008). Oral sexual behavior: Harm reduction or gateway behavior? *Journal of Adolescent Health, 43*(3), 207–208.

Halpern-Felsher, B. L., Cornell, J. L., Kropp, R. Y., & Tschann, J. M. (2005). Oral versus vaginal sex among adolescents: Perceptions, attitudes and behavior. *Pediatrics, 115*(4), 845–851.

Hamilton, B. E., Martin, J. A., & Ventura, S. J. (2010). Births: Preliminary data for 2008. *National Vital Statistics Reports, 58*(16).

Hamilton, B. E., Martin, J. A., & Ventura, S. J. (2011). Births: Preliminary data for 2010. *National Vital Statistics Reports, 60*(2), Table S-2.

Hamilton, B. E., Martin, J. A., & Ventura, S. J. (2012). Births: Preliminary data for 2011. *National Vital Statistics Reports, 61*(5), Table 2.

Hanrahan, C. (2006). Sleep. In K. Krapp & J. Wilson (Eds.), *Gale encyclopedia of children's health: Infancy through adolescence* (Vol. 4, pp.1676–1680). Detroit, MI: Gale.

Hardman, S. (2012) Teen pregnancy: Statistics, risk factors, prevention. http://ezinearticles.com/?Teen-Pregnancy---Statistics,-Risk-Factors,-Prevention&id=6410576

Heibeck, T. H., & Markman, E. M. (1987). Word learning in children: An examination of fast mapping. *Journal of Child Development, 58*(4), 1021–1034.

Herbenick, D., Reece, M., Schick, V., Sanders, S. A., Dodge, B., & Fortenberry, J. D. (2010). Sexual behavior in the United States: Results from a national probability sample of men aged 14–94. *Journal of Sexual Medicine, 7*, 255–265.

Herman-Giddens, M. E. (2006). Recent data on pubertal milestones in United States children: The secular trend toward earlier development. *International Journal of Andrology, 29,* 241–246.

Herman-Giddens, M. E., Wang, L., & Koch, G. (2001). Secondary sexual characteristics in boys: Estimates from the National Health and Nutrition Examination Survey III, 1988–1994. *Archives of Pediatrics & Adolescent Medicine, 155,* 1022–1028.

Hudson, J. A., & Fivush, R. (1991). Planning in the preschool years: The emergence of preschoolers' plans from general event knowledge. *Cognitive Development, 6,* 393–416.

Hudson, J., & Nelson, K. (1983). Effects of script structure on children's story recall. *Developmental Psychology, 19,* 625–635.

Hudson, J. A., & Shapiro, L. R. (1991). From knowing into telling: The development of children's scripts, stories, stories, and personal narratives. In A. McCabe & C. Peterson (Eds.), *Developing narrative structure* (pp. 89–136). Hillsdale, NJ: Erlbaum.

Hudson, J. A., Shapiro, L. R., & Sosa, B. B. (1995). Planning in the real world: Preschool children's scripts and plans for familiar events. *Child Development, 66,* 984–998.

Hudson, J., & Slackman, E. (1990). Children's use of scripts in inferential text processing. *Discourse Processing, 13,* 375–385.

Hudson, J. A., Sosa, B. B., & Shapiro, L. R. (1997). Scripts and plans: The development of pre-school children's event knowledge and event planning. In S.L. Friedman & E. L. Scholnick (Eds.), *The developmental psychology of planning: Why, how and when do we plan?* (pp. 77–102). Mahwah, NJ: Erlbaum.

Itman, C. M., Wong, C., Hunyadi, B. L., Ernst, M. R.., Jans, K. L., & Loveland, K. A. (2011). Smad3 dosage determines androgen responsiveness and sets the pace of postnatal testis development. *Endocrinology, 152,* 2076–2089.

Jackson, K. M., & Nazar, A. M. (2006). Breastfeeding, the immune response, and long-term health. *Journal of the American Osteopathic Association, 106*(4), 203–207.

Jarrell, A. (2000, April 2). The face of teenage sex grows younger, *New York Times.* http://www .nytimes.com/2000/04/02/style/the-face-of-teenage-sex-grows-younger.html

Kaeser, F. (2010). Towards a better understanding of children's sexual behavior. http://www .education.com/reference/article/Ref_Towards_Better/?page=3The effects of increasing sexualization on children

Kaplowitz, P. B. (2010). Precocious puberty. http://emedicine.medscape.com/article/924002-overview

Karmiloff, K., & Karmiloff-Smith, A. (2001). *Pathways to language.* Cambridge, MA: Harvard University Press.

Katchadourian, H. (1990). Sexuality. In S. S. Feldman & G. R. Elliott (Eds.), *At the threshold: The developing adolescent* (pp. 330–351). Cambridge, MA: Harvard University Press.

Klahr, D., & Robinson, M. (1981) Formal assessment of problem solving and planning processes in preschool children. *Cognitive Psychology, 13,* 113–148.

Klees, D. M., Olson, J., & Wilson, R. D. (1988). An analysis of the content and organization of children's knowledge structures in NA. *Advances in Consumer Research, 15,* 153–157.

Kost, K., & Henshaw, S. (2012). U.S. teenage pregnancies, births and abortions, 2008: National trends by race and ethnicity. http://www.guttmacher.org/pubs/USTPtrends08.pdf

Kost, K., Henshaw, S., & Carlin, L. (2010). U.S. teenage pregnancies, births and abortions: National and state trends and trends by race and ethnicity. http://www.guttmacher.org/pubs /USTPtrends.pdf

Kuhl, P. K. (2007). Is speech learning "gated" by the social brain? *Developmental Science, 10*(1), 110–120.

Kutscher, M. (2008). *ADHD: Living without brakes.* Philadelphia, PA: Jessica Kingsley.

Lee, J. M., Appugliese, D., Kaciroti, N., Corwyn, R. F., Bradley, R. H., & Lumeng, J. C. (2007). Weight status in young girls and the onset of puberty. *Pediatrics, 119*(3), 624–630.

Lee, J. M., Appugliese, D., Kaciroti, N., Corwyn, R. F., Bradley, R. H., & Lumeng, J. C. (2010). Body mass index and timing of pubertal initiation in boys. *Archives of Pediatrics & Adolescent Medicine, 164*(2), 139–144.

Leigh, B. C., Morrison, D. M., Trocki, K., & Temple, M. T. (1994). Sexual behavior of American adolescents: Results from a U.S. national survey. *Journal of Adolescent Health, 15*(2), 117–125.

Leitenberg, H., Detzer, M. J., & Srebnik, D. (1993). Gender differences in masturbation and the relation of masturbation experience in preadolescence and/or early adolescence to sexual behavior and sexual adjustment in young adulthood. *Archives of Sexual Behavior, 2*(2), 87–98.

Lescano, C. M., Houck, C. D., Brown, L. K., Doherty, G., DiClemente, R. J., Fernandez, I., et al. (2009). Correlates of heterosexual anal intercourse among at-risk adolescents and young adults. *American Journal of Public Health, 99*(8), 1131–1136.

Lindberg, L. D., Jones, R., & Santelli, J. S. (2008). *Non-coital sexual activities among adolescents.* Journal of Adolescent Health, *43*(3), 231–238.

López, F., Menez, M., & Hernández-Guzmán, L. (2005). Sustained attention during learning activities: An observational study with pre-school children. *Early Child Development and Care, 175*(2), 131–138.

Lozoff, B. M. (2007). Birth: An anthropologic approach to infant care. *Prenatal Care, 5*(4), 192–194.

Malina, R. M., Bouchard, C., & Bar-Or, O. (2004). *Growth, maturation, and physical activity* (2nd ed.). Champaign, IL: Human Kinetics.

Martinez, G. M., Chandra, A., Abma, J. C., Jones, J., & Mosher, W. D. (2006). Fertility, contraception, and fatherhood: Data on men and women from Cycle 6 (2002) of the National Survey of Family Growth. *Vital and Health Statistics, 23*(26). http://www.cdc.gov/nchs/data/series/sr_23/sr23_026.pdf

Martinez, G., Copen, C. E., & Abma, J. C. (2011). Teenagers in the United States: Sexual activity, contraceptive use, and childbearing, 2006–2010. National Survey of Family Growth. National Center for Health Statistics. *National Vital Health Statistics, 23*(31). http://www.cdc.gov/nchs/data/series/sr_23/sr23_031.pdf

Maticka-Tyndale, E. (2008). Sexuality and sexual health of Canadian adolescents: Yesterday, today and tomorrow. *Canadian Journal of Human Sexuality, 17,* 85–95. http://www.sieccan.org/pdf/maticka-tyndale_cjhs2008_commentary.pdf

McKay, A. (2004). Oral sex among teenagers: Research, discourse, and education. *Canadian Journal of Human Sexuality, 13.* http://www.biomedsearch.com/article/Oral-sex-among-teenagers-research/132084927.html

MDhealth.com. (2014). Parts of the brain and their functions. http://www.md-health.com/Parts-Of-The-Brain-And-Function.html

Menyuk, P., Liebergott, J., & Schultz, M. (1995). *Early language development in full-term and premature infants.* Hillsdale, NJ: Lawrence Erlbaum Associates.

Miller, B. C., Norton, M. C., Curds, T., Hill, E. J., Schvaneveldt, P., & Young, M. H. (1997). The timing of sexual intercourse among adolescents: Family, peer, and other antecedents. *Youth & Society, 29,* 54–83.

Miller, J. F. & Paul, R. (1995). The Clinical Assessment of Language Comprehension. Baltimore, MD: Paul H. Brookes.

Moini, J. (2013). *Introduction to pathology for the physical therapist assistant.* Burlington, MA: Jones & Bartlett Learning.

Moses, S. (2013a). Female Tanner stage. *Family Practice Notebook.* http://www.fpnotebook.com /mobile/endo/exam/fmltnrstg.htm

Moses, S. (2013b). Male Tanner stage. *Family Practice Notebook.* http://www.fpnotebook.com/mobile /Endo/Exam/MlTnrStg.htm

Mosher, W. D., Chandra, A., & Jones, J. (2005). Sexual behavior and selected health measures: Men and women 15–44 years of age, United States, 2002. Advance data from *Vital and Health Statistics, 362.* Hyattsville, MD: National Center for Health Statistics.

Muller, O., & Krawinkel, M. (2005). Malnutrition and health in developing countries. *Canadian Medical Association Journal, 173*(3), 279–286.

Mundy, L. (2000 July 16). Young teens and sex: Sex and sensibility. *Washington Post Magazine,* pp. 16–21, 29–34.

National Institute of Mental Health. (1993). *Learning disabilities* (NIH Publication 93-3611). Washington, DC: U.S. Government Printing Office.

Nelson, K. (1986). *Event knowledge: Structure and function in development.* Hillside, NJ: Erlbaum.

Nelson, K., & Gruendel, J. (1986). Children's scripts. In K. Nelson (Ed.), *Event knowledge: Structure and function in development* (pp. 21–46). Hillside, NJ: Erlbaum.

Newcomer, S. F., & Udry, J. R. (1985). Oral sex in an adolescent population. *Archives of Sexual Behavior, 14*(1), 41–46.

O'Donnell, L., O'Donnell, C. R., & Stueve, A. (2001). Early sexual initiation and subsequent sex-related risks among urban minority youth: The Reach for Health study. *Family Planning Perspectives, 33*(6), 268–275.

Piaget, J. (1963). *The origins of intelligence in children* . New York: W. W. Norton.

Pinker, S. (1984). *Language learnability and language development.* Cambridge, MA: Harvard University Press.

Posner, M. I., Rothbart, M. K., & Sheese, B. E. (2007). Attention genes. *Developmental Science, 10*(1), 24–29.

Quigley, M. A., Kelly, Y. J., & Sacker, A. (2007). Breastfeeding and hospitalization for diarrheal and respiratory infection in the United Kingdom Millennium Cohort Study. *Pediatrics, 119*(4), e837–e842.

Reed, V. A. (2005). *An introduction to children with language disorders* (3rd ed.). Boston, MA: Allyn & Bacon.

Rowe, M. L., & Goldin-Meadow, S. (2009). Differences in early gesture explain SES disparities in child vocabulary size at school entry. *Science, 323*(5916), 951–953.

San Francisco Youth Risk Behavior Survey (SFYRBS). (1997). Sexual behavior. http://www.sfdph .org/dph/files/reports/studiesdata/98childhealth/sexual.pdf

Santelli, J. S., Rochat, R., Hatfield-Timajchy, K., Gilbert, B. C., Curtis, K., Cabral, R., et al. (2003). The measurement and meaning of unintended pregnancy. *Perspectives on Sexual and Reproductive Health, 35*(2), 94–101.

Santelli, J. S., Lindberg, L. D., Finer, L. B., & Singh, S. (2007). Explaining recent declines in adolescent pregnancy in the United States: The contribution of abstinence and improved contraceptive use. *American Journal of Public Health, 97*(1), 150–156.

Schneider, W., & Bjorklund, D. F. (1992). Expertise, aptitude and strategic remembering. *Child Development, 63*(2), 461–473.

Schuster, M. A., Bell, R. M., & Kanouse, D. E. (1996). The sexual practices of adolescent virgins: Genital sexual activities of high school students who have never had vaginal intercourse, *American Journal of Public Health, 86*(11), 1570–1576.

Sensory Processing Disorder Foundation (2012). About SPD. http://spdfoundation.net/about-sensory-processing-disorder.html

Shapiro, L. R., & Hudson, J. A. (1997). Coherence and cohesion in children's stories. In J. Costermans & M. Fayol (Eds.), *Processing interclausal relationships: Studies in the production and comprehension of text* (pp. 23–48). Mahwah, NJ: Erlbaum.

Siervogel, R. M., Wisemandle, W., Maynard, L. M., Guo, S. S., Chumlea, W. C., & Towne, B. (2000). Lifetime overweight status in relation to serial changes in body composition and risk factors for cardiovascular disease: The Fels Longitudinal Study. *Obesity Research, 8*(6), 422–430.

Skinner, B. F. (1991). *Verbal behavior.* Action, MA: Copley. (Original work published in 1957).

Spearman, C. (1904). General intelligence: Objectively determined and measured. *American Journal of Psychology, 15,* 201–293.

Stepp, L. S. (1999a, July 8). Parents are alarmed by an unsettling new fad in middle schools: Oral sex. *Washington Post,* p. A1.

Stepp, L. S. (1999b, July 8). Talking to kids about sexual limits. *Washington Post,* p. C4.

Sternberg, R. J. (1985). *Beyond IQ: A triarchic theory of intelligence.* Cambridge, UK: Cambridge University Press.

Sternberg, R. S. (2002). Images of mindfulness. *Journal of Social Issues, 56*(1), 11–26.

Stiles, J. (2008). *The fundamentals of brain development: Integrating nature and nurture.* Cambridge, MA: Harvard University Press.

Stiles, J., Reilly, J., Paul, B., & Moses, P. (2005). Cognitive development following early brain injury: Evidence for neural adaption. *Trends in Cognitive Sciences, 9*(3), 136–143.

Susman, E. J., & Rogol, A. (2004). Puberty and psychological development. In R. M. Lerner & L. D. Steinberg (Eds.), *Handbook of adolescent psychology* (pp. 15–44). Hoboken, NJ: John Wiley & Sons.

Tanner, J. M. (1990). Sequence, tempo, and individual variation in growth and development of boys and girls aged twelve to sixteen. In R.E. Muuss (Ed.), *Adolescent behavior and society: A book of readings* (pp. 39–56). New York, NY: McGraw-Hill.

Tomasello, M. (2006). The social bases of language acquisition. *Social Development, 1*(1), 67–87.

Torff, B., & Gardner, H. (1999). The vertical mind: The case for multiple intelligences. In M. Anderson (Ed.), *The development of intelligence* (pp. 139–159). Hove, UK: Psychology Press.

Tulving, E. (1972). Episodic and semantic memory. In E. Tulving & W. Donaldson (Eds.), *Organization of memory* (pp. 381–403). New York, NY: Academic Press.

University of North Carolina at Chapel Hill. (2001, September 18). Research: U.S. boys also reaching puberty earlier than in past years. *ScienceDaily.* http://www.sciencedaily.com/releases/2001/09/010914074455.htm

Volpe, J. J. (2008). Neurological examination: Normal and abnormal features. In *Neurology of the newborn* (5th ed., pp. 121–153). Philadelphia, PA: Saunders Elsevier.

Weiss, R. E. (2014). How newborn reflexes help babies survive. http://pregnancy.about.com/od/newborntesting/a/Newborn-Reflexes.htm

Welti, K., Wildsmith, E., &, Manlove, J. (2011). *Trends and recent estimates: Contraceptive use among U.S. teens and young adults.* Washington, DC: Child Trends.

Williams, K., Haywood, K., & Painter, M. (1996). Environmental and biological influences on gender differences in the overarm throw for force: Dominant and non-dominant arm throws. *Women in Sport and Physical Activity Journal, 5,* 29–50.

Woodward, A. L., Markman, E. M., & Fitzsimmons, C. M. (1994). Rapid word learning in 13- and 18- month-olds. *Developmental Psychology, 30*(4), 553–566.

Chapter 3

Emotional and Social Development

This chapter describes healthy emotional and social development to assist professionals in understanding what is expected from children and adolescents in normal situations. Human beings are social by nature. Through their interactions with one another, they form strong emotional relationships, initially with their caregivers and subsequently with their peers, which allow them to express their feelings and participate in reciprocal interactions. The types of attachments they form in infancy (Ainsworth & Bell, 1970) will influence their attachments in childhood and beyond (i.e., adolescence and adulthood). Some children have temperaments and personalities that facilitate the formation of close bonds (i.e., they act in ways to engage caregivers and elicit nurturing behaviors from them), whereas some find interacting with others difficult. Adult responses to children's needs and problems will affect the development of their self-concepts, their ability to regulate their emotions and behaviors in social contexts, and their acculturation in society.

Emotions

It is generally believed that human infants are able at birth to experience simple emotions of distress, contentment, and interest. Between 2 and 6 months of age, they become capable of recognizing and expressing basic emotions, such as happiness (joy), sadness, frustration (anger), fear, surprise, and disgust (Ekman, 1992; Izard, 2007). Complex emotions, such as pride, guilt, and shame, emerge initially between 18 and 24 months as the toddlers' understanding of self-concept develops; further development occurs between ages 3 and 5 years as the children's sense of self merges with their higher-order cognitive abilities to give deeper meaning to their experiences (Izard & King, 2009; Tracy & Robins, 2006, 2008).

Caregivers regulate basic positive emotions through nurturing and play, but will need to employ refocusing and calming techniques when young children exhibit high intensity of these emotions, such as extreme excitement (Kochanska, Murray, & Harlan, 2000). In contrast, caregivers must choose regulating techniques based on the specific negative emotion a young child expresses. For example, when sadness is exhibited, failure of the infant to engage in self-soothing (e.g., thumb sucking) will require the caregiver to apply comfort, typically in the form of picking up and holding the child. According to Izard, Stark, Trentacosta, and Schultz (2008), caregivers must use both perceptual and cognitive tools to control complex children's emotions, as these feelings involve a combination of children's previously learned thoughts, their appraisal of the experience eliciting the emotion, and their understanding of their own and others' reactions (attribution process). The preschooler's ability to self-regulate emotions is tied to social and cognitive competence in childhood, adolescence, and adulthood (Goleman, 1995; Izard, 2007; Mischel & Ayduk, 2004).

Emotions encompass our physiological responses, our subjective interpretation and understanding of our experiences, the process of communicating our experiences to others, and our reactions to the experiences (Greenspan & Greenspan, 1985). Emotions serve four main functions:

- Emotions help to *socialize* us by binding us to those we love (e.g., we spend our time with friends and family) and disassociating us from those we despise (e.g., we avoid our enemies).
- Emotions *motivate* us to achieve our goals. For example, we may perform feats and tasks that we would not normally do because it is for a loved one.
- Emotions help us *organize* our world by influencing how we perceive situations and experiences and how we interpret interactions with others and associated feelings stemming from those relationships. People relate their experiences to others, particularly those they like, to get feedback about whether their reactions were logical and appropriate.
- Emotions aid in *communication*. Individuals rely on a combination of verbal messages and nonverbal body language—specifically, whether they match— to assess interactions and experiences. For example, if someone is offering an apology and his or her nonverbal and verbal cues match, then we believe the person is being truthful; conversely, if they do not match, then we believe the person is lying.

Human understanding and display of emotions is not universal, but rather is mediated by one's culture, language, gender, temperament, and personality (e.g., Izard, 2007; Matsumoto, 1992, 2006). Consider the differences between the expression of emotion in individualist and collectivist societies. Individualist cultures believe that the autonomy of the individual is paramount (Lustig & Koester, 1999), personal time and achievement are valued, and strategies and practices tend to be both innovative and novel (Nath & Murthy, 2004). The United States, for example, is an individualist society. In U.S. culture, it is not acceptable for boys and men to express sadness or pain through crying, but it is acceptable for them to show anger. Thus, American boys often have difficulty processing sadness, often expressing anger instead.

By contrast, collectivist societies are "characterized by tight social networks in which people strongly distinguish between their own groups (in-groups, such as relatives, clans, and organizations) and other groups" (Royer & van der Velden, 2002, p. 8). Collectivists hold common goals and objectives, rather than individual ones that focus primarily on self-interest (Adler, 2002). Consequently, collectivist cultures believe in obligations to the group, dependence of the individual on organizations and institutions, a "we" consciousness, and an emphasis on belonging (Lustig & Koester, 1999). Individuals in "collectivist cultures expect members of their particular in-groups to look after them, protect them, and give them security in exchange for their loyalty to the group" (Adler, 2002, p. 53). Children in collectivist cultures (e.g., Japan) are less likely than those in individualistic cultures (e.g., the United States, the United Kingdom) to show openly how they feel, such as through a smile, and consequently will interpret this behavior by others differently (e.g., Matsumoto, Consolacion, & Yamada, 2002). Interpretation and understanding of emotion are also filtered through temperament and personality, as indicated in the next section.

Temperament and Personality

Temperament and personality are integrally linked. Temperament refers to a general, inherent (genetic) disposition evident at birth that affects our responses to environmental and emotional experiences and, as such, typifies our *behavioral style* (Goldsmith, Lemery, Aksan, & Buss, 2000). According to Thomas, Chess, and Birch (1970), the experiences children have as a consequence of their temperaments contribute to the formation of their personality (how they usually think, feel, and act in various situations). To better understand temperament, Thomas et al. (1970) identified nine dimensions in infants, each of which was assigned a score of low, average, or high. Several of these dimensions, according to the Fullerton Longitudinal Study, showed stability from ages 2 through 12 years and from ages 14 through 16 years (Guerin, Gottfried, Oliver, & Thomas, 2003). By combining the nine characteristics, Thomas and Chess (1977, as cited in Firchow, n.d.) were able to classify participants in their sample as having one of three overall temperament dispositions (Table 3-1): easygoing (40%), slow to warm up (15%), and difficult (10%). Some children showed a mixture of characteristics that did not fit into any of these profiles (35%).

Interestingly, the child–caregiver relationship affected the temperament categories in which children were placed (Thomas & Chess, 1977; Thomas et al., 1970). That is, reactions of infants to the demands of their environments and the expectations of the caregivers in their lives were influenced by compatibility—the *goodness of fit*—between the child and caregiver (Chess & Thomas, 1999). It is important, therefore, that caregivers be particularly sensitive to their infants' temperament to assist in the adaption of their children's temperamental traits to the world. In other words, they cannot change children's inborn

Table 3-1 Temperament characteristics organized into three profiles

Temperament characteristic	Easy going	Slow to warm up	Difficult
Activity level	Varies from fidgets/restless to placid	Varies from sits for extended time to placid	Varies from fidgets/restless to placid
Adaptability	Very adaptable even when transitions are rapid	Slow to adapt following transitions	Difficulty adapting to even slight transition; needs high consistency
Approach/withdrawal to new situations	Curious and approaches new experiences with positive attitude	Initially will hold back, then approaches with positive attitude	Withdraws from new experiences; difficulty sometimes with all situations
Persistence	Low (difficult to complete tasks) or high (can return and follow through; at extreme is a perfectionist), especially after a distraction	Low (difficult to complete tasks) or high (can return and follow through; at extreme is a perfectionist), especially after a distraction	Low (difficult to complete tasks) or high (can return and follow through; at extreme is a perfectionist), especially after a distraction
Distractibility (extraneous stimuli affects behavior)	Varies, either easily distracted or good concentration	Varies, either easily distracted or good concentration	Varies, either easily distracted or good concentration
Intensity (energy) of reaction	Low/mild emotional responses to stimuli	Low emotional responses to stimuli	Intense emotional responses to stimuli
Mood (typical demeanor)	Cheerful, pleasant	Somewhat unpleasant	Leary, but often unpleasant (e.g., glum, grumpy)
Rhythmicity in eating, sleeping, elimination	Regular and predictable with bodily functions	Moderate irregularity	Irregular/difficulty with bodily functions
Threshold (intensity needed to evoke response)	Low (ignore)/High (sensitive) response to environmental flux	Low (ignore)/High (sensitive) response to environmental flux	Low (ignore)/High (sensitive) response to environmental flux

Data from Chess, S., & Thomas, A. (1999). *Goodness of fit: Clinical applications from infancy through adult life*. Philadelphia, PA; Brunner/Mazel; Thomas, A., & Chess, S. (1977). *Temperament and development*. New York, NY: Brunner/Mazel.

traits, but they can teach children to manage their impulses and to respond in socially acceptable ways by using strategies to avoid potentially stressful situations (e.g., structure and schedules). For example, parenting a difficult infant who has trouble falling asleep in general requires the caregiver to establish a routine naptime and to avoid noisy environments during that time period. In some situations infants have temperaments (e.g., active child) that are consistent with their caregiver's expectations (e.g., the parents want an active child), whereas in others they are inconsistent (e.g., the parents want a quiet child).

For many infants, temperament tends to remain the same throughout their lives (Rothbart, Derryberry, & Hershey, 2000), but smaller changes do occur (Goldsmith et al., 2000). The caregivers' ability to meet difficult and slow-to-warm-up infants' needs and to manage their behaviors may be key to these children's eventual ease in adapting to different environments. In the case of intense, difficult children, it is important that the caregiver differentiate between intentional misbehavior and temperamentally related behavior (e.g., impulsiveness, high energy) so as to provide appropriate responses that guide the children's future responses and do not damage their self-esteem.

All socioemotional relationships begin with attachment. Social interactions between children and caregivers are bidirectional, meaning that children are as active as their caregivers in moderating this socialization process by encouraging, discouraging, motivating, and redirecting the other party (Bell, 1974). Additionally, children's temperament will mediate their ability to self-soothe or to respond to the caregiver's attempts to soothe them, as well as their ability to increase or decrease the caregiver's reactions to them (e.g., pleasure, displeasure).

Attachment

Human beings require a social and emotional relationship with others (attachments) that involves physical touch. Infants simply cannot survive without attachments, which are developed through the child's daily interactions with primary (e.g., parents, babysitters) and secondary caregivers (e.g., siblings, grandparents). Research has shown that infants who are rarely held or touched by their caregivers will fail to thrive (i.e., fail to grow and gain weight) and may die (e.g., Poland & Ward, 1994). However, physical stimulation promotes human growth hormone and immunization: Field and her colleagues (2010), for example, found that massaging premature infants results in weight gain and growth. Survival is enhanced by children's ability to form multiple attachments to those who provide care to them—parents, siblings, grandparents, and babysitters, among others.

In the past, two explanations of attachment competed for support. The first, known as the *behavioral theory of drive reduction*, stated that caregivers satisfied the child's primary needs, but was later disproved by Harlow (1958). Harlow, through his Rhesus monkey experiments, showed that babies chose to be comforted by a cloth mother who was soft rather than by a wire mother who provided food. The second explanation, known as *socio-psychological theory* (Erikson, 1963), suggested that immediate and consistent care by caregivers built infants' internal sense of trust and confidence that their needs would be met. This theory has been criticized as it employed scientifically unmeasurable concepts, such as "ego."

More recently, the most widely accepted view of why infants form emotional ties to caregivers has been derived from joint work by Ainsworth and Bowlby (1991), which is based on an expansion of *ethological theory* (Lorenz, 1952). According to ethological theory, all babies are endowed with a set of built-in behaviors (e.g., smile, cry, cute face) that help keep the caregiver close, thereby increasing children's protection from harm and enhancing their overall chance of survival. Thus, attachment serves two functions—to provide a secure base for exploration of environment (after all, the sole job of an infant/toddler and preschooler is to learn about the world) and to provide a haven from threat (provide safety and comfort).

Bowlby's (1969) theory explains the formation of attachment in terms of the infant's goal to keep the caregiver close:

- Initially (from birth to 6 weeks), the child is in the *preattachment* stage and uses innate mechanisms (e.g., cuteness, high-pitched distress cry) to engage adult caregivers and keep them nearby. At this time, infants are able to recognize the mother's smell and voice, but will allow anyone to care for them.

- Between 6 weeks and 6–8 months, infants enter the *attachment in the making* phase. Infants 8 to 10 weeks become capable of using rudimentary *social referencing,* in which they seek information from the caregiver about how to respond emotionally about ambiguous situations, and at 3 months can differentiate visually between their caregivers and strangers.

- A third phase, *attachment,* occurs between 6–8 months and 18–24 months, and the special relationship with the caregiver is clear-cut and evident. It is not until 6 to 8 months that infants show a preference for specific caregivers and will act displeased, often by crying and clinging, when the caregiver leaves (known as separation anxiety) and an unfamiliar person or caregiver enters (e.g., fear of strangers). Consequently, it is important to introduce the child to the "substitute" caregiver at the earlier part of this phase before the specific attachment forms.

- In the final phase, *reciprocity or goal corrected partnership,* the 2-year-old uses internal working models or mental representation to portray nonpresent objects (i.e., missing caregiver) and to communicate through language. Accordingly, the relationship between infant and caregiver is changed and improved, as the child can now predict the parent's leaving and returning and can negotiate with the caregiver through requests and persuasion to alter goals (e.g., read me a story before the babysitter comes).

Ainsworth's (1979) assessment of the attachment relationship is an extension of Bowlby's work. According to this theory, children form attachment relationships during the first two years of life, the quality of which depends on the caregiver's sensitivity and responsiveness to the infant's signals and physical needs (e.g., food, diaper change, temperature regulation, fatigue, protection). To assess the quality of the attachment relationship between mobile infants (12–24 months) and their caregivers, Ainsworth created the *strange situation.* Table 3-2 identifies each element of this test and associated behaviors for each attachment type (Ainsworth & Bell, 1970). This particular test focuses on the child's exploration of environment, the way in which the child handles separation from the caregiver (to evaluate separation anxiety), the child's interactions with strangers (to

Table 3-2 Four types of attachment with their associated behaviors in the strange situation

Evaluation	Secure	Insecure: anxious/ avoidant	Insecure: anxious-ambivalent/ resistant	Insecure: disorganized
Safe base behaviors in strange situation	Child explores environment using caregiver as safe base; child demonstrates distress when care-giver leaves	Explores a little; not distressed when caregiver leaves	Limited exploration, if any; remains near caregiver	Random exploration or frozen
Alone and with stranger in strange situation	Comfortable with stranger in caregiver's presence; distressed when left alone; not comforted by stranger	As comfortable with stranger as with mother; not distressed by being alone	Very distressed alone; refuses com-fort from stranger	Unpredictable, odd actions when alone or with stranger
Reunion in strange situation	Signals need to be close to caregiver; demonstrated care-giver soothes anxiety	Avoids or slow to greet care-giver; does not cling if caregiver picks up child	Simultaneously signals need for caregiver and rejects caregiver contact; continues to cry and cannot be soothed	Avoids eye contact with caregiver even on approach; child expresses confusion and fear rather than relief

Data from Ainsworth, M. D. S. (1979). Infant-mother attachment. *American Psychologist, 34,* 932–937; Sroufe, L.A. (2005). *Emotional development.* Cambridge, United Kingdom: Cambridge University Press.

evaluate fear of strangers), and the child's *reunion* behavior with the caregiver (Levine & Munsch, 2011).

Ainsworth (Ainsworth & Bell, 1970) examined the child's behaviors in the strange situa-tion and then classified the attachment relationship as either secure (70%), anxious/avoidant insecure (15%), or anxious ambivalent/resistant insecure (15%). A fourth category, disorga-nized insecure, was added subsequently (Main & Solomon, 1990). The type of attachment a child forms with the primary caregiver will be the same type forged in subsequent social and emotional relationships with secondary caregivers (e.g., siblings, grandparents, babysitters, teachers, coaches) and peers. Table 3-3 lists the observed behaviors in the strange situation associated with each of the four types of attachment patterns, as well as the long-term out-comes based on various studies (e.g., Sroufe, Egeland, Carlson, & Collins, 2009).

The increase in the proportion of working women in the United States who have chil-dren younger than the age of 6 (from 40% in 1975 to 63% in 2005) has prompted societal concern that nonparental care may inhibit infants' formation of secure attachments and, consequently, have negative effects on their social, emotional, and cognitive devel-opment. Fortunately, research has shown that it is the type of caregiving—rather than

Table 3-3 Mothering, models, and long-term social, emotional, and cognitive developmental outcomes

Evaluation	Secure	Insecure: anxious/ avoidant	Insecure: anxious-ambivalent/ resistant	Insecure: disorganized
Type of mothering	Emotionally responsive to child's cues and fulfills needs	Emotionally non-responsive to cues; perceives child as needy	Inconsistent responses to child's needs because unable to read child's cues, sometimes interacts in positive ways, but at parent's desire	Indiscreet; withholds affection; induces fear; responds erratically and capriciously; abusive and/or neglectful
Internal working models	People can be trusted; I can rely on others; People will love me; I am capable and valued; The world is a safe place	People are inaccessible and will reject me; I can protect myself by denying my needs, and instead care for others to avoid rejection and get love	People are unpredictable—alternating between love and hostility; If I leave my caregiver to explore, I may miss an opportunity for love and to get my needs met.	Caregiver cannot provide my needs regularly and sometimes gets angry at me; People are not to be trusted because they harm me; I can't protect myself
Long-term outcome	Able to express distress at separation at age 3; Greater concentration in play; Better achievement, language, conflict resolution, school adjustment, and social competence	Low externalizing; Less socially competent; Likely to be rejected by teachers; Victimized by peers; Difficulty with emotional closeness	High externalizing behavior; Pampered by teachers; Victimized by peers at school; Cognitive and social problem-solving difficulty	Problems at school; Substantial aggression; Self-injury; Dissociative and conduct disorders

Data from Ainsworth, M. D. S., & Bowlby, J. (1991). An ethological approach to personality development. *American Psychologist, 46*, 331-341. 1; Bowlby, J. (1969). *Attachment and loss: Vol. 1. Attachment.* New York, NY: Basic Books; Henninghausen, K.H., & Lyons-Ruth, K. (2005). Disorganization of behavioral and attentional strategies toward primary attachment figures: From biologic to dialogic processes. In C. S. Carter, L.Ahnert, K. E. Grossman, S. B. Hardy, M. E. Lamb, S.W. Porges, & N. Sachser (Eds.), *Attachment and bonding: A new synthesis* (pp. 269-300). Cambridge, MA: MIT Press; Sroufe, L.A. (2005). *Emotional development.* Cambridge, United Kingdom: Cambridge University Press.

who the caregiver is (e.g., mother versus childcare provider)—that affects whether secure attachments develop (Eliker, Fortner-Wood, & Noppe, 1999), although this process may be easier in home-based than in center-based care facilities (Ahnert, Pinquart, & Lamb, 2006). Children will form insecure attachments when they receive insensitive caregiving (i.e., poor quality), the effect of which will be worse when the child spends a lot of time in this type of care situation or when multiple caregivers are used during the child's first 15 months of life, such that there is little consistency in caregiving (National Institute of Child Health and Human Development Early Child Care Research Network, 1997).

The caregiver's attentiveness and responsiveness to the infant's needs affect the development of secure attachment, whereas the infant's temperament (e.g., irritability), particularly a difficult one, mediates the type of insecure attachment formed (Susman-Stillman, Kalkose, Egeland, & Waldman, 1996). Attachment is also influenced by other factors related to the infant's health (e.g., medical complications) and colicky behavior (i.e., when the infant cries for extended periods), both of which are linked to caregiver sensitivity (Sroufe, 2005). New parents, in particular, need a supportive system (i.e., positive partner relationship, adequate finances, good mental health, good parenting in own childhood) to help them to become sensitive, responsive caregivers (Cox, Paley, Payne, & Burchinal, 1999; Crockenberg & Leerkes, 2003; Martins & Gaffan, 2000). Of course, caregiving is also simpler when parents have an easygoing infant.

A connection between the type of caregiving and the resulting attachment profile has been found in a variety of cultures (Posada et al., 2002). Cross-cultural studies using the strange situation have found that approximately two-thirds of infants have secure attachments, although the percentages of children assigned to insecure attachment classes differ (Svanberg, 1998). Specifically, anxious/ambivalent insecure attachment is most common in collectivist cultures (e.g., Japan) in which cooperation is valued, whereas avoidant insecure attachment is most common in individualistic cultures (e.g., Europe) in which independence and self-reliance are prized. The end result of this socialization process in infancy is that the child develops an identity and sense of self.

Identity and Self-Concept

Infants begin the individuation process of understanding "self" as separate from the caregiver around 5 months of age, when they learn that they can activate change intentionally (e.g., the mobile turns if the child kicks his or her leg), and later through self-awareness around 18 months and continuing with independence through age 3 years. Toddlers express their new knowledge in various ways, including how they refer to themselves and others (e.g., I, you), learning that other people's perspectives are different from their own, recognizing themselves in the mirror, and not wanting to share their possessions. Toddlers use categorical information to describe themselves as boys and girls. According to Erikson (1963), the young toddler struggles with autonomy/self-reliance (versus shame and doubt).

Preschoolers' self-assessments are unrealistically confident and overly optimistic, as they believe that they are capable of doing the impossible (e.g., climbing a building). Their descriptions focus on *concrete and observable characteristics*, such as possessions (e.g., I have three dolls), names (e.g., I am Nicole), looks (e.g., I have brown hair), roles (e.g., I am a sister), and some psychological characteristics (e.g., I am nice). Erikson (1963) believed that preschoolers develop a sense of purpose/initiative (versus guilt) as they learn how to perform daily tasks and help around the house with various chores.

During middle childhood, children's self-descriptions include reference to their competencies (e.g., I am good at math); their dispositions (e.g., I am a sourpuss); and their academic, social, and physical selves (e.g., I am smart and athletic and everyone likes me). They can do this because, unlike preschoolers, they have developed an ability to perform *social comparison* (Harter, 1999, 2006)—that is, they can compare themselves to others in terms of their skills and abilities (e.g., I am better than John at swimming). At these ages, Erikson (1990) described children as capable/industrious workers (versus inferior) who understand their competencies by completing tasks in and out of school and by receiving evaluations from teachers, coaches, and tutors who provide advice to them on how to improve their skills.

Strang's (1957) theory described four types of self that develop in adolescence:

- The *general self-concept* involves an overall perception of abilities, roles, and status in world (e.g., "I am smart and I am a daughter and granddaughter").
- The *temporary self-concept* consists of changing perceptions based on current experiences (e.g., when berated by teacher, the child thinks, "I am stupid").
- The *social self-concept* involves the perception of self in relation to others (e.g., "Everyone is nice to me so they like me").
- The *ideal self-concept* consists of projected images of one's best, imagined self, but not necessarily the realistic self (e.g., "I was the first to wear my pants backward, and then everyone copied me").

Adolescents are able to conceive of themselves as a whole, despite seeming incongruities in their self-concepts.

How do adolescents work toward identity? Erikson (1990) claimed that adolescents undergo a process of identification (identity versus role confusion), trying to figure out who they are and who they want to become, whereas young adults struggle with making connections to others while maintaining their own sense of self (e.g., intimacy versus isolation). Marcia's (1990) *identity status theory* assumes that various aspects of identity are formed (such as political ideas, religious beliefs, and career path) on the basis of commitments preceded by a period of exploration of roles and identity during moratorium. The most developed status is *identity achievement* (IA), in which alternatives are explored and commitments made. *Moratorium* is a phase that precedes IA, in which exploration is undertaken prior to commitments being made. *Foreclosure status* occurs when there is no exploration, but rather the person commits to childhood-based values and determines to follow preset ideologies. The least developed status is *identity diffusion*, in which the person is uncommitted to definite directions in his or her life. This process of identity will continue to evolve during adulthood, particularly when undergoing a significant life event (e.g., marriage). This process of identity formation occurs concurrently with the development of children's self-esteem, which is discussed in the next section.

Self-Esteem

Self-esteem refers to one's sense of internal worth and self-confidence. Positive self-esteem means that a person made a good self-evaluation (i.e., one likes and respects oneself), whereas negative self-esteem means that a person made a bad self-evaluation. Self-esteem is important because it affects the willingness of a child to try and welcome challenges, master new skills, and learn new material, despite the fact that the child is unlikely to succeed initially (e.g., tie shoelaces). Self-esteem is derived from four sources: (1) a person's emotional relationship with his or her parents; (2) a person's social competence with peers; (3) a person's intellectual prowess at school as evaluated by teachers; and (4) the attitudes of society and community toward the individual as evidenced by neighbors and community leaders (Wigfield et al., 1997). Through interactions with the people in their lives, children determine whether these adults respect and like them. Adults who use "unconditional positive regard" with children show them approval and acceptance while correcting their mistakes and misbehavior. Positive self-esteem is fostered through honest recognition of children's actions and praise for specific behaviors (e.g., "You worked hard to tie your shoelaces") rather than generic praise (e.g., "Good job") and is related to positive developmental outcomes, such as academic performance (Baumeister, Campbell, Krueger, & Vohs, 2003). Through these external sources, children develop internal sources of satisfaction, respect, value, and competence.

Physical changes in puberty, school environmental changes, cognitive and academic expectations, and social challenges all influence adolescents' self-esteem, often in a negative way. Their newfound abilities allow them to be cognizant of the discrepancy between their self-assessed abilities and their ideal selves in various important areas, which may result in disappointment, sadness, or depression (Eccles et al., 1997; Fenzel, 2000; Harter, 2006). Differences in self-esteem are especially evident in boys and girls who begin puberty early (Newman & Newman, 2009). Girls may become self-conscious of their additional fat, due to critical evaluation from peers raised in a society that worships thinness, and their breast development, which is likely to draw extra attention from older boys. Boys, in contrast, are treated by both peers and adults in positive ways as their bodies become more muscular and athletic, which drives them to engage in sports (such participation is highly valued in American society). By comparison, late-developing boys are at a disadvantage, experiencing lower status and popularity than their peers, whereas late-developing girls are at somewhat of an advantage because they fit in with their female and male peers and garner societal admiration of their thinness, but are treated by others as children despite having a high maturity level. Self-esteem is also reduced by the discrepancy between middle school academic expectations, which require adolescents to do large amounts of work independently and to comply with strict rules, and students' actual developmental capacities to cope and succeed (Eccles, 1999). The impact of family and peers on the child's social development is discussed in the next section.

Social Interactions: Family and Peers

Types of Families

A variety of family types exist within the United States today. A nuclear family consists of two parents with children. A single-parent family has one parent who is divorced or has never been married with children. There are two types of stepfamilies: the blended one in which a spouse joins the family and a binuclear one in which two families merge (*Brady Bunch* style). Extended families include parents, grandparents, uncles, aunts, and cousins (in some combination) with children. Alternative lifestyles include those that are commonly found in American society, such as co-habitators (e.g., homosexual or heterosexual unmarried couples), as well as less common styles, such as communes (i.e., group of unrelated people living together) and other arrangements (e.g., foster homes, group homes).

Benefits of having two people as caregivers include having two views; allowing one person to compensate for shortcomings in the other and to enhance the other's strengths; providing children with love, attention, and discipline; having a higher likelihood of being financially sound; and being able to afford good, safe housing. The problems associated with a two-caregiver household include the fact that not all biological or step-parents are good and not every marriage nurturing. A disturbed or negative parent and/or marital conflict between the caregivers can create psychological harm for the children. Often there are sibling disputes in extended and stepfamilies, and the non-biological parent may be rejected, have different and perhaps conflicting childrearing practices, or be seen as an intruder.

Benefits of having one caregiver include a close, harmonious family relationship and emotional stability, but these benefits also depend on the reason for single parenthood (i.e., never married, divorced, partner death). Single parents may compensate for not having a partner by requiring children to take on household responsibilities (i.e., instrumental parentification) or by relying on extended family to assist in the care of their children (Asmussen & Larson, 1991; Jurkovic, Thirkield, & Morrell, 2001). Another problem often associated with having one caregiver is financial instability (and associated stress), most often because it is difficult to raise children on one income regardless of the reason for single parenthood and because, with the exception of spousal loss, there are few social, economic, and therapeutic support systems in place for single parents. Single-parent families are more likely than two-parent families to be at or below poverty level (U.S. Census Bureau, 2007).

Divorce may have some specific negative results. In particular, if there had been marital discord prior to the divorce, then it is likely that some conflict will persist. Also, divorce always brings a change in socioeconomic lifestyle (e.g., movement from middle-class to lower-class status). Several factors affect adjustment after divorce, including the custodial parent's mental health (dealing with stress), the child's age (younger children blame themselves, older children become disruptive), the child's temperament (dealing with stress), the child's sex (sons under mothers' custodial care often have problems), and the support systems available to parents and children (coping mechanisms and extended family care).

Parenting Styles, Control, and Discipline

Based on her work with preschoolers, Baumrind (1967) proposed a combination of four dimensions of parenting to explain various interactive styles—that is, the responsiveness to the child's needs, expectations, communication, and discipline strategies/control (Baumrind, 1967, 1991; Maccoby, 1992; Maccoby & Martin, 1983):

- The *authoritarian/coercive style* is characterized by parents being unresponsive to children's needs, having high expectations/being demanding of children, showing low communication of parental guidelines (aloof), and using high-discipline strategies/control. Parents with this style require absolute rule obedience without explaining the reasons for the rules, and they often deride, demean, or diminish the child by using mocking, put-downs, and punitive/physical or psychologically controlling means to show absolute power over the child.

- The *indifferent/uninvolved* style is characterized by unresponsive, undemanding/ low expectations, no or low communication, and low control. Such a parent has limited interactions with the child, is emotionally detached when the child is present, and shows indifference to the child's basic needs (e.g., in extreme cases to the point of maltreatment), point of view, and decisions about his or her life.

- The *permissive style* is characterized by high responsiveness, nurturing, and communication, but is lenient and makes few demands and sets few behavioral limits (i.e., no or lax discipline, allowing the child to decide). Parents indulge the child in every whim and desire, allowing the child to engage in whatever activity he or she wants with little expectations of self-regulation or maturity.

- The *democratic/authoritative style* is characterized by high responsiveness, expectations, communication (i.e., children may ask questions, receive explanations), and control (i.e., sets rules and limits but enforces with reasoning and advice). Parents foster warm, positive emotional connections with children; are patient, nurturing, and forgiving; provide reasonable, fair, and consistent limits and decisions; are assertive without being intrusive; and attempt to instill a sense of cooperation, social responsibility, self-regulation, and assertiveness in their children.

Parents also use these styles of parenting with older children and adolescents (Cherry, 2011), but Duncan (n.d.) has shown that the use of a particular style results in different outcomes (Table 3-4). Although an authoritarian style is acceptable for preschool-age children, the parenting style should be adapted in accordance with the age and mental capacity of the child. In middle childhood, parents co-regulate or guide children's behaviors by allowing children to take a bigger role in adapting their own behaviors. Parents should adjust their expectations accordingly, while setting boundaries that are clear and reasonable. During adolescence, parents should foster autonomy by involving their children in developing family rules and establishing consequences that are enforceable and realistic (i.e., outcomes that the parent can control and that directly affect the child). This strategy encourages adolescents' compliance by making it clear what is and is not negotiable, without the parents getting into an argument with them about the rules/consequences each time a violation occurs. Adolescents typically make parenting difficult because they are trying to express themselves, often by contradicting their parents' ways of acting, dressing,

Table 3-4 Childhood and adolescent outcomes for each parenting style

Parenting style	Childhood outcomes	Adolescent outcomes
Democratic/ authoritative	Happy; self-confident; can regulate emotions; persists at tasks; competent; capable; works well with others	Positive self-worth; good social interaction skills; highly developed morality; high achiever
Authoritarian/ coercive	Overly submissive and obedient; socially inept; low self-esteem; apprehensive; inhibited; unhappy; reacts aggressively	Some social and emotional competence; some academic achievement
Permissive	Immature responses; unhappy; noncompliant; defiant with authority; difficult; overly reliant on adults; fails to persevere at tasks and in school	Impulsive; low academic achievement; insolent; destructive
Rejecting/ uninvolved	Interrupted attachment; low cognitive abilities; difficulty in peer interactions, regulating emotions, and expression through play; low self-esteem; unhappy; withdrawn; impulsive	Difficulty in peer interactions and in regulating emotions; poor academic achievement; destructive

Data from Baumrind, D. (1967). Child-care practices anteceding three patterns of preschool behavior. *Genetic Psychology Monographs, 75,* 43–88.; Cherry, K. (2011). Parenting styles: The four styles of parenting. Retrieved from http://psychology. about.com/od/developmentalpsychology/a/parenting-style.htm; Duncan, S.F. (n.d.). Styles of parenting. Retrieved from http:// realfamiliesrealanswers.org/?page_id=78.

and talking, and testing limits using their advanced cognitive skills. Parents must decide which confrontations to engage in and which to avoid, particularly as adolescents have incomplete control over their emotions, and they should be sure that their children are listening when discussing or negotiating with them. Additionally, parental expectations should include that the children be respectful (e.g., perform chores for the family), responsible (e.g., get the best grades you are capable of earning), and pleasant (e.g., someone enjoyable to be around).

One of the toughest tasks of parenting is controlling the child's behavior, while striving to help the child develop self-control. Good parenting dictates that the parent make the rules and require the child to follow them (Fisher, 2006). As the adult, the parent sets an example of how the child should behave. Children follow what they see from their role models—they do what those models do more often than they do what those models say. Children should be rewarded (typically with praise) for complying with parental standards to motivate them to continue making good choices. Routine helps in this process of learning. The parent's job is not to be the child's friend, but rather to guide the child's behaviors, teaching what is expected and why it is necessary.

Inevitably, there will be situations in which children misbehave, and the rationale for such behavior will vary. Some children are seeking attention, and perceive that even negative attention is better than none. Other children feel inadequate; that is, they feel helpless so they want to show others that they do not need to rely on them. Some children seek revenge; in particular, they desire to hurt others because they feel hurt. Others seek power, trying to prove that they are strong and that no one can boss them around.

In response to misbehavior, parents can use a variety of behavioral control and discipline techniques. Experts advise parents to reward good behavior, set a limited number of clear rules, and talk to their child about problems. They also recommend that parents choose alternatives to *power assertive* techniques, which typically use physical force/punishment (e.g., spanking), threats, and deprivations often resulting in negative repercussions. Instead, experts advocate non-spanking techniques for three main reasons. First, spanking sends a message of violence as a way of solving problems and of getting compliance. Second, spanking sends a message that the parent dislikes the child or rejects him or her when the parent is angry. Third, spanking reduces the value of the parent as a positive influence because children avoid people who punish them physically.

Alternative, noncoercive techniques for controlling behavior include parents' use of *time-out* for very young children, in which the child is temporarily removed from a situation, and *commands* (e.g., stop), in which requests are made without threats of harm or punishment. Parents of preschoolers and elementary school–age children should also use *induction* or reasoning with the child from ethical or religious principles, explaining the consequences of children's actions as gains/losses to the child and others, and *withdrawal of privileges*, which involves preventing the child from accessing a source of pleasure, such as television. Parents of older children and adolescents may also include *advice* as a technique, such that they provide potential solutions for their children and identify the consequences that each choice may have for the child's situation/problem. Another technique that may be used, *love withdrawal*, in which parents apply temporary coldness or rejection to gain compliance from the child, has mixed support from experts (see Levine & Munsch, 2011).

Experts recommend that the parents adapt their discipline techniques to their children consistent with their ages and abilities to exercise self-control, responsibility, and independence (Goodman, 2013). Regardless of which control technique a parent chooses to use, discipline will be effective only if the following principles are implemented (Fisher, 2006):

- First, parents must be fair. This goal does not require that parents treat each child in the same way because each child is not the same (fair does not mean equal); that is, children have different needs based on their personality, age, and circumstances, and parents must respond accordingly. Additionally, parents should make the punishment fit the misbehavior (i.e., logical) or, at best, the consequences should be meaningful and appropriate (i.e., natural). For example, suppose your son refuses to clean up his room, leaving books, toys, and laundry scattered on the floor. He trips over an object and hurts his foot (i.e., natural consequence). Alternatively, if the clothes are not placed in the laundry bin, they do not get washed; consequently, the child has no clean clothes available to wear to school (i.e., logical consequence).

- Second, whatever decision they make, parents must be firm and follow through with it. Often parents will blurt out a consequence (e.g., no television for the rest of the child's life), only to later rethink it, evaluate it to be the wrong decision, and thus be discouraged to implement it. If parents are not sure, they should wait until they are calm, telling the child they will inform him or her later of the consequence.
- Third, parents should be consistent each and every time. In other words, they should hand out the same punishment for the same misbehavior so the child can make the connection.
- Fourth, all discipline should be based on an established loving relationship with the children.
- Fifth, discipline should be administered by a person who has control over his or her temper—never in anger. If necessary, step away or send the child to his or her room and return a few minutes later.
- Sixth, parents should never threaten the child's self-esteem. Doing so will merely make it more difficult for the child to learn (or want) to control his or her behavior. In this way, the caregivers' ability to guide children during emotional outbursts (and to prevent them) is related subsequently to children's self-control.

Development of Self-Control in Children

Self-control involves the ability to deal with negative feelings without misbehaving and to accept situations even when they are not what was wanted or expected (Bronson, 2000). At birth, brain regions associated with self-control are undeveloped, but they begin to mature during the preschool years to allow children to control their impulses, refocus their attention, and delay gratification; development of these parts of the brain is completed by the end of adolescence to young adulthood (Tarullo, Obradovic, & Gunnar, 2009). Both intrinsic factors, such as temperament and cognitive abilities (e.g., attention, inhibition), and extrinsic factors, such as caregiving, family and peer relationships, and cultural expectations, affect children's development of self-control (Fox & Calkins, 2003). Parents who provide discipline that guides and externally controls the emotions and behaviors of their infants, toddlers, and preschoolers while establishing clear and consistent rules and routines, moral boundaries, and positive self-esteem will help their children to learn how to engage in self-control and to make good choices (Gliebe, 2011). Specifically, with age, children will become patient, control their anger, empathize with others, and react in positive ways to frustrating situations (Honig & Lansburgh, 1991; Lemmon & Moore, 2007).

Self-control is affected by secure attachment (Bronson, 2000); that is, children with this type of attachment are not defensive, angry, and hopeless in negative situations (Honig, 2002, 2010) and learn to persist despite obstacles (Sroufe et al., 2009). Authoritative parents use warmth and nurturing to support their children, focusing on problem solving rather than on punishment, while providing consistency and enforcing rules, making this style conducive to the child's development of self-regulation (Bronson, 2000; Honig & Lansburgh, 1991). Keeping in mind that not every decision is negotiable, parents need to provide opportunities for their children to make choices and realize consequences, and should allow (and respect) their children's decisions. The parents' role is to guide this process, encouraging their children to adhere to acceptable choices (by the parents' standards) so that children will learn the connection between their own decisions and the ensuing consequences. For example, parents who stay calm when children are having a tantrum will show that they—and not the children—are in control; they teach the children that the tantrum was not only unacceptable behavior, but also an ineffective tool for accomplishing their desired goals.

Likewise, parents need to teach children coping strategies to allow them to regain control of their emotions and behavior in frustrating and disappointing situations. Infants, toddlers, and preschoolers have difficulty controlling their feelings and actions when there is a large gap between what they want and what they can do/have (Zero to Three, 2012). Parents can try to redirect their attention, distract them, or simply give them a time-out to allow them to regain their composure. Infants can develop self-soothing techniques, such as sucking fingers or a pacifier, or can be soothed by the caregiver through contact, such as hugging, rocking, and swaddling. School-age children are capable of understanding the consequences of bad behavior and can use various techniques to remain calm, such as walking away from an irritating situation. Early adolescents are good at identifying their feelings and should learn how to recognize when they lose control and figure out why it happened. They may also be able to analyze which techniques are effective in keeping them calm. Older adolescents should be able to control their actions most of the time, but may need to be reminded of long-term consequences when upset about a situation so they will not respond inappropriately (e.g., slam doors, yell). Peers often help their friends to find socially appropriate ways to control their negative emotional responses. In the next section, peers and friendship will be discussed.

Peers, Play, and Friendship

The peer group consists of individuals who are the same age and have the same social status, and who play, work, and learn together. They form the society of children or the subculture of peers that dictate the group's rules for how to talk, dress, and act (also known as social codes). Peer interactions provide children with voluntary and egalitarian opportunities to interact with others of their own level of social and cognitive ability, often resulting in fun activities (Dunn, 2004). Peer relationships begin in infancy/toddlerhood with use of engaging behaviors, such as smiling (Hay, Nash, & Pedersen, 1983), simple imitation of interesting behaviors (Asendorpf & Baudonniere, 1993; Eckerman & Peterman, 2001), and words geared toward helping to plan and coordinate play (Eckerman & Didow, 1996). Peer groups can form in schools, neighborhoods, or other contexts (e.g., sport teams).

Peers evaluate each other through the lens of an "in-group/acceptance and out-group/rejection" mentality of social status (Brown, 1990). Social status of individual children is measured by various types of sociometric techniques (e.g., nominate several peers whom they like and whom they dislike; indicate pairs whom they want to play with on a scale from 1 to 5). Typically, acceptance is based on physical appearance and social behavior, such as athletic skills. According to Coie, Dodge, and Coppotelli (1982), four types of children can be distinguished in terms of peer acceptance, likeability, and social impact: (1) The popular child gets many positive votes (high peer acceptance and social preference); (2) the controversial child gets both positive and negative votes (high social impact); (3) the neglected child (loner) is seldom chosen for positive or negative votes (low social impact); and (4) the rejected child is actively disliked as indicated by many negative votes, either because the child is withdrawn/passive and socially awkward or aggressive/suffers from severe conduct disorders (low peer acceptance); La Greca & Prinstein, 1999. Such an assessment tool can be used to predict psychological adjustment, particularly for the rejected children, who often demonstrate poor school performance, and are at risk for dropping out, antisocial behavior, and delinquency in adolescence (Bagwell, Newcomb, & Bukowski, 1998). Hymel, Vaillancourt, McDougall, and Renshaw (2002) suggest that popularity is related to both power and dominance, and even adolescents perceived to be popular may perform risky acts, have difficulty academically, and externalize their problems. While popular children are often seen as helpful, cooperative, and good problem solvers, another group of antisocial popular boys earn this high social status while being disruptive and bullying others (Rodkin, Farmer, Pearl, & Van Acker, 2000). For unpopular children, rejection by the group can be countered through friendship with one child. Loners tend to be psychologically capable over time of learning the social skills of friendship, whereas rejected children often remain friendless and disliked by their peer groups (Zettergren, 2005).

Play is important in any culture, as it provides an opportunity for children to develop skills they will need as adults (Scarlett, Naudeau, Salonius-Pasternak, & Ponte, 2005). Often play imitates adult work, but children play because it is fun and keeps them engaged. Play, especially in unstructured activities such as recess, is important because it allows children to develop physically and emotionally, gain social skills, and advance cognitive skills (problem-solving); it also provides motivation for learning because it is intrinsically rewarding and provides an outlet for releasing stress created by cognitive overload (Barros, Silver, & Stein, 2009; Pellegrini, 2005; Smith, 2010). Often boys and girls choose to play in same-sex groups, at least when there are many children available, and this preference is particularly strong in middle childhood (Maccoby, 1990; Maccoby, 1992; Munroe & Romney, 2006) as boys and girls adopt very different play styles.

Children's self-control and peer status can be evaluated through play. According to Fantuzzo, Sekino, and Cohen (2004), children who are capable of regulating their emotions (i.e., play interaction) may engage in prosocial play activities with their peers, whereas those who are impulsive or cannot modulate their emotions (i.e., play disruption) or simply avoid play (i.e., play disconnection) may behave aggressively with their peers. Parten (1932) described different types of play that she had observed, suggesting that interactive, cooperative play occurs more often with age as social, cognitive, linguistic, and emotional skills emerge:

- *Unoccupied* and *onlooker behaviors* occur when the child is observing what is going on without participating.

- In *solitary independent play*, the child plays his or her own game or plays with a toy.
- In *parallel play*, children play the same type of game or with a similar toy, but do not interact.
- In *associative play*, children interact in a game or with a toy, but without any organized goal in mind.
- In *cooperative play*, children work together to fulfill a specific plan or goal.

Friendships (defined as close and affectionate relationships) begin in the preschool years as children select certain companions for the day, weeks, months, or years (Dunn, 2004). Preschoolers and children often select friends from among those in their neighborhoods and schools. However, once children enter school, the way that friends are defined and valued changes. Overall, the child becomes more choosy in regard to expectations of loyalty, self-disclosure, and reciprocity, and the groups of friends/peers get smaller as children between ages 6 and 12 years pair up with a "best friend" with whom they engage in various mutual activities. In adolescence, friends serve a multitude of roles, including being someone from whom to learn social skills to maintain the friendship (i.e., negotiate, compromise, discuss, empathize); helping to understand oneself; achieving independence from parents; establishing sexual relationships; being an important source of companionship and fun; sharing advice and possessions; serving as trusted confidants and critics; providing stability in time of stress; and acting as a source of emotional support (Brown, 1990; Dunphy, 1990). Girls prefer to have smaller, more exclusive and intimate friendships characterized by equality and loyalty than do boys (Clark & Ayers, 1992). Friends also are similar in demographic characteristics, attitudes, values, and activities, because people select others who are like them, and friends' influence over each other becomes stronger with age and over time (Clark & Ayers, 1992; Kandel, 1978; Solomon & Knafo, 2007).

Adolescent Peer Pressure and Support

Adolescents rely on the advice and socioemotional support from the people around them—parents, peers, teachers, and others (Steinberg, 2005). Although they adopt their parents' educational, political, religious, and personal values, peers have more influence on them regarding the peer group's preferences, such as hairstyles, music, and leisure activities. Adolescents join a particular clique (a small group spending time together) and crowd (a larger, reputation-based group such as jocks, nerds, druggies, and brains) as a way of defining themselves and trying out different identities (Brown & Klute, 2003). Many adolescents have multiple friends, some of whom are long term and others fleeting, and belong to various cliques consistent with their varied interests. Thus, children start out in individual unisex playgroups prior to adolescence and then these groups merge into opposite-sex "crowds," offering opportunities for them to learn how to interact appropriately in transition from friendship to dating (Dunphy, 1990).

Despite parental concerns that adolescents will not resist peer pressure to engage in antisocial behaviors (e.g., drugs, delinquency, sex), they show greater resistance for these activities than for neutral or prosocial ones (Clasen & Brown, 1985). Peer pressure refers to direct (e.g., rewarding compliance) or indirect (e.g., modeling desired behavior) influences that children of the same or similar age have on one another. Whether an adolescent is pressured to engage in antisocial or prosocial activities depends on the selected peer group. For example, adolescents who belong to antisocial peer groups are likely to engage in these activities because of the groups' direct and indirect pressure (influence) and their own inclination to do so (selection), which is the reason they joined the group and were motivated to stay (e.g., Dishion, Spracklen, Andrews, & Patterson, 1996; Steinberg, 2005). In contrast, having academically high-achieving peers will pressure adolescents to do well in their schoolwork (Mounts & Steinberg, 1995).

Eventually the crowd, which consists of opposite-sex members, disintegrates into groups of couples (Dunphy, 1990). That is, emotional connections between members often result in pairing off for dating and influence whether adolescents will engage in early or delayed initiation into sexual behavior (Billy & Udry, 1985; Brown, 1993). Girls are vulnerable to peer pressure to have sex because they are duped into thinking that boys will honor and respect intimacy and commitment, which is the hallmark of their friendships with other girls (Brown, 1982, 1993; Savin-Williams & Berndt, 1993). Moreover, girls' ability to resist peer pressure reflects their level of self-confidence (Brown, 1993), which may be low in those who enter into puberty early; consequently, these girls are likely to begin dating before they are emotionally ready. Several researchers indicate that girls (between 60% and 75% prior to age 15 years) are less likely than boys (92%) to report that their first experience of penile–vaginal intercourse was voluntary or wanted (Alan Guttmacher Institute, 1994; Lauman, Gagnon, Michael, & Michaels, 1994). When the first sexual intercourse experience occurs prior to age 13 years, 20% of girls report it was coerced and nonvoluntary and 50% of girls report that it was voluntary but unwanted (SIECUS, 1997, as cited in Crockett, Raffaelli, & Moilanen, 2003). Similarly, sex differences in social and emotional responses to oral sex have been reported. Specifically, the consequences for boys are positive, as they are motivated by pleasure and receive it; in contrast, the consequences for girls may be negative, as they are motivated by improving relationships and instead get "dumped" (i.e., the relationship ends) after performing the sexual act.

Chapter Summary

Children's understanding of who they are, what they are feeling, and which behavior they should expect from others is central to their emotional and social development. These aspects, in turn, contribute to children's self-image, self-esteem, self-actualization, ability to empathize, and even development of healthy, lasting, and meaningful relationships with others. In particular, emotions have four main functions: to help individuals socialize with others by binding them to those they love; to motivate them to achieve their goals; to organize worldviews; and to aid in communication. Socioemotional relationships begin with attachment. Through socialization, children develop an identity and a sense of self. Families, parenting style, and peers play a vital role in developing children's emotional and social well-being (Maccoby, 1992). Children's emotional and social development also influences their cognitive, language and motor development.

Review Questions

1. Why is knowledge of emotional and social development necessary for professionals working in the field of child maltreatment?

2. How did Ainsworth's theory of attachment build on work by Bowlby?

3. What are the four sources that contribute to self-esteem?

4. How do adolescents strive for self-identity?

5. Name and describe the four parenting styles. Name at least one benefit and one consequence of each type in childhood and adolescence.

6. Which factors affect the development of children's self-control?

7. How does the relationship between parents and their children affect friendship and intimacy with peers in childhood and adolescence?

References

Adler, N. (2002). *International dimensions of organizational behavior* (4th ed.) Cincinnati, OH: South-Western College Publishing.

Ahnert, L., Pinquart, M., & Lamb, M. E. (2006). Security of children's relationships with nonparental care providers: A meta-analysis. *Child Development, 77,* 664–679.

Ainsworth, M. D. S. (1979). Infant–mother attachment. *American Psychologist, 34,* 932–937.

Ainsworth, M. D. S., & Bell, S. M. (1970). Attachment, exploration, and separation: Illustrated by the behavior of one-year-olds in a strange situation. *Child Development, 41,* 49–67.

Ainsworth, M. D. S., & Bowlby, J. (1991). An ethological approach to personality development. *American Psychologist, 46,* 331–341.

Alan Guttmacher Institute. (1994). *Sex and America's teenagers.* New York, NY: Author. http://www.guttmacher.org/pubs/FB-ATSRH.html

Asendorpf, J. B., & Baudonniere, P. (1993). Self-awareness and other-awareness: Mirror self-recognition and synchronic imitation among unfamiliar peers. *Developmental Psychology, 29,* 88–95.

Asmussen, L., & Larson, R. (1991). The quality of family time among young adolescents in single-parent and married-parent families. *Journal of Marriage and Family, 53,* 1021–1030.

Bagwell, C. L., Newcomb, A. F., & Bukowski, W. M. (1998). Preadolescent friendship and peer rejection as predictors of adult adjustment. *Child Development, 69,* 140–153.

Barros, R. M., Silver, E. J., & Stein, R. E. K. (2009). School recess and group classroom behavior. *Pediatrics, 123,* 431–436.

Baumeister, R. F., Campbell, J. D., Krueger, J. I., & Vohs, K. D. (2003). Does high self-esteem cause better performance, interpersonal success, happiness, or healthier lifestyles? *Psychological Science in the Public Interest, 4,* 1–44.

Baumrind, D. (1967). Child-care practices anteceding three patterns of preschool behavior. *Genetic Psychology Monographs, 75,* 43–88.

Baumrind, D. (1991). The influence of parenting style on adolescent competence and substance use. *Journal of Early Adolescence, 11*(1), 56–95.

Bell, R. Q. (1974). Contributions of human infants to caregiving and social interaction. In M. Lewis & L. A. Rosenblum (Eds.), *The effect of the infant on its caregiver* (pp. 1–20). New York, NY: Wiley

Billy, J. O., & Udry, J. R. (1985). Patterns of adolescent friendship and effects on sexual behavior. *Social Psychology Quarterly, 48,* 27–41.

Bowlby, J. (1969). *Attachment and loss: Vol. 1. Attachment.* New York, NY: Basic Books.

Bronson, M. (2000) *Self-regulation in early childhood.* New York, NY: Guilford Press.

Brown, B. B. (1990). Peer groups and peer cultures. In S. S. Feldman & G. R. Elliott (Eds.). *At the threshold: The developing adolescent* (pp. 171–198). Cambridge, MA: Harvard University Press.

Brown, B. B. (1982). The extent and effect of peer pressure among high school students: A retrospective study. *Journal of Youth and Adolescence, 11,* 121–133.

Brown, B. B. (1993). Peer groups and peer cultures. In S. S. Feldman & G. R. Elliott (Eds.), *At the threshold: The developing adolescent* (pp. 171–196). Cambridge, MA: Harvard University Press.

Brown, B. B. (2004). Adolescents' relationships with peers. In R. M. Lerner & L. Steinberg (Eds.), *Handbook of adolescent psychology* (2nd ed., pp. 363–394). New York, NY: Wiley.

Brown, B. B., & Klute, C. (2003). Friendships, cliques, and crowds. In G. R. Adams & M. D. Berzonsky (Eds.), *Blackwell handbook of adolescence* (pp. 330–348). Malden, MA: Blackwell.

Cherry, K. (2011). Parenting styles: The four styles of parenting. http://psychology.about.com/od /developmentalpsychology/a/parenting-style.htm

Chess, S., & Thomas, A. (1999). *Goodness of fit: Clinical applications from infancy through adult life.* Philadelphia, PA: Brunner/Mazel.

Clark, M. K., & Ayers, M. (1992). Friendship similarity during early adolescence: Gender and racial patterns. *Journal of Psychology: Interdisciplinary and Applied, 126,* 393–405.

Clasen, D. R., & Brown, B. B. (1985). The multidimensionality of peer pressure in adolescence. *Journal of Youth and Adolescence, 14,* 451–468.

Coie, J. D., Dodge, K. A., & Coppotelli, H. (1982). Dimensions and types of social status: A cross-age perspective. *Developmental Psychology, 18,* 557–570.

Cox, M., Paley, B., Payne, C. C., & Burchinal, M. (1999). The transition to parenthood: Marital conflict and withdrawal and parent–child interactions. In M. J. Cox & J. Brooks-Gunn (Eds.), *Conflict and cohesion in families: Causes and consequences* (pp. 87–104). Mahwah, NJ: Erlbaum.

Crockenberg, S., & Leerkes, E. (2003). Infant negative emotionality, caregiving, and family relationships. In A. C. Crouter & A. Booth (Eds.), *Children's influence on family dynamics* (pp. 57–78). Mahwah, NJ: Erlbaum.

Crockett, L. J., Raffaelli, M., & Moilanen, K. L. (2003). Adolescent sexuality: Behavior and meaning. In G. R. Adams & M. D. Berzonsky (Eds.), *Blackwell handbook of adolescence* (pp. 371–392). Malden MA: Blackwell.

Dishion, T. J., Spracklen, K. M., Andrews, D. W., & Patterson, G. R. (1996). Deviancy training in male adolescents friendships. *Behavior Therapy, 27,* 373–390.

Duncan, S. F. (n.d.). Styles of parenting. http://realfamiliesrealanswers.org/?page_id=78

Dunn, J. (2004). *Children's friendships.* Malden, MA: Blackwell.

Dunphy, D. C. (1990). Peer group socialization. In R. E. Muuss (Ed.), *Adolescent behavior and society: A book of readings* (4th ed., pp. 171–183). New York, NY: McGraw-Hill.

Eccles, J. S. (1999). The development of children ages 6 to 14. *The Future of Children, 9,* 30–44.

Eccles, J. S., Midgley, C., Wigfield, A., Buchanan, C. M., Reuman, D., Flanagan, C., & Iver, D. M. (1997). Development during adolescence: The impact of stage-environment fit on young adolescents' experiences in schools and in families. In J. Nottermann (Ed.), *The evolution of psychology: Fifty years of The American Psychologist* (pp. 475–501). Washington, DC: American Psychological Association.

Eckerman, C. O., & Didow, S. M. (1996). Nonverbal imitation and toddlers' mastery of verbal means of achieving coordinated action. *Developmental Psychology, 32,* 141–152.

Eckerman, C. O., & Peterman, K. (2001). Peers and infant social/communicative development. In G. Bremner & A. Fogel (Eds.), *Blackwell handbook of infant development* (pp. 326–350). Malden, MA: Blackwell.

Ekman, P. (1992). An argument for basic emotions. *Cognition and Emotion, 6,* 169–200.

Eliker, J., Fortner-Wood, C., & Noppe, I. C. (1999). The context of infant attachment in family childcare. *Journal of Applied Developmental Psychology, 20,* 319–336.

Erikson, E. H. (1963). *Childhood and society* (2nd ed.). New York, NY: Norton.

Erikson, E. H. (1990). Youth and the life cycle. In R. E. Muuss (Ed.), *Adolescent behavior and society: A book of readings* (4th ed., pp. 187–193). New York, NY: McGraw-Hill.

Fantuzzo, J., Sekino, Y., & Cohen, H. (2004). An examination of the contributions of interactive peer play to salient classroom competencies for urban Head Start children. *Psychology in School, 41*(3), 323–324.

Fenzel, L. M. (2000). Prospective study of changes in global self-worth and strain during the transition to middle school. *Journal of Early Adolescence, 20,* 93–116.

Field, T., Diego, M., & Hernandez-Reif, M. (2010). Preterm infant massage therapy research: A review. *Infant Behavioral Development, 33,* 115–134.

Firchow, N. (n.d.). Your child's temperament: Some basics. http://www.greatschools.org/special-education/health/788-temperament-traits.gs?page=2

Fisher, H. E. (2006). Broken hearts: The nature and risks of romantic rejection. In A. Booth & C. Crouter (Eds.), *Romance and sex in adolescence and emerging adulthood: Risks and opportunities* (pp. 3–28). Mahwah, NJ: Lawrence Erlbaum Associates.

Fox, N. A., & Calkins, S. D. (2003). The development of self-control of emotion: Intrinsic and extrinsic influences. *Motivation and Emotion, 27,* 7–26.

Gliebe, S. K. (2011). The development of self-control in young children. *Lutheran Education Journal.* http://lej.cuchicago.edu/research-in-education/the-development-of-self-control-in-young-children/

Goldsmith, H. H., Lemery, K. S., Aksan, N., & Buss, K. A. (2000). Temperamental substrates of personality. In V. J. Molfese & D. L. Molfese (Eds.), *Handbook of resilience in children* (pp. 1–32). Mahwah, NJ: Erlbaum.

Goleman, D. (1995). *Emotional intelligence.* New York, NY: Bantam Books.

Goodman (2013). How to discipline children and help them develop self control. NYU Child Study Center. http://www.education.com/reference/article/Ref_About_Discipline/

Greenspan, S. I., & Greenspan, N. (1985). *First feelings: Milestones in the emotional development of your baby and child.* New York, NY: Penguin.

Guerin, D. W., Gottfried, A. W., Oliver, P. H., & Thomas, C. W. (2003). *Temperament: Infancy through adolescence.* New York, NY: Kluwer Academic/Plenum.

Harlow, H. F. (1958). The nature of love. *American Psychologist, 13,* 673–685.

Harter, S. (1999). *The construction of the self.* New York, NY: Guilford.

Harter, S. (2006). The development of self-esteem. In M. H. Kernis (Ed.), *Self-esteem issues and answers: A sourcebook of current perspectives* (pp. 144–150). New York, NY: Psychology Press.

Hay, D. F., Nash, A., & Pedersen, J. (1983). Interaction between six-month-old peers. *Child Development, 54,* 557–562.

Henninghausen, K. H., & Lyons-Ruth, K. (2005). Disorganization of behavioral and attentional strategies toward primary attachment figures: From biologic to dialogic processes. In C. S. Carter, L. Ahnert, K. E. Grossman, S. B. Hardy, M. E. Lamb, S. W. Porges, & N. Sachser (Eds.), *Attachment and bonding: A new synthesis* (pp. 269–300). Cambridge, MA: MIT Press.

Honig, A. (2002). *Secure relationships: Nurturing infant/toddler attachment in early care settings.* Washington, DC: National Association for the Education of Young Children.

Honig, A. (2010). *Little kids, big worries.* Baltimore, MD: Paul H. Brookes.

Honig, A., & Lansburgh, T. (1991). The tasks of early childhood: The development of self-control. Part II. *Day Care and Early Education, 18*(4), 21–22.

Hymel, S., Vaillancourt, T., McDougall, P., & Renshaw, P. D. (2002). Peer acceptance and rejection in childhood. In P. K. Smith & C. H. Hart (Eds.), *Blackwell handbook of childhood social development* (pp. 265–284). Malden, MA: Blackwell.

Izard, C. E. (2007). Basic emotions, natural kinds, emotion schemas, and a new paradigm. *Perspectives on Psychological Science, 2,* 260–280.

Izard, C. E., & King, K. A. (2009). Differential emotions theory. In K. Scherer (Ed.), *Oxford companion to the affective sciences* (pp. 117–119). New York, NY: Oxford University Press.

Izard, C. E., Stark, K., Trentacosta, C., & Schultz, D. (2008). Beyond emotion regulation: Emotion utilization and adaptive functioning. *Child Development Perspectives, 2,* 156–163.

Jurkovic, G. J., Thirkield, A., & Morrell, R. (2001). Parentification of adult child of divorce: A multidimensional analysis. *Journal of Youth and Adolescence, 30,* 245–257.

Kandel, D. B. (1978). Homophily, selection, and socialization in adolescent friendships. *American Journal of Sociology, 84,* 427–436.

Kochanska, G., Murray, K., & Harlan, E. (2000). Effortful control in early childhood: Continuity and change, antecedents, and implications for social development. *Developmental Psychology, 36,* 220–232.

La Greca, A. M., & Prinstein, M. J. (1999). The peer group. In W. K. Silverman & T. H. Ollendick (Eds.), *Developmental issues in the clinical treatment of children and adolescents* (pp. 171–198). Needham Heights, MA: Allyn and Bacon.

Laumann, E. O., Gagnon, J. H., Michael, R. T., & Michaels, S. (1994). *The social organization of sexuality: Sexual practice in the United States.* Chicago, IL: University of Chicago Press.

Lemmon, K., & Moore, C. (2007). The development of prudence in the face of varying future rewards. *Developmental Science, 10*(4), 502–511.

Levine, L. E., & Munsch, J. (2011). *Child development: An active learning approach.* Thousand Oaks, CA: Sage.

Lorenz, K. Z. (1952). *King Solomon's ring.* New York, NY: Crowell.

Lustig, M., & Koester, J. (1999). *Intercultural competence: Interpersonal communication across cultures.* New York, NY: Harper Collins.

Maccoby, E. E. (1990). Gender and relationships: A developmental account. *American Psychologist, 45,* 513–520.

Maccoby, E. E. (1992). The role of parents in the socialization of children: An historical overview. *Developmental Psychology, 28,* 1006–1017.

Maccoby, E. E., & Martin, J. A. (1983). Socialization in the context of the family: Parent–child interaction. In P. H. Mussen (Ed.) & E. M. Hetherington (Vol. Ed.), *Handbook of child psychology: Socialization, personality, and social development* (Vol. 4, 4th ed., pp. 1–101). New York, NY: Wiley.

Main, M., & Solomon, J. (1990). Procedures for identifying infants as disorganized/disoriented during the Ainsworth strange situation. In M. T. Greenberg, D. Cicchetti, & E. M. Cummings (Eds.), *Attachment in the preschool years* (pp. 121–160). Chicago, IL: University of Chicago Press.

Marcia, J. E. (1990). Development and validation of ego-identity status. In R. E. Muuss (Ed.), *Adolescent behavior and society: A book of readings* (4th ed., pp. 194–201). New York, NY: McGraw-Hill.

Martins, C., & Gaffan, E. A. (2000). Effects of early maternal depression on patterns of infant–mother attachment: A meta-analytic investigation. *Journal of Child Psychology and Psychiatry, 41,* 737–746.

Matsumoto, D. (1992). American–Japanese cultural differences in the recognition of universal facial expressions. *Journal of Cross-Cultural Psychology, 23*, 72–84.

Matsumoto, D. (2006). Are cultural differences in emotion regulation mediated by personality traits? *Journal of Cross-Cultural Psychology, 37*, 421–437.

Matsumoto, D., Consolacion, T., & Yamada, H. (2002). American–Japanese cultural differences in judgments of emotional expressions of different intensities. *Cognition and Emotion, 16*, 721–747.

Mischel, W., & Ayduk, O. (2004). Willpower in a cognitive-affective processing system: The dynamics of delay of gratification. In R. F. Baumeister & K.D. Vohs (Eds.), *Handbook of self-regulation: Research, theory, and applications* (pp. 99–129). New York, NY: Guilford.

Mounts, N. S., & Steinberg, L. (1995). An ecological analysis of peer influence on adolescent grade point average and drug use. *Developmental Psychology, 31*, 915–922.

Munroe, R. L., & Romney, A. K. (2006). Gender and age differences in same-sex aggregation and social behavior: A four-culture study. *Journal of Cross-Cultural Psychology, 37*, 3–19.

Nath, R., & Murthy, N. R. V. (2004). A study of the relationship between Internet diffusion and culture. *Journal of International Technology and Information Management, 13*, 123–132.

National Institute of Child Health and Human Development Early Child Care Research Network. (1997). Child care in the first year of life. *Merrill Palmer Quarterly, 43*, 340–360.

Newman, B. M., & Newman, P. R. (2009). *Development through life: A psychosocial approach.* Belmont, CA: Wadsworth/Cengage Learning.

Parten, M. (1932). Social participation among preschool children. *Journal of Abnormal and Social Psychology, 28*, 136–147.

Pellegrini, A. D. (2005). *Recess: Its role in education and development.* Mahwah, NJ: Erlbaum.

Poland, H. J., & Ward, M .J. (1994). Role of the mother's touch in failure to thrive: A preliminary investigation. *Journal of the American Academy of Child & Adolescent Psychiatry, 33*(8), 1098–1105.

Posada, G., Jacobs, A., Richmond, M., Carbonell, O. A., Alzate, G., Bustamante, M. R., & Quiceno, J. (2002). Maternal caregiving and infant security in two cultures. *Developmental Psychology, 38*, 67–78.

Rodkin, P. C., Farmer, T. W., Pearl, R., & Van Acker, R. (2000). Heterogeneity of popular boys: Antisocial and prosocial configurations. *Developmental Psychology, 36*, 14–24.

Rothbart, M. K, Derryberry, D., & Hershey, K. (2000). Stability of temperament in childhood: Laboratory infant assessment to parent report at seven years. In V. J. Molfese & D. L. Molfese (Eds.), *Temperament and personality development across the life span* (pp. 85–119). Mahwah, NJ: Erlbaum.

Royer, R., & van der Velden, R. (2002, December). *Culture's consequences: The work of Geert Hofstede.* Paper presented at the meeting of the Seminar in Organization and International Management on the Theories and Concepts of Internationalization and FDI, Paderborne, Germany.

Savin-Williams, R. C., & Berndt, T. J. (1993). Friendships and peer relations during adolescence. In S. S. Feldman & G. Elliott (Eds.), *At the threshold: The developing adolescent* (pp. 277–307). Cambridge, MA: Harvard University Press.

Scarlett, W. G., Naudeau, S., Salonius-Pasternak, D., & Ponte, I. (2005). *Children's play.* Thousand Oaks, CA: Sage.

Smith, P. K. (2010). *Children and play.* Malden, MA: Wiley Blackwell.

Solomon, S., & Knafo, A. (2007). Value similarity in adolescent friendships In T. C. Rhodes (Ed.), *Focus on adolescent behavior research* (pp. 133–155). Hauppauge, NY: Nova Science.

Sroufe, L. A. (2005). *Emotional development.* Cambridge, UK: Cambridge University Press.

Sroufe, A., Egeland, B., Carlson, E., & Collins, A. (2009). *The development of the person: The Minnesota Study of Risk and Adaptation from Birth to Adulthood.* New York, NY: Guilford.

Steinberg, L. (2005). *Adolescence.* New York, NY: McGraw-Hill.

Strang, R. M. (1957). *The adolescent views himself: A psychology of adolescence.* New York, NY: McGraw Hill.

Susman-Stillman, A., Kalkose, M., Egeland, B., & Waldman, I. (1996). Infant temperament and maternity sensitivity as predictors of attachment security. *Infant Behavior & Development, 19,* 33–47.

Svanberg, P. O. G. (1998). Attachment, resilience, and prevention. *Journal of Mental Health, 7,* 543–578.

Tarullo, A. R., Obradovic, J., & Gunnar, M. R. (2009). Self-control and the developing brain. *Zero to Three, 29,* 31–37.

Thomas, A., & Chess, S. (1977). *Temperament and development.* New York, NY: Brunner/Mazel.

Thomas, A., Chess, S., & Birch, H. G. (1970). The origin of personality. *Scientific American, 109,* 102–109.

Tracy, J. L., & Robins, R. W. (2006). Appraisal antecedents of shame and guilt: Support for a theoretical model. *Personality and Social Psychology Bulletin, 32,* 1339–1351.

Tracy, J. L., & Robins, R. W. (2008). The nonverbal expression of pride: Evidence for cross-cultural recognition. *Journal of Personality and Social Psychology, 94,* 516–530.

U.S. Census Bureau. (2007). Current population survey—POV02. People in families by family structure, age, and sex, iterated by income-to-poverty ratio and race: 2007 below 100% of poverty—all races. http://pubdb3.census.gov/macro/032008/pov/new02_100_01.htm

Wigfield, A., Eccles, J., Yoon, K., Harold, R., Abreton, A., Freedman-Doan, C., & Blumenfeld, P. (1997). Changes in children's competence beliefs and subjective task values across the elementary school years: A 3-year study. *Journal of Educational Psychology, 89,* 451–469.

Zero to Three. (2012). *Effective communication with parents.* http://www.zerotothree.org/early-care-education/family-friend-neighbor-care/effective-communication-with-parents.html

Zettergren, P. (2005). Childhood peer status as predictor of midadolescence peer situation and social adjustment. *Psychology in the Schools, 42,* 745–757.

Section II

The Negative Effects of Maltreatment on Development

In the *Physical and Cognitive Development* and *Emotional and Social Development* chapters, we examined normative development of infants, children, and adolescents (e.g., growth, abilities, accomplishments). The purpose of providing this information was to create a framework against which you can compare the development of maltreated children. The *Signs, Symptoms, and Consequences of Physical and Sexual Abuse* chapter describes child physical abuse along with general information about child victims and their abusers. This chapter also focuses on child sexual abuse, providing specific information on this form of maltreatment as well as on typical characteristics of child victims and their abusers. The *Signs, Symptoms, and Consequences of Psychological Abuse and Neglect* chapter describes child psychological abuse and provides information on common characteristics of child victims and their abusers. This chapter also provides specific information on neglect, and on general characteristics of child victims and their abusers.

The main purpose of the material in this section is to increase your understanding of incidence rates, causes, risk factors and triggers, and protective factors in resilience in regard to various forms of child maltreatment. In both chapters, the specific factors that contribute to exacerbating (i.e., have a risk value) or ameliorating (i.e., have a protective value) children's resilience are identified and discussed. However, our current understanding of resilience suggests that there are general, underlying factors of risk and protection associated with all types of maltreatment.

Researchers in the child maltreatment field have identified three risk factors commonly associated with child maltreatment. The first factor, socioeconomic stressors, includes poverty, unemployment, social isolation, family conflict, domestic violence, attachment problems, and coercive parenting style. The second factor is related to the individual child, including medical problems, prematurity, disability, behavioral problems, and a nonbiological relationship between the child and the caregiver. The third factor includes parental stressors, which are particularly evident when the parent had a past childhood history of abuse and one or more of the following: has low self-esteem, substance abuse problem, or a partner with one, untreated mental illness (e.g., depression, character disorder), has poor parenting skills (e.g., confusing abusive behaviors with discipline), and unrealistic expectations for the child (i.e., misconception of child misbehavior).

Similarly, three main variables seem to offer protective influences against child maltreatment. The first variable involves the degree of maltreatment, which encompasses not only the number of experiences (e.g., one versus multiple), but also the number of different types of maltreatment to which the child is subjected (e.g., neglect versus neglect and physical abuse) and the length of exposure (e.g., one month versus years). The second variable involves those personal characteristics of the child that seem to help in providing a coping mechanism for dealing with the maltreatment. The third variable involves the presence of a social support system—that is, at least one loving caregiver or person who provides a healthy connection to the child.

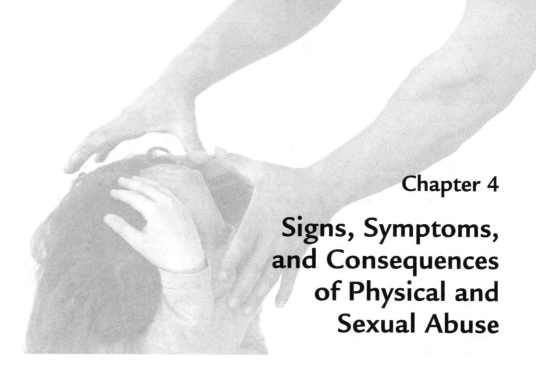

Chapter 4

Signs, Symptoms, and Consequences of Physical and Sexual Abuse

In this chapter, we discuss estimated incidence rates and describe behavioral signs, physical symptoms, and consequences of physically and sexually abusive situations on social, emotional, and cognitive development in infants, children, and adolescents.

Child Physical Abuse

When considering child physical abuse (CPA), it is important to determine whether the definition of such abuse can adequately capture a variety of situations. According to the National Center on Child Abuse and Neglect (NCCAN; U.S. Department of Health and Human Services [U.S. DHHS], 1988), children are physically abused if they have observable injuries that last at least 48 hours (harm standard) or, if children have no observable injuries, they are deemed substantially at risk for injury or endangerment (endangerment standard). That is, all violent acts (i.e., performed intentionally or nonaccidentally to cause injury or pain) towards a child should be considered abusive, regardless of whether the outcome is harm or endangerment (Eisele, Kegler, Trent, & Coronado, 2006; Gelles & Cornell, 1990).

The legal perspective on child physical abuse often encompasses both the harm and endangerment standards, but rather than being uniform across the United States, each state's statute differs in definition and in specificity of acts (Miller-Perrin & Perrin, 2007). The issue of concern, according to Daro (1988), is how to provide state statutes that include objective definitions of abuse that balance the needs of the children with parental rights and how to determine which behaviors meet the legal standards. Hence, most states permit parents to use "reasonable" corporal punishment with children, while focusing on overt abusive acts that result in bruises or broken bones (Myers, 1992).

Official Estimates

The actual rates of physical abuse are estimates at best and are, of course, tied to the definition used (e.g., risk for harm versus observable injuries), which change over time. According to the 2003 National Child Abuse and Neglect Data System (NCANDS; U.S. DHHS, 2005), approximately 149,000 of the 906,000 substantiated cases of child maltreatment reported to child protective services were categorized as physical abuse. This data source revealed that of the 862 deaths reported, 31% were the result of CPA, physical neglect accounted for 38%, and CPA combined with another type of maltreatment for the remainder. Studies using self-reports also disclosed high rates of parents (67–75%) using physical violence/assault with children ranging from minor to severe, albeit with only 1% using very severe physical abuse; approximately half of these adults indicated their own parents had maltreated them as children (e.g., Straus, Hamby, Finkelhor, Moore, & Runyan, 1998; Tjaden & Thoennes, 2002). Various studies performed by NCCAN show an increase in the number of official reports of maltreatment from 1980 to 1993—particularly serious cases—which may be the result of mandatory reporting laws and the way in which abuse was defined (Sedlak & Broadhurst, 1996). Unfortunately, until a national standard is developed, it will be difficult to determine the accuracy of reported rates and to confirm whether the rates are actually changing over time (Leeb, Paulozzi, Melanson, Simon, & Arias, 2008).

Causes of Child Physical Abuse

Different causes of physical abuse and various circumstances that result in a child's injury due to physically abusive behavior have been identified. For example, a caregiver may react angrily and impose an uncontrolled disciplinary response to a real or imagined misbehavior by the child. Caregivers who have psychological impairments or substance abuse problems may react in an uninhibited way or may reject or resent a child based on a distorted perception that the child is different from other children, is purposefully or willfully provoking the caregiver, or is actively rejecting the caregiver (e.g., by crying). Finally, children may be subjected to abuse in situations in which the caregiver is not the parent (e.g., a babysitter) or when the caregiver is involved in a relationship characterized by domestic violence. Most experts in the field would agree that the injuries sustained by the child victims in such cases are due to the caregivers' behaviors, making such physical damage not accidental. However, some abusers may set out purposefully to hurt the child (e.g., burn the child's hand), whereas others may cause injury due to their use of severe discipline, specifically acts that are inappropriate for the child due to his or her age or physical condition (e.g., shake the child vigorously).

The likelihood of unintended injury is increased for children raised in cultures (e.g., United States) in which power-assertive techniques (e.g., spanking) have historically been used as means of correcting a child's (real or perceived) misbehavior (Greven, 1991, as cited in Gershoff, 2002). In a national survey of more than 900 parents in the United States, 94% reported spanking their children by age 4; additionally, 28% of parents of children ages 2–4 years and another 28% of parents of children ages 5–8 years reported using an object to implement spanking (Straus & Stewart, 1999). Corporal punishment has been outlawed in 24 countries and has been prohibited outside the home (e.g., daycare centers, schools) in a small number of countries (e.g., Ethiopia, Canada). Despite the United Nations Committee on the Rights of the Child's (2006) view that corporal punishment is "violence against children" and should be illegal, this principle is accepted by only a minority of countries and is unlikely become an accepted doctrine in the United States (Gershoff, 2002). The main reason why parents choose to apply corporal punishment rather than use other discipline techniques (e.g., denial of privileges) is that they were disciplined themselves in this way as children; that is, the rationale is not based on their children's actual misbehavior (Hoove, Dubas, Eichelsheim, van der Laan, Smeenk, & Gerris, 2009). Certain parental attributes may pose an increased risk for escalation from disciplinary use of corporal punishment to physical abuse, such as overreacting to negative stimuli, having limited and inflexible use and knowledge of disciplinary techniques, and asserting physical power impulsively and in anger to force compliance (Baumrind, Larzelere, & Cowan, 2002).

Characteristics of Child Physical Abuse

Often, abusers insist that they are disciplining the child to gain compliance. Given their small size, children younger than the age of 5 years are the most vulnerable to sustaining serious injury or death due to physical abuse. Table 4-1 describes three key components for helping parents to differentiate abuse from discipline (Smith & Segal, 2013), focusing on parental response to misbehavior in terms of consistency in consequences applied, method of application, and reasoning (e.g., to make the child afraid versus to teach the

Table 4-1 Helping parents differentiate abuse versus discipline

Physical abuse	*Discipline*
Unpredictability: The child cannot predict what is going to trigger a physical assault; the child is continually on alert because rules are unclear.	**Predictability:** There are clear boundaries and rules; consequences for misbehavior are consistently applied.
Lash out in anger: The caregiver responds to the child in anger and maintains constant control over the child; the degree of abuse is contingent upon the parent's degree of anger.	**Calm application:** The motivation is to teach the child proper behavior.
Use of fear to control behavior: Parents think the child will comply only if the child is in fear of them, but instead they are teaching the child ways to escape from being hit rather than how to act properly and maturely.	**Use a loving relationship to control behavior:** There is no need for fear; children change behaviors because they love the parents and want their respect.

Data from Smith, M., & Segal, J. (2013). Child abuse and neglect. Retrieved from http://helpguide.org/mental/child_abuse_physical_emotional_sexual_neglect.htm#recognizing.

child to distinguish right from wrong). Abuse has a negative impact on children and their self-worth, often leading to anger and hatred toward the parent, continuation of the deviant behaviors, and avoidance of the parent. Discipline, in contrast, has a positive impact: It helps children learn a lesson on how to behave properly, which they can then use to guide their behavior in future situations. Abuse makes children feel worthless by imposing shame and guilt for their behaviors and by making them feel resentful and perceive themselves as outcasts. Conversely, discipline enhances the child's self-worth, which in turn increases self-control in both familial and societal situations, because it does not focus on making the child feel ashamed or guilty.

Demographics of Victim and Perpetrator

In reviewing the data on child physical abuse from official reports and surveys conducted as part of empirical and clinical studies, certain demographic features are commonly reported about victims and perpetrators (Black, Heyman, & Smith Slep, 2001).

Victim

Approximately half of physically abused children are aged 7 years and younger. Indeed, this group is at greatest risk for injury from maltreatment (i.e., behavior likely to meet the legal definition of physical abuse), although about one-third are adolescents ages 12–17 years (U.S. DHHS, 1998). Boys are at greater risk for physical abuse than are girls, particularly for serious injuries associated with severe violence (Sedlak & Broadhurst, 1996; U.S. DHHS, 1998; Wolfner & Gelles, 1993). According to U.S. DHHS (2001), girls in adolescence (ages 12–17 years) and boys in infancy through age 11 years have the highest risk of experiencing physical abuse.

Data collected about the effects of race on physical abuse have yielded mixed results. Self-report studies and official reporting statistics report Caucasians and African Americans or mainly African Americans to be at greater risk, whereas child protective services (CPS) agencies report Asian, African American, Latino, and Caucasian children to be almost equally at risk (Straus, Gelles, & Steinmetz, 1980; U.S. DHHS, 2005; Wolfner & Gelles, 1993). Children who come from low-socioeconomic-status families are also vulnerable to child physical abuse, particularly in terms of severe abuse and serious or fatal injuries for those children living in below-poverty-level homes (Wolfner & Gelles, 1993).

Children who have difficult temperaments or personalities and those who had birth complications (Brown, Cohen, Johnson, & Salzinger, 1998) or have some physical, mental, or developmental disability are also at increased risk for physical abuse (Sullivan & Knutson, 1998, 2000). According to CPS agencies, nearly half of their cases of maltreatment involve children with disabilities; in 37% of these cases, the maltreatment created disabilities in children (U.S. DHHS, 1993).

Perpetrator

According to the U.S. DHHS (2001), the majority of abusers are birth parents of the physically abused child victims (85%). This statistic, however, is a product of states' practice of defining child abuse as occurring only when the perpetrator is a caretaker. Child victims were likely to be physically abused by their biologically related mothers rather than by their fathers (60% versus 48%), or by their nonbiological fathers or substitutes rather than by their nonbiological mothers (90% versus 19%) (Sedlak & Broadhurst, 1996). Parental abusers are typically relatively young, often being adolescents when their children were born, which may also be a contributing factor (Brown et al., 1998). Descriptive research and quasi-experimental studies of CPA perpetrators have indicated that many of these adult perpetrators share similar characteristics in terms of emotional and behavioral problems, dysfunctional family and interpersonal relationships, negative parenting perceptions, and physical health issues (Salzinger, Feldman, Hammer, & Rosario, 1993).

Physically abusive parents often have *emotional and behavioral difficulties* that may taint their interpretation of children's behaviors, lower their tolerance for misbehavior, or simply tax their limited parenting abilities (Hillson & Kupier, 1994; Mammen, Kolko, & Pilkonis, 2003; Milner, 1998). Such parents frequently have one or more of the following personal and marital problems, they: are prone to anger; are unable to be empathetic (e.g., do not respond appropriately to the child's pain); are highly moralistic with rigid beliefs; have mental and physical health problems (e.g., high stress, depression, substance abuse); and/or suffer from cognitive deficits (e.g., intellectual impairment, limited problem-solving skills).

Parents who physically abuse their children may also have *family and interpersonal difficulties* (e.g., no social networks with friends and extended family) that limit their ability to build an effective emotional support system. The absence of emotional connections hinders their ability to cope with social and economic stressors in their lives (Coohey, 2000). Correlational studies show a high representation of single parents among samples of abusive caretakers, which may be more a consequence of poverty and stress rather than a risk factor per se (Gelles, 1989; Sedlak & Broadhurst, 1996). Many adults who are physically abusive or at high risk for directing abuse toward children have reported childhood histories in which they themselves had been physically abused (e.g., excessive and harsh physical punishment), typically combined with exposure to domestic violence, and have current dysfunctional families that include domestic violence or high-conflict partner relationships (Appel & Holden, 1998; Cappell & Heiner, 1990; Merrill, Hervig, & Milner, 1996). Often they are suspicious and fearful of other people and have little or no social contact, even from their extended family.

Not surprisingly, physically abusive parents do not perceive their children or their children's behavior in a positive way, label their interactions with their children as unpleasant, and evaluate the parenting task as unsatisfactory (Milner, 2000, 2003; Peterson & Gable, 1998). These parents are easily upset, with low tolerance for frustration and misconduct, and have ineffective child management skills. Additionally, they have unrealistic expectations of their children's actions (i.e., there is a mismatch between the child's developmental ability and the parent's requirements for behavior) that demonstrate insensitivity to the children's needs and a tendency to blame the victim for injuries sustained as a result of the physical abuse (Peterson & Gable, 1998). Consistent with a coercive parenting style, these parents have low communication and interactions with their children, use verbal (i.e., criticism) and physical aggression to discipline them, and have high rates of overly critical and controlling behavior when interacting with them (Caselles & Milner, 2000; Chaffin et al., 2004; Milner, 2000). When asked to explain the child's injuries, these abusers often provide vague, evasive, unconvincing, and inconsistent explanations, resorting to using different hospitals and physicians to conceal multiple injuries and avoid detection.

Finally, physically abusive parents share *biological traits*, *physiological characteristics*, and *neuropsychological deficits* that may predispose them to harming their children (Lahey, Conger, Atkeson, & Treiber, 1984; Milner & Chilamkurti, 1991; Nayak & Milner, 1998). Specifically, abusive parents may react negatively and harshly to their children's actions because they are dealing with their own poor health or physical disabilities (Lahey et al., 1984). In addition, CPA perpetrators may potentially exhibit heightened responses (e.g., increased heart rate and blood pressure) to unpleasant and stress-inducing stimuli, such as crying and noncompliance (Frodi & Lamb, 1980). Finally, caregivers may act physically abusive toward children due to their own limited problem-solving abilities and low cognitive functioning (Nayak & Milner, 1998).

Signs, Symptoms, and Developmental Consequences of Physically Abused Children

Unlike children who experience other forms of maltreatment, child victims of CPA often have specific behavioral signs and physical/emotional symptoms that continue to impact on their lives even when they are adults (Kaplan, Pelcovitz, & Labruna, 1999; Malinosky-Rummell & Hansen, 1993; Wolfe, 1999).

Behavioral Signs

Common signs associated with CPA are that children are uncomfortable with and/or fearful of the caregivers/parents or of returning home, as demonstrated through protesting, crying, cowering, or acting jittery. Additionally, children may be unable to relax in any setting, flinch at noise and at someone's physical contact or closeness to them, show fear when touched, or wear weather-inappropriate clothing as a means of hiding their abuse. Children who are physically abused often exhibit physical aggression and antisocial behaviors in their peer interactions (Fantuzzo, 1990; Kolko, 2002). Long-term outcomes for these children include extreme passivity or aggression, thrill seeking, manipulative behaviors, self-harm and suicide attempts, delinquency, bullying, and fighting in adolescence; and substance abuse, criminal offenses, running away, arrests, prostitution, and abusive interpersonal and intergenerational abusive parenting patterns in adulthood (Coohey & Braun, 1997; Hotaling, Straus, & Lincoln, 1990; Malinosky-Rummell & Hansen, 1993; Rosenbaum & O'Leary, 1981; Widom, 1989; Widom & Kuhns, 1996; Wolfe, 1999). According to an international team of researchers, violent adult behavior is likely to occur subsequent to childhood maltreatment if victims lack a "protective" version of a gene that regulates cerebral control of antisocial behavior (Caspi et al., 2002).

Physical Developmental Consequences/Symptoms

Not surprisingly, numerous medical/health and neurobiological problems—ranging from bruising to physical disfigurements and disabilities (e.g., organ failure) to fatalities—result from CPA (Child Welfare Information Gateway, 2011; Duhaime et al., 1992; Eisele, Kegler, Trent, & Coronado, 2006; Myers, 1992). Most fatalities from CPA injuries are the result of injuries caused when the child suffers head trauma, internal bleeding from punches or kicks to the abdomen, immersion burns, drowning, or smothering (National MCH Center for Child Death Review, 2011).

Head injuries are the most severe trauma experienced by abused children, mainly because such injuries often have negative long-term outcomes (e.g., brain injuries, neurologic deficits; Centers for Disease Control and Prevention, 1997; Ellingson, Leventhal, & Weiss, 2008; Ettaro, Berger, & Songer, 2004; Faul, Xu, Wald, & Coronado, 2010) and are the leading cause of death, particularly for children younger than 1 year of age (Agran, Anderson, Winn, Trent, Walton-Haynes, & Thayer, 2003; Barlow, Thomson, Johnson, & Minns, 2005; Chiesa & Duhaime, 2009; Christian, Block, & Committee on Child Abuse and Neglect, 2009; Dias, Smith, DeGuehery, Mazur, Li, & Shaffer, 2005; Duhaime et al., 1992; Reece & Christian, 2009; Rorke-Adams, Duhaime, Jenny, & Smith, 2009). The majority of the 75% to 85% of abused children who at least initially survive such head injuries suffer various serious health problems (Duhaime, 2008), including "severe learning disabilities, tetraplegia (paralysis of all four limbs), blindness, chronic seizure disorders, and in the most severe cases, persistent vegetative state" (Bonnier, Nassagne, & Evrard, 1995, as cited in Reece, 2011, p. 188).

Work by Barr and his associates (Barr, 1990, 2000, 2006; Barr, Barr, Fujiwara, Conway, Catherine, & Brant, 2009; Barr, Trent, & Cross, 2006; Lee, Barr, Catherine, & Wicks, 2007) has shown that crying is often the most common precursor to head injuries for infants. Consistent with the nomenclature adopted by the American Academy of Pediatrics, "abusive head trauma" and "nonaccidental head injury" have replaced the terms "shaken baby syndrome" and "shaken impact syndrome" to describe infants who have head injuries due to violent shaking accompanied by head impact from contact with hard surface (Barlow & Minns, 2000; Bruce & Zimmerman, 1989; Christian et al., 2009; Duhaime, 2008; Ludwig, & Warman, 1984). Some abusers confess to being frustrated and losing control after failing to console a crying infant (Barr et al., 2009; Catherine, Ko, & Barr, 2008; Starling, Holden, & Jenny, 1995); still others admit to further abusing the infant by punching, kicking, or stomping on the child.

The most common type of physical abuse is skin injuries—specifically, the presence of fresh and fading bruises in areas not commonly injured during play (e.g., buttocks, thighs, neck) or of a specific pattern (e.g., hand, belt) or indicative of choking, smothering, drowning, or hanging (e.g., finger and thumb marks). Other injuries include cuts of inconsistent history, hair-pulling (with thinning hair and bald patches on scalp), black eyes, human bite marks, and burns due to the abuser forcibly holding the child's hands or feet or submerging the child in scalding liquid or dry contact burns from common household

---

Box 4-1 Cultural Practices and CPA

Investigators of CPA should be aware of a variety of cultural traditions that are inconsistent with American beliefs and laws. Specifically, alternative healing practices may result in unusual bruising and scarring patterns that have been misinterpreted as physical abuse. For example, cupping, pinching, coining, and moxibustion have all been used as means of curing headaches or releasing toxins in the body. Cupping involves the placement of a coin on the skin with a lit candle, with the candle then being snuffed out by a glass or jar; it results in a nonraised dark circle caused by ruptured blood vessels (i.e., ecchymosis). Pinching results in a bruise, often between the eyes. Coining, which involves rubbing a coin or spoon over an area, results in an irregularly shaped bruise. Parents may be accused of physical abuse when they use certain substances (e.g., arsenic, lead, urine, feces, slime) in folk remedies given to children, such as moxibustion, which involves burning herbs on acupuncture points of the skin.

---

objects (Miller-Perrin & Perrin, 2007; Reece, 2011). In a review of cases over a four-year period, Showers and Garrison (1988) reported that contact burns (56%) and scalds (38%) most commonly resulted in injuries to children's legs (35%), feet (25%), and hands (23%), particularly for toddlers ages 1 to 2 years (56%), usually under their mothers' care (67%).

Physical abuse may result in soft tissue damage and injury to both hollow and solid organs. Throat injuries occur when an object is forced down the child's throat. In such a case, the child may be hoarse, have a cough or sore throat, or be unable to swallow or eat due to damage to larynx. Both abdominal injuries and thoracic injuries (second highest cause of fatalities) occur when the abuser squeezes, punches, or kicks the child (National MCH Center for Child Death Review, 2011). This action may crush an organ against the spine and chest, resulting in obstruction, internal bleeding, perforated intestines, and infection or in bilateral rib fractures, cardiac arrest, or collapsed lungs (Ledbetter, Hatch, Feldman, Fligner, & Tapper, 1988; Myers, 1992; Reece, 2011).

Similarly, skeletal injuries from physical abuse can result in bone fractures due to the abuser "punching, kicking, twisting, shaking, and squeezing" the child (Reece, 2011, p. 93) or pushing the child from a height, such as down a flight of stairs. In response to child physical abuse, children may also develop disruptions in their neurobiological responses, including reduced stress responses, impairment of cognitive functioning, and poor regulation of emotional and behavioral reactions (De Bellis, 2001; Glaser, 2002).

Emotional Developmental Consequences

The emotional consequences for children who are physically abused stem from failure to develop secure attachment to the parents. That is, the disruption in the parent–child bond results in a disorganized, insecure attachment due to the child being unable to rely on the caregiver as a safe haven and protector because the parent is also the source of danger or harm (Barnett, Ganiban, & Cicchetti, 1999; Hesse & Main, 2000; Salzinger, Feldman, Hammer, & Rosario, 1993). Moreover, these children have poor self-concept and low self-esteem. Approximately 30% of physically abused children develop disruptive behavior disorders, and another 30% to 40% develop post-traumatic stress disorder or internalize symptoms of psychiatric disorders (Famularo, Fenton, Kinscherff, Ayoub, & Barnum, 1994; Famularo, Kinscherff, & Fenton, 1992; Fantuzzo, delGaudio, Atkins, Meyers, & Noone, 1998; Kaplan et al., 1999; Saunders, Berliner, & Hanson, 2004; Widom, 1989, 1999). Emotional reactions include hopelessness and depression, attention-deficit disorder (ADD), and personality disorders. Some evidence indicates that psychiatric diagnoses, such as disruptive disorders (e.g., conduct disorders, ADD or attention-deficit/hyperactivity disorder [ADHD]), personality disorders, anxiety and depressive disorders, and substance abuse, stemming from child physical abuse extend into adulthood and sometimes include self-destructive behaviors, dissociation, and suicidal ideas and behaviors (e.g., Brown, Cohen, Johnson, & Smailes, 1999; Cohen, Brown, & Smailes, 2001; Malinosky-Rummell & Hansen, 1993).

Social Developmental Consequences
The insecure vertical relationship between parent and child stemming from CPA translates into poor horizontal relationships between these child victims and their peers and siblings. Social consequences include peer rejection, low prosocial behavior, and difficulty making and keeping friends (Chu, Frey, Ganzel, & Matthews, 1999; Downs & Miller, 1998; Kaufman & Cicchetti, 1989; Rogosch, Cicchetti, & Abre, 1995; Salzinger, Feldman, Hammer, & Rosario, 1993). Interpersonal interactions of child victims and adult survivors are further hampered by deficits in social-cognitive skills, such as problem solving, perspective taking, and affective regulation (Rogosch et al., 1995; Salzinger et al., 1993).

Cognitive Developmental Consequences
CPA also results in cognitive problems and dissociation, perhaps as a direct result of the physical injury (e.g., head trauma) or environmental deficits (e.g., low stimulation). Physically abused children have shown impairments in neurologic functioning resulting in poor memory, spatial skills, attention, intellectual processing, problem solving, and communication/language ability (Macfie, Cicchetti, & Toth, 2001). Many of these children are given special education services and/or repeat grades due to poor academic performance owing to their learning disabilities, poor school adjustment, and reading and math problems (Eckenrode, Laird, & Doris, 1993).

Mediators for Adverse Effects

Why would children differ in their responses to CPA? The severity (how hard and with which implement) and frequency (whether victims suffer intensely from physical and emotional injuries over long periods of time) of such abuse play large roles in the negative consequences experienced by abused children (Wind & Silvern, 1992). Adverse outcomes have been linked to the number of simultaneous maltreatment episodes experienced by the child (Kurtz, Gaudin, Howing, & Wodarski, 1993). The level of harm caused by maltreatment will be low in children who have high intellectual functioning and good coping skills (Herrenkohl, Herrenkohl, Egolf, & Wu, 1991). Physical coping mechanisms may include becoming aggressive toward others, self-harm (e.g., cutting), or clowning around, whereas emotional coping strategies may include avoiding people and new experiences. The child's age and developmental ability at the onset of CPA affect attributions of blame for maltreatment (i.e., self-blame), which in turn is tied to adolescence maladjustment and psychopathy (Brown & Kolko, 1999). Children who were exposed to CPA prior to age 5 years tend to exhibit internalizing and externalizing problems (e.g., depression and acting out, respectively), whereas those who experience CPA after age 5 tend to demonstrate only externalizing problems (Keiley, Howe, Dodge, Bates, & Pettit, 2001). Thus, children who have access to social supports, such as a parent or extended family member, may have fewer negative outcomes, particularly compared with children whose families are characterized by high stress and parental psychopathology or depression (Herrenkohl, Herrenkohl, Rupert, Egolf, & Lutz, 1995; Kurtz et al., 1993).

Child Sexual Abuse

Sexual abuse definitions are not universally accepted, as the appropriateness of behaviors involved may be influenced by culture and context (Miller-Perrin & Perrin, 2007). Various cultures throughout history have condoned sexual relations between adults and children (Wurtele & Miller-Perrin, 1992). Nevertheless, consistent with the values of Americans since the 20th century, sexualized abuse of children by adults is considered harmful and, therefore, prohibited by our laws (Myers, 1998).

Child sexual abuse (CSA) is defined by the National Center on Child Abuse and Neglect (1978) as follows:

> Contacts or interactions between a child and an adult when the child is being used for the sexual stimulation of the perpetrator or another person. Sexual abuse may also be committed by a person under the age of 18 when that person is either significantly older than the victim or when the perpetrator is in a position of power or control over another child.[1] (p. 2)

This definition provides enough latitude to incorporate both physical contact (e.g., fondling, touching genitals, playing sexual games, coercing sexual activity with animals, sexual penetration) and nonphysical contact types of CSA (e.g., showing pornography, encouraging child to watch/hear sexual acts, exposure, voyeurism, verbally or emotionally abusing in sexual way). It is also applicable to abusers who are within the victim's family (intrafamilial or incestual) or outside of it (extrafamilial), while recognizing that the person is able to abuse the child sexually because he or she is in a position of control and power and has superior cognitive abilities, making it basically impossible for the child to refuse. The law recognizes children's vulnerability by defining the legal age to consent for sexual activity as between 14 and 18 years (depending on the state, but with

---

[1] National Center of Child Abuse and Neglect. (1978). *Child sexual abuse: Incest, assault, and sexual exploitation.* Washington, DC: U.S. Department of Health and Human Services.

the exception of incest), when adolescents are capable developmentally of understanding how sexual involvement may affect them socially, emotionally, cognitively, and physically (Berliner & Elliot, 2002; Miller-Perrin & Perrin, 2007). Finally, the definition allows for prosecution of a child or adolescent perpetrator who sexually abuses a young child (Berliner, 2011; Saunders, Kilpatrick, Hanson, Resnick, & Walker, 1999).

Official Estimates

It is difficult to determine how large a social problem CSA is because the prevalence rates estimated by various sources are inconsistent (U.S. Department of Justice, 2009). Due to stigma concerns and reluctance of victims to divulge these traumatic experiences to friends, family, mandated reporters, or law enforcement agents, it is suspected that a substantial number of CSA incidents are never included in official crime prevalence rates (Smith, Letourneau, Saunders, Kilpatrick, Resnick, & Best, 2000). Information provided by CPS agencies also misconstrues prevalence rates of CSA (which represents approximately 10% of CPS-handled maltreatment cases) because it limits incidents only to abusers who are caregivers or parents (U.S. DHHS, 2010). Another official source used to calculate CSA prevalence rates is a major national crime incidence self-report (i.e., National Criminal Victimization Survey) completed by crime victims, but this collection tool applies only to those ages 12 years and older, who have permanent homes and are not incarcerated.

Thus, prevalence rates vary with each study due to differences in research methodology and definitions of CSA. Nevertheless, general population and nationally representative sample telephone and retrospective prevalence surveys suggest contact CSA incidence ranges from 2% to 62% for female victims and 3% to 16% for male victims (e.g., Finkelhor, Turner, Ormrod, & Hamby, 2009; Saunders et al., 1999; Tjaden & Thoennes, 2000). Evidence from two prospective longitudinal studies shows that more than 30% of victims fail to report their confirmed sexual abuse experiences, so clearly rates are not accurate reflections of the number of actual incidents (Widom & Morris, 1997; Williams, 1994).

A second problem with rate accuracy concerns the different techniques used to perpetrate CSA (e.g., sudden onset, grooming) and variation in the types (contact, noncontact) that make detection difficult. Official incidence rates in the late 1980s and early 1990s indicated an increase in CSA cases, perhaps due to public awareness, legislative changes in mandatory reporting, and changes in willingness to reveal incidents (Miller-Perrin & Perrin, 2007). Subsequently, rates declined and leveled off (Berliner, 2011), which may either represent an actual decrease or be an artifact of current trends in which offenders use extremely young, often preverbal victims (i.e., infants and toddlers) to make CSA detection less likely now than in the past.

A third problem with rate estimates is that some victims do not report their experiences because they view their sexual exploitation by adults as pleasant (i.e., feels good), desirable (e.g., love relationship), or rewarding (i.e., allow them to engage in illegal activities, such as drinking). Many of these "compliant victims" are adolescents (Lanning, 1992) who willingly get involved with adults in trusted positions (e.g., teachers, coaches) or who begin their relationships on the Internet and then culminate that contact in sexual rendezvous (Wolak, Ybarra, Mitchell, & Finkelhor, 2007).

Causes of Child Sexual Abuse

Various theories attempt to explain why perpetrators engage in CSA. In the past, research in this area predominantly focused on male abusers, examining deviant patterns of sexual arousal and the role of disinhibitors, childhood history of abuse, and individual characteristics leading to dysfunctional social interactions. Subsequent thinking has addressed the notion that multiple factors likely contribute to the etiology of CSA, such that several theories have been integrated to provide a complete explanation of such behavior (Marshall & Barbaree, 1990; Quinsey, 1980).

Deviant Sexual Arousal in the Perpetrator

CSA perpetrators may experience deviant sexual arousal in connection with children, either due to biological causes, such as abnormal androgen levels (Bradford, 1990; Ward & Beech, 2006), or because of learned associations reinforced through fantasized sexual activity combined with masturbation (Cortini & Marshall, 2001; Marshall & Eccles, 1993). Unfortunately, research has failed to yield consistent results regarding which of these two causes most accurately explains CSA or whether male child molesters, nonoffenders, and incest offenders can be reliably differentiated in terms of their sexual arousal to children according to a penile plethysmography (Miller-Perrin & Perrin, 2007). Finkelhor (1984) postulated that a person will engage in CSA when he or she is physiologically aroused by a child (e.g., penile erection), is unable to satisfy sexual needs through adult partners, obtains emotional gratification from a child, and is impulsive. Disinhibitors, including substance abuse, which lower offenders' ability to inhibit their sexual impulses toward children, and cognitive distortions, which excuse and provide rationalizations for CSA (e.g., they are teaching children about sex, children enjoy the activities, and children are not harmed), may also influence whether these offenders will engage in CSA (Abel, Becker, & Cunningham-Rathner, 1984; Segal & Stermac, 1990; Thakker, Ward, & Navathe, 2007).

Childhood History of Sexual Abuse in the Perpetrator

Researchers have reported that children with a history of experiencing or witnessing sexual abuse are at risk for becoming CSA abusers themselves in adolescence and/or adulthood (Becker, 1994; Chaffin, Letourneau, & Silovsky, 2002). Four explanations have been proposed to explain this relationship between direct or indirect sexual victimization and subsequent abusive behavior. First, Hartman and Burgess (1988) proposed that CSA provides the offender with an opportunity to release anxiety stemming from his or her own abuse. Second, an alternative suggestion by Ginsburg, Wright, Harrell, and Hill (1989) is that the offender failed to develop empathy for others as a child because he or she was betrayed by the abuser, his or her emotional needs were not met, or his or her parents did not foster sensitivity toward others. Hence, the abuser cannot understand that his or her behaviors are harming the child or that the child is emotionally distressed. A third, related argument is that the offender's exploitation resulted in a need to regain control over his or her life by subjugating the powerless child, just as had been done to him or her (Wurtele & Miller-Perrin, 1992). The fourth notion is derived from learning theories stating that the offender associates children with sexual gratification through fantasies and masturbation (Marshall & Eccles, 1993; Veneziano, Veneziano, & LeGrand, 2000).

Which conditions must occur for people to enact their sexual fantasies with children? According to Finkelhor (1984, as cited in Becker, 1994):

> (1) children are the preferred recipient of the offender's emotional connections; (2) sexual arousal occurs for the offender when in the presence of children; (3) the offender is not capable of sexually satisfaction by adult recipients; and (4) sexual offenses may occur in conjunction with offender's use of drugs or alcohol

Personal and Social Difficulties of the Perpetrator

CSA offenders often have both emotional problems (low self-esteem, insecure familial relationships, poor impulse control and coping strategies) and sociocognitive deficits (difficulty being assertive, lack of social skills, inability to maintain intimate relationships, limited problem-solving ability and judgment, distorted cognitions) that hamper appropriate development of empathetic responses toward others and encourage their use of sexually abusive behavior (Covell & Scalora, 2002; Marshall & Marshall, 2000).

According to Abel et al. (1984), offenders may employ various cognitive distortions: (1) "children want to have sex," as evidenced by their lack of resistance and disclosure; (2) sex between children and adults is natural rather than harmful; (3) sex enhances the emotional relationship; and (4) adults provide a learning experience for children. These thoughts serve as a means for rationalizing and justifying the selfish use of a child to satisfy the offender's own sexual impulses. Their lack of empathy combined with offense-supportive beliefs allows offenders to begin and continue CSA, despite seemingly obvious signs of distress exhibited by their victims (Elsegood & Duff, 2010; Thakker et al., 2007). Instead, CSA offenders interpret victims' mental states (e.g., fear, anxiety) and actions (e.g., crying) using a "theory of mind" (understanding about others' thoughts) that combines their distorted beliefs about people (e.g., children are sexual beings, superior individuals are entitled) and the world (i.e., it is a dangerous place, life is uncontrollable and unchangeable, sex is harmless) despite seemingly obvious incongruent information (Ward, 2000). Such cognitive distortions allow offenders to deny, justify, minimize, and rationalize their actions and continue the cycle of abuse (Howitt & Sheldon, 2007). Accordingly, the offenders do not experience negative feelings of shame, guilt, and anxiety; have a reduced fear of being caught; and do not acknowledge the damage that the sexual abuse does to their victims (Becker, 1994; Marsa, O'Reilly, Carr, Murphy, O'Sullivan, Cotter, & Hevey, 2004; Whittaker, Brown, Beckett, & Gerhold, 2006). Ward and Siegert (2002) believe that a combination of factors co-occur to facilitate abuse, including "distorted sexual scripts," dysfunctional relationship skills, and emotional deficits that prevent abusers from having adult sexual interactions. Clearly, accessibility to a child who does not or cannot resist victimization provides an opportunity for a sufficiently motivated adult (i.e., one who disregards internalized societal mores and externalized laws against CSA) to engage in this criminal activity (Finkelhor, 1984).

Characteristics of Child Sexual Abuse Experiences

Victims' experiences may include noncontact (e.g., exhibitionism) or contact (e.g., penetration) sexual activities, or a combination of the two, over one or multiple sessions. There is a paucity of information about children's exposure to noncontact sexual activities, mainly because it is the contact or combination (rather than noncontact) abuse that comes to the attention of law enforcement officials and CPS. According to Russell (1983), contact sexual activities may be categorized as *very serious abuse* (e.g., vaginal, oral, or anal intercourse), *serious abuse* (e.g., digital penetration, completed and attempted genital fondling), or *least serious abuse* (e.g., sexual touching of buttocks or thighs, kissing). Russell reported that among the 38% of the 930 women she interviewed ($N = 353$) who were victims of CSA, 134 suffered very serious abuse, 120 suffered serious abuse, and 99 suffered least serious abuse. Researchers believe that the majority of children are exposed to multiple episodes of CSA, based on estimates of 50% of cases from nonclinical samples (Saunders et al., 1999) and 75% of cases from clinical samples (Ruggiero, Mcleer, & Dixon, 2000).

Children's exposure to CSA may also be formalized (commercial sexual exploitation of children [CSEC]). That is, sexual maltreatment may occur with groups of children who are used for commercial gain, for sexual pleasure of the abuser, or both, as in child sex rings, pornography, and prostitution. In child sex rings, a single adult (i.e., solo rink) or multiple adults in an organization (i.e., syndicated rinks) recruit children through manipulation, enticement, and deception to join the group. These children are then forced to engage in pornography and provide sexual services (Burgess, Groth, & McCausland, 1981; Burgess & Hartman, 1987). Child pornography (i.e., pictures and movies of children posed seductively or performing sexual actions) constitutes 7% of the pornographic industry in the United States. It presumably makes up an even greater portion of this industry on a worldwide basis, as these products are distributed through the Internet, increasing child exploitation beyond what the law can assess or curtail (Virginia Department of Social Services, 2003). Surveys of adult prostitutes reveal that many of them were forced into the profession prior to age 16, often as runaway adolescents escaping abusive homes or rejected as unwanted burdens to their dysfunctional families (Earls & David, 1990; Nadon, Koverola, & Schludermann, 1998; Silbert & Pines, 1983).

Perpetrators of CSA may victimize children without warning, but the more typical approach is for offenders to sexualize the interactions gradually over time, also known as "grooming" (Berliner & Conte, 1990). Research examining sexual predators reveals that the first step is to befriend the child, by spending time with the child, lavishing attention on the child, and giving gifts to show appreciation often before physical sexual contact is made (for a review, see Leclerc, Proulx, & Beauregard, 2009). This strategy typically works because the offenders target children who are vulnerable; that is, the children have low self-esteem, have family problems that prevent supervision, and are emotionally needy, depressed, or unhappy (Beauregard, Rossmo, & Proulx, 2007; Conte, Wolfe, & Smith, 1989; Elliott, Browne, & Kilcoyne, 1995). In the second step, the sexual predator obtains compliance in sexual touch by desensitizing the child slowly, becoming a little more invasive each time as a way of monitoring whether the child will protest, resist, or disclose seemingly harmless, affectionate touches, while reassuring the child that these behaviors are not immoral (Christiansen & Blake, 1990; Kaufman, Hilliker, & Daleiden, 1988; Lang & Frenzel, 1988). Abusers convince the children that mutual affection in their relationship is normal or may characterize it instead as educational (Berliner, 2011). Overtly sexual acts are initiated in the third step, sometimes after a substantial period of time (e.g., one year). Various strategies, such as bribes, threats, and, in some cases, physical coercion, are used to maintain continued compliance and prevent disclosure (Christiansen & Blake, 1990; Kaufman et al., 1998; Lang & Frenzel, 1988; Smallbone & Wortley, 2001).

Demographics of Victim and Perpetrator

Victim

Victims of child sexual abuse range in age from infancy to 18 years, although researchers disagree as to which is the most vulnerable period. Retrospective studies (e.g., Finkelhor, 1994) indicate that vulnerability reaches its peak in middle childhood (7 to 12 years), whereas clinical studies (e.g., Ruggiero et al., 2000) indicate that this point occurs in pre-adolescence (9 to 11 years). Finkelhor, Hammer, and Sedlak (2004) report that more than half of the child sexual abuse victims are aged 15–17 years. Risk for CSA increases with age, according to Putnam (2003), as incident rates are about 10% for those aged birth to 3 years, 28% for those aged 4–7 years, 25% for those aged 8–11 years, and 36% for those aged 12 years and older. However, the rates for CSA incidents involving very young children are probably underestimated because these victims have limited verbal abilities; this factor makes it unlikely that they would reveal their abuse while simultaneously increasing their desirability as targets because perpetrators can avoid detection (Hewitt, 1998). Similarly, higher incidence rates are found with children who have physical, cognitive, or psychological disabilities, presumably because they are less able or less likely to disclose abuse or may appear less credible than children without disabilities (Skarbek, Hahn, & Parrish, 2009; Tharinger, Horton, & Millea, 1990). Children who are highly compliant, naïve, easygoing, emotionally needy, or passive, and those who are socially and residentially isolated (i.e., few close friends, no extended family members nearby) also have high incidence rates of CSA (e.g., Berliner & Conte, 1990; McCloskey & Bailey, 2000; U.S. DHHS, 2001).

In terms of gender, girls have a higher risk for CSA than do boys, based on official sources and self-report surveys (Snyder, 2000; U.S. DHHS, 2001). However, it is generally believed that the true incidence rates are masked by the fact that boys are less willing than girls to report abuse (Finkelhor, 1981; Larson, Terman, Gomby, Quinn, & Behrman, 1994) due to cultural norms and expectations regarding sexual experiences (Romano & De Luca, 2001). Specifically, boys are afraid that disclosure of CSA by a female perpetrator will be interpreted as them being considered weak (as a victim) or "ungrateful for the sexual experience." Boys may also be afraid to reveal CSA by a male perpetrator for fear that they would be labeled as homosexual. Initial CSA incidents for boys typically occur at older ages than for girls (e.g., Holmes & Slap, 1998).

There is a discrepancy in the incidence rates from clinical and retrospective studies and from official records regarding victim race, ethnicity, and social class, making it unclear what level of risk is associated with these demographics. Some research shows no differences (Finkelhor et al., 2004; Sedlak & Broadhurst, 1996; Tjaden & Thoennes, 2000), whereas other studies have observed an overrepresentation of children of color (Hanson et al., 2003; Newcomb, Munoz, & Carmona, 2009) and those from lower-socioeconomic-status families (Finkelhor et al., 2004).

Perpetrator
Although the majority of child sexual abuse is perpetrated by adult offenders typically aged about 30 years (Douglas & Finkelhor, 2005), evidence from general population surveys and official crime reports indicates that approximately 40% to 50% of all cases of CSA against children 6 years and younger are perpetrated by juvenile offenders (Becker,

---

Box 4-2 Risk Factors for Child Victims of Sexual Abuse

Certain characteristics of the family and the culture render the child more vulnerable to becoming a victim of CSA. Sexual exploitation of children may be the result of a dysfunctional familial milieu in that it provides an opportunity for the perpetrator to be alone and form an emotional relationship with the victim (Miller-Perrin & Perrin, 2007). Initial theories either blamed the mother for not protecting the child victim or for providing infrequent intercourse with her husband or paramour, who in turn sought sexual gratification from the child victim (Justice & Justice, 1979).

However, subsequent research has suggested that children are at an increased risk for CSA when the parent (or parents, although typically it is the mother who provides caregiving) works long hours; is himself or herself typically impaired (i.e., physically disabled, substance abuser, mentally or physically ill); is a co-victim, as in the case of domestic violence (often with a childhood history of maltreatment); or is otherwise unable to care for or to supervise the child adequately (Finkelhor, Moore, Hamby, & Straus, 1997; Strand, 2000). Children who are exposed to high levels of marital conflict; familial instability (e.g., divorce); poor parent–child and sibling relationships, particularly in regard to inflexible parenting styles, poor communication, and low or no emotional bonds; disorganization (e.g., lack of routines); community isolation; or experiences with other child maltreatment are overrepresented in the CSA incidence rates (Boney-McCoy & Finkelhor, 1995; Dadds, Smith, Weber, & Robinson, 1991; Jones et al., 2010; Madonna, Van Scoyk, & Jones, 1991; Walker, Holman, & Busby, 2009). Women survivors of CSA may seek partners who have abuser characteristics, resulting in marital conflict or domestic violence, or who do not require sexual intercourse from them, leaving their children (particularly girls) vulnerable for intrafamilial or extrafamilial CSA (Faller, 1989; Finkelhor, 2009; Gruber & Jones, 1983; Holmes & Slap, 1998). Familial practices of co-bathing and co-sleeping with siblings and parents may repeatedly expose children to sexual activities and sexually explicit content (e.g., movies, magazines, and Internet materials), resulting in sexual acting-out and increased vulnerability to CSA (Friedrich, Fisher, Broughton, Houston, & Shafran, 1998).

Societal perceptions of CSA by those holding extreme perspectives, including the view that adults are falsely accused by children (rather than such accusations are true) or the perception that the consequences of CSA for children are minimal (not understanding how complex and diverse children's reactions can be), actually encourage offenders to continue their abusive behavior unfettered (Conte, 1994). Boys in Western cultures are socialized to be stoic, often not developing empathy, and many male-dominated households advocate a view of women as weak and objectified sexually (Miller-Perrin & Perrin, 2007). By extension, the inequity of those who share minority status in a patriarchal society—namely, women and children who are depicted in various forms of media as sexual objects—may contribute to their sexual victimization by men (Aronson & Plummer, 2010; Ligiero, Fassinger, McCauley, Moore, & Lyytinen, 2009; Rush, 1980; Wurtele & Miller-Perrin, 1992). Sexist beliefs and cultural attitudes toward sexism resulting in gender inequality, often tied to religious beliefs (e.g., Mormon polygamy), are also related to incidences of unreported sexual abuse. The cultural perspective of whether sexual behaviors between adults and children are acceptable, and the corresponding laws regarding such actions, also affect the risk for CSA (Swenson & Chaffin, 2006). For example, parental genital stimulation, predominantly of infant boys, but also of girls, has been noted in more than 70 societies as a means of pacifying, calming, greeting, teasing, gratifying, showing gender-specific pride, or facilitating identity/role (i.e., masculinity) and future virility (Janssen, 2002). These practices, as well as several African cultural practices with female children, such as child brides, chiramu (i.e., sexual intercourse with a female minor to cure sexually transmitted diseases), virginity testing (i.e., inserting a finger inside the vagina to test for hymen presence), and female genital mutilation (in which the clitoris is partially or fully removed), would be considered in the United States to be forms of CSA (Hanzi, 2006).

Kaplan, Cunningham-Rathner, & Kavoussi, 1986; Davis & Leitenberg, 1987; Finkelhor, 2005; National Center for Juvenile Justice, 1999; Saunders et al., 1999). Most of the perpetrators are male, with estimates of their dominance ranging from 75% to 96% (McCloskey & Raphael, 2005; Snyder, 2000; U.S. DHHS, 2005). Some researchers propose that the number of female perpetrators may be underestimated for a variety of reasons, including cultural prescriptions that women are physically incapable of sexual abuse (because they do not have a penis) and society's failure to construe inappropriate sexual contact during the course of childcare routines as anything more than inappropriate affection (see the review by Boroughs, 2004).

The CSA offender's relationship to the child differs depending on the victim's gender (see Table 4-2), but in the majority of cases the victim knows the offender (Bolen, 2000; Finkelhor & Ormrod, 2001; U.S. DHHS, 2005). Research shows that victims are abused

---

Box 4-3 Female Perpetrators of Child Sexual Abuse

Well-known cases of female perpetrators include those in which adult women, often teachers (e.g., Kaufman, Holmber, Orts, McCrady, Rotzien, & Daleiden, 1995), became romantically involved with adolescent boys (e.g., the Mary-Kay LeTourneau case). They also include cases in which women worked with male perpetrators as accomplices (e.g., Wanda Barzee and Brian David Mitchell kidnapped, sexually assaulted, and held Elizabeth Smart captive for 9 months; Nancy and Phillip Garrido kidnapped, raped, and held Jaycee Lee Dugard captive for 18 years; Karla Homolka and Paul Bernardo were serial rapists and killers), perhaps due to their submissive role in the relationship (e.g., willingness to please a lover, fearfulness of repercussions if not cooperative), psychological disturbances, and/or past or current abuse (Margolin & Craft, 1990; Rudin, Zalewski, & Bodmer-Turner, 1995; Saradjian, 1996; Vandiver, 2006). According to an analysis by Wijkman, Bijleveld, and Hendriks (2010), of 111 adult female sex offenders in the Netherlands criminal justice system from 1994 to 2005, 77% of the women were convicted of sexually abusing children and the majority (two-thirds) did so in concert with male co-offenders.

Research shows that male and female offenders are similar in terms of the severity of abuse levied (e.g., overt sexual touching and penetration), but girls and women are more likely than boys and men to have a caretaking role with the victim; consequently, their victims are usually young (Finkelhor, 1994; Rudin et al., 1995; Snyder, 2000; Trocme & Wolfe, 2001). Female offenders may perpetrate abuse in subtle, covert, or seductive ways inconsistent with routine caregiving or medical manners, such as applying medication on a child's penis, using rectal thermometers and suppositories, digitally penetrating genitals while bathing, and exposing themselves with the intention to arouse the child (Denov, 2004; Mitchell & Morse, 1998). Maternal sexual abuse against daughters and sons, such as frequent genital and anal examinations or forcing the child to touch or perform sexual acts on the mother, often escapes notice and, therefore, occurs over an extended period with increased aggression as victims age, causing severe negative consequences (Denov, 2004; Ferguson & Meehan, 2005).

---

more often by extrafamilial abusers, such as friends and neighbors, than by intrafamilial ones, such as parents and other relatives (76% versus 33%), across multiple sessions (Ruggiero et al., 2000; Russell, 1983; Saunders et al., 1999). Extrafamilial abusers are commonly identified in nonclinical samples, whereas official statistics and CPS most often deal with intrafamilial offenders (Bolen, 2000). For example, abusers of nonclinical victims are typically people whom the child knows, usually extrafamilial: 52% involve people whom the victims know, 33% of cases involve relatives, and as many as 15% are initiated by strangers (e.g., Russell, 1983). In contrast, Snyder (2000), using law enforcement data, reported that family members perpetrated CSA in preschool victims aged birth to 5 years (49%) and elementary school-aged victims aged 6–11 years (42%) more than in junior/senior high school victims aged 12–17 years (24%). Acquaintances were the main perpetrators for this oldest group (66%), more so than for preschool (48%) or elementary school-aged victims (53%).

Table 4-2 Relationship of offender to CSA victim

Relation to victim	Girl victim	Boy victim
Family	29%	11%
Acquaintance	41%	44%
Stranger	21%	40%

Data from Finkelhor, D. (1990). Early and long term effects of child sexual abuse: An update. *Professional Psychology: Research & Practice, 21*(5), 325-330.

Abusers tend to exhibit certain signs or characteristics that could serve to warn other adults that they may pose a risk to children. For example, parent or caregiver abusers may be secretive or isolated from others and attempt to curtail the child's interactions with others, particularly individuals of the opposite sex. Abusers may not be capable of understanding social cues about personal boundaries or sexual limits, may combine words and actions about sexuality with aggression, and may encourage adult sexual partners to pretend to be children. They are often uninterested in or incapable of initiating and maintaining adult relationships, instead spending their free time with children, having a special child friend, describing children sexually (e.g., stud, sexy), encouraging children to keep secrets, and attempting to engage children in sexual fantasies and get them to discuss their sexual activities. If confronted with harm caused by their actions, abusers will typically deny it or blame it on others. Finally, they often have sexual obsessions that include Internet sexual activity, downloading and viewing Internet pornography, and excessive masturbation to the point that this practice interferes with their daily activities.

Signs, Symptoms, and Developmental Consequences of Sexually Abused Children

In some children (20% to 40%), no behavioral signs and physical symptoms indicating that they are being or have been sexually abused appear initially or for up to two years later (Bahali, Akgan, Tahiroglu, & Avci, 2010; Kendall-Tackett, Williams, & Finkelhor, 1993). In others, one or more signs and symptoms appear early (see the review by Paolucci, Genuis, & Violato, 2001). Failure to exhibit signs, however, does not provide proof that CSA allegations are false, given that trauma is not always a component of the abuse (Finkelhor, 1990; Kendall-Tackett et al., 1993). A review of the literature (Berliner, 2006; Brierre & Elliott, 1994; Miller-Perrin & Perrin, 2007) suggests that differences in initial and long-term (beyond 2 years) negative outcomes of CSA depend on a combination of risk factors (i.e., preabuse, nature of the abuse, and postabuse responses) and mediating factors (e.g., duration and frequency of sexual abuse, types of sexual activity, age at onset).

Behavioral Signs

The most typical sign of CSA is sexualized behavior, although it is not conclusive without corroborating evidence (e.g., allegations from the child) given that nonabused

Box 4-4 Juvenile CSA Offenders

Almost half of adult CSA offenders began as juveniles, and many juvenile offenders placed in juvenile corrections and human sexuality programs on lesser charges actually have committed serious sexual offenses, some of which went undetected prior to this point (Ryan & Lane, 1991). Moreover, according to national and state law enforcement and CPS statistics, adolescents younger than the age of 18 are responsible for approximately one-third to one-half of all sexual assaults on children (i.e., acts of sexual touching or penetration, however slight, by the use of force or threat of force) each year (Becker et al., 1986; Bonner, Marx, Thompson, & Michaelson, 1998; Davis & Leitenberg, 1987; Weinrott, 1996).

Like their adult counterparts, juvenile child sex abuse offenders have specific psychological or personality flaws, such as poor impulse control and cognitive distortions (Elsegood & Duff, 2010), academic-learning problems that contribute to low sexual knowledge, absent or minimal social experiences (Erooga & Masson, 1999), and exposure to dysfunctional or abusive family lives, such as current or past history of sexual and/or physical abuse (Becker, 1994). These characteristics facilitate juvenile CSA offenders' ability to engage in coercive sexual activities with children so as to satisfy their emotional needs for interpersonal closeness in the absence of the ability to form appropriate relationships with other adolescents (Egan, Kavanagh, & Blair, 2005; Marshall & Laws, 2003).

Several researchers have shown that the absence of social competence, self-esteem, and interpersonal skills contributes to juvenile CSA offending, as these adolescents have few opportunities to establish normal sexual relationships (Elsegood & Duff, 2010). Smith and Israel (1987) reported lack of impulse control in many of the male adolescent CSA offenders that led almost half of them to commit nonsexual offenses even before their first sexual offense occurred. Hunter and Figuerdo (2000) suggested that juvenile CSA offenders who are lacking in social competencies and are competitively disadvantaged relative to their peers may sexually act out as a reflective compensatory behavior rather than from psychopathy and arrested sexual development.

Research has also found that juvenile CSA offenders are able to offend, despite seemingly obvious signs of distress exhibited by their victims, due to a combination of distorted cognition and lack of empathy (Elsegood & Duff, 2010). Cognitive distortions contribute to the promotion of sexually deviant behavior patterns by allowing the juvenile offender to deny, justify, minimize, and rationalize his or her actions (Howitt & Sheldon, 2007). Accordingly, the offender does not experience negative feelings of shame, guilt, and anxiety (Becker, 1994). Many adult sex offenders also do not or choose not to see the damage done to the victim by the sexual abuse (Whittaker et al., 2006). Marsa et al. (2004) found support for this notion in their research: The offenders they studied used cognitive distortion to reduce their feelings of guilt and fear of being caught, thereby allowing the cycle of abuse to continue. As sexually abusive behaviors develop steadily over time, the most effective strategy for reducing CSA recidivism is providing offenders with early treatment (Becker, Kaplan, & Kavoussi, 1988; Grant, 2000).

children show a wide range of sexual behaviors (Besharov, 1990; Friedrich, Grambusch, Broughton, Kuiper, & Beilke, 1991; Kendall-Tackett et al., 1993; Lamb, 1994a, 1994b; Levine & Battistoni, 1991). Preschool and school-aged child victims of CSA may demonstrate precocious sexual knowledge and behavior by attempting to elicit a sexual response (i.e., overt sexual seduction of children and adults), sitting on someone's lap, sexual promiscuity, sex play mimicking intercourse, and compulsive masturbation and/or touching of own and others' genitals (Friedrich et al., 2001; Mannarino & Cohen, 1996). Adolescent victims of CSA often engage in risky sexual behaviors, including having multiple partners and unprotected sex, and for girls, unintended and unwanted pregnancies and abortions (Noll, Shenk, & Putnam, 2009; van Roode, Dickson, Herbison, & Paul, 2009; Wyatt, Newcomb, Reederle, & Notgrass, 1993).

Preschool victims of CSA may show regression by behaving immaturely, becoming socially withdrawn, demonstrating poor relations with family and peers, and engaging in hyperactive behaviors (Wakefield & Underwager, 1991). School-age children not only exhibit these behaviors, but also may engage in delinquency and stealing. In addition, children may inexplicably avoid a person or abruptly change their routine, become shy around others, withdraw from normal activities, become obsessed with cleanliness and good behavior, or refuse to change their clothing, bathe, or play games or sports requiring physical interaction (Access Continuing Education, n.d.; Trocme & Wolfe, 2001). Other behavioral signs include poor academic performance, particularly when the child had been doing well; refusal to attend school; onset or increase in emotional outbursts of anger, including tantrums and overreactions to stimuli from a previously even-tempered or manageable child; and running away from home without a precipitating event (Berliner, 2011; Trocme & Wolfe, 2001). Adolescent victims may display these same behaviors and also become involved in prostitution, run away, seek early marriage, engage in substance abuse, demonstrate truancy, and drop out from high school. Adult survivors of CSA may engage in avoidance behaviors, such as substance abuse and addiction, tension-reducing activities (e.g., self-mutilation, eating disorders, head banging), suicide, and dissociation (Briere & Gil, 1998; Saunders et al., 1999; Smolak & Murnen, 2002).

Physical Developmental Consequences/Symptoms
Child victims of CSA, as well as adult survivors, most commonly show symptoms of reexperiencing trauma (e.g., nightmares, flashbacks, inability to stop intrusive thoughts, feeling guilty), numbing or avoidance (e.g., lack of enjoyment in daily activities, dissociation), and increased arousal (e.g., startling easily, being fearful) consistent with post-traumatic stress (PTS) and post-traumatic stress disorder (PTSD) (Briere & Elliott, 1994; Friedrich, 1993; Friedrich et al., 2001; Kendall-Tackett et al., 1993). Generally, physical symptoms exhibited by victims of CSA vary from individual to individual, depending on the child's developmental level (e.g., Hewitt, 1998; Kendall-Tackett et al., 1993). Bruising and the presence of blood on the child's clothing are more common for preschool victims, whereas encopresis (fecal soiling) and enuresis (urinary incontinence) are seen in both preschool and school-age victims (Finkel, 2011). Child and adolescent victims also present with eating disorders (e.g., binging, purging, overeating); sleep disturbances; sexually transmitted diseases; problems related to the genital or rectal region, including trouble walking or sitting due to injury; stomachaches (e.g., vague complaints); bowel or anal problems (e.g., hemorrhoids, rectal bleeding, painful bowel movements); and genital complaints (e.g., itch, odor, discharge, yeast infections, repeated urinary tract infections,

dysuria [painful urination]) (Miller-Perrin & Perrin, 2007). Adolescent victims may have increased catecholamine levels, dysregulated cortisol, and dysfunctional immune systems (van Roode et al., 2009), whereas adult survivors could exhibit all of these symptoms as well as chronic headaches and migraines, obesity, chronic pelvic pain, and irritable bowel syndrome (Miller-Perrin & Perrin, 2007).

Emotional Developmental Consequences

Some children show severe immediate and long-term disturbed psychological symptoms related to their emotional distress (Kendall-Tackett et al., 1993), such as depression, withdrawal, excessive fears, anxiety, anger, and nervousness (Browne & Finkelhor, 1986; Lanktree, Briere, & Zaidi, 1991). Anxiety develops in children as a reaction to their disrupted sense of security and trust in people when their bodies are violated, often by someone whom they thought would nurture and protect them from harm (Briere, 1992; Gomes-Schwartz, Horowitz, & Cardarelli, 1990). Adult survivors show elevated risk for psychological disorders—particularly depression and anxiety, but also phobias, interpersonal relationship problems that make intimacy difficult, sexual and arousal dysfunction (e.g., anxiety-related difficulties during sexual contact, anorgasmia [inability to experience orgasms]), and somatic difficulties (e.g., headaches, stomach pain, chronic pelvic pain) tied to hyperarousal of the sympathetic nervous system (Beitchman, Zuker, Hood, daCosta, & Akman, 1991; Berliner & Elliott, 2002; Briere & Elliott, 1994; Cunningham, Pearce, & Pearce, 1988; Meiselman, 1978; Stein, Golding, Siegel, Burnam, & Sorenson, 1988). Child victims understandably exhibit anger in both internalized (e.g., depression) and externalized forms (e.g., abusing others), irritability, and behavioral problems (e.g., aggressiveness by fighting, bullying, attacking others), which results in peer rejection and social isolation (Briere & Elliot, 1994; Friedrich, Beilke, & Urquiza, 1988).

Social Developmental Consequences

According to Briere and Elliott (1994, p. 61), social functioning in children and adult survivors of CSA is negatively impacted because of "the immediate cognitive and conditioned responses to victimization that extend into the long term (for example, distrust of others, anger at and/or fear of those with greater power, concerns about abandonment, perceptions of injustice), as well as the accommodation responses to ongoing abuse (for example, avoidance, passivity, and sexualization)." Thus, the violation of the child's body—most commonly by someone whom the child knows and trusts—interrupts the child's ability to form and maintain normative interpersonal relationships (Berliner, 2011). The reduced social competence of child victims further isolates them from peers and adults on whom they could have otherwise relied, using them as sources to reveal their abuse and as emotional supports to calm, soothe, and help them cope during their crises (Friedrich, Urquiza, & Beilke, 1986; Mannarino & Cohen, 1996). Additionally, early and sustained CSA disrupts victims' development of positive self-esteem and sense of self, resulting in both immediate and long-term psychosocial difficulties (e.g., suggestibility, increased risk of exploitation and victimization) and an inability to maintain boundaries in their adult relationships (Briere, 1992; Cole & Putnam, 1992). Lastly, CSA may lead to sexual identity confusion (e.g., homosexual) when the abuser is the same sex as the child victim (Finkelhor & Browne, 1985).

Cognitive Developmental Consequences
Cognitive effects of CSA on the victim include learning difficulties, which become problematic with age as the ability to pay attention and concentrate in school deteriorates, leading to poor grades and negative self-perceptions (Miller-Perrin & Perrin, 2007). CSA alters the victim's belief system and understanding about the self, people, and the world, resulting in the victim underestimating self-worth and overestimating danger (Barahal, Waterman, & Martin, 1981; Williams, 1993). More commonly, the child interprets the abuse using generalized distorted, negative attributions and appraisals (e.g., the child is at fault, no one can be trusted, the world is unsafe) rather than adopting a specific and protective risk-evaluation approach that some adults are not trustworthy (Daigneault, Tourigny, & Hebert, 2006; Feiring, Simon, & Cleland, 2009). Long-term consequences include cognitive distortions, in which survivors attribute negative events to internal causes (i.e., blaming oneself) and positive events to external causes (i.e., undeserving fortune), leading victims to interpret even neutral experiences negatively (Hyman, Gold, & Cott, 2003). Additionally, adult survivors of CSA who have negative appraisals of their maltreatment (e.g., beliefs that it was humiliating, they were at fault, something was wrong with them, no one would believe them, they had no one to give them emotional support) tend to have high levels of maladjustment, such as PTSD symptoms (Barker-Collo & Read, 2003; Hyman et al., 2003).

Meditators for Adverse Effects
Why would children differ in their responses to CSA? A few explanations have been posited. Most obviously, variations in the methodology and definitions used in investigations may yield different results (Miller-Perrin & Perrin, 2007). Another reason is that some children are innately resilient. As such, the sexual trauma to which they are exposed, although devastating to others who are similarly treated (e.g., impaired social and occupational functioning, serious psychological and health outcomes), has seemingly little adverse effect on them (Bonanno & Mancini, 2008; Maniglio, 2009; Turner, Finkelhor, & Ormrod, 2006). Note, however, that although "resilient" children are skilled at coping and can recover naturally, they do not conceive of their sexual abuse experiences, which typically involve unwanted or forced contact, as neutral, but rather as events causing shame, pain, fear, confusion, distrust, and vulnerability (Berliner, 2011). Symptoms and consequences may also differ due to variations in risk factors associated with the sexual trauma itself, including the number of adverse childhood experiences (e.g., death of family member, witnessing domestic violence, physical abuse, accident, disaster), a child's preexisting mental and physical health conditions, the nature of the sexual abuse, and the responses children

receive from their loved ones after disclosure has been made (Deblinger, Mannarino, Cohen, & Steer, 2006; Finkelhor, 2008; Finkelhor, Ormrod, & Turner, 2009).

According to Berliner (2011), "trauma burden" (the number and type of adverse childhood experiences) predicts outcome. Specifically, as the number of negative events (such as multiple forms of maltreatment) accumulates, the likelihood of serious psychological, interpersonal, and health consequences for the victim increases (Dong, Sanchez, & Price, 2004; Finkelhor, 2008; Kinard, 2004; Turner et al., 2006). Children are likely to develop PTSD as a result of CSA if they had already been suffering from anxiety disorders or have parents who have mental illness or who engage in domestic violence (Fitzgerald, Hedtke, Kilpatrick, Resnick, & Zinzow, 2008). The severity and range of negative consequences from CSA are also tied to the nature and seriousness of the abuse; this is particularly true when CSA begins at an early age, occurs over an extended period of time, or involves a parent or parent-figure (Berliner, 2011; Briere & Elliott, 1994). The degree of harm is contingent upon several factors, including the intensity of the emotional relationship between the victim and the perpetrator, whether violence and injury are components of the sexual abuse, and whether the child perceives his or her life (or that of a loved one) as threatened or in danger of serious injury or death (Briere & Elliott, 1994; Ruggerio et al., 2000; Saunders et al., 1999). Finally, researchers (e.g., Bernard-Bonnin, Hebert, Daignault, & Allard-Dansereau, 2008) have found harmful consequences are linked with the absence of belief, support, and protective action—a scenario that often occurs when the offender is a parent or paramour of the nonoffending parent, and most commonly when the offender is the financial provider for the household (Aronson & Plummer, 2010; Briere & Elliott, 1994; Gomez-Schwartz et al., 1990).

Chapter Summary

Child physical abuse is defined on a state-by-state basis. State legislation also varies in terms of its specificity in defining the acts that constitute child physical abuse. Official estimates do not accurately depict the scope of physical abuse. There are several causes of physical abuse. Sometimes circumstances arise that result in a child becoming injured, especially when parents physically punish a child for his or her actual or perceived misbehavior. At other times, physical harm is rendered purposefully, in the absence of any specific precipitating behavior on the part of the child. Children who have suffered from physical abuse often exhibit behavioral signs and physical symptoms, but also experience negatively impacts on their emotional, social, and cognitive development.

The definition of child sexual abuse includes harm caused by physical contact and nonphysical contact. Like physical abuse, the prevalence of child sexual abuse is not accurately depicted by official statistics. This is largely due to victims' general unwillingness to report this crime committed against them, the different types of sexual abuse, and the different types of techniques used by perpetrators to engage in child sexual abuse. Children who are sexually abused show specific behavioral signs and physical symptoms. Such maltreatment also negatively impacts a child's emotional, social, and cognitive development.

Review Questions

1. What are the causes of child physical abuse?

2. What are the causes of child sexual abuse?

3. What are some behavioral signs exhibited by physically and sexually abused children?

4. What are the physical developmental consequences of child physical and sexual abuse?

5. What are the social and emotional developmental consequences of child physical and sexual abuse?

6. What are the cognitive developmental consequences of child physical and sexual abuse?

7. What can mediate the adverse consequences of child physical and sexual abuse?

References

Abel, G. G., Becker, J. V., & Cunningham-Rathner, J. (1984). Complications, consent and cognitions in sex between children and adults. *International Journal of Law and Psychiatry, 7*, 89–103.

Access Continuing Education, Inc. (n.d). *Child abuse and maltreatment/neglect: Identification and reporting.* New York State Mandatory Training. Accessed at: www.accesscontinuingeducation.com

Agran, P. F., Anderson, C., Winn, D., Trent, R. L., Walton-Haynes, L., & Thayer, S. (2003). Rates of pediatric injuries by 3-month intervals for children 0 to 3 years of age. *Pediatrics, 111*(6 Pt 1), e683–692.

Appel, A. E., & Holden, G. W. (1998). The co-occurrence of spouse and physical child abuse: A review and appraisal. *Journal of Family Psychology, 12*(4), 578–599.

Aronson, L., & Plummer, C. (2010). Cultural issues in disclosures of child sexual abuse. *Journal of Child Sexual Abuse, 19*(5), 491–518.

Bahali, K., Akcan, R., Tahiroglu, A. Y., & Avci, A. A. (2010). Child sexual abuse: Seven years in practice. *Journal of Forensic Sciences, 55*(3), 633–636.

Barahal, R., Watennan, J., & Martin, H. (1981). The social cognitive development of abused children. *Journal of Consulting and Clinical Psychology, 49*, 508–516.

Barker-Collo, S., & Read, J. (2003). Models of response to childhood sexual abuse: Their implications for treatment. *Trauma Violence Abuse, 4*(2), 95–11.

Barlow, K. M., & Minns, R. A. (2000). Annual incidence of shaken impact syndrome in young children. *Lancet, 356*(9241), 1571–1572.

Barlow, K. M., Thomson, E., Johnson, D., & Minns, R. A. (2005). Late neurologic and cognitive sequelae of inflicted traumatic brain injury in infancy. *Pediatrics, 116*(2), e174–e185.

Barnett, D., Ganiban, J., & Cicchetti, D. (1999). Maltreatment, negative expressivity, and the development of Type D attachments from 12 to 24 months of age. *Monographs of the Society for Research in Child Development, 64*(3), 97–118.

Barr, R. (1990). The normal crying curve: What do we really know? *Developmental Medicine & Child Neurology, 32*(4), 356–362.

Barr, R. (2000). Excessive crying. In A. J. Sameroff, M. Lewis, & S. M. Miller (Eds.), *Handbook of developmental psychopathology* (pp. 327–350). New York, NY: Kluwer Academic/Plenum Press.

Barr, R. (2006). Crying behavior and its importance for psychosocial development in children. In R. E. Tremblay, M. Boivin, & R. D. Peters (Eds.), *Encyclopedia on early childhood development* (pp. 1–10).

Montreal, QC: Centre of Excellence for Early Childhood Development and Strategic Knowledge Cluster on Early Childhood Development.

Barr, R., Barr, M., Fujiwara, T., Conway, J., Catherine, N., & Brant, R. (2009). Do educational materials change knowledge and behavior about crying and shaken baby syndrome? A randomized controlled trial. *Canadian Medical Association Journal, 180,* 727–733.

Barr, R., Trent, R. B., & Cross, J. (2006). Age-related incidence curve of hospitalized shaken baby syndrome cases: Convergent evidence for crying as a trigger to shaking. *Child Abuse & Neglect, 30*(1), 7–16.

Baumrind, D., Larzelere, R. E., & Cowan, P. A. (2002). Ordinary physical punishment: Is it harmful? Comment on Gershoff (2002). *Psychological Bulletin, 128,* 580–589.

Beauregard, E., Rossmo, K., & Proulx, J. (2007). A descriptive model of the hunting process of serial sex offenders: A rational choice perspective. *Journal of Family Violence, 22*(6), 449–463.

Becker, J. V. (1994). Offenders: Characteristics and treatment. *Future of Children, 4*(2), 176–197.

Becker, J. V., Kaplan, M. S., Cunningham-Rathner, J., & Kavoussi, R. J. (1986). Characteristics of adolescent sexual perpetrators: Preliminary findings. *Journal of Family Violence, 1*(1), 85–87.

Becker, J. V., Kaplan, M., & Kavoussi, R. (1988). Measuring the effectiveness of treatment for the aggressive adolescent sexual offender. In R. A. Prentky & V. L. Quinsey (Eds.), *Human sexual aggression: Current perspectives* (pp. 215–222). New York, NY: New York Academy of Science.

Berliner, D. C. (2006). Educational psychology: Searching for essence throughout a century of influence In P. Alexander & P. Winne (Eds.), *Handbook of educational psychology* (2nd ed., pp. 3–27). Mahway, NJ: Lawrence Erlbaum Associates.

Berliner, L. (2011). *Child sexual abuse: Definition, prevalence, and consequences.* In J. E. B. Myers (Ed.), *The APSAC handbook of child maltreatment* (3rd ed., pp. 215– 232). Thousand Oaks, CA: Sage.

Berliner, L., & Conte, J. R. (1990). The process of victimization: The victims' perspective. *Child Abuse and Neglect, 14,* 29–40.

Berliner, L., & Elliott, D. (2002). Sexual abuse of children in the field of child maltreatment. In J. E. B. Meyers, L. Berliner, J. Briere, C. T. Hendrix, C. Jenny, & T. A. Reid (Eds.), *The APSAC handbook on child maltreatment* (2nd ed., pp. 55–78). London, UK: Sage.

Bernard-Bonnin, A. C., Hebert, M., Daignault, I. V., & Allard-Dansereau, C. (2008). Disclosure of sexual abuse, and personal and familial factors as predictors of post-traumatic stress disorder symptoms in school-aged girls. *Paediatrics and Child Health, 13*(6), 479–486.

Beitchman, J. H., Zucker, K. J., Hood, J. E., daCosta, D. A., & Akman, D. (1991). A review of the short-term effects of child sexual abuse. *Child Abuse & Neglect, 15,* 537–556.

Besharov, D. (1990). *Combating child abuse: Guidelines for cooperation between law enforcement and child protective services.* Washington, DC: American Enterprise Institute.

Black, D. A., Heyman, R. E., & Smith Slep, A. M. (2001). Risk factors for child physical abuse. *Aggression and Violent Behavior, 6,* 121–188.

Bolen, R. M. (2000). Extrafamilial child abuse: A study of perpetrators characteristics and implications for preventions. *Violence Against Women, 6,* 1137–1169.

Bonanno, G. A., & Mancini, A. D. (2008). Resilience. In G. Reyes, J. Elhai, & J. Ford (Eds.), *Encyclopedia of psychological trauma* (pp. 584–585). New York, NY: Wiley.

Boney-McCoy, S., & Finkelhor, D. (1995). The psychological sequelae of violent victimization in a national youth sample. *Journal of Consulting and Clinical Psychology, 63,* 726–736.

Bonner, B., Marx, B., Thompson, J., & Michaelson, P. (1998). Assessment of adolescent offenders. *Child Maltreatment, 3,* 374–383.

Bonnier, C., Nassagne, M., & Evrard, P. (1995). Outcome and prognosis of whiplash shaken infant syndrome: Late consequences after a symptom-free interval. *Developmental Medicine & Child Neurology, 37,* 943–956.

Boroughs, D. S. (2004). Female sexual abusers of children. *Children and Youth Services Review, 26,* 481–487.

Bradford, J. (1990). The antiandrogen and hormonal treatment of sex offenders. In W. L. Marshall, D. R. Laws, & H. E. Barbaree (Eds.), *Handbook sexual assault: Issues, theories, and treatment of the offender* (pp. 297–327). New York, NY: Plenum Press.

Briere, J. (1992). *Child abuse trauma: Theory and treatment of the lasting effects* (Vol. 2). Thousand Oaks, CA: Sage.

Briere, J., & Elliot, D. M. (1994). Immediate and long-term impacts of child sexual abuse. *Future of Children, 4*(2), 54–69.

Briere, J., & Gil, E. (1998). Self-mutilation in clinical and general population samples: Prevalence, correlates, and functions. *American Journal of Orthopsychiatry, 68,* 609–620.

Brown, E. J., & Kolko, D. J. (1999). Child victims' attributions about being physically abused: An examination of factors associated with symptom severity. *Journal of Abnormal Child Psychology, 27,* 311–322.

Brown, J., Cohen, P., Johnson, J. G., & Salzinger, S. (1998). A longitudinal analysis of risk factors for child maltreatment: Findings of a 17-year prospective study of officially recorded and self-reported child abuse and neglect. *Child Abuse and Neglect, 22*(11), 1065–1078.

Brown, J., Cohen, P., Johnson, J. G., & Smailes, E. M. (1999). Child abuse and neglect: Specificity of effects on adolescent and young adult depression and suicidality. *Journal of the American Academy of Child and Adolescent Psychiatry, 38,* 1290–1505.

Browne, A., & Finkelhor, D. (1986). Impact of child sexual abuse: A review of the research. *Psychological Bulletin, 99,* 66–77.

Bruce, D. A., & Zimmerman, R. A. (1989). Shaken impact syndrome. *Pediatric Annals, 18*(8), 482–494.

Burgess, A. W., Groth, A. N., & McCausland, M. P. (1981). Child sex initiation rings. *American Journal of Orthopsychiatry, 51,* 110–119.

Burgess, A. W., & Hartman, C. R. (1987). Child abuse aspects of child pornography. *Psychiatry Annals, 17,* 248–253.

Cappell, C., & Heiner, R. B. (1990). The intergenerational transmission of family aggression. *Journal of Family Violence, 5,* 135–152.

Caselles, C. E., & Milner, J. S. (2000). Evaluations of child transgressions, disciplinary choices, and expected child compliance in a no-cry and a crying infant condition in physically abusive and comparison mothers. *Child Abuse & Neglect, 24,* 477–493.

Caspi, A., McClay, J., Moffitt, T. E., Mill, J., Martin, J., Craig, I. W., Taylor, A., & Poulton, R. (2002). Role of genotype in the cycle of violence in maltreated children. *Science, 297,* 851–854.

Catherine, N., Ko, J. J., & Barr, R. G. (2008). Getting the word out: Advice on crying and colic in popular parenting magazines. *Journal of Developmental & Behavioral Pediatrics, 29,* 508–511.

Centers for Disease Control and Prevention. (1997). Traumatic brain injury—Colorado, Missouri, Oklahoma, and Utah, 1990–1993. *Morbidity and Mortality Weekly Report, 46,* 8–11.

Chaffin, M., Letourneau, E., & Silovsky, J. (2002). Adults, adolescents, and children who sexually abuse children. In J. E. B. Meyers, L. Berliner, J. Briere, C. T. Hendrix, C. Jenny, & T. A. Reid (Eds.), *The APSAC handbook on child maltreatment* (2nd ed., pp. 205–232). Thousand Oaks, CA: Sage.

Chaffin, M., Silovsky, J. F., Funderburk, B., Valle, L. A., Brestan, E. V., Balachova, T., Jackson, S., Lensgraf, J., & Bonner, B. L. (2004). Parent-child interaction therapy with physically abusive parents: Efficacy for reducing future abuse reports. *Journal of Consulting and Clinical Psychology, 72*(3), 500–510.

Chiesa, A., & Duhaime, A. C. (2009). Abusive head trauma. *Pediatric Clinics of North America, 56*(2), 317–331.

Child Welfare Information Gateway. (2011). *Child abuse and neglect fatalities 2009: Statistics and interventions*. Washington, DC: U.S. Department of Health and Human Services, Children's Bureau. http://www.childwelfare.gov/pubs/factsheets/fatality.cfm

Christian, C. W., Block, R., & Committee on Child Abuse and Neglect. (2009). Abusive head trauma in infants and children. *Pediatrics, 123*(5), 1409–1411.

Christiansen, J. R., & Blake, R. H. (1990). The grooming process in father–daughter incest. In A. L. Horton, B. L. Johnson, L. M. Roundy, & D. Williams (Eds.), *The incest perpetrator: The family member no one wants to treat* (pp. 88–98). Newbury Park, CA: Sage.

Chu, J. A., Frey, L. M., Ganzel, B. L., & Matthews, J. A. (1999). Memories of childhood abuse: Dissociation, amnesia and corroboration. *American Journal of Psychiatry, 156*, 749–755.

Cohen, P., Brown, J., & Smailes, E. (2001). Child abuse and neglect and the development of mental disorders in the general population. *Developmental Psychopathology, 13*, 981–999.

Cole, P. M., & Putnam, F. W. (1992). Effects of incest on self and social functioning: A developmental psychopathology perspective. *Journal of Consulting and Clinical Psychology, 60*, 174–184.

Conte, J. R. (1994). Child sexual abuse: Awareness and backlash. *Future of Children, 4*(2), 224–232.

Conte, J. R., Wolfe, S., & Smith, T. (1989). What sexual offenders tell us about prevention strategies. *Child Abuse and Neglect, 13*, 293–301.

Coohey, C. (2000). The role of friends, in-laws, and other kin in father-perpetrated child physical abuse. *Child Welfare, 79*, 373–402.

Coohey, C., & Braun, N. (1997). Toward an integrated framework for understanding child physical abuse. *Child Abuse & Neglect, 21*, 1081–1094.

Cortini, F., & Marshall, W. L. (2001). Sex as a coping strategy and its relationship to juvenile sexual history and intimacy in sexual offenders. *Sexual Abuse, 13*, 27–43.

Covell, C. N., & Scalora, M. J. (2002). Empathic deficits in sexual offenders: An integration of affective, social, and cognitive constructs. *Aggression and Violent Behavior, 7*, 251–270.

Cunningham, J., Pearce, T., & Pearce, P. (1988). Childhood sexual abuse and medical complaints in adult women. *Journal of Interpersonal Violence, 3*, 131–144.

Dadds, M., Smith, M., Weber, Y., & Robinson, A. (1991). An exploration of family and individual profiles following father–daughter incest. *Child Abuse & Neglect, 15*, 575–586.

Daigneault, I., Tourigny, M., & Hebert, M. (2006). Self-attributions of blame in sexually abused adolescents: A mediational model. *Journal of Traumatic Stress, 19*, 153–157.

Daro, D. (1988). *Confronting child abuse*. New York, NY: Free Press.

Davis, G. E., & Leitenberg, H. (1987). Adolescent sex offenders. *Psychological Bulletin, 101*, 417–427.

De Bellis, M. D. (2001). Developmental traumatology: The psychobiological development of maltreated children and its implications for research, treatment, and policy. *Development and Psychopathology, 13*, 539–564.

Deblinger, E., Mannarino, A. P., Cohen, J. A., & Steer, R. A. (2006). A multisite, randomized controlled trial for children with sexual abuse–related PTSD symptoms: Examining predictors of treatment response. *Journal of the American Academy of Child and Adolescent Psychiatry, 45*, 1474–1484.

Denov, M. S. (2004). The long-term effects of child sexual abuse by female perpetrators: A qualitative study of male and female victims. *Journal of Interpersonal Violence, 19*, 1137–1156.

Dias, M. S., Smith, K., DeGuehery, K., Mazur, P., Li, V., & Shaffer, M. L. (2005). Preventing abusive head trauma among infants and young children: A hospital-based, parent education program. *Pediatrics, 115*, e470–e477.

Dong, C., Sanchez, L. E., & Price, R. A. (2004). Relationship of obesity to depression: A family based study. *International Journal of Obesity, 28*, 780–795.

Douglas, E. M., & Finkelhor, D. (2005). Childhood sexual abuse fact sheet. http://www.unh.edu/ccrc/factsheet/pdf/CSA-FS20.pdf

Downs, W. R., & Miller, B. A. (1998). Relationships between experiences of parental violence during childhood and women's psychiatric symptomatology. *Journal of Interpersonal Violence, 13*, 438–455.

Duhaime, A. C. (2008). Demographics of abusive head trauma. *Journal of Neurosurgery: Pediatrics, 1*(5), 349–350.

Duhaime, A. C., Alario, A. J., Lewander, W. J., Schut, L., Sutton, L. N., Seidl, T. S., Nudelman, S., Budenz, D., Hertle, R., Tsiaras, W., & Loporchio, S. (1992). Head injury in very young children: Mechanisms, injury types, and ophthalmologic findings in 100 hospitalized patients younger than 2 years of age. *Pediatrics, 90*(2 Pt 1), 179–185.

Earls, C. M., & David, H. (1990). Early family and sexual experiences of male and female prostitutes. *Canada's Mental Health, 38*(4), 7–11.

Eckenrode, J., Laird, M., & Doris, J. (1993). School performance and disciplinary problems among abused and neglected children. *Developmental Psychology, 29*, 53–63.

Egan, V., Kavanagh, B., & Blair, M. (2005). Sexual offenders, personality and obsessionality. *Sexual Abuse, 17*, 223–240.

Eisele, J. A., Kegler, S. R., Trent, R. B., & Coronado, V. G. (2006). Nonfatal traumatic brain injury-related hospitalization in very young children—15 states, 1999. *Journal of Head Trauma Rehabilitation, 21*(6), 537–543.

Ellingson, K. D., Leventhal, J. M., & Weiss, H. B. (2008). Using hospital discharge data to track inflicted traumatic brain injury. *American College of Preventive Medicine, 34*(4 suppl), S157–S162.

Elliott, M., Browne, K. D., & Kilcoyne, J. (1995). Child sexual abuse: What offenders tell us. *Child Abuse & Neglect, 19*, 579–594.

Elsegood, K. J., & Duff, S. C. (2010). Theory of mind in men who have sexually offended against children: A U.K. comparison study between child sex offenders and nonoffender controls. *Sexual Abuse: A Journal of Research and Treatment, 22*(1), 112–131.

Erooga, M., & Masson, H. (1999). *Children and young people who sexually abuse others: Challenges and responses.* London, UK: Routledge.

Ettaro, L., Berger, R. P., & Songer, T. (2004). Abusive head trauma in young children: Characteristics and medical charges in a hospitalized population. *Child Abuse & Neglect, 28*(10), 1099–1111.

Faller, K. C. (1989). Why sexual abuse? An exploration of the interrogational hypothesis. *Child Abuse & Neglect, 13*, 543–548.

Famularo, R., Fenton, T., Kinscherff, R., Ayoub, C., & Barnum, R. (1994). Maternal and child post-traumatic stress disorder in cases of child maltreatment. *Child Abuse and Neglect, 18*, 27–36.

Famularo, R., Kinscherff, R., & Fenton, R. (1992). Psychiatric diagnoses of maltreated children: Preliminary findings. *Journal of the American Academy of Child and Adolescent Psychiatry, 31*, 863–867.

Fantuzzo, J. W. (1990). Behavioral treatment of the victims of child abuse and neglect. *Behavior Modification, 14*(3), 316–339.

Fantuzzo, J. W., delGaudio, W. A., Atkins, M., Meyers, R., & Noone, M. (1998). A contextually relevant assessment of the impact of child maltreatment on the social competencies of low-income urban children. *Journal of American Academy of Child & Adolescent Psychiatry, 37*, 1201–1208.

Faul, M., Xu, L., Wald, M. M., & Coronado, V. G. (2010). *Traumatic brain injury in the United States: Emergency department visits, hospitalizations and deaths, 2002–2006.* Atlanta, GA: Centers for Disease Control and Prevention, National Center for Injury Prevention and Control.

Feiring, C., Simon, V., & Cleland, C. (2009). Childhood sexual abuse, stigmatization, internalizing symptoms, and the development of sexual difficulties and dating aggression. *Journal of Consulting and Clinical Psychology, 77*(1), 127–137.

Ferguson, C. J., & Meehan, D. C. (2005). An analysis of females convicted of sex crimes in the state of Florida. *Journal of Child Sexual Abuse, 14*, 75–89.

Finkel, M. A. (2011). Medical issue in child sexual abuse. In J. E. B. Myers (Ed.), *The APSAC handbook on child maltreatment* (3rd ed., pp. 253–266). Thousand Oaks, CA: Sage.

Finkelhor, D. (1981). The sexual abuse of boys. *Victimology, 6*, 76–84.

Finkelhor, D. (1984). *Child sexual abuse: New theory and research.* New York, NY: Free Press.

Finkelhor, D. (1990). Early and long term effects of child sexual abuse: An update. *Professional Psychology: Research & Practice, 21*(5), 325–330.

Finkelhor, D. (1994). Current information on the scope and nature of child sexual abuse. *Future of Children, 4*(2), 311–353.

Finkelhor, D. (2005). The main problem is underreporting child sexual abuse and neglect. In D. R. Loseke, R. J. Gelles, & M. M. Cavanaugh (Eds.), *Current controversies on family violence* (2nd ed., pp. 299–310). Thousand Oaks, CA: Sage.

Finkelhor, D. (2008). *Childhood victimization: Violence, crime, and abuse in the lives of young people.* New York, NY: Oxford University Press.

Finkelhor D. (2009). The prevention of child sexual abuse. *Future of Children, 19*, 169–194.

Finkelhor, D., & Browne, A. (1985). The traumatic impact of child sexual abuse: A conceptualization. *American Journal of Orthopsychiatry, 55*(4), 530–541.

Finkelhor, D., Hammer, H., & Sedlak, A. (2004). *Sexually assaulted children: National estimates and characteristics.* Washington, DC: U.S. Department of Justice, Office of Justice Programs, Office of Juvenile Justice and Delinquency Prevention.

Finkelhor, D., & Ormrod, R. (2001). *Child abuse reported to the police* (NCJ Publication No. 187238). Washington, DC: U.S. Bureau of Justice Statistics.

Finkelhor, D., Ormrod, R. K., & Turner, H. A. (2009). Lifetime assessment of poly-victimization in a national sample of children & youth. *Child Abuse & Neglect, 33*, 403–411.

Finkelhor, D., Turner, H. A., Ormrod, R. K., & Hamby, S. L. (2009). Violence, crime, and exposure in a national sample of children and youth. *Pediatrics, 124*(5), 1411–1423. http://pediatrics.aappublications.org/content/124/5/1411.full

Finkelhor, D., Moore, D., Hamby, S. L., & Straus, M. S. (1997). Sexually abused children in a national survey of parents: Methodological issues. *Child Abuse & Neglect, 21*, 1–9.

Fitzgerald, M. M., Hedtke, K. A., Kilpatrick, D. G., Resnick, H. S., & Zinzow, H. M. (2008). A longitudinal investigation of interpersonal violence in relation to mental health and substance use. *Journal of Consulting and Clinical Psychology, 76*, 633–647.

Friedrich, W. N. (1993). Sexual victimization and sexual behavior in children: A review of recent literature. *Child Abuse & Neglect, 17*, 59–66.

Friedrich, W. N., Beilke, R. L., & Urquiza A. J. (1988). Behavior problems in young sexually abused boys. *Journal of Interpersonal Violence, 3*, 21–28.

Friedrich, W. N., Dittner, C. A., Action, R., Berliner, L., Butler, J., Damon, L., Davies, W. H., Gray, A., & Wright, J. (2001). Child Sexual Behavior Inventory: Normative, psychiatric and sexual abuse comparisons. *Child Maltreatment, 6*, 37–49.

Friedrich, W., Fisher, J., Broughton, D., Houston, M., & Shafran, C. (1998). Normative sexual behavior in children: A contemporary sample. *Pediatrics, 101*(4), e9.

Friedrich, W. N., Grambusch, P., Broughton, D., Kuiper, J., & Beilke, R. L. (1991). Normative sexual behavior in children. *Pediatrics, 88*, 456–464.

Friedrich, W. N., Urquiza, A. J., & Beilke, R. (1986). Behavior problems in sexually abused young children. *Journal of Pediatric Psychology, 11*, 47–57.

Frodi, A., & Lamb, N. (1980). Child abusers' responses to infant smiles and cries. *Child Development, 5*, 238–241.

Gelles, R. J. (1989). Child abuse and violence in single parent families: Parent absence and economic deprivation. *American Journal of Orthopsychiatry, 59,* 492–501.

Gelles, R. J., & Cornell, C. P. (1990). *Intimate violence in families* (2nd ed.). London, UK: Sage.

Gershoff, E. T. (2002). Corporal punishment by parents and associated child behaviors and experiences: A meta-analytic and theoretical review. *Psychological Bulletin, 128,* 539–579.

Ginsburg, H., Wright, L., Harrell, P. M., & Hill, D. W. (1989). Childhood victimization: Desensitization effects in the later lifespan. *Child Psychiatry and Human Development, 20,* 59–71.

Glaser, D. (2002). Psychological aspects of congenital heart disease. In R. H. Anderson, E. J. Baker, F. J. Macartney, M. L. Rigby, E. A. Shinebourne, & M. J. Tynan (Eds.), *Paediatric cardiology* (2nd ed., pp. 1931–1946). Edinburgh, UK: Churchill Livingstone.

Gomes-Schwartz, B., Horowitz, J. M., & Cardarelli, A. P. (1990). *Child sexual abuse: The initial effects.* Newbury Park, CA: Sage.

Grant, A. (2000). The historical development of treatment for adolescent sex offenders. In Australian Institute of Criminology, *Trends and issues in crime and criminal justice.* http://www.aic.gov.au

Gruber, K. J., & Jones, R. J. (1983). Identifying determinants of risk of sexual victimization of youth: A multivariate approach. *Child Abuse & Neglect, 7,* 17–24.

Hanson, K., Gordon, A., Harris, A. J. R., Marques, J. K., Murphy, W., Quinsey, V. L., & Seto, M. C. (2003). First report of the collaborative outcome data project on the effectiveness of psychological treatment for sex offenders. *Sexual Abuse: A Journal of Research and Treatment, 14*(2), 169–194.

Hanzi, R. (2006). *Sexual abuse and exploitation of the girl child through cultural practices in Zimbabwe: A human rights perspective.* Unpublished master's thesis. Pretoria, South Africa: Centre University of Pretoria.

Hartman, C. R., & Burgess, A. W. (1988). Information processing of trauma. *Journal of Interpersonal Violence, 3,* 443–457.

Herrenkohl, E. C., Herrenkohl, R. C., Rupert, L. J., Egolf, B. P., & Lutz, J. G. (1995). Risk factors for behavioral dysfunction: The relative impact of maltreatment, SES, physical health problems, cognitive ability, and quality of parent–child interaction. *Child Abuse & Neglect, 19,* 191–203.

Herrenkohl, R. C., Herrenkohl, E. C., Egolf, B. P., & Wu, P. (1991). The development consequences of abuse: The Lehigh longitudinal study. In R. H. Starr & D. A. Wolfe (Eds.), *The effects of child abuse and neglect: Issues and research* (pp. 57–85). New York, NY: Guilford Press.

Hesse, E., & Main, M. (2000). Disorganized infant, child, and adult attachment: Collapse in behavioral and attentional strategies. *Journal of the American Psychoanalytic Association, 48,* 1097–1127.

Hewitt, S. K. (1998). *Small voices: Assessing allegations of sexual abuse in preschool children.* Thousand Oaks, CA: Sage.

Hillson, J. M. C., & Kupier, N. A. (1994). A stress and coping model of child maltreatment. *Clinical Psychology Review, 14*(4), 261–285.

Holmes, W. C., & Slap, G. B. (1998). Sexual abuse of boys: Definition, prevalence, correlates, sequelae, and management. *Journal of the American Medical Association, 280,* 1855–1862.

Hoove, M., Dubas, J. S., Eichelsheim, V. I., Laan, P. H., Smeenk, W. H., & Gerris, J. R. M. (2009). The relationship between parenting and delinquency: A meta-analysis. *Journal of Abnormal Child Psychology, 37*(6), 749–775.

Hotaling, G. T., Straus, M. A., & Lincoln, A. J. (1990). Intrafamily violence and crime and violence outside the family. In M. A. Strans & R. J. Gelles (Eds.), *Physical violence in American families* (pp. 431–466). New Brunswick, NJ: Transaction.

Howitt, D., & Sheldon, K. (2007). The role of cognitive distortions in paedophilic offending: Internet and contact offenders compared. *Psychology, Crime, & Law, 13,* 469–486.

Hunter, J. A., & Figueredo, A. J. (2000). The influence of personality and history of sexual victimization in the prediction of juvenile perpetrated child molestation. *Behavior Modification, 29*(2), 259–281.

Hyman, S. M., Gold, S. N., & Cott, M. A. (2003). Forms of social support that moderate PTSD in childhood sexual abuse survivors. *Journal of Family Violence, 18*(5), 295–300.

Janssen, M. A. (2002). *Complexity and ecosystem management: The theory and practice of multi-agent systems.* Northampton, MA: Edward Elgar Publishers.

Jones, D. J., Runyan, D. K., Lewis, T., Litrownik, A. J., Black, M. M., Wiley, T., . . . Nagin, D. S. (2010). Trajectories of childhood sexual abuse and early adolescent HIV/AIDS risk behaviors: The role of other maltreatment, witnessed violence, and child gender. *Journal of Clinical Child and Adolescent Psychology, 39,* 667–680.

Justice, B., & Justice, R. (1979). *The broken taboo: Sex in the family.* New York, NY: Human Sciences.

Kaplan, S. J., Pelcovitz, D., & Labruna, V. (1999). Child and adolescent abuse and neglect research: A review of the past ten years, part I: Physical and emotional abuse and neglect. *Journal of the American Academy of Child and Adolescent Psychiatry, 38,* 1214–1222.

Kaufman, J., & Cicchetti, D. R. (1989). The effects of maltreatment on school-aged children's socioemotional development: Assessments in a day-camp setting. *Developmental Psychology, 25,* 516–524.

Kaufman, K. L., Hilliker, D. R., & Daleiden, E. (1988). Subgroup differences in the modus operandi of adolescent sexual offenders. *Child Maltreatment, 1,* 17–24.

Kaufman, K. L., Holmber, J. K., Orts, K. A., McCrady, F. E., Rotzien, A. L., & Daleiden, E. L. (1985). Victim–offender relatedness and age. *Child Maltreatment, 3*(4), 349–361.

Keiley, M. K., Howe, T. R., Dodge, K. A., Bates, J. E., & Pettit, G. S. (2001). The timing of child physical maltreatment: A cross-domain growth analysis of impact on adolescent externalizing problems. *Development and Psychopathology, 13,* 891–912.

Kendall-Tackett, K. A., Williams, L. M., & Finkelhor, D. (1993). Impact of sexual abuse on children: A review and synthesis of recent empirical studies. *Psychological Bulletin, 113,* 164–180.

Kinard, E. M. (2004). Methodological issues in assessing the effects of maltreatment characteristics on behavioral adjustment in maltreated children. *Journal of Family Violence, 19,* 303–318.

Kolko, D. (2002). Child physical abuse. In J. Briere, L. Berliner, J. Bulkley, C. Jenny, & T. Reid (Eds.), *The APSAC handbook on child maltreatment* (pp. 21–50). London, UK: Sage.

Kurtz, P. D., Gaudin, J. M., Howing, P. T., & Wodarski, J. S. (1993). The consequences of physical abuse and neglect on the school age child: Mediating factors. *Children and Youth Services Review, 15,* 85–104.

Lahey, B. B., Conger, R. D., Atkeson, B. M., & Treiber, F. A. (1984). Parenting behavior and emotional status of physically abusive mothers. *Journal of Consulting and Clinical Psychology, 52,* 1062–1071.

Lamb, M. E. (1994a). The investigation of child sexual abuse: An interdisciplinary consensus statement. *Child Abuse & Neglect, 18,* 1021–1028.

Lamb, M. E. (1994b). The investigation of child sexual abuse: An international, interdisciplinary consensus statement. *Family Law Quarterly, 28,* 151–162.

Lang, R. A., & Frenzel, R. R. (1988). How sex offenders lure children. *Annals of Sex Research, 1,* 303–317.

Lanktree, C. B., Biere, J., & Zaidi, L. Y. (1991). Incidence and impacts of sexual abuse in a child outpatient sample: The role of direct inquiry. *Child Abuse & Neglect, 15,* 447–453.

Lanning, K. V. (1992). Ritual abuse: A law enforcement view or perspective. *Child Abuse & Neglect, 15,* 171–173.

Larson, C. S., Terman, D. L., Gomby, D. S., Quinn, L. S., & Behrman, R. E. (1994). Sexual abuse of children: Recommendations and analysis. *Future of Children, 4*(2), 4–30.

Leclerc, B., Proulx, J., & Beauregard, E. (2009). Examining the modus operandi of sexual offenders against children and its practical implications. *Aggression and Violent Behavior, 14*, 5–12.

Ledbetter, D. J., Hatch, E., Feldman, K. W., Fligner, C. L., & Tapper, D. (1988). Diagnostic and surgical implications of child abuse. *Archives of Surgery, 123*, 1101–1105.

Lee, C., Barr, R. G., Catherine, N., & Wicks, A. (2007). Age-related incidence of publicly reported shaken baby syndrome cases: Is crying a trigger for shaking? *Journal of Developmental & Behavioral Pediatrics, 28*(4), 288–293.

Leeb, R., Paulozzi, L., Melanson, C., Simon, T., & Arias, I. (2008). *Child maltreatment surveillance: Uniform definitions for public health and recommended data elements, version 1.0.* Atlanta, GA: Centers for Disease Control and Prevention, National Center for Injury Prevention and Control.

Levine, M., & Battistoni, L. (1991). The corroboration requirement in child sex abuse cases. *Behavioral Sciences and the Law, 9*, 3–20.

Ligiero, D. P., Fassinger, R., McCauley, M., Moore, J., & Lyytinen, N. (2009). Childhood sexual abuse, culture, and coping: A qualitative study of Latinas. *Psychology of Women Quarterly, 33*(1), 67–80.

Ludwig, S., & Warman, M. (1984). Shaken baby syndrome: A review of 20 cases. *Annals of Emergency Medicine, 13*(2), 104–107.

Macfie, J., Cicchetti, D., & Toth, S. L. (2001). The development of dissociation in maltreated preschool-aged children. *Development and Psychopathology, 13*, 233–254.

Madonna, P. G., Van Scoyk, S., & Jones, D. P. H. (1991). Family interactions within incest and nonincest families. *American Journal of Psychiatry, 148*, 46–49.

Malinosky-Rummell, R., & Hansen, D. J. (1993). *Long term consequences of childhood physical abuse.* Paper 99. Faculty Publications, Department of Psychology. http://digitalcommons.unl.edu/psychfacpub/99

Mammen, O. K., Kolko, D. J., & Pilkonis, P. A. (2002). Negative affect and parental aggression in child physical abuse. *Child Abuse & Neglect, 26*, 407–424.

Maniglio, R. (2009). The impact of child sexual abuse on health: A systematic review of reviews. *Clinical Psychology Review, 29*(7), 647–657.

Mannarino, A. P., & Cohen, J. A. (1996). Abuse-related attributions and perceptions, general attributions, and locus of control in sexually abused girls. *Journal of Interpersonal Violence, 11*, 162–180.

Margolin, L., & Craft, J. L. (1990). Child abuse by adolescent caregivers. *Child Abuse & Neglect, 14*, 365–373.

Marsa, F., O'Reilly, G., Carr, A., Murphy, P., O'Sullivan, M., Cotter, A., & Heavy, D. (2004). Attachment styles and psychological profiles of child sex offenders in Ireland. *Journal of Interpersonal Violence, 19*, 1–24.

Marshall, W. L., & Barbaree, H. E. (1990). An integrated theory of the etiology of sexual offending. In W. L. Marshall, D. R. Laws, & H. E. Barbaree (Eds.), *Handbook of sexual assault: Issues, theories, and treatment of the offender* (pp. 257–275). New York, NY: Plenum Press.

Marshall, W. L., & Eccles, A. (1993). Pavlovian coordinating processes in adolescent sex offenders. In H. E. Barbaree, W. L. Marshall, & S. M. Hudson (Eds.), *The juvenile sex offender* (pp. 188–142). New York, NY: Guilford Press.

Marshall, W. L., & Laws, D. R. (2003). A brief history of behavioral and cognitive behavioral approaches to sexual offender treatment: Part 2. The modern era. *Sexual Abuse: A Journal of Research and Treatment, 15*, 93–120.

Marshall, W. L., & Marshall, L. E. (2000). The origins of sexual offending. *Trauma, Violence, & Abuse, 1,* 250–263.

McCloskey, K. A., & Raphael, D. N. (2005). Adult perpetrator gender asymmetries in child sexual assault victim selection: Results from the 2000 National Incident-Based Reporting System. *Journal of Child Sexual Abuse, 14,* 1–24.

McCloskey, L. A., & Bailey, J. A. (2000). The intergenerational transmission of risk for child sexual abuse. *Journal of Interpersonal Violence, 15,* 1019–1035.

Meiselman, K. C. (1978). *Incest: A psychological study of causes and effects with treatment recommendations.* San Francisco, CA: Jossey-Bass.

Merrill, L., Hervig, L., & Milner, J. (1996). Childhood parenting experiences, intimate partner conflict resolution, and adult risk for child physical abuse. *Child Abuse and Neglect, 20,* 1049–1065.

Miller-Perrin, C. L., & Perrin, R. D. (2007). *Child maltreatment: An introduction* (2nd ed.). Thousand Oaks, CA: Sage.

Milner, J. S. (1998). Individuals and family characteristics associated with intrafamilial child physical and sexual abuse. In P. K. Trickett & C. J. Schellenbach (Eds.), *Violence against children in the family and the community* (pp. 141–170). Washington DC: American Psychological Association.

Milner, J. S. (2000). Social information processing and child physical abuse: Theory and research. In D. J. Hansen (Ed.), *Nebraska symposium on motivation 46, 1998: Motivation and child maltreatment* (pp. 39–84). Lincoln, NE: University of Nebraska.

Milner, J. S. (2003). Social information processing in high-risk and physically abusive parents. *Child Abuse & Neglect, 7,* 7–20.

Milner, J. S., & Chilamkurti, C. (1991). Physical child abuse perpetrator characteristics: A review of the literature. *Journal of Interpersonal Violence, 6,* 345–366.

Mitchell, J., & Morse, J. (1998). *From victims to survivors: Reclaimed voices of women sexually abused in childhood by females.* Washington, DC: Accelerated Development.

Myers, J. E. B. (1992). Competencies credentialing and standards for gerontological counselors: Implications for counselor education. *Counselor Education and Supervision, 32,* 34–42.

Myers, J. E. B. (1998). *Legal issues in child abuse and neglect practice* (2nd ed.). Thousand Oaks, CA: Sage.

Nadon, S. M., Koverola, C., & Schludermann, E. H. (1998). Antecedents to prostitution: Childhood victimization. *Journal of Interpersonal Violence, 13,* 206–221.

National Center of Child Abuse and Neglect (NCCAN). (1978). *Child sexual abuse: Incest, assault, and sexual exploitation.* Washington, DC: U.S. Department of Health and Human Services.

National Center for Juvenile Justice. (1999). *Juveniles offenders and victims: 1999 national report.* Washington, DC: Office of Juvenile and Delinquency Prevention.

National MCH Center for Child Death Review. (2011). Child abuse and neglect fact sheet. http://www.childdeathreview.org/causesCAN.htm

Nayak, M. B., & Milner, J. S. (1998). Neuropsychological functioning: Comparison of mothers at high- and low-risk for child abuse. *Child Abuse & Neglect, 22,* 687–703.

Newberger, E. H. (1993). Child physical abuse. *Primary Care, 20,* 317–327.

Newcomb, M. D., Munoz, D. T., & Carmona, J. V. (2009). Child sexual abuse consequences in community samples of Latino and European American adolescents. *Child Abuse & Neglect, 33,* 533–544.

Noll, J. G., Shenk, C. E., & Putnam, K. T. (2009). Childhood sexual abuse and adolescent pregnancy: A meta-analytic update. *Journal of Pediatric Psychology, 34,* 366–378.

Paolucci, E. O., Genuis, M. L., & Violato, C. (2001). A meta-analysis of the published research on the effects of child sexual abuse. *Journal of Psychology, 135*, 17–36.

Peterson, L., & Gable, S. (1998). Holistic injury prevention. In J. R. Lutzker (Ed.), *Child abuse: A handbook of theory, research, and treatment* (pp. 291–318). New York, NY: Plenum Press.

Putnam, F. W. (2003). Ten year research update review: Child sexual abuse. *Journal of the American Academy of Child & Adolescent Psychiatry, 42*, 269–278.

Quinsey, V. L. (1980). The base rate problem and the prediction of dangerousness: A reappraisal. *Journal of Psychiatry and Law, 8*, 329–340.

Reece, R. M. (2011). Medical evaluation of physical abuse. In J. E. B. Myers (Ed.), *The APSAC handbook on child maltreatment* (3rd ed., pp. 183–194). Thousand Oaks, CA: Sage.

Reece, R. M., & Christian, C. W. (2009). *Child abuse: Medical diagnosis and management* (3rd ed.). Elk Grove Village, IL: American Academy of Pediatrics.

Rogosch, F., Cicchetti, D., & Abre, J. L. (1995). The role of child maltreatment in early deviations in cognitive and affective processing abilities and later peer relationships problems. *Development and Psychopathology, 7*, 591–609.

Romano, E., & De Luca, R. V. (2001). Male sexual abuse: A review of effects, abuse characteristics, and links with later psychological functioning. *Aggression and Violent Behavior, 6*, 55–78.

Rorke-Adams, L., Duhaime, A. C., Jenny, C., & Smith, W. L. (2009). Head trauma. In R. M. Reece & C. W. Christian (Eds.), *Child abuse: Medical diagnosis and management* (3rd ed., pp. 53–119). Elk Grove Village, IL: American Academy of Pediatrics.

Rosenbaum, A., & O'Leary, D. K. (1981). Children: The unintended victims of marital violence. *American Journal of Orthopsychiatry, 51*, 692–699.

Rudin, M. M., Zalewski, C., & Bodmer-Turner, J. (1995). Characteristics of child sexual abuse victims according to perpetrator gender. *Child Abuse & Neglect, 19*, 963–973.

Ruggiero, K. J., Mcleer, S. V., & Dixon, J. F. (2000). Sexual abuse characteristics associated with survivor psychopathology. *Child Abuse & Neglect, 24*, 951–964.

Rush, F. (1980). *The best kept secret: Sexual abuse of children*. Englewood Cliffs, NJ: Prentice Hall.

Russell, D. E. H. (1993). The incidence and prevalence of intrafamilial and extrafamilial sexual abuse of female children. *Child Abuse & Neglect, 7*, 133–146.

Ryan, G., & Lane, S. (1991). *Juvenile sexual offending*. Lexington, MA: Lexington Books.

Salzinger, S., Feldman, R. S., Hammer, M., & Rosario, M. (1993). The effects of physical abuse on children's relationships. *Child Development, 64*, 169–187.

Saradjian, J. (1996). *Women who sexually abuse children: From research to clinical practice*. Chichester, UK: Wiley.

Saunders, B. E., Berliner, L., & Hanson, R. F. (Eds.). (2004). *Child physical and sexual abuse: Guidelines for treatment* (Revised Report: April 26, 2004). Charleston, SC: National Crime Victims Research and Treatment Center.

Saunders, B. E., Kilpatrick, D. G., Hanson, R. F., Resnick, H. S., & Walker, M. E. (1999). Prevalence, case characteristics, and long-term psychological correlates of child rape among women: A national survey. *Child Maltreatment, 4*, 187–200.

Sedlak, A., & Broadhurst, D. (1996). *Third national incidence study of child abuse and neglect: Final report*. Washington, DC: U.S. Government Printing Office.

Segal, Z. V., & Stermac, L. E. (1990). The role of cognition in sexual assault. In W. L. Marshall, D. R. Laws, & H. E. Barbaree (Eds.), *Handbook of sexual assault: Issues, theories, and treatment of the offender* (pp. 161–174). New York, NY: Plenum Press.

Showers, J., & Garrison, K. M. (1988). Burn abuse: A four-year study. *Journal of Trauma, 28*, 1581–1583.

Silbert, M., & Pines, A. M. (1983). Early sexual exploitation as an influence in prostitution. *Social Work, 28*, 285–289.

Skarbek, D., Hahn, K., & Parrish, P. (2009). Stop sexual abuse in special education: An ecological model of prevention and intervention strategies for sexual abuse in special education. *Sex Disability, 27*, 155–164.

Smallbone, S. W., & Wortley, R. K. (2001). *Child sexual abuse: Offender characteristics and modus operandi.* In: Australian Institute of Criminology, *Trends and Issues in Crime and Criminal Justice, No. 193.*

Smith, D. W., Letourneau, E. J., Saunders, B. E., Kilpatrick, D. G., Resnick, H. S., & Best, C. L. (2000). Delay in disclosure of childhood rape: Results from a national survey. *Child Abuse and Neglect, 24*, 273–287.

Smith, H., & Israel, E. (1987). Sibling incest: A study of the dynamics of 25 cases. *Child Abuse & Neglect, 11*, 101–108.

Smith, M., & Segal, J. (2013). Child abuse and neglect. Accessed from: http://helpguide.org/mental /child_abuse_physical_emotional_sexual_neglect.htm#recognizing

Smolak, L., & Murnen, S. K. (2002). A meta-analytic examination of the relationship between child sexual abuse and eating disorders. *International Journal of Eating Disorders, 31*, 136–150.

Snyder, C. R. (2000). *Handbook of hope: Theory, measures, and applications.* New York, NY: Academic Press.

Starling, S. P., Holden, J. R., & Jenny, C. (1995). Abusive head trauma: The relationship of perpetrators to their victims. *Pediatrics, 95*(2), 259–262.

Stein, J. A., Golding, J. M., Siegel, J. M., Burnam, M. A., & Sorenson, S. B. (1988). Long-term psychological sequelae of child sexual abuse: The Los Angeles epidemiologic catchment area study. In G. E. Wyatt & G. J. Powell (Eds.), *Lasting effects of child sexual abuse. Sage Focus Editions,* Vol. 100 (pp. 135–154). Newbury Park, CA: Sage.

Strand, V. C. (2000). *Treating secondary victims: Intervention with the nonoffending mother in the incest family.* Thousand Oaks, CA: Sage.

Straus, M. A., Gelles, R. J., & Steinmetz, S. (1980). *Behind closed doors: Violence in the American family.* New York, NY: Doubleday.

Straus, M. A., Hamby, S. L., Finkelhor, D., Moore, D. W., & Runyan, D. (1998). Identification of child maltreatment with the Parent–Child Conflict Tactics Scales: Development and psychometric data for a national sample of American parents. *Child Abuse & Neglect, 22*, 249–270.

Straus, M. A., & Stewart, J. H. (1999). Corporal punishment by American parents: National data on prevalence, chronicity, severity, and duration, in relation to child and family characteristics. *Clinical Child and Family Psychology Review, 2*, 55–70.

Sullivan, P. M., & Knutson, J. F. (1998). The association between child maltreatment and disabilities in a hospital-based epidemiological study. *Child Abuse & Neglect, 22*, 271–288.

Sullivan, P. M., & Knutson, J. F. (2000). Maltreatment and disabilities: A population-based epidemiological study. *Child Abuse & Neglect, 24*, 1257–1273.

Swenson, C. C., & Chaffin, M. (2006). Beyond psychotherapy: Treating abused children by changing their social ecology. *Aggression and Violent Behavior, 11*, 120–137.

Thakker, J., Ward, T., & Navathe, S. (2007). The cognitive distortions and implicit theories of child sexual abusers. In T. A. Gannon, T. Ward, A. R. Beech, & D. Fisher (Eds.), *Aggressive offenders' cognition: Theory, research, and practice* (pp. 11–29). London, UK: John Wiley & Sons.

Tharinger, D. J., Horton, C., & Millea, S. (1990). Sexual abuse and exploitation of children and adults with mental retardation and other handicaps. *Child Abuse and Neglect: The International Journal, 14*, 301–312.

Tjaden, P., & Thoennes, N. (2000). *Full report of the prevalence, incidence, and consequences of violence against women* (Rep. No. NCJ 183781). Rockville, MD: Office of Justice Programs, National Institute of Justice.

Tjaden, P., & Thoennes, N. (2002). The role of stalking in domestic violence crime reports generated by the Colorado Springs Police Department. In K. E. Davis, I. H. Frieze, & R. D. Maiuro (Eds.), *Stalking: Perspectives on victims and perpetrators* (pp. 330–352). New York, NY: Springer.

Trocme, N., & Wolfe, D. (2001). *Child maltreatment in Canada: Canadian incidence study of reported child abuse and neglect: Selected results.* Ottawa, Canada: National Clearinghouse on Family Violence, Health Canada.

Turner, H. A., Finkelhor, D., & Ormrod, R. K. (2006). The effect of lifetime victimization on the mental health of children and adolescents. *Social Science & Medicine, 62,* 13–27.

United Nations Committee on the Rights of the Child (UNCRC). (2006). *General comment on the right of the child to protection from corporal punishment and other cruel or degrading forms of punishment,* CRC/C/GC/8, 2 June 2006. http://www.ohchr.org/english/bodies/crc/docs/co/CRC.C.GC.8.pdf

U.S. Department of Health and Human Services, Administration on Children, Youth and Families. (1988). *Study findings: Study of national incidence and prevalence of child abuse and neglect (DHHS Publication No. ADM 20-01099).* Washington, DC: Government Printing Office.

U.S. Department of Health and Human Services, Administration on Children, Youth, and Families. (1993). A report on the maltreatment of children with disabilities (DHHS Contract No. 105-89-1630). Washington, DC: Government Printing Office.

U.S. Department of Health and Human Services, Administration on Children, Youth, and Families. (1998). *Child maltreatment 1996: Reports from the states to the National Child Abuse and Neglect Data System.* Washington, DC: Government Printing Office.

U.S. Department of Health and Human Services, Administration on Children, Youth, and Family. (2001). *Youth violence: A report of the Surgeon General.* Rockville, MD: Office of the Surgeon General.

U.S. Department of Health and Human Services, Administration on Children, Youth, and Family. (2005). *Child maltreatment 2003.* Washington, DC: Government Printing Office.

U.S. Department of Health and Human Services, Administration on Children, Youth, and Family. (2010). *Child maltreatment 2008.* Washington, DC: Government Printing Office.

U.S. Department of Justice. (2009). *Crime in the United States, 2008.* Federal Bureau of Investigation. http://www.fbi.gov/ucr/cius2008/documents/aboutcius.pdf

Vandiver, D. M. (2006). Female sexual offenders: A comparison of solo offenders and co-offenders. *Violence and Victims, 21,* 339–354.

Van Roode, T., Dickson, N., Herbison, P., & Paul, C. (2009). Child sexual abuse and persistence of risk sexual behaviors and negative sexual outcomes over adulthood: Findings from a birth cohort. *Child Abuse & Neglect, 33,* 161–172.

Veneziano, C., Veneziano, L., & LeGrand, S. (2000). The relationship between adolescent sex offender behavior and victim characteristics with prior victimization. *Journal of Interpersonal Violence, 15,* 363–374.

Virginia Department of Social Services. (2003). Internet crime against children. *Virginia Child Protection Newsletter, 68,* 2–17.

Wakefield, H., & Underwager, R. (1991). Female child sexual abusers: A critical review of the literature. *American Journal of Forensic Psychology, 9,* 43–69.

Walker, E. C., Holman, T. B., & Busby, D. M. (2009). Childhood sexual abuse, other childhood factors, and pathways to survivors' adult relationship quality. *Journal of Family Violence, 24,* 397–406.

Ward, T. (2000). Sexual offenders' cognitive distortions as implicit theories. *Aggression and Violent Behavior, 5,* 491–507.

Ward, T., & Beech, A. (2006). An integrated theory of sexual offending. *Aggression and Violent Behavior, 11,* 44–63.

Ward, T., & Siegert, R. (2002). Toward a comprehensive theory of child sexual abuse: A theory knitting perspective. *Psychology, Crime, and Law, 8,* 319–351.

Weinrott, M. (1996). *Juvenile sexual aggression: A critical review.* Boulder, CO: University of Colorado, Institute for Behavioral Sciences, Center for the Study and Prevention of Violence.

Whittaker, M. K., Brown, J., Beckett, R., & Gerhold, C. (2006). Sexual knowledge and empathy: A comparison of adolescent child molesters and non-offending adolescents. *Journal of Sexual Aggression, 12,* 143–154.

Widom, C. S. (1989). Does violence beget violence? A critical examination of the literature. *Psychological Bulletin, 106,* 3–28.

Widom, C. S. (1999). Posttraumatic stress disorder in abused and neglected children grown up. *American Journal of Psychiatry, 156,* 1223–1229.

Widom, C. S., & Kuhns, J. B. (1996). Childhood victimization and subsequent risk for promiscuity, prostitution, and teenage pregnancy: A prospective study. *American Journal of Public Health, 86,* 1607–1612.

Widom, C. S., & Morris, S. (1997). Accuracy of adult recollections of childhood victimization: Part II. Childhood sexual abuse. *Psychological Assessment, 9,* 34–46.

Wijkman, M., Bijleveld, C., & Hendriks, J. (2010). Women don't do such things! Characteristics of female sex offenders and offender types. *Sexual Abuse, 22,* 135–156.

Williams, L. M. (1994). Recall of childhood trauma: A prospective study of women's memories. *Journal of Consulting and Clinical Psychology, 62,* 1167–1176.

Williams, M. B. (1993). Assessing the traumatic impact of child sexual abuse: What makes it more severe? *Journal of Child Sexual Abuse, 2,* 41–59.

Wind, T. W., & Silvern, L. (1994). Parenting and family stress as mediators of the long-term effects of child abuse. *Child Abuse & Neglect, 18,* 439–453.

Wolak, J., Ybarra, M., Mitchell, K., & Finkelhor, D. (2007). Does online harassment constitute bullying? An exploration of online harassment by known peers and online-only contacts. *Special Issue of the Journal of Adolescent Health, 41,* S51–S58.

Wolfe, D. A. (1999). *Child abuse: Implications for children development and psychopathology* (2nd ed.). Thousand Oaks, CA: Sage.

Wolfner, G. D., & Gelles, R. J. (1993). A profile of violence toward children: A national study. *Child Abuse & Neglect, 17*(2), 197–212.

Wurtele, S. K., & Miller-Perrin, C. L. (1992). *Preventing child sexual abuse: Sharing the responsibility.* Lincoln, NE: University of Nebraska Press.

Wyatt, G. E., Newcomb, M., Reederle, M., & Notgrass, C. (1993). *The effects of child sexual abuse on women's sexual and psychological functioning.* Newbury Park, CA: Sage.

Chapter 5

Signs, Symptoms, and Consequences of Psychological Abuse and Neglect

In this chapter, we discuss estimated incidence rates and describe behavioral signs, physical symptoms, and consequences of psychologically abusive and neglectful situations on social, emotional, and cognitive development in infants, children, and adolescents.

Child Psychological Abuse

Child psychological and emotional abuse (heretofore labeled psychological abuse for simplicity) is often overlooked or marginalized, yet is considered by abuse experts to be the most destructive and pervasive form of maltreatment (Behl, Conyngham, & May, 2003; Hart, Brassard, Davidson, Rivelis, Diaz, & Binggeli, 2011; Hibbard, Barlow, & McMillan, 2012; Miller-Perrin & Perrin, 2007). The reasoning underlying this conclusion is twofold.

First, society failed for many years to conceptualize this type of maltreatment as a social problem (Hart, Brassard, Binggeli, & Davidson, 2002; Kantor & Little, 2003) and subsequently floundered in its struggle to define this kind of abuse (Cicchetti & Nurcombe, 1991). The difficulty stemmed from hesitation on the part of the general public to identify particular behaviors exhibited by parents as psychological maltreatment rather than as suboptimal parenting or even as judgment errors (Miller-Perrin & Perrin, 2007; Trickett, Mennen, Kim, & Sang, 2009). According to Straus and Field (2003), "tolerating a certain level of psychological aggression by parents is part of the cultural norms of American society," such that this behavior is ignored "unless it passes a certain threshold of chronicity and severity" (p. 796). Further evidence of societal misunderstanding of psychological maltreatment is the paucity of state legal statutes specifying psychological maltreatment of children as a criminal (rather than civil) violation (Weaver, 2011). That is, many states bring charges of psychological abuse against parents only in family court proceedings that were begun by child protective services (CPS) workers to investigate other accusations.

Second, detection of psychological abuse is rare or nonexistent. Unlike other forms of abuse, such maltreatment does not have immediate or obvious behavioral signs and physical symptoms that could be documented as evidence. Consequently, the harmful effects of psychological abuse may continue over extended periods of time, culminating in significant damage to children's long-term mental health by slowly eroding their self-worth and self-esteem and contributing to educational failure and criminal behavior (Glaser, Prior, & Lynch, 2001; Greenfield & Marks, 2010).

The severity of consequences associated with psychological abuse is often equal to or greater than that of the other forms of maltreatment (Hart et al., 2011). Psychological abuse is complicated. Although it can occur alone, it often coexists with other forms of maltreatment, which magnifies the negative effects (Finkelhor, 2008; Finkelhor, Ormrod, & Turner, 2007; Glaser, 2002; Schneider, Ross, Graham, & Zielinski, 2005). Professionals who deal with maltreated children (e.g., CPS workers, therapists) purport that, conceptually, children are subjected to psychological abuse when they directly suffer from any form of physical abuse, sexual abuse, or neglect or when they are exposed to domestic abuse (Brassard, Germain, & Hart, 1987, as cited in Pecora, Whittaker, Maluccio, & Barth, 2000). That is, regardless of whether the perpetrator's behavior is physical (e.g., beating, sexually penetrating) or nonphysical (e.g., degrading, ignoring), the violation of the emotionally vulnerable child's trust has psychological consequences (Hart & Brassard, 1991). Unfortunately, even when psychological abuse occurs independently, it is the most difficult form of abuse to identify and prosecute because it lacks "substantial and observable" physical evidence and it takes a long time for psychological harm to become evident (Miller-Perrin & Perrin, 2007). Consequently, CPS, police, and prosecutors rely on standards for emotional neglect to justify emergency removal in family court and to charge the perpetrator in criminal court, but both procedures are most likely to succeed in protecting the child when other forms of maltreatment are also present (Hamarman, Pope, & Czaja, 2002; Hart et al., 2002).

Controversy over psychological abuse rests on disagreement about how to identify it because of the ramifications in terms of its use in legal decisions, inclusion in official incidence estimates, and CPS-initiated interventions for children. Yet, the absence of a uniform or operational definition for psychological abuse has impeded progress in the understanding of its short-term and long-term consequences and in prosecuting offenders. One challenge in regard to this task has been to generate a definition that is not so broad as to nominate everyone as a victim, thereby failing to provide clear guidelines for this unique form of maltreatment. Another problem is that professionals have been torn between focusing on child outcomes versus on parental behaviors. By focusing on the child, the definition must demonstrate mental and psychological consequences for the child's developmental functioning as evidence of harm, which may not occur for a long time (Glaser, 2002). Some researchers have attempted to develop a unique definition for psychological abuse, while clarifying the parenting behaviors that result in negative psychological outcomes for children (e.g., Garbarino & Garbarino, 1994; McGee & Wolfe, 1991). They indicate that psychological abuse occurs when parents' physical (e.g., burning the child with a cigarette) or nonphysical (e.g., withholding affection, lack of supervision, swearing at the child) behaviors yield negative physical (e.g., poisoned, malnourished) and nonphysical (e.g., anxiety, fear, cognitive deficits, low self-esteem) results. The majority of professionals and researchers (Baily & Baily, 2986; Garbarino & Garbarino, 1994; Hamarman & Bermet, 2000; Hart & Brassard, 1991, 2001) have concluded that the focus should be on parental behaviors (and their associated frequency, intensity, and duration), with consideration of the effects on the child victim given secondary consideration.

The first concrete step toward achieving this goal of formulating a definition was to hold an international conference and ask professionals to help. This effort yielded the following definition:

> Psychological maltreatment of children and youth consists of acts of omission and commission, which are judged on the basis of a combination of community standards and professional expertise to be psychologically damaging. Such acts are committed by individuals, singly or collectively, who by their characteristics (e.g., age, status, knowledge, and organizational form) are in a position of differential power that renders a child vulnerable. Such acts damage immediately or ultimately the behavioral, cognitive, affective, or physical functioning of the child. Examples of psychological maltreatment include acts of rejecting, terrorizing, isolating, exploiting, and missocializing.[1]

The next step was for the American Professional Society on the Abuse of Children (APSAC) to create guidelines to define and delineate subtypes of psychological abuse. This organization adopted the following general definition: "Psychological maltreatment means a repeated pattern of caregiver behavior or extreme incident(s) that convey to children that they are worthless, flawed, unloved, unwanted, endangered, or only of value in meeting another's needs" (1995, p. 2).

Table 5-1 displays an organizational framework that identifies nine subtypes of psychological maltreatment specifically aimed at devaluing the child as a means of preventing healthy development of self-esteem and social competence. While these descriptions serve as a general guide, the behaviors must occur in a harsh and repeated fashion prompted by the parents' negative intentions (e.g., isolating a child from friends and family to limit emotional ties with others rather than protecting a child from negative influences of delinquent peers) to warrant such classification.

---

[1] Brassard, M., German, R., & Hart, S. N. (1987). Psychological maltreatment of children and youth. *American Psychologist*, 42(2), 160-165.

Table 5-1 Subtypes of child psychological maltreatment

Subtype	Description
Spurning	Hostile acts (verbal, nonverbal) that relate rejection of the child, often making the child into a scapegoat (e.g., criticizing or punishing; rejecting the child's ideas, wants, and desires)
Degrading	Actions that relate deprecation of that child, even for normative emotional responses (e.g., name-calling, insulting, humiliating, belittling, shaming)
Terrorizing	Threats or actions used to invoke extreme fear and/or anxiety in a child and make the world seem intimidating and unpredictable (e.g., causing loss, harm, or danger to the child or to the child's favorite objects; placing them in dangerous, unpredictable, or chaotic situations)
Isolating	Denying the child the opportunity to have normal social interactions with adults or children, whether in person at home, in school, or other places, by phone, or Internet (e.g., the child cannot use phone, join a sports team, have play dates, or participate in afterschool activities; locking the child in a room; not allowing relatives to interact with the child)
Corrupting	Concerted effort made to missocialize child by allowing, stimulating, and reinforcing deviant behavior (e.g., allowing or not preventing delinquent behaviors, teaching racist values, encouraging use of drugs or alcohol)[1]
Exploiting	Taking advantage of the child to satisfy the caregivers' own needs or to profit through the child (e.g., child prostitution and pornography; being a companion to the caregiver; fulfilling the caregiver's dreams of fame and fortune; satisfying the emotional needs of the caregiver; forcing the child to act as a parent to siblings or to act infantile and needy)
Ignoring	Ignoring, limiting, or depriving the child of stimulation, emotional responses, and interactions to suppress emotional and intellectual growth (e.g., uninvolved and detached; does not express positive emotions or affection toward the child; ignores requests for help or affection)
Binding	Preventing the child from moving arms or legs (e.g., ties the child to an immovable object; ties the child's arms and legs together; keeps the child strapped into a stroller)
Other	Forms of psychological maltreatment other than those previously described (e.g., punishes child by withholding basic needs of food, shelter, sleep, and clothing; overpressuring the child to perform tasks beyond the child's developmental abilities; exposing the child to violence against an intimate partner or child sibling)

[1] Corrupting may also be considered moral turpitude, as encouraging children to commit illegal or criminal acts is likely to result in adjudication.

Data from Hart, S., Brassard, M., Davidson, H., Rivelis, E., Diaz, V., & Binggeli, N. (2011). Psychological maltreatment, In J. Myers (Ed.). *The APSAC handbook on child maltreatment* (pp. 125-144). Los Angeles, CA: Sage; Miller-Perrin, C. L., & Perrin, R. D. (2007). *Child maltreatment: An introduction* (2nd ed.). Thousand Oaks, CA: Sage; and Mitchell, G. (2009). Toxic parenting: how parents and other carers can harm children without laying a hand on them. In T. J. David (Ed.), *Recent Advances in Paediatrics*, 25, 43-64.

Official Estimates of Incidence

Official reports of child maltreatment from 1986 to 2004 estimated the incidence of child psychological abuse, as a distinct form of maltreatment, to be between 5% and 8% (U.S. Department of Health and Human Services [DHHS], 1998, 2005, 2007), although actual rates are unknown due to complications with definitions. Recent reports by the National Child Abuse and Neglect Data System (NCANDS; U.S. DHHS, 2010) similarly found incidence rates of 7.6% for psychological abuse in fiscal year 2009.

Each state has a different legal definition of psychological abuse, with some states requiring proof of mental injury, often using specific and narrow definitions, and other states requiring that injuries be substantial and observable, which may take years to occur (Weaver, 2011). These variations contribute to inconsistencies in identification and reporting of such abuse across the United States and consequently prevent CPS from intervening in an effort to protect and aid children (Weaver, 2011). The National Incidence Studies (NIS-4; Sedlak et al., 2010), therefore, calculated psychological abuse rates using two criteria: (1) the stringent "harm" standard (i.e., a victim was included if the child had already experienced demonstrable harm due to maltreatment, with injuries lasting at least 48 hours) and (2) the lenient "endangerment" standard (i.e., a victim was included if the child was not yet harmed by experiences of maltreatment, but was in danger of being harmed). Harm standard estimated rates were 27.5% in 1993 (204,500 out of 743,200 abused children) and of 26.8% in 2005–2006 (148,500 out of 532,200 abused children), whereas endangerment standard estimated rates were 43.6% in 1993 (532,200 out of 1,221,800 abused children) and 36.2% in 2005–2006 (302,600 out of 835,000 abused children).

In an effort to go beyond official reporting methods, researchers using self-report surveys completed by parents found high incidence rates of 45% to 63% for verbal (e.g., yelling, insulting, swearing) and nonverbal (e.g., unavailability, unresponsiveness, neglect) psychological abuse used in the past year when these parents interacted with their children, averaging 12.6 instances over the year (Straus, Hamby, Finkelhor, Moore, & Runyan, 1998; Vissing, Straus, Gelles, & Harrop, 1991). Psychological abuse by caregivers was also among the most frequently self-reported forms of maltreatment indicated by children; 29% to 41% of children reported being a victim of such abuse (Glaser, Kolvin, Campbell, Glasser, Leitch, & Farrelly, 2001; Reyome, 2010). An examination of psychological maltreatment in childhood as recalled by adults revealed that only a small proportion of them (4% of men and 8% to 9% of women) reported this type of abuse had been severe in their childhood, as exemplified by inadequate affection and multiple incidents degrading their overall emotional well-being (Cawson, Wattam, Brooker, & Kelly, 2000; Gilbert, Widom, Browne, Fergusson, Webb, & Janson, 2009).

Causes of Psychological Abuse

Psychological abuse by caregivers may occur for a variety of reasons. Some abusing caregivers were themselves victims of psychological abuse as children, which subsequently influenced their own parenting strategies (Hemenway, Solnick, & Carter, 1994). In particular, these individuals may fail to develop empathy and, therefore, be unable to recognize how their negative discipline techniques and abusive interactions affect their own children's socioemotional well-being. Moreover, these parents may form unrealistic expectations for their children's behaviors and abilities, which, when combined with deficient child management techniques, such as coercive parenting, results in the parents' psychologically abusive reactions (e.g., isolation, emotional withdrawal) when children consistently fail to attain these ideals (Hart, Germain, & Brassard, 1987; Saunders, Berliner, & Hanson, 2004). Stress may also cause abusive caregivers to maltreat their children psychologically as life stressors (e.g., problems related to jobs, finances, marriage) reduce their ability to cope with the constant needs, wanton desires, and common misbehavior of children. Parents who have difficulties in interpersonal and social interactions may lash out at their children to cover their low self-esteem and feelings of inadequacy (Hickox & Furnell, 1989).

Some abusive caregivers have substance abuse or mental health problems. Caregivers who have drug or alcohol addiction are often unavailable to their children, which in turn increases their propensity to respond inappropriately to their children or to misjudge their children's intended actions, or lowers their own tolerance for dealing with children altogether. Besides physical health problems, abusing caregivers may have undiagnosed mental illnesses, such as a personality disorders (especially narcissistic personality) or manic-depressive disorders, resulting in reduced emotional responses and nurturing and increased verbal rebukes of children (Field, Healy, Goldstein, & Gutherz, 1990; Radke-Yarrow & Klimes-Dougan, 2002). Often, psychologically abusive caregivers experience multiple stresses simultaneously (i.e., mental health problems, physical health problems, substance abuse, marital conflict and domestic abuse), but have few resources to relieve or aid in coping with life; in this scenario, their children will be especially vulnerable to being psychologically abused (Stromwall et al., 2008).

Characteristics of Psychological Abuse

The perpetrator of psychological abuse is empowered by dominating and controlling the child victim. The main strategy employed by these abusers is "gaslighting," a term derived from the 1944 film, *Gaslight*. In this film, a woman is duped by her husband through trickery into believing that she is going crazy. Similarly, parents who engage in psychological abuse use a gaslighting strategy to intimidate their child victims gradually into doubting their own perceptions, memories, and understanding of experiences by discounting, denying, and discrediting their versions. These abusers employ "brainwashing" techniques to monopolize the child victims' perceptions or ideas by accusing them of imagining or distorting the events and requiring that they replace those experiences with the abusers' plausible, but untrue accounts (Loring, 1997). Another component of the gaslighting strategy is for abusers to mix warm and kind interactions with the unrelenting psychological abuse (e.g., trivializing, undermining, judging, diverting) as a way of maintaining bonds with their child victims while making them feel powerless, ashamed, anxious, confused, and doubtful of their ability to know what they experienced (Loring, 1997; Marshall, 1996; Mezey, Post, & Maxwell, 2002). Consequently, when child victims discuss their abusive experiences, they seem unsure of the facts. This hesitancy may make them unreliable witnesses in the minds of CPS and criminal justice professionals, who may then accept the abusers' reality, making it even more difficult than before for children to fight their abusers. Perpetrators successfully present their version of "reality" to their child victims, CPS workers, criminal justice professionals, therapists, and anyone else who interacts with them and the children.

Demographics of Victim and Perpetrator

Victim

Research has failed to provide specific sociodemographic characteristics of the child who is likely to become a victim of psychological abuse (Black, Slep, & Heyman, 2001). As reported in the National Incidence Study (Sedlak et al., 2010), incidence rates of psychological abuse in 2005–2006 were higher among children older than age 6 years (4.1 per 1000 children) than among children aged 0–2 years (1.6 per 1000 children), and for African American children (4.5 per 1000 children) compared to their Caucasian (3.5 per 1000 children) and Latino (2.4 per 1000 children) peers. Findings regarding the sex of the child victim have been inconsistent—sometimes indicating that the risk is greater for girls than for boys (e.g., Tang, 1996; U.S. DHHS, 1998), and at other times reporting that it is greater for boys than for girls (Solomon & Serres, 1999; Vissing et al., 1991) or that it is equal for both sexes (e.g., Sedlak, 1997).

Psychological abuse rates for 2005–2006 also differed in accordance with several family characteristics, including the number of children, socioeconomic status, and marital status of the abusive parent, but were consistent with previous findings reported in the NIS-2 and NIS-3 (Sedlak et al., 2010). Specifically, higher rates were found in larger families than in families consisting of only children (5.8 versus 2.8 per 1000), and in families with lower socioeconomic status (SES; i.e., income less than $15,000) than in families with higher SES (2.6 versus 0.5 per 1000). Rates were also higher when children lived with a single parent (especially if cohabiting with partner) or other married parents than with two married biological parents. Additionally, risk for psychological abuse is high when children are unwanted, have disabilities, or are socially isolated (Hart & Brassard, 1987).

Perpetrator

According to the NIS-4 (Sedlak et al., 2010), biological parents (73%) are more likely than nonbiological parents and partners (20%) or another person (7%) to inflict psychological abuse on children. Additionally, the largest percentage of perpetrators tend to be older than age 35 years (47% biological parents, 62% nonbiological parents), with a smaller percentage being between ages 26 and 35 years (39% biological parents, 31% nonbiological parents) rather than younger than age 26 years (5% biological parents, 36% others). Although research findings are mixed, female caregivers are identified more often than male caregivers as being psychologically abusive toward children

(57% versus 43%; U.S. DHHS, 1998). Many caregivers who psychologically abuse children use an authoritarian or overly coercive parenting style, reflecting low emotional responsiveness to children's needs while demanding complete and immediate obedience to their authority (Baumrind, 1991).[2]

Signs, Symptoms, and Developmental Consequences of Psychologically Abused Children

Behavioral signs and physical symptoms of psychological abuse are often undetectable and indistinguishable from those due to other causes, at least initially.

Behavioral Signs

According to Miller-Perrin and Perrin (2007), child victims of psychological abuse exhibit general and specific behavioral problems, such as "aggression, conduct problems, attention difficulties, disruptive classroom behavior, self-abusive behavior, hostility and anger, and anxiety" (p. 221). Behavioral patterns range from one end of the continuum—that is, extremely compliant, passive, and submissive—to the other end—that is, extremely demanding, impulsive, antagonistic, and aggressive (Tomison & Tucci, 1997; Vissing et al., 1991). Infants may show nonspecific behaviors, such as crying, restlessness, poor sleep patterns, and feeding difficulties. Children may act inappropriately, by exhibiting overly dependent or regressive, infantile (e.g., clingy, thumb-sucking, tantrums, soiling, bedwetting or incontinence), autistic (e.g., head banging, rocking), or caregiving behaviors (i.e., parentification, meaning acting as a parent) to younger children and adults (Boulton & Hindle, 2000; Byng-Hall, 2002; Child Welfare Information Gateway, 2007). Long-term effects in adolescents and adults include juvenile delinquency; relational violence; aggressive, oppositional, and destructive behaviors (e.g., setting fires, animal cruelty); sexual dysfunction; drug and alcohol abuse; suicidal and self-abusive behaviors; and unstable job histories (Kotch et al., 2008; Wekerle et al., 2009).

Physical Developmental Consequences/Symptoms

Physical symptoms of psychological abuse include physical health, growth, and neurobiological problems, including failure to thrive (i.e., underweight, stunted development) and infant mortality, chronic respiratory illnesses (e.g., allergies, asthma), and delayed physical development in infancy and childhood. Long-term symptoms consist of hypertension, somatic complaints, health problems, and high mortality in adulthood (Hart, Binggeli, & Brassard, 1998; Hart et al., 2011). Infants may be irritable, overly complacent (e.g., do not seek attention from caregiver, apathetic), and fail to meet physical developmental milestones (e.g., sitting, standing). The brain is particularly vulnerable to psychological abuse during the period of rapid growth from infancy to the preschool years. Recently obtained evidence suggests that psychological abuse by caregivers alters the structure, organization,

---

[2] Baumrind's model of parenting was developed to explain "normative" parenting and is applied in this context to show how distortions of this parenting style may lead to psychological abuse.

and efficacy of the child's brain and the body's neurobiological systems (e.g., high levels of cortisol and noradrenaline neurotransmitters), keeping the child in an alert and stressful state (Bugental, Martorell, & Barraza, 2003; Yates, 2007). When previously maltreated children were given an intervention of positive child–caregiver interactions, they showed neurophysiological adaptation indicative of a normal state (Dozier, Lindheim, & Ackerman, 2005; Fisher, Gunnar, Chamberlain, & Reid, 2000).

Emotional Developmental Consequences

Like other forms of maltreatment, psychological abuse results in children forming insecure attachment to their parents and having delayed emotional development, which in turn negatively affects their ability to form intimate relationships in adolescence and adulthood (Miller-Perrin & Perrin, 2007). Children subjected to psychological abuse are fearful, angry, anxious, withdrawn, isolated, helpless, and humiliated, and they feel abandoned (Schneider et al., 2005; Tomison & Tucci, 1997; Vissing et al., 1991). The abuse interferes with these children's ability to develop positive self-esteem or sympathy and empathy for others, which will detrimentally affect their subsequent interpersonal interactions, caregiving, and parent-child relationships when they become adults (Hart et al., 1998; Riggs & Kaminski, 2010). Long-term effects of psychological unavailability and maltreatment in childhood may include at least one diagnosis of mental illness (e.g., bipolar disorder, depression), personality disorders (e.g., borderline, narcissistic, obsessive-compulsive, and paranoid), sleeping and eating disorders, and impaired functioning in adolescence and adulthood (Brassard & Donovan, 2006; Johnson, Cohen, & Smailes, 2001; Wright, Crawford, & Del Castillo, 2009).

Social Developmental Consequences

Children who are psychologically abused may have difficulty forming and maintaining bonds with their peers due to their social incompetence—specifically, their weak interpersonal skills and tendency to act in impulsive and inappropriate ways (Brassard, Hart, & Hardy, 1991; Erickson, Egeland, & Piantra, 1989; Vissing et al., 1991). As a result, these children may be isolated even further from interacting with their peers because children of the same age are unlikely to befriend anyone who acts in an emotionally immature (e.g., extremely needy and overly dependent, emotionally unresponsive) or antisocial manner, such as by being physically aggressive and using poor conflict-resolution strategies (Hart et al., 2011; Riggs & Kaminski, 2010). Psychologically abused children often engage in self-blame and self-criticism, consistent with the beliefs endorsed by their abusers that the child victims are deficient and not deserving of love (Hibbard et al., 2012). If child victims do not receive treatment, the long-term effects could include continued social isolation due to interpersonal insensitivity (Kent & Waller, 2000).

Cognitive Developmental Consequences

Not surprisingly, psychological abuse severely impacts children's cognitive abilities (i.e., language and social skills) and academic achievement, while encouraging negative internalized life scripts and dissociation (Iwaniec, 1997; Kendall-Tackett & Eckenrode, 1996; Oddone-Paolucci, Genius, & Violato, 2001; Wright et al., 2009). Effects differ based on the type of psychological abuse. When exposed to verbally abusive caregivers, children may develop low creativity, difficulty learning, and poor problem-solving skills, whereas exposure to psychologically unavailable caregivers may lead to poor educational achievement and low intellectual functioning (Erickson & Egeland, 2011). Many Romanian orphans, who faced the prospect of being raised in a stark environment by caregivers who were emotionally detached, were found to have low IQ, poor cognitive processing, and limited executive function and memory (Zeanah et al., 2009; Zeanah et al., 2003).

Box 5-1   Exposure to Family Violence: A Form of Psychological Abuse

When CPS investigates substantiated cases of child maltreatment, co-occurrence of intimate-partner violence is present in 30% to 60% of these households (Edleson, 2004; Zolotor, Theodore, Coyne-Beasley, & Runyan, 2007). Even when children are not directly maltreated themselves, exposing them to their siblings' maltreatment or to intimate-partner violence involving their parent (e.g., seeing or hearing violence, trying to intervene, calling 911, comforting the battered parent, observing injuries) is a form of psychological abuse (Fantuzzo & Mohr, 1999; Holden, Geffne, & Jouriles, 1998). Each year, an estimated 3 to 10 million children (Carter, Weitnorn, & Behrman, 1999), and perhaps as many as 15.5 million children (McDonald, Jouriles, Ramisetty, Caetano, & Green, 2006), are exposed to family violence in the United States. The detrimental consequences of these experiences are apparent at all levels of development, from infants to adolescents (Osofsky, 1999). Exposing children to violence is the abuser's means of exploiting the child's (and the battered parent's) fears, gaining cooperation and compliance from family members, and intimidating and controlling victims (Mbilinyi, Edleson, Hagemeister, & Beeman, 2007). Drawing on their data from the National Survey of Children's Exposure to Violence (NatSCEV), Hamby, Finkelhor, Turner, and Ormrod (2011) indicated that children responded in similar ways to exposure to intimate-partner violence and to parental assaults of a sibling, respectively—49.9% and 49.3% yelled for the abuser to stop, 43.9% and 41.6% tried to get away, and 23.6% and 20.2% called for help.

In response to their stressful experiences with family violence, children exhibit both internalizing behaviors (e.g., depression, anxiety, insomnia, fears, bedwetting, eating disorders) and externalizing behaviors (e.g., aggression, behavior problems), physical health problems, maladaptive social interactions with peers and adults, impaired concentration, poor intellectual functioning and academic performance, and low empathy and self-esteem (Alaggia, Jenny, Mazzuca, & Redmond, 2007; Amato, 2000; Hinchey & Gavelek, 1982; Wolfe, Crooks, Lee, McIntyre-Smith, & Jaffe, 2003). Other outcomes of exposure to domestic violence include development of post-traumatic stress disorder (PTSD) and the possibility of becoming an abuser as an adolescent or adult (Margolin & Vickerman, 2007).

Unfortunately, this form of psychological abuse has only recently been recognized in American society, as evidenced by the paucity of legal and civil remedies in place. As of November 2012, 23 states plus Puerto Rico had passed criminal statutes related to children's exposure to adult domestic violence (Child Welfare Information Gateway, 2013). Some states elevate misdemeanor crimes to felony charges when an assault takes place in front of a child (e.g., Oregon Revised Statutes §163.160). In five states (Arkansas, Florida, Idaho, Louisiana, and Oregon), perpetrators who expose children to domestic violence receive increased penalties (e.g., California Penal Code §1170.76); another eight states (Alaska, Arizona, California, Hawaii, Mississippi, Montana, Ohio, and Washington) consider it part of aggravating circumstances; and five additional states (Delaware, Georgia, North Carolina, Oklahoma, and Utah) file it as separate crime charged in addition or in conjunction with assault charges (e.g., Utah Code Annotated §76-5-109.1).

Despite criminal recognition of this type of maltreatment, civil courts lag behind in dealing with the problem of children's exposure to family violence. Currently, only four states require abusers to pay for children's counseling, two states require abusers to get counseling, and only one state requires supervised parenting time for abusers at least one year subsequent to a domestic violence incident. When deciding child custody, judges are supposed to consider domestic violence as a rebuttable presumption (10 states have adopted statutes that specify the batterer should not have sole or joint custody) or as part of a factor test in determining the best interests of the child (34 states plus Washington, D.C.), although four states make no mention of it at all (Levin & Mills, 2003). More often than not, family court judges disregard the seriousness of family violence in favor of preserving parental rights and award sole or joint custody to the abuser (Liss & Stably, 1993; Pagelow, 1993) or force children to have unsupervised, mandatory visitation with the abuser, thereby allowing the psychological abuse to continue.

Meditators for Adverse Effects

Why would children differ in their responses to psychological abuse? Two important factors include early caregiving experiences and quantity (i.e., frequency, intensity, and duration) of the psychological abuse (Hibbard et al., 2012; Iwaniec, 1997). Clearly, infrequent, low-intensity, and short exposure will have the least impact, but the child victim will react differently to the abuse if it follows a period of positive parent–child interactions and secure attachment than if the relationship has always been poor (Iwaniec, Larkin, & Higgins, 2006). Another factor that moderates negative effects is the child's own characteristics, such as the victim's coping strategies, disposition, communication skills, and self-esteem (Binggelli, Hart, & Brassard, 2001).

Finally, as with all forms of maltreatment, the impact on development often depends on the availability of social and emotional support from other people in children's lives (Iwaniec et al., 2006). In particular, child victims who have other loving caregivers (e.g., nonabusing parent or extended family members) in their lives are likely to experience fewer destructive consequences. Moreover, educators and classmates provide child victims with both healthy outlets for normal social interactions and opportunities for developing secure attachments (Hart et al., 2002). As children spend several hours per day in school, teachers can nurture children's skills and create a sense of accomplishment in them while modeling positive adult–child interactions that build their self-esteem (Miller-Perrin & Perrin, 2007).

Neglect

Like psychological abuse, neglect has not been given its due by researchers, practitioners, and others who are involved in the investigation of the welfare of children (Erickson & Egeland, 2011; Miller-Perrin & Perrin, 2007). According to these experts, child neglect encompasses the parents' failure to meet a child's basic needs (whether once or as a pattern)—specifically, "physical health care, supervision, nutrition, personal hygiene, emotional nurturing, education, or safe housing" (Gaudin, 1993, p. 67)—resulting in harm or endangerment (i.e., future injury likely). Yet, experts disagree as to how neglect should be defined. Some professionals advocate using a standard based on parents' behaviors toward fulfilling children's needs, or lack thereof, whether intentionally or unintentionally (Greenbaum et al., 2008; Zuravin, 1999), whereas others purport it should be based on the child victim's experience without attributing responsibility, blame, or both to the caregiver, especially when reasons for not meeting those needs are poverty related (Dubowitz & DePanfilis, 2000; Dubowitz et al., 2005). Consequently, definitions differ within and across professionals (e.g., health care), agencies (e.g., Administration for Children Services, law enforcement), disciplines (e.g., psychology, nursing, criminology), and jurisdictions (state, federal), making understanding neglect, in general, and protecting children and prosecuting perpetrators, in particular, difficult at best (DePanfilis, 2006).

The main obstacle for achieving consensus of the components constituting neglect seems to be lack of agreement on which levels of care standards and needs should be employed, which caregiving acts of commission or omission should be included, and whether to consider intentionality of actions to harm the child and/or the actual consequences (e.g., safety, well-being, health). Reasons for caregivers failing to meet children's physical/environmental (food, shelter, supervision), medical/mental health (prevention and treatment), educational (academic or special education), or emotional (inattentive, psychological care, missocializing) needs may be related to cultural or community values, religious beliefs, or poverty. Cultural examples that would fit the criteria for neglect in the United States (but not in their country of origin) include making elementary school–aged children responsible for the care of infant siblings, as is done in some South Asian cultures (Korbin, Coulton, Lindstrom-Ufuti, & Spilsbury, 2000), or denying education for Afghanistan girls, as was done under the Taliban regime (Moreau & Yousafzai, 2006). Thus, practitioners should learn about these cultural practices to better assist and guide parents who must learn alternatives considered both appropriate and acceptable in America. Religiously motivated medical neglect examples would include refusing surgery or blood transfusions for a seriously ill child. Poverty-based neglect might include failing to provide adequate nutrition, failing to take an ill child to the pediatrician, or not purchasing prescriptions. In many cases, these parents care about their children, but cannot afford medical care and food because they do not have health insurance or have limited finances.

Box 5-2 Religiously and Culturally Motivated Medical Neglect

Sometimes parents may choose to not provide medical treatment for their children due to such treatment being prohibited by their religion or against their cultural beliefs. Western medical practices often require drug and body-invasive treatments, such as blood transfusion and surgery, that are at odds with naturalistic remedies provided in Eastern medical practices and faith healing. Not surprisingly, the American Academy of Pediatrics (1997) is vehemently opposed to the state making an exception for providing medical care to children. Delays in medical treatment for potentially lethal and crippling illnesses (e.g., meningitis) and injuries (e.g., internal bleeding) often expose children to unnecessary risk, and sometimes death (Asser & Swan, 1998). State and federal laws provide exemptions to child abuse and neglect laws for parents who use prayer instead of medicine in acknowledgment of citizens' rights to practice their religion freely. However, the state reserves the right to protect children and provide life-saving medical treatment to save their lives, even when it violates their parents' rights to religious practice (e.g., *Jehovah's Witnesses of Washington v. King County Hospital*, 390 U.S. 598 [88 S.Ct. 1260, 20 L.Ed.2d 158];1968). The ruling supporting this notion was made in *Prince v. Massachusetts* (32 US 158, 64 SCt 438, 88 LEd 645; 1944): "The right to practice religion freely does not include the liberty to expose the community or child to communicable disease, or the latter to ill health or death . . . Parents may be free to become martyrs themselves. But it does not follow [that] they are free, in identical circumstances, to make martyrs of their children." Too often, however, the state does not become aware that a child is or had been gravely ill and not receiving medical care until the child dies (Dwyer, 2000).

Neglect itself varies in terms of the behaviors that could or should be delineated, as they actually depend on the child's age and developmental capacity (e.g., age and length of time to allow a child to stay home alone). Despite attempts to provide specific definitions through the Child Abuse Prevention and Treatment Act (CAPTA) of 1996, in the past CPS often relied on their own subjective judgments to determine whether neglect occurred, as laws in place did not specify what was meant by "risk" or "significant harm" (P.L., 104-235; DePanfilis, 2007). Eventually, CAPTA, as part of the Keeping Children and Families Safe Act of 2003 (P.L. 108-36), provided minimum standards for states to use when defining maltreatment in their statutory codes as a requirement for federal funding. The definition for child neglect is caregivers' or parents' actions or failure to act that results in "death, serious physical or emotional harm" or "presents an imminent risk of serious harm" (CAPTA, 42 U.S.C. 5106g, §Sec.111-2).

To help practitioners in determining a family's strengths and weaknesses while investigating a case, DePanfilis (2006) recommends conceptualizing neglect as failure to meet children's needs along a continuum, such that severity of incidents can be classified as mild (i.e., requiring community-based intervention only), moderate (i.e., CPS paired with community-based intervention), or severe (i.e., CPS and legal system involved due to long-term harm). Thus, seriousness would be determined as part of a formula encompassing the amount of actual or potentially harmful consequences combined with the duration and frequency (i.e., chronicity or history of acts and omissions) of neglect-related behaviors (Miller-Perrin & Perrin, 2007). Drawing on this comprehensive definition, Table 5-2 provides a list of types and subtypes of neglect that could be used by practitioners to categorize observed and missing care behaviors and their consequences. Many states (e.g., Tennessee, North Carolina) have incorporated a multiple response systems (MRS) approach to investigating allegations that include various family-centered solutions depending on the reasons for the neglect referral (e.g., lack of resources due to homelessness vs. unwilling to care for child).

Table 5-2 Types and subtypes of neglect

Type and subtypes	Description
1. Physical	Failing to provide basic physiological needs.
a. Abandonment	Physically deserting the child without providing adequate substitute care or supervision in the parent's absence or with no intention to retrieve the child (e.g., leaving the child alone for at least 2 days, leaving the child with a sitter but not providing needed supplies or not returning at the agreed-upon time).
b. Inadequate shelter	Refusing custody (e.g., expulsion of the child on a permanent or indefinite basis without providing for substitute care or without adequately arranging for the child's care by others, denying a runaway permission to return) or failing to provide a stable and permanent home (e.g., homeless;[1] overcrowded home; repeatedly shuttling the child from custody of one person to another for days, weeks, or months).
c. Nutritional	Failing to provide a nutritional and balanced diet (e.g., withholding food to the point of undernourishment or malnourishment for long periods of time; forcing the child to eat stale or spoiled food; gluttonous indulgence of foods high in sugar and/or fat, causing obesity, diabetes, and other health problems).[2]
d. Clothing	Not ensuring the child owns and wears weather- and size-appropriate clothing that, if not new, is at least in good repair.
e. Personal care	Failing to provide basic levels of personal cleanliness (e.g., inadequate bathing, lack of dental hygiene, lack of schedule or provision of bed to allow adequate sleep).

[1] This form of neglect is determined on state-by-state level. However, DePanfilis (2006) indicated that neglect charges should be filed when fiscal mismanagement (rather than unemployment or poverty per se) by the parent due to substance abuse (e.g., using rent money to buy drugs) is the primary cause for homelessness.

[2] Parents may choose to provide children with processed foods low in nutrition rather than healthier options (e.g., fruits, vegetables) despite having sufficient financial resources because they make these poor choices themselves or are not educated about the risks. As pointed out by an anonymous reviewer, parents whose children's poor diets lead to medical conditions, such as obesity and diabetes, may need to be referred to a dietitian rather than to CPS, which is the appropriate option when the child is medically unstable (e.g., repeated fainting and emergency room visits).

Table 5-2 Types and subtypes of neglect

Type and subtypes	Description
2. Environmental	Failing to protect the child or keep the child safe from harm in his or her surroundings or neighborhood; lack of opportunities and resources.
a. Household safety	Lack of prevention to ensure safety in the home (e.g., dilapidation of structures, such as broken steps, railings, windows, flooring, and ceilings); inadequate child-proofing; clutter and other fire threats (e.g., combustible materials close to heating elements, frayed wires, too many wires in one outlet).
b. Household sanitation	Failing to meet basic cleanliness and housekeeping standards (e.g., garbage is not removed and is accumulating in the home, vermin and insects are present and no effort is made to remove them, counter surfaces are dirty, bedding is not changed regularly, no running or clean water).
c. Other	Reckless disregard for the child's safety and welfare (e.g., driving while intoxicated with the child, leaving an infant or young child in a car unattended).
3. Inadequate supervision	Not providing age-appropriate supervision to prevent harm or injury to the child inside or outside the home.
a. No supervision	Although most states do not have a specified age and amount of time a child can be left unsupervised inside or outside of the home, guidelines used by CPS include the age and developmental level of the child (e.g., will not open door to strangers, can handle basic emergencies), circumstances (e.g., 5 minutes, 2 hours after school, overnight), and neighborhood (e.g., crime-ridden, rural).
b. Inappropriate supervision	Leaving the child with caregivers who are not able or willing to provide appropriate care, protection, and supervision (e.g., having a child care for an infant, the caregiver is a known child abuser or addict, the caregiver is too distracted by other activities to address the child's needs).
c. Exposure to hazards	Allowing children to become involved in chronic or extreme intimate-partner abuse and purposefully subjecting them to environmental and health dangers (e.g., prenatal drug use by the mother; lead exposure; leaving loaded guns within reach; allowing an infant in a crib to be attacked by rats; exposing the child to the parent's drug and alcohol use, such as smoking pot in front of children or bringing them to a bar; subjecting children with pulmonary conditions to second-hand smoke; not using age-appropriate car seats or using them incorrectly for the developmental level of the child; riding a bike without a helmet; allowing the child to play in the streets, especially in dangerous, crime-ridden neighborhoods; having a methamphetamine lab in or near the home that exposes the child to toxic chemicals).
4. Emotional	Failing to provide adequate nurturing, affection, emotional support, security, and psychological well-being (e.g., parents ignore their young child's cues and signals, leave the child with inappropriate caregivers).[3]

[3] Many of the emotional neglect behaviors are identical to those described for psychological abuse. CPS often pursues maltreatment cases that involve psychological abuse on the basis of emotional neglect, given that most states have only neglect laws on their books.

(Continues)

Table 5-2 Types and subtypes of neglect (*Continued*)

Type and subtypes	Description
a. Missocializing	Failing to take preventive or interventional measures that would discourage maladaptive/antisocial behavior (e.g., chronic delinquency, fighting, alcohol/drug use, smoking or chewing tobacco).
b. Isolating	Preventing social interaction of the child with peers and other adults.
5. Medical	Denying or delaying essential preventive medical or dental care or therapeutic treatment for a physical injury, illness, medical condition, or impairment that could result in serious harm (e.g., withholding immunizations, not filling prescriptions, failing to follow instructions for care, not taking the child to a doctor or a dentist, not permitting the dentist to fill cavities).[4]
6. Mental health	Denying or delaying mental health assessment and refusing to comply with recommended therapy for children with serious emotional or behavioral disorders.
7. Educational	Failing to comply with laws requiring the child to attend school (e.g., permitting truancy, not enrolling the child, not attending to special education needs).

[4] Although parents are not required by the federal government (see the Child Abuse Prevention and Treatment Act [CAPTA], 42 U.S.C. 5106i, §Sec. 113; Reauthorization Act, 2010) to provide medically indicated treatment that is inconsistent with their religious beliefs, CPS may use state authority to seek legal remedies to obtain such medical treatment or care for children in response to serious injury or life-threatening conditions and to decide whether to file charges for maltreatment against these parents.

Data from DePanfilis, D. (2006). *Child neglect: A guide for prevention, assessment, and intervention.* U.S. Department of Health and Human Services Child Abuse and Neglect User Manual Series. http://www.childwelfare.gov/pubs/usermanuals/neglect/neglect .pdf; Dubowitz, H., Newton, R. R., Litrownik, A. J., Lewis, T., Briggs, E. C., Thompson, R., . . . Feerick, M. M. (2005). Examination of a conceptual model of child neglect. *Child Maltreatment, 10*, 173–189; Erickson, M. F., & Egeland, B. (2011). Child neglect. In J. E. B. Myers (Ed.), *The APSAC handbook on child maltreatment* (3rd ed., pp. 103–124). Thousand Oaks, CA: Sage; Gaudin, J. M. (1993). Effective intervention with neglectful families. *Criminal Justice and Behavior, 20* (1), 66–89; Goldman, J., Salus, M. K., Wolcott, D., & Kennedy, K. Y. (2003). A coordinated response to child abuse and neglect: The foundation for practice. Child Abuse and Neglect User Manual Series. US Dept. of Health and Human Services. http://www.childwelfare.gov/pubs /usermanuals/foundation/foundation.pdf; Miller-Perrin, C. L., & Perrin, R. D. (2007). *Child maltreatment: An introduction* (2nd ed.). Thousand Oaks, CA: Sage.

Official Estimates of Incidence

Official estimates predominantly from CPS records indicate that neglect is the most prevalent form of child maltreatment, increasing from 55% of reported child abuse cases in 1986 to 62.8% in 2005, although increases across years may partially reflect broadened definitions (U.S. DHHS, 2007). According to NCANDS data, 78.3% of maltreatment cases reported in 2010 involved neglect (U.S. DHHS, 2011). Similar estimates using the conservative "harm" standard were indicated in the National Incidence Studies (NIS-2, NIS-3, NIS-4), such that 51% of maltreatment cases in 1986, 56.6% in 1993, and 61.4%

in 2005–2006 were classified as neglect (includes physical, emotional, and educational neglect). Not surprisingly, the more liberal "endangered" standard revealed even higher rates: 64.4% in 1986, 70% in 1993, and 77.5% in 2005–2006.

To understand the severity of outcome from neglect, an evaluation of 2005 fatalities by National Child Abuse and Neglect Data System (NCANDS) revealed that death was caused by "only neglect" in 42.2% of these cases, by physical abuse combined with neglect in 24.1% of these cases, and by multiple maltreatment types in 27.3% of these cases (U.S. DHHS, 2007). Fatalities were the result of medical neglect, chronic physical neglect, inadequate supervision (e.g., fires, falling from unprotected windows), and acute incidents (e.g., drowning, suffocation, poison), often in the bathroom. An assessment of severity of injury or harm reported in the NIS-4 revealed that 50% of children who were neglected suffered fatal or serious injuries, whereas 46% suffered moderate injuries (Sedlak et al., 2010). Neglect is the main cause or a contributory factor in most (67%) of the child maltreatment fatalities in 2010 (U.S. DHHS, 2011), particularly for children younger than 8 years of age (U.S. Government Accountability Office, 2011).

Causes of Neglect

It is difficult to determine the causes of neglect given the paucity of research that differentiates each type of maltreatment or examines families from various socioeconomic backgrounds. Instead, many researchers focus on retrospective data or use high-risk clinical samples, thereby reducing the generalizability of their results (see Gaudin, 1993, for a review). Much of our understanding of inadequate parenting stems from contributions made by practitioners who deal with the families, but thus far no cause–effect relationships have been revealed to explain neglect.

Belsksy and Vondra (1989) proposed a model consisting of three factors that have interactive and reciprocal influences on parenting: individual (e.g., parents' idiopathic history and personality), group (e.g., family and child characteristics), and environmental stressors and supports (e.g., community, neighborhood). In essence, the parents' own childhoods mold their personalities and psychosocial capacity to interact with others and directly impact their parenting skills and beliefs. A caregiver may have certain personality characteristics (e.g., impulsivity) that lead to disorganization in the home, which, when paired with problems (e.g., emotional, substance abuse), deficits (e.g., poor planning and problem-solving skills), and stressors (e.g., unemployment, poverty, child with disabilities or health problems, marital conflict), contribute to neglect. Neglectful parents are less likely to have positive verbal, emotional, and behavioral exchanges with their children than non-neglectful parents (Miller-Perrin & Perrin, 2007). Although parents are expected to know how to care adequately for their children, actual parenting skills are based on emotional maturity, positive attitudes toward children (e.g., seeing children as valuable and enjoyable), knowledge of child development (e.g., having realistic expectations of children's abilities and needs), age-appropriate control and discipline techniques, coping skills, and treatment received from their own parents. These abilities could be supplemented or advanced by members of the parents' extended social support network (e.g., grandparents, friends, neighbors), but could also contribute to the chaotic lifestyle as the combination of adults and children in one household changes to accommodate family members' housing needs.

Reciprocity is apparent in parents' reactions to their children's personalities and in the children's behaviors toward their parents, particularly in the development of secure attachment. Parents who are not capable of developing supportive relationships with their spouses/significant others, children, family members, friends, neighbors, or co-workers, for example, operate alone under a high-stress and low-support environment (Gaudin, 1993). The availability of informal and formal supports (e.g., affordable child care, daycare services at work, safe and clean neighborhood) directly influences stress levels, coping ability, and parenting adequacy. The absence of supportive relationships (e.g., noncritical relatives) combined with stressors (e.g., unemployment, illness) hinders proper enactment of demanding parenting tasks.

Demographics of Victim and Perpetrator

Victim

The research suggests that child neglect victims are predominantly younger than age 5 years (51% of all victims, with 34% being younger than 1 year of age), with serious injuries and fatalities occurring with those younger than age 3 years (Connell-Carrick, 2003). According to the NIS-4 data, endangerment standards were highest for children aged 6–8 years in terms of physical and emotional neglect, but highest for children aged 9–11 and 12–14 years in terms of educational neglect (Table 5-3).

Although there are no significant gender differences in rates of neglect (51% male, 49% female), children of African American descent were most often reported to CPS as victims of neglect. According to the NIS-4 data, 14.7 per 1000 (36.8 per 1000) African American children, 7.5 per 1000 (22.4 per 1000) European American children, and 8.3 per 1000 (23.0 per 1000) Latino American children were estimated to be victims under the harm (endangerment) standard of neglect in 2005–2006. This finding might potentially

Table 5-3 Age differences in incidence rates for endangerment standard of neglect (number of abused children per 1000 children)

Neglect type	Ages					
	0–2 years	3–5 years	6–8 years	9–11 years	12–14 years	15–17 years
Physical	17.6	15.3	18.9	15.7	13.0	8.7
Emotional	13.2	13.4	17.0	15.2	15.1	11.4
Educational	—	2.3	4.9	7.5	7.3	6.4

Data from NIS-4. https://www.nis4.org/.

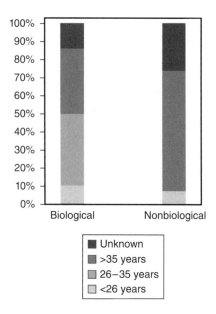

Figure 5-1 Perpetrator's age by perpetrator's relationship to child

reflect socioeconomic class rather than ethnicity, but these two factors often cannot be teased apart in the United States (Miller-Perrin & Perrin, 2007). As suggested by Connell-Carrick (2003), "It could be that neglect is not ethnic-specific, and these results are more reflective of reporting bias within the child welfare system" (p. 409). Relationships found between neglect and disabilities (physical, cognitive, and emotional), physical health problems (e.g., low birth weight, chronic illness), and personality (e.g., passive, withdrawn, nonassertive) may be more a consequence of neglect rather than its contributing agent.

Perpetrator
The primary perpetrators of neglect toward children are the biological parents (Miller-Perrin & Perrin, 2007). According to the NIS-4 data (Sedlak et al., 2010), in 92% of child neglect cases, the biological parents were responsible for the maltreatment; the remaining 8% of cases were attributable to nonbiological parents or partners. The proportion of biological-parent perpetrators did not vary by type of neglect (94% for educational neglect, 91% for physical neglect, and 90% for emotional neglect). Children were subjected to neglect predominantly by their mothers (86%). The age of the perpetrator varied, as shown in Figure 5-1 (which is based on data reported in NIS-4), such that rates of neglect were higher for children who were biologically related rather than unrelated to a caregiver younger than age 35 years. Although less pronounced in the NIS-4 data set, research has shown that children of adolescent mothers are at increased risk of neglect, perhaps

because these women's immaturity, low education, isolation, lack of financial and social support, and high stress detrimentally affect their parenting ability (Lounds, Borkowski, & Whitman, 2006; Murphey & Braner, 2000; Schatz, 2006; Whitman, Borkowski, Keogh, & Weed, 2001).

Many of the perpetrators of child neglect have behavioral and emotional difficulties that make them act irrationally or even be indifferent to their children's needs. Some suffer from mental disorders (e.g., depression) and/or substance abuse, which would also interfere with their parenting functioning (e.g., childrearing style, discipline choices), judgment, and protective capacity (DePanfilis, 2006; Goldman, Salus, Wolcott, & Kennedy, 2003). As a result, their children's health and safety are jeopardized and their basic needs go unmet. Parents who neglect their children may be classified using Baumrind's dimensions as using an uninvolved parenting style and showing low empathy while engaging in verbal aggression. Additionally, these caregivers tend to be coping with a number of stressors simultaneously, such as a single parenthood, a large number of children, extreme poverty, and impoverished neighborhoods (Connell-Carrick, 2003; Dubowitz & DePanfilis, 2000; Goldman et al., 2003; Slack, Holl, McDaniel, Yook, & Bolger, 2004).

Signs, Symptoms, and Developmental Consequences of Neglected Children

The behavioral signs, physical symptoms, and developmental consequences that result from this type of maltreatment depend on the form(s) of neglect to which the child is exposed.

Behavioral Signs

Neglected children may be clumsy, listless, and lethargic, perhaps as a result of their delayed physical development and immature motor skills (DePanfilis, 2006; Roscoe, Peterson, & Shaner, 1983). Most notably, these children are often quiet and submissive, have unusual eating and sleeping behaviors, engage in attention-seeking behaviors, display superficial emotional responses toward others, act impulsively, react to stressful situations passively or aggressively, and hoard, steal, or beg for food (DePanfilis, 2006; Dubowitz et al., 2005). Older children and adolescents may be physically and verbally aggressive with their peers, could be sexually active (often resulting in adolescent pregnancy and parenthood), and may engage in self-abusive and illegal behaviors, such as delinquency, assault, prostitution, drug use, and underage drinking (Miller-Perrin & Perrin, 2007). Long-term consequences of childhood neglect include criminal activities, substance abuse, and intergenerational patterns of neglect in adulthood (DePanfilis, 2006).

Physical Developmental Consequences/Symptoms

Physical symptoms of neglect noted among infants and young children include "nonorganic" failure to thrive (i.e., weight, height, and motor development significantly below age-appropriate ranges without any underlying physiological or medical cause) with related growth delays (e.g., low tone, unemotional, decreased vocalizing, unresponsiveness), dehydration, diarrhea, malnutrition (e.g., emaciated, distended stomach), severe diaper rash and other skin infections, impaired brain development, and even death (DePanfilis, 2006). Infants exposed to harmful substances in utero or whose mothers had minimal prenatal care and poor nutrition are often born prematurely and suffer from birth defects and other complications, including impaired brain functioning (e.g., altered cortical development, fewer neurons, interrupted chemical function) and mental retardation (Frank, Augustyn, Knight, Pell, & Zuckerman, 2001; Shonkoff & Phillips, 2000). The neurobiological problems persist into childhood and, as harm is cumulative, continued (and chronic) neglect is likely to result in stunted brain development by preventing the formation of neural connections and pathways, promoting cortical atrophy, inhibiting signal transfer, and limiting cognitive growth (Perry, 2002). Children also may suffer poor physical health (e.g., visual and hearing problems, short stature), untended injuries (e.g., cuts, bruises, burns, fractures), and serious undiagnosed or untreated illnesses (e.g., childhood diseases that would have been prevented through immunizations, respiratory infections or diabetes left untreated) stemming from nutritional neglect, lack of supervision, medical neglect, and exposure to harmful substances.

It is not uncommon for neglected children and adolescents to have unkempt appearances, including unwashed bodies; soiled, worn, foul-smelling (likely from sweat, urine, and/or feces) and ill-fitting clothing; matted hair with possible lice infestation; and dental caries that lead to tooth decay and gum disease (Lewin & Herron, 2007; Roscoe et al., 2001). Additional evidence of physical neglect presents as stunted growth, listlessness, chronic and infected sores, infections, and untreated injuries, particularly from exposure to cold weather (e.g., redness, swollen limbs, stiff joints). Children exposed to harmful substances may suffer from blood diseases (e.g., anemia), poor immune functioning, cancer, and chronic respiratory illnesses (e.g., asthma). Neglected children also have been diagnosed with psychiatric disorders, such as anxiety and depression; with conduct problems; with attention-deficit disorder; and with personality disorders (e.g., antisocial personality). These problems in emotional regulation tend to persist into adulthood and include mood disorders symptoms (e.g., PTSD, dysthymia, depression).

Emotional Developmental Consequences
Neglected infants often have insecure attachments to parents characterized by either anxiety (e.g., colicky, clingy, overly dependent) or disorganization (e.g., poor coping skills) that continue into childhood (Erickson & Egeland, 2011; Hildyard & Wolfe, 2002). As a result of the inconsistent care and absence of trust, a secure base for exploring, and a safe haven, neglected children form inappropriate social expectations (including that their needs are likely to go unfilled), exhibit disturbed interaction patterns, and demonstrate ineffective coping mechanisms that result in low self-esteem and competence (DePanfilis, 2006). Such children have negative self-concepts, low self-esteem, and little enthusiasm when engaged in enjoyable activities, often appearing disinterested and shy, but not confident enough to engage children in interactions directly (Tyler, Allison, & Winsler, 2006).

Additionally, neglected children display flat or negative affect, are poor at self-regulating their emotions, and have difficulty recognizing and discriminating other people's emotions, which in turn limits their own ability to be remorseful or empathetic, particularly when they behave inappropriately toward peers (DePanfilis, 2006; Pollak, Cicchetti, Hornung, & Reed, 2000). Older children and adolescents have difficulty in controlling their emotions and impulses, display age-inappropriate social and emotional behaviors (especially aggression, wild laughter, immature outbursts and tirades, spitefulness, selfishness, and sexual promiscuity), display apathy or helplessness in stressful situations, and are unresponsive to affection (Tyler et al., 2006).

Social Developmental Consequences

Insecure attachments to peers are manifested in neglected children's poor social interactions, which are marked by high conflict and anger, lack of enthusiasm, unimaginative play, social isolation, few reciprocal friendships, noncompliance, and poor prosocial behavior (Erickson & Egeland, 2011; Hildyard & Wolfe, 2002). In general, these children's impaired social cognition leaves them easily frustrated and stressed by most social situations, which, combined with their difficulty in adjusting to changes in their social environment and delayed social skills (e.g., eating with utensils, toileting, dressing), renders them vulnerable to peer rejection (DePanfilis, 2006; Roscoe et al., 2001). Typically, these children are avoided by their peers because of their appearance (e.g., disheveled clothing, odor) and immature behaviors (e.g., aggressive, fickle, self-centered); but they are also not capable of forming appropriate attachments to adults as evidenced by a needy overdependence and clinginess (Tyler et al., 2006).

Cognitive Developmental Consequences

The development of a variety of cognitive functions is hampered severely by neglect, including language (e.g., comprehension, receptive and expressive capability, verbalization), academic achievement (e.g., math, reading), intelligence, creativity, attention, and problem solving (Erickson & Egeland, 2011; Sullivan, 2000, as cited in DePanfilis, 2006). Moreover, these deficits remain stable over time (Kurtz, Gaudin, Wodarski, & Howing, 1993), beyond the effects contributed by poverty (Erickson & Egeland, 2011), and are more severe among children who are neglected than among children who are physically abused (Hildyard & Wolfe, 2002; Jones & Gupta, 2003, as cited in DePanfilis, 2006).

Children whose parents fail to provide intellectual stimulation, both within and outside the home, show little curiosity, inquisitiveness, or desire to explore the educational and play objects and activities in their school environment and demonstrate few of the basic skills needed to be academically successful (Roscoe et al., 2001). Perhaps as a reflection of their parents' disinterest in their education (e.g., not attending parent–child activities, not keeping scheduled appointments with school personnel, not seeking or procuring tutoring or special education), neglected children demonstrate chronic truancy, habitual tardiness, a high number of failing and below-average grades, and a high likelihood of being retained to repeat grade levels. Even when neglected children are present in school, they are easily discouraged and resigned to their poor academic performance, as their abilities to self-structure, initiate, focus, understand, and persist at scholarly endeavors are limited at best and often require a lot of assistance and approval from teachers (Gaudin, 1993; Tyler et al., 2006). The Minnesota Longitudinal Study found that when neglected children become adolescents, their learning problems continue, resulting in low achievement scores and high expulsion and school dropout rates (Erickson & Egeland, 2011).

Meditators for Adverse Effects

As in every form of maltreatment, the severity of problems stemming from neglect depends on multiple factors. Children's responses to neglect vary. One protective factor is the child's personal characteristics, as those individuals who are optimistic, highly intelligent, hopeful, and self-confident tend to suffer few negative consequences. Another factor is whether the child has a supportive and secure relationship with an adult, preferably one of the caregivers. A third factor is the realization of harm from neglect (i.e., actual versus potential). Although neglect can be quite harmful or deadly (e.g., when a stomach-ache caused by appendicitis goes untreated), it is not always serious (e.g., an ear infection resolves on its own).

A fourth factor is the length of harm (e.g., short versus long term). In some cases, the parent may engage in neglect due to his or her own illness or problems, but then recovers (e.g., stress is reduced to a manageable amount, medicine is used to treat mental illness, the parent attends a program to increase his or her knowledge of children and parenting techniques) to allow proper parenting and care to occur. However, if neglect has been the mode of parenting from infancy, then serious harm is likely to occur. The intergenerational transmission of neglect is interrupted when neglected children have few stressors as adults, have supportive intimate partners and stable relationships, are interested and excited about impending procreation, and give birth to healthy babies (Gaudin, 1993).

Chapter Summary

The consequences of child psychological abuse are often equal to or greater than those noted with other forms of maltreatment. Child psychological abuse occurs when an abuser makes the victim feel worthless and inadequate. There is significant disagreement about the definition of psychological abuse, and this lack of a universally accepted definition has impeded authorities in prosecuting offenders and understanding the short-term and long-term consequences of this form of abuse. Official estimates do not accurately capture the scope of psychological abuse. Psychological abuse by caregivers may occur for a variety of reasons. Children who have suffered from psychological abuse exhibit certain behavioral signs and physical symptoms.

Child neglect encompasses parents' failure to meet their children's basic needs, which results in harm or endangerment. Definitions of this type of abuse differ within and across professionals, agencies, disciplines, and jurisdictions; this variation, in turn, makes understanding and assessing the nature and extent of neglect, protecting children, and prosecuting perpetrators particularly challenging. Official estimates show that child neglect is the most prevalent form of maltreatment, but this prevalence may, in part, be attributed to the broad definitions of neglect. Similarly to psychological abuse, neglect negatively impacts a child's emotional, social, and cognitive development.

Review Questions

1. What are the causes of child psychological abuse?

2. What are the causes of child neglect?

3. What are some behavioral signs that psychologically abused and neglected children exhibit?

4. What are the physical developmental consequences of child psychological abuse and neglect?

5. What are the social and emotional developmental consequences of child psychological abuse and neglect?

6. What are the cognitive developmental consequences of child psychological abuse and neglect?

7. Why do children differ in their responses to psychological abuse?

References

Alaggia, R., Jenny, A., Mazzuca, J., & Redmond, M. (2007). In whose best interest? A Canadian case study of the impact of child welfare policies in cases of domestic violence. *Brief Treatment and Crisis Intervention, 7*(4), 275-290.

Amato, P. R. (2000). The consequences of divorce for adults and children. *Journal of Marriage and the Family, 62,* 1269-1287.

American Academy of Pediatrics, Committee on Bioethics. (1997). Religious objections to medical care. *Pediatrics, 99,* 279-281.

American Professional Society on the Abuse of Children (APSAC). (1995). *Guidelines for psychosocial evaluation of suspected psychological maltreatment of children and adolescents.* Elmhurst, IL: Author.

Asser, S. M., & Swan, R. (1998). Child fatalities from religion-motivated medical neglect. *Pediatrics, 101,* 625-629.

Baily, T. F., & Baily, W. H. (1986). *Operational definitions of child emotional maltreatment: Final report* (DHHS Publication No. 90-CA-0956). Washington, DC: U.S. Government Printing Office.

Baumrind, D. (1991). The influence of parenting style on adolescent competence and substance use. *Journal of Early Adolescence, 11*(1), 56–95.

Behl, L. E., Conyngham, H. A., & May, P. F. (2003). Trends in child maltreatment literature. *Child Abuse & Neglect, 27,* 215–229.

Belsksy, J., & Vondra, J. (1989). Lessons from child abuse: The determinants of parenting. In D. Cicchetti & V. Carlson (Eds.), *Child maltreatment: Theory and research on the causes and consequences of child abuse and neglect* (pp. 153–202). New York, NY: Cambridge University Press.

Binggelli, N., Hart, S., & Brassard, M. (2001). *Psychological maltreatment of children.* Thousand Oaks, CA: Sage.

Black, D. A., Slep, A. M. S., & Heyman, R. E. (2001). Risk factors for child psychological abuse. *Aggression and Violent Behavior, 6,* 203–209.

Boulton, S., & Hindle, D. (2000). Emotional abuse: The work of a multidisciplinary consultation group in a child psychiatric service. *Clinical Child Psychology and Psychiatry, 5*(3), 439–452.

Brassard, M. R., & Donovan, K. L. (2006). Defining psychological maltreatment. In M. M. Feerick, J. F. Knutson, P. K. Trickett, & S. M. Flanzer (Eds.), *Child abuse and neglect: Definitions, classifications, and a framework for research* (pp. 151–197). Baltimore, MD: Paul H. Brookes.

Brassard, M. R., Germain, R., & Hart, S. N. (Eds.). (1987). *Psychological maltreatment of children and youth.* New York, NY: Pergamon Press.

Brassard, M. R., Hart, S. N., & Hardy, D. (1991). Psychological and emotional abuse of children. In R. T. Ammerman & M. Hersen (Eds.), *Case studies in family violence* (pp. 55–270). New York, NY: Plenum Press.

Bugental, D. B., Martorell, G. A., & Barraza, V. (2003). The hormonal costs of subtle forms of infant maltreatment. *Hormones and Behavior, 43,* 237–244.

Byng-Hall, J. (2002). Relieving parentified children's burdens in families with insecure attachment patterns. *Family Process, 41*(3), 375–388.

Carter, L. S., Weitnorn, L. A., & Behrman, R. E. (1999). Domestic violence and children: Analysis and recommendations. *Domestic Violence and Children, 9,* 4–20.

Cawson, P., Wattam, C., Brooker, S., & Kelly, G. (2000). *Child maltreatment in the United Kingdom.* London, UK: NSPCC.

Child Welfare Information Gateway. (2007). Child abuse and neglect fatalities: Statistics and interventions. http://www.childwelfare.gov/pubs/factsheets/fatality.cfm#children

Child Welfare Information Gateway. (2013). Child abuse and neglect fatalities: Statistics and interventions. http://www.childwelfare.gov/pubs/factsheets/fatality.cfm#children

Cicchetti, D., & Nurcombe, B. (Eds.). (1991). *Development and psychopathology, special issue: Defining psychological maltreatment: Reflections and future directions.* New York, NY: Cambridge University Press.

Connell-Carrick, K. (2003). A critical review of the empirical literature: Identifying risk factors for child neglect. *Child and Adolescent Social Work, 20*(5), 389–425.

DePanfilis, D. (2006). Child neglect: A guide for prevention, assessment, and intervention. U.S. Department of Health and Human Services Child Abuse and Neglect User Manual Series. http://www.childwelfare.gov/pubs/usermanuals/neglect/neglect.pdf

DePanfilis, D. (2007). Risk factors and risk assessment in child welfare. In P. R. Popple & F. J. Vecchiolla (Eds.), *Child welfare social work* (pp. 85–118). Boston, MA: Allyn & Bacon.

Dozier, M., Lindheim, O., & Ackerman, J. P. (2005). Attachment and biobehavioural catch-up: An intervention targeting empirically identified needs of foster infants. In L. J. Berlin, Y. Ziv, L. Amaya-Jackson, & M. T. Greenberg (Eds.), *Enhancing early attachments: Theory research, intervention, and policy* (pp. 178–194). New York, NY: Guilford Press.

Dubowitz, H., & DePanfilis, D. (Eds.). (2000). *Handbook for child protection practice.* Thousand Oaks, CA: Sage.

Dubowitz, H., Newton, R. R., Litrownik, A. J., Lewis, T., Briggs, E. C., Thompson, R., . . . Feerick, M. M. (2005). Examination of a conceptual model of child neglect. *Child Maltreatment, 10*, 173–189.

Dwyer, J. G. (2000). Spiritual treatment exemptions to child medical neglect laws: What we outsiders should think. Paper 169. *Faculty Publications.* http://scholarship.law.wm.edu/facpubs/169

Edleson, J. L. (2004). Should childhood exposure to adult domestic violence be defined as child maltreatment under the law? In P. G. Jaffe, L. L. Baker, & A. Cunningham (Eds.), *Protecting children from domestic violence: strategies for community intervention* (pp. 8–29). New York, NY: Guilford Press.

Erickson, M. F., & Egeland, B. (2011). Child neglect. In J. E. B. Myers (Ed.), *The APSAC handbook on child maltreatment* (3rd ed., pp. 103–124). Thousand Oaks, CA: Sage.

Erickson, M. F., Egeland, B., & Pianta, R. (1989). The effects of maltreatment on the development of young children. In D. Cicchetti & V. Carlson (Eds.), *Child maltreatment: Theory and research on the causes and consequences of child abuse and neglect* (pp. 647–684). New York, NY: Cambridge University Press.

Fantuzzo, F., & Mohr, W. (1999). Prevalence and effects of child exposure to domestic violence. *Future of Children, 9*(3), 21–31.

Field, T., Healy, B., Goldstein, S., & Gutherz, M. (1990). Behavior-state matching and synchrony in mother–infant interactions of nondepressed versus depressed dyads. *Developmental Psychology, 26*, 7–14.

Finkelhor, D. (2008). *Childhood victimization: Violence, crime, and abuse in the lives of young people.* New York, NY: Oxford University Press.

Finkelhor, D., Ormrod, R. K., & Turner, H. A. (2007). Poly-victimization: A neglected component in child victimization trauma. *Child Abuse & Neglect, 31*, 7–26.

Fisher, P., Gunnar, M., Chamberlain, P., & Reid, J. (2000). Preventive intervention for maltreatment preschool children: Impact on children's behavior, neuroendocrine activity, and foster parent functioning. *Journal of the American Academy of Child and Adolescent Psychiatry, 39*, 1356–1364.

Frank, D. A., Augustyn, M., Knight, W. G., Pell, T., & Zuckerman, B. (2001). Growth, development, and behavior in early childhood following prenatal cocaine exposure: A systematic review. *Journal of the American Medical Association, 285*, 1613–1626.

Garbarino, J., & Garbarino, A. (1994). *Emotional maltreatment of children* (2nd ed.). Chicago, IL: National Committee to Prevent Child Abuse.

Gaudin, J. M. (1993). Effective intervention with neglectful families. *Criminal Justice and Behavior, 20*(1), 66–89.

Gilbert, R., Widom, C. S., Browne, K., Fergusson, D., Webb, E., & Janson, S. (2009). Burden and consequences of child maltreatment in high-income countries. *Lancet, 373*(9657), 68–81.

Glaser, D. (2002). Emotional abuse and neglect (psychological maltreatment): A conceptual framework. *Child Abuse & Neglect, 26*, 97–714.

Glaser, D., Prior, V., & Lynch, M. (2001). *Emotional abuse and emotional neglect: Antecedents, operational definitions and consequences.* York, UK: British Association for the Study and Prevention of Child Abuse and Neglect.

Glasser, M., Kolvin, I., Campbell, D., Glasser, A., Leitch, I., & Farrelly, S. (2001). Cycle of child sexual abuse: Links between being a victim and becoming a perpetrator. *British Journal of Psychiatry, 179*, 482–494.

Goldman, J., Salus, M. K., Wolcott, D., & Kennedy, K. Y. (2003). *A coordinated response to child abuse and neglect: The foundation for practice. Child Abuse and Neglect User Manual Series.* US Dept. of Health and Human Services. http://www.childwelfare.gov/pubs/usermanuals/foundation/foundation.pdf

Greenbaum, J., Dubowitz, H., Latzker, J. R., Johnson, K. D., Orn, K., Kenniston, J., Butler, P., Parrish, R., Feldman, K., Kornblum, L., O'Connor, A., Faller, K., Hodges, L., & Moeser, M. (2008). *Practice guidelines: Challenges in the evaluation of child neglect.* Elmhurst, IL: American Professional Society on the Abuse of Children.

Greenfield, E., & Marks, N. (2010). Identifying experiences of physical and psychological violence in childhood that jeopardise mental health in adulthood. *Child Abuse & Neglect, 34,* 161–171.

Hamarman, S., & Bernet, W. (2000). Evaluating and reporting emotional abuse in children: Parent-based, action-based focus aids in clinical decision-making. *Journal of the American Academy of Child and Adolescent Psychiatry, 39,* 928–930.

Hamarman, S., Pope, K. H., & Czaja, S. J. (2002). Emotional abuse in children: Variations in legal definitions and rates across the United States. *Child Maltreatment, 7,* 303–311.

Hamby, S., Finkelhor, D., Turner, H., & Ormrod, R. (2011). *Children's exposure to intimate partner violence and other family violence* (pp. 1–12). Juvenile Justice Bulletin: NCJ 232272. Washington, DC: U.S. Government Printing Office.

Hart, S. N., Binggeli, N. J., & Brassard, M. R. (1998). Evidence of the effects of psychological maltreatment. *Journal of Emotional Abuse, 1*(1), 27–58.

Hart, S. N., & Brassard, M. R. (1987). A major threat to children's mental health: Psychological maltreatment. *American Psychologist, 42,* 160–165.

Hart, S. N., & Brassard, M. R. (1991). Psychological maltreatment: Progress achieved. *Development and Psychopathology, 3,* 61–70.

Hart, S. N., & Brassard, M. R. (1991, 2001). Definition of psychological maltreatment. Indianapolis: Office for the Study of the Psychological Rights of the Child. Indiana University School of Education.

Hart, S. N., Brassard, M. R., Binggeli, N. J., & Davidson, H. A. (2002). Psychological maltreatment. In J. E. B. Myers, L. Berliner, J. Briere, C. T. Hendrix, C. Jenny, & T. A. Reid (Eds.), *The APSAC handbook on child maltreatment* (2nd ed., pp. 79–103). Thousand Oaks, CA: Sage.

Hart, S., Brassard, M., Davidson, H., Rivelis, E., Diaz, V., & Binggeli, N. (2011). Psychological maltreatment, In J. Myers (Ed.), *The APSAC handbook on child maltreatment* (pp. 125–144). Los Angeles, CA: Sage.

Hart, S. N., Germain, R., & Brassard, M. R. (1987). The challenge: To better understand and combat psychological maltreatment of children and youth. In M. R. Brassard, R. Germain, & S. N. Hart (Eds.), *Psychological maltreatment of children and youth* (pp. 3–24). New York, NY: Pergamon Press.

Hemenway, D., Solnick, S., & Carter, J. (1994). Child-rearing violence. *Child Abuse & Neglect, 18,* 1011–1020.

Hibbard, R., Barlow, J., & MacMillan, H. (2012). Psychological maltreatment. *Pediatrics (UK), 130*(2), 372–378 (0031–4005).

Hickcox, A., & Furnell, J. R. G. (1989). Psychosocial and background factors in emotional abuse of children. *Child: Care, Health and Development, 15,* 227–240.

Hildyard, K. L., & Wolfe, D. A. (2002). Child neglect: Developmental issues and outcomes. *Child Abuse & Neglect, 26,* 679–695.

Hinchey, F. S., & Gavelek, J. R. (1982). Empathic responding in children of battered women. *Child Abuse and Neglect, 6,* 395–401.

Holden, G. W., Geffne, R., & Jouriles, E. N. (1998). *Children exposed to marital violence: Theory, research, and applied issues.* Washington, DC: American Psychological Association.

Iwaniec, D. (1997). Evaluating parent training for emotionally abusive and neglectful parents: Comparing individual versus individual and group practice. *Research on Social Work Practice, 7*(3), 329–349.

Iwaniec, D., Larkin, E., & Higgins, S. (2006). Research review: Risks and resilience in cases of emotional abuse. *Child & Family Social Work, 11,* 73–82.

Johnson, J. G., Cohen, P., & Smailes, E. M. (2001). Childhood verbal abuse and risk for personality disorders during adolescence and early adulthood. *Comprehensive Psychiatry, 42,* 16–23.

Kantor, G. K., & Little, L. (2003). Defining the boundaries of child neglect: When does domestic violence equate with parental failure to protect? *Journal of Interpersonal Violence, 18,* 338–355.

Kendall-Tackett, K. A., & Eckenrode, J. (1996). The effects of neglect on academic achievement and disciplinary problems: A developmental perspective. *Child Abuse & Neglect, 20,* 161–169.

Kent, A., & Waller, G. (2000). Childhood emotional abuse and eating psychopathology. *Clinical Psychology Review, 20,* 887–903.

Korbin, J. E., Coulton, C. J., Lindstrom-Ufuti, H., & Spilsbury, J. (2000). Neighborhood views on the definition and etiology of child maltreatment. *Child Abuse & Neglect, 24*(12), 1509–1527.

Kotch, J. B., Lewis, T., Hussey, J. M., English, D., Thompson, R., Litrownik, A.J., . . ., Dubowitz, H. (2008). Importance of early neglect for childhood aggression. *Pediatrics, 121,* 725–731.

Kurtz, P. D., Gaudin, J. M., Wodarski, J. S., & Howing, P. T. (1993). Maltreatment and the school-aged child: School performance consequences. *Child Abuse & Neglect, 17*(5), 581–589.

Levin, A., & Mills, L. G. (2003). Fighting for child custody when domestic violence is at issue: A survey of state laws and a call for more research. *Social Work, 48*(4), 463–470.

Lewin, D., & Herron, H. (2007). Signs, symptoms, and risk factors: Health visitors' perspectives of child neglect. *Child Abuse Review, 16*(2), 93–107.

Liss, M. B., & Stably, G. B. (1993). Domestic violence and child custody. In M. Hansen & M. Harway (Eds.), *Battering and family therapy: A feminist perspective* (pp. 175–187). Newbury Park, CA: Sage.

Loring, M. T. (1997). *Stories from the heart: Case studies of emotional abuse.* Amsterdam, Netherlands: Harwood Academic Publishers.

Lounds, J. J., Borkowski, J. G., & Whitman, T. L. (2006). The potential for child neglect: The case of adolescent mothers and their children. *Child Maltreatment, 11*(3), 281–294.

Margolin, G., & Vickerman, K. A. (2007). Post-traumatic, stress in children and adolescents exposed to family violence: I. Overview and issues. *Professional Psychology: Research and Practice, 38,* 613–619.

Marshall, W. L. (1996). Assessment, treatment and theorising about sex offenders: Developments during the past twenty years and future directions. *Criminal Justice and Behaviour, 23*(1), 162–199.

Mbilinyi, L. F., Edleson, J. L., Hagemeister, A. K., & Beeman, S. K. (2007). What happens to children when their mothers are battered? Results from a four city anonymous telephone survey. *Journal of Family Violence, 22,* 309–317.

McDonald, R., Jouriles, E. N., Ramisetty, M. S., Caetano, R., & Green, C. E. (2006). Estimating the number of children living in partner-violent families. *Journal of Family Psychology, 20*(1), 137–142.

McGee, R. A., & Wolfe, D. A. (1991). Psychological maltreatment: Toward an operational definition. *Development and Psychopathology, 3,* 3–18.

Mezey, N. J., Post, L. A., & Maxwell, C. D. (2002). Redefining intimate partner violence: Women's experience with physical violence and non-physical abuse by age. *International Journal of Sociology and Social Policy, 22*(7/8), 122–154.

Miller-Perrin, C. L., & Perrin, R. D. (2007). *Child maltreatment: An introduction* (2nd ed.). Thousand Oaks, CA: Sage.

Mitchell, G. (2009). Toxic parenting: How parents and other carers can harm children without laying a hand on them. *Recent Advances in Paediatrics, 25,* 43–64.

Moreau, R., & Yousafzai, S. (2006). A war on schoolgirls. *Newsweek, 147*(26), 34–35.

Murphey, D. A., & Braner, M. (2000). Linking child maltreatment retrospectively to birth and home visit records: An initial examination. *Child Welfare, 79,* 711–729.

Oddone-Paolucci, E., Genius, M., & Violato, C. (2000). A meta-analysis of the published research on the effects of pornography. In *The changing family and child development* (pp. 48–55). Aldershot, UK: Ashgate.

Osofsky, J. D. (1999). The impact if violence on children. *Future of Children, 9*(3), 33–49.

Pagelow, M. D. (1993). Justice for victims of spouse abuse in divorce and child custody cases. *Violence and Victims, 8,* 69–83.

Pecora, P., Whittaker, J., Maluccio, A., & Barth, R. (2000). *The child welfare challenge.* New York, NY: Aldine de Gruyter.

Perry, B. D. (2002). Childhood experience and the expression of genetic potential: What childhood neglect tells us about nature and nurture. *Brain and Mind, 3,* 79–100.

Pollak, S. D., Cicchetti, D., Hornung, K., & Reed, A. (2000). Recognizing emotion in faces: Developmental effects of child abuse and neglect. *Developmental Psychology, 36,* 679–688.

Radke-Yarrow, M., & Klimes-Dougan, B. (2002). Parental depression and offspring disorders: A developmental perspective. In S. H. Goodman & I. H. Gotlib (Eds.), *Children of depressed parents: Mechanism of risk and implications for treatment* (pp. 155–173). Washington, DC: American Psychological Association.

Reyome, N. D. (2010). Childhood emotional maltreatment and later intimate relationships: Themes from the empirical literature. *Journal of Aggression, Maltreatment & Trauma, 19,* 224–242.

Riggs, S., & Kaminski, P. (2010). Childhood emotional abuse, adult attachment, and depression as predictors of relational adjustment and psychological aggression. *Journal of Aggression, Maltreatment & Trauma, 19*(4), 75–104.

Roscoe, B., Peterson, K. L., & Shaner, J. M. (1983). Guidelines to assist educators in identifying children of neglect. *Education, 103,* 395–398.

Saunders, B. E., Berliner, L., & Hanson, R. F. (Eds.). (2004). *Child physical and sexual abuse: Guidelines for treatment* (Revised Report: April 26, 2004). Charleston, SC: National Crime Victims Research and Treatment Center.

Schatz, J. N. (2006). Preventing child maltreatment. In J. G. Borkowski & C.M. Weaver (Eds.), *The culture of prevention: Using science and art to promote healthy child and adolescent development* (pp. 83–112). Baltimore, MD: Paul H. Brooks.

Schneider, M. W., Ross, A., Graham, J. C., & Zielinski, A. (2005). Do allegations of emotional maltreatment predict developmental outcomes beyond that of other forms of maltreatment? *Child Abuse & Neglect, 29,* 513–532.

Sedlak, A. J. (1997). Risk factors for the occurrence of child abuse and neglect. *Journal of Aggression, Maltreatment, & Trauma, 1,* 149–187.

Sedlak, A. J., Mettenburg, J., Basena, M., Petta, I., McPherson, K., Greene, A., & Li, S. (2010). *Fourth National Incidence Study of Child Abuse and Neglect (NIS–4): Report to Congress.* Washington, DC: U.S. Department of Health and Human Services, Administration for Children and Families.

Shonkoff, J. P., & Phillips, D. A. (2000). *From neurons to neighborhoods: The science of early childhood development.* Washington, DC: National Academy Press.

Slack, K. S., Holl, J. L., McDaniel, M., Yook, J., & Bolger, K. (2004). Understanding the risks of child neglect: An exploration of poverty and parenting characteristics. *Child Maltreatment, 9,* 395–408.

Solomon, C. R., & Serres, F. (1999). Effects of parental verbal aggression on children's self-esteem and school marks. *Child Abuse Neglect, 23,* 339–351.

Straus, M. A., & Field, C. J. (2003). Psychological aggression by American parents: National data on prevalence, chronicity, and severity. *Journal of Marriage and Family, 65*(4), 795–808.

Straus, M. A., Hamby, S. L., Finkelhor, D., Moore, D. W., & Runyan, D. (1998). Identification of child maltreatment with the Parent–Child Conflict Tactics Scales; Development and psychometric data for a national sample of American parents. *Child Abuse & Neglect, 22,* 249–270.

Stromwall, L., Larson, N., Nieri, T., Holley, L., Topping, D., Castillo, J., & Ashford, J. (2008). Parents with co-occurring mental health and substance abuse conditions involved in child protection services: Clinical profile and treatment needs. *Child Welfare, 87*(3), 95–113.

Tomison, A. M., & Tucci, J. (1997). Emotional abuse: The hidden form of maltreatment. *Issues in Child Abuse Prevention, 8.* Melbourne, Australia: National Child Protection Clearinghouse. http://www.aifs.org.au/nch/issues8.html

Trickett, P. K., Mennen, F. E., Kim, K., & Sang, J. (2009). Emotional abuse in a sample of multiply maltreated, urban young adolescents: Issue of definition and identification. *Child Abuse and Neglect, 33,* 27–35.

Tyler, S., Allison, K., & Winsler, A. (2006). Child neglect: Developmental consequences, intervention, and policy implications. *Child & Youth Care Forum, 35*(1), 1–20.

U.S. Department of Health and Human Services (DHHS). (2007). *Funding opportunity: Using comprehensive family assessment to improve child welfare outcomes* [Funding Opportunity Number HHS-2007-ACF-ACYF-CA-0023; CFDA Number 93.670]. Washington, DC: U.S. Government Printing Office.

U.S. Department of Health and Human Services (DHHS), Administration on Children, Youth and Families. (1998). Child maltreatment 1996: Reports from the states to the National Child. Washington, DC: U.S. Government Printing Office.

U.S. Department of Health and Human Services (DHHS), Administration on Children, Youth and Families. (2005). *Child maltreatment 2003.* Washington, DC: U.S. Government Printing Office.

U.S. Department of Health and Human Services (DHHS), Administration on Children, Youth and Families. (2010). *Child maltreatment 2008.* Washington, DC: U.S. Government Printing Office.

U.S. Department of Health and Human Services (DHHS), Administration for Children and Families, Administration on Children, Youth and Families, Children's Bureau. (2011). *Child maltreatment 2010.* Washington, DC: U.S. Government Printing Office.

U.S. Government Accountability Office. (2011). Child maltreatment: Strengthening national data on child fatalities could aid in prevention. http://www.gao.gov/assets/330/320774.pdf

Vissing, Y. M., Straus, M. A., Gelles, R. J., & Harrop, J. W. (1991). Verbal aggression by parents and psychosocial problems of children. *Child Abuse & Neglect, 15,* 223–238.

Weaver, J. D. (2011). The principle of subsidiarity applied: Reforming the legal framework to capture the psychological abuse of children. *Virginia Journal of Social Policy and the Law, 18,* 247–318.

Wekerle, C., Leung, E., Wall, A. M., MacMillan, H., Boyle, M., Trocmé, N., & Waechter, R. (2009). The contribution of childhood emotional abuse to teen dating violence among child protective services involved youth. *Child Abuse and Neglect, 33,* 45–58.

Whitman, T. L., Borkowski, J. G., Keogh, D., & Weed, K. (2001). *Interwoven lives: Adolescent mothers and their children.* Mahwah, NJ: Lawrence Erlbaum Associates.

Wolfe, D. A., Crooks, C. V., Lee, V., McIntyre-Smith, A., & Jaffe, P. G. (2003). The effects of children's exposure to domestic violence: A meta-analysis and critique. *Clinical Child and Family Psychology Review, 6,* 171–187.

Wright, M. O., Crawford, E., & Del Castillo, D. (2009). Childhood emotional maltreatment and later psychological distress among college students: The mediating role of maladaptive schemas. *Child Abuse & Neglect, 33,* 59–68.

Yates, T. M. (2007). The developmental consequences of child emotional abuse: A neurodevelopmental perspective. *Journal of Emotional Abuse, 7*(2), 9–34.

Zeanah, C. H., Egger, H. L., Smyke, A. T., Nelson, C. A., Fox, N. A., Marshall, P. J., & Guthrie, D. (2009). Institutional rearing and psychiatric disorders in Romanian preschool children. *American Journal of Psychiatry, 166,* 777–785.

Zeanah, C. H., Nelson, C. A., Fox, N. A., Smyke, A. T., Marshall, P., Parker, S. W., & Koga, S. (2003). Designing research to study the effects of institutionalization on brain and behavioral development: The Bucharest Early Intervention Project. *Development and Psychopathology, 15,* 885–907.

Zolotor, A. J., Theodore, A. D., Coyne-Beasley, T., & Runyan, D. K. (2007, September 11). Intimate partner violence and child maltreatment: Overlapping risk. *Brief Treatment and Crisis Intervention: A Journal of Evidence-Based Practice.* 10.1093/brief-treatment/mhm021

Zuravin, S. J. (1999). Child neglect: A review of definitions and measurement research. In H. Dubowitz (Ed.). *Neglected children: Research, practice and policy* (pp. 24–46). Thousand Oaks, CA: Sage.

Section III

Investigation and Substantiation of Child Maltreatment

The main goal of this section is to provide professionals with guidelines on how to investigate and gather evidence to substantiate child maltreatment. In the *Investigation of Maltreatment* chapter, a framework and specific steps for evaluating the validity of a maltreatment report are provided. Specific techniques for investigating each type of maltreatment, examining the child, and differentiating injuries caused by nonaccidental versus accidental means are explained. As testimony is a key element in the investigation, the *Interviewing* chapter describes the conduct and content of the fact-finding interview. Additionally, it reviews advantages and disadvantages of various techniques that have been used to elicit recall for maltreatment and provides recommendations for best practices in interviewing.

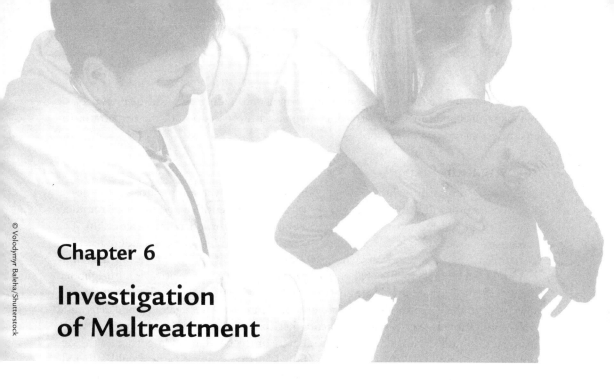

Chapter 6

Investigation of Maltreatment

In this chapter, we focus on investigations of maltreatment overseen by child protective services (CPS), often in conjunction with law enforcement officers and other agencies as part of the multidisciplinary team (MDT). The advantage of using the MDT over solitary investigation is that the former ensures that each case is given full consideration. As stated by Pence (2011), "The MDT's wealth of training, experience, and perspectives leads to increased accuracy in decision making, better evidence collection and stronger accountability for offenders" (p. 326). The overall goal of an investigation is to obtain sufficient forensic evidence from a variety of sources to document, based on agency guidelines and state laws, the existence and severity of maltreatment and/or risk of future maltreatment. Evidence often consists of reports from CPS workers and the police (when available), testimony by direct and indirect witnesses (e.g., the victim, parents, neighbors), and examination reports by medical and psychological personnel, used in concert to confirm or refute suspicions of maltreatment reported to the abuse hotline or to police.

Most states rely on a two-tier system (substantiated/unsubstantiated or founded/unfounded) or three-tier system (substantiated/indicated/unsubstantiated) in making the final determination for a particular case. An investigation will help CPS workers consider which risk factors may be present that increase chances for maltreatment and evaluate the situation. A risk assessment includes examining risk factors, special risk factors (e.g., substance abuse, domestic violence), past and present actions to protect the child, and protective factors (i.e., family's strengths and resources, available resources of CPS and community agencies). Finally, the investigator must decide how to proceed once the maltreatment and/or risk is verified, such as keeping the child in the home with family services provided by CPS or its community partners to reduce risk and ensure safety, or removing the child or the perpetrator combined with prosecution of the perpetrator for maltreatment, among other options.

Investigation Plan

The investigation plan includes several components. First, the investigator should devise an interview protocol in which the relevant witnesses are identified and the order for interviewing them is determined (see the *Interviewing* chapter for a detailed description). The investigator should also obtain testimony from various professionals, including teachers, pediatricians, and police officers who responded to the 911 call or intake call, as well as community members, such as babysitters and other caretakers, relatives, and neighbors. Second, the investigator should arrange to observe individual family members while they are interacting in the home and in the neighborhood. Third, the investigator should determine which professionals (e.g., physicians, mental health counselors) are needed to help verify maltreatment and to gauge the risk to and safety of the child, including whether the victim should remain in the current care situation. Fourth, the investigator should gather all relevant secondary or supportive data, such as academic reports, pediatric health records, the report from the current medical examination (if conducted), police reports, and so on. Fifth, the investigator should develop different hypotheses corresponding to alternative, plausible explanations for the injuries and behaviors that led to the report of suspected maltreatment. Sixth, the investigator should analyze all data to assess which hypothesis is best supported in an effort to make a determination whether the maltreatment claim is valid and substantiated (i.e., is there credible evidence of maltreatment and/or risk of future maltreatment?), while ensuring that this process is performed within the required time frame allowed by the state (which varies and could be 30, 60, or 90 days). Finally, the last stage in the investigation, known as closure, will vary. In some situations, the case is closed immediately. In other cases, the family is monitored for a short time while intervention is provided and then the case is closed. In still other instances, the case remains open while the child either remains at home or is removed from the home, and the family is monitored and given services. Such a case may proceed to family court for civil remedy, but sometimes is also processed criminally. Only after all these steps are complete is the case closed.

Observations

Part of the process of gathering adequate information includes the caseworker's responsibility to observe the identified child alone as well as while the child interacts with peers, with other family members, and in different environments (e.g., home, school, neighborhood). Specific foci for observation include the physical condition of the child, the emotional status of the child, the reactions of the parents to the agency's concerns, the emotional and behavioral reactions during interviewing, the physical condition of the home, and the climate of the neighborhood.

The caseworker should visually examine the child physically, to determine if maltreatment is visible, as well as behaviorally and emotionally, to ascertain observable signs of maltreatment (e.g., fear, nervousness). In the case of physical abuse and neglect that have resulted in injury or physical malady, caseworkers should ask children to raise their sleeves or lift their shirts so as to make a better assessment. Before and after the interview, caseworkers should observe child victims' interactions with toys during play (or note the lack thereof) both inside and outside of the home, alone, and with others to determine if their behaviors and reactions are appropriate for their age and developmental stage.

Caseworkers should also observe parents' and caregivers' verbal and nonverbal interactions with the child victims and others in the home. During the interview process, caseworkers should note emotional reactions and behavioral signs of child victims, parents/caregivers, siblings, and others in the home, particularly in light of the concerns being raised. The home environment and neighborhood should be assessed in terms of cleanliness, potential hazards, danger signs related to drug and alcohol use, violence, and accessibility for communication and public transportation.

Pitfalls of the Investigation

Investigations of child maltreatment are vulnerable to three pitfalls. The first prospective obstacle is that each professional member of the MDT has a different perspective and legal mandate, which may sometimes result in turf battles. The team approach to the investigation should reduce the problems associated with this issue, as the collective goal should be to ensure the child's safety and welfare. The second potential impediment is that interviewers often have a confirmation bias when asking and interpreting questions (i.e., the answers confirm their preconceived notions), blinding them from considering other possibilities outside of their working hypothesis of maltreatment. For this reason, it is critical that the investigator develop more than one hypothesis for the data, including alternative explanations of nonabuse. Examples of nonabusive hypotheses include accidental and medical causes for bruises, rather than physical abuse, or the parent's experiencing of an unexpected medical condition emergency, such as a seizure, rather than willful neglect. The third possible problem is known as source monitoring bias. In other words, some interviewers may not differentiate between what they were told, heard, or inferred and what the child actually experienced.

Possible solutions for these issues involve ensuring the MDT has the appropriate training and experience, which should result in enhanced listening skills for the interviewer. In addition, a recording device may be used during the interview; the recording can then be viewed or heard later and transcribed as a means of increasing the accuracy of the report.

Investigation of Child Physical Abuse

CPS investigators must consider the possibility that a physical injury or marking on the child may have occurred in a nonabusive manner. During the data-gathering phases of the investigation, explanations of the physical findings will likely be given by the child, other witnesses, and the suspected perpetrator. Three questions must be considered in making the determination of abuse versus nonabuse:

- *Is an explanation provided?* Some suspected offenders choose not to explain, as a way of denying responsibility or hiding abuse. In some cases, a simple examination of the injury may show that the bruise or burn is of a particular shape.
- *Is the explanation plausible?* In other words, is the explanation consistent with the injury or marking? It is important to consider the child's age and developmental ability in determining plausibility of the explanation, often in light of medical professional's opinion and examination of the child.
- *Was there a delay in medical care?* Oftentimes, abusers fail to obtain or will delay medical care as a way of denying the injury's seriousness, hoping that it will heal on its own, or as a means of covering it up, including avoiding the child's pediatrician or going to different urgent care or emergency room facilities.

According to Reece (2004), physicians must determine the source of a child's injuries using a variety of factors. The first step is to rule out pathologic and accidental causes of physical findings (see Tables 6-1 and 6-2). Physicians make this determination by learning about the social context surrounding the injury, listening to the explanations given by different witnesses/reports, and considering the reporters' biases and motives. Next, they should conduct a thorough physical examination (e.g., assess the presenting injury, past injuries in healing stages, patterns in injury, multiplanar injuries, assault-location of injury), keeping in mind the age and developmental capacity of the child and his or her general well-being. It is recommended that physicians include an assessment of the scalp, ears (i.e., tympanic membranes, auricles), mouth (i.e., frenulum), abdomen (particularly all hollow organs), and inner arms and legs. If suspicious findings emerge, physicians

Table 6-1 Physical findings that may be confused with physical abuse

Examination findings in newborns that are due to birth trauma

- Facial or other petechiae[1] or bruises up to one week after birth
- Skull fractures
- Clavicle fractures
- Erb's palsy due to positioning of the child's arm during birth
- Retinal hemorrhages may be normal up to six weeks

Examination findings in infants through adolescents

- Congenital pigmented lesions (Mongolian blue spots[2])
- Bruising due to other causes (hematologic disorders[3] or syndromes such as Ehlers-Danlos syndrome[4])

[1] Small dots indicative of bleeding under the skin.
[2] Birthmarks that are common in persons of African, Asian, and East Indian descent.
[3] Disorders that primarily affect the blood.
[4] A disorder that affects connective tissues (i.e., blood vessel walls, joints, and skin).
Botash (2005-2013), Appendix G. Reprinted with permission.

Table 6-2 Clinical findings leading to differential diagnosis by test

Clinical findings	Differential diagnosis	Differential tests
Ocular findings		
Retinal hemorrhage[1]	Shaking or other trauma	
	Bleeding disorder	Coagulation studies
	Neoplasm	
	Resuscitation	History
Conjunctival hemorrhage[2]	Trauma	Culture, Gram stain[3]
	Bacterial or viral conjunctivitis[4]	History
	Severe coughing	
Orbital swelling[5]	Trauma	
	Orbital or periorbital cellulitis[6]	Complete blood count, culture, sinus radiographs
	Metastatic disease[7]	Radiograph, CT scan, CNS examination
	Epidural hematoma[8]	Radiograph, CT scan, CNS examination
Sudden Infant Death Syndrome	Unexplained death	Autopsy
	Trauma	Autopsy
	Asphyxial[9] (including, aspiration, nasal obstruction, laryngospasm, sleep apnea[10])	"Near-miss" history
		Cultures, bacterial and viral
	Infection (e.g., botulism[11])	Immunoglobulins
	Immunodeficiency	Autopsy
	Cardiac arrhythmia	Electrolytes, ACTH stimulation test
	Hypoadrenalism[12]	Ca^{++}, Mg^{++}, other
	Metabolic abnormality	
	Hypersensitivity to cow's milk protein	

[1] Bleeding in the retina (the membrane along the back of the eye).
[2] Bleeding in the transparent tissue covering the whites of the eyes.
[3] A procedure in which dye is used to enhance the clarity of the microscopic image.
[4] Inflammation of the clear membrane covering the whites of the eye and lining the eyelids (also known as pink eye), caused by virus or bacteria.
[5] Swelling of the eye.
[6] Infection of the eyelid or skin surrounding the eye. Symptoms include redness around the eye or in the whites of the eyes and swelling of the eyelid.
[7] Cancer, typically associated with cancer in other organs. Intraocular metastasis affects the optic nerve, the macula, and the anterior part of the eye.
[8] Bleeding leads to accumulation of blood between the skull and dura mater (the thick membrane that covers the brain). Symptoms include brief loss of consciousness, and the bleeding may result in a coma.
[9] Lack of oxygen caused by interruption to respiration.
[10] A sleep disorder in which breathing in temporarily, but repeatedly, interrupted (i.e., stops and starts).
[11] A serious illness resulting in paralysis, caused by a nerve toxin being ingesting or entering the body through open wounds.
[12] Impaired adrenal gland function. The adrenal gland regulates metabolic function, particularly hormone production and distribution.
Notes: ACTH = adrenocorticotropic hormone; CNS = central nervous system; CT = computed tomography.
Botash (2005–2013), Appendix H. Reprinted with permission.

should order and examine laboratory and imaging results (i.e., bone x-rays, magnetic resonance imaging [MRI], computed tomography [CT] scan), and review the child's medical history (specifically, nutritional status and growth parameters indicated in pediatric examination records and notes) and changes in that history by the caregivers. Next, physicians should produce differential diagnoses accounting for the injury (nonabusive versus abusive probabilities). Sometimes the history is absent, inconsistent, or not a logical mechanism for the injury (e.g., it is impossible for trauma to occur in that fashion, the child is not developmentally advanced enough to self-inflict injury, there is no evidence for medical explanation, such as illness or genetic condition, no corroboration is available). Finally, the physician should examine the evidence provided by law enforcement or social services personnel (also see recommendations made in Injury Surveillance Workgroup, 2003, 2007, 2008).

Abusive Head Injuries

The leading causes of head injuries in children are accidents due to motor vehicle crashes and falls and, secondarily, abuse (Centers for Disease Control and Prevention, 1997, 2010; Dennison & Pokras, 2000). Abusive head injuries, particularly in infants younger than 1 year of age (Agran, Anderson, Winn, Trent, Walton-Haynes, & Thayer, 2003; Alexander, Levitt, & Smith, 2001), commonly present with subtle subacute or chronic symptoms (e.g., vomiting, lethargy, irritability, increasing head circumference without visible trauma) or acute critical illness (e.g., unresponsiveness, apnea, seizures, slow heart rate [bradycardia], cardiopulmonary arrest, respiratory distress) that may result in morbidity (e.g., severe, permanent brain injury) and death (Bishop, 2006; Christian, Block, & Committee on Child Abuse and Neglect, 2009; Covington, Foster, & Rich, 2005; Duhaime, 2008; Heron, Hoyert, Murphy, Xu, Kochankek, & Tejada-Vera, 2009; Hoyert, Heron, Murphy, & Kung, 2006; Kung, Hoyert, Xu, & Murphy, 2008; Parks, Kegler, Annest, & Mercy, 2012; Parks, Sugerman, Xu, & Coronado, 2012). Infants and toddlers may present to the physician with nonaccidental head injury or abusive head trauma (previously called "shaken baby syndrome") when they have been subjected to severe shaking or impact against a hard surface (Barlow & Minns, 2000; Chiesa & Duhaime, 2009; Dennison & Pokras, 2000; Dias, Smith, DeGuehery, Mazur, Li, & Shaffer, 2005; Duhaime, Alario, Lewander, Schut, Sutton, Seidl, et al., 1992). The severe shaking (forceful, jerking, side-to-side or up-and-down motions) and sudden deceleration (abrupt stopping) causes the infant's brain to move quickly inside the skull, with his or her breathing then shutting down (Barlow & Minns, 2000; Barlow, Thomson, Johnson, & Minns, 2005; Bishop, 2006). Further brain damage is caused by the concomitant stretching and tearing of the brain tissue and blood vessels, continued oxygen deprivation due to damage to the respiratory center of the brain, and the breakdown of the dying brain cells (Eisele, Kegler, Trent, & Coronado, 2006; Reece, 2011).

Children who have inflicted head trauma usually also have specific external injuries (Annest et al., 2008; Jayawant et al., 1998; Keenan, Runyan, Marshall, Nocera, Merten, & Sinal, 2003; Parks et al., 2012; Parks, Sugerman, et al., 2012; Reece, 2011; Sirotnak &

Krugman, 1994), including scalp bruising, lacerations, ecchymoses (skin hemorrhages), subscapular hematoma (bleeding under the scalp outside the skull), subgaleal hematomas (intracranial bleeding), skull fractures, subarachnoid hemorrhages (bleeding between the brain and the tissues covering it), subdural hematomas (breaks in the brain's blood vessels), cerebral edema (extra fluid in the tissues), increased head circumference, or a bulging fontanelle (the soft spot in an infant's skull). They may also experience a change in mental status, white matter injuries, hypoxic brain injuries, and parenchymal brain injuries (concussion caused by impact of the moving head on a rigid surface). Certain characteristics coexist with abusive head trauma, including retinal hemorrhages (i.e., burst blood vessels in the retina), intracranial trauma, diffuse axonal injury (tearing of the long nerve axons), secondary cerebral edema (brain swelling), and rib and skull fractures (i.e., posterior and anterolateral ribs, metaphyseal). Retinal hemorrhages, especially those that are high in number (e.g., 20 to 30), are extensive, and involve multiple layers of the retina, are often present in abuse (Reece, 2011). Moreover, many victims of abusive head trauma (up to 90%) present with retinal hemorrhages; such bleeding does not occur in accidental trauma and is not the result of cardiopulmonary resuscitation or seizures (Duhaime et al., 1992; Reece, 2011). Additionally, the child may have periorbital bruising (black eye) indicative of globe injury or orbital fracture and bruising of the pinna (outer ear) suggestive of serious ear trauma (Duhaime et al., 1992; Duhaime, 2008; Sirotnak & Krugman, 1994).

Physicians who suspect head trauma in children younger than age 2 years should use a head CT scan to assess soft-tissue and brain injury with acute blood accumulation, scalp swelling, complex or depressed skull fractures, or injury to the face; this imaging modality may be supplemented by ultrasound imaging to assess the anterior fontanelle or by plain skull films to assess any small fractures in the same plane as the imaging beam (American College of Radiology, 1997; Bishop, 2006). To evaluate for subacute or chronic injury, a head MRI offers a complete soft-tissue image of the brain and should be performed if the head CT is positive or if it is negative but accompanied by two or more fractures without history (e.g., medically relevant or accidental explanation). Skull fractures that are multiple, are bilateral, or cross suture lines are most consistent with abuse. Dating of skull fractures is difficult because they do not show typical radiological signs of healing. If head trauma presents with bleeding (e.g., petechiae, retinal hemorrhages), then the physician should request the following lab tests: complete blood count,[1] prothrombin,[2] partial thromboplastin time,[3] and platelet count.[4] To identify retinal hemorrhages presenting with intracranial bleeding or when abuse is suspected, it is recommended that retinal examinations be performed by an

---

[1] A complete blood count assesses the number and average size of red and white blood cells, the amount of hemoglobin, and the fraction of red blood cells and hemoglobin in the blood.

[2] The prothrombin test assesses clotting of blood to determine if it is normal.

[3] Partial thromboplastin time assesses the amount of time it takes for the blood to clot, in case the individual has a bleeding disorder.

[4] A platelet count assesses the number of platelets in the blood; these cells are needed for clotting.

ophthalmologist. In contrast, children who have accidental head and birth injuries may have the following symptoms: multiple lesions; intracranial epidural hematomas; simple linear skull fractures; diffuse, severe brain injury (due to deceleration forces to the head either with or without head impact); or asymptomatic subdural hematomas (SDH) in the posterior fossa and in the occipital lobe following labor (which resolves between 1 and 3 months after birth).

Abdominal Injuries

Abusive abdominal injuries may present with bruising, fever, vomiting, hematuria (blood in the urine), abdominal pain, tenderness and distention accompanied by the absence of bowel sounds signifying dysfunction, shock, neurological impairment, and low red blood count (Sirotnak & Krugman, 1994). Table 6-3 provides a list of clinical findings and their associated abdominal injury diagnoses. Approximately 40% to 50% of abusive abdominal injuries result in child fatalities due to blood loss and sepsis, typically bacterial infection from the perforation (Child Welfare Information Gateway, 2011; Reece, 2011; Schnitzer, Covington, Wirtz, Verhoek-Oftedahl, & Palusci, 2008).

According to Ledbetter, Hatch, Feldman, Fligner, and Tapper (1988), abusive abdominal injuries should be suspected in very young children (e.g., preschoolers) who (1) have little history to account for the injury (e.g., motor vehicle accident, falls); (2) were given delayed medical treatment; (3) had injuries involving hollow organs rather than solid organs (e.g., the small intestine rather than the liver); and (4) suffered injuries resulting in a high mortality rate (53%). A CT scan or ultrasound (rather than plain film) should be used to determine whether the intra-abdominal injury resulted in free fluid or blood, which organ was injured, and the extent of the injury.

Throat Injuries

Abusive injuries may occur to the pharynx, back of the throat, trachea, and esophagus due to traumatic insertion of objects, such as a fork or spoon. Oropharynx injuries may include tears in the frenulum (the mucous membrane under the tongue that attaches it to the mouth floor) and dental trauma (Sirotnak & Krugman, 1994). According to Reece (2011), throat injuries symptoms include "vomiting blood, coughing, gagging, poor feeding, respiratory distress, cyanosis,[5] and fever" (p. 189). Physicians must obtain history to determine whether these injuries are consistent with accident or abuse.

Thoracic (Chest) Injuries

Young children who present with rib fractures are likely to be victims of abuse, particularly when no accident is confirmed and the injuries occur in both the anterior (front) and posterior (back) rather than laterally (left or right side of the abdomen) (Reece, 2011). Rib fractures are highly unlikely to occur during birth (Reece, 2002). When the abuser grabs a

---

[5] A bluish discoloration of the skin and mucous membranes caused by lack of oxygen.

Table 6-3 Clinical findings leading to differential diagnosis for abdominal injuries

Clinical findings	Differential diagnosis	Differential tests
Acute abdomen	Trauma	Rule out other disease
	Intrinsic gastrointestinal disease (e.g., peritonitis, obstruction, inflammatory bowel disease, Meckel's diverticulum[1])	Radiographs, stool tests, and others
	Intrinsic urinary tract disease (infection, stone)	Culture, ultrasound, intravenous pyelogram (x-ray exam of kidneys, bladder, and ureters)
	Genital problems (e.g., torsion of spermatic cord, ovarian cyst)	History, physical examination, ultrasound, radiograph, laparoscopy (surgical procedure to insert thin tube into incision in abdominal wall)
	Vascular accident, as in sickle cell crisis	Angiography, sickle cell studies
	Other: mesenteric adenitis (inflammation of lymph nodes), strangulated hernia (blood supply to organ inhibited), anaphylactoid purpura (inflamed blood vessels resulting in a rash and pain in the joints and stomach), pulmonary disease (lung disorder), pancreatitis (inflammation of pancreas), lead poisoning, diabetes	As appropriate
Hematuria	Trauma	Rule out other disease
	Urinary tract infection	Culture
	Acute or chronic forms of glomerular injury (e.g., glomerulonephritis, in which kidneys fail to filter toxins)	Renal function tests, biopsy
	Hereditary or familial renal disorders (e.g., familial benign recurrent hematuria—a kidney disease that causes blood to appear in the urine)	History
	Other: vasculitis (inflammation of blood vessels), thrombosis (blood clot in vessel), neoplasm (abnormal tissue mass/tumor), bacteremia (bacterial blood infection), may be caused by anomalies, stones, or exercise)	History, cultures, radiologic studies

[1] A bulge on the lower wall of intestine accompanied by stomach pain and bloody stools.

Botash (2005–2013), Appendix H. Reprinted with permission.

child just below the arms and squeezes his or her chest, rib fractures occur bilaterally and near the child's spine, but may be difficult to detect without a bone scanning imaging technique.

Blunt trauma does not always result in bruising, but the child may develop costo-chondral tenderness (due to inflammation in the cartilage around the ribcage) or a chest deformity (Sirotnak & Krugman, 1994). Typically, the ribs are not displaced or fragmented, nor do they show external signs of trauma. Direct blows to the chest may result in cardiac arrest, lacerations, and rupture, as well as bruising of the lung and pneumothorax or collapsed lung (Reece, 2011). Plain films can be used to assess ribs for fractures and lungs for injuries (e.g., pulmonary contusion), but this damage may be undetectable for 7 to 10 days following injury until collus formation occurs. When there is evidence of vessel injury, however, a CT scan should be used to assess chest and abdomen injuries, especially to determine the presence of small pneumothoraces (gas formed in cavity between lung and chest wall that interferes with breathing) and to identify the extent of lung injury.

Skeletal Injuries: Fractures

The American Academy of Pediatrics (1991) recommends that physicians conduct a full skeletal survey in every anatomic region (appendicular and axial skeleton) to detect acute and previous injuries. Scintigraphy (bone scan) can be used to supplement skeletal surveys of infants up to age 12 months or in place of skeletal surveys for children ages 1–5 years (but should be supplemented with skull x-ray for cranial injuries). Plain x-rays are most often used to evaluate significant clinical findings of skeletal injuries, but may be supplemented by CT scans for pelvis injuries. MRI can also be used to evaluate spinal cord injuries.

The American College of Radiology (1997) advises that radiologists include several perspectives to determine whether maltreatment is indicated. Anteroposterior (taken from the front toward the back) images of the appendicular skeleton should include the humeri, forearms, femurs, lower legs, and feet. The oblique (slanted) and posteroanterior (taken from the back toward the front) images of the hands should be included as well. The anteroposterior and lateral images of the axial skeleton should include the thorax, abdomen, lumbar spine, cervical spine, and skull. Frontal projections of each extremity should also be performed. Additionally, two projections of abnormalities and additional views of definite and possible fractures should be made, as well as oblique views when rib or thorax fractures are suspected. When head trauma is suspected, four views of the skull should be made. Physicians should assess unseen and old, healing fractures of all bones and the skull using a bone x-ray. They should perform a CT scan or MRI when skull fracture, bleeding in the eye, severe bruising, neurological symptoms, headaches, and loss of consciousness have occurred.

Bony injuries evolve through four healing stages (Botash, 2005–2013). First, induction occurs within 3 to 7 days and is characterized by inflammation, pain, and soft-tissue swelling. Second, the soft callus state occurs 7 to 10 days after the injury in infants and 10 to

Table 6-4 Three categories of radiological findings due to inflicted skeletal injury

High-specificity injuries	Moderate-specificity fractures	Common, low-specificity fractures
• Classic metaphyseal lesions (CMLs)	• Multiple fractures (especially if bilateral)	• Clavicle fractures,
• Metaphyseal fractures	• Fractures of different ages	• Long-bone shaft fractures
• Rib fractures	• Epiphyseal separations	• Linear skull fractures
• Scapular fractures	• Vertebral body fractures	
• Spinous process fractures	• Digital fractures	
• Sternal fractures	• Complex skull fractures	

Botash (2005–2013). Reprinted with permission.

14 days after the injury in older children. It involves new bone formation (periosteal), with callus formation occurring around the fracture site. Third, the hard callus stage occurs 2 to 3 weeks after injury (peaking in infants between 21 and 42 days); during this stage, union occurs at the fracture site. Fourth, remodeling occurs 3 to 12 months after injury, during which woven bone is converted to lamellar bone and the original bone configuration is restored. A 2-week follow-up skeletal survey is recommended for infants to obtain precise assessment of injuries due to suspected abuse.

Three categories of inflicted fractures are distinguished: low, moderate, and high specificity (Table 6-4). In the absence of accidental history, particularly for infants, the low- and moderate-specificity fractures are classified as highly specific. Inflicted fractures are difficult to distinguish from accidental bone breakage; thus, estimates of abuse average 30% but range from 11% to 55% of all fractures and are as high as 70% in infants due to their limited mobility. Long bone fractures in the arms and legs (i.e., classic metaphyseal lesions [CMLs],[6] also called corner or bucket handle fractures[7]), particularly in children younger than 2 years of age, are often cited as abuse, as such injuries occur when the child's limb is grabbed and jerked or flailed (Kleinman, Marks, Richmond, & Blackbourne, 1995). Although accidental falls from heights of 3 or 4 feet or less may result in fractured collarbones or even simple linear fractures in infants, abuse is suspected in case of humeral and femoral fractures, particularly when the child is younger than 18 months. Additionally, the location of the long bone fracture (e.g., midshaft spiral or transverse of femur) combined with the age and mobility of the child (3-year-old versus 6-month-old) helps differentiate accident from abuse. Table 6-5 provides examples of the various types of diaphyseal fractures that are commonly considered as resulting from accident, as well as characteristics that the physician may use to distinguish among them (Giardino,

---

[6] A planar fracture occurring in the metaphysis (the wide portion of a long bone—part of the growth plate) involving the distal end of one or both femurs (thighs), the proximal and distal tibias (knee and ankle), or proximal humerus (shoulder).

[7] The term "corner fracture" reflects the fact that the corner of the bone is chipped; the "bucket handle" is used because the lesion ends in a crescent shape (the same fragment, but the perceived shape depends on the radiology angle).

Table 6-5 Diaphyseal fractures in children

Causes	Type	Characteristics
Accidental (Uncommon from Abuse)		
Common between the ages of 1 and 3 Occurs with routine play activities. May result from running and slipping, jumping and falling, and even sliding with a difficult landing. There may be a delay in seeking medical care because the injury does not initially appear significant.	Toddler's fracture 	**A nondisplaced spiral fracture of the tibia** Initial radiographs may miss the fracture. The fracture is diagnosed by bone scan at the time of presentation or on plain films repeated in approximately 2 weeks.
Occurs secondary to plasticity of a child's bone Commonly accidental and rarely reported in the abused child.	Greenstick fracture 	**An incomplete fracture** The compressed side of the bone is bowed, but not completely fractured.
Results from forces applied parallel to long axis of the bone Seen in Both Accidental and Nonaccidental Injuries	Impacted fracture Torus (buckle) fracture 	**Involves entire bone** **Localized buckling of the cortex of the bone** Injuries located toward the metaphysis of the bone. Caused by anatomy of the developing bone.
Indirect twisting or torsion forces to the bone May be associated with abusive injuries, primarily in infants and young toddlers. Seen with accidental injury in ambulatory (able to walk) children with a history of twisting injury.	Spiral fracture 	**Fracture line curves around a portion of the bone**

Table 6-5 Diaphyseal fractures in children (*Continued*)

Causes	Type	Characteristics
Indirect twisting forces, similar to spiral fractures	Oblique fracture	Fracture line angled across long axis of the bone
Direct force to bone	Transverse fracture	Fracture line perpendicular to long axis of the bone

Botash (2005–2013), Appendix F. Reprinted with permission.

Christian, & Giardino, 1997). As indicated in Table 6-6, the clinical findings may lead to different diagnoses, depending on evidence from specific tests.

According to Reece (2011, pp. 190–191), the physician should consider nonabusive explanations, such as "accidental trauma, obstetric trauma, prematurity leading to low bond mass (osteopenia), nutritional deficiencies (rickets,[8] scurvy[9]), metabolic disorders, T-cell disease,[10] drug toxicity, infections, neuromuscular disorders, skeletal abnormalities, neoplasms, genetic bone disease, and rare inherited bone disorders, such as osteogenesis imperfecta." Children who have osteogenesis imperfecta present with fractures during accidents that normal children would not incur.

Skin Injuries

To differentiate abuse and accidental infliction resulting in skin injuries (e.g., bruises, burns, bites), both the location and pattern of injuries must be considered. Table 6-7 provides alternative diagnoses and tests to consider for cutaneous lesions (Vandeven & Knight, 2001). One type of skin injury children receive is a bruise, which may occur during the normal course of play and of being active. It is not possible to ascertain the age of bruises by simple observation (Maguire, Mann, Sibert, & Kemp, 2005). Notably, some children are less coordinated than others and may have more bruises, abrasions, and lacerations than their playmates. However, bruising is suspicious in infants and nonmobile children, particularly on the neck, buttocks, and hands (Sugar, Taylor, & Feldman, 1999).

[8] Rickets is a nutritional disease caused by inadequate intake of vitamin D in the diet. It leads to weak, soft bones and slow growth and skeletal development.

[9] Scurvy is a nutritional disease caused by inadequate intake of vitamin C in the diet. It leads to muscle weakness, joint and muscle aches, and tiredness.

[10] A disease involving recurrent infections due to a low T-cell count.

Table 6-6 Clinical findings leading to differential diagnosis for skeletal injuries

Clinical findings	Differential diagnosis	Differential tests
Osseous lesions		
Fractures (multiple or in various stages of healing)	Trauma	
	Osteogenesis imperfecta[1]	Radiographic and blue sclerae[2]
	Rickets	Nutritional history
	Birth trauma	Birth history
	Hypophosphatasia[3]	Decreased alkaline phosphatase
	Leukemia[4]	Complete blood count, bone marrow
	Neuroblastoma[5]	Bone marrow, biopsy
	Status after osteomyelitis[6] or septic arthritis[7]	History
	Neurogenic sensory deficit[8]	Physical examination
Metaphyseal lesions, epiphyseal lesions, or both	Trauma	
	Scurvy	Nutritional history
	Menkes syndrome[9]	Decreased copper, decreased ceruloplasmin
	Syphilis[10]	Serology
	"Little League" elbow[11]	History
	Birth trauma	History
Subperiosteal ossification	Trauma	
	Osteogenic malignancy[12]	Radiograph and biopsy
	Syphilis	Serology tests
	Infantile cortical hyperostosis[13]	No metaphyseal irregularity
	Osteoid osteoma[14]	Response to aspirin
	Scurvy	Nutritional history

[1] A genetic disorder in which the bones easily break with little to no pressure.
[2] A condition in which the outer coat of the eyeball appears blue due to retention of normal fetal transparency (prominent feature of osteogenesis imperfecta).
[3] An inherited metabolic (chemical) bone disorder due to low levels of the enzyme alkaline phosphatase (ALP).
[4] Cancer of the blood-related tissues, particularly the lymphatic system and bone marrow. It begins with destruction of white blood cells.
[5] A rare form of cancer in which a tumor forms from nerve cells (neuroblasts).
[6] Inflammation of the bones due to a bacterial infection, which leads to destruction of bones.
[7] A joint infection (especially of the knees and hips) that is very painful. The infection spreads through the bloodstream from other parts of the body and leads to severe damage to cartilage and bones.
[8] Problems with the senses resulting from injury to the brain or abnormally altered nervous tissue.
[9] A disorder affecting the level of copper in the body, one symptom of which is weak muscle tone.
[10] A sexually transmitted disease caused by bacterial infection, which in the later stages causes irreversible heart and nervous system damage.
[11] A syndrome in which overstress (e.g., repetitive throwing motions) leads to injury of the elbow.
[12] Cancer in the bone, usually in the section where new bone tissue forms (e.g., thigh, upper arm, shin).
[13] A self-limited inflammatory disorder in infants leading to soft-tissue swelling and bone changes.
[14] A noncancerous bone tumor, typically present in the long bones (thigh and leg), which causes dull, aching pain.

Botash (2005-2013), Appendix H. Reprinted with permission.

Table 6-7 Clinical findings leading to differential diagnosis for skin injuries

Clinical findings	Differential diagnosis	Differential tests
Bruising	Trauma	Rule out other disease
	Hemophilia	Prothrombin time, partial prothromboplastin time
	Von Willebrand's disease	Von Willebrand's panel
	Henoch-Schönlein purpura	Typical distribution of lesions
	Purpura fulminans[1]	Rule out sepsis
	Ehlers-Danlos syndrome	Hyperextensibility
Local erythema or bullae	Burn, frostbite, contact dermatitis, allergic, irritant	Clinical history and characteristics
	Bacterial cellulitis, pyoderma gangrenosum,[2] staphylococcal impetigo[3]	Culture, Gram stain
	Photosensitivity (reaction to ultraviolet light) and phototoxicity reactions (skin damage caused by chemicals)	History of sensitizing agent, oral or topical reactions
	Herpes, zoster (chickenpox, shingles) or simplex (oral, genital herpes)	Scraping, culture
	Epidermolysis bullosa[4]	Skin biopsy

[1] A life-threatening disorder presenting with discoloration of skin from blood clots, bruising, and blood spots and resulting in skin necrosis and interrupted tissue blood flow, leading to multiple-organ damage.
[2] A condition that leads to tissue necrosis and causes ulcers, typically on the legs. It results in chronic wounds.
[3] A common staphylococcus bacterial infection that causes the skin to be inflamed and infected.
[4] An inherited connective tissue disease that causes blisters to form on mucosal membranes and the skin.
Botash (2005-2013), Appendix H. Reprinted with permission.

The areas that are bruised *most commonly* during normal play include the leading or bony edges of the body, such as knees, elbows, shins, hips, forearms, forehead, and brows. Thus, bruises not on the bony prominences, particularly those in soft-tissue areas (e.g., cheeks, buttocks, thighs) as well as those on the back, trunk (i.e., chest and abdomen), hands, arms, external ear, lower jaw, and feet, are suggestive of abuse. It is also highly unlikely that multiple bruises would be similar in size and shape or be found in a cluster or group. Finally, imprints of an implement or distinct shape inside the bruise, such as a hand, belt buckle, or teeth marks, are not accidental.

Bruises should be distinguished from artifact (dirt, dye, paint), skin discoloration such as birth marks (Mongolian blue spots, hemangiomata[11]), striae (stretch marks), and photosensitive or contact dermatitis (which may show a pattern similar to that of a weapon imprint). Abnormal bruising patterns can also be the result of alternative healing practices or be caused by various medical conditions, including genetic blood coagulation disorders that prevent proper clotting (e.g., hemophilia, Christmas disease, Von Willebrand's disease); meningococcal sepsis (which causes meningitis and sepsis conditions) except if localized; Henoch-Schönlein purpura (HSP)[12]/idiopathic thrombocytopenic purpura (ITP);[13] connective tissue disorders affecting the skin, joints, and blood vessel walls (e.g., Ehlers-Danlos syndrome); accidental asphyxia; accidental drug poisoning (e.g., aspirin, nonsteroidal anti-inflammatory drugs, warfarin); or liver disease. It is also possible, within a few days after an accident, for a child to have two black eyes; this symptom is caused by blood being tracked down from the forehead (Craft, 2006).

Another type of skin injury to child victims is human bite marks, which may signify that they are in imminent danger from the perpetrator(s). Human bite arches are U-shaped due to the paired crescent combination of canines and incisors (i.e., not prominent canine teeth). Consequently, it is imperative for medical personnel—preferably a forensic odontologist—to measure and document a bite, photograph it at 12- to 24-hour intervals with a millimeter ruler (i.e., right angle) and scale positioned parallel to the injury, and swab the area to obtain saliva for use in DNA testing (Craft, 2006; Reece, 2011). Although the size of the injury may be informative, it is often difficult to determine whether the bite is from an adult or a child due to the short intercanine distance between the primary teeth. An odontologist may be able to compare the lesions to the dentition of the suspect to confirm identity.

A third type of skin injury—burns of the feet, hands, legs, buttocks, and face—accounts for approximately 10% of physical abuse (see publications by Core Info [2014] for an up-to-date review). Child victims, typically ages 13–24 months, suffer from predominantly grease burns, hot-water scalding, and dry contact burns (e.g., irons, cigarettes and lighters, light bulbs), but may also experience burns from chemicals, electricity, and microwaves (Rosenberg & Marino, 1989). Punishment using scalding liquid (e.g., boiled water in a pot, hot water in bathtub) may result in stocking or glove burns, due to immersion of the feet or hands, or in doughnut or doughnut hole burns to the buttocks, lower back, genitals, and anus when the child is dipped and forcibly held in place. The absence of splash marks and the demarcation of burned and normal skin provide evidence of inflicted (rather than accidental) burns. A child's skin will burn in 10 seconds at temperatures of 127–130 degrees Fahrenheit, 1 second at 140 degrees Fahrenheit, and less than 1 second at temperatures of 150 degrees Fahrenheit

---

[11] Red or purple birth marks, usually on head or neck.

[12] Henoch-Schönlein purpura appears as purple spots on the skin and causes gastrointestinal problems, joint pain, and kidney disorder (glomerulonephritis).

[13] Idiopathic thrombocytopenic purpura is a bleeding disorder that causes the immune system to destroy platelets needed for blood clotting.

and higher (Moritz & Henriques, 1947). Dry contact burns could be caused by a number of household items, but most frequently come from appliances (e.g., iron) and cigarettes. Initially, intentional cigarette burns cause circular blisters that later heal into craters with hyperpigmented edges, whereas accidental cigarette burns are oval and superficial (Reece, 2011).

It may be possible for medical personnel experienced in burns to estimate the approximate age of burns (Craft, 2006). Physicians should include in the report a detailed drawing and photographs (close-up, distant) of the burn, providing information on the burn's dimensions, site, pattern, and depth, while considering the position of the child and effects of clothing during the injury. When evaluating the injury to determine the cause as abuse or accident, the physician should consider whether the history provided about how the incident occurred is plausible given the child's current development and ability. For example, a parent may explain a rib injury experienced by a 1-month-old as resulting from the child rolling from back to front and falling off the bed; however, this motor ability is beyond the development of such an infant (i.e., it typically occurs around 4 months). This information can supplement the police investigation of the home. Physicians should rule out skin pathology, such as infections (e.g., *Staphylococcus aureus* infection results in "scalded skin syndrome") and noninflicted burns from car seats or belts on a hot, sunny day.

Academic Performance

Children who suffer from physical abuse often have problems in school. Investigators should request an education evaluation, if one has not been done already by the school, and review the individual education plan (IEP) if the child has special education accommodations. Additionally, past and present teachers should be consulted to ascertain the child's academic and related problems (e.g., speech, occupational therapy). School records and report cards should indicate whether the child has frequent absences and tardiness, grade retention and repeat, poor marks, learning problems, or behavioral problems.

Investigation of Child Sexual Abuse

CPS investigators must consider the possibility that an allegation of sexual abuse may not be the truth or that recanting an allegation may be a lie. During the data-gathering phases, it is important to determine whether a child or an adult made the initial allegation. A "red flag" should go up when sexual abuse allegations arise during separation or divorce proceedings, although this context should not immediately negate their validity. Even when the allegation is made by a professional on the behalf of the child, his or her qualifications should be considered. Some healthcare providers conducting genital examinations may believe that abuse occurred when it did not (and vice versa), particularly when they are inexperienced in this type of evaluation. In contrast, medical personnel at child advocacy centers (CAC) are usually capable of making this assessment. Although it is preferable to bring a child to a CAC (such facilities are available in most states, but not in every town or city), realistically this is not always possible. Specifically, authorities may not become aware of the possible abuse until after the child is brought into a hospital emergency center.

Three aspects must be considered in making a determination that child sexual abuse occurred. First, CPS must obtain an accurate record of what the child stated. It is possible that the child's words were misconstrued by the adult to whom the statement was made. Genital touching that is not sexual in nature can occur in the course of caregiving. For example, the child may have been describing touching during a bath (e.g., "Daddy touched my butt"), but the adult thought it occurred in another context (at bedtime). The child may have been unintentionally exposed to adult sexual acts (e.g., watched a sexually explicit movie, walked in on parents having sex). Oftentimes, the description of what happened is at the child's level of development in terms of the wording used, and the child may or may not be able to provide details of chronology and location, depending on whether he or she had one experience or multiple experiences. Second, CPS personnel must consider whether the statement of suspected abuse was made spontaneously, particularly after the child exhibited suspicious behaviors or symptoms. Third, CPS workers must consider whether circumstantial evidence exists that corroborates the allegation. That is, was it possible that abuse could have occurred at a particular location or time when it was alleged? Are there artifacts that corroborate the story (e.g., pornographic DVDs, used condoms)?

The roles of the physician are to collect and document physical evidence of child sexual abuse (CSA), provide treatment for trauma and related issues (e.g., sexually transmitted infection [STI], pregnancy), obtain a history (i.e., statements made by the child during a physical examination, observation of affect, review of preexisting medical conditions), provide feedback about the child's body to reassure him or her, aid CPS in making a determination of the validity of abuse claims, and aid criminal justice personnel in deciding whether criminal actions occurred (Finkel, 2011; Kerns, Terman, & Larson, 1994). According to Adams (2011), the physician draws a conclusion about suspected sexual abuse by interpreting the history (i.e., none, behavioral change, nonspecific history by child, history by parent only, clear statement), physical findings (i.e., normal, nonspecific, specific findings), and laboratory results (i.e., none; positive culture or serologic test; STI; presence of semen, sperm, and acid phosphatase (enzyme primarily found in prostate gland). It is important for the physician to rule out benign medical conditions, non-sexually transmitted infections in newborns (i.e., from an infected mother during pregnancy, birth, and breastfeeding), and physical symptoms that may be confused with sexual abuse. As indicated in Table 6-8, it is possible for newborns to contract STIs (e.g., HIV, gonorrhea,[14] chlamydia,[15] syphilis, herpes) from their infected mothers during pregnancy, at birth, and from breastfeeding.

The kind of findings varies considerably with the nature of the abuse, the involvement of objects (or not), the degree of force used, the age of the child, and the frequency of the abuse. In two studies, the time since the last incident and a history of pain and/or

---

[14] Gonorrhea is a bacterial disease that is spread through sexual contact. Its symptoms include discharge, abdominal pain, burning while urinating, and conjunctivitis (pink eye).

[15] Chlamydia is a bacterial disease that is spread through sexual contact. Although it is the most common STI, affected individuals rarely have symptoms.

Table 6-8 Physical findings that may be confused with sexual abuse

1. Prepubertal genital bleeding (includes newborns)
    a. Tumors (e.g., ovarian, hemangioma, endodermal carcinoma)
    b. Endometrial shedding (due to estrogen withdrawal)
    c. Vaginitis (e.g., poor hygiene, foreign body, non-STI)
    d. Urinary tract (e.g., hematuria, infection, urethral prolapse)
    e. Accidental trauma (e.g., straddle injury)
    f. Gastrointestinal tract (e.g., Crohn's disease [inflammatory bowel disease], anal fissure, hematochezia from hemorrhoids [passage of blood in stools], colon cancer)
    g. Metabolic (e.g., liver cirrhosis, precocious puberty, McCune-Albright syndrome [disorder of bones, skin, and endocrine tissue], ovarian cyst, hypothyroidism, coagulopathy [clotting and bleeding disorder])
    h. Dermatosis (condition of the glands, hair, skin, and nails)

2. STIs in newborns infected during delivery
    a. Gonorrhea: vaginal and rectal infections possible, but not past newborn period
    b. Chlamydia: asymptomatic vaginal and rectal perinatal infections (but not pharyngitis), up to age 3 years
    c. Syphilis: perinatal infection occurs, but often is prevented by screening the mother
    d. Human immunodeficiency virus (HIV)/acquired immunodeficiency syndrome (AIDS): infection through contact with infected semen, blood, cervical secretions, and human milk
    e. Trichomonas: perinatal vaginal infection possible, but not past newborn period

3. STIs transmitted nonsexually: perinatal or person-to-person
    a. Molluscum contagiosum (viral skin infection): need direct contact for transmission; incubation is 2 weeks to 6 months
    b. Candida (yeast overgrowth): perinatal infection or person-to-person transmission; unknown incubation period
    c. Scabies (parasite infestation): person-to-person transmission; incubation of 4–6 weeks
    d. Hepatitis B virus (liver disease): perinatal infection or transmission from living with HBV carriers by infected blood, wound secretions, and saliva; incubation is 45–160 days after contact but can be prevented through vaccination
    e. Human papillomavirus (HPV; viral STI): caregiver with hand wart transmits during genital/anal diaper changes or assisting with toileting

4. Genital complaints
    a. Urinary tract infection
    b. Perianal or perivaginal pinworms
    c. Group A Streptococcus or streptococcal perianal cellulitis or vaginitis
    d. Lichen sclerosus et atrophicus (chronic inflammatory dermatosis presenting on the genital and extragenital regions)
    e. Acute or healed laceration or ecchymosis (bleeding) on the hymen with history of abdominal/pelvic compression injury, known infection, or coagulopathy

5. Variations of normal hymen configurations
    a. Crescentic
    b. Annular/cuff

(Continues)

Table 6-8 Physical findings that may be confused with sexual abuse (*Continued*)

    c. Collar/cuff-like

    d. Septate

    e. Fimbriated

    f. Redundant

    g. Cribiform

    h. Microperforate

    i. Imperforate

6. Variations in genitalia

    a. Hymenal tags or septal remnants

    b. Hymenal bumps and mounds

    c. Thickened hymen

    d. Periurethral or vestibular bands

    e. Intravaginal or external hymenal ridges or columns

    f. Labial adhesions

    g. Friability of the posterior fourchette or commissure

    h. Hyperpigmentation of the skin of the labia minora

    i. Clefts or notches in anterior half (between 9 o'clock and 3 o'clock positions)

    j. Erythema of the genitalia (reddish lumps)

7. Variations in perianal and anal areas

    a. Erythema of the anus or perianal tissues (reddish lumps)

    b. Perianal skin tags

    c. Perianal groove, partial or complete

    d. Hyperpigmentation of the perianal tissues

    e. Anal fissures

    f. Partial or complete anal dilation less than 2 cm (with/without stool in the ampulla)

    g. Venous congestion or pooling in the perianal area

Data From Botash (2005–2013); Finkel (2011); Lahoti, McClain, Girardet, McNeese, & Cheung (2001).

bleeding were the only two factors that significantly increased the likelihood of detecting abnormal physical findings (Adams, Harper, Knudson, & Revilla, 1994; Kerns et al., 1994). In more than 95% of CSA cases, no physical findings are revealed in the medical examinations (Heger, Ticson, Velasquez, & Bernier, 2002) because of one or more of the following: no penetration was involved, no damage was done, the injuries were minor or had already healed (usually 2–3 days), or delays in medical care decreased probability of finding semen, often because the child had washed or used the toilet (Bays & Chadwick, 1993).

Acute symptoms of CSA include various skin injuries, such as active genital and/or anal bleeding, ecchymosis, superficial abrasions, irritation, and lacerations in the genital or anal tissues, caused by friction and penetration. The child may have ecchymosis on the inner thighs, buttocks, neck, throat, and back of the ears as a result of the perpetrator applying force during the sexual assault either to restrain the child and thereby gain compliance or to keep the child in place. Throat injuries may also occur as a result of forcing the penis into the victim's mouth to perform fellatio, which may produce a torn frenulum, ecchymosis of the gums, or petechiae (red dots indicative of bleeding under the skin) on the roof and back of the child's mouth as a result of ruptured capillaries (Finkel, 2011). Additionally, examination may reveal presence of pregnancy in pubertal girls and discharge, sperm, and STIs in boys and girls at any age. Frequently, stress-induced somatic symptoms, such as recurring stomachaches and headaches, or medical problems, such as dysuria, encopresis, enuresis, and urinary tract infections, are also reported by children (Lahoti et al., 2001).

Rape and sexual abuse of infants and toddlers may result in severe, often irreversible, and sometimes fatal physical injuries: tears in the anus and vaginal linings; displacement, damage, and rupture of internal organs; fractured and broken bones; and oropharynx tears in the frenulum, caused by penile, digital, and object insertion into the infant's small openings. An erect penis averages 5 to 7 inches (127 to 178 mm) in length and is approximately 25 to 40 mm in diameter, whereas the average index or middle finger is at least 4 inches (102 mm) in length and approximately 15 to 20 mm in diameter (Goodyear-Smith, 1994). Other potentially lethal injuries associated with infant/toddler sexual abuse include skeletal, abdominal, and rib fractures, which are caused when the perpetrator holds the infant to perform the rape; asphyxiation, caused by the penis blocking the infant's airway during fellatio and/or ejaculation; and head injuries, which occur when the perpetrator crushes the infant's skull by pressing on the head during ejaculation.

Genital and Perianal Findings Involving Penetration

For a prepubertal girl, a visual inspection involves labial separation and tracking with her in the supine frog leg position (Figure 6-1) and is supplemented, at times, with the prone knee–chest position (Figure 6-2) to check the hymen and for secondary confirmation of CSA (Bays, Chewning, Keltner, Steinberg, & Thomas, 1990). The labial traction technique (i.e., thumb and forefinger exerts pressure downward and laterally) allows the examiner

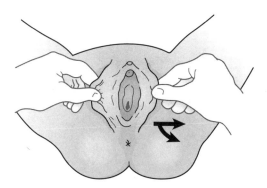

Figure 6-1 Labial traction in the supine frog leg position

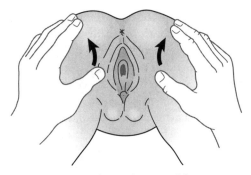

Figure 6-2 Labial traction in the prone knee chest position

to see foreign bodies, discharge, or trauma in the vagina and to determine if the hymen has tears or scars. Examination of a pubertal girl also involves labial separation and traction while she is in the supine frog leg position with supplemental investigation of the hymenal membrane edge. A vaginal speculum is not usually indicated in prepubertal girls, unless there is severe genital trauma or a foreign object is (or is suspected to be) inside, with decisions made on a case-by-case basis for pubertal girls when the history indicates penetration and to assess for STIs (Finkel, 2011).

Physicians should note the child's Tanner stage and document all findings using anatomic drawings to note the location and explanation of lesions with the 12 o'clock position being defined as anterior (Figure 6-3). Penetration through the hymen and into the vagina can be detected more easily in prepubertal girls than pubertal ones due to the absence of elasticity of the unestrogenized hymenal membrane, except when acute injuries occur in the hymen and/or intravaginal area (Adams, Botash, & Kellogg, 2004). The presence of

Figure 6-3 Clock face superimposed on female genital area

semen inside the vagina (quite uncommon) or pregnancy in a pubertal girl younger than the age of consent or without a history of consent signifies child sexual abuse. The absence of semen does not negate the contention that sexual abuse occurred, as the perpetrator may not have ejaculated, may not have ejaculated inside the victim (e.g., on body, clothing, or a washcloth), may have sexual dysfunction, or may have used a prophylactic.

Vaginal examinations revealing abrasions, tears, and bruises between the 3 o'clock and 9 o'clock positions or to the posterior are believed to be penile penetration injuries, whereas those between the 9 o'clock and 3 o'clock positions or anterior are believed to be due to digital penetration (Steinberg & Westhof, 1988). Vaginal examinations in the supine position that reveal acute and healed hymenal injuries at the 4 and 8 o'clock positions, a torn or missing hymen (in any portion of the posterior half), vaginal injury with or without bleeding or scarring from serious lacerating wounds, and a large vaginal opening (more than 5 mm) are considered diagnostic of blunt-force penetrating trauma (McCann, Miyanmoro, Boyle, & Rogers, 2007). However, findings of notches or clefts in the posterior half of the hymen in all positions, especially when they extend to the vaginal floor, and presence of condylomata acuminate in a child older than 2 years (without history of sexual contact) are highly suspicious, but not conclusive of sexual abuse (Lahoti et al., 2001).

For boys, a complete examination of the perineum and penis, including the shaft, scrotum, testicles, and epididymis, is made in the sitting, standing, or supine position for adenopathy (i.e., enlargement of the lymph nodes), hernias, bite marks, bruises, abrasions, STI lesions, edema, dried secretions, hematomas, discharge, bleeding, or suction ecchymosis[16] (Finkel, 2011). Any of these injuries to the penis or scrotum and the surrounding areas is considered to be highly indicative of sexual abuse.

Physicians should examine the buttocks and perianal skin of both boys and girls (Botash, 2005–2013; Lahoti et al., 2001) for dried secretions, rashes, STI lesions, ecchymosis, fresh or healed lacerations and fissures (particularly extending across pectinate line or internal to the sphincter), mucosal tears, and handprints or fingerprints (used to hold the child in place). A visual inspection of the perianal region involves manual separation of the buttocks while the child is in the supine frog leg position or lateral decubitus position (on the child's side, with legs pulled up). The physician should examine the anal verge, folds, and rugae to determine first whether the sphincter skin folds are normal, prominent, or flattened while the child is relaxed, and then determine whether both the tone and laxity of the anus are within the normal range (Lahoti et al., 2001). With only gentle buttocks traction applied to the gluteal folds, physicians should measure the diameter of anal dilation and indicate the length of time to reach maximum amount (Botash, 2005–2013). A digital rectal examination is not recommended in a child without significant intra-abdominal or rectal trauma, or when a foreign body is lodged inside (which may necessitate assessment by anoscopy); additionally, a guaiac exam (test for blood in the urine or

---

[16] Ecchymosis is ruptured blood vessels caused by blood escaping into the tissues due to sucking.

feces) should be performed to determine the extent of injuries in the case of acute trauma (Botash, 2005–2013; Finkel, 2011).

The degree of damage and risk of injury to the anus depend on the degree of force, use of lubrication, and victim "cooperation," as the anus already functions to allow large-diameter stools to pass through regularly with little to no residual trauma, barring frictional injury caused by the penis rubbing between the buttocks (McCann & Voris, 1993). Penetration from a finger, penis, or foreign object may cause internal damage to the anus beyond the external sphincter that, when indicated, can be assessed using an anoscope or sigmoidoscope (Finkel, 2011). Although inconclusive, marked anal dilation and anal scarring are highly suspicious of sexual abuse, whereas deep anal laceration is diagnostic of penetrating trauma (Lahoti et al., 2001). Specifically, anal dilation greater than 15–20 mm in diameter resulting from gentle buttocks traction is significant given that this amount of elasticity is needed for penetration by a finger or erect penis (Botash, 2005–2013).

Table 6-9 Physical findings of STIs that are diagnostic of sexual abuse

Infection	Incubation and transmission	Diagnostic tests
Gonorrhea	Vaginal discharge: 2–7 days Rectal, throat, and cervix asymptomatic; infection of infant during delivery; sexual abuse if beyond the newborn period	Bacterial culture using a modified Thayer-Martin medium in a CO_2-rich environment *plus* confirm positive culture with 2 other ID tests. Note: NAAT tests not diagnostic.
Syphilis	Primary: 10–90 days after contact Secondary: 1–2 months later; perinatal infection, otherwise sexual abuse	Microscopic ID; serologic blood test with positive non-treponemal test (RPR, VDRL, ART) or positive treponemal test (FTA-ABS, MHA-TP)
Chlamydia	5–7 days after contact Perinatal infection, otherwise sexual abuse if after age 3	Positive bacterial tissue culture N.B. NAAT tests not diagnostic
Trichomoniasis[1]	4–28 days after contact Perinatal infection, otherwise sexual abuse if after age 1	Microscopic ID or bacterial culture of vaginal secretions; also stool or urine analysis, but differentiate from other types
HIV/AIDS	6–12 weeks after exposure 6 months up to 6 or more years; contact with infected semen, blood, cervical secretions, milk; blood transfusions or IV drug use; otherwise, sexual abuse	HIV antibodies in blood is presumptive diagnosis; if the infant is younger than 18 months *and* the mother is HIV positive, use other tests

[1] A sexually transmitted disease caused by an infection from a parasite, *Trichomonas vaginalis*.

Data From Botash (2005–2013); Lahoti et al. (2001).

Findings of STIs in the Throat, Genital, and Perianal Regions

When the examination reveals a diagnosis of STI, the physician must determine whether sexual contact was highly likely (Table 6-9). Prima facie or confirmatory evidence of vaginal, rectal, and throat infections of gonorrhea and syphilis in victims beyond the newborn period, Trichomonas vaginalis infection in victims older than 1, and Chlamydia infection in victims older than 3 are diagnostic of sexual abuse (Botash, 2005–2013). Herpes simplex virus type 2 infection and condyloma acuminate of the genitalia or anus region in victims beyond the newborn period are suggestive of sexual abuse, as are hepatitis B, C, and E infections and pubic lice (typically in the eyelash), once other modes of transmission have been ruled out (Botash, 2005–2013). For example, children may be infected with herpes virus when a caretaker touches their genital or perianal regions, or when the caretaker kisses them, or with pubic lice through contact with contaminated bedding and towels.

Evaluation of Sexually Explicit Behaviors as Index of Child Sexual Abuse

A description of normative sexual development is provided in the *Physical and Cognitive Development* chapter to aid in evaluating whether sexually explicit behaviors are concerning, are problematic, and/or require therapy. Sexual acting-out provides children with an outlet to cope with unresolved trauma caused by sexual abuse. It is uncommon for children

---

Box 6-1 Sexual Assault: Female Genital Mutilation

Female circumcision or female genital mutilation (FGM), involving the cutting of female genitals, is commonly practiced in Sub-Saharan and Northeastern Africa, Indonesia, Asia, and immigrant communities around the world (including in the United States). According to the World Health Organization (2010), girls (right after birth, but more commonly between ages 4 and 12) and women (by the seventh month of the first pregnancy) may have one of four procedures performed that remove (1) the prepuce and sometimes the clitoris; (2) the prepuce and clitoris and part or all of the labia minora; (3) part or all of the external genitalia; or (4) part or all of the external genitalia with a reduction in the vaginal opening. This procedure is not usually performed in a hospital or by medical personnel and recovery is not monitored by health practitioners, resulting in serious immediate health complications (e.g., severe pain, shock, uncontrolled bleeding, infections) and long-term problems (e.g., clitoral cysts, chronic urinary or pelvic infection, infertility, pregnancy complications) for these girls and women. Despite FGM being a social custom or ritual practiced by a variety of religions, this practice was federally outlawed in 1996 by the United States (18 U.S.C. §116), and subsequently by 20 other states. For example, in 1997 New York (Section 130.85 of New York Penal Law) made FGM punishable as a class E felony with up to 4 years in prison. However, the federal law and many of the state laws (except in Florida, Georgia, and Nevada) do not include penalties for transporting the girls and women to have FGM performed overseas (i.e., "vacation provisions"). To date, there have been no federal and only one state prosecution against implementers of FGM in the United States (Anderson, 2013). Moreover, despite claims that more than 20,000 girls younger than 15 and 66,000 women victims living in England and Wales have had the FGM procedure performed on them, and the 2003 update making it illegal to bring a U.K. child abroad for the procedure, not one perpetrator has been convicted in the United Kingdom (Torjesen, 2013).

and adolescents to attempt to engage others in adult-like sexual interactions (i.e., oral-genital or intercourse), to masturbate openly in public (but not in their homes), to talk to peers about particular sexual acts using explicit sexual language, or, in adolescence, to have sexual interests in young children (Botash, 2005–2013). However, children in American culture are often exposed to sexually explicit media and music, giving them awareness of sexual terms and acts beyond their understanding. It is also plausible that some children may be advanced in their awareness, knowledge, and understanding about sex, particularly if they have older siblings. For example, a 4-year-old boy, while sitting with his preschool group at a picnic table and eating lunch, looked up at his teacher, smiled, and announced, "I have a boner" (a slang term for an erection).

The behaviors listed in Table 6-10 necessitate intervention by an adult, whether it is discussing the behavior with a parent or teacher, seeking professional help, or contacting CPS and/or police. It is important that these actions be considered in the context

Table 6-10 Juvenile sexual behaviors

Behaviors that require adult response:
- Sexual preoccupation/anxiety that interferes with daily functioning
- Pornographic interest
- Promiscuity/multiple sexual partners
- Sexually aggressive themes/obscenities
- Sexual graffiti that is chronic or affects others
- Embarrassment of others with sexual themes
- Violation of another person's body and privacy (e.g., pulling down pants, pulling up shirts, snapping brassieres)
- Single occurrence of peeping, exposing, or frottage

Behaviors that require correction and may require professional help:
- Compulsive masturbation
- Degradation/humiliation of self or others with sexual themes
- Attempting to expose another person's genitals
- Chronic preoccupation with sexually aggressive pornography
- Sexually explicit conversation with significantly younger children
- Touching genitals without permission (grabbing, "goosing")
- Sexually explicit threats, either verbal or written

Illegal behaviors that require immediate intervention:
- Obscene phone calls, voyeurism, exhibitionism, frottage, or sexual harassment
- Sexual contact with someone with a significant age difference (differential in size, power, popularity, or intellect may also play a part)
- Forced sexual contact (sexual assault)
- Forced penetration (rape)
- Sexual contact with animals
- Genital injury to others

Botash (2005–2013). Reprinted with permission.

of the age and development of the child, the situation in which the acts occurred, and the culture in which they were performed. A preschooler who pulls down his pants and wiggles his butt toward a peer while changing for swimming class should be corrected by the teacher, but this act alone would not signify he had been sexually abused. In contrast, a preschooler who corners another boy in the bathroom, pulls down the other child's pants, and places his mouth on the child's penis is demonstrating behavior suspicious of sexual abuse. Additionally, it should be recognized that preadolescents and adolescents commonly engage in some inappropriate sexual behavior. For example, it is not uncommon in social settings for children of these ages to perform frottage (rubbing against others as a sexual gesture), to expose their genitals or posterior and attempt to expose others by pulling down their pants/underwear, to "goose" someone (poke the person in the posterior), to embarrass someone by using lewd language, and to show pornographic interest. Rather than correcting them, adults will shrug and recite, "Boys will be boys," as they believe that these behaviors are simply part of growing up. Unfortunately, this attitude and its response contribute to an atmosphere in which girls and boys who are sexually molested may feel that adults will not help or protect them.

Investigation of Psychological Abuse

CPS investigators must consider the possibility that children who are psychologically abused may not exhibit overt signs of harm or that accusations of psychological abuse are, in fact, psychological disturbances from organic sources.

Medical and Psychological Evaluation of Psychological Abuse

Unfortunately, there is no simple psychological test that can be administered to determine whether a child is being psychologically abused (Hart, Brassard, Davidson, Rivelis, Diaz, & Binggeli, 2011). As recommended by American Professional Society on the Abuse of Children (APSAC, 1995), investigators should obtain whatever information is available regarding the psychological abuse of the child, particularly from a variety of sources (e.g., child, siblings, peers, family, neighbors, relatives, school), employing different measures, such as interviews and observations, and constructing a comprehensive report that delineates specific experiences gathered in the course of the investigation and based on advice from experts in the field.

Investigators should speak to the child privately—that is, outside of the caregivers' hearing, in case they are involved in psychological maltreatment (Hibbard, Barlow, & MacMillan, 2012). In addition, professionals who interact with the child, such as babysitters, coaches, teachers, and medical staff, should be consulted whenever possible, as they may help determine the timing and degree of impairment in the course of interacting and working with the child or evaluating the child's health. Specifically, they may have witnessed interactions or obtained history that documents parental psychological illness, intimate-partner violence, or direct psychological maltreatment of the child, including inappropriate discipline or parenting techniques that may harm the child's well-being, self-worth, and feelings of being loved (Hibbard et al., 2012). Psychological maltreatment, if severe, can result in psychosocial short stature or dwarfism due to growth failure that can be assessed by a pediatrician (Muñoz-Hoyos et al., 2011). Finally, cultural expectations may guide how parents and children interact (e.g., emotional distance) and whether adult responsibilities to children (e.g., assume parenting roles with younger siblings) may be deemed to be psychological abuse in the United States.

Investigation of Child Neglect

A variety of professionals will need to be involved to help the MDT evaluate suspected neglect. With the MDT approach, a pediatrician would assess the child's physical symptoms and health problems due to physical, environmental, inadequate supervision, or medical neglect. A psychologist would assess psychological problems due to environmental, inadequate supervision, psychological, or mental health neglect. Finally, a teacher would assess academic problems due to educational neglect.

Medical and Psychological Evaluation of Child Neglect

A medical examination will be needed to assess some of the child neglect symptoms associated with physical problems, particularly in regard to growth (e.g., non-organic failure to thrive, malnourishment), health (e.g., STIs, obesity, diabetes, asthma, substance abuse), and injuries. When the child has been seen by a pediatrician regularly, history and records can be used initially to assess health and medical issues. When the child has not been under pediatric care or simply for purposes of documentation, an independent physician may be consulted to collect current history (e.g., height, weight, head circumference); review birth history (e.g., complications during pregnancy and birth), medical records (e.g., growth rates, medical problems, feeding and nutrition problems, family history), and notes indicating missed appointments and lack of compliance for medical treatment; and obtain physical findings through a comprehensive physical examination (e.g., iron-deficiency anemia, infectious diseases). With young infants, examiners should check whether they are alert, have proper feeding responses (e.g., good suck), and demonstrate positive responses to cuddling. An assessment of injuries to determine whether they resulted from an accident; were due to neglect; or occurred from sexual abuse, physical abuse, or both should be performed by the physician (Child Welfare Information Gateway, 2011). Dental examinations are needed to review past history of dental care and problems, as well as to treat dental caries (tooth decay) and related problems. Psychological and educational examinations concerning social and emotional adjustment (e.g., psychiatric problems), psychologically related problematic behaviors (e.g., aggression), and academic problems should also be performed.

Chapter Summary

The purpose of the child maltreatment investigation is to collect and examine evidence, consider possible mechanisms for injuries and death, and determine whether there is support to substantiate one or more forms of abuse or neglect. To do so, medical personnel conducting the examination and others associated with the investigation (e.g., child protective services workers and law enforcement officers) must be able to distinguish between physical and psychological consequences that were accidental and those that were purposely done. Investigations of physical abuse must rule out medical explanations and accidents, and the provided history from caregivers explaining the injuries must be logical and consistent with children's development. With regard to child sexual abuse, investigators should be cognizant of the signs and symptoms of this type of abuse. Research shows that there may be common explanations for certain sexual behaviors and even infections typically associated with sexual transmission. In reference to child psychological abuse, there is no simple psychological test that can be administered to determine whether such abuse has occurred. Furthermore, with respect to child neglect, often medical examinations are performed that seek to determine if any physical problems, health issues, or injuries are present.

Review Questions

1. What is the investigation plan for child maltreatment? What are its components?

2. What are potential obstacles in a child maltreatment investigation?

3. What is the role of a physician in child abuse and neglect investigations?

4. Which behavioral signs and physical symptoms are exhibited by a child who has been physical abused?

5. Which behavioral signs and physical symptoms are exhibited by a child who has been sexually abused?

6. How is the psychological abuse of a child determined?

7. Which tests are used to determine child neglect?

References

Adams, J. A. (2011). Medical evaluation of suspected child sexual abuse: 2011 update. *Journal of Child Sexual Abuse, 20,* 588–605.

Adams, J. A., Botash, A. S., & Kellogg, N. (2004). Differences in hymenal morphology between adolescent girls with and without a history of consensual sexual intercourse. *Archives of Pediatric Adolescent Medicine, 158,* 280–285.

Adams, J. A., Harper, K., Knudson, S., & Revilla, J. (1994). Examination findings in legally confirmed child sexual abuse: It's normal to be normal. *Pediatrics, 94*(3), 310–317.

Agran, P. F., Anderson, C., Winn, D., Trent, R. L., Walton-Haynes, L., & Thayer, S. (2003). Rates of pediatric injuries by 3-month intervals for children 0 to 3 years of age. *Pediatrics, 111*(6 Pt 1), e683–e692.

Alexander, R., Levitt, C., & Smith, W. (2001). Abusive head trauma. In R. Reece & S. Ludwig (Eds.), *Child abuse: Medical diagnosis and management* (pp. 47–80). Philadelphia, PA: Lippincott, Williams & Wilkins.

American Academy of Pediatrics Committee on Child Abuse and Neglect. (1991). Guidelines for the evaluation of sexual abuse of children (RE9202). *Pediatrics, 87*(2), 81–87.

American College of Radiology. (1997). American College of Radiology standard for skeletal surveys in children. *ACR Standards, 23*, 1–4. Reston, VA: Author.

American Professional Society on the Abuse of Children (APSAC). (1995). *Guidelines for psychosocial evaluation of suspected psychological maltreatment of children and adolescents.* Elmhurst, IL: Author. http://www.apsac.org/mc/page.do?sitePageId=54514&orgId=apsac

Anderson, L. (2013). Female genital mutilation on the rise in the United States: Report of the Thomson Reuters Foundation. http://www.trust.org/item/?map=female-genital-mutilation-on-the-rise-in-the-united-states-report

Annest, J. L., Fingerhut, L. A., Gallagher, S. S., Grossman, D. C., Hedegaard, H., Johnson, R. L., Kohn, M., Pickett, D., Thomas, K. E., & Trent, R. B. (2008). Strategies to improve external cause-of-injury coding in state-based hospital discharge and emergency department data systems: Recommendations of the CDC Workgroup for Improvement of External Cause-of-Injury Coding. *MMWR Recommendations and Reports, 57*(RR-1), 1–13.

Barlow, K. M., & Minns, R. A. (2000). Annual incidence of shaken impact syndrome in young children. *Lancet, 356*(9241), 1571–1572.

Barlow, K. M., Thomson, E., Johnson, D., & Minns, R. A. (2005). Late neurologic and cognitive sequelae of inflicted traumatic brain injury in infancy. *Pediatrics, 116*(2), e174–e185.

Bays, J., & Chadwick, D. (1993). Medical diagnosis of the sexually abused child. *Child Abuse and Neglect, 17*, 91–110.

Bays, J., Chewning, M., Keltner, L. R., Steinberg, M., & Thomas, P. (1990). Changes in hymenal anatomy during examination of prepubertal girls for possible sexual abuse. *Adolescent Pediatric Gynecology, 3*, 34–46.

Bishop, N. B. (2006). Traumatic brain injury: A primer for primary care physicians. *Current Problems in Pediatric and Adolescent Health Care, 36*(9), 318–331.

Botash, A. S. (2005–2013). Child abuse evaluation and treatment for medical providers. http://childabusemd.com

Centers for Disease Control and Prevention. (1997). Traumatic brain injury—Colorado, Missouri, Oklahoma, and Utah, 1990–1993. *Morbidity and Mortality Weekly Report, 46*, 8–11.

Centers for Disease Control and Prevention. (2010). Vision, mission, core values, and pledge. http://www.cdc.gov/about/organization/mission.htm

Chiesa, A., & Duhaime, A. C. (2009). Abusive head trauma. *Pediatric Clinics of North America, 56*(2), 317–331.

Child Welfare Information Gateway. (2011). *Child abuse and neglect fatalities 2009: Statistics and interventions.* Washington, DC: U.S. Department of Health and Human Services, Children's Bureau. http://www.childwelfare.gov/pubs/factsheets/fatality.cfm

Christian, C. W., Block, R., & Committee on Child Abuse and Neglect. (2009). Abusive head trauma in infants and children. *Pediatrics, 123*, 1409–1411.

Core Info. (2014). Cardiff child protection systematic reviews. http://www.core-info.cf.ac.uk

Covington, T., Foster, V., & Rich, S. (Eds.). (2005). *A program manual for child death review.* Okemos, MI: National Center for Child Death Review.

Craft, A. (2006). *Child protection companion.* London, UK: Royal College of Paediatrics and Child Health.

Dennison, C., & Pokras, R. (2000). Design and operation of the National Hospital Discharge Survey: 1988 redesign. *Vital Health Statistics, 1*(39). http://www.cdc.gov/nchs/data/series/sr_01/sr01_039.pdf

Dias, M. S., Smith, K., DeGuehery, K., Mazur, P., Li, V., & Shaffer, M. L. (2005). Preventing abusive head trauma among infants and young children: A hospital-based, parent education program. *Pediatrics, 115*(4), e470–e477.

Duhaime, A. C. (2008). Demographics of abusive head trauma. *Journal of Neurosurgery: Pediatrics, 1*(5), 349–350.

Duhaime, A. C., Alario, A. J., Lewander, W. J., Schut, L., Sutton, L. N., Seidl, T. S., Nudelman, S., Budenz, D., Hertle, R., Tsiaras, W., & Loporchio, S. (1992). Head injury in very young children: Mechanisms, injury types, and ophthalmologic findings in 100 hospitalized patients younger than 2 years of age. *Pediatrics, 90*(2 Pt 1), 179–185.

Eisele, J. A., Kegler, S. R., Trent, R. B., & Coronado, V. G. (2006). Nonfatal traumatic brain injury-related hospitalization in very young children—15 states, 1999. *Journal of Head Trauma Rehabilitation, 21*(6), 537–543.

Finkel, M. A. (2011). Medical issues in child sexual abuse In J. E. B. Myers (Ed.), *The APSAC handbook on child maltreatment* (3rd ed., pp. 253–266). Los Angeles, CA: Sage.

Giardino, A. P., Christian, C. W., & Giardino, E. R. (1997). *A practical guide to the evaluation of child physical abuse and neglect.* Thousand Oaks, CA: Sage.

Goodyear-Smith, F. (1994). Medical considerations in the diagnosis of child sexual abuse. *Institute for Psychological Therapies, 6.* http://www.ipt-forensics.com/journal/volume6/j6_2_1.htm

Hart, S. N., Brassard, M. R., Davidson, H. A., Rivelis, E., Diaz, V., & Binggeli, N. J. (2011). Psychological maltreatment. In J. E. B. Myers (Ed.), *The APSAC handbook on child maltreatment* (3rd ed., pp. 125–144). Los Angeles, CA: Sage.

Heger, A., Ticson, L., Velasquez, O., & Bernier, R. (2002). Children referred for possible sexual abuse: Medical findings in 2,384 children. *Child Abuse and Neglect, 26,* 645–659.

Heron, M. P., Hoyert, D. L., Murphy, S. L., Xu, J. Q., Kochankek, K. D., & Tejada-Vera, B. (2009). Deaths: Final data for 2006. *National Vital Statistics Reports, 57*(14), 1–135.

Hibbard, R., Barlow, J., & MacMillan, H. (2012). Clinical report: Psychological maltreatment. *Pediatrics, 130,* 372–378.

Hoyert, D. L., Heron, M. P., Murphy, S. L., & Kung, H. (2006). Deaths: Final data for 2003. *National Vital Statistics Reports, 54*(13), 1–120.

Injury Surveillance Workgroup. (2003). *Consensus recommendations for using hospital discharge data for injury surveillance.* Marietta, GA: State and Territorial Injury Prevention Directors Association.

Injury Surveillance Workgroup. (2007). *Consensus recommendations for injury surveillance in state health departments.* Atlanta, GA: State and Territorial Injury Prevention Directors Association.

Injury Surveillance Workgroup. (2008). *Assessing an expanded definition for injuries in hospital discharge data systems.* Atlanta, GA: State and Territorial Injury Prevention Directors Association.

Jayawant, S., Rawlinson, A., Gibbon, F., Price, J., Schulte, J., Sharples, P., . . ., Kemp, A.M. (1998). Subdural haemorrhages in infants: Population based study. *British Medical Journal, 317*(7172), 1558–1561.

Keenan, H. T., Runyan, D. K., Marshall, S. W., Nocera, M. A., Merten, D. F., & Sinal, S. H. (2003). A population-based study of inflicted traumatic brain injury in young children. *Journal of the American Medical Association, 290*(5), 621–626.

Kerns, D. L., Terman, D. L., & Larson, C. S. (1994). Role of physicians in reporting and evaluating child sexual abuse cases. *Sexual Abuse of Children, Future of Children, 4*(2), 119–134.

Kleinman, P. K., Marks, S. C. Jr., Richmond, J. M., & Blackbourne, B. D. (1995). Inflicted skeletal injury: A post mortem radiologic–histopathologic study. *American Journal of Roentgenology, 165,* 647–650.

Kung, H. C., Hoyert, D. L., Xu, J. Q., & Murphy, S. L. (2008). Deaths: Final data for 2005. *National Vital Statistics Reports, 56*(10), 1–121.

Lahoti, S., McClain, N., Girardet, R., McNeese, M., & Cheung, K. (2001). Evaluating the child for sexual abuse. *American Family Physician, 63*(5), 883–892.

Ledbetter, D. J., Hatch, E. I. Jr., Feldman, K. W., Fligner, K. L., & Tapper, D. (1988). Diagnostic and surgical implications of child abuse. *Archives of Surgery, 123,* 1101–1105.

Maguire, S., Mann, M. K., Sibert, J., & Kemp, A. (2005). Can you age bruises accurately in children? A systematic review. *Archives of Disease in Childhood, 90*, 187–189.

McCann, J., Miyanmoro, S., Boyle, C., & Rogers, K. (2007). Healing of hymenal injuries in prepubertal and adolescent girls: A descriptive study. *Pediatrics, 119*, e1094–e1106.

McCann, J., & Voris, J. (1993). Perianal injuries resulting from sexual abuse: A longitudinal study. *Pediatrics, 91*, 390–397.

Moritz, A. R., & Henriques, F. C. (1947). Studies of thermal injury: The relative importance of time and surface temperature in the causation of cutaneous burns. *American Journal of Pathology, 23*, 695–720.

Muñoz-Hoyos, A., Molina-Carballo, A., Augustin-Morales, M. C., Contreras-Chova, F., Naranjo-Gómez, A., Justicia-Martínez, F., & Uberos, J. (2011). Psychological dwarfism: Psychopathological and putative neuroendocrine markers. *Psychiatric Research, 188*, 96–101.

Parks, S., Kegler, S., Annest, J., & Mercy, J. (2012). Characteristics of fatal abusive head trauma among children in the U.S.—2003-2007: An application of the CDC operational case definition to national vital statistics data. *Injury Prevention, 18*(3), 193–199.

Parks, S., Sugerman, D., Xu, L., & Coronado, V. (2012). Characteristics of non-fatal abusive head trauma among children in the U.S.—2003-2008: An application of the CDC operational case definition to national hospital inpatient data. *Injury Prevention, 18*(6), 392–398.

Pence, D. M. (2011). Child abuse and neglect investigation. In J. E. B. Myers (Ed.), *The APSAC handbook on child maltreatment* (3rd ed., pp. 325–336). Los Angeles, CA: Sage.

Reece, R. M. (2002). What the literature tells us about rib fractures in infancy. National Conference on Shaken BS. *SBS Quarterly, 2–3*, 6.

Reece, R. M. (2004). Child abuse. In R. M. Kliegman, L. A. Greenbaum, & P. S. Lye (Eds.), *Practical strategies in pediatric diagnosis and therapy* (2nd ed., pp. 611–629). Philadelphia, PA: Elsevier.

Reece, R. M. (2011). Medical evaluation of physical abuse. In J. E. B. Myers (Ed.), *The APSAC handbook on child maltreatment* (3rd ed., pp. 183–194). Los Angeles, CA: Sage.

Rosenberg, N. M., & Marino, D. (1989). Frequency of suspected abuse/neglect in burn patients. *Pediatric Emergency Care, 5*, 219–221.

Schnitzer, P. G., Covington, T. M., Wirtz, S. J., Verhoek-Oftedahl, W., & Palusci, V. J. (2008). Public health surveillance of fatal child maltreatment: Analysis of 3 state programs. *American Journal of Public Health, 98*, 296–303.

Sirotnak, A., & Krugman, R. (1994). Physical abuse of children: An update. *Pediatrics in Review, 15*, 394–399.

Steinberg, M., & Westhoff, M. (1988). Behavioral characteristics and physical findings: A medical perspective. In K. C. Faller (Ed.), *Child sexual abuse: An interdisciplinary manual for diagnosis, case management, and treatment* (pp. 244–264). New York, NY: Columbia.

Sugar, N., Taylor, J., & Feldman, K. (1999). Puget Sound Pediatric Research Network. Bruises in infants and toddlers: Those who don't cruise rarely bruise. *Archives Pediatric Adolescence Medicine, 153*, 399–403.

Torjesen, I. (2013). First UK prosecution for female genital mutilation moves a step closer. *BMJ, 346*, f2981.

Vandeven, A., & Knight, J. R. (2001). Physical abuse: The father's hand print. In J. R. Knight, C. Frazer, & S. J. Emans (Eds.), *Bright Futures case studies for primary care clinicians: Child development and behavior*. Boston, MA: Bright Futures Center for Education in Child Growth and Development, Behavior, and Adolescent Health. http://www.pedicases.org

World Health Organization (WHO). (2010). *International classification of diseases* (10th rev.). Geneva, Switzerland: Author.

Chapter 7

Interviewing

Interviewing relevant witnesses is a key component in the investigation process, as it provides insight, understanding, and evidence regarding the abuse allegations. Researchers recommend that maltreated children have as few investigative interviews as possible because these sessions are distressful and may result in children making inconsistent statements across interviews due to the different questioning styles employed by each interviewer (American Prosecutors Research Institute, 2004). Initially, children should have a minimal fact-finding interview with a first responder (e.g., child protective services [CPS] worker, emergency hospital intake nurse). If this person deems it necessary, a follow-up investigative fact-finding interview can then be conducted by a formally trained investigator—typically someone who is part of a multidisciplinary team (MDT). In other words, the mandated reporter or first responder uses the victim's answers to assess the severity of maltreatment and decides whether the child's immediate safety is at risk, including the need to take the child into emergency protective custody; an immediate medical examination and care (preferably at a child advocacy center for sexual and physical abuse) and/or therapeutic counseling services should be provided; and a follow-up investigative fact-finding interview is required.

This chapter describes the linguistic and cognitive abilities needed by children during interviews to recall personal experiences, as well as findings from the developmental literature on event memory and interviewing. It also examines components of the interview, alternative forensic assessments, and interviewer techniques; reviews advantages and disadvantages of various interview techniques in light of the developmental capacity of children and adolescents; and provides recommendations. Finally, it focuses on the advantages and disadvantages of nonverbal assessments that sometimes are used to supplement interviews and the corresponding indicators (e.g., lying) that may affect witness reliability.

Fact-Finding Interview Protocol

The fact-finding interview protocol provides the best practices approach to gathering evidence through testimony. It is very important that the interviewer considers the interviewee's cognitive and linguistic abilities when designing the questions used to elicit information about the alleged maltreatment (Saywitz & Snyder, 1996). The interviewer will need to determine the developmental ability of the interviewee regardless of that person's chronological age and to find a way to make the interviewee comfortable with the interview process. The ideal interview setting for any interviewee is a neutral room that contains few distractions, particularly as the victim will feel vulnerable and stressed by the discussion of maltreatment. Typically the room for investigative interviews will be clean and uncluttered and will have either a child-sized table and chairs or rugs and pillows on the floor to allow the child and interviewer to stay at eye level. Although the first responder rarely has the option of where to interview the child victim, an attempt should be made to emulate closely the described ideal setting. Most importantly, the interviewer must stay attuned to the child's comfort and anxiety levels, providing breaks and snacks whenever the child becomes restless or unfocused (but should never use these as bribes to gain compliance). Another key element is that the investigative interview room should have either a closed-circuit monitor or a one-way mirror to allow the MDT to observe the interview.

The investigative interview plan focuses on decisions that interviewers need to make in the interview protocol. As such, it is relevant for anyone who will need to question a child victim. Specifically, a mandated reporter or first responder will conduct a minimal fact-finding interview with the child victim(s) to determine what harm (if any) has been done, evaluate the risk to safety for the child victim(s) immediately and in the future (such as the need for emergency protective custody), identify which services (if any) may be needed (e.g., medical examination and care), and decide whether further investigation should be conducted. Additionally, an investigator will interview the child victim(s) and anyone else who could provide information relevant to the case (i.e., investigative fact finding).

Investigative Interview Plan

Who should be interviewed and in which order? The first decision the interviewer must make is to determine who should be interviewed. The interviewer should speak with the person who made the report, the child victim, witnesses (e.g., family members, acquaintances, neighbors, peers), collateral sources (e.g., professionals, such as teachers, coaches, law enforcement officers, medical personnel, and psychologists), the nonoffending parent/guardian(s), and the suspect (Pence, 2011).

Once the list of relevant parties is compiled, the second decision is to determine the order in which to interview them. This requires careful thought, as the outcome of the investigation may be affected by the evidence gathered during each interview (Pence & Wilson, 1994). It is desirable for the interviewer to speak directly with the person who made the report, but this may depend on availability of the reporter, the jurisdiction, use of a coordinated MDT to conduct the investigation, and the means by which the report was made (e.g., child abuse hotline, agency, police). The goal of the interview with the reporter is to ascertain the person's motive and credibility, details of the abuse as described by the child, the means by which the abuse was disclosed (e.g., spontaneously, in response to direct questions), additional witnesses to the abuse and/or disclosure, the reporter's concerns about the child's and others' safety, other agencies or individuals contacted, and any information necessary to enhance understanding of the abuser's motives (Pence, 2011).

Recommendations for interview order dictate that the interviewer obtain testimony from the child victim(s) first, but there are two options for how to proceed beyond this point. One option is to interview the alleged perpetrator as a means of keeping the suspect unbalanced and ill prepared to respond to questions. The other option is to gather evidence about the maltreatment and learn about the alleged perpetrator, thus, ending with the interview of the suspect (Pence, 2011). Regardless of which option is selected, the interview procedure should continue with children who live in the same home as the victim (siblings, relatives, nonrelatives), followed by nonoffending adults who live in the home (e.g., caregiver/parent, relatives, nonrelatives), and then by collateral parties and professionals (e.g., neighbors, schoolmates, friends, teachers, pediatricians, psychologists, medical personnel conducting maltreatment assessment).

Which documentation option should you select? A third decision the interviewer must make is which documentation option to use—interviewer and observer note-taking, audio recording, and/or video recording (Pence & Wilson, 1994). It is recommended that interviewers obtain detailed, accurate verbal statements and record the accompanying emotions and behavioral indices from children who witness or allege abuse, as well as the investigative questions and both behavioral and verbal responses by the interviewer. Although ideally more than one method should be used for documentation, such an approach is not always practical. Therefore, the advantages and disadvantages of the various options must be considered:

- Notes have the advantage of not making the interview process subject to evaluation, but the disadvantage of not accurately representing all that the child stated or nonverbal cues perceived by the interviewer/observer.
- Audio provides an accurate recording of what the child stated and the questions asked by the interviewer, but have the disadvantages of exposing errors in the interview procedure, missing nonverbal cues, or misconstruing statements made by the child.
- Video has several advantages, including producing an accurate recording of the child's statements and nonverbal responses (e.g., facial expressions, body language, physical reactions), reducing the number of interviews needed because other agencies will have access to the recording, providing a record for the nonoffending parent to review, encouraging plea bargains, allowing the child to watch may refresh his or her memory for the testimony, and using

the video for grand jury inquiry instead of live testimony (Myers, 1993; Perry & McAuliff, 1993; Perry, McAuliff, Tam, Claycomb, Dostal, & Flanagan, 1995). Disadvantages of video are that juries become overly concerned with using them rather than other evidence, and the defense can use the video to expose inconsistencies in statements made by the victim, point out problems with interview techniques, and highlight these problems so as to raise doubts about the credibility of the victim.

In some jurisdictions, policies dictate which interview documentation option interviewers must use. Nevertheless, this decision varies within the same state or even from city to city, and depends on whether the case is being considered for prosecution in criminal court or will be retained in family court. For example, the five boroughs of New York City (considered separate counties) vary in their requirements for investigation of potential criminal cases. In Brooklyn, the interviewer videos the interview in the child advocacy center while simultaneously sending a live feed to the district attorney (DA)/prosecutor, who, in turn, at the recommendation of the investigating officer, presents the video to the grand jury. In the Bronx, only the DA/prosecutor interviews the child at the child advocacy center, recording the exchange through notes, which are then used to present evidence to the grand jury.

Fact-Finding Investigative Interview Goals

The goal of the investigative interviews with the child victim(s) and witness(es) is to obtain information about the alleged maltreatment against the victim(s). Consequently, these interviews should address the circumstances surrounding the maltreatment (e.g., which activities were performed prior to and subsequent to the maltreatment), the causal mechanism for physical injuries (e.g., explain how injuries occurred, which weapon or implement was used and its current location), who perpetrated the harm (i.e., reveal the offender), the degree of harm (e.g., was there bleeding, pain, or any bloody or stained clothing), supplemental information (e.g., the names of other witnesses, the name of the person to whom the child disclosed information about the incident, whether coercion was used to prevent the child from reporting any incident and/or to keep the child from resisting the maltreating incident), and the general quality of the parent–child relationship (e.g., determine who is the main caretaker and disciplinarian, which parenting style is used, how this child and other children in the household are disciplined, what the results of discipline have been in the past for this victim and for siblings). Interviews of siblings and other children and adults in the home should similarly ascertain the surrounding circumstances; descriptions and observations of the alleged perpetrator, maltreatment, and consequences; and confirmation of the parent–child relationship for the victim and themselves.

The overall goals of interviewing the parents/caregivers are to determine each one's strengths and weaknesses and to understand the relationship between the parent and the child so as to assess present and future risk for maltreatment. Parents should be asked to provide a description of their parent–child relationship with the child victim and with other children in the household, their parenting style, the discipline techniques typically used and sometimes used for specific infractions, and the misbehaviors of the child victim and other children. This information will allow the interviewer to determine the nonoffending parent's ability to protect children against future incidents (which will become important when CPS is deciding whether to leave the child in the home). Interviewers should also obtain a social history, including the current family characteristics and dynamics. Attempts should be made to learn the parents' past (i.e., family) and current (e.g., neighborhood) cultural influences, as these factors will impact their parenting, as well as whether they have relationships (and which type of relationships they have) with their own parents and siblings. Other factors that affect family functioning and risk for abuse should be assessed, such as academic and vocation history, military service, legal history, physical history, substance use, emotional/psychological issues, and a detailed marital history.

In the interview with the nonoffending caregiver who was present during the maltreatment, the goal is to obtain corroboration of the circumstances, causal mechanism, person who perpetrated the maltreatment, and degree of harm. Even if the nonoffending caregiver was not present during the incident, this person may be able to provide a timeline of when the injuries were first noticed, what type of care was provided, and the explanation provided by the child victim (and by the alleged perpetrator) for the symptom or injury. This person may also be able to provide his or her own observations, report past incidents of a similar nature with explanations of how these events occurred, and give his or her interpretations and suggestions for questioning the perpetrator and protecting the child. If this person was the one to whom the child disclosed maltreatment, then obtain information regarding the circumstances under which the disclosure occurred, the wording of the disclosure itself, and the reaction and questioning following disclosure, as well as previous incidents that were observed and their explanations. The interviews of collateral parties and professionals should be geared toward gleaning information that will aid in confirming or disconfirming maltreatment, including, but not limited, to these persons' observations of the child's physical and mental health prior to and subsequent to the maltreatment incident, disclosures of maltreatment (if any), and evaluations and descriptions of the child's socioemotional interactions with the caregivers, family members, and others (e.g., friends, peers).

The goal of the suspect interview is to obtain preliminary statements regarding the suspect's perception of the event leading to alleged maltreatment. The investigator will inform the suspect of his or her role in this process, build rapport, and then progress to interviewing the suspect based on already obtained information from other parties. Investigators should ask the suspect to describe his or her relationship with the child, responsibilities (if any) the person has in providing care, and activities he or she engaged in prior to, during, and subsequent to the alleged maltreatment. These statements may indicate a plausible, alternative account (e.g., "He bruises easily because of a medical condition");

reasons (e.g., "She wanted me to do it"); or excuses (e.g., "I was drunk") for the child's statements, injuries, and/or symptoms to confirm or disconfirm maltreatment.

Recommended Fact-Finding Interview

The primary purpose of the fact-finding interview is to gather facts related to the incident as a means of ascertaining whether the child's safety is at risk, either imminently or in the future. A secondary purpose is to determine whether the perpetrator of the maltreatment should be prosecuted criminally. Consequently, questions should focus on the events, including their location and timing, and the identification of the alleged perpetrator(s), other witnesses, and other victims. For both types of fact-finding interviews, only general, open-ended questions should be asked. Minimal fact-finding interviewers should avoid follow-up questions to obtain details while acknowledging that they are taking the child's allegations seriously. It is imperative that the interviewer be respectful and listen to the child victim rather than interrupting and challenging what is stated (even if the story is fragmented), keeping in mind that the topic being discussed is a traumatic experience. Many jurisdictions have established their own minimal and investigative fact-finding forensic interview protocols and require their staff to be trained in how to use them properly.

Types of Questions

Various types of questions could be used in a fact-finding interview to elicit information about an experience. The best questions to ask are open-ended ones in which no information is provided (e.g., "What happened?" or "Tell me everything you can about what happened"), thereby allowing the child to determine what should be reported about the experience. These should be followed up with general prompts to obtain additional details (e.g., "What else?" or "Then what?" or "What happened next?") and to get clarification (e.g., "You said _____. Tell me more about that _____."). Interviewers could also use neutral acknowledgments, such as "uh huh" or "hmm," to encourage the child to expand or to continue with what is being said. Specific, nonleading questions are also appropriate to ask children as a follow-up to their statements as these can address temporal sequencing of the event (e.g., "Start with the first thing that happened from the beginning to the end."). Prompts can be used, when needed, to get additional details of the sequence (e.g., "What happened after your father left the room?") and people, events, and objects associated with the event (e.g., "You said the babysitter hit you. What is the name of the babysitter?" or "You said you were wearing pajamas. What color were your pajamas?").

Three types of questions—namely, closed-ended, yes/no, and leading questions—should be avoided. Multiple-choice, closed-ended questions provide a set of limited options from which the child may choose (e.g., "Were you attacked at home or in school?"). There are four problems with this type of question. First, it produces options that may not include the correct answer (e.g., "Were the pajamas red, blue, or green?" when they were yellow). Second, it creates pressure for children to select one of the options, particularly if the information is not remembered. Third, simply mentioning these choices may prevent children from remembering the actual information or, even worse, may replace it. Fourth, closed-ended questioning assumes that children will state the correct answer spontaneously or will be able to inform the interviewer when the correct answer is not present among the choices.

Yes/no questions may provide general (e.g., "Did he tell you anything?") or specific (e.g., "Did he tell you to keep the game a secret?" and "Did that happen to you after school?") information to which children must respond yes or no. Such questions make it difficult for children to respond, "I don't know," when they do not know, remember, or understand the question because they feel pressure to produce a response (Poole & Lindsay, 2001). It is also possible that children may get locked into a "response bias," in which they keep responding the same way, with only yes or only no (they may even "sing" it: "Yes, Yes, Yes") to every question.

Four specific types of yes/no questions are possible. A negative format is used for both *negative-term* yes/no questions (e.g., "Didn't he tell you to keep the game a secret?" and "Isn't it true that your mother knew Tom would hurt you if he stayed") and for *double-negative* yes/no questions (e.g., Didn't he tell you not to tell anyone?" and "Is it true that your mother didn't know that Tom would not hurt you if he stayed?"). Children may feel pressure to answer "yes" even if they do not know what they are affirming (i.e., "He didn't tell me" or "He did tell me"). *Tag-ending* yes/no questions also require a response, but are worded as a statement followed by a question for children to answer (e.g., "You are scared to go to your Dad's home, aren't you?" and "This happens to you after school, doesn't it?"). This order of words may be confusing for children to understand and answer (i.e., does "yes" mean "I am scared" or "I am not scared"?). *Compound/double-barrel* yes/no questions contain more than one question within the structure (e.g., "Isn't it true that your mother knew Tom would hurt you if he stayed and she did so because you made her angry?"). It is impossible to know whether the child's answer of yes or no is in response to the first or second question. Moreover, such a structure does not necessarily provide an opportunity for the child to inform the interviewer that the question contained a mixture of true and false information. That is, the child may agree with information in one question, but disagree with information in the other question. In addition, this format requires children to hold two or more pieces of information in their minds simultaneously and to consider all the parts before responding, yet either task alone is difficult for them to do.

Leading questions suggest information that the child has not yet provided (hence, they are also called suggestive questions). If the information in the question is correct, it is considered a positive leading question (e.g., "Were the pajamas yellow?" when they were yellow). If the information in the question is incorrect, it is considered a negative or misleading question (e.g., "Were the pajamas blue?" when they were yellow). These types of questions are inherently problematic, as interviewers could not possibly know which information is correct or incorrect. Children may not be capable of resisting the suggestions, and the suggestions can become incorporated into their memories.

Investigative Interview Format

The Step-wise Interview (SI; Yuille, Hunter, Joff, & Zaparniuk, 1993) attempts to minimize inaccurate reporting by gradually increasing specificity in questions, starting with free recall and progressing to directive questions for clarification and elaboration of already mentioned information (without inquiring about anything that was not indicated directly by the child). The Enhanced Cognitive Interview (ECI; Geiselman & Fisher, 1997) was designed to enhance field interviews with crime victims and witnesses who often show emotional signs of their trauma and have difficulty in providing critical information. It was modified for use with children (e.g., Saywitz, Geiselman, & Bornstein, 1992) and has been adopted by the United Kingdom as the formal investigative interviewing procedure for children (see Bull, 1996; Bull & Corran, 2002).). The ECI begins with an introduction and rapport-building phase that sets up the social dynamics of the interchange between the witness, who actively generates testimony, and the interviewer, who actively listens and provides support. This procedure seems effective in increasing the amount of correct information in reports by older children and adults, but the retrieval methods require perspective taking that is beyond the limited cognitive capacity of preschoolers (Qin, Quas, Redlich, & Goodman, 1997).

The recommendations for interviewing strategies presented here are based on training obtained by Lauren Shapiro under the auspices of Peter Ornstein at the University of North Carolina in Chapel Hill and on interviewing and interrogation practices used by Marie-Helen Maras during U.S. Navy investigations. The authors recommend a combination of these two interview protocols as the ideal investigative interview format to obtain testimony for all forms of maltreatment, regardless of whether an episode occurred only once or repeatedly (also see Bull & Corran, 2002; Price & Roberts, 2007; Saywitz & Snyder, 1996). The following description organizes the best practice approach into five phases.

Phase 1: Rapport development and narrative practice. The interviewer talks to the child about neutral topics to encourage him or her to relax, establish credibility, and develop rapport. A few toys can be kept in the room, as allowing the child to play with them should reduce some of the distress from being interviewed. To determine the child's ability to describe personal experiences completely, accurately, and with detail, the child should be asked about two past experiences, unrelated to the maltreatment, using nonleading, open-ended questions (e.g., "Tell me more" and "What happened next?"). The interviewer should ask the child about a recent or personally relevant event (e.g., birthday party, trip to the zoo). A chronological narrative of the experience may be obtained by requesting, "Tell me what happened from the time you got out of bed until the time you went home." Nonleading prompts should be given until the child indicates he or she is finished as a way for the interviewer to model the questioning format. The goal is to obtain information about the people who participated in the event, the location, and other details. This phase of the questioning provides the interviewer with an opportunity to assess the child's developmental skills and adjust questions as needed.

Phase 2: Transition and interview preparation instructions. The interviewer prepares the child in a few ways. First, an explanation of the expectations, rules, and role the child has in the interview process is provided. Specifically, the child is informed that the interviewer was not there, so only the child knows what happened and the interviewer needs the child to tell him or her everything that the child remembers. The child should be told, "I want you to tell me only what you really remember" and given permission to (1) state "I don't know" and "I don't remember," when he or she does not know or forgot; (2) state "I don't understand/know what you mean," when the child is confused about the question; (3) state "I don't want to tell you," if the child is uncomfortable providing the information or otherwise does not want to respond; and (4) correct the interviewer when a question or statement is incorrect. Second, the child should be told that sometimes the interviewer will ask a question more than one time, but that does not mean the child should change the answer; instead, the child should be reminded to state simply what he or she remembers. This is also an opportunity to determine the child's ability to distinguish between truth/lie and fantasy/reality through the use of specific questions. Finally, ask the child to promise to tell the truth.

Phase 3: Narrative of maltreatment. The interviewer informs the child of the purpose of the interview. To introduce the topic, the interviewer will state, "Tell me the reason you came to talk to me today." If the child is unresponsive, the interviewer can provide various focused questions based on the child's previous disclosure or reasons for abuse without using suggestive statements, such as "I heard that you saw/spoke to a police officer/social worker/doctor/teacher today/yesterday/last week. Tell me what you talked about." The interviewer could also state, "My job is to talk to children about things that happened to them. It is very important that I understand why you are here today."

Once the topic is introduced, the interviewer will ask the child to "Picture that time as if you were there right now. Think about what it was like there. Tell me out loud." The interviewer should help the child to focus on people and any sense-related information (e.g., sounds, feelings, smells). The interviewer should then elicit information in a free narrative format, allowing the child to describe the event from beginning to end without interruption (i.e., do not correct or challenge, simply listen), waiting for a lull to use general, open-ended prompts (e.g., "What else happened? Then what?") and clarification prompts (e.g., "Tell me more about that"). Avoid repeating questions unless you need clarification, and do not ask questions that may be answered yes/no without elaboration (e.g., "Can you . . . ?" "Do you . . . ?" "Is there . . . ?"). To obtain information about individual episodes in recurrent maltreatment, avoid present-tense language that elicits what generally happens rather than what happened during a particular time.

Phase 4: Specific questions. Make sure you use plain language and simple sentence structure, checking periodically for comprehension. Specific nonleading questions about the event may be used to elicit additional details about a person, object, or action (e.g., "You told me X was there. Tell me more." "You saw Y on the desk? What is Y?" "You said that P came over to you. Tell me everything about that."). To determine if the child's description was complete, the interviewer should ask the child to recall the events in reverse order (bearing in mind this task is difficult for young children to do), starting at the end and then proceeding toward the middle and the beginning, as prompted ("What happened right before that?"). It is *not* recommended that the interviewer use memory jogging techniques to produce additional details, such as going through the alphabet one letter at a time to recall a forgotten name or asking the child if anyone's voice or characteristics remind them of the perpetrator, as these suggestive techniques can backfire (i.e., make the child think the wrong information introduced in the interview had instead been experienced). If the child is capable of understanding perspective taking, he or she may be able to provide the report from another's point of view (e.g., "What would your teddy bear say happened last night?" when a child is hesitant to report child sexual abuse). The interviewer should conclude with final fact checking to give the child one last opportunity to clarify or provide additional details.

Phase 5: Closure. At this point, you need to return to discussing neutral topics (e.g., television, movies, music). It is also important that you inform the child of the procedure from this point forward (e.g., if someone else will be talking to the child) and provide the child with an opportunity to ask questions. The child may have developed false conceptions of what happened in the experience or what will happen to him or her and to his or her family that you are obligated to dispel. Finally, thank the child for his or her time and for talking with you.

Forensic Assessment Tools: Advantages and Disadvantages

Young children, who typically are the only witnesses to their maltreatment, often have difficulty providing detailed descriptions of their traumatic experiences (Ceci & Bruck, 1995). However, because their exhibited physical symptoms and behavioral signs are not always considered definitive evidence of abuse, their testimony becomes the prime source used to prosecute their perpetrator. Additionally, children may be hesitant to recount details of their maltreatment or their emotional reaction to it, choosing instead to show what happened to them (Boat & Everson, 1988). Consequently, several nonverbal, forensic investigative tools have been developed to facilitate testimony, including simple free drawing, playhouses, conventional dolls, puppets, projective cards, play dough, games, and anatomically detailed body drawings and dolls (Kendall-Tackett, 1992). These tools may help children to express behaviorally what they cannot verbalize because they do not know the names for the body parts that were touched or the actions performed on them (Everson & Boat, 1994). However, researchers warn that these tools are not valid or reliable diagnostic assessment techniques and are likely to taint testimony when the interviewer lacks training, does not use the instruction manual, does not follow standard protocol (see the practice guidelines developed by the American Professional Society on the Abuse of Children, 2012), or encourages the child to pretend (Boat & Everson, 1988; Pence & Wilson, 1994; Underwager & Wakefield, 1995).

The controversy is greatest regarding the use of anatomically correct dolls—which are soft and have clothes that are easily disrobed, hands with individual fingers, and penises that can be inserted into holes in the mouth, anus, and vagina (mature dolls have pubic hair and protruding breasts)—to investigate alleged sexual abuse (Koocher, Goodman, White, Friedrich, Sivan, & Reynolds, 1995; Pence & Wilson, 1994; Yates & Terr, 1988). Proper use entails that children are given a limited play period (an ice breaker) prior to using the dolls in the interview. The dolls serve as valuable communication aids: allowing the child to feel comfortable identifying body parts using whatever labels he or she has for them and showing the interviewer where touching may have occurred; as a demonstration aid to show described behaviors or to enhance the interviewer's understanding of the child's experience, particularly when he or she has limited verbal skills; and as a memory trigger for the child's recall of the sexual abuse (Everson & Boat, 1994). Likewise, critics indicate that drawings—such as free drawings, outlines of the front and back of a boy and a girl, or the house–tree–person and kinetic family drawings—have not been shown to support the assumption that abused children will reliability produce qualitatively different pictures than nonabused children in terms of colors or body shape and size (Underwager & Wakefield, 1995).

These tools (particularly anatomically correct dolls) are likely to trigger play, be distractions, or elicit fantasy rather than reflect reality of actual abuse (Cohn, 1991; Maan, 1991). For example, children are just as likely to insert their fingers into a doll's vaginal hole as they would into a doughnut hole (Ceci & Bruck, 1995), given the perceptual affordances presented by both items (Gibson, 1977). Research findings examining whether abused (confirmed or suspected) and nonabused children play with dolls in a standardized test setting have been mixed, with some studies indicating there are differences (August & Forman, 1989; Jampole & Weber, 1987; White, Strom, Santili, & Halpin, 1986) and others yielding no significant differences (Cohn, 1991; Kenyon-Jump, Burnette, & Robertson, 1991; McIver, Wakefield, & Underwager, 1989; Realmuto, Jensen, & Westcoe, 1990; Realmuto & Wescoe, 1992).

More importantly, findings by DeLoache and her colleagues (e.g., DeLoache, 1994; DeLoache & Marzolf, 1995; DeLoache, Miller, & Rosengren, 1997) clearly contradict the basic assumption that young children can use dolls to represent their experiences. Ironically, the concept that the doll represents the self is understood best by older children, who already have the linguistic skills necessary to verbalize their experiences (e.g., Gordon, Ornstein, Nida, Follmer, Crenshaw, & Albert, 1993; Greenhoot, Ornstein, Gordon, & Baker-Ward, 1999; Murachver, Pipe, Gordon, Owens, & Fivush, 1996; Saywitz, Goodman, Nicholas, & Moan, 1991; Shapiro & Waymire, 2001). The development of the "self" forms the basis for children's autobiographical memories. Autobiographical memory refers to people's recall of personal experiences that not only hold significant meaning for them, but also collectively make up their self-identity (Nelson & Gruendel, 1981). In the next section, an explanation of how autobiographical memories may operate is provided.

Autobiographical Memory Processes

Unlike filmed documentaries of past events, neither one's memory for pleasant and traumatic personal experiences nor its report constitutes a complete and detailed set of recordings that can be produced upon request. It is not surprising that errors occur when children relate what happened to them as their general event knowledge and specific memory for episodes are part of the same cognitive system (Nelson & Gruendel, 1981). Our current understanding of autobiographic experiences was summed by Ornstein, Larus, and Clubb (1991) as: not all information is encoded, stored memory changes over time and with knowledge, the strength of the memory varies, and retrieval is not perfect. That is, Ornstein et al. suggested several explanations for why children do not always have accurate memory recall for events they have experienced or witnessed. First, "not everything gets into memory" during the encoding stage (p. 151). Some information will never be registered in children's minds, simply because they do not understand the event, are not interested in what is going on, or are too stressed by the event to pay attention to it. Second, if the child does encode the information, the impression of the event may not be strong enough to ensure long-term storage. Depending on how much involvement or participation the child has in the event, the strength of the memory trace may vary. For instance, a child who undergoes a medical procedure repeatedly is more likely to recall details than a child who experiences it only once. Finally, even if the information is encoded and stored, those factors do not guarantee a "perfect retrieval." The memory can be altered during the time between the encoding and the retrieval effort—a span called the post-event period. Inaccurate recall can be the result of changes in children's knowledge or cognitive abilities, exposure to similar events, or even a suggestive interview (through the "misinformation effect"). Over time, as forgetting becomes more likely, children become more vulnerable to suggestions (i.e., to accept false information). A review of theories explaining post-event effects (i.e., phenomena that occur after the original event, such as discussion of the experience or occurrence of similar experiences) is therefore warranted.

Theories Explaining Effects of Post-Event Suggestions on Memory

Interviewers must be concerned with how event memory can be changed by post-event interviews and intervening experiences. Information disclosed during informal conversations with participants and nonparticipants as well as formal question-and-answer interviews of past experiences create opportunities for bits and pieces, or even whole sections of information, to be misremembered (i.e., false memory) during reconstruction (Principe & Schindewolf, 2012). Various theories have been proposed to explain this misinformation effect, with researchers contending that the original memory is lost and replaced by, blended with, or less accessible than the false memory.

Loftus and her colleagues (Ceci, Crotteau-Huffman, Smith, & Loftus, 1994; Loftus & Hoffman, 1989; Loftus & Loftus, 1980; Loftus, Miller, & Burns, 1978) argue that original memories are erased or permanently changed due to suggestions used to elicit recall. The process of changing a memory can be considered an unconscious procedure on the person's part. That is, suggestions given to the person cause him or her to truly come to believe that the information is correct. According to this theory, false information presented after an event occurs either overwrites the person's original memory with the new false one or fuses the memories together into a blend of true and false information. The post-event information becomes incorporated into memory, making the false information either "all or part of the truth." Subsequently, witnesses asked about the event in subsequent interviews retrieve the misinformation.

An alternative explanation by Bekerian and Bowers (1983) proposes that the new, false information does not replace the original memories. Instead, both the original and the new information coexist in memory, but post-event suggestions make retrieval of the original information difficult, whereas retrieval from the new (wrong) source is more easily achieved (also see Brainerd & Poole, 1997). According to this theory, the change may be either a conscious or an unconscious procedure. For example, an interviewer might ask a witness whether the man in the blue sweater hit the cashier during the robbery. An example of unconscious memory interference would be when a witness reports in the original interview that the sweater was blue (as this memory was readily available), but in a later interview states that the sweater was red; this inconsistency weakens the person's reliability from a legal perspective. In contrast, in the conscious memory interference process, the witness agrees with the suggestion of the blue sweater, but is cognizant that he or she either never knew or temporarily cannot access the color of the sweater.

McCloskey and Zaragoza (1985) also believe that the memory for the original event still exists, but they suggest that people accept/report false information either because the demand characteristics of the interview pressure them to accept it (or fail to reject it) or because post-event information is used to fill in the missing gaps about aspects of the event that were never encoded or are already forgotten. The misinformation effect may also be the result of the person failing to discriminate between the sources of the remembered information—as witnessed or as discussed (Zaragoza & Lane, 1994).

In line with the findings from several empirical studies, Qin et al. (1997) proposed that the misinformation effect is derived from multiple mechanisms (i.e., all or some of the previously mentioned theories), with changes in memory being the product of misinformation after a long delay. The eyewitness literature indicates that regardless of which theory is used to explain the "misinformation effect," both adult and child witnesses fall victim to it, albeit to different degrees.

Factors Influencing Amount and Accuracy in Recall

Three main factors have been indicated by researchers to influence the amount and accuracy of children's recall about personally experienced events: developmental ability (Batterman-Faunce & Goodman, 1993; Fischer & Bullock, 1984), stress, and the interview itself (e.g., type of questions, format).

Developmental Differences in Memory and Reporting

Investigations of child maltreatment often hinge on children's ability and willingness to provide accurate and detailed descriptions of their own or others' maltreatment. The youngest children may first show cognitive and linguistic competence for a particular task, such as remembering and reporting details about a past experience, under nonstressful and supportive contexts (Hudson & Shapiro, 1991). Consequently, researchers and psychologists who provide developmental guidelines may actually overestimate children's ability to recall traumatic experiences of maltreatment, particularly when maltreated children have disabilities, come from deprived home environments and diverse backgrounds, and are in stressful, unsupportive situations (Lyon, 2005). Interviewers should familiarize themselves with differences in eyewitnesses'/victims' ability to remember and report experiences of maltreatment, as well as learn how to best elicit unbiased descriptions from them of the abusive perpetrators and the traumatic experiences they endured, given their level of development, language, and mental capacity.

The task of describing one's past experiences in informal conversations and in formal interviews requires several specific cognitive and linguistic skills. In particular, children must have knowledge (e.g., event knowledge, coherent organization strategies), memory (e.g., memory strategies for storing and retrieving autobiographical experiences), and language (e.g., cohesive reference devices, comprehension of the question) appropriate for this task. Children must develop and have under their control different strands of knowledge—content (i.e., generalized event representations, social interactions, specific episodes), structural (i.e., macrolinguistic components of storytelling to create coherence), microlinguistic (i.e., connectives, tense, pronouns, and other linguistic elements to create cohesion), and contextual (i.e., knowledge of the function of the narrative for particular elicitation)—which they translate into the telling of their experience (Hudson & Shapiro, 1991; Shapiro & Hudson, 1997). Differences in children's competence in producing a cohesive and coherent retelling of a past experience occur when they are forced to provide evidence in a question-and-answer interview rather than allowed to self-select which memories they want to reminisce about during the course of a conversation (Peterson & McCabe, 1983).

Of course, children are capable of performing elicited-recall tasks as long as their event knowledge is accessible and the structure of their experiences is closely related to the format in which the information is elicited—that is, when the memory requires little translation from "knowing to telling" to convert it into a coherent report (Hudson & Shapiro, 1991; Shapiro & Hudson, 1991, 1997). Initially, their performance is highly contextualized, meaning that young children rely on support from the environment to cue their memory, resulting in more detailed reports about their experience when they are in the situation (or a close facsimile) rather than elsewhere in a decontextualized location (i.e., not where the maltreatment occurred). That is, children's failure to report critical information cannot be attributed to their lack of awareness of the listener's need; indeed, even preschoolers are able to tailor their language to different audiences. Rather, the child's omission of such information reflects the interviewer's failure to provide context-specific prompts to elicit these details (Menig-Peterson, 1975).

Infants (Birth to Age 2 years)
Research has shown that infants by 6 to 8 months of age are capable of forming memories of specific experiences, which they can recall weeks and months later as demonstrated

nonverbally with elicited imitation (see Rovee-Collier & Gerhardstein, 1997, for a review). Toddlers will even produce spontaneous speech while enacting previously shown events with props (see Bauer, 2007, for a review). From a linguistic perspective, most toddlers know a lot of words (approximately 500–600); recognize names of people, objects, and body parts; and can point to named objects or pictures. Although they are not able to produce complete sentences, toddlers understand simple instructions and requests, such as "Give me the spoon" (and may even comply if they so desire). Comprehension can be hampered when sentences do not follow the active form of subject–verb–object order (e.g., "The boy kicked the dog") and instead use the passive form (e.g., "The dog was kicked by the boy") as they will misinterpret it (e.g., "The dog kicked the boy").

Between 2 and 3 years of age, children's ability to represent and discuss past events emerges with the development of general event knowledge and discourse skills. Parents are instrumental in teaching their children how to remember and recount their experiences through jointly constructed conversations of the past (Hudson, 1990). Initially, they take complete responsibility in conversations with their 20- to 30-month-olds, teaching the child how to use discourse skills, which aspects of events are important, and how to search and retrieve information from memory using cues. The child can respond to only yes/no questions at the beginning, but over time, at around age 2½ years, the child can offer information as well. By the end of the second year of life, the child will be able to initiate and direct the conversation about his or her own past experiences. The quality and quantity of the recall seem to be influenced by the type of conversation style employed by the parent, with an elaborative elicitation style resulting in a longer, detailed, and more complete report than that derived from a repetitive elicitation style (Fivush & Fromhoff, 1988).

Preschool Children (Ages 3–6 years)

Preschoolers (ages 3 to 6 years) are capable of speaking in short full sentences using a variety of one- and two-syllable words and idiomatic expressions; can differentiate terms, such as "same" and "different"; have rudimentary mastery of a referential system of pronouns and articles (e.g., relying on pronouns to refer to various people); and can use simple intraclausal and interclausal cohesive devices (e.g., "and," "then") to link ideas within and between sentences, respectively. However, there is still a discrepancy between their receptive and expressive language (i.e., what they understand and what they produce linguistically) as evidenced by their grammatical errors (e.g., over-regularization of nouns and verbs, using incorrect terms such as "gooses" or "goed"), confusion in using prepositions (e.g., "before" versus "after"), and substitution of present tense (used to express general knowledge about events—that is, what typically happens at the beach) for past tense when describing a particular past experience (Saywitz, 1995). Preschoolers have developed sufficient conversational skills to allow them to discuss their past experiences (Hudson & Shapiro, 1991) and are in the process of learning how to respond in an intelligible and credible way to the type of complex questions asked by police and prosecutors during investigative interviews and cross-examinations (Goodman et al., 1992; Perry, McAuliff, Tam, Claycomb, Dostal, & Flanagan, 1995; Saywitz & Goodman, 1996). However, in general, this mode of responding is foreign to them because question-and-answer interview formats solicit specific answers rather than allowing children to choose their own topics to discuss, forces them to wait to speak until asked a question, and rudely interrupts them when it is their turn and they are already providing information, which is a violation of conversational rules.

Preschoolers, and even some 2-year-olds, are able to report neutral or highly stressful experiences for up to 2 years later accurately, especially when given specific, nonleading cues (see Fivush, 1997, for a review; Howe, Courage, & Peterson, 1994). In general, such young children provide incomplete, but accurate information about their experiences in response to general, open-ended questions (Baker-Ward, Gordon, Ornstein, Larus, & Clubb, 1993; Lamb, Hershkowitz, Sternberg, Boat, & Everson, 1996; Roberts & Blades, 1998; Shapiro, Blackford, & Chen, 2005). For example, Lamb, Sternberg, Orbach, Esplin, Stewart, and Mitchell (2003) showed that preschoolers produced about 50% of forensically relevant information (e.g., Who? What? When?) in response to a free-recall prompt.

Interviewers may attempt to obtain omitted details by using closed-ended questions, not realizing that young children are vulnerable to suggestions and will submit to coercion, resulting in inaccurate reports (e.g., Goodman & Aman, 1990; Goodman et al., 1992; Poole & Lindsay, 1998). Their ability to provide an accurate account of a particular episode is more likely when the event is unique or the incident differs significantly from those typically experienced in a recurring event (Fivush, Hudson, & Nelson, 1984; Graesser, Gordon, & Sawyer, 1979). However, when the event is not unusual, the report given by the child will likely be script-like—that is, a general description of what usually happens (Hudson & Nelson, 1986; Pillemer, Picariello, & Pruett, 1994). Naturally, scripted versions of children's past experiences will contain knowledge-based errors of commission (i.e., typical aspects not experienced will be reported), particularly for very specific and/ or peripherally related details that were not remembered by the child. Defense attorneys often use these types of mistakes to impeach the child's testimony.

Young children's thinking is egocentric, concrete, and literal, meaning it is easier for them to understand and discuss the "here-and-now" rather than abstract or logical concepts (e.g., truth). Consequently, they do not grasp the notions of irony, metaphor, and analogy. Although most interviews are done with an interviewer questioning the child alone, this strategy is not recommended for very young preschoolers because they are unlikely to talk to unfamiliar adults without the presence of a support person, such as a parent. The interviewer can try to separate the child from the parent at a later time if the child becomes comfortable, but should remain flexible within the guidelines of the agency.

Preschoolers basically know the difference between fact/fiction and lie/truth, but can get confused (e.g., believing in Santa Claus or the tooth fairy). They may lie when they are afraid their behaviors will result in punishment, to impress or avoid hurting or angering someone, or if they want attention from adults. Preschoolers have limited attention spans and difficulty with space (e.g., over, under), number (e.g., many, few), distance (e.g., 3 blocks, 2 miles), time (e.g., yesterday, 2 months ago, 5:00 P.M.), and sequencing in a linear progression (e.g., before, first), making it difficult for them to provide these types of information in regard to their maltreatment. Investigations require specific details, such as the number of times an event occurred, but young children who are asked to report this type of information are likely to pick a number at random, such as hundreds or 62, and to be inconsistent across interviews because estimation is also a difficult task for them.

Knowledge serves as a framework for memory. Consequently, children have difficulty discussing experiences that are novel, unfamiliar, confusing, and abstract, particularly when they are out of context or decontextualized (i.e., the child is not currently at the location or involved in the event). Their recounting reflects an inability to portray their experience logically under these conditions, instead stating whatever comes to mind and mixing irrelevant and relevant details together. Also, because their receptive language skills (understanding words) are more advanced than their expressive language skills (producing words), even when young children understand and know the answers to the questions they were asked, they may be unable to respond verbally. To maximize the amount, organization, and orientation of information provided, interviewers should tell a young child that unlike him or her, they were not there and do not know what happened (Menig-Peterson, 1975).

Recommended strategies for eliciting accurate information take into consideration these limitations of children. Consistent with the National Institute of Child Health and Human Development (NICHHD) protocol, the interviewer can ask the child to indicate whether the disclosed abuse incident happened one time or more than one time. If multiple incidents occurred, then the interviewer should begin by asking about the one "remembered best" (Price & Roberts, 2007); they may then target the first incident and the last one (Powell, Thomson, & Ceci, 2003; Saywitz, Lyon, & Goodman, 2010).

Inferences about time are similarly difficult to estimate, usually because young children have not learned how to tell time or simply do not know how to figure out the passage of time. Temporal terms are also beyond their understanding; instead, they generalize "the past" as yesterday and "the future" as tomorrow regardless of the number of days, weeks, or months (Harner, 1982). The interviewer must find specific reference points (e.g., birthday, vacation, lunchtime, bedtime) and references to location of the maltreatment (e.g., in the shed) and significant others (e.g., "My mother was working") that will help the child to discuss and sequence chronologically a particular incident among many similar ones. The interview session should consist of several short sessions, with breaks taken to keep the child's interest and attention.

School-Aged Children (Ages 7–11 years) and Adolescents (Ages 12–17 years)

When children and adolescents are 7 to 17 years of age, episodic autobiographical memory (e.g., school event, trip, vacation) shows gradual improvement, and seems to be supported by earlier development of semantic autobiographical memory (e.g., names of childhood friends) (Mishkin, Suzuki, Gadian, & Vargha-Khadem, 1997; Picard, Reffuveille, Eustache, & Poilino, 2009; Willoughby, Desrocher, Levine, & Rovet, 2012). It is believed that these improvements correspond to the extended maturation of the prefrontal cortex, which guides retrieval and executive processes (Levine, 2004; Piolino, Hisland, Ruffeveille, Matuszewski, Jambaqué, & Eustache, 2007). Studies of sex differences in episodic and semantic autobiographical memory have shown that girls are able to provide more information about an event, including time and perceptual details, than boys, demonstrating girls' more efficient prefrontal memory retrieval and organization processes in memory tasks that are unstructured and have little support (Bloise & Johnson, 2007; Willoughby et al., 2012).

School-aged children are capable of understanding complex syntax and words in sentences. However, they still interpret meaning literally—that is, in a very broad or very narrow use of a term. Thus, in a sexual abuse case, when a female victim is asked whether a male abuser "touched" her, she may "deny" it because he used his mouth rather than his hand to assault her (Schumann, Bala, & Lee, 1999). School-aged children can recall and sequence information in a logical progression for both familiar and unfamiliar events in response to open-ended questions (Reese, Haden, Baker-Ward, Bauer, Fivush, & Ornstein, 2011). They are capable of discussing personal experiences outside of the moment, but still reason in concrete ways about causes and consequences. Yet, between ages 9 and 11 years, their personal narratives are coherently organized around a "high point" theme (i.e., the most important and interesting component of the story), similar to the accounts given by adults (Peterson & McCabe, 1983; Trabasso, Secco, & van den Broek, 1984; van den Broek, Lorch, & Thurlow, 1996). At the same time, children's reports may be inaccurate as a result of incorporating misinformation introduced by investigators during the interview or because their recall was distorted by their misunderstanding of certain aspects of an event (Terr, 1994).

From age 7 years through early adolescence, the ability to understand current events based on past experiences develops (Montangero, 1996) as a by-product of the youth's emerging person (Selman, 1980) and personal continuity concepts (Chandler, Boyes, Ball, & Hala, 1987). By mid-to late adolescence, an individual is capable of thinking logically and abstractly; understanding causes, motives, and rationales for people's behaviors; drawing on inferences and interpretation to construct past experiences; and conceptualizing events within temporal or biographical contexts (Feldman, Bruner, Kalmar, & Renderer, 1993; Habermas & Bluck, 2000; Habermas & Paha, 2001; Montangero & Pons, 1995). Researchers examining early and middle adolescent witnesses' immediate recall have shown it is complete and accurate for theft (Saywitz, 1987; Shapiro, 2009) and kidnapping (Coxon & Valentine, 1997), surpassing the recall exhibited by children (Davies, Tarrant, & Flin, 1989; Sutherland & Hayne, 2001) and preadolescents (Cohen & Harnick, 1980). In Shapiro (2009), children and adolescents reported 82% of the central crime features and 48% of the peripherally related crime features for a theft they witnessed. In contrast, accuracy in immediate recall by high school students has been shown to be lower than that demonstrated by college students (Marin, Holmes, Gruth, & Kovak, 1979; Sutherland & Hayne, 2001).

Stress Effects on Memory and Reporting

Researchers and those involved in the justice system agree that children who witnessed or experienced traumatic events (e.g., domestic violence, killing of a parent or sibling, sexual abuse, physical abuse) are likely to suffer adverse psychological effects (Pynoos & Eth,

Box 7-1 General Advice to Interviewers

a. Language of interview

1. Make it clear and understandable in accordance with the child's age, developmental level, and method of communication (e.g., sign language, primary language).
2. Explain legal words and phrases.
3. Check the child's understanding of the concepts he or she used.
4. Use specific names and places rather than pronouns.
5. Use nouns rather than deictics ("in your room" rather than "there").
6. Use an item (e.g., gun) rather than a category (weapons).
7. Use subject–object–verb sentence structure.

b. Proper composition of questions and guidelines for interview

1. Avoid compound and "why" questions.
2. Avoid leading or coercive questions and forced choice/multiple-choice questions that hint at a particular response.
3. Avoid yes/no questions; replace them with "Tell me" or "Why?" questions (see Table 7-1).
4. Avoid recognition questions ("did," "was," "were").
5. Phrase questions in a general (e.g., "Where were his hands?" or "Where were your clothes?") rather than in a specific way (e.g., "Were your clothes off or on?" or "Did he hit you?").
6. Use a simple sentence structure.
7. Ask about one thought at a time.
8. Warn the child before shifting from the present to the past in topic discussion.
9. Allow the child time to organize his or her story.
10. Give the child concrete examples to demonstrate the difference between the truth and a lie.
11. Do not interpret the child's answers. If not sure about the response, ask the child to repeat it or "Tell me more about that."
12. Use elaboration questions to prompt justification for answers: "What makes you think so?" and "What made _____ do that?"
13. Do not randomly probe; instead, ask for elaboration of what the child states.
14. Allow the child to indicate his or her feelings or responses rather than suggesting what those feelings are or were.
15. Ask the child to repeat information you had difficulty hearing (e.g., "What did you say?") instead of guessing (e.g., "Did you say _____?").
16. As long as the child is responding appropriately to your requests for information (and not doing anything dangerous, such as tipping the chair back), it is not necessary to correct the child's fidgety or nervous behaviors, such as squirming in the chair or getting up to walk around the room.

Table 7–1 Type of information children are capable of providing at each age

Type of information	3 years	4 years	5–6 years	7–8 years	9–10 years	11–12 years
Who	Y	Y	Y	Y	Y	Y
What	Y	Y	Y	Y	Y	Y
Where	?	Y	Y	Y	Y	Y
When	N	?	Y	Y	Y	Y
How	N	N	?	Y	Y	Y
Frequency	N	N	N	?	Y	Y
Circumstances	N	N	N	N	?	Y

Key: Y = yes, N = no, ? = maybe.

1984; Terr, 1991). Of utmost importance is determining how this stress—both from the abuse itself and from revealing facts about the child's own victimization to others—affects accuracy in his or her memory. Clinically based theories purport that a negative relationship exists between memory and trauma (e.g., high stress, low recall) due to repression or dissociation preventing victims from processing and having access to their own trauma. Therapy is the proposed solution for recovering repressed memories according to clinicians, but scientific researchers claim many therapy techniques (e.g., imaging, hypnosis) induce false memories of trauma (Qin et al., 1997). Similarly, children who experience trauma may not encode it completely (i.e., the memory may be incoherent) or may form a separate, fragmented memory dissociated from their consciousness (McNally, 2003), although this notion cannot be assessed objectively.

Empirically based explanations tested with naturally occurring stressors, such natural disasters and medical examinations, posit that an inverted "U" relationship exists between stress and recall (Yerkes & Dodson, 1908) or that centrality of to-be-remembered information prevails in conjunction with the stressor (e.g., Christianson, 1992; Easterbrook, 1959). The Yerkes-Dodson law predicts that children's memory performance should be enhanced by arousal at some optimal or moderate level (perhaps in accordance with personal preferences of stimulation), whereas arousal that is low (e.g., boredom) or high (e.g., trauma) is predicted to result in low memory performance.

In an investigation of these concepts, Bahrick, Parker, Fivush, and Levitt (1998) examined autobiographical recall by preschool children whose families' homes suffered low, moderate, or high damage in a major hurricane. When children were interviewed 2 to 6 months after the storm, those in the moderate-damage group reported more information about their experience than those in the low- or high-damage groups. However, in a follow-up study (Fivush, Sales, Goldberg, Bahrick, & Parker, 2004) conducted 6 years later, children provided detailed accounts of their experiences regardless of their damage grouping, almost twice as much as originally. The implication is that verbal ability may moderate reporting level; children are able to provide additional information about past experiences with age because of their increased linguistic skills. Fivush and her colleagues (Fivush, Berlin, Sales, Mennuti-Washburn, & Cassidy, 2003; Fivush, Hazzard, Sales, Sarfati, & Brown, 2002; Sales, Fivush, & Peterson, 2003) reasoned that parents discussed this fear-inducing event and the associated negative responses with their children, helping them to understand the causes and consequences and to regulate their emotional and behavioral expressions. Thus, reminiscing with their parents facilitated children's organization of their memories into a coherent story. Building on this notion, children exposed to various forms of maltreatment may have disjointed and incoherent memories of these stressful experiences because they lack the knowledge to understand them and the ability to cope with their feelings without adult assistance.

Although some researchers have reported that children have high recall of stressful, traumatic, or violent experiences (e.g., Bahrick et al., 1998; Burgwyn-Bailes, Baker-Ward, Gordon, & Ornstein, 2001; Oates & Shrimpton, 1991) and that children demonstrate coherence in the information provided in regard to these experiences (Fivush et al., 2002), other studies have described low recall of such events (Ceci & Bruck, 1993; Kassin, Ellsworth, & Smith, 1989; Merritt, Ornstein, & Spicker, 1994) and poor coherence of information provided (Peterson & Biggs, 1998). To explain this discrepancy in the findings, centrality extends the Yerkes-Dodson law by indicating arousal enhances central information while inhibiting peripheral information (Yuille & Tollestrup, 1992). Yuille and Tollestrup claim that in "high-impact" events (i.e., stressful and emotionally arousing incidents), witnesses who constrict their attention focus inward will likely have poor central feature recall, but good internal state recall (e.g., "I was so scared"), due to them being emotionally overwhelmed. Owing to this reaction, a witness would have little cognitive effort available for encoding. In contrast, keeping the attention focus outward in "high-impact" events would allow witnesses to represent central features at the expense of encoding/remembering peripheral details. Research has confirmed this proposed relationship, particularly with the "weapon focus" phenomenon resulting in adverse memory effects for peripheral aspects, such as the face of the assailant (e.g., Cutler, Penrod, & Martens, 1987). In contrast, for "low-impact" events that engender no or low stress, central and peripheral features will be attended, encoded, stored, and retrieved equally well.

In an alternative approach, Poole (cited in Goodman & Quas, 1997) explains—using Brainerd, Reyna, Howe, and Kevershan's (1991) fuzzy-trace theory—that stress enhances children's recall for the gist (i.e., relational) of the experience, while impairing recall for verbatim information (i.e., perceptual). Reyna's (1995) review of children's suggestibility literature concludes that delayed introduction of misleading information negatively impacts verbatim information (i.e., misremembered as witnessed/experienced), which likely had been forgotten by that point, at least in part, whereas immediate exposure to misleading information fails to impair verbatim memory, which remains strong shortly after the event occurred.

Individual differences in how children react to stress and neurobiological changes in response to trauma, particularly over time, may also help us to understand the stress-memory relationship. Ornstein and his colleagues (e.g., Ornstein, Shapiro, Clubb, Follmer,

& Baker-Ward, 1997) have proposed that children's temperament affects attention and encoding of a stressful experience, leading to differences in storage and retrieval. General findings showed that recall for a novel, stressful, medical procedure (e.g., voiding cystourethrogram [VCUG]) was good both initially (88%) and after a 6-week delay (86%); however, a negative association was found between the amount of stress exhibited and recall, particularly at the delayed interview. Similarly, children exposed to prolonged high stress through maltreatment may have permanent memory problems due to hippocampal atrophy from elevated cortisol levels (showing stress), which in turn inhibit consolidation and retrieval of implicit memory, spatial memory, and autobiographical memory (Elzinga, Baka, & Bremner, 2005; Kitayama, Vaccarino, Kutner, Weiss, & Bremner, 2005). It is also possible that trauma-related memory problems may be the result of one's conscious efforts to avoid intrusive ruminative thoughts (i.e., repeatedly thinking about the event), which reduces cognitive energy and truncates memory search and retrieval of specific episodes (Greenhoot, Johnson, Legerski, & McCloskey, 2009).

Much of the literature has focused on recall for a one-time arousing, stressful, or traumatic experience. However, victims of maltreatment are often exposed to emotionally arousing, personally threatening, physically and psychologically painful experiences on a repeated basis (Connolly & Read, 2006). In most cases of maltreatment, the basic facts are not known, making it difficult to determine whether the child victim's report is complete or accurate. There have been a few forensic cases in which the information reported was corroborated independently by the perpetrator (i.e., Jones & Krugman, 1986), audiotape (Orbach & Lamb, 1999), and a combination of audiotapes and photographs (Bidrose & Goodman, 2000). In the last situation, four girls who were victims of a sex ring were able to provide detailed information about their repeated abuses for 85% of their sexual allegations that corresponded to audio or photographic evidence.

The experimental literature has shown that children differ in their recall of repeated and single experiences of events (Connolly & Lindsay, 2001; Connolly & Price, 2006; Fivush & Hudson, 1990; Hudson, 1990). Repetition may create a memorial advantage by improving recall for fixed details that stay constant across instances (Quas, Goodman, Bidrose, Pipe, Craw, & Ablin, 1999). Alternatively, events that are repeatedly experienced by children tend to be transformed into abstract cognitive representations, or scripts, of what usually happens, which then serve to inform them of what to expect in future occurrences (Nelson, 1986). Under supportive conditions, children are able to report details about a specific episode of an event, but may rely on their general knowledge as a framework to organize their memory and fill in missing information (Fivush, 2002; Powell et al., 2003). Hence, repeated experiences may potentially contain errors as one episode blends with the next or gaps are filled in with schema-consistent information. Nevertheless, several studies indicate that children's reports of a traumatic medical procedure (VCUG) are not less accurate as a result of repeated versus one-time experience (Goodman & Quas, 1997; Goodman, Quas, Batternman-Faunce, Riddlesberger, & Kuhn, 1997; Salmon, Price, & Pereira, 2002).

Interview Factors Affecting Memory and Reporting

In particular, children's inaccurate reporting of information they never experienced (i.e., false memory) seems to stem from a combination of strategies used by interviewers—interviewer bias; repeated questions within interviews and repeating misinformation across interviews; source confusion; and coercion through emotional tone and peer pressure, high status, and stereotype inducement. The false information reported by children in the mass-allegation daycare cases and in research designed to simulate these real-life interview blunders is more often a consequence of the techniques used to question the children rather than naturalistic memory errors on their part.

Interviewer Bias

One technique is for interviewers to develop a line of questioning consistent with a single hypothesis (Bruck & Ceci, 1995), that of maltreatment, even when alternative explanations are just as valid, the evidence is inconsistent with maltreatment, or the testimony is incomprehensible or simply bizarre, such as a boy testifying that the couple who owned Country Walk Daycare forced him to drink poison that killed him (Ceci & Bruck, 1995, p. 98). The rationale employed by investigators in such circumstances is that their job to speak for the children who may not admit abuse because they are embarrassed or have been intimidated into silence by their abusers. Research confirms that interviewers' preconceived beliefs about what occurred (i.e., maltreatment) influence the types of questions they ask witnesses (specifically, those suggestive or reflective of maltreatment), the strategies employed to elicit testimony (e.g., bribes, threats, repetitive and suggestive questioning, coercion), and, consequently, the reliability of the information witnesses provide (Clarke-Stewart, Thomson, & Lepore, 1989; Pettit, Fegan, & Howie, 1990). In a study by White, Leichtman, and Ceci (1997), preschoolers participated in game-like events and then 1 and 2 months later were questioned by interviewers, who were given either a correct or an incorrect one-page summary of activities performed by children (i.e., some were physically touched, some performed unusual acts, some observed others' actions). Interviewers used their preconceived beliefs to guide their questions, resulting in inaccurate reporting of some activities by children (e.g., someone licked their knees, someone put marbles in their ears). Despite their initial denial or reluctance to provide these inaccurate reports, the children stated them convincingly over time.

These findings reflect those from real-life legal cases. Ceci and Bruck (1995) reviewed the transcripts containing the line of questioning by prosecutors in the Wee Care Nursery School case for Kelly Michaels [*New Jersey v. Michaels*, WL 278424 (N.J.), 1994]. Their pursuit of a single hypothesis tainted children's testimony, as their questions ignored children's testimony that was contrary with their primary beliefs, inconsistent with or discrepant from physical evidence, or unintelligible. Moreover, the statements in response to the interviewer were never clarified or challenged, despite allegations that these bizarre acts occurred in public locations during the day. Single-hypothesis pursuit in the line of police questioning has contributed to approximately 25% of the 303 wrongful convictions of post-conviction DNA exonerees who pleaded guilty to crimes they did not commit (The Innocence Project, n.d.).

Repeated Questions

A second technique is to ask the same questions repeatedly, particularly suggestive ones that require a dichotomous response (yes or no), within an interview. This strategy may be used to elicit additional details or to check consistency of information already provided (Ceci & Bruck, 1995). In general, repetition operates by strengthening storage and retrieval of memory, regardless of whether the information provided is factual (Poole & White, 1995). When interviewers repeat open-ended questions, children provide essentially the same or elaborated responses presumably because this is consistent with their everyday experiences. However, they interpret repetition of closed-ended questions as a request to produce a different answer (Siegal, Waters, & Dinwiddy, 1988). Children may assume that the interviewer persistently and repeatedly asks the same specific question that has already been answered unambiguously because their response was not correct (Bruck & Ceci, 1995). In turn, they may succumb to the inherent pressure and change their answers (Cassel & Bjorklund, 1995; Shapiro, Blackford, & Chen, 2005), even if it is based on mere speculation, but now state it confidently despite their initial uncertainty (Poole & White, 1991).

Krähenbühl and Blades (2006) reported that children (5, 7, and 9 years old) maintained their responses only three-fourths of the time when asked repeated questions, changing their responses more for unanswerable questions than answerable ones. Moreover, children kept the changes in response to the second repeated question for all subsequent repeats of that query within the same interview. In Shapiro et al.'s (2005, Experiment 2) examination of recall for a simulated bicycle theft, age effects in compliance with repeated questions introduced in the 7-week delayed interview were mediated by the type of feature (e.g., 4/5-year-olds complied with misinformation concerning the central crime features; 9/10-year-olds complied with misinformation about the bicycle) and the temperament of the child (e.g., higher rates for active 4/5-year-olds regarding central crime features and active 9/10-year-olds for the bicycle). Additionally, studies show that children are particularly vulnerable to the influence of repeated questions when given explicit negative feedback (e.g., "You did not get all of those questions exactly right") about their performance (e.g., Warren, Hulse-Trotter, & Tubbs, 1991).

The children in the Little Rascals, Wee Care, and Country Walk daycare cases were asked the same questions repeatedly (e.g., "Did they have their clothes on or off?"; Ceci & Bruck, 1995, p. 98), particularly when the answers were inconsistent with maltreatment or when the children outright denied these suggestive prompts (Bruck & Ceci, 1995). In contrast, La Rooy and Lamb's (2011) evaluation of 37 transcripts of forensic interviews alleging abuse revealed that despite an average of eight repeated questions per interview, children basically provided the same response (54% of the time) or an elaborated response (27% of the time). Unlike the mass-allegation cases, the interviewers in this study were trained in best practices and mainly repeated questions as a challenge for a previous response, making it unlikely that they were pressuring children to change their answers. In general, the literature shows that repetition facilitates the incorporation of false information into memory, which children are likely to include in subsequent interviews as discussed in the next section.

Repeating Misinformation Across Interviews

A third technique is for the interviewer to repeat questions containing misinformation from the initial interview in subsequent interviews. Although repeated general, open-ended/nonleading interviewing across short delays results in accurate and complete reports (e.g., Howe, Courage, & Bryant-Brown, 1993; La Rooy, Pipe, & Murray, 2005; Shapiro, Blackford, & Chen, 2005), often with new (previously unrecalled) details (Hershkowitz & Terner, 2007; La Rooy, Katz, Malloy, & Lamb, 2010; La Rooy, Lamb, & Pipe, 2009), repeated suggestive interviewing has the opposite effect (Bruck, Ceci, & Hembrooke, 2002; Ceci et al., 1994). Researchers have found that a single exposure to misleading questions in the first interview does not necessarily bias free recall in later interviews (Shapiro et al., 2005), but can cause a decline in the proportion of peripherally related event features reported (Shapiro, Russell, & Henry, 2005). In contrast, introducing the misleading information in a delayed interview or having two or more misleading interviews can have deleterious effects on recall accuracy, including accepting misinformation as correct, incorporating misinformation into reports, and making inferences from suggestions (Bruck, Ceci, Francoeur, & Barr, 1995; Lewis, Wilkins, Baker, & Woobey, 1995; Warren & Lane, 1995), even for central event features (Shapiro et al., 2005). Suggestibility can even affect reports of central features of an event when misinformation is initially introduced in delayed interviews.

Ceci and Bruck (1995) explain that the increased suggestibility is the concomitant result of long delays between the original event and the individual's reporting of it (which by itself increases the chances of forgetting) and repeated exposure to misleading information (which increases familiarity and source monitoring errors). In many of the mass-allegation daycare cases, the initial interviews were not taped, but recordings of subsequent interviews showed heavy reliance on suggestive, forced-choice probes and questions, worded in complicated ways, that increased the opportunities to implant and sustain false reports.

Source Confusion or Source Attribution Error

In the fourth technique, the interviewer employs suggestive, misleading questions combined with mild or extreme social pressure to conform to expected answers (Ceci & Friedman, 2000). Consequently, this practice leads to source misattribution errors because children inaccurately report the suggested misinformation as witnessed, form false memories, and have difficulty in determining the source of misinformation as their own memory or the interrogator's suggestive remarks (Ackil & Zaragoza, 1995; Bruck & Ceci, 1997; Lindsay, Gonzales, & Eso, 1995; Shapiro & Purdy, 2005). Confabulated events become confused with experienced ones (Winningham & Weaver, 2000) because perceptual elaboration makes the mental representation of the fictitious information as rich or as clear in quality and details as true memories (Thomas, Bulevich, & Loftus, 2003) or because it forces people to process the information at a deeper, more meaningful level, allowing synthesis of false information in memory (i.e., depth-of-processing theory; see Craik & Lockhart, 1986).

Children in the daycare cases rarely contradicted incorrect statements by interviewers (Bruck & Ceci, 1997; Hunt & Borgida, 2001), resulting in them telling bizarre tales on the witness stand, such as stating that the teacher licked peanut butter off of children's genitals, made them drink the teacher's urine and eat her feces, or raped and assaulted them with knives, forks, spoons, and Lego blocks (see additional examples in Ceci & Bruck, 1995). Despite the 115 counts of sexual abuse supposedly being performed during the daytime by Kelly Michaels at the Wee Care Nursery School over the course of several months, none of them were witnessed by staff members or parents, children did not report any of them during this time frame, and no parents observed genital trauma or problems, food remnants, or strange behavior in their children as a result of this alleged prolonged abuse.

Over the past 30 years (e.g., Ceci et al., 1994; Ceci, Loftus, Leichtman, & Bruck, 1994; Foley & Johnson, 1985; Roberts, 2000, 2002; Roberts & Blades, 2000; Thierry, Spence, & Memon, 2001), researchers have examined children's ability to distinguish real from imagined events (i.e., reality monitoring) and investigated whether they can determine the origin of their recollections for real experiences (i.e., source monitoring). As stated by Ceci and Bruck (1995, p. 216), "The concepts of reality and source monitoring are sometimes indistinguishable when we try to remember whether something actually happened to us or whether someone merely told us that something happened to us." Children's reality monitoring ability may be reduced when they are exposed to misleading suggestions and forced confabulation (Ackil & Zaragoza, 1995, 1998; Shapiro & Purdy, 2005), making them vulnerable to linking personally relevant information to confabulated events, resulting in blurring sources (Foley, Santini, & Sopasakis, 1989).

Shapiro and Purdy (2005) examined source attribution errors in 5- to 8-year-old children who had false events merely suggested to them or were forced to produce false details; these children were reinterviewed after a 1-week delay using the same or different interviewers, who provided warnings that mistakes might have been made in the initial interview. The researchers found children's compliance in the forced confabulation group was near the ceiling for the six items, whereas children in the suggestive group showed resistance, with 16 of the 30 children not complying with any items, 11 of the 30 complying with 1 item, and 3 of the 30 complying with 2 to 6 items in the initial interview. Despite the disclaimer and in the absence of social pressure in the delayed interview, children failed to distinguish between interviewer-introduced information and their own memories for both true-event and false-event items. Ceci and Bruck (1995) similarly reported that 27% of the children in their mousetrap study accepted the fictitious events they described as real, despite debriefing informing them the incidents never happened.

In regard to the source-amnesia findings showing group differences, Shapiro and Purdy (2005) explain that self-generated confabulations are more susceptible to this misattribution effect than false-event information generated by the interviewer. Moreover, despite any misgivings children had about confabulating in the initial interview, as evidenced by their resistance to prompts and outright statements of denial, many of them failed to distinguish the source of the confabulations as occurring in the interview when talking to the same interviewer again (also see Lindsay, Johnson, & Kwon, 1991). In contrast, the suggestive group had difficulty remembering that the initial interview was the source of false information when a different interviewer asked them about it. The research demonstrates the difficulty children from the various daycare center cases (e.g., Old Cutler, Little Rascals, Wee Care, Country Walk) would have had in differentiating their own experiences from information gained in multiple interviews with many people, counseling sessions using a variety of questionable techniques (e.g., imagining role playing), and books with abusive themes read to them over the course of months and years (Ceci & Bruck, 1995).

Coercion Through Emotional Tone of Interview

In the fifth technique, interviewers use a coercive emotional tone delivered through implicit or explicit threats, bribes, and rewards to pressure victims into producing a particular response, often a false statement that supports maltreatment. For example, the interviewer may use an accusatory probe implying that the child was involved in a socially unacceptable event (e.g., "We know Mr. Bob did something bad to you") and then encourage the child to report it as a form of release (e.g., "Once you admit it, you'll feel better").

Interviewing conditions may lead children to report fantasy events as their real experiences (Principe & Smith, 2007), as was done by child witnesses in the Little Rascals Day Care and Wee Care Nursery School child abuse cases (Pendergrast, 1995; Rabinowitz, 1990). These children uttered fantastical statements such as "I peed in her penis" and "We chopped our penises off" (Ceci & Bruck, 1995, p. 158). In everyday conversations, adults are accepting, encouraging, and even complicit in children's embellishments of their personal experiences (e.g., invisible friend, monsters, fairies, aliens), as these devices make the story interesting and amusing (Principe & Schindewolf, 2012). Hence, interviewers may inadvertently prompt preschool and elementary school children, who commonly and naturally pretend in their storytelling and play, to invent tales or acquiesce to suggestions of bizarre acts (e.g., licking peanut butter from genitals, stabbing babies and throwing them into the river), such as had been demonstrated in real forensic interviews (see Ceci & Bruck, 1995).

Researchers have also found that children may fabricate participation in events they do not recall, even when the suggested events involve sexually abusive acts (e.g., hugged or kissed, given a bath, photographed in the bathroom), when the children are pressured by interviewers (see the review in Ceci & Bruck, 1993; Goodman, Wilson, Hazan, & Reed, 1989). Social coercion to comply with false statements can also be applied by using verbal reinforcers, such as telling the child "You are good;" bribes, such as giving toys or dessert or even promising to end the interview if a confession is made; or other comments to encourage children's cooperation, such as telling the child that she is special (see the Wee Care interviews by Detective McGrath described in Bruck & Ceci, 1995). Demonstrating the danger of such enticements, Garven, Wood, and Malpass (2000) reported that 50% of the children (4- to 7-year-olds) in their study who were given praise and encouragement made false accusations about Paco, a stranger who visited them briefly, including that they flew in a helicopter with him to a farm.

Coercion Through Peer Pressure
The sixth technique involves peer pressure to obtain information about maltreatment. Interviewers may attempt to convince children to reveal their victimization by indicating that their peers have already provided the requested information (e.g., "Johnny already told me that Mr. Bob touched your penis"), as though they are part of a conspiracy (Bruck et al., 2002). They may also explicitly threaten uncooperative children that they will be reported to the peers for not wanting to help or to protect the rest by revealing information about the group's maltreatment (e.g., "You don't want me to tell the other kids that you won't help them").

Peer pressure can also occur naturally when co-witnesses interact and discuss their own versions of the event, resulting in changes to each witness's memory. This process was demonstrated in the Wee Care Nursery School case, as revealed by a witness who stated that her friend was the source of her allegation rather than her own experience (Ceci & Bruck, 1995). Credibility is often assessed through similarity of allegations across victims, naively assuming that each witness is producing an independent representation of the event. In reality, children may insist that they were active participants in an event they did not directly experience, but rather simply heard about it from their peers (Pettit et al., 1990; Pynoos & Nader, 1989). Research by Principe and her colleagues (Principe, Guiliano, & Root, 2008) found that overheard rumors about an event discussed with peers, particularly classmates (Principe, Daley, & Kauth, 2010), can become falsely incorporated into memory as experienced, regardless of whether the rumor was adult generated (Principe, Kanaya, Ceci, & Singh, 2006) or child generated (Principe & Ceci, 2002; Principe, Guiliano, & Root, 2008). Preschoolers are particularly susceptible to false memories when the rumor helps to explain a confusing event they have experienced (Principe, Tinguely, & Dobkowski, 2007). However, older children (9 to 11 years) will revise their event memory reports, after learning of another person's perspective, to make them reflect the new information at a minimum, or to integrate their recollections into a coherent version reflecting both perspectives (Tsethlikai & Greenhoot, 2006).

High Status/Power Interviewer
In the seventh technique, the interviewer attempts to intimidate the child through his or her job status, such as in law enforcement. Children are cognizant that they should comply with the implicit and explicit beliefs of adults, particularly requests by adults who have status or power (Ceci & Bruck, 1995). Research has shown that children are more likely to

be swayed to provide false testimony when questioned by police officers than by neutral interviewers who use accusatory statements (e.g., Tobey & Goodman, 1992). In many of the nursery school abuse cases (e.g., Country Walk, Little Rascals, Wee Care) described by Ceci and Bruck, high-status adults (sometimes with more than one in a room) imposed intimidating interview contexts by informing children of their status (e.g., "I'm a policeman") and their power (e.g., "I'm going to introduce to one of the men who arrested Kelly and put her in jail") to obtain testimony from the child witnesses/victims (p. 152).

Stereotype Inducement
An eighth technique is the use of negative stereotypes induction to influence the child's interpretation, encoding, and recall of an actor's behaviors in an event (Bigler & Liben, 1993; Greenhoot, 2000; Greenhoot, Tsethlikai, & Wagoner, 2006). Researchers have found that children can be swayed to accept incriminating statements (e.g., "He wasn't supposed to do/say that. That was bad.") as factual when these statements are consistent with their prior expectations (Leichtman & Ceci, 1995; Lepore & Sesco, 1994). Lepore and Sesco reported that in response to suggestions ("Did Dale ever touch other kids at the school?"), children even provided additional false details of incrimination (e.g., "He touched Jason, he touched Tori, and he touched Molly."), including how (e.g., kissed) and where they were touched (e.g., legs) and whether clothing was removed, both in the immediate and delayed interviews. Similarly, Leichtman and Ceci reported on preschoolers ages 3 to 6 years who were subjected to four suggestive interviews over a 10-week period, after being told negative stereotypes about a person whom they met (Sam Stone) briefly at their daycare center (e.g., Sam gets into accidents, Sam breaks things). A high percentage of the children (72%) subsequently claimed that this person did one or two of the misdeeds (i.e., rip book, soil teddy bear) of which he was accused by a new interviewer who used general prompts (i.e., "Did anything happen to a book?") to elicit this information during the delayed interview.

Children rely on their social knowledge to understand and remember behaviors and experiences, which could be induced simply by an interviewer's negative stereotype (Thompson, Clarke-Stewart, & Lepore, 1997), particularly when the event discussed is ambiguous (Dodge & Frame, 1982). Many of the interviews in the childcare abuse cases, such as the Wee Care case, used stereotype induction, such as indicating that the alleged perpetrator was "bad" and "was in jail because he or she did bad things." For example, this technique was used by the investigator when interviewing 15 of the 34 children in the Wee Care case (Bruck & Ceci, 1995, p. 287).

Nonverbal Indicators of Lying

It is possible for interviewers to determine whether people providing information about their experiences are lying. The detection of lies may rest on nonverbal cues emitted through the interviewees' own actions, despite their efforts to conceal the lie. According to Eckman (1997), lies fail because people do not prepare sufficiently the falsehood they intend to relate or because their emotions reveal their deception. One consequence of this "thinking" failure is that when interviewed repeatedly, liars fail to provide the same information, often contradicting themselves about the details. Eckman cautions that reports by truth tellers may also contain contradictions; however, there are no particular signs in contradiction that reliably distinguish liars from truth tellers (also see Orcutt, Goodman, Tobey, Batterman-Faunce, & Thomas, 2001).

A second consequence of this "thinking" failure is that liars lose voice intonation, reduce hand expression to supplement their words, and produce specific nonverbal cues, such as long pauses, increased speech mannerisms and speech disfluencies (e.g., revisions, hesitations, repetitions of multisyllable words and phrases), and extended aversion of their gaze. These behaviors, although not signs of lying per se, signify that people are attempting to devise answers to questions for which they had not anticipated or prepared, none of which would have been necessary if they had responded with the truth.

There are also consequences of "emotion" failure. People fail when feigning the feelings associated with the deception. Eckman (1997) believes that certain behavioral signs indicate emotional lying, such as the absence of "narrowing of the red margins of lips in anger" (p. 343). The other deception involved, besides creating false emotions, is concealing true emotions. The liar may attempt to stop or disguise feelings, which escape nonetheless, through a process called "leakage." Additionally, the liar's behaviors may change due to the amount of effort involved in concealing emotions. Liars may have feelings about how their lies may be discovered and they will be punished; feel guilty about lying, particularly if they think it may hurt someone; or feel a thrill for duping the interviewer. Importantly, if a person does not believe that the statement being made is a lie, then these lie-associated feelings (e.g., fear, guilt) will not occur. In this way, a person who committed a crime may pass a lie-detector test, as this machine measures certain physiological reactions (i.e., blood pressure, pulse, and respiration) in response to fear or guilt from lying. Finally, despite individual differences in how lies are nonverbally expressed, most people channel their lies through their face, voice, and body.

Leach, Talwar, Lee, Bala, and Lindsay (2004) reported that adults' ability to detect children's deception visually is poor (Experiment 1), even when they had additional exposure to them (Experiment 4), but improved somewhat when children promised to tell the truth (Experiment 3). Law enforcement officers are only slightly better than chance (54%) at detecting lies visually (Eckman, O'Sullivan, & Frank, 1999; Mann, Vrij, & Bull, 2004), despite their overconfidence in their ability to do so. Some people may possess certain traits that allow them to be good at reading emotions and detecting behavioral cues of liars (Edelstein, Luten, Ekman, & Goodman, 2006) or may simply differ in their inclination to assess statements as truthful (Bond & DePaulo, 2008).

Another strategy for detecting false information involves examining children's statements for consistency within and across interviews and the amount of details provided in these reports. For example, statement validity analysis (SVA) has been used to differentiate truthful and deceptive reports (Vrij, 2005), but it has substantial error rates (e.g., higher than 22%), cannot distinguish lies from implanted memories, and is compromised by repeated events (see Gilstrap, Fritz, Torres, & Melinder, 2005, for a review). Low consistency and provision of few details in allegations of abuse is often interpreted as the child being unreliable (e.g., Leippe, Romanczyk, & Manion, 1991), yet research has shown that both of these markers are controlled by the interviewer. Specifically, different interviewers may draw out different types of information from children, but this inconsistency does not mean the information given was inaccurate (Fivush, Hamond, Harsch, Singer, & Wolf, 1991). Similarly, the number of details a child provides often reflect the interviewer's ability to produce specific enough cues to signal recall.

Chapter Summary

Interviewing is a critical component in the investigative process. The interview should aim at fact finding and should follow established valid and reliable protocols. Before conducting the interview, the investigator must establish a plan. In this plan, the interviewer determines who will be interviewed and in which order they will be interviewed. The interviewer also determines how to record the interview—for example, notes, audiotape, and/or videotape. The pros and cons of each option are considered before selection.

Concerning the format of the interview, a combination of the Step-wise Interview and the Enhanced Cognitive Interview is recommended. With this best practice approach, the interview consists of five phases: (1) rapport development and narrative practice; (2) transition and interview preparation instructions; (3) narrative of maltreatment; (4) specific questions posed by interviewer; and (5) closure. The use of forensic assessment tools, such as anatomically correct dolls and drawings, during interviews has drawn significant criticism from courts, practitioners, academicians, and researchers in the field.

Several theories seek to explain the autobiographical memory process and the effects of post-event suggestions on memory. Certain factors affect the recall of events, particularly in terms of the amount and accuracy of recall—namely, stress, developmental ability, and the interview itself. Specifically, for children, experiencing or witnessing a traumatic event can have adverse psychological effects on the child, such as creating stress. Children's development also influences their memory and reporting of events. Moreover, children may inaccurately report information due to improper interviewer techniques and tactics. The following factors all adversely impact a child's report of abuse: interviewer bias; repeated questioning; repeated misinformation across interviews; source confusion; coercion through the emotional tone of the interviewer; coercion through peer pressure; use of the interviewer's high status or power to influence child; and use of negative stereotypes to influence the child. Furthermore, interviewers can attend to certain nonverbal indicators to determine whether the person providing information is intentionally lying.

Review Questions

1. What is the interview protocol? Why is it important?

2. What is the most appropriate format for an interview? Why do you think so?

3. What are the essential stages of an interview? What occurs in each stage?

4. Name and describe the factors that influence the amount and accuracy of recall.

5. In which ways does child development influence memory and reporting? Give specific examples in your response.

6. Name and describe the tactics that an interviewer uses that can adversely impact a child's reporting of an event.

7. How can an interviewer determine if an interviewee is lying?

References

Ackil, J. K., & Zaragoza, M. S. (1995). Developmental differences in eyewitness suggestibility and memory for source. *Journal of Experimental Child Psychology, 60*(1), 57–83.

Ackil, J. K., & Zaragoza, M. S. (1998). Memorial consequences of forced confabulation: Age differences in susceptibility to false memories. *Developmental Psychology, 34*(6), 1358–1372.

American Professional Society on the Abuse of Children (APSAC). (2012). *Guidelines for psychosocial evaluation of suspected sexual abuse in young children*. Chicago, IL: Author.

American Prosecutors Research Institute. (2004). *Investigation and prosecution of child abuse* (3rd ed.). Thousand Oaks, CA: Sage.

August, R. L., & Forman, B. D. (1989). A comparison of sexually abused and nonsexually abused children's behavioral responses to anatomically correct dolls. *Child Psychiatry and Human Development, 20*(1), 39–47.

Bahrick, L. E., Parker, J. F., Fivush, R., & Levitt, M. (1998). The effects of stress on young children's memory for a natural disaster. *Journal of Experimental Psychology: Applied, 4*(4), 308–331.

Baker-Ward, L., Gordon, B. N., Ornstein, P. A., Larus, D. M., & Clubb, P. A. (1993). Young children's long-term retention of a pediatric examination. *Child Development, 64*(5), 1519–1533.

Batterman-Faunce, J. M., & Goodman, G. S. (1993). Effects of context on the accuracy and suggestibility of child witnesses. In G. S. Goodman & B. L. Bottoms (Eds.), *Child victims, child witnesses: Understanding and improving testimony* (pp. 301–330). New York, NY: Guildford Press.

Bauer, P. J. (2007). *Remembering the times of our lives: Memory in infancy and beyond*. Mahwah, NJ: Lawrence Erlbaum Associates.

Bekerian, D. A., & Bowers, J. M. (1983). Eyewitness testimony: Were we misled? *Journal of Experimental Psychology: Learning, Memory, & Cognition, 9*(1), 139–145.

Bidrose, S., & Goodman, G. S. (2000). Testimony and evidence: A scientific case study of memory for child sexual abuse. *Applied Cognitive Psychology, 14*(3), 197–213.

Bigler, R. S., & Liben, L. S. (1993). A cognitive-developmental approach to racial stereotyping and reconstructive memory in Euro-American children. *Child Development, 64*(5), 1507–1518.

Bloise, S. M., & Johnson, M. K. (2007). Memory for emotional and neutral information: Gender and individual differences in emotional sensitivity. *Memory, 15*, 1192–1204.

Boat, B. W., & Everson, M. D. (1988). Use of anatomical dolls among professionals in sexual abuse evaluations. *Child Abuse & Neglect, 12*, 171–179.

Bond, C. F. Jr., & DePaulo, B. M. (2008). Individual Differences in judging deception: Accuracy and bias. *Psychological Bulletin, 134*(4), 477–492.

Brainerd, C. J., & Poole, D. A. (1997). Long term survival of children's false memories: A review. *Learning and Individual Differences, 9*(2), 125–151.

Brainerd, C. J., Reyna, V. F., Howe, M. L., & Kevershan, J. (1991). Fuzzy-trace theory and cognitive triage in memory development. *Developmental Psychology, 27*(3), 351–369.

Bruck, M., & Ceci, S. J. (1995). Amicus brief for the case of *State of New Jersey v. Michaels* presented by Committee of Concerned Social Scientists. *Psychology, Public Policy, and Law, 1*(2), 272–322.

Bruck, M., & Ceci, S. J. (1997). The description of children's suggestibility. In N. L. Stein, P. A. Ornstein, B. Tversky, & C. Brainerd (Eds.), *Memory for everyday and emotional events* (pp. 371–400). Mahwah, NJ: LEA.

Bruck, M., Ceci, S. J., Francoeur, E., & Barr, R. (1995). "I hardly cried when I got my shot!": Influencing children's reports about a visit to their pediatrician. *Child Development, 66*(1), 193–208.

Bruck, M., Ceci, S. J., & Hembrooke, H. (2002). The nature of children's true and false narratives. *Developmental Review, 22*, 520–554.

Bull, R. (1996). Good practice for video-recorded interviews with child witnesses for use in criminal proceedings. In G. Davies, S. Llyod-Bostock, M. McMurran, & C. Wilson (Eds.), *Psychology, law, and criminal justice* (pp. 101–117). Berlin, Germany: de Gruyter.

Bull, R., & Corran, E. (2002). Interviewing child witnesses: Past and future. *International Journal of Police Science and Management, 4*(4), 315–322.

Burgwyn-Bailes, E., Baker-Ward, L., Gordon, B. N., & Ornstein, P. A. (2001). Children's memory for emergency medical treatment after one year: The impact of individual difference variables on recall and suggestibility. *Applied Cognitive Psychology, 15*(7), S25–S48.

Cassel, W. S., & Bjorklund, D. F. (1995). Developmental patterns of eyewitness memory and suggestibility: An ecologically based short-term longitudinal study. *Law and Human Behavior, 19*(5), 507–532.

Ceci, S. J., & Bruck, M. (1993). Suggestibility of the child witness: A historical review and synthesis. *Psychological Bulletin, 113*(3), 403–439.

Ceci, S. J., & Bruck, M. (1995). *Jeopardy in the courtroom: A scientific analysis of children's testimony.* Washington, DC: American Psychological Association.

Ceci, S. J., Crotteau-Huffman, M. L., Smith, E., & Loftus, E. F. (1994). Repeatedly thinking about a non-event. *Consciousness & Cognition, 3*, 388–407.

Ceci, S. J., & Friedman, R. D. (2000). The suggestibility of children: Scientific research and legal implications. *Cornell Law Review, 86*, 33–108.

Ceci, S. J., Loftus, E. F., Leichtman, M., & Bruck, M. (1994). The possible role of source misattributions in the creation of false beliefs among preschoolers. *International Journal of Clinical & Experimental Hypnosis, 42*(4), 304–320.

Chandler, M. J., Boyes, M., Ball, S., & Hala, S. (1987). The conservation of selfhood: Children's changing conceptions of self-continuity. In T. Honess & K. Yardley (Eds.), *Self and identity: Perspectives across the life-span* (pp. 108–120). London, UK: Routledge & Kegan Paul.

Christianson, S. -A. (1992). Emotional stress and eyewitness memory: A critical review. *Psychological Bulletin, 112*(2), 284–309.

Clarke-Stewart, A., Thomson, W. C., & Lepore, S. (1989). *Manipulating children's interpretation through interrogation.* Paper presented at the 1989 Society for Research in Child Development meetings, Kansas City, MO.

Cohen, R. L., & Harnick, M. A. (1980). The susceptibility of child witnesses to suggestion: An empirical study. *Law and Human Behavior, 4*(3), 201–210.

Cohn, D. S. (1991). Anatomical doll play of preschoolers referred for sexual abuse and those not referred. *Child Abuse & Neglect, 15*(4), 455–466.

Connolly, D. A., & Lindsay, D. S. (2001). The influence of suggestions on children's reports of a unique experience versus an instance of a repeated experience. *Applied Cognitive Psychology, 15*, 205–223.

Connolly, D. A., & Price, H. L. (2006). Children's suggestibility for an instance of a repeated event versus a unique event: The effect of degree of association between variable options. *Journal of Experimental Child Psychology, 93,* 207–223.

Connolly, D. A., & Read, J. D. (2006). Delayed prosecutions of historic child sexual abuse: Analyses of 2064 Canadian criminal complaints. *Law and Human Behavior, 30*(6), 409–434.

Coxon, P., & Valentine, T. (1997). The effects of age of eyewitness on the accuracy and suggestibility of their testimony. *Applied Cognitive Psychology, 11*(5), 415–430.

Craik, F. I. M., & Lockhart, R. S. (1986). CHARM is not enough: Comments on Eich's model of cued recall. *Psychological Review, 93*(3), 360–364.

Cutler, B. L., Penrod, S. D., & Martens, T. K. (1987). The reliability of eyewitness identification: The role of system and estimator variables. *Law and Human Behavior, 11*(3), 233–258.

Davies, G. M., Tarrant, A., & Flin, R. (1989). Close encounters of the witness kind: Children's memory for a simulated health inspection. *British Journal of Psychology, 80*(4), 415–429.

DeLoache, J. S. (1994). The use of dolls in interviewing young children. In M. S. Zaragoza, J. R. Graham, G. C. N. Hall, & Y. S. Ben-Porath (Eds.), *Memory and testimony in the child witness* (pp. 160–178). Thousand Oaks, CA: Sage.

DeLoache, J. S., & Marzolf, D. P. (1995). The use of dolls to interview young children. *Journal of Experimental Child Psychology, 60,* 155–173.

DeLoache, J. S., Miller, K. F., & Rosengren, K. S. (1997). The credible shrinking room: Very young children's performance with symbolic and nonsymbolic relations. *Psychological Science, 8,* 308–313.

Dodge, K. A., & Frame, C. L. (1982). Social cognitive biases and deficits in aggressive boys. *Child Development, 53*(3), 620–635.

Easterbrook, J. A. (1959). The effect of emotion on cue utilization and the organization of behavior. *Psychological Review, 66*(3), 183–201.

Eckman, P. (1997). What we have learned by measuring facial behavior. In P. Eckman & E. L. Rosenberg (Eds.), *What the face reveals: Basic and applied studies of spontaneous expression using the Facial Action Coding System* (FACS) (pp. 469–486). Oxford, UK: Oxford University Press.

Eckman, P., O'Sullivan, M., & Frank, M. G. (1999). A few can catch a liar. *Psychological Science, 10,* 263–266.

Edelstein, R. S., Luten, T. L., Ekman, P., & Goodman, G. S. (2006). Detecting lies in children and adults. *Law and Human Behavior, 30*(1), 1–10.

Elzinga, B. M., Baka, M., & Bremner, J. D. (2005). Stress-induced cortisol elevations are associated with impaired delayed, but not immediate recall. *Psychiatry Research, 134*(3), 211–223.

Everson, M. D., & Boat, B. W. (1994). Putting the anatomical doll controversy in perspective: An examination of the major uses and criticisms of the dolls in child sexual abuse evaluations. *Child Abuse & Neglect, 18*(2), 113–129.

Feldman, C., Bruner, J., Kalmar, D., & Renderer, B. (1993). Plot, plight, and dramatism: Interpretation at three ages. *Human Development, 36*(6), 327–342.

Fischer, K. W., & Bullock, D. (1984). Cognitive development in school-age children: Conclusions and new directions. In W. A. Collins (Ed.), *Development during middle childhood: The years from six to twelve* (pp. 70–146). Washington, DC: National Academy Press.

Fivush, R. (1997). Event memory in childhood. In N. Cowan (Ed.), *The development of memory in childhood* (pp. 139–162). Sussex, UK: Psychology Press.

Fivush, R. (2002). The development of autobiographical memory. In H. L. Westcott, G. M. Davies, & Ray H. C. Bull (Eds.), *Children's testimony: A handbook of psychological research and forensic practice* (pp. 55–68). Chichester, UK: Wiley.

Fivush, R., Berlin, L. J., Sales, J. M., Mennuti-Washburn, J., & Cassidy, J. (2003). Functions of parent-child reminiscing about emotionally negative events. *Memory, 11*(2), 179–192.

Fivush, R., & Fromhoff, F. A. (1988). Style and structure in mother-child conversations about the past. *Discourse Processes, 11*(3), 337–355.

Fivush, R., Hamond, N. R., Harsch, N., Singer, N., & Wolf, A. (1991). Content and consistency of young children's autobiographical recall. *Discourse Processes, 14*(3), 373–388.

Fivush, R., Hazzard, A., Sales, J. M., Sarfati, D., & Brown, T. (2002). Creating coherence out of chaos? Children's narratives of emotionally negative and positive events. *Applied Cognitive Psychology, 16,* 1–19.

Fivush, R., & Hudson, J. A. (1990). *Knowing and remembering in young children.* New York, NY: Cambridge University Press.

Fivush, R., Hudson, J. A., & Nelson, K. (1984). Children's long-term memory for a novel event: An exploratory study. *Merrill-Palmer Quarterly, 30*(3), 303–316.

Fivush, R., Sales, J. M., Goldberg, A., Bahrick, L., & Parker, J. (2004). Weathering the storm: Children's long-term recall of Hurricane Andrew. *Memory, 12*(1), 104–118.

Foley, M. A., & Johnson, M. K. (1985). Confusions between memories for performed and imagined actions: A developmental comparison. *Child Development, 56*(5), 1145–1155.

Foley, M. A., Santini, C., & Sopasakis, M. (1989). Discrimination between memories: Evidence for children's spontaneous elaborations. *Journal of Experimental Child Psychology, 48,* 146–169.

Garven, S., Wood, J. M., & Malpass, R. S. (2000). Allegations of wrongdoing: The effects of reinforcement on children's mundane and fantastic claims. *Journal of Applied Psychology, 85,* 38–49.

Geiselman, R. E., & Fisher, R. P. (1997). Ten years of cognitive interviewing. In D. Payne & F. Conrad (Eds.), *Intersections in basic and applied memory research* (pp. 291–310). Mahwah, NJ: Lawrence Erlbaum Associates.

Gibson, J. J. (1977). The theory of affordances. In R. Shaw & J. Bransford (Eds.), *Perceiving, acting and knowing* (pp. 67–82). Hillsdale, NJ: Lawrence Erlbaum Associates.

Gilstrap, L. L., Fritz, K., Torres, A., & Melinder, A. (2005). Child witnesses: Common ground and controversies in the scientific community. *William Mitchell Law Review, 32,* 59–79.

Goodman, G., & Aman, C. (1990). Children's use of anatomically detailed dolls to recount a recent event. *Child Development, 61,* 1859–1871.

Goodman, G. S., & Quas, J. A. (1997). Trauma and memory: Individual differences in children's recounting of a stressful experience. In N. L. Stein, B. Tversky, & C. Brainerd (Eds.), *Memory for everyday and emotional events* (pp. 267–294). Mahwah, NJ: Lawrence Erlbaum Associates.

Goodman, G. S., Quas, J. S., Batterman-Faunce, J. M., Riddlesberger, M. M., & Kuhn, J. (1997). Children's reactions to and memory for a stressful event: Influences of age, anatomical dolls, knowledge, and parental attachment. *Applied Developmental Science, 1*(2), 54–74.

Goodman, G. S., Taub, E. P., Jones, D. P., England, P., Port, L. K., Rudy, L., & Prado, L. (1992). Testifying in criminal court: Emotional effects on child sexual assault victims. *Monographs of the Society for Research in Child Development, No. 229, 57*(5), 1–142.

Goodman, G. S., Wilson, M. E., Hazan, C., & Reed, R. S. (1989, April). *Children's testimony nearly four years after an event.* Paper presented to the Eastern Psychological Associates, Boston, MA.

Gordon, B. N., Ornstein, P. A., Nida, R., Follmer, A., Crenshaw, M., & Albert, G. (1993). Does the use of dolls facilitate children's memory of visits to the doctor? *Applied Cognitive Psychology, 7,* 459–474.

Graesser, A. C., Gordon, S. E., & Sawyer, J. D. (1979). Recognition memory for typical and atypical actions in scripted activities: Tests of a script point+tag hypothesis. *Journal of Verbal Learning and Verbal Behavior, 18,* 319–332.

Greenhoot, A. F. (2000). Remembering and understanding: The effects of changes in underlying knowledge on children's recollections. *Child Development, 71*(5), 1309–1328.

Greenhoot, A. F., Johnson, R., Legerski, J. P., & McCloskey, L. (2009). Chronic stress and autobio-graphical memory functioning. In R. Fivush & J. Quas (Eds.), *Stress and memory in development: Biological, social, and emotional considerations* (pp. 86–117). Oxford, UK: Oxford University Press.

Greenhoot, A. F., Ornstein, P. A., Gordon, B. N., & Baker-Ward, L. (1999). Acting out details of a pediatric check-up: The effects of interview condition on individual differences in children's memory reports. *Child Development, 70*, 363–380.

Greenhoot, A. F., Tsethlikai, M., & Wagoner, B. (2006). The relations between children's past experi-ences, social knowledge, and memories for social situations. *Journal of Cognition and Development, 7*(3), 313–340.

Habermas, T., & Bluck, S. (2000). Getting a life: The emergence of the life story in adolescence. *Psychological Bulletin, 126*(5), 748–769.

Habermas, T., & Paha, C. (2001). The development of coherence in adolescents' life narratives. *Narrative Inquiry, 11*, 35–54.

Harner, L. (1982). Talking about the past and the future. In W. J. Friedman (Ed.), *The developmental psychology of time* (pp. 141–170). New York, NY: Academic.

Hershkowitz, I., & Terner, A. (2007). The effects of repeated interviewing on children's forensic state-ments of sexual abuse. *Applied Cognitive Psychology, 21*(9), 1131–1143.

Howe, M. L., Courage, M. L., & Bryant-Brown, L. (1993). Reinstating preschoolers' memories. *Devel-opmental Psychology, 29*(5), 854–869.

Howe, M. L., Courage, M. L., & Peterson, C. (1994). How can I remember when I wasn't there: Long term retention of traumatic experiences and convergence of the cognitive self. *Consciousness & Cognition, 3*, 327–355.

Hudson, J. A. (1990). Constructive processes in children's event memory. *Developmental Psychology, 26*(2), 180–187.

Hudson, J. A., & Nelson, K. (1986). Repeated encounters of a similar kind: Effects of familiarity on children's autobiographic memory. *Cognitive Development, 1*, 253–271.

Hudson, J. A., & Shapiro, L. R. (1991). From knowing to telling: The development of children's scripts, stories, and personal narratives. In A. McCabe & C. Peterson (Eds.), *Developing narrative structure* (pp. 89–136). Hillsdale, NJ: Lawrence Erlbaum Associates.

Hunt, J. S., & Borgida, E. (2001). Is that what I said?: Witnesses' responses to interviewer modifica-tions. *Law and Human Behavior, 25*(6), 583–603.

The Innocence Project. (n.d.). Causes and remedies of wrongful convictions. http://www.innocen-ceproject.org/fix/947/Causes-and-Remedies.php

Jampole, L., & Weber, M. K. (1987). An assessment of the behavior of sexually abused and nonsexu-ally abused children with anatomically correct dolls. *Child Abuse and Neglect, 11*(2), 187–192.

Jones, D. P. H., & Krugman, R. D. (1986). Can a three-year-old child bear witness to her sexual assault and attempted murder? *Child Abuse and Neglect, 10*(2), 253–258.

Kassin, S. M., Ellsworth, P. C., & Smith, V. L. (1989). The "general acceptance" of psychological research on eyewitness testimony: A survey of experts. *American Psychologist, 44*(8), 1089–1098.

Kendall-Tackett, K. A. (1992). Beyond anatomical dolls: Professionals' use of other play therapy techniques. *Child Abuse & Neglect, 16*, 139–142.

Kenyon-Jump, R., Burnette, M., & Robertson, M. (1991). Comparison of behaviors of suspected sexually abused and nonsexually abused preschool children using anatomical dolls. *Journal of Psychopathology and Behavioral Assessment, 13*, 225–240.

Kitayama, N., Vaccarino, V., Kutner, M., Weiss, P., & Bremner, J. D. (2005). Magnetic resonance imaging (MRI) measurement of hippocampal volume in posttraumatic stress disorder: A meta-analysis. *Journal of Affective Disorders, 88*, 79–86.

Koocher, G. P., Goodman, G. S., White, S., Friedrich, W. N., Sivan, A. B., & Reynolds, C. R. (1995). Report of the anatomical doll task force. *Psychological Bulletin, 118*, 199–222.

Krähenbühl, S., & Blades, M. (2006). The effect of question repetition within interviews on young children's eyewitness recall. *Journal of Experimental Child Psychology, 94*(1), 57–67.

Lamb, M. E., Hershkowitz, I., Sternberg, K. J., Boat, B., & Everson, M. D. (1996). Investigative interviews of alleged sexual abuse victims with and without anatomical dolls. *Child Abuse and Neglect, 20*(12), 1239–1247.

Lamb, M. E., Sternberg, K. J., Orbach, Y., Esplin, P. W., Stewart, H., & Mitchell, S. (2003). Age differences in young children's responses to open-ended invitations in the course of forensic interviews. *Journal of Consulting and Clinical Psychology, 71*(5), 926–934.

La Rooy, D., Katz, C., Malloy, L. C., & Lamb, M. E. (2010). Do we need to rethink guidance on repeated interviews? *Psychology, Public Policy and Law, 16*(4), 373–392.

La Rooy, D., & Lamb, M. E. (2011). What happens when interviewers ask repeated questions in forensic interviews with children alleging abuse? *Journal of Police and Criminal Psychology, 26*(1), 20–25.

La Rooy, D., Lamb, M. E., & Pipe, M. (2009). Repeated interviewing: A critical evaluation of the risks and potential benefits In K. Kuehnle & M. Connell (Eds.), The evaluation of child sexual abuse allegations: A comprehensive guide to assessment and testimony (pp. 327–361). Hoboken, NJ: Wiley.

La Rooy, D., Pipe, M. -E., & Murray, J. E. (2005). Reminiscence and hyperamnesia in children's eyewitness memory. *Journal of Experimental Child Psychology, 90*, 235–254.

Leach, A., Talwar, V., Lee, K., Bala, N., & Lindsay, R. C. L. (2004). Intuitive lie detection of children's deception by law enforcement officials and university students. *Law and Human Behavior, 28*(6), 661–685.

Leichtman, M. D., & Ceci, S. J. (1995). The effects of stereotypes and suggestions on preschoolers' reports. *Developmental Psychology, 31*(4), 568–578.

Leippe, M. R., Romanczyk, A., & Manion, A. P. (1991). Eyewitness memory for a touching experience: Accuracy difference between child and adult witnesses. *Journal of Applied Psychology, 76*(3), 367–379.

Lepore, S. J., & Sesco, B. (1994). Distorting children's reports and interpretations of events through suggestion. *Journal of Applied Psychology, 79*(1), 108–120.

Levine, B. (2004). Autobiographical memory and the self in time: Brain lesion effects, functional neuroanatomy, and lifespan development. *Brain and Cognition, 55*(1), 54–68.

Lewis, C., Wilkins, R., Baker, L., & Woobey, A. (1995). "Is this man your daddy?" Suggestibility in children's eyewitness identification of a family member. *Child Abuse and Neglect, 19*(6), 739–744.

Lindsay, D. S., Johnson, M. K., & Kwon, P. (1991). Developmental changes in memory source monitoring. *Journal of Experimental Child Psychology, 52*, 297–318.

Lindsay, J. S., Gonzales, V., & Eso, K. (1995). Aware and unaware uses of memories of postevent suggestions. In M. S. Zaragoza, J. R. Graham, C. N. Gordon, R. Hirschman, & Y. Ben-Porath (Eds.), *Memory and testimony in the child witness* (pp. 86–108). Newbury Park, CA: Sage.

Loftus, E. F., & Hoffman, H. G. (1989). Misinformation in memory: The creation of new memories. *Journal of Experimental Psychology: General, 118*(1), 100–104.

Loftus, E. F., & Loftus, G. R. (1980). On the permanence of stored information in the human brain. *American Psychologist, 35*, 409–420.

Loftus, E. F., Miller, D., & Burns, H. (1978). Semantic integration of verbal information into a visual memory. *Journal of Experimental Psychology: Human Learning and Memory, 4*(1), 19–31.

Lyon, T. D. (2005). Speaking with children: Advice from investigative interviewers. In P. F. Talley (Eds.), *Handbook for the treatment of abused and neglected children* (pp. 65–82). Binghamton, NY: Haworth.

Maan, C. (1991). Assessment of sexually abused children with anatomically detailed dolls: A critical review. *Behavioral Sciences & the Law*, 9(1), 43–51.

Mann, S., Vrij, A., & Bull, R. (2004). Detecting true lies: Police officers' ability to detect deceit. *Journal of Applied Psychology*, 89(1), 137–149.

Marin, B. V., Holmes, D. L., Gruth, M., & Kovak, P. (1979). The potential of children as eyewitnesses. *Law and Human Behavior*, 3(4), 295–305.

McCloskey, M., & Zaragoza, M. (1985). Misleading post-event information and memory for events: Arguments and evident against memory impairment hypotheses. *Journal of Experimental Psychology: General, 114*(1), 1–16.

McIver, W., Wakefield, H., & Underwager, R. (1989). Behavior of abused and nonabused children in interviews with anatomically correct dolls. *Issues in Child Abuse Accusations*, 1(1), 39–48.

McNally, R. (2003). *Remembering trauma*. Cambridge, MA: Belknap Press/Harvard Press.

Menig-Peterson, C. L. (1975). The modification of communicative behavior in preschool aged children as a function of the listener's perspective. *Child Development*, 46(4), 1015–1018.

Merritt, K. A., Ornstein, P. A., & Spicker, B. (1994). Children's memory for a salient medical procedure: Implications for testimony. *Pediatrics*, 94(1), 17–23.

Mishkin, M., Suzuki, W. A., Gadian, D. G., & Vargha-Khadem, F. (1997). Hierarchical organization of cognitive memory. *Philosophical Transactions of the Royal Society of London Series B: Biological Sciences, 352*, 1461–1467.

Montangero, J. (1996). Understanding things along the time dimension: An adequate developmental approach can provide partial explanations of behavior. *Swiss Journal of Psychology*, 55(2–3), 104–111.

Montangero, J., & Pons, F. (1995). Introduction of past and future events in the description of a current situation: Developmental study of the diachronic tendency. *L'Anee Psychologique, 95*, 621–644.

Murachver, T., Pipe, M. E., Gordon, R., Owens, J. L., & Fivush, R. (1996). Do, show, and tell: Children's event memories acquired through direct experience, observation, and stories. *Child Development, 67*, 3029–3044.

Myers, J. E. B. (1993). Expert testimony regarding psychological syndromes. *Pacific Law Journal, 24*, 1449–1464.

Nelson, K. A. (1986). *Event knowledge: Structure and function in development*. Hillsdale, NJ: Lawrence Erlbaum Associates.

Nelson, K., & Gruendel, J. (1981). Generalized event representations: Basic building blocks of cognitive development. In M. E. Lamb & A. L. Brown (Eds.), *Advances in developmental psychology* (Vol. 1, pp. 21–46). Hillsdale, NJ: Lawrence Erlbaum Associates.

Oates, K., & Shrimpton, S. (1991). Children's memories for stressful and non-stressful events. *Medicine, Science, and the Law, 31*, 4–10.

Orbach, Y., & Lamb, M. E. (1999). Assessing the accuracy of a child's account of sexual abuse: A case study. *Child Abuse & Neglect*, 23(1), 91–98.

Orcutt, H. K., Goodman, G. S., Tobey, A. E., Batterman-Faunce, J. M., & Thomas, S. (2001). Detecting deception in children's testimony: Factfinders' abilities to reach the truth in open court and closed-circuit trials. *Law and Human Behavior*, 25(4), 339–372.

Ornstein, P. A., Larus, D. M., & Clubb, P. A. (1991). Understanding children's testimony: Implications of research on the development of memory. In R. Vasta (Ed.), *Annals of child development* (Vol. 8, pp. 145–176). London, UK: Jessica Kingsley.

Ornstein, P. A., Shapiro, L. R., Clubb, P. A., Follmer, A., & Baker-Ward, L. (1997). The influence of prior knowledge on children's memory for salient medical experiences. In N. L. Stein, P. A.

Ornstein, C. J. Brainerd, & B. Tversky (Eds.), *Memory for everyday and emotional event* (pp. 83–111). Mahwah, NJ: Lawrence Erlbaum Associates.

Pence, D. M. (2011). Child abuse and neglect investigation. In J. E. B. Myers (Ed.), *The APSAC handbook on child maltreatment* (3rd ed., pp. 325–336). Thousand Oaks, CA: Sage.

Pence, D. M., & Wilson, C. A. (1994). Reporting and investigating child sexual abuse. *The Future of Children, 4*(2), 70–83.

Pendergrast, M. (1995). *Victims of memory: Incest accusations and shattered lives.* Hinesburg, VT: Upper Access.

Perry, N. W., & McAuliff, B. D. (1993). The use of videotaped child testimony: Public policy implications. *Notre Dame Journal of Law, Ethics & Public Policy, 7*(2), 387–422.

Perry, N. W., McAuliff, B. D., Tam, P., Claycomb, L., Dostal, C., & Flanagan, C. (1995). When lawyers question children: Is justice served? *Law and Human Behavior, 19*(6), 609–629.

Peterson, C., & Biggs, M. (1998). Stitches and casts: Emotionality and narrative coherence. *Narrative Inquiry, 8*(1), 51–76.

Peterson, C., & McCabe, A. (1983). *Developmental psycholinguistics: Three ways of looking at a child's narrative.* New York, NY: Plenum.

Pettit, F., Fegan, M., & Howie, P. (1990, September). *Interviewer effects on children's testimony.* Paper presented at the International Congress on Child Abuse and Neglect, Hamburg, Germany.

Picard, L., Reffuveille, I., Eustache, F., & Piolino, P. (2009). Development of autonoetic autobiographical memory in school-age children: Genuine age effect or development of basic cognitive abilities? *Consciousness and Cognition, 18*(4), 864–876.

Pillemer, D. B., Picariello, M. L., & Pruett, J. C. (1994). Very long term memories of a salient preschool event. *Journal of Applied Cognitive Psychology, 8*(2), 95–106.

Piolino, P., Hisland, M., Ruffeveille, I., Matuszewski, V., Jambaqué, I., & Eustache, F. (2007). Do school-age children remember or know the personal past? *Consciousness and Cognition, 16*(1), 84–101.

Poole, D. A., & Lindsay, D. S. (1998). Assessing the accuracy of young children's reports: Lessons from the investigation of child sexual abuse. *Journal of Applied and Preventative Psychology, 7*, 1–26.

Poole, D. A., & Lindsay, D. S. (2001). Children's eyewitness reports after exposure to misinformation from parents. *Journal of Experimental Psychology: Applied, 7*(1), 27–50.

Poole, D., & White, L. (1995). Tell me again and again: Stability and change in the repeated testimonies of children and adults. In M. S. Zaragoza, J. R. Graham, C. N. Gordon, R. Hirschman, & Y. Ben-Porath (Eds.), *Memory and testimony in the child witness* (pp. 22–43). Newbury Park, CA: Sage.

Poole, D. A., & White, T. W. (1991). Effects of question repetition on the eyewitness testimony of children and adults. *Developmental Psychology, 27*(6), 975–986.

Powell, M. B., Thomson, D. M., & Ceci, S. J. (2003). Children's memory of recurring events: Is the first event always the best remembered? *Applied Cognitive Psychology, 17*, 127–146.

Price, H. L., & Roberts, K. P. (2007). A practical guide to interviewing child witnesses. *The Canadian Journal of Police & Security Services, 5*, 1–9.

Principe, G. F., & Ceci, S. J. (2002). "I saw it with my own ears": The influence of peer conversations and suggestive questions on preschoolers' event memory. *Journal of Experimental Child Psychology, 83*(1), 1–25.

Principe, G. F., Daley, L., & Kauth, K. (2010). Social processes affecting the mnemonic consequences of rumors on children's memory. *Journal of Experimental Child Psychology, 107*(4), 479–493.

Principe, G. F., Guiliano, S., & Root, C. (2008). Rumormongering and remembering: How rumors originating in children's inferences can affect memory. *Journal of Experimental Child Psychology, 99*(2), 135–155.

Principe, G. F., Kanaya, T., Ceci, S. J., & Singh, M. (2006). Believing is seeing: How rumors can engender false memories in preschoolers. *Psychological Science, 17*(3), 243–248.

Principe, G. F., & Schindewolf, E. (2012). Natural conversations as a source of false memories in children: Implications for the testimony of young witnesses. *Developmental Review, 32*, 205–223.

Principe, G. F., & Smith, E. (2007). The tooth, the whole tooth, and nothing but the tooth: How belief in the tooth fairy can engender false memories. *Applied Cognitive Psychology, 22*(5), 1–18.

Principe, G. F., Tinguely, A., & Dobkowski, N. (2007). Mixing memories: The effects of rumors that conflict with children's experiences. *Journal of Experimental Child Psychology, 98*, 1–19.

Pynoos, R. S., & Eth, S. (1984). The child as witness to homicide. *Journal of Social Issues, 40*(2), 87–108.

Pynoos, R. S., & Nader, K. (1989). Children's memory and proximity to violence. *Journal of the American Academy of Child and Adolescent Psychiatry, 28*(2), 236–241.

Qin, J., Quas, J., Redlich, A., & Goodman, G. S. (1997). Children's eyewitness memory. In N. Cowan (Ed.), *Memory development in childhood* (pp. 301–342). London, UK: Psychology.

Quas, J., Goodman, G. S., Bidrose, S., Pipe, M. -E., Craw, S., & Ablin, D. (1999). Emotion and memory: Children's remembering, forgetting, and suggestibility. *Journal of Experimental Child Psychology, 72*(4), 235–270.

Rabinowitz, D. (1990, May). From the mouths of babes to a jail cell: Child abuse and the abuse of justice. *Harper's Magazine*, 52–63.

Realmuto, G., Jensen, J., & Wescoe, S. (1990). Specificity and sensitivity of sexually anatomically correct dolls in substantiating abuse: A pilot study. *Journal of the American Academy of Child Adolescent Psychiatry, 29*(5), 743–746.

Realmuto, G., & Wescoe, S. (1992). Agreement among professionals about child's sexual abuse status: Interviews with sexually anatomically correct dolls as indicators of abuse. *Child Abuse and Neglect, 16*(5), 719–725.

Reese, E., Haden, C. A., Baker-Ward, L., Bauer, P., Fivush, R., & Ornstein, P. A. (2011). Coherence of personal narratives across the lifespan: A multidimensional model and coding method. *Journal of Cognition and Development, 12*(4), 424–462.

Reyna, V. F. (1995). Interference effects in memory and reasoning: A fuzzy-trace theory analysis. In F. N. Dempster & C. J. Brainerd (Eds.), *Interference and inhibition in cognition* (pp. 29–59). San Diego, CA: Academic.

Roberts, K. P. (2000). An overview of theory and research on children's source monitoring. In K. P. Roberts & M. Blades (Eds.), *Children's source monitoring* (pp. 11–57). Mahwah, NJ: Lawrence Erlbaum Associates.

Roberts, K. P. (2002). Children's ability to distinguish between memories from multiple sources: Implications for the quality and accuracy of eyewitness statements. *Developmental Review, 22*, 403–435.

Roberts, K. P., & Blades, M. (1998). The effects of interacting with events on children's eyewitness memory and source monitoring. *Applied Cognitive Psychology, 12*, 489–503.

Roberts, K. P., & Blades, M. (2000). *Children's source monitoring*. Mahwah, NJ: Lawrence Erlbaum Associates.

Rovee-Collier, C., & Gerhardstein, P. (1997). The development of infant memory. In N. Cowan (Ed.), *The development of memory in childhood* (pp. 5–39). Hove, UK: Psychology.

Sales, J. M., Fivush, R., & Peterson, C. (2003). Parental reminiscing about positive and negative events. *Journal of Cognition and Development, 4*(2), 185–209.

Salmon, K., Price, M., & Pereira, J. K. (2002). Factors associated with young children's long-term recall of an invasive medical procedure: A preliminary investigation. *Journal of Developmental and Behavioral Pediatrics, 23*(5), 347–352.

Saywitz, K. J. (1987). Children's testimony: Age related patterns of memory error. In S. J. Ceci, M. P. Toglia, & D. F. Ross (Eds.), *Children's eyewitness memory* (pp. 36–52). New York, NY: Springer-Verlag.

Saywitz, K. (1995). Improving children's testimony: The question, the answer, the environment. In M. S. Zaragoza, J. R. Graham, G. C. Hall, R. Hirschman, & Y. S. Ben-Porath (Eds.), *Memory and the child witness* (1st ed., pp. 109–113). Thousand Oaks, CA: Sage.

Saywitz, K. J., Geiselman, R. E., & Bornstein, G. K. (1992). Effects of cognitive interviewing and practice on children's recall performance. *Journal of Applied Psychology, 77*(5), 744–756.

Saywitz, K., & Goodman, G. S. (1996). Interviewing children in and out of court: Current research and practice implications. In J. Briere, L. Berliner, J. A. Bulkley, C. Jenny, & T. Reid (Eds.), *The APSAC handbook of child maltreatment* (pp. 297–318). Thousand Oaks, CA: Sage.

Saywitz, K. J., Goodman, G. S., Nicholas, E., & Moan, S. (1991). Children's memories of physical examinations involving genital touch: Implications for reports of child sexual abuse. *Journal of Consulting and Clinical Psychology, 59*(5), 682–691.

Saywitz, K. J., Lyon, T. D., & Goodman, G. S. (2010). Interviewing children. In J. E. B. Myers (Ed.), *The APSAC handbook on child maltreatment* (3rd ed., pp. 337–360). Los Angeles, CA: Sage.

Saywitz, K. J., & Snyder, L. (1996). Narrative elaboration: Test of a new procedure for interviewing children. *Journal of Consulting and Clinical Psychology, 64*(6), 1347–1357.

Schumann, J. P., Bala, N., & Lee, K. (1999). Developmentally appropriate questions for child witnesses. *Queen's Law Journal, 25*, 251–304.

Selman, R. L. (1980). *The growth of interpersonal understanding: Developmental and clinical analyses.* New York, NY: Academic.

Shapiro, L. R. (2009). Eyewitness testimony for a simulated juvenile crime by male and female perpetrators with gender-role consistent or inconsistent characteristics. *Journal of Applied Developmental Psychology, 30*(6), 649–666.

Shapiro, L. R., Blackford, C., & Chen, C. -F. (2005). Eyewitness memory for a simulated misdemeanor crime: The role of age and temperament in suggestibility. *Applied Cognitive Psychology, 19*(3), 267–289.

Shapiro, L. R., & Hudson, J. A. (1991). Tell me a make-believe story: Coherence and cohesion in young children's picture-elicited narratives. *Developmental Psychology, 27*(6), 960–974.

Shapiro, L. R., & Hudson, J. A. (1997). Coherence and cohesion in children's event narratives. In J. Costerman & M. Fayol (Eds.), *Processing interclausal relationships in the production and comprehension of text* (pp. 23–48). Hillsdale, NJ: Lawrence Erlbaum Associates.

Shapiro, L. R., & Purdy, T. (2005). Suggestibility and source monitoring errors: Blame the interview style, interviewer consistency, and the child's personality. *Applied Cognitive Psychology, 19*(4), 489–506.

Shapiro, L. R., Russell, C., & Henry, C. (2005, April). *The timing and number of suggestive interviews on child eyewitness memory.* Society for Research and Child Development, Atlanta, GA. Also presented at the 2005 Research and Creativity Forum, Emporia State University.

Shapiro, L. R., & Waymire, A. R. (2001, October). *Children's knowledge for pediatric check-ups.* Virginia Beach, VA: Cognitive Development Society.

Siegal, M., Waters, L. J., & Dinwiddy, L. S. (1988). Misleading children: Causal attribution for inconsistency under repeated questioning. *Journal of Experimental Child Psychology, 45*, 438–456.

Sutherland, R., & Hayne, H. (2001). Age-related changes in the misinformation effect. *Journal of Experimental Child Psychology, 79*(4), 388–404.

Terr, L. (1991). Childhood trauma: An outline and overview. *American Journal of Psychiatry, 148*(1), 10–20.

Terr, L. (1994). True memories of childhood trauma: Flaws, absences, and returns. In K. Pezdek & W. P. Banks (Eds.), *The recovered memory/false memory debate* (pp. 69–80). San Diego, CA: Academic.

Thierry, K. L., Spence, M. J., & Memon, A. (2001). Before misinformation is encountered: Source monitoring decrease child witness suggestibility. *Journal of Cognition and Development, 2*(1), 1–26.

Thomas, A. K., Bulevich, J. B., & Loftus, E. F. (2003). Exploring the role of repetition and sensory elaboration in the imagination inflation effect. *Memory & Cognition, 31*(4), 630–640.

Thompson, W. C., Clarke-Stewart, K. A., & Lepore, S. J. (1997). What did the janitor do? Suggestive interviewing and the accuracy of children's accounts. *Law & Human Behavior, 21*(4), 405-426.

Tobey, A. E., & Goodman, G. S. (1992). Children's eyewitness memory: Effects of participation and forensic context. *Child Abuse and Neglect, 16*, 779-796.

Trabasso, T., Secco, T., & van den Broek, P. (1984). Causal cohesion and story coherence. In H. Mandl, N. L. Stein, & T. Trabasso (Eds.), *Learning and comprehension of text* (pp. 83-111). Hillsdale, NJ: Lawrence Erlbaum Associates.

Tsethlikai, M., & Greenhoot, A. F. (2006). The influence of another's perspective on children's recall of previously misconstrued events. *Developmental Psychology, 42*(4), 732-745.

Underwager, R., & Wakefield, H. (1995). Special problems with sexual abuse cases. In J. Ziskin (Ed.), *Coping with psychiatric and psychological testimony* (5th ed., pp. 1315-1370). Los Angeles, CA: Law and Psychology Press.

van den Broek, P., Lorch, E. P., & Thurlow, R. (1996). Children's and adults' memory for television stories: The role of causal factors, story-grammar categories, and hierarchical level. *Child Development, 67*(6), 3010-3028.

Vrij, A. (2005). Criteria-based content analysis: A qualitative review of the first 37 studies. *Psychology, Public Policy, and Law, 11*(1), 3-41.

Warren, A., Hulse-Trotter, K., & Tubbs, E. C. (1991). Inducing resistance to suggestibility in children. *Law and Human Behavior, 15*(3), 273-285.

Warren, A. R., & Lane, P. (1995). Effects of timing and type of questioning on eyewitness accuracy and suggestibility. In M. S. Zaragoza, J. R. Graham, G. C. N. Hall, R. Hirschman, & Y. S. Ben-Porath (Eds.). *Memory and suggestibility in the child witness* (pp. 44-60). Thousand Oaks, CA: Sage.

White, S., Strom, G. A., Santili, G., & Halpin, B. (1986). Interviewing young sexual abuse victims with anatomically correct dolls. *Child Abuse and Neglect, 10*, 519-529.

White, T. L., Leichtman, M. D., & Ceci, S. J. (1997). The good, the bad, and the ugly: Accuracy, inaccuracy, and elaboration in preschoolers' reports about a past event. *Applied Cognitive Psychology, 11*(7), S37-S54.

Willoughby, K. A., Desrocher, M., Levine, B., & Rovet, J. F. (2012). Episodic and semantic autobiographical memory and everyday memory during late childhood and early adolescence. *Frontiers in Psychology, 3*. http://www.ncbi.nlm.nih.gov/pmc/articles/PMC3289112/

Winningham, R. G., & Weaver, C. A. (2000). The effects of pressure to report more details on memories of an eyewitness event. *European Journal of Cognitive Psychology, 12*(2), 271-282.

Yates, A., & Terr, L. C. (1988). Debate forum: Anatomically correct dolls: Should they be used as a basis for expert testimony. *Journal of the American Academy of Child and Adolescent Psychiatry, 27*, 254-257.

Yerkes, R. M., & Dodson, J. D. (1908). The relation of strength of stimulus to rapidity of habit-formation. *Journal of Comparative Neurology and Psychology, 18*(5), 459-548.

Yuille, J. C., Hunter, R., Joff, R., & Zaparniuk, J. (1993). Interviewing children in sexual abuse cases. In G. S. Goodman & B. L. Bottom (Eds.), *Child victims, child witnesses: Understanding and improving children's testimony* (pp. 95-115). New York, NY: Guilford.

Yuille, J. C., & Tollestrup, P. A. (1992). A model of the diverse effects of emotion on eyewitness memory. In S. -A. Christianson (Ed.), *The handbook of emotion and memory: Research and theory* (pp. 201-215). Hillsdale, NJ: Lawrence Erlbaum Associates.

Zaragoza, M. S., & Lane, S. M. (1994). Source misattributions and the suggestibility of eyewitness memory. *Journal of Experimental Psychology: Learning, Memory, and Cognition, 20*(4), 934-945.

Section IV

Roles, Responsibilities, and Perspectives of Those Involved in Child Maltreatment Cases

This section focuses on the roles, responsibilities, and perspectives of parents, child protective services (CPS) workers, law enforcement officers, and other criminal justice agents in child abuse and neglect cases. In the *Parental Experiences of Child Protective Services, the Criminal Justice System, and Family Court* chapter, parents' experiences with the investigation and allegation of child maltreatment are covered. The *Child Protective Services* chapter examines the investigation of and response to child maltreatment by CPS personnel. Family court proceedings are also examined in this chapter. In the *Law Enforcement, Probation, and Parole Officers* chapter, the legal approach to investigating child maltreatment is described, whereas the *Agents of the Courts: Roles and Perspectives* chapter covers the prosecution of maltreatment in criminal court. Finally, the *Advice and Conclusions: Recommendations for Those in the Field* chapter makes suggestions for readers who are researching and/or working in the area of child maltreatment.

Chapter 8

Parental Experiences of Child Protective Services, the Criminal Justice System, and Family Court

This chapter examines the experiences and perspectives of the parents of allegedly maltreated children. The literature on child abuse and neglect focuses almost exclusively on the maltreating parent, while ignoring the nonabusive parent's interactions with child protective services (CPS). CPS is a state agency within the department of social services whose mission is to investigate reports of child maltreatment; it is known by different names in each state (e.g., Administration for Children's Services [ACS] in New York; Department of Children and Families [DCF] in New Jersey).

This chapter explores the rights of the family, but also considers the countervailing interests of the state in protecting children. It examines the experiences of parents who are forced to interact with CPS, family courts, and the criminal justice system, with a primary focus on those who are accused of perpetrating the maltreatment. It also covers special considerations in parental experiences of child abuse and neglect cases, such as cultural differences and allegations made to sway temporary and final custody decisions during legal separations and divorces.

Familial Rights: Reigning Supreme?

Familial rights are enshrined in international law, constitutions, and jurisprudence. Each of these areas is explored separately here.

International Law

The private life of the family is protected under international law and enshrined in human rights instruments. According to Article 12 of the Universal Declaration of Human Rights: "No one shall be subjected to arbitrary interference with his privacy, family, home or correspondence, nor to attacks upon his honor and reputation. Everyone has the right to the protection of the law against such interference or attacks." The exact same definition of this right is provided in Article 17 of the International Covenant on Civil and Political Rights (ICCPR). Article 16 of the Universal Declaration of Human Rights and Article 23 of the ICCPR also state that "the family is the natural and fundamental group unit of society and is entitled to protection by society and the State." Likewise, Article 11(2) of the American Convention on Human Rights holds that: "No one may be the object of arbitrary or abusive interference with his private life, his family, his home, or his correspondence, or of unlawful attacks on his honor or reputation."

These rights, however, are qualified rights; that is, they are not absolute and can be interfered with if there is a legitimate reason to do so. Nevertheless, the actions of the state in these instances must be necessary and proportionate. Proportionality requires that there is a rational connection between the objective of the state and the means the state employs to achieve that objective. To be proportionate, a state and its agents must demonstrate that the actions they take do not go beyond what is necessary to achieve their objectives. Without the concept of proportionality, the state would be allowed to deprive individuals of human rights so long as it was for a legitimate reason and in accordance with existing law. Proportionality also serves as a check to ensure that the interference with this right is not "arbitrary or abusive."

As a signatory to these human rights instruments, the United States is bound by them, bound to respect the rights prescribed in them, and required to enforce the protection of these rights. International law also protects the rights of children. The preamble of the Convention on the Rights of the Child (CRC), which has the force of customary international law and to which the United States is a signatory, holds that "the family, as the fundamental group of society and the natural environment for the growth and well-being of all its members and particularly children, should be afforded the necessary protection and assistance [and] the child . . . should grow up in a family environment." Article 7 of the CRC further states that "a child has, as far as possible, the right to know and be cared for by his or her parents." Therefore, in addition to familial rights, the child has the right to remain within his or her family without undue interference from the state.

U.S. Constitution and Jurisprudence

In *Duchesne v. Sugarman* (1997, p. 824), the court stated that the "existence of a private realm of family life which the state cannot enter [(*Prince v. Commonwealth of Massachusetts*, 1944, p. 166)] has its source not in state law, but in the intrinsic human rights ([(*Moore v. City of East Cleveland*, 1977, p. 503)]." Indeed, the constitutional right of children and their families to live together free from government intrusion is a well-established right (*Wallis v. Spencer*, 2000). Courts have consistently found that parents have a constitutionally protected interested in controlling how they raise their children without interference from the government. For example, in *Parham v. J.R.* (1979), the court found that parents have the right to decide and choose the medical treatment for their children. In *Pierce v.*

Box 8-1 Parental Rights: Do They Extend to Corporal Punishment?

Parents have the right to discipline their children using corporal punishment—an implied right derived from familial rights. Yet, this right, like others encompassed within family rights, is a qualified right; that is, it must be exercised only in a reasonable manner (*In re B.B.*, 1999; *In re J.P.*, 1998; *People ex rel. C.F.*, 2005; *P.R. v. Department of Public Welfare*, 2002). Some courts have found corporal punishment unreasonable if the parent did not seek to intervene in another manner before resorting to physical discipline. Put another way, jurisprudence reveals that corporal punishment is found to be reasonable when parents use it as a last resort (*In re T.A.*, 2003). Corporal punishment, therefore, is unreasonable if it is deemed unnecessary or excessive (*In re Horton*, 2004). Furthermore, punishment is unreasonable if it creates a "substantial risk of serious physical harm" (*In re Horton*, 2004, p. 7).

Society of Sisters (1925), the court held that parents have the right to make decisions concerning their children's education.

In addition to rights related to child-rearing, there exists a right to the preservation of familial integrity, which "encompasses the reciprocal rights of both parent and children. It is the interest of the parent in the 'companionship, care, custody and management of his or her children,' [quoting *Stanley v. Illinois* (1972, p. 651)] and of the children in not being dislocated from the 'emotional attachments that derive from the intimacy of daily association' with the parent [quoting *Smith v. Organization of Foster Families for Equality and Reform* (1977, p. 844)]" (*Duchesne v. Sugarman*, 1997, p. 825). In short, family rights—particularly decisions made in regard to the raising of children—including "choices about marriage, family life, and the upbringing of children are among associational rights the [c]ourt has ranked of 'basic importance in our society'" (*M. L. B. v. S. L. J.*, 1996, p. 116).

States' interference with family life and the exercise of familial rights primarily impacts two amendments to the U.S. Constitution: the Fourth Amendment and the Fourteenth Amendment. Usually, claims of violations of these amendments are made when a child is removed from his or her household by CPS. When a child is unjustly removed from his or her household, he or she can challenge the constitutionality of the government's decision to remove them pursuant to the Fourth Amendment, which holds that: "The right of the people to be secure in their persons, houses, papers, and effects, against unreasonable searches and seizures, shall not be violated, and no Warrants shall issue, but upon probable cause, supported by Oath or affirmation, and particularly describing the place to be searched, and the persons or things to be seized." In fact, in *Tenenbaum v. Williams* (1999), the court found that the removal of a child by CPS amounted to a seizure. In addition, the court in *Meyer v. Nebraska* (1923) held that the Fourth Amendment includes both the right of individuals to establish a home and the right to bring up children. Moreover, in its application of the Fourth Amendment to family rights, the court in *Duchesne v. Sugarman* (1997) concluded that the "right of the family to remain together without the coercive interference of the awesome power of the state" is "the most essential and basic aspect of familial privacy" (p. 825).

The Fourteenth Amendment is also impacted by governmental intrusions into the private life of the family. The due process clause of the Fourteenth Amendment holds that: "No State shall make or enforce any law which shall abridge the privileges or immunities of citizens of the United States; nor shall any State deprive any person of life, liberty, or property, without due process of law; nor deny to any person within its jurisdiction the equal protection of the laws." The court in *Troxel v. Granville* (2000) concluded that: "it cannot . . . be doubted that the Due Process Clause of the Fourteenth Amendment protects the fundamental right of parents to make decisions concerning the care, custody, and control of their children" (p. 66). Furthermore, in *M. L. B. v. S. L. J.* (1996), the court held that family rights are "sheltered by the Fourteenth Amendment against the State's unwarranted usurpation, disregard, or disrespect" (pp. 116–117). The manner in which these rights are sheltered has been prescribed by case law. For instance, a plurality of the court in *Troxel* held that the due process clause of the Fourteenth Amendment does not allow a "state to violate the fundamental right of parents to make child rearing decisions simply because a state judge believes that a 'better' decision could be made" (pp. 72–73).

Fourteenth Amendment violations may occur when governments unjustifiably interfere with the right of a family not to be forcibly separated. Specifically, in *Quilloin v. Walcott* (1978), the court stated, "We have little doubt that the Due Process Clause would be offended [if] a State were to attempt to force the breakup of a natural family, over the objections of the parents and their children, without some showing of unfitness and for the sole reason that to do so was thought to be in the children's best interest" (quoting *Smith v. Organization of Foster Families*, 1977, pp. 862–863). In other words, the state must meet specific requirements if it is to legitimately violate these family rights.

State Interference in Family Life: Is it Justified?

In *Tenenbaum*, the court held that "society's interest in the protection of children is, indeed, multifaceted, composed not only with concerns about the safety and welfare of children from the community's point of view, but also with the child's psychological well-being, autonomy, and relationship to the family" (quoting *Franz v. Lytle*, 1993, pp. 792–793). The state's pursuit in protecting children encounters two countervailing interests. On the one hand, there is a need to respect familial rights. On the other hand, the state is entitled to take legally appropriate actions to protect the child within his or her family setting. This power of the state stems from the *parens patriae* doctrine rooted in English common law. *Parens patriae* affords states the ability to protect judicially recognized interests in the well-being of its populace (*Snapp & Son, Inc. v. Puerto Rico*, 1982). In the case of children, it refers to the ability of the state to intervene into the private realm of family life when a parent or legal guardian has engaged in child abuse or neglect.

Basically, the *parens patriae* doctrine refers to the power of the state to act as a parent to any child who is in need of protection.

In line with this reasoning, the court, in *Prince v. Commonwealth of Massachusetts* (1944), held that there is a "private realm of family life which the state cannot enter. But the family itself is not beyond regulation in the public interest. . . . Acting to guard the general interest in youth's well-being, the state as parens patriae may restrict the parent's control. . . . The state has a wide range of power for limiting parental freedom and authority in things affecting the child's welfare" (p. 166). This power of state was reiterated in other court cases as well. For instance, in *Croft v. Westmoreland County Children and Youth Services* (1997), the court concluded that "this liberty interest in familial integrity is limited by the compelling governmental interest in the protection of children particularly where the children need to be protected from their own parents" (p. 1125).

Parents' due process rights do not and have not barred the state from altering the custodial rights of their children (*Weller v. Department of Social Services*, 1990). Case law has provided states with guidance as to when they can intervene or interfere with the exercise of familial rights. In *Lassiter v. Department of Social Services* (1981), for example, the court found that these rights require protection "absent a powerful countervailing interest" (p. 27). A review of jurisprudence further reveals that "when the government intrudes on choices concerning family living arrangements, [the court] must examine carefully the importance of the governmental interests advanced and the extent to which they are served by the [action taken]" (*Griswold v. State of Connecticut*, 1965, p. 502; *Moore v. City of East Cleveland*, 1977, p. 499). The state's interests in intervening and the ability to intervene stem solely from the existence of definitive and articulable evidence resulting in reasonable suspicion that a child has been abused or that there is an immense risk that the child will be abused (*Croft v. Westmoreland County Children and Youth Services*, 1997). To determine the proportionality of the intrusion, the court examines whether a fair balance was struck between the state's interest in protecting children from abuse or neglect and the right of individuals to maintain a family unit (*Miller v. City of Philadelphia*, 1999). This balance must also occur when Fourth and Fourteenth Amendment claims are being made for the removal of children from their household (*Darryl H. v. Coler*, 1986; *Wallis v. Spencer*, 2000).

According to existing case law, there must be "an objectively reasonable basis" for removing the child without first seeking judicial authorization (*Croft v. Westmoreland County Children and Youth Services*, 1997; *Gottlieb v. County of Orange*, 1996). To make a removal decision on an objectively reasonable basis, a preliminary investigation must be conducted after a report alleging abuse has been obtained (*Croft v. Westmoreland County Children and Youth Services*, 1997). This, however, does not always occur. Consider the case of Crystal Rhodes. Rhodes was a victim of domestic violence. She was battered by her children's father, Alfonso Washington, and had obtained orders of protection against him in the past. ACS visited the home of Rhodes after she failed to extend the order of protection against the children's father. When the ACS caseworker went to the apartment and knocked, a male voice asked who was at the door, but he did not respond after the caseworker identified herself and asked to speak with Rhodes. The caseworker never confirmed whether the male voice was, in fact, Washington. Nonetheless, ACS subsequently removed the children, charging Rhodes with child neglect because she engaged in domestic violence (*Nicholson v. Williams*, 2002). Other less severe alternatives that were available for the situation were not pursued by ACS caseworkers. Yet, the courts have deemed such actions by CPS workers as unjustified. Specifically, the court has stated that the due process clause of the Fourteenth Amendment would certainly be violated "if children are taken away from their parents without sufficient investigation" (*Strail v. Department of Children, Youth & Families of Rhode Island*, 1999, p. 529).

In *Tenenbaum* (1999), the court stated that "even a temporary removal of a child '[deprives] the parents of the care, custody, and management of their child' so that judicial authorization is necessary unless the child is immediately threatened with harm" (p. 594). The removal of the child from his or her family, therefore, is justified in emergency situations. In *Tenenbaum*, emergency situations were considered those "circumstances in which the child is immediately threatened with harm. The mere possibility of danger is not enough" (p. 594). In *Nicholson v. Scoppetta* (2004), the court elaborated on the requirement set out in *Tenenbaum* by stating that emergency removal is only "appropriate where the danger is so immediate, so urgent that the child's life or safety will be at risk before an ex parte order can be obtained. The standard obviously is a stringent one" (p. 853).

Emergency removals that last a few hours, but no more than a day, may be justified in limited circumstances. Specifically, in *Tenenbaum* (1999), the court held that an investigative removal that lasted less than one day did not violate the familial rights of the nonabusive parent. Nevertheless, other courts have concluded that rights of familial association can be and have been violated when the length of the investigative removal lasted less than 24 hours. Specifically, in *J.B. v. Washington County* (1997), the court concluded that the rights of familial association were violated when the parent's child was "physically removed from her home and from her parents for a period of almost 18 hours, which included an overnight stay in a pre-arranged shelter home" (*Griffin v. Strong*, 1993, p. 1548). Thus, courts have recognized that forced separation of parents from their children, "even for a short time, represents a serious infringement upon both the parents' and [children's] rights" (*J.B. v. Washington County*, 1997, p. 925). As the court in *Santosky* concluded, "When the State initiates a parental rights termination proceeding, it seeks not merely to infringe that fundamental liberty interest, but to end it" (p. 759).

The greatest of care must be taken to ensure that decisions of removal—both temporary and permanent—are not made in a capricious manner. Especially when a removal is permanent, it is imperative that just cause for this action exists. The state must first prove that a parent is unfit before a child can be permanently removed from the parent's care (*Santosky v. Kramer*, 1982). Unfortunately, these standards for child removal have not always been followed in practice. Violations of these standards by agents enforcing child protection mandates have been recorded, and these unjustified actions have negatively affected the parents of children who were removed from their care.

CPS Enforcement: Parents' Experiences

Parents who are accused of child abuse or child neglect often face a very serious dilemma. On the one hand, if they cooperate with CPS, they are more likely to maintain custody or contact with their child (or children)—but the information they provide may be used against them by a prosecutor in criminal court should charges be brought. On the other hand, if they do not cooperate with CPS, they will most likely lose custody or be denied contact with their child—but they preserve their privilege against self-incrimination. The privilege against self-incrimination can be applied to criminal and civil proceedings and can be invoked by participants in these proceedings. For example, the parents or guardians can refuse to cooperate fully in psychological and psychiatric evaluation processes mandated by dependency courts if, by participating, they may incriminate themselves. Case law has revealed that "an individual may not be compelled to testify absent a grant of immunity from use of the statements in any subsequent prosecution" (*Matter of the Welfare of S.A.V. and S.M.V.*, 1986, p. 261). Given that parents can be prosecuted for child abuse and neglect, it is imperative that attorneys be made available to assist parents in family court or civil dependency proceedings to protect their rights and interests adequately. These lawyers should be prepared to assist parents in understanding the nature of the proceedings, their rights, and the consequences of various legal directives (Scahill, 1999).

CPS, criminal justice agents, and family court personnel serve the interests of the state in protecting children. Parents accused of child abuse and neglect respond to interventions applied to their families by these individuals in a variety of ways. Primary reactions to such intrusions have included hostility, anger, fear, embarrassment, humiliation, shame, and sadness. In terms of specific actions taken in response to interventions, some parents have moved to different states or out of the country when allegations have been made against them by CPS to prevent the state agency from being able to take their children away from them.

Others have committed crimes to try to keep their families intact. A case in point is that involving Nephra and Shanel Payne. The Paynes abducted their own children from foster care in Queens, New York, during a supervised visit, after being informed that their eight children would not be returned to them, but instead would be put up for adoption (Nir, 2011). Eventually, the couple was arrested and ACS regained possession of their children. The Paynes claimed that they unlawfully removed their children from foster care because ACS had unfairly taken custody of their children, accusing them of child maltreatment. The Paynes also stated that some of their children were being medicated for psychological disorders, such as attention-deficit/hyperactivity disorder, against their wishes, and that two of their children revealed they were being sexually abused and neglected, showing bruises and split lips during their visits with their parents. For their illegal interference with CPS, the Paynes pleaded guilty to second-degree custodial interference, and each received 60 days in jail and 3 years' probation ("NY Parents Get 60 Days Jail," 2011). In this case, the abuse alleged by the parents to have occurred in foster care was not substantiated.

In other cases, however, children have suffered horrific abuse in foster care. For example, in *Doe v. New York City Department of Social Services* (1981), a child was physically assaulted and raped by her foster father. Likewise, in *Thomas v. City of New York* (1992), siblings who had been placed in foster care were repeatedly raped and beaten. Specifically, the mother in this case, Ivonne Thomas, had eight children removed from her home after a report was made alleging that one of her children was sexually abused by Thomas' paramour (a term used by ACS to refer to an unmarried live-in lover). The children were placed in various foster care homes. During their foster care stay, three of Thomas' children were subjected to various forms of emotional, physical, and sexual abuse. After Thomas was informed of this abuse, she contacted city officials. The children were subsequently placed in other foster homes. In these new homes, the children were again subjected to emotional and physical abuse.

When parents find out about sexual abuse perpetrated against their children, their reactions are often shock, fear, anger, and a general concern for the well-being of their children. There are, however, exceptions to these reactions. In fact, some parents may not believe their children and may blame them for their own abuse. For instance, one parent, such as the mother, may deny sexual abuse occurred against her child or even dismiss it as something temporary or minor, particularly when that parent is financially dependent on the perpetrator.

The reactions of parents and responses to intrusions caused by investigations of the family by CPS (and police officers) do not depend on whether the parents were the alleged abusers. In fact, nonoffending parents have sometimes suffered similar or even more severe consequences than the offender; that is, the nonoffending parents have had adverse experiences interacting with the police and CPS when their child has been reportedly abused or neglected. This outcome is most pronounced in households containing children where domestic violence occurs. Research has shown links between child maltreatment and intimate-partner abuse (Barnett, Miller-Perrin, & Perrin, 1997; Browne & Hamilton, 1999; Straus & Gelles, 1988; Straus, Gelles, & Steinmetz, 1988; Truesdell, McNeill, & Deschner, 1986). The extent of these links, however, is difficult to gauge accurately because of the different types of research methods used to assess this relationship (Geffner, Rosenbaum, & Hughes, 1988; Widom, 1988).

Domestic Violence: Intimate Partner and Child Maltreatment in the Same Household

There are serious child abuse and neglect cases in which a swift and punitive response against parents is required. A case in point is Brian and Shannon Gore. The Gores, who were residents of Virginia, kept their daughter in a crib modified as a cage and essentially starved her, feeding her so little that the child ate her own skin to satisfy her hunger (Lohr, 2011). When the child was found by police officers, she was filthy and was covered in bed sores and her own feces (Goldman, 2011). In this case, both parents were complicit in the abuse of the child.

Not all cases, however, are as clear cut. Consider the case of Lisa Steinberg. Joel Steinberg, a resident of New York, had adopted a girl named Elizabeth (or Lisa, as she was known to many). When police officers responded to Steinberg's house, a woman, Hedda Nussbaum, answered the door. She had numerous cuts and bruises on her face. In one of the home's rooms, the police officers observed an infant who was tied to his crib by a rope around his waist. His body and clothes were soaked in urine and covered in dirt. They also found a little girl, Lisa; like her brother, she was dirty and unkempt, lying on the floor of the home barely breathing. She also had burns and cuts all over her body. The transcripts of Joel Steinberg's trial revealed that after Lisa was beaten, she was left lying on the bathroom floor unattended and alone (*People v. Steinberg*, 1992). Nussbaum did not call anyone to help her.

During her trial, Nussbaum stated that she did not contact anyone because "Joel said he would take care of her, he would get her up when he got back . . . and I didn't want to show disloyalty or distrust to him, so I didn't call" ("Girlfriend Thought Lawyer Would Heal Dying Child," 1988). Hedda Nussbaum, who was severely beaten by Joel Steinberg throughout her marriage, had suffered from broken bones, teeth, ribs, and nose; black eyes; burns; and other injuries. On June 16, 2003, Nussbaum appeared on *Larry King Live*. During her interview, Nussbaum was asked by King, "Why do a lot of people blame you?" to which she responded, "Well, because people believe that a mother has to protect her child no matter what. And a lot of people just don't understand what it's like to be a battered woman, unless they've been through it."

Cases like this one demonstrate how domestic violence poses unique challenges to long-held notions of parental responsibilities, especially societal beliefs regarding the role of the mother in child abuse and neglect cases. They also pose significant challenges to the police and CPS in terms of the appropriate execution of their respective duties to ensure public safety and the protection of children's well-being.

The Role of Police

The agency primarily responsible for responding to domestic violence is the police. Literature has shown that victims of domestic violence "all too frequently continue to encounter denials of their rights to equal protection and equal justice in the criminal justice system" (De Santis, 2000, para. 2). Particularly in cases of domestic violence, "police officers, prosecutors, and judges have been described as holding victim-blaming attitudes, believing that women provoke abuse, and/or should be able to control their abusers on their own" (Hart, 1993, cited in Byrne, Kilpatrick, Howley, & Beatty, 1999, p. 277). In addition, male victims of heterosexual domestic violence incidents are normally met by criminal justice agents with indifference and insensitivity. Nonetheless, "men who are punched, slapped, kicked, bitten, or otherwise assaulted by their wives or partners are no less deserving of compassion and understanding than are women who are so assaulted" (Kimmel, 2001, p. 23).

Victims of same-sex couples' domestic violence similarly encounter indifference and insensitivity by criminal justice agents. In fact, this historical response of the criminal justice system has caused many lesbians and gay men to be reluctant about reporting crimes of intimate-partner violence (Christopher et al., 1991, as cited in Kuehnle & Sullivan, 2003; Richardson & May, 1999). Unfortunately, these individuals may experience secondary victimization by the very system on which they relied and trusted to provide them with assistance and support for the crimes committed against them. Moreover, victims of same-sex battering often receive fewer protections and services than victims of opposite-sex battering because many jurisdictions define domestic violence in such a way as to exclude same-sex relationships (Lundy, 1993, as cited in Kuehnle & Sullivan, 2003).

Police intervention in domestic violence cases is believed to deter abuse and reoffending. The reasoning is that arrests send the following message: Domestic violence is illegal and unacceptable to society, and those engaging in it will be punished. For the victims, an arrest of the perpetrator signifies the protection of the victim and his or her family. Police play another important role in these cases: They refer the victims, perpetrators, and any children in the household to appropriate treatment and support services.

When domestic violence victims or another person who suspects or has witnessed the crime calls the police, the responding officers must determine whether to arrest one or both of the parties involved in the incident. Some states have mandatory arrest laws concerning domestic violence, whereas other states have preferred arrest laws or discretionary arrest laws (Table 8-1). Mandatory arrest laws require law enforcement agents to make an arrest when responding to incidents in which they have probable cause to believe that domestic violence has occurred. If the police officers are considering arresting both of the parties involved in domestic violence incidents, most of these laws require that police officers attempt to identify a "primary aggressor." Some states also permit police officers responding to the scene to consider other factors, such as future dangerousness, in determining whether the individual involved in the incident was acting in self-defense, and to consider the nature and extent of the injuries sustained by one or both parties, when deciding whom to arrest (Haviland, Frye, Rajah, Thukral, & Trinity, 2001; McMahon & Pence, 2003). The benefit of this procedure is that it removes the burden from the victim of making allegations or reports against the abuser and allows the police and district attorney to proceed even when the victim wants to recant or to prevent the abuser from experiencing legal repercussions. By contrast, in states with preferred arrest laws, while arrest in domestic violence cases is preferred, police officers can exercise their discretion and use options other than arrest to handle the situation. Discretionary arrest laws enable officers to make an arrest if an officer has probable cause to believe that domestic violence has occurred.

A study conducted by the National Institute of Justice (2008) of the Department of Justice based on information retrieved from the National Incident Based Reporting System

Table 8-1 States with mandatory, preferred, and discretionary arrest laws

Mandatory arrest laws	Preferred arrest laws	Discretionary arrest laws
Arizona	Arkansas	Alabama
Colorado	California	Delaware
Connecticut	Massachusetts	Florida
District of Columbia	Montana	Georgia
Iowa	North Dakota	Hawaii
Kansas	Tennessee	Idaho
Louisiana		Illinois
Maine		Indiana
Mississippi		Kentucky
Missouri		Maryland
Nevada		Michigan
New Jersey		Minnesota
New York		Nebraska
Ohio		New Hampshire
Oregon		New Mexico
Rhode Island		North Carolina
South Carolina		Oklahoma
South Dakota		Pennsylvania
Utah		Texas
Virginia		Vermont
Washington		West Virginia
Wisconsin		Wyoming

Data from Hirschel, D. (2008). Domestic violence cases: What research shows about arrest and dual arrest rates. National Institute of Justice. Retrieved from http://www.nij.gov/nij/publications/dv-dual-arrest-222679/contents.htm

(NIBRS) revealed that in states with mandatory arrest laws, police officers were more likely to arrest both parties in a domestic violence incident. Mandatory arrests in domestic violence cases have been lauded as prompting fair and equitable treatment of parties in these cases (Stark, 1993), empowering the victim (Forell, 1991), ending the abuse of the victim in the short term, and deterring future instances of abuse against the victim (Sherman, 1992). There are, however, serious adverse consequences to the victim who is arrested during these incidents. Dual arrests often result is secondary victimization of the abused and may even deter them from reporting future incidents of abuse. Moreover, this practice may deter others from reporting abuse if they believe they will be arrested for defending themselves against their abuser. When battered partners are arrested pursuant to dual arrest practices, they are also denied victim services (due to their perpetrator status) and are often mandated to participate in batterer intervention programs (Osthoff, 2002).

To prevent the further victimization of battered partners, some states do not have dual arrest laws. Instead, these states have preferred or discretionary arrest provisions in domestic violence cases (Table 8-1). Overall, in states with either mandatory or discretionary arrest laws, several factors influence a law enforcement officer's decision to arrest the parties involved, including any injuries sustained by the victim and the extent of these injuries, the presence or use of drugs or alcohol, the presence of children or witnesses in the household, the perpetrator's demeanor, and the victim's demeanor (Bachman & Coker, 1995; Buzawa & Austin, 1993; Mignon & Holmes, 1995; Trujillo & Ross, 2008). Police decisions in domestic violence cases are also influenced by previous incidents between the parties involved. A police officer will check whether any other calls have been made to the residence and whether a protection order exists against the perpetrator. Protection (or restraining) orders are often obtained by victims to prevent the offenders from contacting them in the future. Unfortunately, restraining orders may not reduce family violence. The order, which is essentially a piece of paper, may not deter an offender from seeking to harm the victim. In fact, the restraining order may further aggravate the situation, resulting in other types of harm to the victim, such as financial or psychological abuse.

A violation of a restraining order also carries with it a small penalty—a misdemeanor charge with little, if any, jail time, which is unlikely to deter the offender. Consider the case of Ekaete Udoh. After she was physically abused, Udoh called the police, but her husband was never arrested (*Nicholson v. Williams*, 2002). She eventually obtained an order of protection and moved out of the house with her children. Her husband soon violated the protective order by making threatening calls to his wife. He spent only one day in jail for violating the order.

In some states, harsher punishments have been sought for repeat domestic violence offenders. For instance, in New York, a new statutory offense was created known as the "aggravated family offense"—a felony charge that applies to perpetrators who have a history of domestic violence abuse such that they have previously committed misdemeanor offenses (Englebright, 2012). Many victims of domestic violence have died at the hands of their abusers, however, making the effectiveness of arrests and restraining orders in deterring and reducing family violence questionable at best (Schmidt & Sherman, 1996).

The Role of Child Protective Services

In addition to police officers, CPS workers become involved in domestic violence cases when children live in the household. In determining whether the child can remain at home with the nonoffending parent in domestic violence cases, CPS workers examine existing relationships in the household. Specifically, two types of relationships must be assessed in cases of child abuse and neglect: the parent–child relationship and the parent–perpetrator relationship. When a mother is overly dependent socially and financially on the perpetrator, she is prone to devastating consequences when that person is removed from the household. In addition, if the mother believes the perpetrator to be innocent of the allegations, she (and other family members) is (are) unlikely to empathize with the child. In addition, if the perpetrator was the sole breadwinner and provider in the household, then the mother may blame the child for the family's current involvement with CPS and impoverished state of affairs (e.g., homelessness). In these situations, the child may suffer serious consequences if allowed to remain in the care of the mother. By contrast, if the mother shows genuine horror and disgust when the abuse against the child is disclosed to her and bans the perpetrator from the household, then the child should remain there so as to allow the relationship with the mother to aid in the child's recovery.

Battered mothers have had mixed experiences dealing with CPS workers who removed their children in the aftermath of domestic violence incidents. In a study conducted by Johnson and Sullivan (2008), some participants reported that caseworkers were extremely helpful and treated them in a fair manner. These women also claimed that CPS workers provided them with information about their cases and their children throughout the entire process. Moreover, they reported that CPS kept them abreast of progress by informing them not only about their cases, but also about the location and well-being of their children. These caseworkers were also reported to have advocated on behalf of the mothers and implemented measures to hold abusers accountable for their behavior. In addition, they placed the removed children with relatives whom the mother trusted. Instead of referring battered women to shelters alone, these CPS workers referred battered women to areas where affordable housing could be obtained.

Yet, in practice, this type of response is not always observed. For example, other participants in the study by Johnson and Sullivan (2008) claimed that they were deliberately misinformed about the progress of their cases by CPS workers, given no information, and/or not informed about the whereabouts or well-being of their children. Furthermore, battered mothers have been blamed for the violence perpetrated against them, had stricter requirements and harsher penalties placed on them than on their abusers, have been mandated to fulfill certain requirements that others in similar situations have not been required to complete, and had their children used as leverage to force them to complete the required services.

Blaming the Victim   Literature has shown that some CPS workers hold victim-blaming attitudes. For example, a study by Johnson and Sullivan (2008) revealed that battered women with children were actually blamed by the CPS workers for the abuse perpetrated against them. When mothers asked about their children, their requests were often dismissed by CPS personnel. In fact, this study revealed that the women were scolded for not ensuring the protection of their own children, which demonstrates ignorance of the realities of domestic violence and its implications. Another study similarly found that mothers in child sexual abuse investigations received minimal, if any, services; were criticized by those involved in the investigation; were met with insensitivity toward their concerns; and were accused falsely of being complacent or participating in the abuse (Plummer & Eastin, 2007).

In some jurisdictions, it is common practice to substantiate a claim of the parent's neglect of a child on the sole basis that the parent failed to protect child from exposure to domestic violence. Such child neglect is substantiated even when the parent did not mistreat the child in any way. In these cases, a "failure to protect" allegation is made. This accusation holds that a parent placed the child at risk due to action or inaction during a domestic violence incident perpetrated against the parent-victim. These practices serve to revictimize the battered parent, who in essence is unable to prevent the domestic abuse from occurring.

According to O'Hagan (1998), "A powerful commitment from a mother who otherwise may have been providing a reasonable degree of care, and who accepts some responsibility for the crime committed against her child is potentially far more effective than removing the child to strangers, and subjecting her to the latest fashions in child sexual abuse therapy" (p. 179). But why should a mother have to accept even partial responsibility for the crime committed against her? Why must she first admit guilt to be able to keep her child?

In domestic violence cases, the nonoffending parent is more often than not charged with child abuse or neglect when the child was exposed to the abuse. This is especially true for mothers. In Florida, a "special condition" voluntary foster care placement program exists that "allows battered mothers to place their children for up to three months in foster care to avoid charges of abuse or neglect" ("Failure to Protect" Working Group, 1999, p. 863). Why are battered mothers being charged as if they were the perpetrators? Unfortunately, this practice does not exist solely in Florida: Many states have treated exposure of the child to domestic violence as a form of child neglect that requires intervention by CPS (Edleson, 2004).

Indeed, in *People United for Children, Inc. v. City of New York* (2000), the court found that ACS blamed the mother in domestic violence cases. In fact, at the time, ACS had a policy in place that dictated children should be removed from households where domestic violence was perpetrated. Consider the case of Sharwline Nicholson. She experienced a domestic violence attack by the father of one of her children, a man named Barnett with whom she was in a relationship (*Nicholson v. Williams*, 2002). Specifically, Barnett assaulted Nicholson, causing her to suffer broken bones, broken ribs, and head injuries. During the assault, Nicholson's 8-year-old son was at school, but her 3-year-old daughter was in her crib in another room. Following the incident, Nicholson called 911 and went to the hospital to treat her injuries. When ACS was contacted, its personnel removed her children and placed them in foster care. The case manager for Nicholson's family testified that he placed the children in foster care because he believed that the children's safety was at imminent risk if they remained in the care of their mother because "she was not, at that time, able to protect herself nor her children because Mr. Barnett had viciously beaten her" (p. 170).

Nicholson was one of the named plaintiffs in *Nicholson v. Williams* (2002), a case that consolidated the complaints of several parents who had been victims of domestic violence and had their children removed from them and placed in foster care for that reason alone. This case revealed that ACS had a long-standing policy in place wherein personnel would remove children from the household where domestic violence had occurred and would charge the battered mother with child neglect. A review of jurisprudence before the *Nicholson* case revealed that courts have held that the notion of neglect pursuant to the Family and Domestic Violence Intervention Act of 1994 was sufficiently broad to include a child's exposure to domestic violence. Specifically, in *In re Lonell J.* (1998), the court accepted "domestic violence in the child's presence as [a form of child] neglect" (p. 118). The reasoning of this court was applied to future cases. For instance, in *In re Athena M.V.* (1998), the court concluded that "acts of severe domestic violence between respondents in the presence of their children is sufficient to show 'as a matter of common sense' that the children were in imminent danger of harm" (p. 12).

In supporting these claims of child neglect when domestic violence is involved, courts have relied on the findings of the studies conducted to support the passage of the Family and Domestic Violence Intervention Act of 1994, which showed that children were harmed when exposed to domestic violence (*In re Lonell J.*, 1998). In particular, the studies showed that children exposed to domestic violence may exhibit various emotional, behavioral, and developmental problems. This type of evidence was included in subsequent cases as well. In *In re Deandre T.* (1998), evidence was presented showing that when a father perpetrates abuse against the mother, this exposure emotionally and mentally impairs the health of the child. However, every child's case is unique. In fact, other studies have revealed that some children who have been exposed to domestic violence are not adversely affected by it. For instance, Edleson (2004) found that at least half of the children who participated in his studies experienced few, if any, problems after exposure to domestic violence. Nevertheless, even when immediate effects of a child's exposure to domestic violence are not readily apparent, damage may be present and cumulative (Bragg, 2003).

When domestic violence occurs in a household that includes children, both parents are charged with child neglect, regardless of who perpetrated the crime. The plaintiffs named in *Nicholson v. Williams* (2002) were all charged with child neglect. For example, ACS filed petitions against these individuals claiming that each "engaged in domestic violence" with the perpetrator in the presence of their children. This practice further victimizes women (because domestic violence victims are overwhelmingly female). In these cases, when petitions are filed against the mother by CPS, they hold nonabusive parents equally responsible for the harm to the child ("Failure to Protect" Working Group, 1999). This practice has several implications. First, removing children from the care of the nonabusive parent may discourage the victim from seeking assistance for fear that his or her children will be removed as a consequence. Second, the publicizing of instances in which battered parents have had their children removed from them could lead to reticence in seeking assistance. In short, in both of these instances, a chilling effect has occurred in which "individuals otherwise interested in engaging in a lawful activity are deterred from doing so in light of perceived or actual government regulation of that activity" (Horn, 2005, p. 49).

Furthermore, blaming the adult victim may adversely affect the livelihood of that victim. More specifically, when battered partners are named in "indicated" reports, where a CPS worker concludes that evidence supports the alleged failure to protect their children from exposure to abuse, this can have serious consequences—especially in terms of employment. If the battered individual is seeking employment involving working with children, he or she may not be able to do so. Employers in this field are required to submit an inquiry to the State Central Register (SCR) to find out if the individual seeking employment has been the subject of an indicated report. An employer is not allowed to hire someone with an SCR report for these positions unless the employer provides a detailed report in writing as to why it is hiring such a person with a history of child abuse or neglect for the position. Accordingly, indicated reports make employment in certain positions extremely difficult.

Increased Services and Greater Penalties for Nonabusive Parents   Participants in a study conducted by Johnson and Sullivan (2008) reported that CPS placed extensive requirements on the nonabusive mother and few, if any, requirements on the abusive father. In this study, many of the participants were required to take parenting classes as a condition of retaining physical custody, but the abusive father was not required to do so; even in cases where the abuser had joint custody. In fact, the mothers (who often had physical custody of the children) were the ones whom CPS monitored to ensure that they were capable of raising their own children. The majority of participants further reported that no meaningful sanctions were placed on the abuser in an attempt to change his behavior.

However, the domestic violence guiding principles of CPS agencies, such as ACS, hold that "the nonabusive parent and the abusive parent must be engaged in appropriate services to help maximize the safety and stability of the home for the child. These services must be provided separately when indicated by the assessment" (NYC ACS, 2003, para. 8). In many cases involving domestic violence with children in the household, CPS has required nonoffending parents—particularly mothers—to take part in and complete several programs before their children are returned to them. Indeed, studies reveal that domestic violence victims are approximately twice as likely as their abusers to be referred for such services by CPS ("Failure to Protect" Working Group, 1999). It should be recognized that it is inappropriate to require the victim to attend services for anger management or to take parenting classes. It is also inappropriate to have both parties attend couples' counseling, particularly given that this practice is likely to prove dangerous to the victim. The practice of joint visitation for children who have been removed from a household characterized by domestic violence should also be avoided, as it can endanger the welfare of the domestic violence victim.

A case in point was the requirements placed on April Rodriguez, another parent named in the *Nicholson* case. Like Nicholson, Rodriguez was the victim of domestic violence by the father of her children, Michael Gamble. During a verbal argument, Gamble pushed her to the floor, causing her to be injured. Rodriguez notified the police the next day, and Gamble was subsequently arrested. Following his arrest, Gamble served Rodriguez with a notice seeking legal custody of their children (*Nicholson v. Williams*, 2002). ACS held a conference with Gamble, Rodriguez, and her two children; the CPS caseworker, Ms. Williams; and the CPS manager, Mr. Bentil. Rodriguez was informed by ACS workers "that we needed to come up with an agreement between me and Mr. Gamble about my children, or [ACS] would go to court" (p. 174). In the presence of ACS staff, an agreement was signed transferring custody to Gamble for 6 months or until Rodriguez was able to secure an apartment and daycare services for her children, whichever came first. Following the construction of this agreement, ACS filed a petition against both Rodriguez and Gamble for child neglect. Two significant issues arise in this case. First, ACS pressed Rodriguez to sign a custody agreement to have her children live with her abuser, Gamble. Second, ACS placed numerous requirements on Rodriguez to regain custody of her children. Why did it not place any requirements on Gamble, who perpetrated the abuse?

It is not uncommon for a child to be placed with an abuser or with a relative of the abuser. These actions, however, are not without consequence for the victim of domestic violence. In these situations, the child and visitations with the child may be withheld by the batterer or his or her relatives to punish the victim. The child and visitations to the battered victim may also be used as leverage to gain concessions, including dropping the charges against the batterer.

Another case in which similar actions by CPS adversely impacted a domestic abuse victim involved Sharlene Tillett. Tillett was subjected, on a few occasions, to domestic violence throughout her marriage. Because of this abuse, she separated from her husband and moved to California to live with her family. While residing in California, she began a relationship with Jamie Gray and later moved to New York with him. During the relationship, she was assaulted by Gray on more than one occasion. After giving birth to her daughter (whom she named Uganda) with Gray, Tillett confided to the staff at the hospital where her daughter was born that there was a history of domestic violence in her household. The hospital staff subsequently contacted ACS. ACS decided to remove her daughter from Tillett's home. The reason provided for this removal was as follows: ACS believed that Uganda was in "'imminent danger' because the apartment that Tillett was living in was being paid for by Gray (even though Tillett had informed the caseworker that Gray had moved out on August 19), and because Tillett was unemployed and dependent on Gray for financial support (even though Tillett had told the caseworker that she was expecting support from her family in California)" (*Nicholson v. Williams*, 2002, p. 181). Court transcripts, however, revealed that the case manager admitted that the child was not removed due to Tillett's financial situation, but rather because of the ongoing domestic violence perpetrated in the household. In this case, a child neglect petition was filed against both Tillett and Gray.

Tillett was required to take part in and complete several programs, such as domestic violence classes and one-to-one counseling (*Nicholson v. Williams*, 2002). But what about the perpetrator of abuse? The case makes no mention of any services being required of

Gray, the father of the child and the abuser in this case. Likewise, the *Nicholson* court transcript revealed that other mothers in the case were required to take part in several programs before their children were returned to them. For instance, Michelle Norris was required to take a variety of programs to get her son back. She was also required to obtain a job and a two-bedroom apartment to receive custody of her son from ACS. However, ACS did not provide her with any services that would help her to achieve these requirements.

Similar requirements were observed in the case of Jane Doe (*Nicholson v. Williams*, 2002). ACS was contacted after Doe's husband tried to pick up her child from school while he was intoxicated. While the caseworker found no evidence that the child was harmed by Doe, the report of the caseworker focused almost entirely on how she was subjected to domestic violence during her marriage, consequently neglecting her responsibilities as a mother. Specifically, the preliminary report by the caseworker stated: "The [m]other must be an active participant in trying to help herself and her [child]. She needs to get her husband help" (*Nicholson v. Williams*, 2002, p. 190).

Despite the history of domestic violence in the household, ACS mandated that both Mr. and Mrs. Doe jointly participate in family counseling. Such referrals to joint counseling are not an uncommon practice. Indeed, in the past, CPS often referred families in which domestic violence had occurred to marriage or couples counseling and family therapy. Programs in which the victim and the abuser must cooperatively participate should be avoided. Moreover, Mr. and Mrs. Doe's case was closed after the mother fulfilled the mandated services. The ACS report did not mention if the father completed any services (*Nicholson v. Williams*, 2002). In this instance, just as in the aforementioned ones, ACS personnel placed the entire burden for compliance on the nonabusive parent.

In many cases of domestic violence, the victim's financial assets are limited or nonexistent (perhaps because the abuser prevented access to bank accounts) and the victim is prevented from using the family home (usually because the abuser remains there or still has access). Consequently, mothers may be forced to live in a domestic violence shelter—at least temporarily until permanent housing can be found ("Failure to Protect" Working Group, 1999). However, these options may be unavailable to the victim; that is, the victim may not be able to stay at the domestic violence shelter without children because space is limited at the shelter and priority is given to those with families ("Failure to Protect" Working Group, 1999). The viability of these options depends on the victim and the case at hand.

A frequent argument brought forward for removing children is the failure of the victim to complete required services. One such service is being placed in a domestic violence shelter. Victims of domestic violence have complained that they have been forced to leave their jobs to go to a domestic violence shelter, as this step is usually mandated by CPS. Consider, once again, the case of April Rodriguez. After the domestic violence incident, Rodriguez fled to the home of her relatives with her biological children (she was the stepmother to another child, who remained in the care of the biological father, Michael Gamble). Rodriguez did not go to a domestic violence shelter, but instead went to live with relatives (*Nicholson v. Williams*, 2002). In *Nicholson*, it was revealed that Ms. Rodriguez was forced to quit her job because a strict curfew existed in the facility that conflicted with her work hours. Accordingly, Rodriguez resorted to using public assistance in the form of welfare to support herself and her children.

Furthermore, there have been instances in which the nonoffending parent in domestic violence cases with children in the household has received a harsher sentence than the offending parent. Indeed, the criminal justice system has unfairly punished nonabusive parents by providing them with more punitive sentences than the punishments doled out to their abusers. A prime example was observed in the Nixzmary Brown case. Nixzmary was beaten to death in 2006 by her stepfather (Fahim & Kaufman, 2006). Her biological mother, Nixzaliz Santiago, was sentenced to 43 years in jail, whereas her stepfather, Cesar Rodriguez, received 29 years (Fahim, 2008). The mother received the additional 14 years for failing to heed the cries of her daughter for help, even though it was the stepfather's direct violent actions that caused the child's death.

Double Standards?   Some cases have shown that CPS requires families to fulfill certain obligations that they do not require of their foster families or, at the very least, do not monitor whether foster families have completed. Consider the case of Ekaete Udoh. Like others in the *Nicholson* case, Udoh was a victim of intimate-partner physical abuse by her husband, as were their children. When Ms. Udoh witnessed this abuse, she would intervene either by trying to calm her husband down or calling the police when her attempts to soothe him failed. Eventually, both the police and CPS became involved in her case.

A report by CPS revealed that Mr. Udoh believed that "under Nigerian cultural upbringing, he was allowed to engage in corporal punishment as a means of controlling the 'so-called unruly behavior of his children, and that this even extends to the disciplining of his wife's behavior'" (*Nicholson v. Williams*, 2002, pp. 177–178). This report also revealed that Mr. Udoh admitted that he was "verbally and physically abusive for the cardinal reason of maintaining order and good behavior among his family members" (*Ibid.*, p. 178). ACS informed Mr. Udoh that if he continued to live in the apartment he shared with his wife and children, the police would be called again and would arrest him. He subsequently fled to Nigeria.

After the incident, ACS ordered immediate removal of Ms. Udoh's children for the following reason: The "children were in 'imminent danger' because Mr. and Ms. Udoh might 'be in [family] court at the return of the children from school and [the children] wouldn't have parents to come home to'" (*Nicholson v. Williams*, p. 179). The ages of Ms. Udoh's children were as follows: 12, 13, 16, and 17 years old. Children of that age can reasonably and legally be allowed to stay home by themselves for several hours. Despite this fact, the children were removed. During the trial, the case manager revealed that another reason for the children's removal and placement in foster care was that she was concerned that the children might not have keys to enter their home. In fact, no inquiry was ever conducted to determine whether the children had keys. Curiously, this fate is exactly what befell the Udoh children while in foster care: They were locked out of their house after returning from school.

A similar occurrence was observed in the case of Michele Garcia (*Nicholson v. Williams*, 2002). Garcia was in a 7-year relationship with one of her children's father, Benjamin Hunter, Sr. One day, Hunter returned his son to Garcia and found her at home with a male friend who was visiting her. Enraged at seeing another man in her house, even though they were separated and not living together, Hunter attacked Garcia and her male friend. Garcia was kicked so hard in the stomach that she required hospitalization. Her male friend was attacked with a meat cleaver and required 24 stitches for the wounds he sustained in the attack by Hunter.

As a result of this incident, Hunter was charged with assault; however, he was not arrested (*Nicholson v. Williams*, 2002, p. 183). In addition, ACS removed Garcia's children because there was a "long history of domestic violence" in the household (*Ibid.*, p. 184). In *Nicholson*, the case manager also testified in court that one of the reasons why the children were removed from Garcia's care was because ACS was concerned about their well-being, as they were not receiving mandatory counseling. Oddly, while the children were in foster care they also did not receive any counseling. Why was ACS not concerned about the children's well-being in this instance? The cases of Ms. Udoh and Garcia demonstrate that CPS sometimes holds biological parents to different standards than are applied to foster care parents.

Treatment of male and female nonoffending parents may also differ. In the past, CPS personnel have not pursued dual charges of child abuse or neglect when the non-offending parent was the father. In *C.C. v. J.S.* (2009), a man brought a case against his wife in divorce court, alleging that she was physically, verbally, and psychologically abusing him. He also stated that he had witnessed her abuse their children. He sought an order of protection and CPS workers filed a neglect petition against the mother. But what about the father? Why was he not also charged? In the other cases described in *Nicholson*, both abusive and nonabusive parents were charged with child neglect. The difference was that in the case of *C.C. v. J.S.*, the father made allegations of domestic violence against the mother, rather than the reverse. Hence, CPS was unjustly charging mothers in domestic violence cases with neglect, but did not do the same to fathers in similar situations.

The literature shows that mothers face greater scrutiny than do fathers in terms of parenting. Epstein (1999) described the most common maternal stereotypes as follows: Women are all-knowing, all-supportive, and/or all-nurturing. Frequently, one or more of these stereotypes inform responses—often negative in nature—to abused mothers. In contrast, fathers do not face similar scrutiny because they "are not expected to be the primary caretakers of their children, and thus the quality of their parenting does not face as much scrutiny" (Murphy, 1998, p. 708; see also, Fugate, 2001, pp. 287–300). CPS personnel also find it easier to deal with nonabusive parents, as they are often the ones who remain with the children and are willing to be compliant with CPS requirements in an effort to retain custody of the children (Goodmark, 2004). This, however, is unfair and places an unjust and disproportionate burden on the victim of domestic violence.

Children as "Leverage" In the *Nicholson* trial, it was revealed that the case manager for Ms. Nicholson delayed filing a petition to family court until 5 days after placing her children in foster care. However, ACS policy requires that CPS workers file a petition in court the next business day after removing a child from a household and placing them in foster care (*Nicholson v. Williams*, 2002). In *Nicholson*, the caseworker stated that he delayed the filing because "he was hoping Ms. Nicholson would cooperate with his demands in order to avoid going to court" (p. 170). Basically, the process was purposely stalled in an attempt to force Nicholson to concede to the demands of ACS. Eight days after having her children taken from her and placed in foster care, she was finally allowed to see her children. According to the trial transcript, both of her children were in a dreadful state when she saw them. Her son had a swollen eye, the result of being slapped by his foster parent, and her daughter had a rash on her face and yellow pus running from her nose.

This tactic of stalling the return of children placed in foster care was not applied only to Nicholson. In fact, the caseworker acknowledged that it was "common in domestic violence cases for ACS to wait a few days before going to court after removing a child because, after a few days of the children being in foster care, the mother will usually agree to ACS's conditions for their return without the matter ever going to court" (p. 170). What is most troubling about this case was the filed petition alleged that Nicholson neglected her children, even though the case manager admitted in court that ACS did not believe that Nicholson was neglectful. According to the case manager, the petition was filed merely to put pressure on the mother to agree to the terms and services of ACS so that she could have her children returned to her.

Comparable actions were taken by ACS against Michelle Norris (*Nicholson v. Williams*, 2002). Norris decided to end her relationship with her son's father, Angel Figueroa. When she was collecting her things, Figueroa attacked her. Police were called to the scene. Norris then filed a report with police and obtained an order of protection against Figueroa. According to Norris, she needed to collect certain things from her apartment. She went to the apartment when Figueroa was not there. However, while in the apartment, he unexpectedly arrived and attacked her again. Police were called again to the scene. After the police arrived, Figueroa took his son and locked himself in the bathroom and refused to leave. Despite Norris' protest, the police removed her from the apartment without returning her child to her (*Nicholson v. Williams*, 2002). ACS later contacted her and stated she had engaged in domestic violence and neglected her child by leaving her child with an abusive man. When Norris informed ACS that the police forced her to leave, the ACS caseworker stated that this fact was irrelevant to the case. Norris was then mandated to surrender her child to ACS within 24 hours. Court transcripts also revealed that Norris's child was being used as leverage for her to make an untrue admission or suffer an undue delay for failing to do so. In particular, Norris was informed that if she "went into court and made an admission to domestic violence," she would probably receive her child back right away; however, if she did not make this admission, her child would not be returned to her for several weeks (p. 187).

Domestic violence victims' requests for placement with relatives may also be ignored in an attempt to obtain concessions from them. Specifically, for domestic violence victims, the policy of CPS may be to allow victims of this crime to make decisions about who will care for their children. Court approval is not required for this decision. However, in practice, some caseworkers have ignored the recommendations of parents—even though they were viable options. For example, Nicholson had provided police with the names of relatives with whom her children could stay while she was in the hospital (*Nicholson v. Williams*, 2002). Instead of placing the children with those relatives, the CPS manager decided to place them in foster care, even though other viable alternatives could have been pursued.

To try to prevent these incorrect practices in the future, in *Nicholson*, the judge ruled that removal of a child would be authorized only in limited circumstances with a court order. The CPS caseworker, to obtain such a court order, would have to demonstrate the child's need for removal and explain why other, less drastic steps, such as the removal of the abusive parent or placement of the child with a relative, was not a viable option. According to the court ruling in *Yuan v. Rivera* (1999), "a non-abusing parent clearly retains some rights in her child's custody, although these may be contingent on separating the child from the abuser" (p. 346). As such, when CPS removes a child from or unnecessarily delays the return of a child to a mother against whom the agency has no evidence of child abuse or neglect, on the sole basis that the mother was a victim of domestic violence, then the mother's rights have been violated (*Tenenbaum v. Williams*, 1999). Hence, abused victims now have legal recourse—which would not have been necessary if societal attitudes toward domestic abuse victims reflected by ACS did not impede these personnel's work with nonabusive parents toward facilitating family cohesion.

Lessons from *Nicholson* Cases preceding Nicolson, such as *In re Lonell J.* (1998) and *In re Glenn G.* (1992), set a precedent for charging battered nonabusive parents with neglect on two grounds: for failure to prevent their own abuse and for their child's exposure to it. In these cases, the court did not evaluate whether the mother took any steps to remove herself and her child from the abuser and the harmful situation. Actions of the mother to protect her children have been ignored in other cases as well. In fact, the court in *In re Glenn G.* (1992) held that any such actions have no bearing on the mother's culpability for neglecting her children. Consider, once again, Tillett. Tillett had taken steps to protect her children, yet her actions were not considered by ACS. Specifically, Tillett sent her son back to California to stay with her family so he would not be exposed to the abuse perpetrated against her. In contrast to the rulings that preceded it, the court in *Nicholson v. Williams* (2002) concluded that any actions the mother took to mitigate the risks to children should be considered. In addition, in *Nicholson*, the court ruled that domestic violence victims who are physically abused in front of their children cannot be charged with child neglect. The caveat here is that this action is prohibited if the charge stems solely from the fact that the child was exposed to the abuse. The court further concluded that caseworkers are required to consider the risks to the victim and the children associated with leaving the abuser, the risks to the victim and the children associated with remaining and suffering continuous perpetrated abuse against them by the abuser, the risks to the victim and the children that are associated with them seeking assistance through the criminal justice system, and the victim's ability and attempts to remove herself/himself and children from the abusive situation.

In CPS, there is a "growing consensus that helping the non-offending parent protect herself and her children and holding the offender accountable is the preferred strategy for obtaining child safety and reducing future risk" (*Nicholson v. Williams*, 2002, p. 201). Expert testimony provided in *Nicholson* also revealed that the "general opinion in the field and the best practice recognizes that the single most effective strategy in protecting children in homes where there is domestic violence is removal and sanctioning of the offending party" (p. 204). Best practice, therefore, is removal of the perpetrator—not the children—and requirement of at least temporary child support (and perhaps alimony) to provide the victim and children with financial resources.

Nevertheless, even though both CPS and experts have acknowledged the removal of children from domestic violence victims is bad practice case law following *Nicholson* shows that battered mothers are still being prosecuted for child neglect. *In re Aiden L.* (2008), a mother was charged by CPS for neglect because she allowed her child to be exposed to an incident of domestic violence. In particular, the court in *In re Aiden L.* (2008) concluded that CPS failed to "consider, or at least to articulate their consideration of, the 'clearly attributable' causation requirement and the 'risk' factors necessary to determine whether a domestic violence victim has provided a minimum degree of care to her children" (Copps, 2009, p. 515). In addition, in the *In re David G.* (2010) case, the judge admonished CPS for removing a child from the victim because she was exposed to domestic violence. In this case, the child was removed because CPS believed that the mother would return to the abuser or the father would violate the order of protection. The court concluded that mere speculation is grossly inefficient to establish that the child was at imminent risk, warranting the child's removal from the home and placement in foster care.

In the *In re David G.* (2010) case, the court concluded that CPS had not met its burden of proof and had contravened the principles set out in *Nicholson* by removing David from the care of his mother based solely on the rationale that she was a domestic violence victim. As a policy, children should be removed from the care of the nonoffending parent only as a last resort—that is, if no other means to ensure the child's safety exists. Yet, this has not always been seen in practice. When this occurs, domestic violence victims are revictimized by being blamed not only for their own abuse but also for the abuse perpetrated by the offender.

The Case of Child Custody

Parents can seek several types of custody of children: legal, physical, sole, joint, and divided custody. With legal custody, parents have the right to make major decisions about their children's lives. If parents have physical custody of children, then the children reside with them on a daily basis. A parent with sole custody of the children has both legal and physical custody rights. If parents have joint custody, then legal and physical custody is shared by both parents. In these cases, one parent is designated as being primarily responsible for the physical custody and the child primarily resides with this parent. Finally, divided custody is sought and obtained when there is more than one child in the household. In this arrangement, each parent has primary legal and physical custody (i.e., sole custody) of at least one child.

Under the Uniform Marriage and Divorce Act of 1970, judges are required to consider the child's wishes in regard to the parent with which the child is to be placed. This practice has been required by all states either through existing jurisprudence or law. Overall, when making custody decisions, judges are required to consider the best interests of the child. In assessing the best interest of the child, the following factors are considered: the parents' wishes regarding child custody; the child's wishes regarding custody; the relationships among the child, parents, and siblings; the mental and physical health of the parents; the ability of the parents to provide a stable home for the child; and any other factors that would affect the child's best interest (Wallace & Koerner, 2003).

A study conducted by Felner, Terre, Farber, Primavera, and Bishop (1985) revealed that parental characteristics (e.g., mental health, emotional ability to provide for the child, ability to care for the child), situational characteristics (e.g., financial resources, stability of the household, time available to spend with the child), and family functioning (e.g., the relationship between the parent and the child) primarily affected judges' decisions in child custody cases. As such, decisions on primary physical custody were often made by a judge based on each of the parents' relationship with the child (Wallace & Koerner, 2003). Judges principally tend to award custody to the parent who had mainly provided for the child's emotional and physical needs before the separation of the parents (Wallace & Koerner, 2003).

Domestic violence has also factored in judges' decisions on child custody. In domestic violence cases, child custody, the receipt of child support, and visitation rights have served as means for the perpetrator to control the victim further. The issues have become more pronounced given that more than two-thirds of the states in the United States have passed mandatory joint custody laws; under such laws, joint custody is required unless evidence is presented that proves that this should not occur. In certain states, where domestic violence is proven (i.e., typically through criminal charges resulting in sentencing), it must be considered in courts when making child custody and visitation decisions; for example, this requirement is noted in § 240(1)(a) of the New York Domestic Relations Law. In custody cases, assessments of allegations of domestic violence are often quite challenging. Sometimes there may be no documented abuse to help substantiate the claims. The individual responsible for evaluating this factor—a child custody investigator—has a very important role to play. Usually, the investigator's opinion can have a significant impact on the final decision in custody cases. Some research criticizes child custody investigators on the basis of their lack of knowledge of domestic violence, overreliance on psychological testing, tendency to assume allegations are exaggerated or fabricated, and severe bias that is regularly exhibited in favor of fathers (Bancroft & Silverman, 2002; Bow & Boxer, 2003; Dalton, 1999; Jaffe & Geffner, 1998; Walker & Edwall, 1987).

In other instances, domestic violence allegations have been used to limit or deny custody or visitation for vindictive reasons and not because such violence was perpetrated. Research has shown that "[f]alse accusations of sexual abuse may also be made by a child who is the subject of a custody dispute" (Paquette, 1991, p. 1421). Equally problematic is when a judge finds allegations of abuse to be false, when they are actually true. In these cases, the nonoffending parent might by denied contact with the child and the offending parent might be awarded sole custody. This has been observed in custody cases. For example, "a four-year-old child . . . told her mother of sexual abuse by her father, but the judge found her story to be inconsistent, and awarded custody to the father with no visitation to the mother, all based on a theory of Parental Alienation Syndrome" (*Karen B. v. Clyde M.*, 1991, as cited in Wood, 1994, p. 1367). Parental alienation syndrome (PAS) is a term coined by child psychologist Richard Gardner; it refers to a disorder in which the child alienates one parent because he or she has been coached by another parent to do so (Gardner, Sauber, & Lorandos, 2006). In such situations, it is argued that child custody should be transferred to the alienated parent. This so-called disorder is not recognized by the medical community. Despite being criticized in the field of psychology, it has been introduced into the legal system in child custody cases and has been used by parents to obtain custody decisions in their favor (Williams, 2001).

Chapter Summary

Family rights are prescribed in international, constitutional, and case law. Yet, these rights are not absolute: The state has a legitimate interest in protecting children. Those tasked with child protection include CPS, criminal justice agents, and family court personnel.

Domestic violence cases in which children are present in the households are referred to CPS, and both parents may be charged with child neglect, regardless of who perpetrates the crime. Charging the battered nonoffending parent with child neglect for failing to protect the child from exposure to violence places the blame on the victim of domestic abuse and not on the abuser. Moreover, society revictimizes the person for his or her own abuse through the loss of the children. Instead of blaming the victim of domestic violence, CPS workers and agents of the criminal justice system should assign sole responsibility to the abusers for their behaviors.

Child custody decisions in favor of the offender have also contributed to the victimization of domestic violence victims. As a policy, children should be removed from the care of the nonoffending parent only as a last resort, if no other legitimate means exists to protect the child.

Review Questions

1. Family rights are enshrined in which international human rights instruments?

2. Which amendments to the U.S. Constitution are violated by the state's interference with family life and exercise of familial rights?

3. In which circumstances can a state legitimately interfere with family life?

4. When are emergency removals of children justified?

5. How have parents experienced interventions by child protective services?

6. Prior to the *Nicholson* ruling, how were domestic violence victims with children treated by child protective services? How are they treated after the *Nicholson* decision?

7. What was the past policy and practice of child protective services when domestic violence occurs in the household with children? What is the practice now?

References

Bachman, R., & Coker, A. L. (1995). Police involvement in domestic violence: The interactive effects of victim injury, offenders' history of violence, and race. *Violence and Victims, 10*(2), 91–100.

Bancroft, L., & Silverman, J. G. (2002). *The batterer as parent: Addressing the impact of domestic violence on family dynamics.* Thousand Oaks, CA: Sage.

Barnett, O. W., Miller-Perrin, C. L., & Perrin, R. D. (1997). *Family violence across the lifespan.* Thousand Oaks, CA: Sage.

Bow, J. N., & Boxer, P. (2003). Assessing allegations of domestic violence in child custody evaluations. *Journal of Interpersonal Violence, 18*(2), 1394–1410.

Bragg, L. H. (2003). Child protection in families experiencing domestic violence: Chapter 2: The overlap between child maltreatment and domestic violence. U.S. Department of Health and Human Services, Administration for Children and Families, Administration on Children, Youth and Families, Children's Bureau, Office on Child Abuse and Neglect. https://www.childwelfare.gov/pubs/usermanuals/domesticviolence/domesticviolenceb.cfm

Browne, K. D., & Hamilton, C. E. (1999). Police recognition of the link between spouse abuse and child abuse. *Child Maltreatment, 4*(2), 136–147.

Buzawa, E. S., & Austin, T. L. (1993). Determining police response to domestic violence: The role of victim preference, *American Behavioral Scientist, 36*(5), 610–623.

Byrne, C. A., Kilpatrick, D. G., Howley, S. S., & Beatty, D. (1999). Female victims of partner versus non-partner violence: Experiences with the criminal justice system. *Criminal Justice and Behaviour, 26*(3), 257–292.

C.C. v. J.S., 2009 N.Y. Misc. LEXIS 2697 (N.Y. Sup. Ct. June 4, 2009).

Christopher, W., Arquellas, J., Anderson, R., Barnes, W., Estrada, L., Kantor, M., & Tranquada, R. E. (1991). *Report of the independent commission on the Los Angeles Police Department.* Los Angeles, CA: Diane.

Copps, K. A. (2009). The good, the bad, and the future of *Nicholson v. Scoppetta*: An analysis of the effects and suggestions for further improvements. *Albany Law Review, 72*(2), 497–526.

Croft v. Westmoreland County Children and Youth Services, 103 F.3d 1123 (3d Cir. 1997).

Dalton, C. (1999). When paradigms collide: Protecting battered parents and their children in the family court system. *Family and Conciliation Court Review, 37*, 273–296.

Darryl H. v. Coler, 801 F.2d 893 (7th Cir. 1986).

De Santis, M. (2000). Online handbook: Advocating for women in the criminal justice system in cases of rape, domestic violence and child abuse. Women's Justice Centre. http://www.justice-women.com/handbook/intro.html

Doe v. New York City Department of Social Services, 649 F.2d 134 (2d Cir. 1981), cert. denied, 464 U.S. 864 (1983).

Duchesne v. Sugarman, 566 F.2d 817 (2d Cir. 1977).

Edleson, J. L. (2004). Should child exposure to domestic violence be defined as child maltreatment under the law? In P. G. Jaffe, L. L. Baker, & A. Cunningham (Eds.), *Protecting children from domestic violence: Strategies for community intervention.* New York, NY: Guilford Press. http://www.mincava .umn.edu/link/documents/ shouldch/shouldch.shtml

Englebright, S. (2012). Legislation strengthening New York's domestic violence laws passes legislature. http://assembly.state.ny.us/mem/Steve-Englebright/story/48482/

Epstein, D. (1999). Effective intervention in domestic violence cases: Rethinking the role of prosecutors, judges, and the court system. *Yale Law Journal, 11,* 3–39.

Fahim, K. (2008, November 12). Mother gets 43 years in death of child, 7. *New York Times.* http:// www.nytimes.com/2008/11/13/nyregion/13nixzmary.html

Fahim, K., & Kaufman, L. (2006, January 12). Girl, 7, found beaten to death in Brooklyn. *New York Times.* http://www.nytimes.com/2006/01/12/nyregion/12child.html?pagewanted=all

"Failure to Protect" Working Group of Child Welfare Committee of New York City Inter-agency Task Force Against Domestic Violence. (1999). Charging battered mothers with "failure to protect": Still blaming the victim. *Fordham Urban Law Journal, 27*(3), 849–873.

Felner, R. D., Terre, L., Farber, S. S., Primavera, J., & Bishop, T. A. (1985). Child custody: Practices and perspectives of legal professionals. *Journal of Clinical Child Psychiatry, 14,* 27–34.

Forell, C. (1991). Stopping the violence: Mandatory arrest and police tort liability for failure to assist battered women. *Berkeley Women's Law Journal, 6,* 215–263.

Franz v. Lytle, 997 F.2d 784 (10th Cir. 1993).

Fugate, J. A. (2001). Who's failing whom? A critical look at failure-to-protect laws. *New York University Law Review, 76,* 272–308.

Gardner, R. A., Sauber, S. R., & Lorandos, D. (2006). *The international handbook of parental alienation syndrome: Conceptual, clinical and legal considerations.* Springfield, IL: Charles C. Thomas.

Geffner, R., Rosenbaum, A., & Hughes, H. (1988). Research issues concerning family violence. In V. B. Van Hasselt, R. Morison, A. S. Bellack, & M. Hersen (Eds.), *Handbook of family violence* (pp. 457–481). New York, NY: Plenum Press.

Girlfriend thought lawyer would heal dying child. (1988, December 2). *Houston Chronicle.* http://www .chron.com/CDA/archives/archive.mpl/1988_588106/girlfriend-thought-lawyer-would-healdying-child.html

Goldman, R. (2011, May 4). Virginia parents accused of murder, keeping starving child in cage. *ABC News.* http://abcnews.go.com/US/virginia-parents-accused-murder-keeping-starving-child-cage /story?id=13528448#.UDGIVaN_UeU

Goodmark, L. (2004). Achieving batterer accountability in the child protection system. *Kentucky Law Journal, 93,* 613–657.

Gottlieb v. County of Orange, 84 F.3d 511 (2d Cir. 1996).

Griffin v. Strong, 983 F.2d 1540 (10th Cir. 1993).

Griswold v. State of Connecticut, 381 U.S. 479 (1965).

Hart, B. (1993). Battered women and the criminal justice system. *American Behavioral Scientist, 36,* 624–638.

Haviland, M., Frye, V., Rajah, V., Thukral, J., & Trinity, M. (2001). *The Family Protection and Domestic Violence Intervention Act of 1995: Examining the effects of mandatory arrest in New York City.* New York, NY: Urban Justice Center.

Hirschel, D. (2008). Domestic violence cases: What research shows about arrest and dual arrest rates. National Institute of Justice. http://www.nij.gov/nij/publications/dv-dual-arrest-222679 /contents.htm

Horn, G. (2005). Online searches and offline challenges: The chilling effect, anonymity, and the new FBI guidelines. *New York University Annual Survey of American Law, 60,* 735–778.

In re Aiden L., 850 N.Y.S.2d 671 (3d Dep't 2008).

In re Athena M.V., 678 N.Y.S.2d 11, 12 (App. Div. 1998).

In re B.B., 598 N.W.2d 312 (Iowa Ct. App. 1999).

In re David G., 909 N.Y.S.2d 891 (Fam. Ct. 2010).

In re Deandre T., 676 N.Y.S.2d 666 (App. Div. 1998).

In re Glenn G., 587 N.Y.S. 2d 464 (Fam. Ct. 1992).

In re Horton, 2004 WL 2674562, at 7 (Ohio Ct. App. Nov. 23, 2004).

In re J.P., 692 N.E.2d 338 (Ill. App. Ct. 1998).

In re Lonell J., 673 N.Y.S.2d 116 (App. Div. 1998).

In re T.A., 663 N.W.2d 225, 230 (S.D. 2003).

Jaffe, P. G., & Geffner, R. (1998). Child custody disputes and domestic violence: Critical issues for mental health, social service, and legal professionals. In G. W. Holden, R. Geffner, & E. N. Jouriles (Eds.), *Children exposed to marital violence: Theory, research, and applied issues* (pp. 371–408). Washington, DC: American Psychological Association.

J.B. v. Washington County, 127 F.3d 919 (10th Cir. 1997).

Johnson, S. P., & Sullivan, C. M. (2008). How child protection workers support or further victimize battered mothers. *Affilia, 23*(3), 242–258.

Karen B. v. Clyde M., 574 N.Y.S.2d 267 (Fam. Ct. 1991).

Kimmel, M. S. (2001). Male victims of domestic violence: A substantive and methodological research review. http://www.xyonline.net/downloads/malevictims.pdf

Kuehnle, K., & Sullivan, A. (2003). Gay and lesbian victimization: Reporting factors in domestic violence and bias incidents. *Criminal Justice and Behaviour, 30*(1), 85–96.

Larry King Live. (2003, June 16). Interview with Hedda Nussbaum. *CNN.* http://transcripts.cnn.com /TRANSCRIPTS/0306/16/lkl.00.html

Lassiter v. Department of Social Services, 452 U.S. 18 (1981).

Lohr, D. (2011, May 2). Brian and Shannon Gore arrested after child found in cage-like crib, another buried in Trailer Court. *Huffington Post.* http://www.huffingtonpost.com/2011/05/02/brian-and-shannon-gore_n_856502.html

Lundy, S. (1993). Abuse Dare not Speak its Name: Assisting Victims of Lesbian and Domestic Violence in Massachusetts. *New England Law Review, 20*, 273–311.

Matter of the Welfare of S.A.V. and S.M.V., 392 N.W.2d 260 (Minn. App. 1986).

McMahon, M., & Pence, E. (2003). Making social change: Reflections on individual and institutional advocacy with women arrested for domestic violence. *Violence Against Women, 9*, 47–74.

Meyer v. Nebraska, 262 U.S. 390 (1923).

Mignon, S. I., & Holmes, W. M. (1995). Police response to mandatory arrest laws. *Crime & Delinquency, 41*(4), 430–442.

Miller v. City of Philadelphia, 174 F.3d 368 (3d Cir. 1999).

M. L. B. v. S. L. J., 519 U.S. 102 (1996).

Moore v. City of East Cleveland, 431 U.S. 494 (1977).

Murphy, J. C. (1998). Legal images of motherhood: Conflicting definitions from welfare "reform," family, and criminal law. *Cornell Law Review, 83*, 688–766.

National Institute of Justice. (2008). Domestic violence cases: What research shows about arrest and dual arrest rates. U.S. Department of Justice. http://www.nij.gov/publications/dv-dual-arrest-222679/ch1/Pages/findings.aspx

Nicholson v. Scoppetta, 3 N.Y.3d 357, 820 N.E.2d 840, 787 N.Y.S.2d 196 (*2004*)

Nicholson v. Williams, 203 F. Supp. 2d 153 (E.D.N.Y. 2002).

Nir, S. M. (2011, November 29). Recalling days on the run with abducted children. *New York Times.* http://www.nytimes.com/2011/11/30/nyregion/parents-who-abducted-their-8-children-say-they-feared-adoption-plans.html?pagewanted=all

NY parents get 60 days jail in abduction case. (2011, November 23). *ABC News*. http://abclocal.go.com/wtvd/story?section=news/local/new_york&id=8443590

NYC ACS. (2003). ACS's domestic violence principles. http://www.nyc.gov/html/acs/html/about/domestic_violence.shtml

Office on Child Abuse and Neglect. (2003). Child protection in families experiencing domestic violence. http://www.childwelfare.gov/pubs/usermanuals/domesticviolence/domesticvioleceb.cfm

O'Hagan, K. (1998). Child sexual abuse: A social work categorization. *Social Work in Action*, 2(2), 176–183.

Osthoff, S. (2002). But Gertrude, I beg to differ, a hit is not a hit is not a hit: When battered women are arrested for assaulting their partners. *Violence Against Women*, 8, 1521–1544.

Paquette, C. (1991). Handling sexual abuse allegations in child custody cases. *New England Law Review*, 25, 1415–1446.

Parham v. J.R., 442 U.S. 584 (1979).

People ex rel. C.F., 708 N.W.2d 313 (S.D. 2005).

People v. Steinberg, 584 N.Y.S.2d 770 (1992).

People United for Children, Inc. v. City of New York, 108 F. Supp. 2d 275 (S.D.N.Y. 2000).

Pierce v. Society of Sisters, 268 U.S. 510 (1925).

Plummer, C. A., & Eastin, J. A. (2007). System intervention problem in child abuse investigation: The mothers' perspectives. *Journal of Interpersonal Violence*, 22(6), 775–787.

P.R. v. Department of Public Welfare, 801 A.2d 478 (Pa. 2002).

Prince v. Commonwealth of Massachusetts, 321 U.S. 158 (1944).

Quilloin v. Walcott, 434 U.S. 246 (1978).

Richardson, D., & May, H. (1999). Deserving victims?: Sexual status and the social construction of violence. *Sociological Review*, 47(2), 308–331.

Santosky v. Kramer, 455 U.S. 745 (1982).

Scahill, M. (1999). Prosecuting attorneys in dependency proceedings in Juvenile Court: Defining and assessing a critical role in child abuse and neglect cases. *Journal of the Center for Children & the Courts*, 1, 73–99.

Schmidt, J. D., & Sherman, L. W. (1996). Does arrest deter domestic violence? In E. S. Buzawa & C. G. Buzawa (Eds.), *Do arrest and restraining orders work?* (pp. 43–53). Thousand Oaks, CA: Sage.

Sherman, L. (1992). *Policing domestic violence*. New York, NY: Free Press.

Smith v. Organization of Foster Families for Equality and Reform, 431 U.S. 816 (1977).

Snapp & Son, Inc. v. Puerto Rico, 458 U.S. 592 (1982).

Stanley v. Illinois, 405 U.S. 645 (1972).

Stark, E. (1993). Mandatory arrest of batterers: A response to its critics. *American Behavioral Scientist*, 36(5), 651–680.

Strail v. Department of Children, Youth & Families of Rhode Island, 62 F. Supp. 2d 519 (D. R. I. 1999).

Straus, M., & Gelles, R. J. (1988). How violent are American families? Estimates from the National Family Violence Resurvey and other studies. In G. Hotaling, D. Finkelhor, J. Kirkpatrick, & M. Straus (Eds.), *Family abuse and its consequences: New directions in research* (pp. 14–37). Newbury Park, CA: Sage.

Straus, M. A., Gelles, R. J., & Steinmetz, S. K. (1988). *Behind closed doors: Violence in the American family* (rev. ed.). Newbury Park, CA: Sage.

Tenenbaum v. Williams, 193 F.3d 581 (2d Cir. 1999).

Thomas v. City of New York, 814 F. Supp. 1139 (E.D.N.Y. 1992).

Troxel v. Granville, 530 U.S. 57 (2000).

Truesdell, D. L., McNeill, J. S., & Deschner, J. P. (1986). Incidence of wife abuse in incestuous families. *Social Work, 31*, 138–140.

Trujillo, M. P., & Ross, S. (2008). Police response to domestic violence: Making decisions about risk
and risk management. *Journal of Interpersonal Violence, 23*(4), 454–473.

Walker, L. E. A., & Edwall, G. E. (1987). Domestic violence and determination of visitation and custody in divorce. In D. J. Sonkin (Ed.), *Domestic violence on trial: Psychological and legal dimensions of
family violence* (pp. 127–152). New York, NY: Springer.

Wallace, S. R., & Koerner, S. S. (2003). Influence of child and family factors on judicial decisions in
contested custody cases. *Family Relations, 52*(2), 180–188.

Wallis v. Spencer, 202 F.3d 1126 (9th Cir. 2000).

Weller v. Department of Social Services, 901 F.2d 387 (4th Cir. 1990).

Widom, C. S. (1988). Sampling biases and implications for child abuse research. *American Journal of
Orthopsychiatry, 58*, 260–270.

Williams, R. J. (2001). Alienated children in divorce: Should judges close the gate on PAS and PA?
Family Court Review, 39, 267–281.

Wood, C. L. (1994). The parental alienation syndrome: A dangerous aura of reliability. *Loyola of Los
Angeles Law Review, 27*, 1367–1416.

Yuan v. Rivera, 48 F. Supp. 2d 335 (S.D.N.Y. 1999).

Chapter 9

Child Protective Services

Cases, such as that of *Doe v. New York City Department of Social Services* (1981), *Nelson ex rel. Wharton v. Missouri Division of Family Services* (1983), *Brodie v. Summit County Children Services Board* (1990), and *Thomas v. City of New York* (1992), among others, have brought forward a rush of public criticism of child protective services (CPS). In an attempt to prevent such failures in the future, an understanding of the processes and requirements of CPS is needed. The focus of this chapter is on each stage of the CPS process, looking in particular at: intake, the preliminary investigation, family assessment, case plan, service provision, and case closure. Particular emphasis is placed on the ramifications of deciding to keep the children with the family versus removing them from their homes.

Child Protective Services

CPS is the agency responsible for protecting children and investigating cases of child maltreatment. Usually, CPS is responsible for intervening in situations where the offender in a case of child abuse or neglect is the parent or guardian of the victim. Typically, police officers are responsible for investigating cases of child abuse or neglect where the offender is not the parent or guardian of the victim. However, CPS has been involved in cases in which the offender was not the victim's parent or guardian. In these cases, CPS usually conducts an investigation when the parent or guardian seemingly failed to protect the child from the alleged offender.

CPS agencies obtain information about families and their members to examine situations and provide appropriate assistance to enable families to resolve the issues that led to the need for agency intervention and court supervision. To make appropriate decisions in child abuse and neglect cases, CPS workers must be able to conduct interviews properly; collect, organize, and analyze the information they obtain; and draw accurate conclusions.

When the wrong decisions are made in regards to interventions and as a result a child is severely harmed or dies, these actions or inactions make headlines in the news media. A case in point is the death of Elisa Izquierdo in New York. Elisa was beaten to death by her mother, Awilda Lopez. Elisa had been born addicted to cocaine owing to her mother's use of this illicit drug. Her father won primary custody of Elisa, and her mother was allowed to see her during the weekend. Her father petitioned to have Lopez's parental rights terminated because Elisa was being abused during her visits with her mother. Elisa's father died of cancer before the court heard his case. A custody fight for Elisa occurred shortly after. Her father's cousin, Elsa Canizares, petitioned for custody (Van Biena, Epperson, & Rivera, 1995). However, the Brooklyn Family Court judge, Phoebe Greenbaum, gave custody of Elisa to her mother.

On November 22, 1995, Elisa was murdered by her mother. Specifically, Lopez smashed Elisa's head against a cement wall and left her unattended to die (Leduff, 1996). Lopez also later confessed to making Elisa eat her own feces and mopping the floor with Elisa's head (Van Biena et al., 1995). When Elisa's body was discovered, she was covered in bruises. Elisa and her family had been provided numerous social services by the Child Welfare Administration (CWA), which at the time was responsible for all issues of child welfare in New York City (NYC ACS, 1996). Caseworkers of this agency had many opportunities to respond, but failed to do so. Lopez was allowed to maintain custody of Elisa, even with numerous reports that were made against her concerning the physical abuse of her daughter.

The death of Elisa Izquierdo led to a reorganization of child welfare services. Particularly, in response to her murder, the Administration of Children's Services (ACS) was created in New York. The mission of ACS includes protecting children by investigating reports of child abuse and neglect; assisting families in obtaining services, such as drug rehabilitation programs; recruiting and training parents or guardians in the provision of foster care; ensuring children in foster care have a safe home; and providing permanent homes for children.

In addition to the creation of ACS, changes were made to CPS to insert openness and accountability in the process. At the time of Elisa's death, confidentiality laws existed that shielded the CWA from having to disclose the number of reports it had received concerning the alleged abuse. After her death, CPS was reformed with the passage of the Child Protective Services Reform Act of 1996, referred to as Elisa's Law (Section 422-a, New York Social Services Law). Elisa's Law required public accountability in deaths of children in which child abuse or neglect have been reported prior to their death. This law

> permits the disclosure of child protective services information—when it is not contrary to the best interest of the child—in four limited circumstances in which the public has a legitimate interest in the case: 1) the subject of the report has been

charged with a crime relating to the report, 2) the case has been made public by law enforcement officials, a district attorney, a state or local investigative agency, or by a judge, 3) the case has been made public by the subject of the report, or 4) the child has died (NYC ACS, 1996).

Similar requirements exist for CPS agencies in other states as well, including, but not limited to, Florida, Nevada, and Washington (Williams-Mbengue, 1998, p. 2).

To prevent failures such as those that occurred in the case of Elisa, it is imperative that CPS workers adhere to their guidelines and requirements. This chapter examines the stages of a CPS worker's job—intake, preliminary investigation, comprehensive family evaluation, case planning, provision of services, assessment of progress, and case closure—and the obligations of CPS workers in each area (DePanfilis & Salus, 1992).

Intake

The Child Abuse Prevention and Treatment Act of 1974 made the reporting of child abuse and neglect mandatory for certain individuals. The individuals required to report instances of child abuse and neglect when brought to their attention include doctors, other healthcare professionals (e.g., nurses), mental health professionals (e.g., psychologists and psychiatrists), schools (e.g., teachers and school counselors), childcare workers, clergy, members of government agencies, and law enforcement personnel. For those persons who have a duty to report suspected child abuse or neglect, failure to do so can result in criminal prosecution. However, in such situations, most states require the prosecution to show that there was a "willful failure" to report, which is a standard that is quite difficult to prove.

For failure to report cases, civil liability is likely to be the result. As an example, consider the educational system. In the educational system, teachers, school counselors, and principals can be held liable for monetary damages if they do not report suspected maltreatment of children. In civil cases of this nature, the plaintiffs often argue educator negligence is present. To substantiate a claim of negligence, the court will consider various aspects. First, it examines whether the educator had a duty to report. Second, it explores whether the educator failed to exercise this duty. Third, it looks at any harm or injury suffered by the child. Finally, it evaluates whether the failure of an educator to report was the proximate cause of the child's injuries. To avoid liability, individuals should familiarize themselves with federal and state laws governing mandatory reporting. In addition, given that these laws usually have a time limit on disclosing child abuse or neglect, reports of maltreatment should be made in a timely manner. Absolute proof of child maltreatment is not required before reporting. In fact, waiting to report an incident may endanger the child.

If child abuse and neglect is suspected, mandatory reporters are required to submit a report to the appropriate agency. This report should not be mistakenly construed as being an accusation of maltreatment; it is instead a request for further investigation. A case is opened when a report of suspected child abuse or neglect is made. In *Angela R. v. Huckabee*

(1993), the court mandated that CPS maintain a 24-hour intake process for accepting complaints of child abuse and neglect. Many states currently have such processes in place. In New York, reports are received by the State Central Register (SCR) and then sent to the appropriate ACS branch depending on the location of the case. An exception to this, for example, is if someone walks into an ACS location and reports suspected abuse or neglect. A CPS worker is then assigned to the case.

The job of the CPS worker begins with intake. During the intake process, reports of maltreatment are received and then screened. Jurisprudence reveals that actions must be taken at this stage to ensure that bona fide reports are not screened out inappropriately (*David C. v. Leavitt*, 1995; *Marisol v. Pataki*, 1996; *Sheila A. v. Finney*, 1993). During intake, the credibility of the report is assessed. Issues to be considered include whether the reporter is willing to provide contact information, the relationship of the reporter to the family, the nature and extent of the knowledge the reporter has of the family, the nature and extent of the knowledge of the incident, the means by which the reporter came to find about the maltreatment, and the demeanor and behavior of the reporter. Basically, as much information as possible is gathered about the person reporting the child abuse or neglect and the incident, including information about what led the reporter to believe that the child was maltreated (i.e., the behavior or demeanor of the child) and whether the reporter knows of anyone else who might be able to provide further information on the incident. This will significantly assist the CPS personnel in determining whether intervention is required. It also assists CPS caseworkers in planning their investigation of the incident. If the report involves a family that has been the subject of previous child abuse and neglect reports, the report is often assigned to the caseworker for the family, regardless of whether the allegation of neglect or abuse was made against this family.

One of the primary decisions that is made during intake is whether to accept an incoming report for further investigation. This type of decision is based on the existing policies, state law, and the characteristics of the case (which are received from the reporter). After an intake decision is made, a supervisor reviews this decision. The decision is then approved or disapproved. If disapproved, an appropriate response to the report should be provided.

Preliminary Investigation

After receiving a report, the CPS caseworker conducts a preliminary investigation of the allegations that have been made. The caseworker is also responsible for substantiating the alleged child abuse or neglect. The circumstances of the case determine who will intervene along with CPS. For example, the police are usually called if an incident of domestic violence occurs. If substance abuse or mental illnesses are involved, other agencies are usually tasked with dealing with the situation. The types of cases that are usually handled solely by CPS include those cases that the police and prosecutors do not consider serious enough to pursue for criminal investigation and prosecution, respectively, and those that can be justifiably handled outside the criminal justice system. In some instances, CPS workers have handled cases because the victims or adults of the household have refused to contact and give any information to the police. In other cases, parents have willingly handed over guardianship of a child or children who have been neglected or abused to CPS by signing a voluntary agreement. Nonetheless, such cases by no means constitute the norm.

One of the responsibilities of CPS is to determine whether a child is safe in the household. This is done via face-to-face contact by a member of CPS or another professional who is trained in risk assessment. During the preliminary investigation, the CPS worker assigned to the case must determine whether it is in the best interest of the child for an unannounced visit to occur with the parent(s) or whether the best option is to contact the parent(s) and schedule an appointment for an interview. This decision will be based on the circumstances of the case and any prior history of abuse or neglect in the household.

By law, CPS is required to respond immediately in situations where the injury of a child is severe or the treatment of the child could result in serious harm, such as locking a child in small enclosed spaces, pushing a child down the stairs, or locking a child outside the house without supervision. To determine how imminent a response must be, the CPS worker must assess the existing risks to the child, such as exposure to drug and alcohol abuse. The response time, therefore, will depend on the situation. Consider a scenario in which a woman tells her psychiatrist that she hears voices telling her to kill her children. This patient currently is refusing to continue taking her medication and coming to her psychiatric sessions. This situation would require an immediate intervention and response by CPS caseworkers.

In this stage of the investigation process, the CPS caseworkers must first identify and interview the child victim. The caseworker must meet with the child within a certain amount of time—usually, within 24 hours of the report. After that, CPS workers interview any siblings of the child, the nonoffending adults in the household, and the offending parent or legal guardian (preferably in that order).

During the preliminary investigation, information is sought that either refutes or supports the allegations of abuse or neglect that have been made in the initial report. Accordingly, it is important to interview the nonoffending parent and any other persons (adults and children) in the household. These individuals can provide additional information concerning the likelihood of maltreatment and can help the CPS caseworker understand the causes and dynamics leading to the abuse. Interviews with them can also reveal the role of these individuals, if any, in the child's disclosure or nondisclosure of the abuse or neglect. Such interviews can further assist the CPS caseworker in determining whether these individuals support the child and believe the allegations made against the perpetrator.

Certain factors can determine whether a nonoffending parent (and any other adults in the household) will act or is acting in the child's best interests. These factors include the quality of the individual's relationship with the child, the level of dependency of the person on the offender, and the willingness and capability of the individual to protect the child. It is important to note any antagonistic relationships between the alleged offender and other nonoffending individuals in the household. These relationships can shed light

---

Box 9-1 Alcohol or Drug Screening During the Preliminary Investigation

Given the correct circumstances, the CPS caseworker will look for signs of drug and alcohol abuse when visiting the family during his or her investigation. This is especially true if alcohol and substance abuse by a parent or guardian has been disclosed in the initial report received during intake or during the preliminary investigation. To assess substance or alcohol abuse, CPS caseworkers observe members of the household, interview them, review available medical histories and arrest records, and obtain reports from other members of the household or relatives outside the household. In addition, to determine drug and/or alcohol abuse, CPS workers look for visual and olfactory indications of abuse, such as the smell of alcohol or drugs, the presence of drug paraphernalia or alcohol bottles in the home, and the appearance of drug or alcohol abuse from the parents (e.g., needle marks on arm, slurred speech, or excessively missing teeth).

Moreover, screening tests may be conducted to determine whether further drug and/or alcohol evaluation is required. The screening of individuals for drug or alcohol abuse is an important part of the CPS investigation, as the results affect risk assessments and the achievement of effective outcomes from interventions (when case plans are developed). If CPS drug tests of the parents yield positive results, this is not necessarily indicative of patterns of abuse, and does not prove that the parent is dependent upon drugs of abuse. Rather, it simply shows that the individual used drugs before the test was administered. Tests that are commonly used (e.g., breathalyzer) do not provide accurate information because alcohol is usually metabolized within 8 hours and is not easily detected. In addition, whether drugs are detected depends on the individual and the type of drug used. If a positive result is found, the CPS caseworker must carefully follow up with the family in this regard and determine the appropriate services for the family.

In general, if one or both parents engage in drug or alcohol abuse, the CPS worker must include the following elements in the assessment: the effects of substance abuse on the ability of the parent to properly raise the children, the type of intervention that would be most appropriate for the parent, and the steps that the parent needs to take to be able to show that he or she is able to safely raise a child in light of the parent's problem with alcohol or drugs.

---

on the veracity of the claims being made, although this is not always the case. Some examples of problematic relationships include divorce, when the nonoffending parent is in the process of divorcing the alleged offending parent, and child custody, particularly when physical custody and parental visitation disputes exist.

During this stage of the CPS process, the investigation is conducted to determine if the child is safe in his or her current environment; if the child is at risk of future harm; and what response, if any, is required. These assessments are made by the CPS caseworker and reviewed by his or her supervisor. The remainder of this section explores how safety evaluations are made by CPS caseworkers and how they respond to cases in which abuse or neglect has been substantiated.

Ensuring Child Safety

The preliminary investigation is designed to identify safety risks to the child in the household. Apart from signs of child abuse, CPS caseworkers look for more general signs of neglect. They make an assessment as to whether the neglect was the result of physical harm, lack of supervision, or a combination of the two. They must also determine which areas in the child's life were neglected (e.g., nutrition, hygiene, medical, clothing, substitute care, or supervision) and how extensive the neglect was (DePanfilis & Salus, 1992). Neglect may involve the failure of parents to provide the requisite care after injury, illness, or in response to a disability or chronic disease. The failure to attend to the child's basic hygiene needs is also assessed by CPS. Are the living conditions unsanitary and/or dangerous? The stability of the child includes the number of times a child changed residences and/or the number of evictions from apartments or homes due to the parent's or guardian's poverty, substance abuse, or mental illness.

Moreover, parents' pattern of leaving the child at home for extended periods of time might be considered neglect. Many states do not have specific laws regarding the particular age at which a child may be left home alone or the number of hours for which a child may be left unsupervised. Instead, CPS is responsible for making a determination regarding a child's ability to be unsupervised. For instance, CPS tends to view children younger than the age of 8 who are left alone as being neglected (Fairfax County Virginia, n.d.), whereas children older than 12 can spend approximately 2 hours at home alone (New York State Office of Children and Family Services, FAQ, n.d.). Nevertheless, in determining neglect, CPS primarily looks at maturity, competence, and mental ability of the child, particularly whether the child has knowledge of what to do in an emergency (Ohio Department of Job and Family Services, n.d.; Fairfax County Virginia, n.d.; New York State Office of Children and Family Services, FAQ, n.d.). The length of time and frequency of episodes during which the child is left alone also plays a role in the assessment of neglect (Ohio Department of Job and Family Services, n.d.). In making this determination, CPS workers also check for any indirect supervision of the child, including whether the parents checked in or had a relative check on the well-being of the child (Fairfax County Virginia, n.d.). Furthermore, CPS workers examine whether the neighborhood and home environment are safe (New York State Office of Children and Family Services, FAQ, n.d.).

Psychological or emotional abuse is very difficult for the caseworker to assess. To determine whether this type of abuse has occurred, a CPS worker would need to have access to information concerning the behavior of the parent or guardian and the child over time. Specifically, a behavioral pattern of psychological abuse (rather than an isolated incident or two) must be established. This may include making continuous derogatory and critical comments to the child, placing unrealistic expectations on the child based on his or her developmental level, and threatening to abandon the child or send him or her away. To assess this type of abuse, the CPS worker must observe several interactions of the parent with the child and obtain information in this regard from relatives and other sources, such as friends, coaches, babysitters, and neighbors. This type of abuse is very difficult to establish, as it must be demonstrated that the actions of the parent or guardian are a direct cause of harm to the child (e.g., depression).

If the child's safety is at risk, a plan must be devised to rectify the situation. Before removing the child or the alleged perpetrator, CPS workers assess how this removal will affect the unity of the family, the relationship between the child and the family, the relationship between the child and his or her siblings (if any), and the relationship of the child at school and with and his or her community. Protecting a child, however, does not necessarily imply that instant removal of the child or suspect from the house is required. The CPS worker is responsible for ensuring the safety of the child by either providing services to the family to mitigate the existing risks to the child's safety, removing the offender from the household, returning the child to the parent at a safe location, taking the child to a safe location that has been identified by the parent (such as the home of a relative), or taking the child to another safe place such as a foster care.

Accordingly, during the preliminary investigation, the CPS caseworker must determine both if maltreatment has occurred and if the child is at imminent risk of future harm. In the latter case, the caseworker must determine whether certain family services would reduce the risk of harm to the child. If it is decided that provision of such services would not create a safer environment for the child, the caseworker will most likely remove the child from the home—if, of course, other alternatives are not available. If services are provided to the family and child, the caseworker is required to monitor the situation to see if it improves. If the situation at home does not improve, then the caseworker would file a petition of neglect or abuse to a family or dependency court to have the child removed.

In the preliminary investigation, if the allegations of abuse or neglect are substantiated, then appropriate action is taken in criminal, civil, or family courts. In addition, during this stage, the CPS caseworker may remove a child if it is determined that the child is or will be in danger if he or she is left in the household. Sometimes CPS workers will intervene in a less intrusive manner by removing one parent from the household, if that parent is the offending parent. However, this step is taken only if the CPS caseworker is reasonably certain that the offending parent will not have contact with the child. If a CPS caseworker believes that the offending parent will try to contact the child and will be allowed to do so by the nonoffending parent, the caseworker will have the child removed from the home. However, jurisprudence has revealed that a mere assumption that the child is at imminent risk is insufficient grounds for removal (*In re David G.*, 2010). Indeed, removal should occur only as a last resort, as it has a significant adverse impact on the child, parents (or legal guardians), and the family as a whole.

Removal

A CPS caseworker, after investigating claims of child abuse and neglect, has several options that he or she can pursue to ensure the child's safety, all of which depend on the case at hand. The venues in which most legal proceedings on child abuse and neglect are heard are family (or dependency) and criminal courts. The focus of this chapter is family courts, whereas the *Agents of the Courts: Roles and Perspectives* chapter covers criminal courts. Each proceeding has different standards of proof, rules of evidence and discovery, and time restrictions. These two types of courts also have different and often mutually exclusive goals, such as preserving families, protecting children, ensuring children's well-being, punishing offenders, and protecting families from unwarranted state intrusion (Sedlak, 2005, p. 390).

Family courts hear cases that involve child abuse and neglect. They focus on serving the best interests of the child by taking action to ensure the well-being of the child by, wherever possible, rehabilitating the parent or guardian. Thus such courts do not seek to punish the parent or guardian; rather, their primary goal is to preserve the family. To do so, the family court identifies the issues that led to the removal of the child from the family. After identifying the issues at hand, the court seeks to find the appropriate remedy—such as counseling or education for the parents—to provide parents with an opportunity to remedy the issues that led to the child's removal. If the situation is such that the child cannot be returned to his or her family, the court seeks out the most appropriate permanent home for the child. The court considers various options in this situation: adoption; foster care; guardianship; or placement with the child's family, which includes individuals other than the parents such as grandparents, aunts, and uncles.

If the CPS worker removes the child from the home, the individual is required by law to have a court hearing very quickly (1 to 3 days) after removal; this proceeding is also known as a removal hearing or shelter care. The CPS agency that removed the child must also file a petition that includes fact-specific information concerning how the alleged parent or legal guardian offender abused or neglected the child. The judge hears the petition and decides whether to return the child to his or her parent or parents, place the child with a suitable relative, or place the child temporarily in foster care. In this process, courts have emphasized the requirement that CPS caseworkers first seek to place children with relatives wherever possible and appropriate (*LaShawn A. v. Dixon*, 1991). When children are placed with relatives, these homes must be licensed and approved in a comparable manner similar to foster homes (*G.L. v. Stangler*, 1983). In some instances, a child may be placed in a group home or residential treatment center instead of with a foster family. This usually occurs when the child exhibits severe emotional and behavioral problems that a typical foster family may not be able to handle.

Foster care programs and practices are governed by statutes and case law. In West Virginia, the court held that foster homes must also meet standards established by CPS, which assure adequate food, clothing, and shelter for the child (*Gibson v. Ginsberg*, 1981). Additionally, in Kansas, the court held that children cannot be placed in an unlicensed foster home (*Sheila A. v. Finney*, 1993). Despite this licensing requirement, there is a need to improve the existing quality of foster care and coordination of the delivery of family services. In addition, children have suffered from abuse and neglect in the foster care system. A notorious case involved foster parents Warren and Melody Tripp. These individuals were annually recertified by the Department of Human Services to serve as foster parents despite numerous allegations against them concerning the physical and sexual abuse of children while in their care (Cole, 2009). After a report was made by a 15-year-old girl who was placed in his care, Warren Tripp was charged with and pleaded guilty to sodomy and first-degree sexual abuse (Cole, 2009).

Those persons seeking to serve as foster or adoptive parents are subjected to a criminal background check. An individual who has been convicted of a felony that involves crimes against children, domestic violence, or violent crimes (e.g., homicide, sexual assault, or rape) cannot be a foster or adoptive parent. In addition, any individual who has engaged in a drug-related offense, battery, or other form of physical assault in the preceding five years cannot be a foster or adoptive parent.

The case of Janie Buelna illustrates the importance of conducting background investigations into the individuals who serve as foster parents, even when they are relatives of the child or children. Janie and her brother were living in Phoenix, Arizona, with her grandmother, Juanita Rodriguez; the grandmother's boyfriend, Humelio Dominiquez-Vazquez; and a man named Christopher Lopez (Roberts, 2011). A CPS worker conducted a cursory investigation of reported abuse, but missed three very important facts. First, in a different state (Nevada), Rodriguez had lost custody of her six children. Second, the CPS worker did not conduct a criminal background investigation. Had this occurred, the CPS worker would have found that the grandmother had served a 13-month sentence for child abuse. Third, had CPS conducted a background check on the males living in the household, the caseworker would have found that one of them had lost custody of his own child. When Janie was found dead in her grandmother's home, she had scars all over her body, severe burns on one of her legs, broken teeth, and a deformed forehead (Roberts, 2011). This case, and other cases like it, demonstrate the critical importance of conducting background investigations before child placement.

The Adoption and Safe Families Act of 1997 provides incentives for ensuring that children are adopted. Pursuant to Section 437, an adoptive incentive program was developed, where states receive "$4,000, multiplied by the amount (if any) by which the number of foster child adoptions in the State during the fiscal year exceeds the base number of foster child adoptions for the State for the fiscal year" and "(B) $2,000, multiplied by the amount (if any) by which the number of special needs adoptions in the State during the fiscal year exceeds the base number of special needs adoptions for the State for the fiscal year." An agency loses its commission if a child is removed from placement. There is, however, a risk in providing monetary incentives to CPS workers for placing children in foster care. Specifically, they may be overly lenient in their decisions when they evaluate foster families and may be predisposed toward the intervention of child removal from the household and placement with a foster or adoptive family.

States require CPS personnel to create a case plan when a child is removed from a home and placed in foster care, with a relative, in a group home, or other residential area. For those children placed in foster care, § 409(e) of the New York Social Services Law requires that a plan be developed that includes a description of the reasonable efforts made by CPS to prevent the need for placement or the reasons why such efforts were not required. The CPS worker is also required to identify the alternatives that existed for placement and explain why such alternatives were unsuitable. If family reunification is sought, the anticipated duration of the child in out-of-home care and the conditions that must be met for the child to be returned must be stipulated. This plan, wherever feasible and in the best interests of the child, should also include visitation plans for the parents and other members of the family with the child. Moreover, according to § 16.1-281 of the Code of Virginia, foster care plans must document in writing the support services provided to the child and his or her family members.

According to the Adoption and Safe Families Act of 1997, all reasonable efforts must be made to preserve and reunify families. However, there are three exceptions noted in this act: (1) if the child has been subjected to aggravating circumstances (e.g., torture, sexual abuse, chronic physical abuse, abandonment); (2) if a parent has assaulted the child or has previously killed or assaulted one of his or her children; and (3) if the parent has had his or her parental rights involuntarily terminated in the past for another child. In these situations where reunification is not required, a permanency hearing must be held within 30 days and the child must be placed with adoptive parents, a legal guardian, or another form of permanent placement. It is the responsibility of CPS workers to not only find a permanent home for the child, but also to document all of the steps they took in this regard and to ensure that adoption or legal guardianship is finalized.

When family reunification is infeasible, a petition is filed to terminate parental rights immediately. In cases where a child has been in foster care for 18 months, the child was abandoned as an infant, or the parents assaulted the child or assaulted a sibling of the child, a qualified adoptive family must be found and approved for the child. A petition to terminate parental rights can be granted 15 to 22 months after its filing. This time limit starts 60 days after a child has been removed from his or her household or 60 days after the court finds that a child has been abused or neglected, whichever of these occurs earlier.

After the preliminary investigation is conducted, it is the responsibility of the CPS caseworker to determine if the harm inflicted on the child is severe enough to constitute child abuse and neglect and if sufficient evidence exists to prove this charge. The entire investigation is required to be completed within a specific amount of time. Typically, the investigation should not last more than a couple of months. The time frame within which to complete an investigation is specified by state law. For example, in New York, under § 424(6) and § 424(7) of the Social Services Law, ACS is responsible for completing investigations that are referred to this agency by the State Central Register within 60 days of their receipt.

When preparing a child abuse or neglect report, the following information must be included, whenever available (New York State Office of Children and Family Services, CPS Manual, n.d.):

- The name and location of the child
- Any imminent risk to the child
- Disclosures made by the child, if any
- Information about the alleged offender
- Any available information on the parents, guardians, and other family members

- Whether any other children reside in the household
- Any prior instances of abuse or neglect
- The names and contact information of any other individuals who may have information about the incident

Caseworkers are required to document everything about the case: every phone call they made that is relevant to the case; every visit made to the family; and every conversation held with the child, family members, medical professionals, neighbors, or teachers. Even unsubstantiated cases must be thoroughly documented. These cases may be important in future incidents of child abuse and neglect if the same individuals are involved in a report. Records of unsubstantiated reports may not be kept by CPS for a significant period of time or even at all. The length time for which unsubstantiated reports are kept depends on the jurisdiction, the state laws, and the policies of the CPS branch that is responsible for the case.

Failure to assess accurately the risks to a child's safety can have catastrophic consequences. In some instances, CPS workers have failed to investigate a case of suspected child abuse and neglect thoroughly; occasionally they failed to investigate a case at all (*Brodie v. Summit County Children Services Board*, 1990; *Nelson ex rel. Wharton v. Missouri Division of Family Services*, 1983). Consider the case of Joseph Wallace, a 2-year-old boy who was murdered by his mother in Chicago in 1993 (Kiernan, 1996). Public outcry ensued following his death, calling for changes to the child welfare system in Illinois. Joseph and his brother Joshua had been removed from his mother on more than one occasion. Joseph's mother, Amanda Wallace, was mentally ill and had repeatedly threatened to kill her children. Her physician and the child welfare system were fully aware of her condition and the threat of harm to her children. Despite this knowledge, on several occasions Joseph and his brother were removed from the foster families with whom they had been placed and returned to their mother. Amanda Wallace eventually killed Joseph by hanging him.

Another example of CPS caseworkers' failure to properly pursue a case involved Nixzmary Brown, who was beaten to death by her stepfather in New York when she was 7 years old (Hearn & Mattingly, 2007). ACS had not made meaningful contact with her family even after Nixzmary's school had notified them of the girl's injuries and absences from school. In fact, ACS had received two prior reports, but did not take sufficient action. Upon receiving the second report of abuse from the school, a caseworker showed up to Nixzmary's house to investigate the incident but Nixzmary's stepfather did not let the caseworker in. The caseworker did not make any attempts to obtain a court order to gain entry to the house, nor did ACS investigate the incident further. Following the death of Nixzmary Brown, another overhaul of ACS was undertaken (the first large-scale change of child welfare had occurred after Elisa Izquierdo's death). More individuals were hired and the caseloads of ACS workers were reduced from the national average, from 16.5 cases per worker to 9 cases per worker (Buckley & Secret, 2011). ACS also implemented an accountability program known as ChildStat (Buckley & Secret, 2011). The principle behind ChildStat is similar to the New York City Police Department's CompStat, which seeks to hold NYPD commanders accountable for controlling crime. In ChildStat, ACS officials hold regular meetings in which they evaluate statistics and cases.

CPS caseworkers can be held liable for failing to conduct adequate investigations into allegations of suspected abuse and neglect. In fact, courts have declined to extend immunity to social workers for negligence in child abuse and foster placement cases (*Department of Health & Rehabilitative Services v. Yamuni*, 1988; *Jensen v. South Carolina Department of Social Services*, 1988; *Turner v. District of Columbia*, 1987). For example, consider the case of Marchella Pierce. In 2010, in New York, Marchella, a 4-year-old girl, died from being beaten to death by her mother, Carlotta Brett-Pierce (Associated Press, 2012). When the child died, she was horribly malnourished—in fact, the only food in her stomach at the time of her death was a single kernel of corn. According to the testimony of a medical examiner, the girl's body had more than 70 marks of physical abuse. Brett-Pierce was ultimately convicted of drugging, beating and starving Marchella to death and was given a prison sentence of 32 years to life (Associated Press, 2012).

ACS personnel had not followed through in monitoring the family as they were supposed to. ACS started to monitor the family after Brett-Pierce tested positive for drugs when giving birth. Accordingly, Brett-Pierce was informed that she would have to undergo regular drug testing; failure to do so would put her at risk of losing her baby. The case was assigned to the Child Development Support Corporation, but this agency did not provide a plan for assessment or follow through with any kind of assessment. On a different matter, Brett-Pierce went to the hospital for help with her daughter's tracheal tube but left without receiving instructions on how to care for it. A concerned medical staff member contacted CPS because hospital personnel were unsure that the woman could properly care for her child. However, no new investigation of this matter was pursued, although one was required by agency protocol, nor did any further contact with the family occur. This case led to the prosecution of two CPS caseworkers for the murder of a child (Associated Press, 2012). The CPS caseworkers, Damon T. Adams and Chereece M. Bell, ultimately pleaded guilty to lesser misdemeanor charges (Secret, 2013).

Several valid arguments can be made both opposing and supporting the imposition of liability for CPS caseworkers. The most compelling argument brought forward for not holding CPS caseworkers liable is that over-intervention may occur as a consequence. Specifically, CPS caseworkers may place children in protective custody even in situations where this may not be necessary. The looming threat of liability may also serve as a disincentive for those seeking to enter into this field. The issue that leads to a child protection intervention error often lies not at the caseworker level, however, but rather at the levels responsible for the current understaffing and underfunding of CPS. Nevertheless, there are equally valid reasons for holding CPS caseworkers liable for failing to execute their duties properly. Being open to liability claims can serve as an incentive to ensure that caseworkers are properly trained. It may also induce supervisors to appropriately monitor caseworkers and verify that their cases have been meticulously investigated. Nevertheless, the court has restricted the imposition of liability to only those situations "when the [individual] decision by [a] professional is such a substantial departure from accepted professional judgment, practice, or standards as to demonstrate that the person responsible actually did not base the decision on such a judgment" (*Youngberg v. Romeo*, 1982, p. 323).

Family Evaluation

After the maltreatment has been substantiated, the family is evaluated to determine their needs and strengths. Before family assessment occurs, it is important to develop a plan for this process. The CPS worker must consider the following details in preparing for the family evaluation: the frequency of the meetings with the family, the dates and times of these meetings, the location of the meetings, who will be involved in the meetings, whether the services of other professionals will be needed in the meetings (e.g., drug or alcohol abuse assessments), and the date when the assessment and final report will be completed. To achieve outcomes beneficial to the family and the child, the interviews must be purposeful and well planned.

This prior planning helps ensure that the requisite information is retrieved to assist the caseworker in determining the type of treatment that the family needs. To obtain the information, the CPS worker meets and talks with the family as a group, members of the family separately, and parents or guardians together (if possible). Sometimes mental health or other healthcare providers are contacted if the child or family members exhibit a medical condition or behaviors that require clinical assessment. After gathering this information and evaluating it, if significant questions still exist about the risks in the household, CPS workers can contact their supervisor to ask if outside consultation on the issue can be obtained; this is especially appropriate when special information is sought that cannot be obtained by the caseworker alone.

In contrast to a preliminary investigation, which is purely designed to identify problems, the family assessment is designed to evaluate and compare the strengths and risks in the family, identify the changes that need to be made to ensure the safety of the child, mitigate or prevent the risk of future child abuse and neglect, and enhance the well-being of the child victim and his or her family. The family assessment, therefore, goes beyond identifying problems; it also promotes family understanding of the issues that impair the family's proper functioning as a unit and the ways in which these problems can be remedied through the development and implementation of an intervention plan.

During the family assessment, CPS workers review all of the information collected during the preliminary investigation and, on this basis, develop an appropriate plan to assess properly the needs of the family and the services they require. To conduct the family assessment, all members of the child's household are interviewed. If family members identify other individuals who have an important role in the life of the child, those individuals are interviewed as well; the goal is to get to know the family being assessed well enough to draw accurate conclusions regarding their needs. Usually, this takes approximately 4 weeks. However, the length of the duration of the assessment depends on state laws.

Case Plan

Once all of the relevant information is obtained, the CPS worker will analyze this information. If a specific evaluation is sought, the reason for this assessment must be given. It is imperative that the caseworker identify the most critical risks in the household and determine what is causing these risks. To do so, the CPS worker examines all available information in respect to the cause, nature, and extent of the risk and the perception of the members of the household of these risks. This enables the CPS worker to create an individualized response for the child and for other members of the household.

The plan will include several different outcomes. Each desired outcome is tailored to the specific participant. For parents or legal guardians, the outcomes would be different than those for the child and the family unit as a whole. For parents or legal guardians, examples of desired outcomes are the successful completion of drug and alcohol abuse treatment and improved parenting skills. For the child, desired outcomes would include adverse behavior control, improved physical health, and better performance at school. For the family unit as a whole, desired outcomes might include improved communication and understanding of roles and responsibilities of each member of the household.

The tasks that are provided in the plan must include the specific intervention needed to assist the family members in achieving the set goals and desired outcomes. Before these tasks can be identified, the CPS worker must confirm which services are appropriate and available at that time. Specifically, some factors that CPS workers consider when making these decisions include the cost of services, the waiting time to attain these services, the eligibility of the individuals for these services, and the suitability of these services for the family in question. CPS workers also assess whether any services are required to prevent future instances of child abuse and neglect, or at the very least mitigate the risk of such incidents occurring sometime in the future.

The Adoption and Safe Families Act of 1997 made a variety of services available to families, such as drug and alcohol treatment, domestic violence victims' assistance, counseling services, mental health services, temporary child care, and transportation of parents to and from these services. These services have one overarching goal: improving the family situation. Even so, these services are time limited. Services also are available that enhance the quality of child care and early education through programs such as Head Start. Head Start offers free educational programs for children between the ages of 3 and 5 years, as well as support services for their families (Administration for Children and Families, 2010). In addition, Head Start enables children and their families to obtain free health services in their community. For parents, Head Start offers, among other things, job training, education, and housing assistance.

Treatment is often offered to improve relationships within the family. Treatment may be considered the optimal outcome in a case. It can, however, take many different forms. Specialized treatment may be required not only for the victim or the offender, but also for the nonoffending parent(s) or guardian(s). If the enhancement or reparation of a relationship between family members is sought, dyadic treatment may be recommended

(Faller, 1993). Usually, this form of treatment occurs after participants have undergone individual therapy treatment. Such multiple-participant treatment seeks to address issues that arose concerning the relationship in individual treatment sessions. Treatment is sought to deal with the effects of maltreatment on the victim and reduce the risk of future incidents of maltreatment against the child. Family therapy is also mandated, but only if the case is such that child reunification with the family is sought by the state (Faller, 1993).

If drug or alcohol use is identified during the preliminary investigation, these issues need to be included in the case plan. The case plan must also include the means with which to address this issue. It is the responsibility of the CPS caseworker to explain to the household how substance or alcohol use has impacted their proper functioning as a family. If a parent or legal guardian has been ordered to take part in substance abuse treatment, the CPS caseworker can coordinate with the treatment provider to monitor the progress of the individual. This coordination allows for the development of ongoing support and intervention during times of crises. In addition, it permits the modification of the plans as necessary.

Once these services and tasks have been identified, the CPS worker develops a plan. Several states require that a case plan be created when a child and his or her family receive in-house services to prevent the placement of a child in foster care.[1] For example, Title 110 of the Code of Massachusetts Regulations requires a service plan to be created for any family that is receiving services from the Department of Children and Families. According to this law, the services must be aimed at strengthening the family unit, reunifying a family unit whose child or children have been removed from the home, and providing an alternative out-of-home placement for the child or children if necessary. This plan must also include the type of placement (e.g., foster care), any family history of out-of-home placement (e.g., if the child has been previously removed from the home or his or her siblings have been), the reasons why the child was removed from the home, and visitations with parents or siblings. If no visitations are allowed, the reasons for this decision must be noted. A permanency plan for the child must be included as well. How will permanency (end result) be achieved? For example, will permanency be attained through reunification with the family, placement with other family members, or adoption?

Many states require parental involvement in case planning unless specific circumstances exist that prevent their participation. If the parents are not involved, the reasons for the lack of participation must be documented (see, for example, Massachusetts Code 110, Section 6.07). Many states have a time limitation within which a case plan must be developed, which is triggered when the child is placed in out-of-home care. For instance, in Alabama, under Chapter 660-5-28-.06 of the Administrative Code, "a written case plan must be developed for the child within 30 days from the time of placement. For children

---

[1] Alaska, Arizona, Arkansas, California, Colorado, Florida, Hawaii, Kansas, Massachusetts, Missouri, Montana, New Hampshire, New Jersey, Ohio, Oklahoma, Oregon, Pennsylvania, Rhode Island, South Carolina, Vermont, Virginia, and West Virginia.

in foster care or related care less than 30 days, this case plan requirement is waived. A brief case plan statement will suffice." New York has a similar requirement: "upon completion of any assessment of a family's needs and circumstances, and no later than 30 days after a child is removed from his or her home or is placed in foster care, the local social services district shall establish or update and maintain a family service plan based on an assessment of the family's needs and circumstances" (New York Social Services Laws § 409-e). According to the policies of the Family Services Division in Vermont, the case must be designed and aimed at protecting the child and reducing the risks to which the child is exposed at home (Policy #71).

In short, the plan must include the goals for the family members, the means with which to achieve them, and the specific tasks that need to be completed to achieve the desired outcomes. Benchmarks must be included against which to measure the progress of the family in achieving the necessary results. It is imperative that the CPS worker communicates the plan to the household: what needs to be done, why it needs to be done, and which time limits apply to the achievement of these requirements. It is also important that the goals set are realistic and achievable within the amount of time specified, given the dynamics and capability of the family.

After the plan is completed, the next stage is implementation. The preferred outcome in cases involving intervention is that after services have been rendered and treatment completed by victims, offenders, and family members, the family can and will be allowed to remain intact. To ensure that this permanency plan occurs, cases must be continuously monitored.

Monitoring and Managing the Case

After the investigation has been completed and services have been provided to the victim and the family, it is important that the CPS workers continue to monitor the case. A different unit than the one that carried out the investigation will be in charge of making a continual assessment to determine the progress of the family and the efficacy of these services on the family and the child. It is, indeed, the CPS caseworker's responsibility to monitor the situation to determine that improvement occurs as a result of these services (as outlined in the plan). If the situation does not improve, the CPS worker may file a petition of neglect at a dependency court and ask for the removal of the child from the home. When faced with such a petition, the judge is required to assess and make a finding as to whether the CPS worker made reasonable efforts to prevent the removal of the child from the home. Consider the following example: A CPS worker investigates a case of child sexual abuse. In particular, the stepfather of a 7-year-old boy sexually abused him. A court order may be obtained in this case both to prevent the stepfather from contacting the victim and to have the stepfather removed from the home. A court would view this step as a reasonable effort on behalf of the CPS caseworker to have the child remain at home safely.

CPS workers are additionally responsible for managing their case. That is, they are required to ensure continuity of care by monitoring the progress of the family and keeping detailed records in this regard to ensure accountability. Case management encompasses several different activities.

- First, case management involves monitoring treatment and intervention services. CPS workers monitor cases as soon as treatment and intervention services are under way. Such monitoring of progress should be ongoing and last until the case is closed, at which point each member of the family and the family as a whole should have achieved the desired outcomes.
- Second, CPS workers obtain and organize information about family progress as part of case management. During this stage, CPS workers review the existing case plan and acquire information from all of the treatment and intervention service providers concerning the progress of the members of the family.
- Third, CPS workers analyze and evaluate the progress of the family. To do so, they examine family progress in the following areas: what has been done to alter the behaviors and conditions that were conducive to abuse and neglect and the extent to which the set tasks and outcomes that were laid out in the plan had been accomplished. Such an evaluation is also required to determine whether other services need to be provided or alternative action needs to be taken.
- Finally, CPS workers are required to comprehensively document the progress of the family since the preliminary investigation was completed, the family assessment was conducted, the case plan was created, and the services were provided. After the report is complete, the CPS worker consults with his or her supervisor regarding which additional actions need to be taken in the future.

Case Closure

Case closures can occur for several reasons. A case can be closed if the child is safe and the outcomes have been achieved. A case can also be closed if the family accepts participating in other services with other agencies or providers to fulfill the outcome. In addition, a case can be closed and can be picked up by another CPS worker. Finally, the family may wish to voluntarily discontinue service. This cannot occur, however, if these services have been legally mandated by the court.

If the court is involved in the case closure, then the court must first approve the closure of the case and terminate any existing court orders. To determine whether the case should be closed, CPS caseworkers will examine which steps were taken to reduce the risk to the child and whether any other concerns remain to be addressed by the family. In so doing, CPS workers should assist families in planning to maintain the changes so as to ensure a safe environment for the child and discuss with them any anticipated obstacles they may encounter when trying to sustain these changes. As part of this effort, CPS workers should provide the means with which the family can overcome these barriers. Moreover, CPS workers should inform the family that they can contact them should they need services in the future.

There are, however, dangers in closing a case too soon. Consider the case of Nadine Lockwood (McFadden, 1996; Sullivan, 1997). Nadine was murdered by her mother, Carla. Before her murder, Nadine was systematically starved by her mother *(People v. Dickerson,* 2007). Among her other siblings, Nadine was singled out for the abuse. Her mother expressed hatred for her daughter and would refer to her as "it." Carla already had six children when she gave birth to Nadine. According to the mother, she blamed Nadine for being kicked out of her father's house. More specifically, Carla was told by her father that she must leave the house because she had too many children. She also blamed Nadine for the family having to live in a shelter from time to time.

As in the case of Elisa Izquierdo, an internal investigation that was conducted after Nadine's murder revealed that CPS failed to check on reports of neglect (Sexton, 1996). In addition, individuals who were aware of the situation and were required by law to report the incident failed to do so. When caseworkers visited Carla's apartment, they did not interview any of the children in the house, which is standard protocol; they interviewed only the mother. Even though the caseworker noted in her report on the incident that Carla's children were being subjected to education neglect and inadequate guardianship, the same caseworker followed up on the case only via telephone. Before the death of Nadine, the CPS caseworker had closed the case. To prevent such occurrences in the future, as a general rule, cases should be closed only when families have achieved the desired outcomes of the plan and the risk to the child has been mitigated or eliminated.

Chapter Summary

Child protective services is a public social service agency that is mandated by the law to protect children. The CPS process has several stages: intake, preliminary investigation, family evaluation, case plan, service provision, and case closure. During the initial evaluation, the CPS worker is required to substantiate whether maltreatment occurred. If the maltreatment is substantiated, the CPS worker must determine the risk of future harm (abuse or neglect) to the child. A CPS worker, after investigating a claim of child maltreatment, has several options that depend on the case at hand.

Intervention may involve removing the offending caregiver from the household. Another form of intervention involves removing the child from the home and placing the child with either another relative or a foster family. If the child is removed from the family, CPS workers can concurrently place the child with a legal guardian or for adoption while engaging in family reunification. When family reunification is infeasible, CPS workers seek to provide a permanent home for the child either through foster care or by the placement of a child with a relative.

When family reunification is feasible, the CPS caseworker should assess the family and develop a case plan. The case plan itself must address issues regarding the proper functioning of the family. Additionally, it must contain the steps that are required to ensure the betterment of existing families functioning as a unit. A plan must be devised that includes the desired outcomes and the steps that the family members must take to achieve the desired outcomes. It must specify the goals to be achieved and the time frame to achieve them. The case plan must also include the responsibilities of the CPS worker and family members for the assigned tasks. Benchmarks should additionally be included in the plan to monitor the progress of family members. To determine which services the family requires, the caseworker will analyze all of the information obtained in earlier stages of the CPS process.

After the case plan is completed, the next stage is implementation. Family assessment during this process is continuous. Meetings with the family are set up to evaluate their progress and reports from other professionals are sought as well, until closure is made.

Review Questions

1. What happens during intake?

2. Which individuals are required by law to report child maltreatment?

3. When is a child removed from his or her home?

4. What are the criticisms of the Adoption and Safe Families Act of 1997? Do you agree or disagree with these criticisms? Why?

5. What is included in a family assessment?

6. What is included in a case plan?

7. When is a case closed? Why is this stage important?

References

Administration for Children and Families. (2010). The Head Start child development and early learning framework. U.S. Department of Health and Human Services. http://eclkc.ohs.acf. hhs.gov/hslc/tta-system/teaching/eecd/Assessment/Child%20Outcomes/HS_Revised_Child_ Outcomes_Framework(rev-Sept2011).pdf

Angela R. v. Huckabee, 999 F.2d 320 (8th Cir. 1993).

Associated Press. (2012, June 6). Prison term for mother of a girl, 4, found dead. *New York Times.* http://www.nytimes.com/2012/06/07/nyregion/mother-gets-prison-term-in-marchella-pierces-death.html

Brodie v. Summit County Children Services Board, 554 N.E.2d 1301 (Ohio 1990).

Buckley, C. & Secret, M. (2011, March 24). Caseworkers dispirited over charges in girl's death. *New York Times.* http://www.nytimes.com/2011/03/25/nyregion/25acs.html?_r=0

Cole, M. (2009, September 2). Abuse in children's foster care: State officials call for outside review. *The Oregonian.* http://www.oregonlive.com/politics/index.ssf/2009/09/abuse_in_foster_care_state_off.html

David C. v. Leavitt, 900 F. Supp. 1547 (D. Utah 1995).

DePanfilis, S. & Salus, M. K. (1992). Child protective services: A guide for caseworkers. U.S. Department of Health and Human Services, Administration for Children and Families Administration

on Children, Youth and Families National Center on Child Abuse and Neglect. http://www
.hawaii.edu/hivandaids/Child%20Protective%20Services%20%20% 20%20A%20Guide%20for%20
Caseworkers.pdf

Department of Health & Rehabilitative Services v. Yamuni, 529 So. 2d 258 (Fla. 1988).

Doe v. New York City Department of Social Services, 649 F.2d 134 (2d Cir. 1981), cert. denied, 464 U.S. 864 (1983).

Fairfax County Virginia. (n.d.). Child Supervision Guidelines. http://www.fairfaxcounty.gov/dfs /childrenyouth/supervision_eng.htm

Faller, K. C. (1993). Child sexual abuse: Intervention and treatment issues. U.S. Department of Health and Human Services, Administration of Children and Families. http://www.childwelfare. gov/pubs/usermanuals/sexabuse/sexabuse.pdf

Gibson v. Ginsberg, No. 78-2375 (S.D.W.Va. Sept. 28, 1981).

G. L. v. Stangler, 564 F. Supp. 1030 (W.D. Mo. 1983).

Hearn, R. G. & Mattingly, J. B. (2007, August). A Department of Investigation examination of eleven fatalities and one near fatality. A joint report. by the New York City Department of Investigation and the Administration for Children's Services. http://www.nyc.gov/html/doi/downloads /pdf/acsreport_pdfaug2007.pdf

In re David G., 909 N.Y.S.2d 891 (Fam. Ct. 2010).

Jensen v. South Carolina Department of Social Services, 377 S.E.2d 102 (S.C. Ct. App. 1988).

Kiernan, L. (1996, July 26). Last act in a tragedy: Life in prison for Amanda Wallace. *Chicago Tribune*. http://articles.chicagotribune.com/1996-07-26/news/9607260193_1_mentally-ill-mother-death-hand

LaShawn A. v. Dixon, 762 F. Supp. 959 (D.D.C. 1991).

Leduff, C. (1996, August 1). Woman sentenced in daughter's death. *New York Times*. http:// www.nytimes.com/1996/08/01/nyregion/woman-sentenced-in-daughter-s-death. html?ref=awildalopez

Marisol v. Pataki, 929 F. Supp. 660 (S.D.N.Y. 1996).

McFadden, R. D. (1996, September 2). Girl, 4, is dead in Manhattan and her mother is charged. *New York Times*. http://www.nytimes.com/1996/09/02/nyregion/girl-4-is-dead-in-manhattan-and-her-mother-is-charged.html

Nelson ex rel. Wharton v. Missouri Division of Family Services, 706 F.2d 276 (8th Cir. 1983).

New York City Administration for Children's Services (NYC ACS). (1996). Elisa's Law. http://www .nyc.gov/html/acs/html/about/elisaslaw.shtml

New York State Office of Children and Family Services. (n.d.). Child Protective Services Program Manual (CPS Manual). http://www.ocfs.state.ny.us/main/cps/cps_manual.asp

New York State Office of Children and Family Services. (n.d.). Frequently asked questions (FAQ). http://ocfs.ny.gov/main/cps/faqs.asp

Ohio Department of Job and Family Services, Office of Families and Children. (n.d.). Child abuse and neglect: A reference for educators. http://www.odjfs.state.oh.us/forms/file .asp?id=398&type=application/pdf

People v Dickerson (Leroy), 2007 NY Slip Op 04718 [42 AD3d 228]

Roberts, L. (2011, March 30). CPS had time to help girl before it was too late. *The Arizona Republic*. http://www.azcentral.com/arizonarepublic/news/articles/2011/03/30/20110330cps-roberts. html

Secret, M. (2013, December 17). Ex-child welfare caseworkers plead guilty in death of a 4-year-old. *New York Times*. http://www.nytimes.com/2013/12/18/nyregion/ex-child-welfare-caseworkers-plead-guilty-in-death-of-a-4-year-old.html

Sedlak, A. J., Doueck, H. J., Lyons, P., Wells, S., Schultz, D., and Gragg, F. (2005). Child maltreatment and the justice system: Predictors of court involvement. *Research on Social Work Practice, 15*(5), 389-403.

Sexton, J. (1996, October 9). Report says city missed chances to save girl. *New York Times.* http://www.nytimes.com/1996/10/09/nyregion/report-says-city-missed-chances-to-save-girl.html

Sheila A. v. Finney, 861 P.2d 120 (Kan. 1993).

Sullivan, J. (1997, March 8). From jailed mother's lips, how child lived and died. *New York Times.* http://www.nytimes.com/1997/03/08/nyregion/from-jailed-mother-s-lips-how-child-lived-and-died.html

Thomas v. City of New York, 814 F. Supp. 1139 (E.D.N.Y. 1992).

Turner v. District of Columbia, 532 A.2d 662 (D.C. 1987).

Van Biena, D., Epperson, S. E., & Rivera, E. (1995, December 11). Elisa Izquierdo: Abandoned to her fate. *Time.* http://www.time.com/time/magazine/article/0,9171,983842,00.html

Williams-Mbengue, N. (1998). Confidentiality of child protective records. *National Conference of State Legislatures: Legisbrief, 6*(29), 1-2. http://www.ncsl.org/Portals/1/documents/cyf/29nina.pdf

Youngberg v. Romeo, 457 U.S. 307 (1982).

© Kzenon/Shutterstock

Chapter 10

Law Enforcement, Probation, and Parole Officers

Most child abuse and neglect cases are handled in family or dependency courts by child protective services (CPS) alone. Police involvement occurs when criminal maltreatment is suspected; thus, it depends on the severity of the reported abuse or neglect. Generally, CPS calls the police to investigate a criminal act against a child, place the child in emergency care, or assist with the placement of the child in emergency care. In some instances, the police officers may have to take control of the child, at least until CPS workers arrive. Most commonly, sexual abuse and serious cases of physical abuse are investigated by the police in coordination with CPS, but law enforcement officers may proceed independently when the child victim does not live or have contact with the alleged perpetrator. In criminal child maltreatment cases, particularly those resulting in death and severe medical conditions, law enforcement officers investigate the crime(s) committed, and identify and arrest the offender(s).

Child abuse cases are markedly different from other criminal cases. Most notably, they are more difficult to investigate and prosecute than are other criminal cases, mainly because children frequently are unable to protect themselves physically, delay disclosure, and do not reveal many details about their abuse. Such a crime is also typically committed outside of the purview of witnesses and rarely leaves any visible traces of evidence. The motivations of the victim can be affected by loyalty to or fear of the alleged perpetrator, further complicating the investigation. The police officers handling these cases should have specialized knowledge of child abuse and ways to assist these victims, as well as knowledge of child interview protocols, child development, forensic and medical evidence (for both physical and sexual abuse cases), sex offender knowledge, and the ability to interview suspects in these types of cases. They must also learn psychological (e.g., battered child syndrome, dissociation) and medical terms, and familiarize themselves with professional and slang terms for body parts and sexual acts, as this information will be needed during the interview with the child victim.

This chapter focuses on issues addressed by law enforcement personnel during the course of investigating allegations of abuse and neglect. First, it examines the role of law enforcement agents as sole investigators in child neglect and abuse. Second, it explores the role of multidisciplinary teams in child neglect and abuse investigations. Third, it provides information about how police conduct maltreatment investigations. Fourth, it covers certain child maltreatment laws, with special attention paid to the laws of New York. Fifth, it considers special issues in child sexual abuse related to alleged perpetrators, such as sex offenders, pedophiles, and child traffickers. Finally, it examines criminal justice procedures in place to oversee convicted offenders, such as probation and parole.

Dealing with Child Abuse: Sole Investigators or Multidisciplinary Teams

Child abuse has long been considered solely as a social welfare issue. However, this perspective deflects attention from one very important truth: Child abuse is a crime and should be dealt with accordingly. In reality, child abuse is both a social welfare issue and a crime problem that is investigated along both spheres—that is, by both CPS and law enforcement. And herein lies the problem: How is it addressed concurrently from both spheres?

In the 1990s, some states, frustrated by the increasing number of child deaths, lack of prosecution of child abuse cases, improper investigations of child neglect and abuse cases, and deficiencies within CPS, decided to transfer responsibility for these investigations to the police. The two most notable cases involved Arkansas and Florida. In 1997, through the passage of legislation, Arkansas had transferred all investigative responsibility for crimes against children to a newly created Family Protection Unit (FPU) of the Arkansas State Police (Cross, Finkelhor, & Ormrod, 2005). The creation of the FPU resulted in confusion as to the role of the state police, local police, and CPS workers in investigations. Initially, relationships between the civilian investigators of CPS and state police were strained and local police resisted state involvement. Originally, the emphasis of the FPU (now known as the Crimes Against Children Division) was on a criminal justice response, where investigators' training focused largely on interviewing the alleged offender. Child interviewing techniques, in contrast, were not emphasized. After the passage of new legislation and the implementation of protocols for collaboration among agencies, the process for investigating child maltreatment improved.

In 1998, as an experiment, Florida also transferred lead responsibility for serious child neglect and abuse cases to the sheriff's offices in three counties (Cross et al., 2005; Kinnevy et al., 2003). In doing so, state officials hoped to improve the efficiency and effectiveness of these investigations. A 2007 evaluation by Crist and Butterworth (2008) revealed that sheriff-led investigations with cooperation from the Department of Children and Families (DCF) not only enhanced local coordination of protection and prevention services, but also improved "dependency investigations for the families served; and . . . applicable criminal investigations linked to crimes committed against children" (p. 7).

In general, law enforcement agencies are concerned when CPS takes the lead in an investigation. Sometimes the actions of CPS personnel interfere with investigations because the CPS agenda (i.e., assessing whether the child is currently in danger or at risk while maintaining family relationships) differs from that of law enforcement (i.e., determining if a crime occurred, and identifying and arresting perpetrators). According to Walsh (1993), "When police do not take the lead in cases of CSA [child sexual abuse], they allow the offender, once notified of an allegation, to destroy evidence, pressure the child to recant their testimony, construct an alibi, secure legal counsel or flee the location" (p. 120). Despite law enforcement officers' general belief that their efforts to obtain evidence against abusers are hampered when CPS controls the investigation, no research exists to either confirm or disconfirm this notion (Pence & Wilson, 1992; Tjaden & Anhalt, 1994). For their part, CPS workers are concerned that law enforcement officers will scare the alleged perpetrator or family into noncooperation and defensiveness. In certain cases, intervention without the involvement of the criminal justice system is possible, desirable, and even necessary.

Law enforcement agencies clearly have very different goals in child maltreatment cases than do CPS. Specifically, police are focused on identifying and apprehending the alleged perpetrator, whereas CPS workers are interested in protecting the child. The primary goal of the police is to investigate whether a particular act occurred and the law was violated. The responsibility of the police officer is to conduct a criminal investigation of the case. Based on the outcome of the investigation, the prosecutor then determines whether to file charges against the offender. Involvement of only police (and not CPS) in child abuse investigations raises concerns about the emphasis on a criminal justice response as opposed to a responsibility to protect the child. Studies have revealed that police are more likely to remove a child from the home if they respond to an incident first, irrespective of how this action will affect the child and his or her family (Maguire, 1993; Shireman, Miller, & Brown, 1981; Tjaden & Anhalt, 1994; Winterfield & Sakagawa, 2003).

Due to the different orientations of CPS workers and agents of the criminal justice system and their competing interests in child maltreatment cases, coordination in managing cases of child abuse and neglect can be endangered. Multidisciplinary teams are important in this respect, because they enable professionals working on these cases to coordinate their responses, collaborate toward common goals, and conduct joint forensic interviews. In fact, when conducting an investigation into a child abuse case, the law enforcement officer and the CPS worker assigned to the case may jointly determine how best to handle the case, where the investigation should occur, and which role each party will assume in this particular case. These investigations are coordinated with the dual objective of determining what happened and how best to meet the needs of the child.

The multidisciplinary team members should appreciate the roles that other members of the team are fulfilling; learn the goals, missions, and plans that members have for the victim and his or her family in the case; and understand how the activities of each member on the team interrelate. Clear guidelines must exist for the team members in their investigations of child neglect and abuse cases. Accordingly, for such teams, certain common protocols are established to enable their proper functioning and success. The mandate for these multidisciplinary teams is to strive for efficient and effective investigation and prosecution of child abuse cases. In addition, these multidisciplinary teams should provide all necessary services for victims and their families. Such teams use a skilled forensic interviewer and team members observe the interview with the victim, thereby eliminating duplication of efforts. Prior to the existence of these teams, social workers, CPS workers, law enforcement agents, and prosecutors would conduct separate interviews of the child. Reducing the number of times a child is interviewed lessens the trauma and stress experienced by the victim and his or her family during the investigation. The use of multidisciplinary teams also promotes the proper and expedient collection of evidence relative to the case. As such, joint investigations shorten the response times of all participants in these cases and the length of time investigators spend on cases. Moreover, the use of such teams helps reduce the duplication of services provided by each agency. Finally, joint investigations promote accountability, as each individual conducts his or her investigation under the view of others.

Child Advocacy Centers

In addition to creation of specialized units within law enforcement departments, child advocacy centers (CACs) have been set up either within hospitals or as stand-alone facilities to investigate child maltreatment, in particular, and crimes against children, in general (e.g., sexual exploitation of children) in the United States. CACs are designed to be more child and family friendly than traditional methods and avenues used to interview child abuse victims and their family members. One of the primary goals of CACs is to improve the process of forensic interviewing and minimize the number of times that a child is interviewed by CPS workers, medical professionals, and agents of the criminal justice system. Another aim of CACs is to coordinate child abuse investigations involving CPS, law enforcement, medical, and other agencies, by making a single interviewer responsible for providing information to all of the members of the multidisciplinary team.

In addition, CACs often provide links to therapeutic services for victims and victim advocacy services. Victim services can offer emotional support to the child; provide information about support services; give referrals to therapeutic services; accompany the victim during a medical exam; and update the victim and his and her family about the police investigation, outcomes of the case, and information concerning the release conditions of the alleged perpetrator. CACs also offer specialized medical evaluations and treatment in on-site facilities or through referrals to specialized treatment providers.

Law Enforcement Involvement in Child Neglect and Abuse Cases

Police involvement in child neglect and abuse cases includes conducting investigations and interviewing witnesses, victims, and suspects.

Conducting the Investigation

The police conduct investigations of cases that involve crimes committed against children. If CPS workers have not been alerted initially, the law enforcement officer should contact them to determine whether a child protection investigation will also be required. If the parents are not taking reasonable steps to protect the child from the alleged perpetrator, the police officer will report this information to CPS. If CPS is involved or will be involved in the case, the police should consult with them about how to best coordinate the investigation given the child protection and criminal issues at stake. In the majority of cases, timing is of the essence because the child or children may be at risk and important evidence may potentially be disposed of if the investigation is delayed. If removal of the child is sought, the CPS caseworker and the police officer should meet beforehand to discuss a plan of action. Both the CPS caseworker and the police officer should review the facts of the case (if not already known), the layout of the house (if the CPS worker or police officer has been there), the number of individuals in the house (if known), and any other pertinent information. Collectively, they need to ensure that extraction of the child occurs in the least traumatic way possible. Any necessary items that the child needs, such as medication, should also be brought with the child at the time of removal.

Interviews

When interviewing witnesses, victims, and suspects, direct evidence of the crime is sought. Direct evidence establishes a fact. For example, eyewitness testimony or a confession from a suspect that he or she actually committed the alleged offense constitutes direct evidence that the person committed the crime.

Circumstantial evidence is further sought from these interviews. This type of evidence allows someone to infer the truth of a given fact. A prime example of circumstantial evidence is providing the motive for committing a crime.

Overall, the quality and methods of the interview process are similar for both types of governmental agencies—law enforcement and CPS—so interviewers follow many of the same rules and guidelines. However, the main purpose of interviews conducted by law enforcement personnel is to obtain proof of a crime; the burden of proof rests on the prosecution in criminal court, which is held to a higher standard than family court.

Witness Interview

In terms of witnesses, if the parents or guardians are not the alleged offenders, the police should interview them to obtain information about the victim, any knowledge of abuse, and any information about the offender, if known. If one of the parents or guardians is the alleged offender, the nonoffending parent or guardian should be asked questions about the victim's knowledge of the incidents and information about the offender. Other witnesses, if available, should also be interviewed. The types of people who might have information about the abuse and could be interviewed include any other children in the household, other family members, neighbors, friends, school officials, and daycare center workers. Any information that is relevant to CPS should be communicated to the caseworker. Therefore, witnesses, if any are available, should be interviewed to obtain corroborative evidence to support or refute the alleged abuse.

Victim Interview

Child victims should never be interviewed at home, even in cases where family members are not suspects in the abuse. Children may feel uncomfortable disclosing abuse in front of their parents. Additionally, any adverse reaction to the disclosure by their parents (e.g., screening, crying) could affect the child's cooperation and further disclosure during an investigation.

Before the child is interviewed, the parents, if present, should be informed that their child has made allegations of abuse. There is one exception to this rule: Parents are not notified if they are the alleged offender. If the parents are not believed to be the suspects, the police officer will inform them that the child will be interviewed to find out the facts about the alleged abuse. The police officer should also inform the parents that the officer will tell them about what the child discloses during the interview. Parents should be discouraged from being present during the interview because the child may be reluctant to disclose or may not fully disclose abuse in their presence. However, parents do have the right to be present and can exercise that right should they choose to do so.

Child victims should be taken to an interview room that is specially designed for them. The best site to conduct the interview is a neutral location. The police officer and the CPS caseworker are both usually present for the interview, and the best practice is for them to interview the child victim jointly. Ideally, the primary role in interviewing should be assumed by the police officer when criminal charges are likely to be brought. It would be best if an officer interviews the child victim while the officer is wearing plain clothes, as the uniform itself (and the sight of the officer's gun) might intimidate the child. It is extremely important for those conducting the investigation to spend some time establishing trust and rapport with the victim. The interviewer (or interviewers) needs to make sure that the child is comfortable speaking with him or her.

Ideally, the interview should be conducted in the victim's native language, but if the interviewer does not speak that language, a translator should be used. This translator should not only know the language, but also be familiar with the victim's culture, which in turn will help the interviewer build rapport with the child. Preferably, the translator will work in the criminal justice or related field (e.g., police officer, social worker) and have experience conducting forensic interviews. These individuals should also have knowledge regarding the type of evidence needed for the investigation; as such, they will be able to ask the appropriate questions without tainting the interview. Only neutral third parties should be considered. Under no circumstances should a parent, sibling, relative, or friend of the victim or family be used as the translator.

In most cases, the district attorney monitors and/or reviews the initial interview and determines whether to file charges against the alleged perpetrator. In some jurisdictions, the district attorney interviews the child (particularly when criminal charges are anticipated); in other jurisdictions, the interview is either recorded and sent to the district attorney's office for review or watched by the district attorney via live feed or through a one-way mirror. The exact process used is dictated by state, county, and city regulations and procedures, and may even differ within a city by jurisdiction. For example, in New York City, the process varies by borough at the discretion of the district attorney.

Suspect Interview

All denials made by the suspect during the interview should be confronted. The purpose of the interview is to obtain testimonial evidence confirming maltreatment of the child victim. A complete background check should also be conducted on the alleged perpetrator. All familial relationships (i.e., spousal, parental) with the suspect should be examined. That is, if the alleged perpetrator is currently or was formerly married or in an intimate-partner relationship with the child's parent, the suspect's relationship to the current/ former spouse/partner should be explored. Additionally, if the suspect has children, regardless of whether the victim is a full, half-, or step-sibling to them, the interviewer should assess these parent–child relationships. Law enforcement officers should further determine whether the alleged perpetrator has a past history as a child sexual predator. Moreover, the interview with the suspect will be important even if a confession is not obtained. The narrative provided by the suspect often includes details that can help the police in their investigation, especially if dubious explanations are provided.

When the police receive a report about a suspected child abuse case and the alleged perpetrator is known, the law enforcement officer should check police records and other sources regarding the suspect. Furthermore, the police should try to obtain a DNA sample from the suspect. If the suspect has committed a crime in the past, his or her DNA sample may already be in the Combined DNA Index System (CODIS), which allows both storage of and searches for DNA profiles at local, state, and federal levels. If it is not in CODIS, then the police officer can ask the suspect's permission to obtain a DNA sample (voluntary) or the police officer can obtain a search warrant to retrieve the sample (if there is probable cause). Alternatively, the police officer can retrieve DNA from evidence obtained with a search warrant from the alleged perpetrator's house. For example, the crime scene investigators can retrieve items that may have the alleged perpetrator's DNA on them. In sexual abuse cases, police protocol dictates that DNA evidence be obtained from the suspect or suspects.

The Crime Scene

During an investigation, the police are required to gather any evidence that can be used to establish the facts of the case. The first step in processing a crime (or incident) scene is to secure the scene. An investigator is responsible for controlling the scene and the individuals on or near the scene. To secure the crime scene, all nonessential personnel (especially news media and other bystanders) are removed and the boundaries of the scene are set (e.g., using barricades or tape). The area to be secured should encompass the entire crime scene. If this does not occur, any potential evidence outside of the boundaries can be contaminated—for example, by pedestrian traffic—or laboratory findings may be discredited in court.

After the boundaries are set, a single path of entry and exit is established to protect the crime scene and to preserve the evidence. The personal information (e.g., name, phone number, work and home addresses) of all those who enter and exit the crime scene are recorded. This is either done in a separate log or documented in an investigator's notebook. Any changes to the crime scene due to emergency personnel (e.g., removing an injured person) or police actions (e.g., opening a door) should be recorded and reported to the investigators/superiors.

After the scene is secured, the next step is to establish a clear search pattern for the evidence to ensure that all areas of the crime scene are thoroughly searched and vital evidence within these areas is not overlooked. Subsequently, the investigator documents the crime scene in its entirety; that is, the investigator records the conditions of the scene and identifies all relevant physical evidence (e.g., fingerprints, blood, semen), direct or prima facie evidence (i.e., proof of a fact), indirect or circumstantial evidence (i.e., incriminating data that are inconclusive, such as a packaged condom), and trace evidence (e.g., hair, clothing fibers) within it (Lyman, 2008). The evidence for which an investigator looks will depend on the type of crime committed. In the final step, the investigator decides which evidence can be lawfully collected from the crime scene. All seized evidence should then be documented.

Documentation

Documentation is important for several reasons (Gardner, 2005). First, it helps police officers to corroborate or to refute the testimony of a witness, suspect, or victim. Second, documentation allows investigators to corroborate, refute, or modify an existing hypothesis, particularly in regard to what occurred at the crime scene. Third, it facilitates forensic scientists' understanding of how the evidence found relates to the crime (e.g., what the evidence reveals about the suspect's modus operandi or method of operation). Fourth, documentation proves that data collected at the scene remain unaltered. This step is particularly important because evidence presented to support prosecution may be questioned by the defense and the prosecutor must show that the chain of custody for the evidence was not broken. The chain of custody seeks to preserve evidence throughout the life of a case. During a criminal trial, if the prosecutor fails to show that the chain of custody was maintained, the evidence will not be admitted in the court proceedings (Gardner & Anderson, 2007). Specifically, all people who had possession of the physical evidence (in the chain of custody) must provide information regarding the location, the means by which the evidence was obtained, and the evidence's authenticity—that is, proof that it has not been contaminated, substituted, or tampered with (p. 339). Finally, documentation illustrates to the court the conditions of the crime scene, including how the crime occurred and who was involved. The five ways in which a scene can be documented are field notes, sketches, photographs, digital recordings, and reports (Gardner, 2005; Girard, 2008; Saferstein, 2011). Each of these is explored individually below.

Field Notes   The police officer is trained to document the crime scene and evidence. Individuals at the crime scene and their location at the time of an investigator's arrival should be identified in the field notes. Investigators should include the who, what, when, where, why, and how aspects of the case in their notes (Lyman, 2008). Specifically, a description of the victim (including wounds) and the crime scene must be made. With respect to the evidence, the type and location of each piece should be documented, along with the time and date it was found. The details of the individual who discovered the evidence should also be recorded. Anything (e.g., a piece of evidence) or anyone (e.g., a dead body) that was moved or removed prior to the investigator's arrival should be documented as well. The physical condition of the evidence should also be noted. For instance, any distinguishing aspects or marks on the evidence (e.g., blood, mud, chip) should be included in the notes.

Additionally, if any evidence is damaged, this fact should be documented. The suspect may have tried to damage these items to prevent the extraction of incriminating evidence (e.g., broken a CD, crushed a computer hard drive). Regardless of why the evidence was damaged, its condition should be recorded to protect the investigator and his or her department from subsequent allegations that the suspect's property was mishandled or damaged by the investigator or other individuals working on the case. In sum, anything relevant to the investigation at hand should be included in the investigator's notes. When taking these notes, an investigator should keep in mind the following rules (Girard, 2008):

- Notes must be made in ink in a bound notebook whose pages are numbered sequentially.
- No spaces or empty pages should be left with the intention to go back and make any additions to previous entries.
- If a mistake is made, it needs to be crossed out.
- Under no circumstances should an entry be erased, nor should another entry be written over an erased one.

Notes are important because if an investigator is called to testify in court, he or she must be able to recall what was observed and which actions were taken at the crime scene. Notes should be supplemented by sketches, photographs, and, wherever possible, digital recordings.

Sketches   Sketches include the measurements taken by an investigator to provide accurate dimensions of the crime scene and the location of the evidence in relation to that scene. Lyman (2008) recommends that each crime scene have a rough sketch (i.e., drawn initially with true dimensions and showing distances between items) and a finished sketch (i.e., one drawn to scale and complete or, if unscaled, one with measurements). A compass direction should be included in the sketch. Moreover, the sketch should contain the case number, the name of the individual who prepared the sketch, the date of the sketch, the type of crime, the location of the crime, and the name of the victim (or victims) depicted in the sketch (if any). The artistic skill displayed in such sketches is less important than the information being depicted.

Sketches help document the exact position of the evidence—something that cannot be done with use of photographs or digital recordings. With the measurements given in the sketches, an investigator can recreate the crime scene in a controlled environment. By doing so, the investigator seeks to determine which events took place at the crime scene and in what order. The investigator also recreates the scene to make sense of the evidence found within it.

Photographs Photographs are used to supplement and provide a visual depiction of the crime scene and evidence illustrated in an investigator's sketches and described in an investigator's notes. Photographs are taken to preserve the crime scene and evidence. Evidence may also be contaminated by officers who, unbeknownst to them, bring items into the crime scene (e.g. dirt from a police officer's shoes) and take items out of the crime scene (e.g., fibers attached to their shoes).

Photographs must be taken in such a way that they do not disturb the crime scene or the evidence within it. Some changes are unavoidable, but they must be both valid and thoroughly documented (e.g., where the item was moved to, by whom, and for what reason it was moved). Failure to do so may render the evidence inadmissible in court. Ideally, a crime scene should be photographed before any changes are made. One notable exception to this rule occurs when it is necessary to render assistance to any injured parties.

Photographs provide a much-needed visual representation of the crime for those persons who were not physically present at the scene (e.g., judge, jury, forensic scientists, behavioral profilers). They can also bring to light information that was initially overlooked by an investigator when he or she was physically at the crime scene. Investigators should include a general view (i.e., overall perspective at a distance), a medium-range view (i.e., broad panoramic or closer view around 20 feet away from the subject), and a close-up view (i.e., a perspective of less than 5 feet away) of the crime scene (Lyman, 2008). In addition, photographs should include markers (e.g., a ruler, coin) to direct attention to specific objects or to indicate the size and distance of objects.

Photographs are required for other reasons as well. Depending on the crime committed, law enforcement agencies may require assistance from other agencies—state or federal. Specifically, photographs may be required for criminal profiling, which refers to the process by which the traits of individuals responsible for committing criminal acts are inferred (Turvey, 2008). Indeed, crime scene photographs may be sent to the Behavioral Analysis Unit of the Federal Bureau of Investigation (FBI) so that profilers there can construct a profile of the alleged perpetrator of the crime.

A photograph log of crime scene photos should be maintained. It should include photographs of the overall scene, medium-range photos of parts of the crime scene and any evidence included in it, and close-range photographs of the evidence and victims (the latter are necessary if a homicide has taken place). The photograph log should include the case number, the name of the photographer, the date and time when the photograph was taken, the location of the evidence, the type of case (e.g., homicide, rape, stalking), and camera specifications (e.g., make and model of camera, lens used, shutter speed).

Digital Recordings Digital recordings are used to document the overall crime scene. They complement the photographs of the crime scene and evidence. Similar to photographs, such recordings provide a visual depiction of the crime to those involved in the case (e.g., investigators, forensic scientists, prosecution, defense teams, relevant experts, judges and juries). Sometimes digital recordings may reveal a vital clue that an investigator (or investigators) initially missed while at the crime scene. Given that cases may take anywhere from several months to years to be resolved, digital recordings can refresh an investigator's memory of what happened during the event.

In addition, digital recordings may provide an audio narrative of what is observed at the crime scene. With visual and audio narration, investigators can transcribe what is recorded in the digital recordings to their report at a later time. However, audio recordings are often discouraged because the comments made by investigators may be considered unprofessional, inappropriate, or prejudicial by a defense team or jury. Furthermore, questions that may arise in court about the proper execution of a warrant may be resolved by digital recordings of the actions of investigators at the crime scene.

Reports

Reports provide a narrative of what happened at the crime scene and how the investigation of the scene was conducted. All evidence should be included in the report. Moreover, the steps that the investigator took to document, collect, package, label, transport, and preserve the evidence should be noted. The names of the victims, witnesses, and suspects and their contact information should be included as well. In addition, these individuals' statements should be included in the report. Any observations made by the police officer concerning any of the parties involved should be included in the report as well. However, reports should include only the facts of the case—the personal opinions of the investigators should not be included under any circumstances.

Steps After Documenting the Scene

Once the crime scene and the evidence within it have been thoroughly documented, the investigator must properly collect the evidence (while wearing gloves), label (tag) it, and package (bag) it for its later transport to a forensic laboratory. Once the evidence has been transported to the lab, all seized items need to be inventoried, recorded, analyzed, and secured in a locked room or container in a climate-controlled environment; otherwise, the evidence will not be admissible in court. All of the information that is gathered during the investigation is disclosed to the defendant before his or her case is heard at trial.

Penal Laws on Maltreatment

Child maltreatment is a crime; it also can encompass other crimes, such as murder, manslaughter, assault, battery, and mayhem. Child maltreatment is criminalized by statutes covering sex offenses as well. Other laws criminalize failure to protect children and, in some states, failure to notify authorities of missing children.

The criminalization of the latter behavior—failure to notify—was largely due to the outcome of the infamous Casey Marie Anthony trial. Casey lived in Florida with her parents, George and Cindy Anthony, and her daughter, Caylee Marie Anthony. On July 15, 2008, Cindy informed a 911 operator that her granddaughter had been missing for 31 days and that the trunk of her daughter's car smelled like a body had decomposed there (Lohr, 2011). News media extensively covered details of how Casey failed to report that her daughter was missing for more than a month and, instead of searching for her, went out partying (e.g., Banfield & Hopper, 2011; Bello & Welch, 2011; Richey, 2011). Casey Anthony was arrested and provided authorities with numerous false explanations about Caylee's whereabouts. For instance, at one point during the investigation, she told police that her daughter was missing because a nanny had kidnapped her. A massive search ensued, during which Caylee's body was eventually found; however, because her remains were in an advanced state of decomposition, the cause of death could not be determined.

During the trial of Casey Anthony, prosecutors argued that she had killed her daughter by dosing her with chloroform and suffocating her with duct tape (Alvarez, 2011). They also argued that Casey hid Caylee's body in the trunk of her car for a few days and then dumped her body in a wooded area close to her home (Richey, 2011). The defense argued that Caylee had accidentally drowned in her grandparents' pool and that Casey and her father, George Anthony, had covered up this incident to prevent Casey from facing child neglect charges. The defense further argued that Casey's emotionless response to what happened to her daughter was the result of sexual abuse she had endured from her father (Richey, 2011). On July 5, 2011, Casey Anthony was convicted of providing false information to a law enforcement officer, but was acquitted of the other charges against her: first-degree murder, aggravated child abuse, and aggravated manslaughter for the death of her daughter (Hayes, 2011).

The legislation that was drafted in various states after this outcome, collectively referred to as Caylee's Law, criminalizes the failure to report a missing or dead child. For instance, according to South Dakota Code Annotated § 22-11-37, "Any parent, legal guardian, or caretaker who knowingly fails to notify law enforcement within forty-eight hours of learning that a child, in his or her care and less than thirteen years of age, is missing is guilty of a Class 1 misdemeanor" (National Conference of State Legislatures, 2012).

New York Child Maltreatment Laws

To illustrate the types of laws covering child maltreatment, this section focuses on legislation passed in New York. The laws used in New York family courts for child maltreatment cases are social services and family laws.

Neglected Children

Under New York Social Services Laws § 371(4-a):

"Neglected child" means a child less than eighteen years of age (i) whose physical, mental or emotional condition has been impaired or is in imminent danger of becoming impaired as a result of the failure of his parent or other person legally responsible for his care to exercise a minimum degree of care (A) in supplying the child with adequate food, clothing, shelter, education, medical or surgical care, though financially able to do so or offered financial or other reasonable means to do so; or (B) in providing the child with proper supervision or guardianship, by unreasonably inflicting or allowing to be inflicted harm, or a substantial risk thereof, including the infliction of excessive corporal punishment; or by misusing a drug or drugs; or by misusing alcoholic beverages to the extent that he loses self-control of his actions; or by any other acts of a similarly serious nature requiring the aid of the court; provided, however, that where the respondent is voluntarily and regularly participating in a rehabilitative program, evidence that the respondent has repeatedly misused a drug or drugs or alcoholic beverages to the extent that he loses self-control of his actions shall not establish that the child is a neglected child in the absence of evidence establishing that the child's physical, mental, or emotional condition has been impaired or is in imminent danger of becoming impaired as set forth in paragraph (i) of this subdivision; or (ii) who has been abandoned by his parents or other person legally responsible for his care.

Laws against child abandonment are also relevant to child maltreatment. Specifically, under New York Social Services Laws § 384-b:

A child is "abandoned" by his or her parent if such parent evinces an intent to forgo his or her parental rights and obligations as manifested by his or her failure to visit the child and communicate with the child or agency, although able to do so and not prevented or discouraged from doing so by the agency. In the absence of evidence to the contrary, such ability to visit and communicate shall be presumed.

However, abandonment or endangerment charges are not made against parents when the child is left for fewer than 30 days and provisions for care are made by dropping the infant off at a safe haven (e.g., hospital).

Other laws that are relevant to child neglect that are associated with criminal trial and prosecution of such cases include the following:

- NY Penal Law § 260.10, which defines endangering the welfare of a child (a Class A misdemeanor) as "knowingly act[ing] in a manner likely to be injurious to the physical, mental or moral welfare of a child less than seventeen years old or authoriz[ing] such child to engage in an occupation involving a substantial risk of danger to . . . life or health."

- NY Penal Law § 120.20, which refers to reckless endangerment in the second degree (a Class A misdemeanor). Pursuant to this law, "A person is guilty of reckless endangerment in the second degree when he or she recklessly engages in conduct which creates a substantial risk of serious physical injury to another person."
- NY Penal Law §120.25, which covers reckless endangerment in the first degree (a Class D felony). Under this law, "A person is guilty of reckless endangerment in the first degree when, under circumstances evincing a depraved indifference to human life, he recklessly engages in conduct which creates a grave risk of death to another person."

Abused Children

Under New York Social Services Laws § 371(4-a):

> [An] "abused child" means a child less than eighteen years of age whose parent or other person legally responsible for his care (i) inflicts or allows to be inflicted upon such child physical injury by other than accidental means which causes or creates a substantial risk of death, or serious or protracted disfigurement, or protracted impairment of physical or emotional health or protracted loss or impairment of the function of any bodily organ, or (ii) creates or allows to be created a substantial risk of physical injury to such child by other than accidental means which would be likely to cause death or serious or protracted disfigurement, or protracted impairment of physical or emotional health or protracted loss or impairment of the function of any bodily organ, or (iii) commits, or allows to be committed, an act of sexual abuse against such child as defined in the penal law.

Another law that is relevant to child abuse cases in family court relates to emotional abuse. Pursuant to the New York Family Court Act § 1012:

> "Impairment of emotional health" and "impairment of mental or emotional condition" includes a state of substantially diminished psychological or intellectual functioning in relation to, but not limited to, such factors as failure to thrive, control of aggressive or self-destructive impulses, ability to think and reason, acting out, or misbehavior, including incorrigibility, ungovernability, or habitual truancy; provided, however, that such impairment must be clearly attributable to the unwillingness or inability of the respondent to exercise a minimum degree of care toward the child.

The following New York penal laws cover physical abuse:

- NY Penal Law § 120.00 (a Class A misdemeanor), assault in the third degree. A person is guilty of this crime when "1. With intent to cause physical injury to another person, he causes such injury to such person or to a third person; or 2. He recklessly causes physical injury to another person; or 3. With criminal negligence, he causes physical injury to another person by means of a deadly weapon or a dangerous instrument."

- NY Penal Law § 120.02 (a Class D felony), reckless assault of a child. A person 18 years of age or older is guilty of this crime when "such person recklessly causes serious physical injury to the brain of a child less than five years old by shaking the child, or by slamming or throwing the child so as to impact the child's head on a hard surface or object."
- NY Penal Law § 120.05(8-9) (a Class D felony), assault in the second degree. A person 18 years of age or older is guilty of this crime when "with intent to cause physical injury to a person less than eleven years old, the defendant recklessly causes serious physical injury to such person; or . . . Being eighteen years old or more and with intent to cause physical injury to a person less than seven years old, the defendant causes such injury to such person."
- NY Penal Law § 120.10 (a Class B felony), assault in first degree. A person is guilty of this crime when "1. With intent to cause serious physical injury to another person, he causes such injury to such person or to a third person by means of a deadly weapon or a dangerous instrument; or 2. With intent to disfigure another person seriously and permanently, or to destroy, amputate or disable permanently a member or organ of his body, he causes such injury to such person or to a third person; or 3. Under circumstances evincing a depraved indifference to human life, he recklessly engages in conduct which creates a grave risk of death to another person, and thereby causes serious physical injury to another person . . ."
- NY Penal Law § 120.12 (a Class E felony), aggravated assault upon a person less than 11 years old. A person 18 years of age or older is guilty of this crime when "the defendant commits the crime of assault in the third degree as defined in section 120.00 of this article upon a person less than eleven years old and has been previously convicted of such crime upon a person less than eleven years old within the preceding three years."

The following New York penal laws cover sexual offenses against children and adults:

- NY Penal Law § 130.05: Sex offenses; lack of consent
- NY Penal Law § 130.10: Sex offenses; limitations; defenses
- NY Penal Law § 130.16: Sex offenses; corroboration
- NY Penal Law § 130.20: Sexual misconduct (Class A misdemeanor)
- NY Penal Law § 130.25: Rape in the third degree (Class E felony)
- NY Penal Law § 130.30: Rape in the second degree (Class D felony)
- NY Penal Law § 130.35: Rape in the first degree (Class B felony)
- NY Penal Law § 130.40: Criminal sexual act in the third degree (Class E felony)
- NY Penal Law § 130.45: Criminal sexual act in the second degree (Class D felony)
- NY Penal Law § 130.50: Criminal sexual act in the first degree (Class B felony)
- NY Penal Law § 130.52: Forcible touching (Class A misdemeanor)
- NY Penal Law § 130.53: Persistent sexual abuse (Class E felony)
- NY Penal Law § 130.55: Sexual abuse in the third degree (Class B misdemeanor)

- NY Penal Law § 130.60: Sexual abuse in the second degree (Class A misdemeanor)
- NY Penal Law § 130.65: Sexual abuse in the first degree (Class D felony)
- NY Penal Law § 130.65-a: Aggravated sexual abuse in the fourth degree (Class E felony)
- NY Penal Law § 130.66: Aggravated sexual abuse in the third degree (Class D felony)
- NY Penal Law § 130.67: Aggravated sexual abuse in the second degree (Class C felony)
- NY Penal Law § 130.70: Aggravated sexual abuse in the first degree (Class B felony)
- NY Penal Law § 130.75: Course of sexual conduct against a child in the first degree (Class D felony)
- NY Penal Law § 130.80: Course of sexual conduct against a child in the second degree (Class D felony)
- NY Penal Law § 130.85: Female genital mutilation (Class E felony)
- NY Penal Law § 130.90: Facilitating a sex offense with a controlled substance (Class D felony)
- NY Penal Law § 130.96: Predatory sexual assault against a child (Class A-II felony)

In all of these laws, there is the implication that the sexual act was performed without the victim's consent. According to NY Penal Law § 130.05, "lack of consent results from: (a) forcible compulsion; or (b) incapacity to consent; or (c) where the offense charged is sexual abuse or forcible touching . . .; or (d) where the offense charged is rape in the third degree . . ." As defined in #3 of that statute, a child younger than 17 years of age "is deemed incapable of consent." Adult offenders aged 21 and older are guilty of rape when they engage in sexual intercourse or criminal sexual acts including oral or anal sexual conduct with a child younger than 17 years (third degree, § 130.25 and § 130.40) or the perpetrator is 18 years or older and the victim is younger than 15 years (second degree, § 130.30 and § 130.45) or younger than 13 or 11 years (first degree, § 130.35 and § 130.50). The rest of these laws can be applied to child sexual abuse, including forcible touching (i.e., sexually, with intent to gratify the actor and/or degrade the victim); forcible touching and/or insertion of "a foreign object . . . or a finger into the vagina, urethra, penis, rectum, or anus"; and sexual conduct. The criminal charges are defined by specific acts, and classification is based on the age of the victim.

Sentencing

NY Penal Law § 70.00 provides for imprisonment for felonies depending on the class, such that the sentence fixed for: Class E is 1.5 to 4 years, Class D is 2 to 7 years, Class C is 3.5 to 15 years, Class B is 5 to 25 years, and Class A-II is life imprisonment. Sentencing of imprisonment for misdemeanors in New York is up to 1 year for Class A crimes and up to 90 days for Class B crimes.

Special Issues in Child Abuse: Sex Offenders, Pedophiles, and Child Trafficking

Child abuse is not always a stand-alone crime. In fact, it has been connected with other serious crimes, such as crimes committed by sexual predators, pedophiles, child traffickers, and persons responsible for commercial sexual exploitation of children. This section focuses on three of these crimes: sexual predation (including the tactics these individuals used in the online environment), pedophilia, and child trafficking.

Pedophilia and Commercial Sexual Exploitation of Children

A pedophile is a person—either a man or a woman—who is sexually aroused by prepubescent girls, boys, or both. According to the *Diagnostic and Statistical Manual of Mental Disorders, Fourth Edition (DSM-IV)*, pedophilia is "a recurrent, intense, sexually arousing fantasy, sexual urge, or behavior involving prepubescent children." There are pedophile organizations, such as NAMBLA (North American Man/Boy Love Association), that argue for the right of sexual determination for children: not for altruistic motives, such as for the best interests of the child, but rather for self-serving purposes, to have the age at which children can have sex reduced or to have the consent laws (Table 10-1) abolished (Richardson, 2000).

Under Article 3(a) of the United Nations' Protocol to Prevent, Suppress and Punish Trafficking in Persons, Especially Women and Children (2003), human trafficking refers to

> the recruitment, transportation, transfer, harboring or receipt of persons, by means of the threat or use of force or other forms of coercion, of abduction, of fraud, of deception, of the abuse of power or of a position of vulnerability or of the giving or receiving of payments or benefits to achieve the consent of a person having control over another person, for the purpose of exploitation. Exploitation shall include, at a minimum, the exploitation of the prostitution of others or other forms of sexual exploitation, forced labor or services, slavery or practices similar to slavery, servitude or the removal of organs.[1]

The Trafficking Victims Protection Act of 2000 (TVPA) defines "severe forms of human trafficking" as the recruitment, harboring, transportation, provision, or obtaining of a person for the following purposes:

Table 10-1 Age of consent laws in the United States

Age of consent	States
16	Alabama, Alaska, Arkansas, Connecticut, District of Columbia, Georgia, Hawaii, Indiana, Iowa, Kansas, Kentucky, Maine, Maryland, Massachusetts, Michigan, Minnesota, Mississippi, Montana, Nebraska, Nevada, New Hampshire, New Jersey, New Mexico, North Carolina, Ohio, Oklahoma, Pennsylvania, Rhode Island, South Carolina, South Dakota, Vermont, Washington, West Virginia, Wyoming
17	Colorado, Illinois, Louisiana, Missouri, New York, Texas
18	Arizona, California, Delaware*, Florida, Idaho**, North Dakota, Oregon, Tennessee, Utah, Virginia, Wisconsin

* Sexual acts with youths at least 16 years of age are illegal if the defendant is 30 years of age or older.

** "Sexual acts not amounting to penetration" are legal under limited circumstances in cases where the victim is at least 16 years of age.

[1] https://www.unodc.org/southeastasiaandpacific/en/topics/illicit-trafficking/human-trafficking-definition.html. Reprinted by permission of United Nations Publications.

- Sex trafficking, in which a commercial sex act is induced by force, fraud, or coercion (e.g., threats of physical or psychological harm to children and/or their families), or in which the person induced to perform such act has not attained 18 years of age
- Labor or services, through the use of force, fraud, or coercion, for the purpose of subjection to involuntary servitude, peonage, debt bondage, or slavery

The commercial sexual exploitation of children (CSEC) is defined by the First World Congress against Commercial Sexual Exploitation of Children as "sexual abuse by the adult and remuneration in cash or kind to the child or a third person or persons. The child is treated as a sexual object and as a commercial object. The commercial sexual exploitation of children constitutes a form of coercion and violence against children, amounts to forced labor and a contemporary form of slavery" (Adams, Owens, & Small, 2010, p. 1). CSEC includes the prostitution of children, sex tourism, and any type of transactional sexual activity performed by a child for remuneration or the fulfillment of the child's basic needs within this definition.

According to Klain, Kloer, Eason, Lieberman, Smolenski, and Thompson (2009), signs of child trafficking include: a lack of access to identification documents; knowledge of the commercial sex industry; inferences to sexual situations that are not age appropriate; truancy; frequent travel to other cities, states, or countries; an increase in expensive possessions; signs of physical abuse; exhibiting fearful or withdrawal behaviors; drug addiction or exhibiting behaviors associated with drug use; and a significantly older boyfriend or girlfriend. Individuals that engage in commercial exploitation of children may include traffickers, pimps, boyfriends/girlfriends, parents, relatives, family acquaintances, and strangers (Estes & Weiner, 2001). In the United States, child trafficking occurs in multiple ways: children may be prostituted on streets, in private residences, or in private businesses (e.g., spas, massage parlors, hotels and clubs); sold to homes or businesses for labor; used by others to receive money from begging; and utilized to sell drugs (Raymond & Hughes, 2001).

In the United States, victims of commercial sexual exploitation with no parent, guardian, or relative in the United States are eligible for the Unaccompanied Refugee Minors (URM) program. Children placed in this program "receive the full range of services available to other foster children in the State, as well as special services to help them adapt to life in the United States and recover from their trafficking experience" (Administration for Children and Families, 2012). A primary goal of the URM program is the safe reunification of the child with his or her family. An unfortunate truth is that such reunification may not be possible, as many children are initially sold into sexual slavery by their families.

The extent to which child sexual exploitation occurs in the United States is difficult to assess due to the low visibility of this industry. Laws have been passed to decriminalize prostitution for all youths younger than the age of 18. Prior to enactment of these laws, children were being charged with prostitution even though the law holds that children of certain ages cannot consent to sexual encounters. In New York, the Safe Harbor for

Exploited Children Act of 2007 did just that—that is, it relabeled prostitutes younger than the age of 18 as sexually exploited children (SEC). In Illinois, the Safe Children Act of 2010 similarly decriminalized prostitution, even for repeat offenders. Other states have similar laws in place, including Connecticut (Safe Harbor for Exploited Children Act of 2010) and Minnesota (Safe Harbor for Sexually Exploited Youth Act of 2011). Unfortunately, not all of the states have revised their laws to be consistent with the federal guidelines set in the Trafficking Victims Protection Reauthorization Act (2013) that define youth engaged in the sex trade as victims rather than as criminals.

Sexual Predators

Internet resources can be used to gather evidence on sex offenders. Specifically, monitoring of the Internet can assist investigators and members of the public in identifying predators and child molesters. The National Sex Offender Registry is one such website that can provide investigators with information on sexual predators. The Family Watchdog website (http://www.familywatchdog.us) provides access to such a registry; it also offers many essential tools for parents, concerned citizens, and law enforcement agencies. Parents and concerned citizens can search this site for registered sex offenders in their neighborhoods. In addition, investigators can type in a victim's address and locate any sex offenders who live close by using the website. If an incident occurs at a school, an investigator can locate both the school and nearby sex offenders' residences and employment on the map from this website.

Another very important tool for investigations is reverse email lookup. This tool scans various social and picture sites to see where email addresses have been registered. Investigators can use this information to track down any profiles created by sex offenders on these social sites and ascertain whether these individuals have contacted children by looking at their "friends" lists. Examples of websites that provide reverse email searches include the following:

- AnyWho (http://www.anywho.com/rl), which provides reverse phone lookup
- People Search Pro (http://www.peoplesearchpro.com/resources/email-search /reverse-email-lookup/), which provides reverse email lookup
- Reverse Records (http://www.reverserecords.org/?hop=haskinsmic), which provides reverse email, phone, cell phone, and home address lookups

Additionally, the Dru Sjodin National Sex Offender Public Website provides real-time access to state and territory sex offender registries, including those from all 50 states and the District of Columbia, the U.S. territories of Guam and Puerto Rico, and participating tribes (U.S. Department of Justice, n.d.). This registry was named after Dru Sjodin, a young woman who was kidnapped, brutally raped, and murdered by a three-time convicted sex offender, Alfonso Rodriguez, Jr. The public outcry over this crime led to "Dru's Law," which called for creation of a national sex offender registry.

Dru's Law became part of the Adam Walsh Child Protection and Safety Act of 2006, which was passed in response to the abduction from a mall in Florida and subsequent murder of Adam Walsh, the son of John Walsh, the former host of *America's Most Wanted*. Adam's killer was never caught. Title I of the Adam Walsh Child Protection and Safety Act is the Sex Offender Registration and Notification Act (SORNA). SORNA created a national sex offender register, in which each offender's photograph, full name and any aliases, home and work addresses, date of birth, and offenses committed are posted.

The Adam Walsh Child Protection and Safety Act also strengthened the national sex offender registry by requiring additional data to be included about sex offenders, such as their physical description, fingerprints, palm prints, DNA samples, criminal history, and a detailed summary of the crimes committed. This law was passed to harmonize and standardize state sex offender laws nationwide. It further provided for development of a three-tier system within which sex offenders are placed. Tier 1 offenders must be registered for 15 years and update their information annually. Individuals in this tier have a low risk of reoffending. Tier 2 offenders must be registered for 25 years and update their information biannually; they have a moderate risk of reoffending. Tier 3 offenders—the most dangerous offenders—must register for life and are required to update their information in the database every 3 months (to ensure that it remains up-to-date). Individuals in Tier 3 have a high risk of reoffending and pose a threat to public safety.

Prior to passage of the Adam Walsh Child Protection and Safety Act, several other laws had paved the way for national registration of sex offenders. These laws were triggered by the abduction and murder of children by sexual offenders. In particular, in 1994, Megan Kanka was raped and murdered by a neighbor who was a sex offender. Her parents were unaware that a sex offender lived in their neighborhood. Her death triggered the passage of state and federal laws (e.g., Megan's Law) that focused on sex offender registration and notification of residents of neighborhoods when sex offenders move into the area (e.g., Pennsylvania State Police, 2003-2008). The Jacob Wetterling Crimes Against Children and Sexually Violent Offender Act (codified in 42 U.S.C. § 14071) was enacted as part of the Violent Crime Control and Law Enforcement Act of 1994 and required states to implement a sex offender registry. Some state sex offender registries also provide users with the option to track sexual predators. For instance, Florida has implemented an offender alert system, which is a free service providing email alerts when an offender or predator moves close to any address in Florida that an individual chooses to monitor (Florida Department of Law Enforcement, n.d.).

Furthermore, AMBER (America's Missing: Broadcasting Emergency Response) alerts were developed to alert the public to child abductions. This alert system was named after Amber Hagerman, who was abducted in 1996 outside of a Winn-Dixie grocery store in her hometown of Arlington, Texas, as she was riding her bike. Four days after her abduction, her lifeless body was found in a drainage ditch. According to the U.S. Department of Justice (January 2010), as of 2009, AMBER alerts had helped rescue 495 children. For an AMBER alert to be issued, the following criteria must be met:

- Law enforcement agents must confirm that the child has been abducted.
- The abducted child must be at risk of serious harm or death.

- A sufficient description of the child, the child's abductor, or the abductor's vehicle must exist.
- The abducted child must be 17 years old or younger.

Apart from televisions, radios, websites, and highway traffic boards, AMBER alerts can be issued through messages sent to wireless devices, should users opt to receive such alerts relative to their geographical location.

Sexual predators have been known to frequent chat rooms and monitor ongoing online conversations in search of their next victim. Once they find a potentially suitable target, they engage in conversation with him or her. Sometimes they attempt to engage the target in a private conversation. Slowly they develop a relationship of trust with their victim—encouraging the victim to confide in the predator by convincing the victim to share his or her personal information (e.g., age, home address, phone number, relationship status). They may also try to convince the minor to engage in sexually explicit conduct. For example, Ivory Dickerson persuaded and enticed "female minors into engaging in sexually explicit conduct for the purpose of manufacturing child pornography" (United States Attorney, Middle District of Florida, 2007). His computer also contained more than 600 child pornography images. Another case involved Mark Wayne Miller, who posed as a young male to persuade his victims—young girls—to engage in sexually explicit conduct (United States Attorney, Southern District of Ohio, 2006). Miller recorded these sessions and even distributed some of them to third parties via active webcams.

Eventually, sexual predators try to set up a meeting with their victim. Some even travel across states to meet a victim. One such example involved an individual who violated 18 U.S.C. § 2423(b), which prohibits a "person from traveling in interstate commerce, or conspiring to do so, for the purpose of engaging in criminal sexual activity with a minor," when he traveled across state lines (from Minnesota to Wisconsin) to meet with a minor (a 14-year-old girl) whom he had met in an online chat room and engage in sexual acts (Working Group on Unlawful Conduct on the Internet, 1999).

Adults may identify themselves as children on websites to lure children into dangerous situations. One cannot definitively know that the person with whom an individual is communicating in chat rooms and social networking sites or through emails and instant messages is not a sexual predator. To remedy this situation, the Keeping the Internet Devoid of Sexual Predators (KIDS) Act of 2008 was enacted. The KIDS Act requires sex offenders to submit their email addresses and online screen names to the national sex offender registry.

The Internet also provides these predators with a cloak of anonymity. They can pretend to be any age; for example, some have even entered into chats among 10-year-olds pretending to be the same age. When predators pretend to be children or teenagers, the victim is more likely to develop friendships and online relationships with the offender. At other times, predators have pretended to be a different gender. William Ciccotto, a 51-year-old male, posed as a young girl (between the age of 13 and 14 years) on the Internet to find victims (United States Attorney's Office, Middle District of Florida, 2010). Specifically, he opened a Hotmail account and a MySpace account under the name

"Cindy Westin," through which he proceeded to send friend requests to young girls and chatted with them within this site and via AOL instant messages. Under this persona, Ciccotto convinced the girls to send nude photos of themselves to "Cindy"—sometimes persuading them to take photos of themselves engaging in sexually explicit conduct and send them to "her." Ciccotto then distributed the photos through a private peer-to-peer (P2P) network.

Child Pornography: Are Laws More Lenient in the United States?

U.S. case law and statutes have outlawed the manufacture, possession, and distribution of child pornography. For instance, the Sexual Exploitation of Children Act of 1978 made it illegal for someone to manufacture and commercially distribute obscene materials that involve minors younger than age 16 years. Ten years later, the Child Protection and Obscenity Enforcement Act of 1988 was enacted. Under this act, it is illegal for an individual to use a computer to depict or advertise child pornography. Additionally, in 1990, the courts, in *Osborne v. Ohio* (495 U.S. 103, 1990), ruled that private possession of child pornography was illegal.

In 1996, the Child Pornography Protection Act was passed. The sections of this federal legislation that explicitly criminalize the exploitation of children online include, but are not limited to, the following:

- 18 U.S.C. § 2251: Prohibits the sexual exploitation of children
- 18 U.S.C. § 2251A: Provides severe penalties for those who buy and sell children for sexual exploitation
- 18 U.S.C. § 2252: Covers activities relating to material involving the sexual exploitation of minors
- 18 U.S.C. § 2252A: Prohibits activities relating to material constituting or containing child pornography

In electronic media, child pornography can be found in numerous places (Wortley & Smallbone, 2006):

- *Newsgroups.* Members may share child pornography images and information on child pornography websites through this medium to avoid unwanted attention by Internet service providers (ISPs) and attention by authorities. They may use code to discuss child pornography websites or hide the images of child pornography among legal adult pornographic images.
- *Bulletin boards.* Discussions of child pornography often occur in such forums, and websites containing child pornography are rated and shared among child pornographers. These forums may be password protected to avoid infiltration by undercover law enforcement agents and individuals who oppose the collection and distribution of child pornography.
- *Chat rooms.* These areas are used to exchange child pornography images and find minors to sexually exploit and victimize.

- *Peer-to-peer networks.* These networks enable the file sharing of child pornography images to closed groups, thereby enabling perpetrators to avoid detection.
- *Email.* This method is rarely used by seasoned sexual predators because of their fear that they might unwittingly transfer child pornography material to undercover law enforcement agents.

In 1998, the Child Protector and Sexual Predator Punishment Act was enacted, which required ISPs to report incidents of child pornography to authorities when they come across them. ISPs are not actively required to monitor their websites or customers. Additionally, Section 508 of the Prosecutorial Remedies and Other Tools to End the Exploitation of Children Today (PROTECT) Act of 2003 amended

> [the] Victims of Child Abuse Act of 1990 to authorize a provider of electronic communication or remote computing services that reasonably believes it has obtained knowledge of facts and circumstances indicating a State criminal law child pornography violation to disclose such information to an appropriate State or local law enforcement official.

The PROTECT Act further prohibited the use of a misleading domain names with the intent to deceive a minor into viewing material that is harmful to minors online. John Zuccarini, for example, had used the Internet domain names of a famous amusement park, celebrity, and cartoons to deceive minors into logging into pornography websites (United States Attorney, Southern District of New York, 2004). Specifically, he intentionally misspelled versions of a domain name (e.g., www.dinseyland.com) owned by Walt Disney (www.disneyland.com). He also used 16 misspellings and variations of the legitimate website of the popular female singer Britney Spears to attract children. He further used misspellings and variations of the domain names of legitimate websites depicting two popular cartoon characters: Bob the Builder (www.bobthebiulder.com) and Teletubbies (www.teltubbies.com).[2]

The Securing Adolescents from Exploitation Online (SAFE) Act of 2007 expanded the definition of ISPs to include wireless hot spots, such as libraries, hotels, and municipalities. It also required such service providers to "provide information relating to the Internet identity of any individual who appears to have violated a child exploitation or pornography law, including the geographic location of such [an] individual and images of any apparent child pornography." It further required these ISPs to preserve images of child pornography that were observed for evidentiary purposes. Failure to do so or to report instances of child pornography will result in significant penalties to the ISPs. If civilians find websites that exhibit child pornography, the Child Exploitation and Obscenity Section (CEOS) website states that these individuals should contact the National Center for Missing and Exploited Children (NCMEC).

According to Wortley and Smallbone (2006), ISPs can also help fight against the proliferation of child pornography by performing the following tasks:

---

[2] The legitimate websites were www.bobthebuilder.com and www.teletubbies.com.

- Removing illegal sites wherever and whenever they encounter them.
- Establishing websites and hotlines where individuals can complain about any child pornography images or websites encountered.
- Making ISPs responsible for the content of sites they host by requiring them to notify authorities when child pornography is encountered.
- Preserving their records to make them available for law enforcement agencies during investigations of child pornography manufacture, collection, and distribution.
- Requiring the verification of personally identifying information given by individuals to open up accounts. Individuals can use fake names, home addresses, and phone numbers to open up accounts if this information is not authenticated by service providers. This practice makes it extremely difficult for law enforcement authorities to trace and find those persons responsible for these illegal activities.

Further, Wortley and Smallbone (2006) recommend that law enforcement responses to child pornography should include the following measures:

- Locating and taking down child pornography websites.
- Finding out who is signed up to download and post child pornography from these websites.
- Conducting undercover sting operations. For instance, an undercover FBI agent downloaded child pornography images from P2P networks from a user known as "Boys20096" (U.S. Department of Justice, March 16, 2010). The undercover agent traced the IP address of "Boys20096" to a residence in Wheaton, Illinois. A laptop seized at the residence was believed to belong to a live-in nanny, Lubos Albrecht. The laptop contained approximately 6000 images and videos of child pornography. The FBI eventually linked Albrecht to the laptop and the P2P sharing network from which the child pornography images were obtained.
- Creating honeypots (i.e., a trap set to detect criminal activity), such as a fake child pornography website monitored by the police, to lure child pornographers so as to identify them. Honeypots also seek to discourage other child pornographers from visiting these websites for fear that they are not legitimate child pornography websites, but rather fake websites designed to bait and catch them.

In a landmark but controversial case, *Ashcroft v. Free Speech Coalition* (535 U.S. 234, 2002), the U.S. Supreme Court held that virtual (i.e., computer-generated) images of child pornography were legal—as long as a real child was not used to produce the image. This ruling raised significant issues for prosecutors of child pornography cases because the burden of proof is now on the government to show that the images actually depict children and are not adult models made to look like children. The Child Victim Identification Program, which houses the largest database of child pornography for the purpose of identifying victims of child exploitation and abuse, was developed in the aftermath of the Supreme Court's ruling in *Ashcroft.*

The United States does not make all simulated child pornography illegal, only that which "lacks serious literary, artistic, political, or scientific value" (18 U.S.C. § 1466A). In contrast to the United States, both real and virtual images of child pornography have been outlawed in other countries. Sexual images of fictional characters that appear or have been described as being younger than 18 years of age are also illegal in several countries, including, but not limited to, the United Kingdom (see the Coroners and Justice Act of 2009), Canada (see the ruling in *R v. Sharpe*, 1 S.C.R. 45, 2001), and the Netherlands (Bulletin of Acts and Decrees 470).

Policing Sex Offenders

The criminal justice system's involvement in child abuse cases extends beyond the investigative component. Specifically, sex offenders are monitored after conviction by probation and parole officers. Probation and parole officers also monitor offenders who are involved in child abuse cases.

Probation and Parole

Probation is a sentence provided to a convicted offender that entails the individual's conditional release into the community under the supervision of a probation officer. This type of sentence serves as an alternative to incarceration and usually involves specific conditions that must be followed by the offender for a particular amount of time. Moreover, this sentence may be revoked and the individual sent to jail or prison if he or she violates the terms of his or her probation.

The probation officer assigned to the case is responsible for ensuring that the probationer is in compliance with the conditions of probation; providing referral services for employment, drug, or family problems; conducting home visits; effectuating arrests (when necessary); writing reports to the court to update it on the status of the probationer, as well as notifying the court of any violations of probation when they occur. Some

---

Box 10-1 New York City Probation Department's Halloween Initiative

A large portion of the limited resources of the Probation Department of the City of New York is dedicated to protecting the community from sex offenders, such as pedophiles, by implementing intensive supervision measures. One innovative measure by the NYC Probation Department was implemented on Halloween and targeted pedophiles. A curfew was imposed on pedophiles for that day and probationers were warned not to open up their doors to any children who were trick-or-treating. Officers from the Probation Department, as well as police officers from the New York City Police Department (NYPD), conducted surveillance of the pedophiles' residences to ensure that they abided by the curfew, were not opening up their doors to children, and did not have any lures (e.g., toys, teddy bears) in their possession.

probation officers work in a geocoding system, in which a probation officer is assigned to probationers in a specific area. This approach enables the probation officers to not only familiarize themselves with the area, but also to build working relationships with the local precincts in these areas. What is more, the travel times of the probation officers to the probationers are significantly reduced because the probationers assigned to the probation officer are located in a specific geographic area of a county, borough, or city.

Probation officers, if appropriate, may subject a probationer to drug testing if this is a stipulation of his or her sentence. Probationers are usually given an order that prohibits them from threatening or harassing their victims. For child abuse offenders, another requirement for probationers may include participation in some form of child abuse treatment program. When serious probation violations occur, probation officers have the authority to arrest probationers, but such arrests require supervisory approval; additionally, there are instances where probationers have been arrested even for minor violations (e.g., not meeting the probation officer at the scheduled time and place).

Sometimes probationary sentences have been given to individuals against whom allegations of child abuse were confirmed with independent corroborating evidence, even in severe cases. A case in point is David Zimmer. In this case, "prosecutors seemed in a strong position, with a handwritten confession from Mr. Zimmer. Initially charged with more than 24 counts of sex offenses, he [later] pleaded guilty to one count of sexual abuse in the first degree and received five years' probation" (Rivera & Otterman, 2012, para. 30). Despite the confession and a diary delineating each abuse, the prosecutor's plea agreement with Zimmer was the only option available to the government because the parents of the victims refused to allow them to testify. In another case where abuse was suspected over a period of 30 years, the alleged perpetrator, a rabbi, received only 3 years' probation (Rivera & Otterman, 2012). As in the Zimmer case, the prosecution cited parents' reluctance to have their children testify. It is likely that pressure was exerted on the families to have the victims recant, as members of the ultra-Orthodox close-knit Jewish community typically prefer to discipline abusers themselves rather than report them. However, the refusal to testify could also be due to the embarrassment of the families caused by the stigma associated with the abuse. Either way, prosecutors are loath to go to trial when cases rest solely on testimony by very young children or by those whose maltreatment occurred several years ago.

In contrast to probation, parole is the early, conditional release of an offender from prison. The conditions of the prisoner's release are set by the parole board. Parole officers determine how to handle offenders once they are released. These officers supervise parolees, visit them, and conduct random searches to ensure that the conditions of parole are being followed by the parolee. For instance, one special condition of parolees convicted of sex offenses against children is that they are prohibited from having children's toys. Judges tend not to revoke parole for minor violations; however, technically, violations should result in revocation. This decision is made at the judge's discretion. As with probation, other conditions placed on an individual's parole may include attendance of a treatment program for sex offenders and a prohibition against contacting the victim—specifically, no correspondence, no phone calls, and the exact minimum distance the offender must keep from the victim, among other restrictions.

Wherever available, needed, and economically feasible, both probationers and parolees may be subjected to electronic monitoring (EM). EM requires that an offender is fitted with a bracelet or anklet, which has the capabilities of regularly checking on (or in the case of global positioning system [GPS] technology, continuously tracking) the individual's whereabouts. The most common form of EM is used for curfew orders, which require an offender to be at home between certain hours of the day as a condition for parole or early release. This technology can be used for probation as well. EM may be implemented as a community penalty, a means of early release from prison, part of an intensive supervision program, and an alternative for young offenders who would otherwise have been remanded into custody (Nellis, 2003).

In a study conducted by Padgett, Bales, and Blomberg (2006) using data on offenders placed on home confinement in Florida, the researchers' aim was to determine the effect of EM on the likelihood of revocation of probation/parole and absconding from supervision. Two types of EM were evaluated: radio-frequency (RF) and GPS monitoring. The first type of EM to be introduced was RF technology; it was mostly used to ensure that offenders were at home in compliance with curfew orders. RF technology indicates whether the person is home at any given time, but does not reveal the actual location of the offender if he or she is not at home. The second type of EM, GPS, was introduced at a later date to enable the tracking of the offender's exact geographic location.

These measures diverted individuals from prison, "while providing a greater level of offender accountability and surveillance than would be provided by traditional probation supervision" (Padgett et al., 2006, p. 62). What has yet to be determined, however, is to what extent intermediate sanctions, such as EM, have fulfilled their formal goals of reducing prison populations and protecting public safety. In terms of protecting public safety, Padgett et al. found EM to be effective in reducing the likelihood of reoffending and absconding while offenders were on home confinement. Regarding the decisions concerning which offenders should be placed on EM, their study showed that EM works for serious offenders and that it works equally well for all "types" of serious offenders (Mair, 2006; Padgett et al., 2006).

The use of either GPS or RF monitoring had virtually the same inhibiting effect on revocations and absconding for violent, property, and drug offenders on home confinement (Mair, 2006; Padgett et al., 2006). Research also suggests that "there is a reduced likelihood of reoffending and absconding associated with the use of EM" (Mair, 2006, p. 57). In summary, "EM works to suppress crime during the period offenders are subjected to it" (Padgett et al., 2006, pp. 61, 83). However, Padgett, Bales, and Blomberg noted that their findings were limited to the effectiveness of EM while offenders were actually being monitored, not after they had completed the program. Due to the cost of implementing these technologies, in light of the dwindling budgets of parole and probation, they are simply not used in many cases.

Chapter Summary

Joint investigations of child abuse investigations are conducted by many states. For instance, sheriff's offices in many Florida counties have developed a common protocol on how to respond to child abuse investigations. Joint interviews tend to minimize the number of times that the child victim is interviewed concerning the alleged abuse. Those personnel typically involved in the forensic interviews are social workers, CPS workers, police, medical personnel, and prosecutors. Unfortunately, crimes against children remain very hard to investigate.

Sexual predators may use the Internet to stalk their victims under the cloak of anonymity afforded to them by the online environment. In this setting, a predator may use multiple personas to lull the victim into a false sense of security. Many laws have been created to prohibit the sexual exploitation of children and the manufacture, collection, and distribution of child pornography online. In the absence of online boundaries and single jurisdictions in cases, the regulation of child pornography, prevention of child exploitation, and investigation of child sexual predators pose unique challenges to law enforcement agencies worldwide.

The criminal justice system's involvement in child sexual abuse cases extends beyond the investigative component. Specifically, sex offenders are monitored after conviction by probation and parole officers. Technology has also been utilized to aid probation and parole officers in monitoring offenders.

Review Questions

1. Is probation an appropriate sentence for child abuse cases? Why or why not?
2. What are the advantages of using a multidisciplinary team to investigate child abuse?
3. What is the police officer's role in child abuse cases?
4. What is geocoding?
5. How can probation and parole be monitored?
6. Where can an investigator find information on sexual predators?
7. What is being done to combat the spread of child pornography?
8. Provide an example of child exploitation. What is a law enforcement officer's role in this crime?

References

Adams, W., Owens, C., & Small, K. (2010, July). Effects of federal legislation on the commercial sexual exploitation of children. U.S. Department of Justice, Office of Justice Programs. https://www.ncjrs.gov/pdffiles1/ojjdp/228631.pdf

Administration for Children and Families. (2012). Fact sheet: Child victims of human trafficking. http://www.acf.hhs.gov/programs/orr/resource/fact-sheet-child-victims-of-human-trafficking

Alvarez, L. (2011, July 5). Casey Anthony not guilty in slaying of daughter. *New York Times*. http://www.nytimes.com/2011/07/06/us/06casey.html?pagewanted=all

American Psychiatric Association. (1994). *Diagnostic and Statistical Manual of Mental Disorders*, Fourth Edition (DSM-IV). Washington DC.

Banfield, A., & Hopper, J. (2011, May 25). Casey Anthony trial: Former boyfriend describes Casey Anthony romance. *ABC News*. http://abcnews.go.com/US/casey-anthony-trial-tony-lazzaro-describes-romance-caylee/story?id=13682814#.UbXrKJzAbqw

Bello, M., & Welch, W. M. (2011, July 6). How the Casey Anthony case came apart. *USA Today*. http://usatoday30.usatoday.com/news/nation/2011-07-05-Casey-Anthony-Caylee-Anthony-acquittal-murder-case-Florida_n.htm

Crist, C., & Butterworth, R. A. (2008, January 31). Sheriff's child protective investigations: Program performance evaluation report. Broward, Hillsborough, Manatee, Pasco, Pinellas, & Seminole County Sheriff's Offices and the Florida Department of Children and Families. http://www.dcf.state.fl.us/initiatives/childsafety/docs/ 120109/2007 PeerReviewReportFINAL013108.pdf

Cross, T. P., Finkelhor, D., & Ormrod, R. (2005). Police involvement in child protective services investigations: Literature review and secondary data analysis. *Child Maltreatment, 10*(3), 1–21.

Estes, R. J., & Weiner, N. A. (2001). The commercial sexual exploitation of children in the U.S., Canada, and Mexico. http://www.sp2.upenn.edu/restes/CSEC_Files/Exec_Sum_020220.pdf

Florida Department of Law Enforcement. (n.d.). Florida Offender Alert System. http://www.nsopw.gov/Core/ResultDetails.aspx?index=3&x=0AD7C0B4-EA7E-41C9-AD1D-C0BDF0167096

Gardner, R. S. (2005). *Practical crime scene processing and investigation: Practical aspects of criminal and forensic investigations*. New York, NY: CRC Press.

Gardner, T. J., & Anderson, T. M. (2007). The crime scene, the chain of custody requirement, and the use of fingerprints and trace evidence. In *Criminal evidence: Principles and cases* (6th ed., pp. 330–353). Australia: Thomson/Wadsworth.

Girard, J. E. (2008). *Criminalistics: Forensic science and crime*. Sudbury, MA: Jones and Bartlett.

Hayes, A. (2011, July 5). Casey Anthony not guilty of murder, other charges in daughter's death. *CNN*. http://www.cnn.com/2011/CRIME/07/05/florida.casey.anthony.trial/index.html

Kinnevy, S., Cohen, B., Huang, V., Gelles, R., Bae, H., Fusco, R., Dichter M. (2003). *Evaluation of the transfer of responsibility for child protective investigations to law enforcement in Florida: An analysis of Manatee, Pasco, and Pinellas counties*. Report of the Center for Research on Youth and Social Policy, School of Social Work, University of Pennsylvania. Philadelphia, PA: Center for Research on Youth and Social Policy.

Klain, E., Kloer, A., Eason, D., Lieberman, I., Smolenski, C., & Thompson, R. (2009). An introduction for children's attorneys and advocates. http://www.americanbar.org/content/dam/aba/migrated/2011_build/domestic_violence/child_trafficking.authcheckdam.pdf

Lohr, D. (2011, July 3). Casey Anthony trial: Guilty or innocent? You be the 13th juror. *Huffington Post*. http://www.huffingtonpost.com/2011/07/03/casey-anthony-trial-verdict-poll_n_889038.html

Lyman, M. D. (2008). *Criminal investigation: The art and the science* (5th ed.). Upper Saddle River, NJ: Pearson.

Maguire, E. R. (1993). The professionalism of police in child sexual abuse cases. *Journal of Child Sexual Abuse, 2*, 107–116.

Mair, G. (2006). Electronic monitoring, effectiveness, and public policy. *Criminology and Public Policy, 5*(1), 57–60.

National Conference of State Legislatures. (2012, November 16). Caylee's Law. http://www.ncsl.org/issues-research/justice/caylees-law.aspx

Nellis, M. (2003). News media, popular culture and the electronic monitoring of offenders in England and Wales. *Howard Journal of Criminal Justice, 42*(1), 1–31.

Padgett, K. G., Bales, W. D., & Blomberg, T. G. (2006). Under surveillance: An empirical test of the effectiveness and consequences of electronic monitoring. *Criminology and Public Policy, 5*(1), 61–92.

Pence, D., & Wilson, C. (1992). *The role of law enforcement in the response to child abuse and neglect.* Washington, DC: National Center on Child Abuse and Neglect.

Pennsylvania State Police. (2003–2008). Megan's Law website. Commonwealth of Pennsylvania. http://www.pameganslaw.state.pa.us/History.aspx?dt=

Raymond, J. G., & Hughes, D. M. (2001). Sex trafficking women in the United States: International and domestic trends. Coalition Against Trafficking in Women. http://www.uri.edu/artsci/wms /hughes/sex_traff_us.pdf

Richardson, D. (2000). Constructing sexual citizenship: Theorizing sexual rights. *Critical Social Policy, 20*(1), 105–135.

Richey, W. (2011). Casey Anthony murder trial: What did her "Bella Vita" tattoo mean? *Christian Science Monitor.* http://www.csmonitor.com/USA/Justice/2011/0614 /Casey-Anthony-murder-trial-What-did-her-Bella-Vita-tattoo-mean

Rivera, R., & Otterman, S. (2012, May 10). For ultra-Orthodox in abuse cases, prosecutor has different rules. *New York Times.* http://www.nytimes.com/2012/05/11/nyregion/for-ultra-orthodox-in-child-sex-abuse-cases-prosecutor-has-different-rules.html?pagewanted=all&_r=0

Saferstein, R. S. (2011). *Criminalistics: An introduction to forensic science* (10th ed.). New York, NY: Prentice Hall.

Shireman, J., Miller, B., & Brown, H. F. (1981). Child welfare workers, police, and child placement. *Child Welfare, 55,* 413–422.

Tjaden, P. G., & Anhalt, J. (1994). *The impact of joint law enforcement child protective services investigations in child maltreatment cases.* Denver, CO: Center for Policy Research.

Turvey, B. E. (2008). *Criminal profiling* (3rd ed.). New York, NY: Elsevier.

United States Attorney, Middle District of Florida. (2007, November 30). North Carolina man sentenced to 110 years for computer hacking and child pornography. U.S. Department of Justice, Computer Crime & Intellectual Property Section. http://www.justice.gov/criminal/cybercrime /dickersonSent.pdf

United States Attorney, Southern District of New York. (2004, February 26). "Cyberscammer" sentenced to 30 months for using deceptive Internet names to mislead minors to X-rated sites. U.S. Department of Justice, Computer Crime & Intellectual Property. http://www.justice.gov /criminal/cybercrime/zuccariniSent.htm

United States Attorney, Southern District of Ohio. (2006, January 19). Dayton man pleads guilty to sexual exploitation crimes involving minors. U.S. Department of Justice, Computer Crime & Intellectual Property Section. http://www.justice.gov/criminal/cybercrime/millerPlea.htm

United States Attorney's Office, Middle District of Florida. (2010, April 30). Brevard man pleads guilty to producing child pornography. Federal Bureau of Investigation Tampa. http://tampa .fbi.gov/dojpressrel/pressrel10/ta043010.htm

U.S. Department of Justice. (2010, January). AMBER alert timeline. http://www.ojp.usdoj.gov/newsroom/pdfs/amberchronology.pdf

U.S. Department of Justice. (2010, March 16). Wheaton nanny arrested for distribution of child pornography. Federal Bureau of Investigation Chicago. http://chicago.fbi.gov/pressrel/pressrel10 /cg032610.htm

U.S. Department of Justice. (n.d.). Dru Sjodin national sex offender public website. http://www
.nsopw.gov/Core/Conditions.aspx?AspxAutoDetectCookieSupport=1

Walsh, B. (1993). The law enforcement response to child sexual abuse cases. *Journal of Child Sexual
Abuse, 2,* 117–121.

Winterfield, A. P., & Sakagawa, T. (2003). *Investigation models for child abuse and neglect: Collaboration
with law enforcement.* Englewood, CO: American Humane Association.

Working Group on Unlawful Conduct on the Internet. (1999, August 5). Appendix C: Online child
pornography, child luring, and related offenses. http://www.cybercrime.gov/append.htm

Wortley, R., & Smallbone, S. (2006, May). Child pornography on the Internet. U.S. Department
of Justice, Office of Community Oriented Policing Services, Problem-Oriented Guides Series
No. 41. http://www.cops.usdoj.gov/files/RIC/Publications/e04062000.pdf

Chapter 11

Agents of the Courts: Roles and Perspectives

Child maltreatment cases are heard in both family and criminal courts. In some circumstances, a prosecutor may decide to press criminal charges when child maltreatment occurs. A prosecuting attorney is responsible for prosecuting all criminal violations on behalf of the state or county for which he or she is appointed or elected. Ideally, prosecutors should be trained to handle crimes against children in general, and child abuse in particular. In other circumstances, a prosecutor may decide not to pursue a case that is currently being handled in family (or dependency) courts. This decision, however, may not serve the best interests of the child. It is important for prosecutors to consider the impact on the child, his or her parent or parents (particularly when one or both are accused of maltreatment), and the subsequent treatment of the child during the process when criminal charges against a suspect are pursued (Melton & Limber, 1989; Schroeder, Gordon, & Hawk, 1983). Generally, prosecutors decide a case on the basis of whether they actually have sufficient evidence to win that case. If the prosecutor decides to start criminal proceedings against the alleged offending parents or guardians, the family courts and criminal courts often hear the case simultaneously.

The types of cases that are heard in criminal courts are those involving extreme cases of physical abuse and neglect that resulted in death, long-term trauma, or permanent injuries, as well as cases of sexual abuse. A criminal case is initiated by the state, and the burden of proof is then on the state to prove that a defendant (the individual charged with a crime) is guilty beyond a reasonable doubt (the highest standard of proof). Criminal law deals with public offenses—that is, actions that are harmful to society as a whole. These actions are prohibited by law. Individuals who violate criminal law are assigned a punishment, which may consist of a fine given to the court, community service, probation, a term of incarceration in a penal institution (such as a jail or prison), or capital punishment (i.e., the death penalty).

This chapter examines the prosecutor's decision to pursue a case and the critical issues that arise in child eyewitness testimony and abuse investigations from the perspective of agents of the court. First, this chapter explores prosecutorial discretion. It then considers factors that play a role in the decision to prosecute, considering, in particular, a victim's credibility and competency and the availability of corroborative evidence in a child sexual abuse case. It further covers the manner in which children are prepared for trial and the impact of a trial on children. Finally, this chapter analyzes the experiences of the child in the courtroom. Special emphasis is placed on expert testimony, children's testimony, hearsay evidence, the use of videotaped interviews in the courtroom in lieu of the live testimony of a child, and the testimony of a child victim given via closed-circuit television.

Prosecutorial Discretion: Plea Bargaining and Case Attrition

Child abuse cases should be investigated and prosecuted by specially trained prosecutors. The National Center for Prosecution of Child Abuse was created by the American Prosecutors Research Institute to do just that: to improve the investigation and prosecution of child abuse cases. It provides expert training and legal assistance to investigators and prosecutors tasked with handling criminal child abuse cases.

The prosecutor should proceed first by making an in-depth review of the initial report of abuse, for the purposes of determining the types and number of crimes that have occurred in the case, identifying individuals within the case and their roles, obtaining the school records of the victim, retrieving and reviewing evidence related to the case, and conducting criminal history checks for the suspects and witnesses in the case. The prosecutor should also contact child protective services (CPS) to determine whether CPS has made contact with the child.

The prosecutor's next responsibility is to review any evidence of child abuse and to request any additional information from the police, if necessary, that will provide clarity regarding the decision of whether to move forward with the charges. Types of information that are sought by prosecutors to make a determination as to whether to initiate prosecution include the location of the abuse; when the abuse occurred; what the victim was wearing; what the offender was wearing; whether any clothes were removed during maltreatment (if clothes were removed, then which clothes must be specified); the frequency of the abuse; the length of time over which the abuse occurred; the location of other members of the family at the time of the abuse; anything that the offender might have said to the child; if the offender talked to the child about not disclosing the abuse; whether the child disclosed the abuse to anyone; and, if the abuse was disclosed, to whom was it disclosed and what was the person's reaction (e.g., statements, questions, emotional responses). In particular, for a child's disclosure of sexual abuse, the prosecutor examines the interview to determine whether the child's sexual knowledge is beyond that expected for his or her age and developmental stage.

Prosecutors have discretion to drop a case, reject a case, dismiss charges against an offender, or *nolle prosequi* (in which the prosecutor enters on the record to the court that he or she will not process the case any further). Prosecutors also have broad discretion in several other areas, such as which charges, if any, to bring forward; whether to offer a plea bargain; and which recommendations to make on sentencing. Two major forms of prosecutorial discretionary decision making are explored here: plea bargaining and case attrition. Plea bargaining is the process whereby the defendant agrees to plead guilty to an existing charge or to a lesser charge in exchange for a concession on the part of the prosecution, ranging from a more lenient sentence to dropping of the charges. Case attrition occurs when individuals have been arrested, but their cases do not go to trial. In this situation, a prosecutor makes the decision that there is no probable cause to pursue any formal court action against the alleged perpetrator of child maltreatment. Attrition additionally occurs in various ways, including arrests that law enforcement agencies do not present for prosecution, arrests made that are declined by the prosecutor for prosecution, and charges filed and cases taken to court that are later dismissed by the judge or in which the suspect is acquitted.

Certain scholars, such as Murray (1989), define attrition as including only those instances of the initial screening of cases and their dismissal; that is, their definition is limited to the initial decision not to prosecute the case or forward it for further action in the criminal justice system. When prosecution does not occur in rejected cases, sometimes other informal sanctions are implemented instead. Examples of informal dispositions for nonprosecuted cases include removing the alleged perpetrator out of the home; removing the child from the home; placing the victim in foster care; obtaining a restraining order against the suspected perpetrator; providing the victim with counseling; mandating that the perpetrator receive counseling and treatment; and, if the offender is a parent, having the nonoffending parent separate from the offending parent and banning the offending parent's visitation rights with that child (Murray, 1988).

Deciding to Prosecute

Successful convictions of perpetrators of child sexual abuse are important because they remove the offenders from the community, thereby preventing them from engaging in similar conduct with another child (at the very least during the duration of their incarceration); acknowledge publicly that harm was done to the victim and his or her family; hold the perpetrator accountable for his or her crimes; and encourage other victims and their families to report crimes and to cooperate with the prosecution. However, studies have shown that the majority of reported cases of abuse are not pursued in court (e.g., Berliner & Barbieri, 1984; Joa & Edelson, 2004; Murray, 1989; Parkinson, Shrimpton, Swanston, O'Toole, & Oates, 2002). Why does this occur? There are many reasons why cases that have been substantiated by initial investigations of CPS workers might be dropped at later stages of the criminal justice process.

The main reason why cases are dropped is due to the lack of uniformity on the substantiation of abuse. Particularly, in regards to child abuse cases, CPS workers, law enforcement personnel, mental health professionals, prosecutors, and others involved tend to substantiate abuse differently. Studies have shown that in only a minority of cases substantiated by health professionals, and where the offenders' identity was known, have charges been pursued and a conviction obtained against an offender (Parkinson et al., 2002). What is disconcerting is that the same level of proof for substantiation of abuse is not required for those outside the criminal justice system. It is not surprising, then, that cases initially deemed as substantiating abuse do not proceed to prosecution or conviction.

Berliner and Barbieri (1984) have suggested that child sexual abuse cases are difficult to prosecute for four reasons:

1. The evidence of abuse often depends on how believable the child's testimony is. This credibility reflects not only on the age of the child, but also the competency of the child to testify in court.

2. Many individuals believe that sexual abuse should be dealt with outside the criminal justice system. Specifically, they believe that sexual abuse is a mental health issue and should be treated therapeutically instead of punitively.

3. Some people believe that a child is further victimized during court proceedings.

4. Prosecutors are reluctant to pursue cases that rely solely on the testimony of the child without corroborating evidence.

Some members of society believe that other forms of maltreatment, such as emotional abuse, psychological abuse, and neglect, should be dealt with as mental health issues and that offenders should be given both treatment and punishment. Alternatively, some people may prefer that these suspects be dealt with in family courts. Of the many reasons why cases are not prosecuted, two of them are explored further here: the victim's credibility and competency and a lack of corroborating evidence.

Victim's Credibility and Competency

Murray (1989) noted that the age and maturity of the victim play major roles in the decision of a prosecutor to charge a suspect with child abuse. Research has shown that of the cases referred to the prosecution, the ones most likely to be tried in court are those in which the child victim is in middle childhood rather than early childhood (Joa & Edelson, 2004; Stroud, Martens, & Barker, 2000). Another factor that affects the legal outcome of a child abuse case is the perceived credibility of the child as a witness (Fivush, Peterson, & Schwarzmueller, 2002; Joa & Edelson, 2004; Perry & Wrightsman, 1991).

The competency of the child to participate in a trial and the child's credibility as a witness are two different issues. As shown by Perry and Wrightsman (1991, as cited in Joa & Edelson, 2004), the rendering of a child as a competent witness to stand trial does not ensure that the child will be perceived as credible by the judge and jury. Young children may not pass the competency exams or assessment, and many of them may not understand the role of the trier of fact[1] (Saywitz, Goodman, & Lyon, 2002). Accordingly, young children

---

[1] The trier of fact (i.e., the finder of fact) is the person or persons (e.g., judge and or jury) who determine the facts of a case.

may not be able to testify. Cases that are often referred for prosecution typically involve witnesses in middle childhood (Stroud et al., 2000) because they are more likely than those in early childhood to comprehend the role of the court as a trier of fact and to pass the competency exam, which allows them to testify (Joa & Edelson, 2004; also see Saywitz et al., 2002).

Lack of Corroborative Evidence

Cases are often rejected due to issues with witnesses and evidence (Murray, 1988). Some of the challenges that prosecutors encounter when dealing with child abuse cases include identifying the suspect(s) in the case, the date of the disclosure, inconsistent statements by the victim or witness, uncooperative victims (e.g., children who refuse to disclose or subsequently recant their abuse[2]), victims who seek to protect the perpetrator, incomplete investigations, lack of physical and biological evidence of the crime, and situations in which the parents or legal guardians are the suspects. Given these challenges, a major reason why child abuse cases do not proceed toward prosecution is that the offender cannot be identified and arrested. Moreover, when parents and/or children are unwilling to cooperate with police in a case of extra-familial abuse, the prosecutor is unable to pursue the case effectively. Furthermore, an investigation cannot be completed when the family and the child have left the state or when the parents or the child do not want to proceed with pressing charges. For cases in which the parents or the child refuses to press charges, the prosecutor cannot proceed with the case, as the child's statement on maltreatment or abuse is critical for proceedings.

As the testimony provided by the child's interview is key for the case, it is imperative that the initial (and any subsequent) interview to be conducted by a skilled interviewer. This requirement not only bolsters and strengthens a prosecutor's case, but also enhances the credibility of the child witness. The questions asked and the answers given during a forensic interview form the basis for whether a prosecutor decides to pursue a case. Several high-profile cases have not resulted in conviction or have been overturned for exactly this reason—improper interviewing tainted the child's testimony.

Suspect confessions are sought in child abuse cases. There are many benefits to obtaining an offender's confession of the crime. In child abuse cases, they confirm the allegations, facilitate a speedy criminal justice response, and lessen the burden on the victim to provide testimony, particularly in open court (Lippert, Cross, Jones, & Walsh, 2010). Nonetheless, even if a confession is not obtained, the interview with the suspect is important. The narrative given often provides details that help the prosecution in its investigation. During the interview, any denials made by the suspect should be confronted. Some of the best approaches involve recording the victim and the defendant interviews, then examining both to find any inconsistencies offered by the victim, witness, or suspect, while addressing each of them accordingly.

Courts and the police place greater emphasis on the need for corroborative evidence in child abuse cases and on the credibility of witnesses in the cases. In many instances, cases

---

[2] Recanting means that the victim denies the abuse occurred, often stating that he or she made a mistake or lied.

have been dismissed for lack of evidence; this rationale entails either the provision of an insufficiently descriptive statement by the child (which is especially likely when children are younger than 7 years old) or the lack of corroborative evidence. One difficulty encountered in finding evidence of the crime is establishing proof beyond a reasonable doubt, which is the required standard in criminal law. It is rare that someone other than the victim witnesses child sexual abuse. Indeed, this crime is usually committed outside of the purview of witnesses and rarely leaves any visible or indisputable traces of evidence. Consequently, corroborating evidence to support the victim's report of the crime is often lacking.

In addition, the motivations of the victims can be affected by loyalty to or fear of the alleged perpetrator, further complicating cases. Sometimes children will refuse to testify. At other times, they have been intimidated or threatened by the perpetrators (or family members), resulting in subsequent refusal to testify in court or recanting of the abuse. If the perpetrator is a family member or a friend of the family, it may be quite difficult for the child to talk about the abuse, especially if the child or parents have a special affiliation with the offender. However, difficulties in proceeding with the child testifying may arise even when the perpetrator is not a member or friend of the family, simply due to social stigma (e.g., embarrassment). In fact, research has shown that in most cases, irrespective of who the perpetrator is, it is difficult for children to disclose abuse (Back, Gustafsson, & Berterö, 2013; Back, Gustafsson, Larsson, & Berterö, 2011).

Corroborative evidence can be obtained through suspect confessions, witness interviews, medical records, school records, and crime scene evidence. This type of evidence includes "developmentally unusual sexual behavior by the victim, unusual psychological symptoms (e.g., severe nightmares), medical evidence, eyewitnesses to the alleged crime, witnesses who can confirm some aspect of the victim's testimony, offender confessions, physical or material evidence, or an additional complaint against the offender that supports the victim's testimony" (Walsh, Jones, Cross, & Lippert 2010, p. 438; see also Lanning, 2002; Myers, 2005). The existence of corroborative evidence increases the likelihood that the offender will plead guilty or will accept a negotiated plea agreement, and decreases the chance that the child will have to testify.

In many situations, little, if any, corroborative evidence exists, so that the case boils down to the child's word against the word of the perpetrator. Corroborative evidence confirms or adds to a child's statement, such as a sperm identified as belonging to the perpetrator found inside the child's vagina, mouth, or anus (Veith, 1999). Studies have also shown that cases with a corroborating witness were more likely to be brought to court (Walsh et al., 2010). Abuse usually occurs in private, so corroboration is needed because the victim is often the only witness to the crime. Additionally, disclosure of abuse is often delayed, which further reduces the probability of obtaining physical evidence of the crime. Moreover, as the offender typically denies the child's claim of abuse, undue burden and pressure are placed on the child to ensure that his or her account of the crime is consistent and reliable because it is the only piece of evidence used to prove the case.

Studies confirm that "evidence besides child disclosure improves the chance of successful prosecution. Most of the research in this area has focused on medical evidence, although such evidence of sexual abuse is rare" (Heger, Ticson, Velasquez, & Bernier, 2002, as cited in Walsh et al., 2010, p. 438). Although some studies have shown that medical evidence introduced into a case increased the likelihood of prosecution (e.g., Bradshaw & Marks, 1990), other studies have failed to confirm this relationship (Cross, De Vos, & Whitcomb, 1994; Whitcomb et al., 1994). By contrast, cases with medical evidence, physical evidence, eyewitness testimony, and hearsay evidence are most likely to be accepted for prosecution (Cross et al., 1994).

Overall, those cases that are often accepted for prosecution tend to be characterized by the presence of strong evidence (Freyd, 2003; Murphy, 2003; Walsh et al., 2010). For example, Miller and Rubin (2009, as cited in Adams, 2009) found that cases with lower rates of prosecution often involved younger victims, no medical findings of abuse, an offender who lives in the home, and an unsupportive nonoffending parent or guardian. In addition, a study conducted by Walsh, Jones, Cross, and Lippert (2010, as cited in Back et al., 2013) revealed that cases in which an offender confessed, the child disclosed the abuse, evidence existed of the abuse, and other charges existed against the offender were more likely to be brought to court. The same study indicated that even when strong evidence did not exist (e.g., physical evidence was lacking and no confessions were obtained from the suspect), cases in which a corroborating witness was available were most likely to proceed to court. Furthermore, research suggests that child distress during courtroom proceedings is lessened when corroborating evidence of child sexual abuse is available (Goodman et al., 1992; Lipovsky, 1994; Walsh et al., 2010).

Trial Preparations

The child must be prepared for court, but by no means is this practice exclusive to child witnesses. Preparation is key to providing testimony that will stand up in court. Consequently, all witnesses who are scheduled to testify should be prepared for this experience; this is true even for expert witnesses, first responders, and reporters of the abuse. The attorney will prepare the witness for trial through the following activities, among other things:

- Discussing the witness' testimony with him or her
- Reviewing the witness' notes or reports, and highlighting any inconsistencies between those documents and the witness' oral testimony of the events, evidence, procedures used, observations, and/or opinions
- Discussing the possible line of questioning that the witness can expect from both parties
- Rehearsing witness testimony through, for example, role playing[3]

If the witness has never testified in court before this case (as is usually true for children), then the attorney must explain the pretrial and courtroom proceedings to this individual. Children must become familiar with legal proceedings.

It is important to reduce the number of statements a child makes concerning his or her alleged abuse. As the number of times that the child discloses his or her abuse to others

---

[3] Richard C. Wydick, *The Ethics of Witness Coaching,* 17 CARDOZO L. REV. 1 (1995), 4-5. Reprinted by permission.

increases, the likelihood of the statement becoming contaminated (and inconsistent, and hence unreliable) also increases (Ceci & Bruck, 1995; Lanning, 2002). Research has shown that the risk of contaminating a child's testimony can be decreased by limiting the number of times a child discloses the abuse (Ghetti, Alexander, & Goodman, 2002). This, in turn, can limit the child's stress during the proceedings.

How is a child prepared for court? The child is first informed of all of the individuals (e.g., judge, jury, prosecutor, defense attorney, bailiff) involved in courtroom proceedings and their roles in the process. The child is also taken to a courtroom to familiarize the child with this environment. The location of each individual within the court is pointed out. Next, the procedures followed during the trial are explained. This can be demonstrated via role playing to walk the child through each step of the courtroom proceedings. Courtroom-specific behaviors of the prosecutor, defense, and judges should be explained as well. For instance, the child should be informed of what it means for the prosecutor or defense to say, "objection." In addition, the examination and cross-examination process should be explained. The child should be instructed to dress appropriately and to tell the truth at all times during the proceedings. Several tools are "available to familiarize children with courtroom layout (e.g., court models) and procedures (e.g., videotapes, court notebooks)" (Lipovsky & Stern, 1997, p. 157).

The child should be made aware of the time and date of the courtroom proceedings, as well as when the testimony of the child is expected to occur during those proceedings. Depending on the age of the child, the prosecutor should take into account any times that would not be ideal for a testimony to occur. For example, if a child takes a nap between 1 and 2 P.M., the testimony of the child should ideally be scheduled for the morning. The child and his or her family (except any offending parties in the family) should be informed of the location in which they will wait before they testify.

Additionally, it is important that the prosecutor gains the child's trust. The preparation of a child witness can help "enhance the ability of the fact finders to make an accurate determination of the truth, improving the quality of the evidence that the child provides" (Saywitz & Snyder, 1993, as cited in Lipovsky & Stern, 1997, p. 152). Finally, the child should have input as to the nature and extent of his or her involvement in the courtroom process. The input of the child should be considered when determining whether to pursue the case, how to pursue it, and whether a settlement should be negotiated. While the child's input is considered, in reality, it does not dictate the outcome of the case. Ultimately, the final decision lies exclusively with the prosecutor; the victim and his or her family should be made aware of this fact.

In the Courtroom

This section reviews all aspects of the courtroom process, including the role of testimony in prosecution and the implications of interviewing techniques on the stand for witness reliability. The impact of scientific evidence from expert witnesses is also presented.

Finally, research on a jury's understanding and interpretation of the reliability of children's testimony, particularly when various techniques are used (e.g., closed-circuit television) to shield the child from psychological harm, is presented.

Testimony

Testimony is provided either to give an opinion to assist the court in understanding a piece of evidence or to establish a fact that is presented in court. According to the Federal Rule of Evidence 704, ultimate opinion testimony is not automatically objectionable "just because it embraces an ultimate issue." An exception to this is as follows: "In a criminal case, an expert witness must not state an opinion about whether the defendant did or did not have a mental state or condition that constitutes an element of the crime charged or of a defense. Those matters are for the trier of fact alone" (Federal Rule of Evidence 704). Two types of testimony are explored here: expert testimony and the child's testimony.

Expert Testimony

An expert witness can be allowed to testify in child abuse cases. According to Rule 702 of the Federal Rules of Evidence:

> If scientific, technical, or other specialized knowledge will assist the trier of fact to understand the evidence or to determine a fact in issue, a witness qualified as an expert by knowledge, skill, experience, training, or education may testify thereto in the form of an opinion or otherwise, if (1) the testimony is based upon sufficient facts or data, (2) the testimony is the product of reliable principles and methods, and (3) the witness has applied the principles and methods reliably to the facts of the case.

Basically, in this role, the expert witness collects, analyzes, and evaluates evidence and forms an opinion on it. This opinion is then communicated to the court, meaning the judge and/or jury. Expert witnesses are the only witnesses in court who can give their opinion about the case without having been present physically during the crime or civil wrongdoing, or involved in it in any way thereafter. The opinion, however, must be supported by facts. In particular, Rule 703 of the Federal Rules of Evidence states:

> [T]he facts or data in the particular case upon which an expert bases an opinion or inference may be those perceived by or made known to the expert at or before the hearing. If of a type reasonably relied upon by experts in the particular field in forming opinions or inferences upon the subject, the facts or data need not be admissible in evidence in order for the opinion or inference to be admitted.

Moreover, Rule 705 of the Federal Rules of Evidence holds: "The expert may testify in terms of opinion or inference and give reasons therefor[e] without first testifying to the underlying facts or data, unless the court requires otherwise. The expert may in any event be required to disclose the underlying facts or data on cross-examination."

Testimony for the Defense   Expert testimony can be given for the defense and for the prosecution. For the defense, the types of testimony used are as follows:

1. Testimony on improper interviewing techniques
2. Testimony on child suggestibility and memory
3. Admissibility of scientific testimony
4. Credentials and credibility of an expert witness

Testimony on Improper Interviewing Techniques   An expert can "inform jurors about the influence of misleading information on the accuracy of child's self-report" (McAuliff & Kovera, 1998, p. 195). At times, expert testimony has been provided in child abuse cases on the use of anatomically detailed dolls during forensic interviewing. More specifically, sometimes "props" (e.g., regular or anatomically correct dolls and drawings) are used to facilitate the child's accounts of abuse. The dolls/drawings are often used to aid in the discussion of abuse when children do not have the proper vocabulary to explain abuse (Kovera, Levy, Borgida, & Penrod, 1994). Even though some courts have excluded anatomically detailed dolls testimony (e.g., *In re Amber B.*, 1987; *In re Jennifer*, 1988), this type of expert testimony has been admitted in other cases (e.g., *D.A.H. v. G.A.H.*, 1985; *In re Christine C.*, 1987; *In re J.K.*, 1987; *In re Rinesmith*, 1985) (Kovera et al., 1994).

Other than the props used, the court will look at the manner in which the interview was conducted and the questions that were asked. Particularly, the court will look for the following issues (*New Jersey v. Margaret Kelly Michaels*, 1994):

- The failure of law enforcement agents and forensic interviewers to videotape or to record digitally the initial interview with a child witness
- If the interviewer failed to control for outside (e.g., family) influences
- If the interviewer used suggestive questions, pursued only one hypothesis, or otherwise influenced the direction pursued
- If the interviewer was biased or had a preconceived notion that the accused "did it"
- If the interviewer or families engaged in incessant questioning
- The presence of the transmission of suggestion to children (e.g., through the interviewer's or family member's tone of voice and body language)
- The use of positive reinforcement for inculpatory statements
- The use of negative reinforcement or punishment for exculpatory statements
- The use of mild threats, bribes, or cajoling for disclosure
- If the interviewer or the family member vilified the alleged wrongdoers

Without a videotape, audiotape, or digital recording of the interviews of victims and suspects, the defense has the opportunity to attack the reliability and credibility of the investigator or interviewer of the victim or suspect. Despite this occurrence, most police and prosecutors still do not use these means of documenting interviews.

McGough (1995) reported that videotaping confessions does more harm than good, as it often provides defense attorneys with the information they needed to obtain acquittals for offenders. In addition, according to McGough (1995), the videotape could be used to exaggerate a child's inconsistencies in an effort to discredit the child. However, in the interests of justice, it is important to remember that the suppression of information because it may discredit the child cannot be justified. The court must have all relevant evidence and testimony at its disposal. It is up to the trier of fact (or fact finders)—that is, the judge and jury—to determine the reliability of evidence and the credibility of a witness. Besides, expert testimony could be introduced to show that retractions and inconsistencies are typical patterns of reactions by child abuse victims, without such events implying that the child's testimony is unreliable.

Another negative facet of the inclusion of the recordings is that it shifts the focus of the court from the victim's account of the abuse to the interviewer's mistakes. A further argument against recording child accounts of abuse is their potential for release to the press due to their availability. Such recordings have been published in the past, causing embarrassment to both the family and the victim and further victimizing the victim. To prevent this inappropriate use of recordings in the future, protective orders can be sought to preserve their confidentiality.

There are, however, notable benefits to recording interviews (McGough, 1995). One advantage is that this practice decreases the number of interviews and interviewers. Additionally, it motivates interviewers to use proper interview techniques. Moreover, it provides prosecutors with a tool with which to assess the strength of the witnesses' testimony and facilitates decisions on whether to pursue a case.

Some proponents argue that recorded interviews aid in refreshing the child's memory when preparing him or her for their testimony in court. By recording a child's verbal and nonverbal statements, the truthfulness of the child's account of the abuse can be assessed. Finally, other advantages of recording an interview include preserving the questions asked of the child and his or her answers to the questions, the child's account of the incident before his or her memory fades, the child's exact statement and nonverbal behaviors (e.g., demeanor and emotions) during initial disclosure, and the child's appearance at the time of the disclosure (McGough, 2002; Pence & Wilson, 1994).

Testimony on Child Suggestibility and Memory   Experts can testify about research findings on the causes and extent of suggestibility in children and the issues that arise concerning memory, particularly over time, given the length of time between the abuse and trial. "In cases claiming repressed or recovered memory, a defense witness can testify about how false memories can be implanted in children and adults" (Loftus, 1993; Loftus & Hoffman, 1989; Loftus & Ketchman, 1994; Loftus & Rosenwald, 1995; Pezdek & Banks, 1996). Memories can be falsely implanted because of interviewer bias, repeated questioning, repeating misinformation across interviews, source confusion, coercion through emotional tone of interview, coercion through peer pressure, reference to the high status or the power of the interviewer, and stereotype inducement.

Admissibility of Scientific Testimony   Experts "can refute the testimony of a prosecution witness, and, particularly, they can question whether the procedures used by prosecution experts meet the standards for admissibility of scientific testimony specified in" a well-known court case, *Daubert v. Merrell Dow Pharmaceuticals, Inc.* (1993). According to the *Daubert* ruling, four criteria are used to determine the reliability of a particular scientific theory or technique:

1. Testing (Has the method in question undergone empirical testing?)

2. Peer review (Has the method been peer reviewed?)

3. The potential rate of error (What is the error rate in the results produced by the method?)

4. Acceptability (Has the method gained general acceptance in the relevant scientific community?)

The *Daubert* standard requires an independent, judicial assessment of the reliability[4] of the scientific test or evidence. A "reliability assessment does not require, although it does permit, explicit identification of a relevant scientific community and an express determination of a particular degree of acceptance within that community" (*United States v. Downing*, 1985, p. 1238, quoted in *Daubert v. Merrell Dow Pharmaceuticals Inc.*, 1993). Moreover, in *Daubert*, the court ruled that the fact that a theory or technique that has not been subjected to peer review or has not been published does not automatically render the method in question inadmissible. In so doing, the court recognized that the inquiry must be flexible and must focus on the principles and methodology in question.

Credentials and Credibility of an Expert Witness   To establish the competency of a technical or expert witness to stand trial, a thorough examination of that individual's background and credentials is required. This occurs through a process known as *voir dire*.[5] Before an expert witness can provide testimony, he or she must be qualified in the *voir dire* process—a process in which the individual makes statements under oath. To verify that a witness is qualified to provide testimony, the party that is seeking to call the expert as a witness questions him or her. The goal of this line of questioning is to validate (or refute) the background and credentials of the witness.

During this process, the following information about the witness must be verified:

- Name
- Title
- Employment history (positions held, length of positions, and duties in each position)
- Current occupation (or occupations), including the position (or positions) held, duties performed, and length of time in that position (or positions)

---

[4]Reliability concerns when a measure "yields consistent scores or observations of a given phenomenon on different occasions" (Bachman & Schutt, 2003, p. 72).

[5]*Voir dire* is French. It means "to speak the truth."

- Any specializations in the current field of employment (e.g., in the computer forensics field, an individual may specialize in network forensics)
- Employment address
- Education including any degrees held, in which subject(s) and from which college(s) and/or university (or universities)
- Licenses (from which states in the United States and in which fields)
- Specialized training
- Board certification as a specialist in the field
- Any teaching or lectures given, including the date and place where the teaching or lectures took place
- Publications in the individual's field
- Cases where the individual served as a technical or expert witness in pretrial or court proceedings
- Membership in professional societies, organizations, or associations, and which position an individual held (or holds) in them
- Honors, awards, or any other special achievements in the individual's field
- Consulting the individual may have provided to private and/or public agencies

Every aspect of the background of the potential expert witness should be reviewed, beginning with the individual's résumé or curriculum vitae (CV). All of the information included in this document should be verified. An investigator should contact prior employers to determine, among other things:

- If the potential witness actually worked there and, if so, the length of employment
- The position or duties performed by the individual during his or her employment

This verification process is important because some individuals may truthfully identify previous workplaces, but exaggerate their responsibilities or positions there. Both the educational institutions and the degrees earned should also be verified. This can be done by contacting the educational institution and enquiring as to the individual's educational background. Online searches can also be conducted to verify an individual's education background. For instance, the National Student Clearinghouse website (http://studentclearinghouse.com/) can be visited for student degree and enrollment verification. Such websites and public records searches can also provide information about the individual's aliases, maiden names, relatives, criminal record, property, military service (if any), address history, phone numbers, and email address (or addresses). All licenses, professional certificates, and training listed should be checked. This can be done by contacting the institutions, agencies, or organizations that provided them. Professional license information may also be found on websites (free or for a fee) such as Black Book Online (http://blackbookonline.info/).

Moreover, publications should be verified. If the individual has published an article, to search for this publication, the investigator can go directly to the publisher's website and browse for the article in question. If the publication is a book, an online search for it would suffice. Chances are such a search would produce numerous results. Alternatively, the publisher's website could be searched. Other essential sources with which to check published material include the U.S. Copyright Office, the Library of Congress catalog, LexisNexis, HeinOnline, and Westlaw. Additional sites where publications can be found include Amazon.com, Barnes & Noble, and other bookstores.

Insight into the personal and professional lives of the expert witness is sought as well. Some information on these individuals may be found on social and business networking sites (e.g., Twitter, Facebook, LinkedIn). Use of an online search engine (e.g., Google, Bing) could produce information on many of these items, such as education, employment, and publications. Moreover, interviews with the witness should be conducted, both over the phone and in person.

Prior cases in which experts have testified should be checked to reveal, for example, any existing biases or challenges to the testimony they provided, their methods, or their qualifications as experts. The prior testimony (or testimonies) of potential witnesses should also be reviewed to reveal the strengths and weaknesses of these individuals. Legal research websites and self-reports from technical and expert witnesses are inadequate tools for vetting[6] witnesses, so relying solely on these strategies means would-be employers of these experts are not doing their due diligence.[7] One very important, yet sometimes overlooked, informational resource that seeks to aid in verification of credentials is the *Daubert Tracker*. According to its website, this database serves to provide information about challenged expert witnesses, their disciplines and areas of expertise, and the results of these challenges. This database holds information on all reported and numerous unreported state and federal cases in which the methodology or qualifications of a testifying expert witness has been challenged. One can easily search this website using the name of the technical or expert witness.

Attorneys should pay special attention to research regarding whether the potential witness has publications or has provided testimony that conflict with the case at hand. They should also research whether a prospective witness provides testimony for only one particular party (e.g., always testifies for the defense in a criminal trial), illustrating the expert's bias. In contrast, impartial witnesses will testify on behalf of either party in criminal or civil courts.

The interrogation and background check to which the witness is subjected is "quite intense, because acceptance of an unqualified expert (or conversely, exclusion of a qualified expert) is considered grounds for overturning the verdict in a higher court" (Girard, 2008, p. 52). A case in point is the experience of Carolyn Ridling. In 2008, she lied under oath by claiming that she was a certified Sexual Assault Nurse Examiner by the Texas Attorney General's office (Garsee, 2008). Ridling had been certified as a Sexual Assault Nurse Examiner at one point, but her certification had expired on April 18, 2004. As a result, the cases in which which she had testified after the date her certificate expired were reevaluated.

---

[6]Vetting involves researching a person's background to determine the veracity of his or her credentials.

[7]Due diligence refers to systematic research conducted to acquire valid and reliable information with which to make an informed decision on the issue at hand.

Based on the authenticity of the information provided by the potential expert witness and a thorough review of his or her background and qualifications, a decision is made as to whether an individual is competent to serve as a technical or expert witness. This decision is then communicated to the court by the hiring attorney.

The opposing party also has the opportunity to cross-examine the expert witness during the *voir dire* process to highlight any weaknesses in the witness's education or experience. In so doing, the attorney may attack the credibility of the individual providing the testimony. Primarily, the attorney will attack the credentials, methods used, and any oral or written statements made by the witness. Often, the opposing party's attorney (or attorneys) seeks to attack the qualifications of the expert rather than his or her methods or interpretation of the results. The Federal Rules of Evidence include guidelines that explain how an individual's credibility may be attacked. In particular, Rule 607 states that "the credibility of a witness may be attacked by any party, including the party calling the witness." To undermine the witness's credibility, the attorney may provide evidence in support of the untruthfulness of the character of the witness. Evidence showing the truthful character of the witness may be admitted only after this type of attack has occurred (Rule 608(a), Federal Rules of Evidence).

Testimony for Prosecution   For the prosecution, the following types of testimony are most common:

1. Social framework testimony

2. Syndromal evidence testimony

Social Framework Testimony   Social framework testimony uses the "general conclusions from social science research in determining factual issues in a specific case" (Walker & Monahan, 1987, p. 570). According to Berliner (1998, as cited in Fulero & Wrightsman, 2009, p. 192), examples of such testimony include "the nature of sexual abuse of children, the reactions of victims, and the memory abilities and suggestibility of children."

Syndromal Evidence Testimony   One controversial form of expert testimony is testimony on syndrome evidence (e.g., medical and psychological syndromes), especially testimony on child sexual abuse accommodation syndrome (CSAAS) (Bulkley, 1987; Melton & Limber, 1989). CSAAS was first described by Dr. Roland Summit (1983). According to Summit (1983), this syndrome can be broken down into two preconditions—secrecy and helplessness—and three sequential contingencies—entrapment and accommodation; delayed, conflicted, and unconvincing disclosure; and retraction (Gitlin, 2008). Some of the purported indicators of CSAAS have been observed in children who suffer from psychological disorders, but have not been abused.

Existing clinical and empirical studies have failed to establish a universal or uniform response to sexual abuse. Instead, victims may exhibit either no unusual behaviors or a variety of behaviors, including regression, aggression, withdrawal, eating disorders, school-related problems, changes in appearance or dress, nightmares, age-inappropriate sexual behavior, and bedwetting (Underwager & Wakefield, 1991). Among the emotional reactions observed in abused children are unusual or excessive fears, anger, anxiety, disgust, depression, post-traumatic stress disorder (PTSD) symptoms, embarrassment, sexual arousal, and reluctance to disclose. In this regard, experts have provided testimony on the emotional and behavioral impact that sexual abuse had on the child. Some courts have asserted that there is no need for such testimony as it is common knowledge—particularly the point that children may not always report abuse after it occurs because they may be embarrassed and afraid.

Indeed, none of the behaviors identified as part of CSAAS occur solely in sexual abuse cases. A defense attorney, therefore, may cross-examine the expert to vitiate (i.e., impair the quality of) some of the arguments given that young children in the general population also exhibit similar behaviors for other reasons. Nonetheless, one should not consider the absence of behaviors as indicating false reporting of sexual abuse (Lamb, 1994).

CSAAS testimony meets the court requirements of validity, reliability, and relevance; however, as Gitlin (2008) argues, there are instances in which it should be excluded because it might be unfairly prejudicial to the defendant. U.S. courts have varied in their admittance of this type of evidence and the reasons why such testimony can be used, with some judges allowing it[8] and others not.[9]

Courts have similarly varied in their admittance of expert testimony that provides an opinion as to whether the behavior of the child is consistent with the characteristics and behaviors of abused children.[10] During this testimony, experts are not permitted to offer an opinion regarding whether the child in a case has been abused. Indeed, experts' opinions that a child has been sexually abused or has been a victim of abuse have been deemed inadmissible as evidence.[11] Experts' opinions that children are credible or are telling the truth have also largely been excluded.[12] Overall, a review of the jurisprudence reveals that it is more likely than not that this type of evidence is excluded when the prosecutor seeks to show that the child fits the profile and was abused. By contrast, the defense, when this type of testimony is admissible in court, tries to demonstrate how the child does not fit the prescribed profile.

---

[8] Some cases that have allowed the testimony include *Keri v. State*, 1986; *People v. Gray*, 1986; *People v. Luna*, 1988; *People v. Payan*, 1985; *State v. Kim*, 1982; *State v. Myers*, 1984; *People v. Eminger*, 1989; *Powell v. State*, 1987; *Allison v. State*, 1986; *State v. Hall*, 1986; *People v. Keindl*, 1986; *People v. Grady*, 1986; *State v. Bachman*, 1989; and *Scadden v. State*, 1987.

[9] Some cases that have excluded the testimony include *In re Amber B.*, 1987; *Johnson v. State*, 1987; *Lantrip v. Commonwealth*, 1986; *People v. Bledsoe*, 1984; *People v. Roscoe*, 1985; *People v. Leon*, 1989; *People v. Bowker*, 1988; *State v. Milbradt*, 1988; and *State v. Hudnall*, 1987.

[10] Cases permitting such testimony include *U.S. v. Azure*, 1986; *People v. Ronovost*, 1987; *Ward v. State*, 1988; *People v. Server*, 1986; *State v. Dana*, 1987; *State v. Garden*, 1987; *Stale v. McCoy*, 1987; and *In re Nicole V.*, 1987. Cases excluding such testimony include *Russell v. State*, 1986; *Lantrip v. Commonwealth*, 1986; *Bussey v. Commonwealth*, 1985; *State v. Lawrence*, 1988; and *State v. Jensen*, 1987.

[11] See, for example, *Johnson v. State*, 1987; *In re Amber B.*, 1987; *In re Christine C.*, 1987; and *State v. Haseltine*, 1984. Some cases have allowed such testimony. See, for example, *Seering v. Dep't Social Serv.*, 1987; *State v. Hester*, 1988; *Townsend v. State*, 1987; *In re Nicole V.*, 1987; *In re Donna K.*, 1987; *State v. Bailey*, 1988; and *State v. Edward Charles L.*, 1990.

[12] A few cases have allowed such testimony. See, for example, *State v. Butler*, 1986; *State v. Myers*, 1984; *State v. Geyman*, 1986; and *Dunham v. State*, 1988. One of the major rulings for allowing expert testimony on a child's credibility is *State v. Kim*, 1982. This case was overruled in *State v. Batagan*, 1990.

While most U.S. courts generally prohibit the use of syndrome testimony as proof of child abuse, a few courts have been exceptions to this rule. In Indiana, courts have held that "it is permissible to admit evidence of child sexual abuse syndrome to show that sexual contact occurred" (*Turney v. State*, 2001). Cases in which this testimony was used to prove that the child was sexually abused have been reversed. For instance, in *People v. Knupp* (1992), an expert testified about the symptoms associated with CSAAS. The expert then stated that the symptoms were exhibited by the children who claimed to have been sexually abused. The court in *Knupp* found this testimony to be improper. In *Commonwealth v. Dunkle* (1992), the Supreme Court of Pennsylvania held that the syndrome evidence should not be included for any purpose. Specifically, after surveying existing literature on CSAAS, the court concluded that "there is no one classical or typical personality profile for abused children" (*Commonwealth v. Dunkle*, 1992, p. 832).

Often this type of evidence is used to explain any inconsistencies in the child's behavior with respect to the veracity of the child's account of the situation. Testimony involving this syndrome should focus on a specific myth or misconception that is suggested by admitted evidence (Gitlin, 2008; Summit, 1983). Indeed, this type of testimony is often used by some courts to counter certain commonly held myths or misconceptions about sexually abused children (e.g., that delayed reporting is inconsistent with the behavior of a child who has truly been sexually abused).

CSAAS testimony is provided to help shed light on aspects of the victim's behavior that might be confusing to the fact finder. The most common use of this type of testimony is to explain why a child delayed reporting the abuse, particularly in cases where multiple incidents occurred. Expert testimony is also important when a child gives conflicting or confusing reports about his or her abuse or retracts his or her statement of the abuse by the alleged perpetrator. In addition, this type of testimony is often used when the child's credibility is attacked (e.g., in Oklahoma, Illinois, and Iowa). In *People v. Bowker* (1988), the court limited the use of such testimony to its inclusion only to rebut claims of the child's lack of credibility. Certain states allow the introduction of CSAAS testimony before the credibility of a child has been attacked (e.g., New York, District of Columbia, Kansas, and New Hampshire). Additionally, rehabilitative testimony may be admitted in court. In *State v. Michaels* (1993), the court concluded that the appropriate use of this type of testimony is for rehabilitative uses only; it is not allowed as a diagnostic tool to detect sexual abuse.

Jurors' Perspectives on Expert Testimony in Child Abuse Cases A study conducted by Kovera et al. (1994) sought to determine whether different types of expert evidence exert a differential influence on jurors' judgments. The findings of this study revealed that jurors were less influenced by expert testimony based on probability data, such as syndromal evidence, than by expert testimony focused on the case history (e.g., witness credibility and the use of anatomically detailed dolls evidence). Moreover, medical testimony is important in cases involving child sexual abuse where penetration has been alleged. Jurors look at medical experts as individuals tasked with introducing unbiased, clinical facts relevant to a case (Geltz, 1994). If a victim reports sexual abuse, most protocols recommend that the

---

Box 11-1 The Role of Psychologists in the Court

Psychologists' most common role in legal proceedings related to child maltreatment has been in the provision of dispositional evidence in criminal or civil hearings. Psychologists may also become involved in such cases when the court appoints them as clinical evaluators to assess whether a child or family needs services. At the conclusion of trial proceedings, they may execute the court's dispositional orders requiring therapy for particular individuals involved in the process.

Psychologists have several roles in maltreatment abuse cases. In the past, these roles were usually limited to the beginning and the end of the criminal justice process. For example, psychologists may initiate an investigation by reporting suspected maltreatment. They also have testified regarding which past experiences children of varying ages were able to relate and how questions used in the interview may distort recall of these experiences. Other than that, historically they had little, if any, role in the investigation of child maltreatment cases. Often, such cases remain exclusively in the hands of the CPS and law enforcement agencies.

---

victim be examined as quickly as possible if the disclosure of abuse has occurred within 72 hours of the incident. In fact, this rule pertains to child sexual abuse cases because biological evidence (e.g., semen) can best be obtained within this time frame. The type of information that can be obtained from a medical exam includes identification of sexually transmitted diseases (e.g., syphilis, gonorrhea, and HIV) and physical and genetic findings (e.g., absence of a hymen, hymen disruption, healed hymen, abnormal hymenal opening, age of the child, and scars). Nevertheless, it is important to note that most sexually abused children have normal medical physical examinations.

Child Testimony

Professionals have been concerned with the distress caused by children and adolescents having to testify against their perpetrator in open court. Children's ability to provide testimony is affected by a variety of issues (London, Bruck, Ceci, & Shuman, 2005; Lyon & Ahern, 2011; Malloy, Lyon, & Quas, 2007). First, children's expectations associated with disclosure of maltreatment, such as being believed and supported in testifying against the perpetrator, have a big impact on their ability to testify. Second, children's concern that the accused will be found "not guilty," and then will be able to hurt the child again, influences testifying. Third, the child may be embarrassed and shamed into recanting, either by the family or by the suspect.

The main reason for long delays before children reveal their abuse is that these victims have been coerced by the offenders in a variety of ways: blaming the victims for their own maltreatment, making them promise not to tell, giving them warnings, or threatening them and their loved ones with adverse consequences if the maltreatment is revealed (Christiansen & Blake, 1990; Kaufman et al., 1998; Lang & Frenzel, 1988). Many child witnesses fear confronting the defendant, making their testifying stressful to them and reducing their ability to provide responses to questions (Dezwirek-Sas, 1992; Goodman et al., 1992).

Unfortunately, children forced to engage with the criminal justice system often do not have support to meet their needs. Children might be at risk when they go home with their parents during and after a hearing. Also, parents may try to exert their influence over children and have them recant their testimony or encourage them to refuse to testify. Moreover, if one or more of the parents or family members were the abusers, the child may be subjected to punishment for wanting to testify. Furthermore, children may be revictimized through their participation in the court proceedings. That is, if the child's credibility is attacked in the court and the offender is not convicted, the child may experience additional trauma.

Criminal court proceedings in child abuse cases tend to be a very lengthy process (Walsh, Lippert, Cross, Maurice, & Davison, 2008). In addition, court appearances place a great strain on the child victim (Goodman, Quas, Bulkley, & Shapiro, 1999; Lipovsky, 1994; National Center for Prosecution of Child Abuse, 2004; Walsh et al., 2010). The general practice is to have the victim describe the abuse he or she suffered in front of the abuser and other individuals present in the courtroom. Often, child victims break down and become unable to give their testimony. Certain factors have been identified as reducing the level of stress in child witnesses. More specifically, research has identified that children's awareness of court proceedings (Sas, Hurley, Austin, & Wolfe, 1991), the existence of corroborating evidence of abuse, a small number of appearances of the child witnesses in court, and support from a nonoffending parent or guardian may reduce the level of stress children experience in the courtroom (Goodman et al., 1992, cited in Lipovsky & Stern, 1997). Even though the existing literature largely focuses on the child's fear and anxiety about the process, certain studies have shown that "some children find the process of testifying empowering and wish to be active participants in the process" (Berliner & Barbieri, 1984; Goodman et al., 1992, cited in Lipovsky & Stern, 1997, p. 155).

Child witnesses must be confident when testifying about their maltreatment experiences or various facts in the case. They should request that questions be clarified if they do not understand what an attorney is asking them. This is a common instruction by prosecutors. It is also important that questions posed to children are not purposefully untruthful, but instead are formulated carefully to avoid confusing the child. Otherwise, child witnesses will make mistakes that will impeach[13] their testimony, rendering it inadmissible.

The court proceedings in child abuse cases are adversarial in nature. Defense attorneys represent the accused and are responsible for representing the rights of the accused. As a strategy, the defense seeks to find any aspect of the investigation and interview that might have been conducted inappropriately as a means of attacking its validity and reliability. The defense attorney may use sophisticated language designed to confuse the child, which in turn will raise doubts regarding his or her credibility as a witness.

Studies have shown that the language used by defense attorneys to question children in court tends to be developmentally inappropriate and complex (Brennan & Brennan,

---

[13] A witness is considered unreliable when there are inconsistencies (conflicting statements) in his or her testimony.

1988; Cashmore & DeHaas, 1992; Flin, Stevenson, & Davies, 1989; Goodman et al., 1992; Peters & Nunez, 1999) compared to the language used by prosecutors (Cashmore & DeHaas, 1992; Davies & Seymour, 1998; Evans, Lee, & Lyon, 2009; Flin, Bull, Boon, & Knox, 1993; Goodman et al., 1992; Perry, McAuliff, Tam, & Claycomb, 1995; Zajac & Hayne, 2003). The purpose underlying this strategy is to make children seem unreliable. Indeed, research has shown that the accuracy of the child's testimony is influenced by the attorneys' language (Zajac, Gross, & Hayne, 2003; Zajac & Hayne, 2003). In fact, studies have shown that children tend to answer questions that are complex and hard to understand rather than ask for clarification (Zajac et al., 2003). As Wood and Garven (2000, cited in Joa & Edelson, 2004) noted, this language not only is difficult to comprehend, but may also lead the child to provide inaccurate information. Accordingly, attorneys prosecuting a child abuse case must understand the impact of their language on the quality of the child's testimony.

Studies by Walker (1993) and Saywitz (1995) revealed that children often do not understand the rules of communication in the courtroom and are likely to respond to adult questions with incomplete or inaccurate information based on assumed conversational demands. Given this factor, it would be helpful for the child to practice how to answer questions when on the witness stand. A child can be taught how to respond to confusing and misleading questions and what to do if he or she does not remember the answer to a question (Saywitz & Moan-Hardie, 1994). For instance, to prepare children for trial, prosecutors present children with multifaceted questions and show them the appropriate responses to such questions (e.g., "I don't understand" or "Please repeat the question") via role playing (Lipovsky & Stern, 1997).

The age of the victim also determines the credibility of his or her testimony. Compared to older children, younger children are often viewed as less competent to recall their abuse, are more susceptible to leading questions, are more susceptible to suggestibility, and are more likely to have their statements contaminated by repetitive questions (Ceci & Bruck, 1995; Saywitz et al., 2002). Moreover, studies conducted on the perceptions of jurors reveal that juries, in general, do not regard children as credible witnesses (Cobley, 1991; Goodman, 1984). Indeed, Goodman's (1984) study showed that jurors rated children as less credible witnesses compared to adults. The same study also revealed that jurors rated 6-year-old children as less credible than 10-year-old children. Another study, however, indicated that this may not be true with all child abuse cases, as younger children may be perceived as being more credible than older children because they would not have the knowledge of sexual matters needed to fabricate allegations (Cobley, 1991).

Several studies have shown that the increased ability of the witness to narrate improves his or her credibility in court (e.g., Murray, 1998). According to Murray (1998, p. 19), "a victim's age as well as the presence of disabilities, speech problems, and vague, unclear victim statements raise concerns for both the legal competence of a victim to serve as a court witness and the perceived credibility of witnesses and their testimony" (p. 19).

Despite popular belief, the child's testimony is not necessarily the major determinant of a successful child abuse case. For instance, a study conducted by Coulborn Faller and Henry (2000) revealed that successful outcomes of cases were deemed to be the result of suspect confessions and plea bargains, which were the product of collaborative efforts between the prosecutor, CPS, and law enforcement.

Digitally Recorded or Videotaped Testimony Some countries do not require children to testify in court in child abuse cases. For example, in Sweden, videotaped recordings of the interview are used in court for children 15 years or younger. In these cases, there is no chance for the defense to cross-examine the witness in courts. Similarly, in the United States, in the past, prerecorded forensic interviews and the testimony of adults (e.g., police, pediatricians) were used in lieu of the child's live testimony. Legally, both prerecorded child witness testimony and adult testimony about the abuse constitute hearsay.

Rule 801 of the Federal Rules of Evidence defines hearsay as a statement, which can be "an oral of written assertion or . . . nonverbal conduct of a person, if it is intended by the person as an assertion, . . . other than one made by the declarant [i.e., the individual who makes the statement] . . . while testifying at the trial or hearing, offered in evidence to prove the truth of the matter asserted." Hearsay evidence is inadmissible in criminal courts except as provided by the Federal Rules of Evidence, other rules prescribed by the U.S. Supreme Court pursuant to law, or an act of Congress (Rule 802, U.S. Federal Rules of Evidence). The determination as to what constitutes hearsay and whether hearsay is admissible in court has been heavily debated. Hearsay evidence has been admitted when the victim is unavailable or has recanted his or her statement of abuse.

Courts unanimously have held that statements made during interviews that were conducted specifically to investigate and gather evidence for a criminal prosecution are testimonial. The introduction of hearsay evidence and the use of videotaped/digitally recorded or televised child testimony have been considered violations of a suspect's Sixth Amendment rights. More specifically, the introduction of this type of evidence in court-room proceedings violates a defendant's right to confront the witnesses against him or her (known as the Confrontation Clause of the Sixth Amendment of the U.S. Constitution):

> In all criminal prosecutions, the accused shall enjoy the right to a speedy and public trial, by an impartial jury of the State and district wherein the crime shall have been committed, which district shall have been previously ascertained by law, and to be informed of the nature and cause of the accusation; to be confronted with the witnesses against him; to have compulsory process for obtaining witnesses in his favor, and to have the Assistance of Counsel for his defense.

In *Crawford v. Washington* (2004), the court explicitly stated that the framers of the U.S. Constitution "would not have allowed admission of testimonial statements of a witness who did not appear at trial unless he was unavailable to testify, and the defendant had had a prior opportunity for cross-examination" (pp. 53–54). The *Crawford* ruling further noted that the ultimate goal of the Confrontation Clause of the Sixth Amendment is to ensure reliability of evidence, but it is a procedural rather than a substantive guarantee. It commands, not that evidence be reliable, but that reliability be assessed in a particular manner: by testing in the crucible of cross-examination . . . Dispensing with confrontation because testimony is obviously reliable is akin to dispensing with jury trial because a defendant is obviously guilty. This is not what the Sixth Amendment prescribes (pp. 61–62).

Accordingly, when suspects are prevented from confronting witnesses against them, they become unable to test the reliability of the evidence presented against them. However, in *Mattox v. United States* (1895), the court held that the Confrontation Clause included within the Sixth Amendment does not create a per se rule that bars the admission of any prior statements made by a declarant who is unable to testify before the jury during the trial.

Prosecutors need to consider first whether a statement is hearsay and then whether it falls under any of the exceptions. Hearsay may be admissible if it fits one of the existing exceptions to the hearsay rule (i.e., excited utterance, medical diagnosis/treatment, residual and child hearsay, fresh complaint of sexual abuse), as defined in Rule 803. These types of evidence can be admitted even when the declarant is available as a witness to testify. The most common types of evidence introduced in child abuse cases are excited utterance and statements made for medical diagnosis or treatment. Rule 803(2) holds that excited utterance is "a statement relating to a startling event or condition, made while the declarant was under the stress of excitement that it caused." In addition, Rule 803(4) holds that a statement made for medical diagnosis or treatment is "a statement that . . . is made for—and is reasonably pertinent to—medical diagnosis or treatment; and . . . describes medical history; past or present symptoms or sensations; their inception; or their general cause."

In *State v. Scacchetti* (2005), the court held that a child's disclosure of abuse to a nurse was nontestimonial because the primary purpose of the meeting and interview with the child did not involve the pursuit of an investigation. Instead, it occurred to assess and respond to an imminent risk to the child's health and welfare. Other interviews performed by mental health professionals, which were conducted to respond to risk to the child's health and welfare, were similarly considered to be nontestimonial in court (*State v. Bobadilla*, 2006; *State v. Krasky*, 2007; *State v. Vaught*, 2004).[14] For example, in *Idaho v. Wright* (1990), the court admitted the testimony of a pediatrician regarding maltreatment discovered during the course of examining the child on the grounds of the state's hearsay exception. A similar occurrence was observed in *White v. Illinois* (1992). In *White*, a 4-year-old girl, S.G., informed her babysitter, DeVore, that White, a friend of her mother's, had sexually assaulted her. Her mother, Grigsby, testified in court that when she returned home on the day of the alleged abuse, her daughter appeared scared and informed her mother of the assault in detail. Her mother called the police and S.G. repeated the manner in which she was assaulted and identified the assaulter to Officer Lewis. S.G. repeated this

---

[14] See also *State v. Bobadilla*, 709 N.W.2d 243 (Minn. 2006); *State v. Krasky*, 736 N.W.2d 636 (Minn. 2007), *cert denied Krasky v. Minnesota*, 736 N.W.2d 636 (Minn. 2008); and *State v. Vaught*, 682 N.W.2d 284 (Neb. 2004).

information to two medical professionals, RN Reents (an emergency room nurse) and Dr. Meinzen, with whom she came in contact shortly after disclosing the incident of abuse. As S.G. experienced emotional difficulty when asked to testify in court, she did not do so. Nonetheless, DeVore, Grigsby, Officer Lewis, RN Reents, and Dr. Meinzen all testified on her behalf in court. White objected to the introduction of the testimony of these five witnesses on the grounds of hearsay. The court overruled his objections on the grounds that the testimony of DeVore, Grigsby, and Lewis could be admitted under the hearsay rule for spontaneous declarations and the testimony of Reents and Meinzen was admissible under two exceptions to the hearsay evidence rule: the spontaneous declaration exception to hearsay evidence and the exception for statements made during the course of medical treatment. The court concluded that the statements introduced under these two hearsay exceptions did not violate White's Sixth Amendment rights and, in particular, his right to confront his accusers.

However, in some other cases, disclosure to such professionals has been considered testimonial. In *People v. Vigil* (2004), the court held that the statements made by an abused child to a doctor alleging that the offender abused him were testimonial because the doctor was part of a child prosecution team, conducted examinations at certain hospitals when abuse was suspected, had provided expert testimony on several occasions in the past in child abuse cases, performed a forensic sexual abuse examination on the child, and had spoken to the police officer who had accompanied the child prior to the examination. As such, the court concluded that these "statements were made under circumstances that would lead an objective witness reasonably to believe that they would be used prosecutorially" (*People v. Vigil*, 2004, p. 265). The court further noted that "although the doctor himself was not a government officer or employee, he was not a person unassociated with government activity. The doctor elicited the statements after consultation with the police and he necessarily understood that information he obtained would be used in a subsequent prosecution for child abuse" (p. 265)

The results of studies on the impact of hearsay evidence on jurors' decisions of guilt have varied. In some studies that involved mock trials of child abuse cases, the child's testimony compared to hearsay did not differentially affect the juror decision concerning the guilt of the defendant (Golding, Sanchez, & Sego, 1997; Tubb, Wood, & Hosch, 1999, as cited in Goodman et al., 2006). Similar results were found in research conducted on real jurors in criminal court trials (Myers, Redlich, Goodman, Prizmich, & Imwinkelried, 1999, as cited in Goodman et al., 2006). On the whole, the available research reveals that eyewitness (first-hand) testimony is received more positively than hearsay (second-hand) testimony for adult eyewitness, but not for children eyewitnesses (Goodman et al., 2006).

Closed-Circuit Television   During his or her testimony, the child should be made aware of the location of the defendant. The child may want to face away from the defendant during his or her testimony (by having his or her chair turned), may ask the prosecutor to stand in front of the defendant so he or she cannot see the alleged perpetrator during the testimony, or may ask to be in the perpetrator's line of sight to directly face his or her abuser. Other, more controversial methods involve allowing children to testify via closed-circuit television (CCTV) outside of the presence of the defendant and pretrial videotaping of the child's testimony (Myers, 1996). A more common practice in countries such as the United States is to have children follow the courtroom proceedings in a separate room via technology as opposed to being physically present in the courtroom. This choice will depend on the state in which the case is tried (see Table 11-1).[15]

The least controversial alternatives for child testimony involve turning the child so he or she cannot see the defendant directly or placing a screen so the child cannot see the defendant. This method was used in *Coy v. Iowa* (1988). John Coy was accused of sexually assaulting two girls (each was 13 years old). When the girls testified in court, a large screen was placed in front of the defendant so the children would not have to see him when they were testifying. The law at the time in Iowa (Code 910A) afforded victims the opportunity to have this screen put up when testifying in child sexual abuse cases. The jury convicted Coy of the crime. Coy's defense attorney claimed that using this shield violated his Sixth Amendment right and, more specifically, his right to come face to face with his accuser. In fact, in *Coy*, the court held that these procedures, which involved the witness not directly facing the defendant, did not adversely impact the Sixth Amendment rights of defendant.

By contrast, the U.S. Supreme Court held that the screen interfered with the right "to be confronted with the witnesses against him," which is essential to fairness, and could potentially bias the outcome of the trial. The Supreme Court further noted that while "face-to-face presence may, unfortunately, upset the truthful rape victim or abused child," it can also serve to "confound and undo the false accuser, or reveal the child coached by a malevolent adult."

Two years later, the court in *Maryland v. Craig* reached a different decision. In child abuse cases, the court must determine whether child witnesses would be traumatized by being required to testify in the presence of their alleged abuser. Indeed, the U.S. Supreme Court, in *Craig* (1990), held that the "State's interest in protecting the physical and psychological well-being of children . . . could be sufficiently important to outweigh defendants' rights to face their accusers in court." In fact, in *Craig*, the Supreme Court stated that the right provided to the defendant to come face-to-face with the witnesses against him or her at trial by the Confrontation Clause is not an absolute right. The defendant in the case, Sandra Ann Craig, was accused of sexually abusing a 10-year-old child. During the trial, the child victim was allowed to provide testimony via a one-way CCTV. Specifically, the child was placed in a separate room with the prosecutor and the defense attorney and gave testimony via CCTV while the defendant, judge, and jury watched. This was done to avoid—or, at the very least, lessen—the emotional distress for the child witness. This case, and others like it, challenge the necessity of child witnesses to testify in open court (i.e., in front of their abuser).

---

[15] The states included in this table, which exclude North Carolina, North Dakota, Maine, and the District of Columbia, afford a child an alternative means to testify without appearing in court.

Table 11-1 State laws concerning the use of CCTV and other alternatives for child testimony

Alabama	Code of Alabama Section 15-25-3, 15-25-32
Alaska	Alaska Stat. Section 12.45.046
Arizona	A.R.S. Section 13-4251, 13-4253
Arkansas	A.C.A. Section 16-43-1001
California	Cal. Health and Safety Code Section 1596.8871, Cal. Penal Code Section 1347
Colorado	C.R.S. 16-10-402
Connecticut	Conn. Gen. Stat. § 54-86g
Delaware	11 Del. C. §3514
Florida	Fla. Stat. § 92.54, Fla. R. Juv. P. 8.104, Fla. R. Juv. P. 8.255
Georgia	O.C.G.A. § 17-8-55
Hawaii	HRS § 616
Idaho	Idaho Code § 9-1801 to Idaho Code § 9-1809
Illinois	§ 725 ILCS5/106B-5
Indiana	Burns Ind. Code Ann. § 31-34-14-12, Burns Ind. Code Ann. § 31-35-5-2, Burns Ind. Code Ann. §35-37-4-8
Iowa	Iowa Code § 915-38
Kansas	K.S.A. § 22-3434,K.S.A. § 38-2359, K.S,A, § 38-2249
Kentucky	KRS § 26A.140,KRS § 421.350
Louisiana	La. R.S. 15:283, La. Ch.C. Art. 323, La. Ch.Co. Art. 329, La. Ch. C. Art. 1034
Maryland	Md. Criminal Procedure Code Ann. § 11-303
Massachusetts	ALM GL ch. 278, §16D
Michigan	MCLS §712A.17b, MCR 3.923
Minnesota	Minn. Stat. §595.02
Mississippi	Miss. Code Ann. §13-1-405, Miss. R. Evid. Rule 617
Missouri	(§491.680 R.S. Mo., §491.699 R.S. Mo
Montana	Mont. Code Anno., §41-3-110, Mont. Code Anno., §46-10-202, Mont. Code Anno., §46-16-227, Mont. Code Anno., §46-16-229
Nebraska	R.R.S. Neb. §29-1926
Nevada	Nev. Rev. Stat. Ann.§50.500, Nev. Rev. Stat. Ann. 50.520, Nev. Rev. Stat. Ann.§50.530, Nev. Rev. Stat. Ann. §50.540, Nev. Rev. Stat. Ann. §50.570, Nev. Rev. Stat. Ann. §50.580, Nev. Rev. Stat. Ann. §50.590, Nev. Rev. Stat. Ann.§50.600, Nev. Rev. Stat. Ann. §50.610
New Hampshire	RSA 517:13-a
New Jersey	N.J. Stat. § 2A:61B-1, N.J. Stat. § 2-A:84A-32.4

(Continues)

Table 11-1 State laws concerning the use of CCTV and other alternatives for child testimony (*Continued*)

New Mexico	N.M. Stat. Ann. §30-9-17; N.M. Dist. Ct. R. Cr. P.5-504, N.M. Children's Ct. Rule 10-217
New York	NY CLS CPL §65.00, NY CLS Exec §642-a, NY CLS CPL §65.10, NY CLS CPL §65.20, NY CLS CPL §65.30, NY CLS Family Ct. Act §343.1, NY CLS Unif. Civ. Rules, NYC Civ. Ct §208.12, NY CLS Unif. Rules, Family Ct §205.44, NY CLS Standards & Admin Pol §35.1, NY CLS Jud §211
Ohio	ORC Ann. 2152.81, ORC Ann. 2945.481, ORC Ann. 2937.11
Oklahoma	10 Okl. St. §7003-4.3, 10 Okl. St. §7303-1.1, 12 Okl. St. §2611.3, 12 Okl. St. §2611.4 to 12 Okl. St. §2611.110
Oregon	ORS § 40.460 Rule 803 (24), ORS §419C.025
Pennsylvania	42 Pa.C.S. §5982, 42 Pa.C.S. §5984.1, 42 Pa.C.S. §5985
Rhode Island	R.I. Gen. Laws §11-37-13.2, R.I. Gen. Laws § 12-28-8
South Carolina	S.C. Code Ann. §16-3-1550, S.C. Code Ann. §19-1-180
South Dakota	S.D. Codified Laws §26-8A-30, S.D. Codified Laws §26-8A-31
Tennessee	Tenn. Code Ann. §24-7-120
Texas	Tex. Code Crim. Proc. Art. 38.071, Tex. Fam. Code § 104.004, Tex. Gov't Code § 2001.121
Utah	Utah R. Crim. P. Rule 15.5, Utah Code Ann. § 76-5-411, Utah R. Evid. Rule 1102, Utah R. Juv. P. Rule 29A, Utah R. Juv. P. Rule 37A
Vermont	V.R.E. Rule 804, V.R.E. Rule 807
Virginia	Va. Code Ann. §18.2-67.9
Washington	Rev. Code Wash. (ARCW) §9A.44.150
West Virginia	W. Va. Code §62-6B-2, W. Va. Code § 62-6B-3, W. Va. Code §62-6B-4, W. Va. Child Abuse and Neglect Proceedings, Rule 9
Wisconsin	Wis. Stat. §972.11, Wis. Stat. §908.08
Wyoming	Wyo. Stat. §7-11-408, W.R.Cr. P Rule 26

In the United States, the courts in 47 states (excluding North Carolina, North Dakota, Maine, and the District of Columbia) and 3 U.S. territories (Guam, Puerto Rico, and the Virgin Islands) afford a child alternative means to testify without appearing in court. In North Carolina, however, case law exists that could be used to argue for the inclusion of the CCTV testimony of a child in court (*North Carolina v. Jones*, 1988). To determine whether to use live CCTV testimony in lieu of live testimony in court, 8 states (West Virginia, South Carolina, Oklahoma, Nevada, Nebraska, Idaho, Delaware, and Alaska) require the court to first consider the age of the child, the development level of the child, the general physical health of the child, and the effect that testifying in front of the alleged perpetrator would have on the child.

When a child testifies via CCTV, only certain people are allowed in the room during the time that the testimony is given. In 12 states, these individuals are the child, any support person for the child who is legally authorized to be in the room, the prosecutor, defense attorney, and the operators of the CCTV equipment.[16] In these states, the individuals who remain in the courtroom are the defendant, the judge, and the jury. In 14 states, the people allowed in the room during the child's testimony include the child, any support person for the child who is legally authorized to be in the room, the prosecutor, the defense attorney, the judge, and the operators of the CCTV equipment.[17]

Closed-circuit television testimony can be provided via either a one-way or two-way system. With the one-way system, a child is in a separate room and the testimony of the child is viewed on a television in the court. Some states, such as Washington, Minnesota, and Kentucky, have laws that require the use of one-way CCTV systems.[18] With two-way systems, a child is in a separate room and has a monitor on which the child can view and hear what is happening in the courtroom. The child can choose not to look at the monitor. The equipment used must be able to accurately communicate the image and demeanor of the child to the defendant, defense attorney, prosecution, judge, and jury.

Some states have laws that require the use of two-way CCTV systems instead of one-way systems. One such state is West Virginia. According to that state's law, before the testimony of a child is given through the use of a live, two-way CCTV system, the court must have clear and convincing evidence of the following:[19]

- The child is a competent witness.
- The child can testify only with the use of the live, two-way CCTV system.
- Without the use of the live, two-way CCTV, the child would be unable to testify because of the physical presence of the defendant.
- The ability of the prosecution to proceed with the case would be significantly hindered without the testimony via CCTV.

In determining the necessity of affording the child the opportunity to testify by use of two-way CCTV, the courts in West Virginia also consider factors such as the age and maturity

---

[16]Alaska (Alaska Stat. §12.45.046), Alabama (Code of Ala. §15-23-3), Arizona (A.R.S. §13-425), Delaware (11 Del. C. §3514), Kansas (K.S.A. §22-3434, K.S.A. §38-2359, K.S.A. §38-2249), Kentucky (K.R.S. §421.350), Maryland (Md. Criminal Procedure Code Ann. §11-303), Nebraska (R.R.S. Neb. §29-1926), New Jersey (N.J. Stat. §2A:61B-1, N.J. Stat. §2A:84A-32.4), Oklahoma (10 Okl. St. §7003-4.3), Tennessee (Tenn. Code Ann. §24-7-120), Virginia (Va. Code Ann. § 18.2-67-9).

[17]Arkansas (A.C.A. §16-43-1001), Colorado (C.R.S. 16-10-402), Connecticut (Conn. Gen. Stat. §54-86g), Florida (Fla. Stat. §92.54, Fla. R. Juv. P. 8.104), Georgia (O.C.G.A. §17-8-55), Illinois (§725 ILCS5/106B-5), Indiana (Burns Ind. Code Ann. §35-37-4-8), Iowa (Iowa Code §915.38), Louisiana (La. R.S. 15:283, La. Ch. C. Art. 329, La. Ch. C. Art. 1034), Minnesota (Minn. Stat. §595.02), Montana (Mont. Code Anno. §46-10-202, Mont. Code Anno. §46-16-229), Pennsylvania (42 Pa.C.S. §5984.1, 42 Pa.C.S. §5985), Rhode Island (R.I. Gen. Laws §11-37-13.2), Utah (Utah R. Crim. P. Rule 15.5).

[18]Rev. Code Wash. (ARCW) § 5 (A 44.150, Minn. Stat. § 595.02 and KRS § 421.350).

[19]W. Va. Code §62-6B-3.

of the child, any mental or physical handicap of the child, the facts and circumstances of the case, and whether harm was allegedly inflicted or threatened to be inflicted.[20]

A state with a similar law is New York. In New York, if the use of CCTV is authorized, the child witness will provide testimony while having his or her image and voice transmitted to a CCTV in the courtroom. The image projected will show not only the witness, but also any other persons in the room. This method ensures that the child's demeanor and other nonverbal behavior can be observed by those in the court during the testimony. In New York, those persons present in the courtroom during the testimony include the defendant, defense attorney, prosecution, judge, and jury. At the same time, the images of the jury, the defendant, and the defense attorney are transmitted to the child victim in the testimonial room.

California allows for the use of two-way and one-way CCTV systems; one-way CCTV systems can be used only when the use of two-way systems is such that it renders the child witness unable to testify.[21] CCTV (two-way and, if a legal reason exists, one-way) systems can be used for the testimony of children 13 years or younger in California. The age limit for the child to testify via CCTV, however, varies among states. For instance, in New York, for a child to be able to testify via CCTV, one criterion is that the child must be 14 years or younger.[22] By comparison, in Hawaii, the law allows children younger than the age of 18 to testify via CCTV.[23] In Rhode Island, children 17 years or younger are afforded the opportunity to testify via CCTV if it is shown that they would suffer unreasonable and unnecessary mental or emotional harm from testifying in court in the presence of the alleged offender.[24] In fact, if a child is 14 years or younger, there is a "presumption that the child is unable to testify before the court without suffering unreasonable and unnecessary mental or emotional harm."[25]

In other states, such as Missouri, New Hampshire, and New Jersey, children 16 years or younger can testify via CCTV.[26] In New Mexico, North Carolina, and Pennsylvania, children younger than the age of 16 can testify via CCTV.[27] In Idaho, Kansas, Oklahoma, Tennessee, and Texas, CCTV testimony is allowed for those younger than the age of 13.[28] Finally, in Arkansas and Kentucky, this form of testimony is permitted for those 12 years or younger.[29]

---

[20]W. Va. Code §62-6B-3.

[21]See California Penal Code § 1347(B) and § 1347(B)(3)(c).

[22]New York Criminal Procedure - § 65.00 -.

[23]HRS §616.

[24]R.I. Gen Laws § 11-37-13.2 (a).

[25]R.I. Gen Laws § 11-37-13.2 (a).

[26]Miss. R. Evid. 617 (A); N.H. Rev. Stat. Ann. § 517:13-A (I); N.J. Stat. Ann. § 2a:61b-1 (e) (2).

[27]N.M. Dist. Ct. R. Crim. Proc. § 5-504 (2010).(A); N.C. Gen. Stat. § 15a-1225.1 (2010). (A)(1); 42 Pa. Cons. Stat. Ann. § 5982 (2010).

[28]Idaho Code Ann. § 9-1801 (2010); Okla. Stat. Ann. Tit. 12, § 2611.3 (2010); Tenn. Code Ann. § 24-7-117 (2010); Tex. Code Crim. Proc. Ann. Art. 38.071 (2010). Sec. 1.

[29]Ark. Code Ann. § 16-43-1001 (2010). (A) (1); Ky. Rev. Stat. Ann. § 421.350 (2010).(1).

Various shielding strategies (i.e., a screen barrier in the courtroom, prerecorded or contemporaneous videotaped testimony, one-way or two-way CCTV) have been employed by prosecutors as means of reducing child witnesses' stress about testifying while balancing the rights of the defendant to confront the accuser, particularly in regard to fairness and reducing the likelihood of lying. Research using mock jurors has shown that employment of alternative procedures does not create prejudice against the defendant, but rather is likely to reduce conviction rates (Eaton, Ball, & O'Callaghan, 2001), despite jurors' belief that children will be less stressed when allowed to testify using these alternatives rather than in open court (McAuliff & Kovera, 2002). Swim, Borgida, and McCoy (1993) found that in pre-deliberation (but not post-deliberation), the defendant was more likely to be found guilty on criminal sexual assault charges in the first degree when the child witness testified in open court rather than via videotape/digital recording (48% versus 30%). Ross, Hopkins, Hanson, Lindsay, Hazen, and Eslinger (1994) used transcripts of an actual child sexual abuse case as the basis for videotaped trials in which the child testified in open court confronting the defendant, in court with a protective shield, or via closed-circuit television as one of several witnesses (Experiment 1) or as the only witness (Experiment 2). No differences in guilty verdict were found for Experiment 1, whereas a guilty verdict was more likely when the child testified in open court rather than either behind the screen or by closed-circuit television in Experiment 2. Using a similar paradigm comparing open court, protective shield, and closed-circuit television testimony of child witnesses, Lindsay, Ross, Lea, and Carr (1995) found that mock jurors' perceptions of fairness of the trial were not compromised by the use of protective devices in open court. Moreover, these mock jurors were more likely to perceive shields as being fair if the judge warned them that protective devices were not evidence of guilt than if the judge provided no such instructions.

How is testimony affected by using these alternative strategies? Children ages 3, 5, and 9 years old were less likely to report a perpetrator's misdeeds (i.e., breaking a valuable glass) if the person was present than absent (Bussey, Lee & Grimbeek, 1993). However, Bussey and Grimbeek (1995) reported that although older children reported a stranger's transgression regardless of whether he was present, younger children were more likely to do so if the perpetrator was absent rather than present. Testimony is similarly affected. Indeed, in one study, children produced lower amounts of information and fewer facts about a staged robbery when the robber was present during the interview than when he was absent (Peters, 1991). Goodman et al. (1998) also reported that omission errors by young children (5 and 6 years of age) were more likely when testimony was given in open court than by closed-circuit television. Hill and Hill (1987) found that children ages 7 to 9 provided more detailed and accurate testimony and fewer omissions (e.g., no response or "I don't know" response) about a witnessed unpleasant exchange between a father and a daughter from a small room without the father present than in the courtroom with the father present.

Lying by child witnesses, either because their testimony is shielded instead of being presented in open court or at the behest of a parent, has also been examined. Orcutt,

Goodman, Tobey, Batterman-Faunce, and Thomas (2001) reported that children (ages 7 to 9) who were asked to lie about being touched on their body did not differ in their implication of the defendant whether testifying in open court or by closed-circuit television. In one study, Talwar, Lee, Bala, and Lindsay (2004) examined children's testimony regarding a parent's transgression (i.e., breaking a puppet) as an analogy to whether they would lie about alleged abuse by falsely denying it occurred or would fabricate a report of alleged abuse by a parent at the request of another parent. This paradigm closely emulates the social pressures and motivations experienced during real-life situations, such as loyalty and fear of reprisal if caught lying (Lyon, 2000). In Experiment 1, after children ages 3 to 11 years of age agreed to not reveal their parent's misdeed (two of the three groups were in the room at the time of the breakage), they were interviewed either with or without the parent present in the initial fact-finding session, but without the parent in the second interview by a different interviewer following a competence examination emphasizing truth-telling. Results indicated that in response to a general prompt asking what happened and specifically asking if the parent broke the item, children were more likely to reveal that the parent broke the puppet with the parent absent (56% and 80%) and present (46% and 67%) than with the child absent (22% and 51%) conditions for the initial interview. These percentages increased to 85%/89%, 96%/96%, and 60%/69%, respectively, in response to general open-ended/direct closed-ended questions in the second interview. The child absent condition ensured that the child would not be held responsible for the misdeed and may have served as motivation for lying. Experiment 2 varied the child absent condition, but similarly found that children basically did not lie for parents.

Although some research indicates that live or videotaped child testimony does not differentially impact the outcome of cases (Davies, Wilson, Mitchell, & Milsom, 1995), prosecutors believe that a live child witness is the most likely to secure a guilty verdict (Goodman et al., 1999; MacFarlane, 1986). Research on the use of live CCTV testimony exists that has largely confirmed this belief. Indeed, a study found that "children who testified via CCTV in a mock trial were perceived as less believable, less accurate, less attractive, less intelligent, and less confident than children who testified live in court" (Goodman et al., 2006, p. 367).

Chapter Summary

Prosecutors have significant discretion to determine whether to press charges or prosecute cases of child sexual abuse. Crimes against children are very hard to prosecute for many reasons, including the unavailability of evidence substantiating the abuse; the age and maturity of the victim; and the relationship, if any, that exists between the perpetrator and the victim. In addition, prosecutors may not be able to pursue a case because the child cannot or will not testify (e.g., the child is too young or parents do not want to press charges against the offender or place undue stress on their child) or because the offender has not been identified or arrested.

In child abuse cases, the child's testimony and experts' testimony play critical roles in the outcome of the case. A more controversial form of expert testimony involves child sexual abuse accommodation syndrome; such testimony is often used to explain how a child reacts to sexual abuse. Child sexual abuse accommodation syndrome describes the typical behaviors or common reactions of children who have been sexual abused. Some courts allow this type of expert testimony only if it is limited to providing the general characteristics of children who have been sexually abused. In other words, these courts do not permit the expert to testify that these characteristics are observed in the victim.

There is significant debate on how best to accommodate child witnesses during courtroom proceedings. Prosecutors have a support person remain with the child during courtroom proceedings, provide the child with information about the courtroom, give the child a tour of the court to familiarize him or her with these surroundings, and prepare the child to testify. However, several issues may arise during a child's testimony. Attorneys prosecuting a child abuse case must understand the impact of their language on the quality of the child's testimony. Indeed, the language of lawyers has been found to influence the accuracy of the child's response. Depending on state law and the age of the victim, some alternatives to live testimony of children may be available, such as introducing a videotaped/digitally recorded statement of the victim's interview or allowing a child to testify via one-way or two-way CCTV. Furthermore, the manner in which the testimony via CCTV is administered and who is involved in the process varies by jurisdiction.

Review Questions

1. Which factors play a role in prosecutorial discretion to pursue a child sexual abuse case?

2. Which types of testimony are most common in child sexual abuse cases?

3. What is child sexual abuse accommodation syndrome?

4. Is evidence of child sexual abuse accommodation syndrome admissible in court? Why or why not? If it is, when is it admissible?

5. How is a child prepared for court?

6. Are children considered credible witnesses? Why do you think so?

7. For various reasons, children may not be able to provide live testimony. Which alternatives exist for them?

References

Adams, A. (2009). Seen but not heard: Child sexual abuse, incest, and the law in the United States. *Journal of Law and Family Studies 11*, 543–550.

Ahern, E. C., Lyon, T. D., & Quas, J. A. (2011). Young children's emerging ability to make false statements. *Developmental Psychology*, *47*(1), 61–66.

Allison v. State, 346 S.E.2d 380 (Ga. Ct. App. 1986).

Bachman, R., & Schutt, R. K. (2003). *The practice of research in criminology and criminal justice* (2nd ed.). London, UK: Sage/Pine Forge Press.

Back, C., Gustafsson, P. A., & Berterö, C. (2013). Sexually abused children: Prosecutors' experiences of their participation in the legal process in Sweden. *Psychiatry, Psychology and Law*, 20(2), 273–283.

Back, C., Gustafsson, P. A., Larsson, I., & Berterö, C. (2011). Managing the legal proceedings: An interpretative phenomenological analysis of sexually abused children's experience with the legal process. *Child Abuse & Neglect*, 35(1), 50–57.

Berliner, L. (1998). The use of expert testimony in child sexual abuse cases. In S. J. Ceci & H. Hembrooke (Eds.), *Expert witnesses in child abuse cases* (pp. 11–28). Washington, DC: American Psychological Association.

Berliner, L., & Barbieri, M. K. (1984). The testimony of the child victim of sexual assault. *Journal of Social Issues*, 40(2), 125–137.

Bradshaw, T. L., & Marks, A. E. (1990). Beyond a reasonable doubt: Factors that influence the legal disposition of child sexual abuse cases. *Crime and Delinquency*, 36(2), 276–286.

Brennan, M., & Brennan, R. E. (1988). *Strange language: Child victims under cross examination.* Wagga Wagga, Australia: Riverina Murray Institute of Higher Education.

Bulkley, J. (1987). Psychological expert testimony in child sex abuse cases. In B. Nicholson (Ed.), *Allegations of child sexual abuse in custody and visitation disputes* (pp. 191–213). Washington, DC: American Bar Association.

Bussey v. Commonwealth, 697 S.W.2d 139 (Ky. 1985).

Bussey, K., & Grimbeek, E. J. (1995). Disclosure processes: Issues for child sexual abuse victims. In K. J. Rotenberg (Ed.), *Disclosure processes in children and adolescents* (pp. 166–203). Cambridge, UK: Cambridge University Press.

Bussey K., Lee K., & Grimbeek E. J. (1993). Lies and secrets: Implications for children's reporting of sexual abuse. In G. S., Goodman & B. L. Bottoms (Ed.), *Child victims, child witnesses: Understanding and improving testimony* (pp.147–168). New York, NY: Guilford.

Cashmore, J., & DeHaas, N. (1992). *The use of closed-circuit television for child witnesses in the act.* Australian Law Reform Commission Research Paper No. 1.

Ceci, S. J., & Bruck, M. (1995). *Jeopardy in the courtroom: A scientific analysis of children's testimony.* Washington, DC: American Psychological Association.

Christiansen, J. R., & Blake, R. H. (1990). The grooming process in father-daughter incest. A. L. Horton, B. L. Johnson, L. M. Roundy, & D. Williams (Eds.). *The incest perpetrator: A family member no one wants to treat* (pp. 88–98). Newbury Park, CA: Sage.

Cobley, C. (1991). Child victims of sexual abuse and the criminal justice system in England and Wales. *Journal of Social Welfare and Family Law*, 13(5), 362–374.

Commonwealth v. Dunkle, 602 A.2d 830, 837–38 (Pa. 1992).

Coulborn Faller, K., & Henry, J. (2000). Child sexual abuse: A case study in community collaboration. *Child Abuse & Neglect*, 24, 1215–1225.

Coy v. Iowa, 487 U.S. 1012 (1988).

Crawford v. Washington, 541 U.S. 36 (2004).

Cross, T. P., De Vos, E., & Whitcomb, D. (1994). Prosecution of child sexual abuse: Which cases are accepted? *Child Abuse & Neglect*, 18(8), 663–677.

D.A.H. v. G.A.H., 371 N.W.2d 1 (Minn. App.1985).

Daubert v. Merrell Dow Pharmaceuticals Inc., 509 U.S. 579 (1993).

Davies, E., & Seymour, W. F. (1998). Questioning child complainants of sexual abuse: Analysis of criminal court transcripts in New Zealand. *Psychiatry, Psychology and Law*, 5(1), 47–61.

Davies, G., Wilson, C., Mitchell, R., & Milsom, J. (1995). *Videotaping children's evidence: An evaluation.* London, UK: Home Office.

Dezwirek-Sas, L. (1992). Empowering child witnesses for sexual abuse prosecution. In H. Dent & R. Flin (Eds.) *Children as witnesses* (pp.181–200). Chichester: John Wiley & Sons.

Dunham v. State, 762 P.2d969 (Okla. Crim. App. 1988).

Eaton, T. E., Ball, P. J., & O'Callaghan, M. G. (2001). Child-witness and defendant credibility: Child evidence presentation mode and judicial instructions. *Journal of Applied Social Psychology*, *31*(9), 1845–1858.

Evans, A. D., Lee, K., & Lyon, T. D. (2009). Complex questions asked by defense lawyers but not prosecutors predict convictions in child abuse trials. *Law & Human Behavior*, *33*(3), 258–264.

Fivush, R., Peterson, C., & Schwarzmueller, A. (2002). Questions and answers: The credibility of child witnesses in the context of specific questioning techniques. In M. L. Eisen, J. A. Quas, & G. S. Goodman (Eds.), *Memory and suggestibility in the forensic interview* (pp. 331–354). Mahwah, NJ: Lawrence Erlbaum.

Flin, R. H., Bull, R., Boon, J., & Knox, A. (1993). Child witnesses in Scottish criminal trials. *International Review of Victimology*, *2*(4), 309–329.

Flin, R. H., Stevenson, Y., & Davies, G. M. (1989). Children's knowledge of court proceedings. *British Journal of Psychology*, *80*(3), 285–297.

Freyd, J. J. (2003). Memory for abuse: What can we learn from a prosecution sample? *Journal of Child Sexual Abuse*, *12*(2), 97–103.

Fulero, S. M., & Wrightsman, L. S. (2009). *Forensic psychology*. Belmont, CA: Cengage.

Garsee, R. (2008, February). Sex crimes expert lied on the stand. *KTEN News*. http://www.kten.com /global/story.asp?s=7937161&ClientType=Printable

Geltz, R. M. (1994). The Little Rascals' Day Care Center case. *Journal of Child Sexual Abuse*, *3*(2), 103–106.

Ghetti, S., Alexander, K. W., & Goodman, G. S. (2002). Children in the legal system: Consequences and interventions. *International Journal of Law and Psychiatry*, *25*, 235–251.

Girard, J. E. (2008). *Criminalistics: Forensic science and crime*. Sudbury, MA: Jones and Bartlett.

Gitlin, C. (2008). Expert testimony on child sexual abuse accommodation syndrome: How proper screening should severely limit its admission. *Quinnipiac Law Review*, *26*, 497–549.

Golding, J. M., Sanchez, R. P., & Sego, S. A. (1997). The believability of hearsay testimony in a child sexual assault trial. *Law and Human Behavior*, *21*(3), 299–325.

Goodman, G. S. (1984). The child witness: Conclusions and future directions for research and legal practice. *Journal of Social Issues*, *40*(2), 157–175.

Goodman, G. S., Myers, J. E. B., Qin, J., Quas, J. A., Castelli, P., Redlich, A. D., and Rogers, L. (2006). Hearsay versus children's testimony: Jurors' abilities to detect truth and lies. *Law and Human Behavior*, *30*(3), 363–401.

Goodman, G. S., Quas, J. A., Bulkley, J., & Shapiro, C. (1999). Innovations for child witnesses: A national survey. *Psychology, Public Policy, and Law*, *5*(2), 255–281.

Goodman, G., Taub, E. P., Jones, D. P. H., England, P., Port, L. K., Rudy, L., . . . Melton, G. B. (1992). Testifying in criminal court: Emotional effects on child sexual assault. *Monographs of the Society for Research in Child Development*, *57*(5), 1–159.

Goodman, G. S., Tobey, A. E., Batterman-Faunce, J. M., Orcutt, H., Thomas, S., & Shapiro, C. (1998). Face-to-face confrontation: Effects of closed-circuit technology on children's eyewitness testimony and jurors' decisions. *Law and Human Behavior*, *22*(2), 165–203.

Heger, A., Ticson, L., Velasquez, O., & Bernier, B. (2002). Children referred for possible sexual abuse: Medical findings in 2384 children. *Child Abuse and Neglect*, *26*(6–7), 645–659.

Hill, P. E., & Hill, S. M. (1987). Note-videotaping children's testimony. *Michigan Law Review*, *85*, 809–833.

Idaho v. Wright, 497 U.S. 805 (1990).

In re Amber B., 191 Cal. App. 3d 682, 236 Cal. Rptr. 623 (lst. Dist. 1987).

In re Christine C., 236 Cal. Rplr. 630(Cal. Ct. App. 1987).

In re Donna K., 518 N.Y.S.2d 289 (1987).

In re J. K., 49 Wash. App. 670, 745 P.2d 1304 (1987).

In re Jennifer, 517 N.E.2d 187 (Mass. Ct. App. 1988).

In re Nicole V., 524 N.Y.S.2d 19 (N.Y.1987).

In re Rinesmith, 376 N.W.2d 139 (Mich. Ct. App. 1985).

Joa, D., & Edelson, M. G. (2004). Legal outcomes for children who have been sexually abused: The impact of child abuse assessment center evaluations. *Child Maltreatment*, *9*(3), 263–276.

Johnson v. State, 292 Ark. 632,732 S.W.2d 817 (1987).

Kaufman, K. L., Holmberg, J. K, Orts, K. A., McCrady, F. E., Rotzien, A. L., Daleiden, E. L, & Hilliker, D. R. (1998). Factors influencing sexual offenders' modus operandi: An examination of victim-offender relatedness and age. *Child Maltreatment*, *3*(4), 349–361.

Keri v. State, 179 Ga. App. 664, 347 S.E.2d 236 (1986).

Kovera, M. B., Levy, R. J., Borgida, E., & Penrod, S. D. (1994). Expert testimony in child sexual abuse cases: Effects of expert evidence type and cross-examination. *Law and Human Behavior*, *18*(6), 653–674.

Lamb, M. E. (1994). The investigation of child sexual abuse: An international, interdisciplinary consensus statement. *Family Law Quarterly*, *28*(1), 151–161.

Lanning, K. V. (2002). Criminal investigation of sexual victimization of children. In J. E. B. Myers, L. Berliner, J. Briere, C. T. Hendrix, C. Jenny, & T. A. Reid (Eds.), *The APSAC handbook on child maltreatment* (2nd ed., pp. 329–347). Thousand Oaks, CA: Sage.

Lantrip v. Commonwealth, 713 S. W. 2d 816 (Ky. 1986).

Lindsay, R. C. L., Ross, D. F., Lea, J. A., & Carr, C. (1995). What's fair when a child testifies? *Journal of Applied Social Psychology*, *25*(10), 870–888.

Lipovsky, J. A. (1994). The impact of court on children: Research findings and practical recommendations. *Journal of Interpersonal Violence*, *9*(2), 238–257.

Lipovsky, J., & Stern, P. (1997). Preparing children for court: An interdisciplinary view. *Child Maltreatment*, *2*(2), 150–163.

Lippert, T., Cross, T. P., Jones, L., & Walsh, W. (2010). Suspect confession of child sexual abuse to investigators. *Child Maltreatment*, *15*(2), 161–170.

Loftus, E. F. (1993). The reality of repressed memories. *American Psychologist*, *48*(5), 518–537.

Loftus, E. F., & Hoffman, H. G. (1989). Misinformation and memory: The creation of memory. *Journal of Experimental Psychology: General*, *118*(1), 100–104.

Loftus, E. F., & Ketcham, K. (1994). *The myth of repressed memory*. New York, NY: St. Martin's Press.

Loftus, E. F., & Rosenwald, L. A. (1995). Recovered memories: Unearthing the past in court. *Journal of Psychiatry and Law*, *23*(3), 3419–3461.

London, K., Bruck, M., Ceci, S. J., & Shuman, D. W. (2005). Disclosure of child sexual abuse: What does the research tell us about the ways that children tell? *Psychology, Public Policy, & Law*, *11*(1), 194–226.

Lyon, T. D. (2000). Child witnesses and the oath: Empirical evidence. *Southern California Law Review*, *73*, 1017–1074.

MacFarlane, K. (1986). Videotaping of interviews and court testimony. In K. MacFarlane & T. Waterman (Eds.), *Sexual abuse of young children: Evaluation and treatment* (pp. 164–193). New York, NY: Guilford.

Malloy, L. C., Lyon, T. D., & Quas, J. A. (2007). Filial dependency and recantation of child sexual abuse allegations. *Journal of the American Academy of Child and Adolescent Psychiatry, 46*(2), 162–170.

Maryland v. Craig, 497 U.S. 836 (1990).

Mattox v. United States, 156 U.S. 237 (1895).

McAuliff, B. D., & Kovera, M. B. (1998). *Are laypersons' beliefs about suggestibility consistent with expert opinion?* Paper presented at the meeting of the American Psychological Association, San Francisco, CA.

McAuliff, B. D., & Kovera, M. B. (2002). The status of evidentiary and procedural innovations in child abuse proceedings. In B. L. Bottoms, M. B. Kovera, & B. D. McAuliff (Eds.), *Children, social science, and the law* (pp. 412–445). New York, NY: Cambridge University Press.

McGough, L. S. (1995). For the record: Videotaping investigative interviews. *Psychology, Public Policy, and Law, 1*(2), 370–386.

McGough, L. (2002). Good enough for government work: The constitutional duty to preserve forensic interviews of child victims. *Law & Contemporary Problems, 65*(1), 179–208.

Melton, G. B., & Limber, S. (1989). Psychologists' involvement in cases of child maltreatment: Limits of role and expertise. *American Psychologist, 44*(9), 1225–1233.

Miller, A., & Rubin, D. (2009). The contribution of children's advocacy centers to felony prosecutions of child sexual abuse. *Child Abuse & Neglect, 33*(1), 12–18.

Murphy, W. J. (2003). The overlapping problems of prosecution sample bias and systematic exclusion of familial child sex abuse victims from the criminal justice system. *Journal of Child Sexual Abuse, 12*(2), 129–132.

Murray, B. K. M. (1988). Prosecutorial decision making and case attrition for child sexual abuse: A qualitative approach to case rejection decisions. *Prison Journal, 68*(2), 11–24.

Murray, B. K. M. (1989). Criminal determination for child sexual abuse: Prosecutor case-screening judgments. *Journal of Interpersonal Violence, 4*(2), 233–244.

Myers, J. E. B. (1996). A decade of international reform to accommodate child witnesses. In B. Bottoms & G. Goodman (Eds.), *International Perspectives on Child Abuse and Children's Testimony* (pp. 221–266). Newbury Park, CA.: Sage.

Myers, J. E. B. (2005). *Myers on evidence in child, domestic and elder abuse cases: Successor edition to "Evidence in child abuse and neglect"* (3rd ed., Vols. 1–2). New York, NY: Aspen.

Myers, J. E. B., Redlich, A. D., Goodman, G. S., Prizmich, L. P., & Imwinkelried, E. (1999). Jurors' perceptions of hearsay in child sexual abuse cases. *Psychology, Public Policy, and Law, 5*(2), 388–419.

National Center for Prosecution of Child Abuse. (2004). *Investigation and prosecution of child abuse* (3rd ed.). Thousand Oaks, CA: Sage.

New Jersey v. Margaret Kelly Michaels, 642 A 2d 1372, 1377 (June 13, 1994).

North Carolina v. Jones, 89 N.C. App. 584, 367 S.E. 2d 139 (1988).

Orcutt, H. K., Goodman, G. S., Tobey, A. E., Batterman-Faunce, J. M., & Thomas, S. (2001). Detecting deception in children's testimony: Factfinders' abilities to reach the truth in open court and closed-circuit trials. *Law and Human Behavior, 25*(4), 339–372.

Parkinson, P. N., Shrimpton, S., Swanston, H. Y., O'Toole, B. I., & Oates, R. K. (2002). The process of attrition in child sexual assault cases: A case flow analysis of criminal investigations and prosecutions. *Australian & New Zealand Journal of Criminology, 35*(3), 347–362.

Pence, D., & Wilson, C. (1994). *Team investigation of child sexual abuse*. Thousand Oaks, CA: Sage.

People v. Bledsoe, 36 Cal. 3d 236, 203 Cal. Rptr. 450. 681 P.2d 291 (1984).

People v. Bowker, 203 Cal. App.3d 385, 249 Cal. Rptr. 886 (1988).

People v. Eminger, 772 P.2d 674 (Colo. Ct. App. 1989).

People v. Grady, 506 N.Y.S.2d 922 (N.Y. App. Div. 1986).

People v. Gray, 187 Cal.App.3d, 231 Cal. Rptr. 658 (1986).

People v. Keindl, 68 N.Y.S.2d 410 (N.Y. 1986).

People v. Knupp, 179 A.D.2d 1030, 579 N.Y.S.2d 801 (1992).

People v. Leon, 263 Cal. Rpk. 77 (Cal. Ct. App. 1989).

People v. Luna, 204 CaI.App.3d 776, 250 Cal. Rptr. 878 (1988).

People v. Payan, 173 Cal.App.3d 27, 220 Cal.Rptr. 126 (1985).

People v. Ronovost, 756 P.2d 387 (Colo. Ct. App. 1987).

People v. Roscoe, 168 Cal. App. 3d 1093, 215 Cal. Rptr. 45 (5th Dist. 1985).

People v. Server, 499 N.E.2d 1019 (111. App. Ct. 1986).

People v. Vigil, 104 P.3d 258 (Colo. Ct. App. 2004).

Perry, N. W., McAuliff, B. D., Tam, P., & Claycomb, L. (1995). When lawyers question children: Is justice served? *Law and Human Behavior, 19*(6), 609–629.

Perry, N. W., & Wrightsman, L. S. (1991). *The child witness: Legal issues and dilemmas.* Newbury Park, CA: Sage.

Peters, D. P. (1991). The influence of stress and arousal on the child witness. In J. Doris (Ed.), *The suggestibility of children's recollections* (pp. 60–76). Washington, DC: American Psychological Association.

Peters, W. W., & Nunez, N. (1999). Complex language and comprehension monitoring: Teaching child witnesses to recognized linguistic confusion. *Journal of Applied Psychology, 84*(5), 661–669.

Pezdek, K., & Banks, W. P. (Eds.). (1996). *The recovered memory/false memory debate.* San Diego, CA: Academic.

Powell v. State, 527 A.2d 276 (Del. 1987).

Ross, D. F., Hopkins, S., Hanson, E., Lindsay, R. C. L., Hazen, K., & Eslinger, T. (1994). The impact of protective shields and videotape testimony on conviction rates in a simulated trial of child sexual abuse. *Law and Human Behavior, 18*(5), 553–566.

Russell v. State, 712 S.W.2d 916 (Ark. 1986).

Sas, L., Hurley, P. Austin, G., & Wolfe, D. (1991). *Reducing the system-induced trauma for child sexual abuse victims through court preparation, assessment, and follow up (Project #4555-1-125).* Final report to the National Welfare Grants Division, Health and Welfare Canada, London, Ontario.

Saywitz, K. J. (1995). Improving children's testimony: The question, the answer and the environment. In M. S. Zaragoza, J. R. Graham, G. C. N. Hall, R. Hirschman, & Y. S. Ben-Porath (Eds.), *Memory and testimony in the child witness* (pp. 113–140). Thousand Oaks, CA: Sage.

Saywitz, K. J., Goodman, G. S., & Lyon, T. D. (2002). Interviewing children in and out of court: Current research and practice implications. In J. E. B. Myers, L. Berliner, J. Briere, C. T. Hendrix, C. Jenny, & T. A. Reid (Eds.), *The APSAC handbook on child maltreatment* (2nd ed., pp. 349–377). Thousand Oaks, CA: Sage.

Saywitz, K. J., & Moan-Hardie, S. (1994). Reducing the potential for distortion of childhood memories. *Consciousness and Cognition, 3*, 257–293.

Saywitz, K. J., & Snyder, L. (1993). Improving children's testimony with preparation. In G. Goodman & B. Bottoms (Eds.), *Child victims, child witnesses* (pp. 117–146). New York, NY: Guilford.

Scadden v. State, 737 P.2d 1036 (Wyo. 1987).

Schroeder, C. S., Gordon, B. N., & Hawk, B. (1983). Clinical problems of the preschool child. In C. E. Walker & M. C. Roberts (Eds.), *Handbook of clinical child psychology* (pp. 296–334). New York, NY: Wiley.

Seering v. Dep't Social Serv., 239 Cal. Rpu. 422 (Cal. Ct. App. 1987).

State v. Bachman, 446 N.W.2d 271 (N.D. 1989).

State v. Bailey, 365S.E.2d 651 (N.C. 1988).

State v. Batagan, 799 P.2d 48 (Haw. 1990).

State v. Black, 537 A.2d 1154 (Me. 1988).

State v. Bobadilla, 709 N.W.2d 243 (Minn. 2006).

State v. Butler, S.E.M 684 (Ga 1986).

State v. Dana, 416 N.W.2d 147 (Minn Ct. App.1987).

State v. Edward Charles L., 398 S.E.2d I23 (W. Va.1990).

State v. Garden, 404 N.W.2d 912 (Minn. Ct. App. 1987).

State v. Geyman, 729 P.2d 475 (Mont 1986).

State v. Hall, 392 N.W.2d 285. 289 (Minn. Cr. App.. 1986).

State v. Haseltine, 352 N.W.2d 673 (Wis. CL App. 1984).

State v. Hester, 760 P.2d 27(Idaho 1988).

State v. Hudnall, 359 S.E.2d 59 (S.C. 1987).

State v. Jensen, 415 N.W.2d 519 (Wis. Ct. App. 1987).

State v. Kim, 64 Haw. 598, 645 E2d 1330 (1982).

State v. Krasky, 736 N.W.2d 636 (Minn. 2007), cert denied *Krasky v. Minnesota*, 736 N.W.2d 636 (Minn. 2008).

State v. Lawrence, 541 A.2d 1291 (Me. 1988).

State v. McCoy, 404 N.W.2d 807 (Minn. Ct. App. 1987).

State v. Michaels, 625 A.2d 489, 496 (N.J. Super. Ct. App. Div. 1993).

State v. Milbradt, 756 P.2d 620 (Or. 1988).

State v. Myers, 359 N.W.2d 604 (Minn. 1984).

State v. Scacchetti, 690 N.W.2d 393 (Minn. App. 2005).

State v. Vaught, 682 N.W.2d 284 (Neb. 2004).

Stroud, D. D., Martens, S., & Barker, J. (2000). Criminal investigation of child sexual abuse: A comparison of cases referred to the prosecutor to those not referred. *Child Abuse & Neglect, 24*(1), 689–700.

Summit, R. (1983). The child sexual abuse accommodation syndrome. *Child Abuse & Neglect, 7*(2), 177–193.

Swim, J. K., Borgida, E., & McCoy, K. (1993). Videotaped versus in-court witness testimony: Does protecting the child witnesses jeopardize due process? *Journal of Applied Social Psychology, 23*(8), 603– 631.

Talwar, V., Lee, K., Bala, N., & Lindsay, R. C. L. (2004). Children's lie-telling to conceal a parent's transgression: Legal implications. *Law & Hum Behavior, 28*(4), 411–435.

Townsend v. State, 734 P.2d 705 (Nev. 1987).

Tubb, V. A., Wood, J. M., & Hosch, H. M. (1999). Effects of suggestive interviewing and indirect evidence on child credibility in a sexual abuse case. *Journal of Applied Social Psychology, 29*(6), 1111–1127.

Turney v. State, 759 N.E.2d 671 (2001).

Underwager, R., & Wakefield, H. (1991, June 16). *Child sexual abuse and real world research*. Paper presented at the Third Annual Convention of the American Psychological Society, Washington, DC.

United States v. Downing, 753 F.2d 1224 (1985).

U.S. v. Azure, 801 F.2d 336 (8th Cir. 1986).

Vieth, V. I. (1999). When a child stands alone: The search for corroborating evidence. *American Prosecutors Research Institute, 12*(6), 1–4.

Walker, A. G. (1993). Questioning young children in court: A linguistic case study. *Law and Human Behavior, 17*, 59–81.

Walker, L., & Monahan, J. (1987). Social frameworks: A new use of social science in law. *Virginia Law Review, 73*, 559–612.

Walsh, W. A., Jones, L. M., Cross, T. P., & Lippert, T. (2010). Prosecuting child sexual abuse: The importance of evidence type. *Crime & Delinquency, 56*(3), 436–454.

Walsh, W. A., Lippert, T., Cross, T. P., Maurice, D., & Davison, K. (2008). How long to prosecute child sexual abuse for a community using a children's advocacy center and two comparison communities? *Child Maltreatment, 13*(1), 3–13.

Ward v. State, 519 So. 2d 1082 (Fla. Dist. Ct. App. 1988).

Whitcomb, D., Runyan, D., De Vos, E., Hunter, W. M., Cross, T .P., Everson, M. D., et al (1994). *The child victim as a witness*. Washington, DC: Office of Juvenile Justice and Delinquency Prevention.

White v. Illinois, 502 U.S. 346,112 S. Ct. 736,116 L. Ed. 2d 848 (1992).

Wood, J. M., & Garven, S. (2000). How sexual abuse interviews go astray: Implications for prosecutors, police, and child protection services. *Child Maltreatment, 5*(2), 109–118.

Wydick, R. C. (1995, September). The ethics of witness coaching. *Cardozo Law Review, 17*, 1–52.

Zajac, R., Gross, J., & Hayne, H. (2003). Asked and answered: Questioning children in the courtroom. *Psychiatry, Psychology and Law, 10*(1), 199–209.

Zajac, R., & Hayne, H. (2003). "I don't think that's what really happened": The effect of cross-examination on the accuracy of children's reports. *Journal of Experimental Psychology: Applied, 9*(3), 187–195.

Chapter 12

Advice and Conclusions: Recommendations for Those in the Field

Child maltreatment occurs to children of all genders, ages, ethnicities, races, religions, socioeconomic classes, and communities. If they are to be successful, child abuse and neglect prevention efforts should examine risk factors. According to Fraser and Terzian (2005), "Broadly defined, the term *risk factor* relates to any event, condition, or experience that increases the probability that a problem will be formed, maintained or exacerbated" (p. 5). An individual is labeled "at risk" when he or she has characteristics similar to those of a group of individuals who are more likely to develop a problem than others in the general population (Fraser, Galinsky, & Richmond, 1999). It is rare that a risk factor will be experienced in isolation. Indeed, individuals are more commonly considered to be at risk when they experience several risk factors. Risk factors are present in the individual, the family, the community, and society as a whole. These factors are included in the socio-ecological framework (see Figure 12-1) explored in this chapter.

Theoretical Framework for Conceptualizing Child Maltreatment

The socio-ecological model was conceptualized by Bronfenbrenner (1977, 1986). In his model, he divides the social context into four components: *micro*, *meso*, *exo*, and *macro* systems. Each of these components acts and interacts with the others to explain human behavior. The first component, the *micro* system, consists of the individual (the child's biological and psychological makeup) and his or her immediate environment (e.g., family). The second component, the *meso* system, refers to interrelationships between the different social environments experienced by a child. Specifically, the child will interact with peers in the neighborhood and at school, with parents and siblings at home, with teachers at

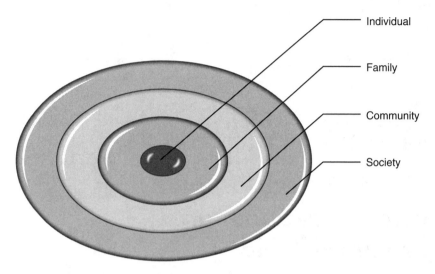

Figure 12-1 Core areas of social ecology

school, and with coaches in the neighborhood, among others. The third component, the *exo* system, includes those informal and formal structures with which a person is directly involved—that is, the community (e.g., neighborhoods). The fourth component, the *macro* system, includes cultural patterns, norms, values, and behaviors that relate to political, economic, social, and legal systems.

Although not a formal part of the model, a fifth component is the *chrono* system, which refers to autobiographic events—that is, experiences that contain special meaning to us across our lifetime and that will influence our behavior. This component provides another dimension to environmental influences, both for a child's chronological time frame and for the historical time frame (Bronfenbrenner, 1994). Bronfenbrenner proposed a bidirectional influence between the child and the different systems and highlighted the importance of examining the child and his or her behavior within the environmental context to understand it.

Belsky (1980) built upon Bronfenbrenner's theory by using the first four components to explain how maltreatment is the product of several factors affecting the child rather than a single cause. In contrast to Bronfenbrenner's (1977) theory, Belsky emphasized the importance of individual factors, which he labeled as ontogenetic development, over contributions of the *meso* and *exo* systems. Like Bronfenbrenner, Belsky (1980) proposed an ecological framework with four levels: (1) the *ontogenetic* system, which includes individual factors of children and parents; (2) the *micro* system, which covers what happens in the family; (3) the *exo* system, which encompasses the larger social system; and (4) the *macro* system, which includes cultural beliefs and influences both the *meso* and *exo* systems.

According to this social–ecological theory (Figure 12-1), child maltreatment is the outcome of individual, family (*micro*), community (*exo*), and society (*macro*) contexts that provide both interpersonal and environmental challenges and supports. The individual factors flow through the system outward towards society (and of course, from society back toward the individual). Individual factors comprise biological and personal history factors that increase the likelihood of someone becoming a victim or perpetrator of child maltreatment (Violence Prevention Alliance, n.d.). Children's age, gender, and vulnerability (such as disability or a difficult temperament) are related to their likelihood of victimization (e.g., DePanfilis & Zuravin, 1999; Fryer & Miyoshi, 1994; Fuller, Wells, & Cotton, 2001; Levy, Markovic, Chaudhry, Ahart, & Torres, 1995; Miller-Perrin & Perrin, 1999).

Additionally, parental features factor into child maltreatment. For instance, parents with a history of maltreatment are more likely to abuse their own children (Cicchetti & Lynch, 1995). Moreover, parents who chronically maltreat their children are more likely to have substance abuse problems (Hamilton & Browne, 1999; Inkelas & Halfon, 1997; Jones, 1987; Murphy, Bishop, Jellinek, Quinn, & Poitrast, 1992; Wolock & Magura, 1996), to have learning disabilities, or to suffer from mental disorders (Hamilton & Browne, 1999; Jones, 1987; Murphy et al., 1992). Here, individual characteristics of the child, such as the child's temperament disposition and health, influence and interact with the individual characteristics of the parent. For example, children with disabilities, children with chronic illnesses, and children with difficult temperaments may be at greater risk of maltreatment (Rycus & Hughes, 1998) due to the overwhelming demands placed on the parents who must care for these children (Goldman, Salus, Wolcott, & Kennedy, 2003). Parents who are alcohol or substance abusers often tend to their own needs first (e.g., buying alcohol or drugs) and neglect the needs of their child (e.g., food and safety).

Individual characteristics interact with family factors as well. Indeed, family factors such as the family size, structure (e.g., single parent), functioning (e.g., marital problems), conflicts and stress, and history of domestic violence (or not) in the household contribute to incidents of child maltreatment and even to repeated child maltreatment incidents (Browne, 1986; DePanfilis & Zuravin, 1999; English, Marshall, Brummel, & Orme, 1999; Hamilton & Browne, 1999; Inkelas & Halfon, 1997; Levy et al., 1995; Marshall & English, 1999). Studies have shown that children who are at greater risk of victimization are from families of low socioeconomic status, with limited financial resources, with one or more parent who is unemployed, with a parent (or parents) with minimal education, and who live in public housing (Browne, 1986; Cicchetti & Lynch, 1993; Levy et al., 1995). According to Belsky (1980), individual and family factors play a more prominent role in child maltreatment than do social and cultural factors.

The family system is further influenced by social factors. Social factors (*exo*) include the socioeconomic characteristics of the family, informal and formal social support, degree of social isolation, and community characteristics. DePanfilis and Zuravin (1999) found that deficits in social support were related to child maltreatment. Social support can include both tangible and emotional support. Those who may provide social support may include relatives, friends, neighbors, employers, school, religious institutions, and other community groups and organizations. The social level affects the everyday activities of both parents and children (Asmussen, 2010).

Lastly, system factors represent "the cultural context within which beliefs, values and societal rules determine the ways in which families and communities interact" (Asmussen, 2010, p. 8). Accordingly, the system includes those factors that create an environment where child maltreatment is either permitted or discouraged. For example, if society is accepting of family punishment, parents will tend to believe that they can physically discipline their children as they see fit.

How do all of these levels interact? Individual characteristics of the child and the parents affect family functioning, including parenting style and the structure of the family. The structure of the family is also influenced by external factors, the social and economic environment, and, more specifically, the community. Their neighborhood and those persons and institutions within it affect the lives of families. The family is also influenced by the system or the societal culture. Beliefs, values, and societal rules impact family functioning as well.

Many risk factors are associated with child maltreatment, making the prevention of child maltreatment particularly challenging (Table 12-1). The presence of these risk factors, however, does not necessarily mean that a child will be maltreated. Protective factors may also be present and operate to ameliorate the negative effects of risks (Table 12-2). Protective factors can be defined as "those influences, characteristics, and conditions that buffer or mitigate a person's exposure to risk" (Jenson & Fraser, 2010, p. 11). These protective factors help explain why some individuals who are considered at risk have the personal resources needed to overcome adversity. Individuals with a history of child maltreatment, therefore, will not necessarily suffer adversity throughout their entire lifetime. Certain protective factors are associated with resilience, which is defined as the person's successful adaptation to risk or adversity.

Evolution of Child Maltreatment

The methods of child maltreatment are evolving; the responses to it should follow suit. Child maltreatment offenders have been and currently are seeking new ways to target and harm children without attracting the attention of authorities. Young children are the most vulnerable to abuse and neglect. Unfortunately, child maltreatment offenders are becoming more sophisticated in their maltreatment of children; nowhere is this more pronounced than in infant and early childhood sexual abuse.

Infant and Early Childhood Sexual Abuse

Infant and early childhood victims are considered "non-ideal" victims by agents of the criminal justice system, because authorities often do not really know what happened to them owing to these victims' inability to provide information about their experiences. Accordingly, authorities often have no corroborating evidence or must rely on circumstantial and often arbitrary evidence to prosecute offenders. For these reasons, perpetrators of such heinous crimes may receive either no sentence, a minimal sentence, or an alternative penalty to incarceration due to plea bargaining. Such outcomes, however, violate children's basic rights as victims.

Table 12-1 Summary of risk factors in child maltreatment

Parents	Young age; upbringing; child maltreatment history; attachment issues; parenting style; presence of mental disorders, learning disorders, alcohol abuse, and substance abuse (Azar, Povilaitis, Lauretti, & Pouquette, 1998; Balge & Milner, 2000; Crittenden & Ainsworth, 1989; Pears & Capaldi, 2001; Rogosch, Cicchetti, Shields, & Toth, 1995; Buchanan, 1998; Zuravin & DiBlasio, 1996)
Children	Young age; gender; presence of mental disorders, chronic illnesses, and disabilities, difficult temperament (Belsky, 1993; Burgess & Draper, 1989; DePanfilis & Zuravin, 1999; Dukewich, Borkowski, & Whitman, 1996; Hawkins & Duncan, 1985; Rogosch et al., 1995)
Family	Structure, size, communication among members, time parents spend with children, relationship between parents, relationship between parent(s) and child, conflicts in the marriage or household, history of domestic violence (Cummings, 1998; DePanfilis & Zuravin, 1999; Finkelhor, Araji, Baron, Browne, Peters, & Wyatt, 1986; Kotch et al., 1997; Miller-Perrin & Perrin, 1999; O'Keefe, 1995; Patterson, DeBaryshe, & Ramsey, 1989; Shaffer, 2000; Sidebotham & Golding, 2001)
Social	Poverty; unemployment, little or no education, living in public housing, crowded living conditions, lack of (or lacking in) social support, existence of social conflict (Christoffersen, 2000; Cicchetti & Lynch, 1993, 1995; Coohey, 1996; Garbarino, 1976; Garbarino & Barry; 1997; Garbarino & Crouter, 1978; Gillham, Tanner, Cheyne, Freeman, Rooney, & Lambie, 1998; Miller-Perrin & Perrin, 1999; Parke & Collmer, 1975; Pianta, Egeland, & Erickson, 1989; Rogosch et al., 1995; Shaffer, 2000; Whipple & Richey, 1997)
Community	High crime neighborhood, poor neighborhood, high rates of unemployment, economic inequality (Cicchetti & Lynch, 1993, 1995; Garbarino & Barry, 1997; Kotch et al., 1997)
System (Society)	Religion; ethnicity; values, norms, and beliefs (e.g., permissive beliefs of physical punishment) (e.g., Belsky, 1980; Belsky & Vondra, 1989; Kamerman & Kahn, 1995; Parke & Collmer, 1975)

Table 12-2 Summary of protective factors in child maltreatment

Child	Positive self-image and high self-esteem; good health, peer relationships, and social skills; above-average intelligence; good problem-solving skills; easy temperament; a positive disposition; hobbies, interests, and sense of humor (Asmussen, 2010; Benard, 1991; DePanfilis, 2006)
Family	Family harmony, close bond with at least one member of the family, good parent–child relationship, nurturing home environment, good emotional and mental health of parents, sufficient financial and material resources (Asmussen, 2010; Benard, 1991; DePanfilis, 2006; Jenson & Fraser, 2010)
Community	Neighborhood support, positive adult role models, good school experiences, ties with religious and/or social institutions in the community, good peer relationships (Asmussen, 2010; Benard, 1991; DePanfilis, 2006; Jenson & Fraser, 2010)

Incidents of infant molestation and sexual assault are believed to be increasing—a belief that stems in large part from the publicity accorded to cases such as the following:

- On September 29, 1998, in Ohio, Steven Smith sexually assaulted the 6-month-old daughter of his girlfriend, resulting in the infant's death (Welsh-Huggins, 2013). In 2013, Smith was executed by lethal injection for his crime (Myers, 2013).
- On July 24, 2000, a 4-month-old infant was raped while in the care of her babysitter, Rosalba Rodriguez (Hanley, 2000). The assailant was believed to be a relative of the babysitter's husband, Marios Patino Cabrera (18 years old).
- In 2011, in Tennessee, Molly Jane Roe was charged with raping and murdering Maleeya Marie Murley, the 17-month-old daughter of her boyfriend (Lohr, 2011).

Media reports of such occurrences make it seem to the public as if these cases are a part of a nationwide epidemic of infant and early childhood maltreatment. The mass media selectively cover risks—specifically, in accordance with how rare or dramatic and newsworthy (marketable) they are.

Recent incidents of infant and early childhood sexual assault have also created headlines. For instance, in January 2013, a registered sex offender in Connecticut, Joseph Lane, was charged with sexually assaulting a 1-year-old child (whose family he knew), causing injuries to the child's pelvic region (Connors, 2013). On May 28, 2013, Jerry Andrew Active, a convicted sex offender, broke into the home of an elderly couple in Alaska; he killed them and raped their 2-year-old great-granddaughter (Shedlock, 2013). Rape is not the only sexual crime perpetrated on infants. In August 2011, Steven Deuman's 15-week-old daughter died when he forced her to perform fellatio on him; she was found with a condom in her mouth ("Steven Deuman Convicted," 2012).

These sexual assaults are not always perpetrated by only one assailant. Indeed, women may be complicit in the assault and rape of their own children, at times for the pleasure of their boyfriends/husbands. In one incident, Felicia and Cody Beemer were accused of raping their own child. Child protective services (CPS) had previously taken all four of Felicia Beemer's children from her custody (as soon as they were born). However, they had allowed her supervised visits. Felicia's husband, Cody, was a registered sex offender—he had sexually assaulted a 3-year-old girl when he was a teenager (Byrd, 2013). Cody had been removed as a child from his own home by CPS due to allegations that sexual abuse was occurring in the home (Ferrise, 2012). The rape allegedly occurred during the couple's supervised visit with one of their children. According to the Executive Director of the Children's Services Board (CSB), Nick Kerosky, "the child's supervision plan began with a caseworker in the room for the entire visit. As the Beemers made progress on the case plan outlined by CSB, the supervision became less restrictive" (Ferrise, 2012). Specifically, CPS caseworkers began conducting 15-minute checks on the couple during the visits; purportedly, however, these checks did not always occur (Byrd, 2013).

The disproportionate media coverage given to these types of incidents explains why the probability of such instances occurring is considered great. However, official statistics do not exist to support this claim. This is not to say that such incidents do not occur; rather, the emphasis here is on the lack of official collection of statistics on the rate of infant sexual abuse and molestation. Usually, such incidents are brought to light only when children suffer serious trauma or even death. Given that victims of such heinous crimes are at an age where they cannot verbally express what happened to them, it is imperative that those involved in the investigation process have knowledge of cognitive, developmental, emotional, and abnormal psychological development of children (infants and older). Without such knowledge, investigators and those involved in child protection may miss important nonverbal cues alerting them to problems.

There are a disproportionate number of abuse victims and a disproportionate fatality rate among infants and young children. The 2011 National Child Abuse and Neglect Data System (NCANDS) report noted that more than one-fourth of all such victims (27.1%) were children younger than 3 years, and 19.6% of the victims were between the ages of 3 and 5 years (Children's Bureau, 2012). These numbers are cause for concern, and they have spurred government efforts to find ways to minimize and prevent such instances of infant and early childhood maltreatment. Specifically, the National Quality Improvement Center on Preventing the Abuse and Neglect of Infants and Young Children (QIC), now known as the National Quality Improvement Center on Early Childhood (QIC-EC), was established pursuant to the criteria set out in Sections 105(b)(5) of the Child Abuse

---

Box 12-1 Risks, the AIDS Myth, and the Infant, Child, and Adolescent Rape Crisis in Africa

In 2000, there was an alarming trend of increased child rapes and assault in South Africa. In fact, 21,000 reports were made of such incidents (McGreal, 2001). That year, the Minister of Health, Dipuo Peters, stated that he suspected "that at least part of the reason these children were raped is because of the myth held in rural areas by men with HIV that they can cleanse themselves by having sex with a virgin" (para. 4). Peters further noted that he frequently provides "AIDS education; [but] this myth is firmly entrenched and [the country is] doing [its] best to dispel it" (para. 5). Due to their status of no HIV infection, rapes of infants, children, and adolescents in the region have increased, thereby causing an increase in the number of infants, children, and adolescents who are HIV positive.

Today, the child rape crisis in Africa still exists, although its proliferation has occurred largely due to the ongoing conflicts in the Democratic Republic of Congo, Somalia, and Kenya, among other African nations. The United Nations envoy on sexual violence in conflict, Zainab Hawa Bangura, was informed of several cases of infant (as young as 6 months of age), child, and adolescent sexual abuse (Nichols, 2013). For example, in "the Ituri district in turbulent eastern Congo on its border with Uganda, 59 children aged between 1 and 3, and 182 children between 5 and 15 years old had been raped" in 2012 (Nichols, 2013).

Prevention and Treatment Act (first authorized in 1974), as amended, and the Abandoned Infants Assistance Act of 1988. The primary goal of the QIC-EC is as follows:

> [To] advance innovative approaches to child abuse/neglect prevention research and support several projects implementing and evaluating these approaches. Children of parents with HIV/AIDS or substance abuse issues are a particular focus. The work focuses on building conditions or qualities–known as Protective Factors–that can reduce the likelihood of abuse and neglect when present (Zero to Three, n.d.-a).

The QIC-EC's main task is to create and disseminate information concerning ways to prevent child maltreatment for infants and young children (up to the age of 5 years). More generally, the goals of the QIC-EC include the following (Children's Bureau, 2012):

- Creating an information-sharing network concerning the maltreatment of infants and young children
- Distributing knowledge on how to reduce risk and prevent child maltreatment
- Strengthening family functioning
- Assisting infants and children where HIV/AIDS, alcohol abuse, and/or substance abuse are present in the household
- Supporting innovative collaboration and effective prevention efforts at the local and state levels to improve outcomes for the target population

Zero to Three is another organization tasked with meeting the developmental and mental health needs of infants and toddlers. Zero to Three (n.d.-b) has a project in place, called the Court Teams for Maltreated Infants and Toddlers, that "emphasizes the development of a coordinated response to very young children in foster care, in order to improve their immediate and long-term outcomes."

Recommendations

The following recommendations are based on a review of the literature and suggestions from those in the field with whom the authors spoke during the writing of this text.

Professional Training

All those involved in child abuse cases should have the requisite training and qualifications to participate effectively in the investigation and interviewing of victims, witnesses, and suspects. From the literature and the authors' interviews with key personnel involved in child abuse cases, such as parents, CPS workers, law enforcement agents, and agents of the courts (e.g., judges, prosecutors, and defense attorneys), it is clear that more rigorous and frequent training of new and existing personnel is needed. This training of professionals should be provided in the child advocacy center (CAC).

CPS workers, law enforcement officers, prosecutors, and others who are often part of a multidisciplinary team (MDT) should receive training on forensic interviewing, preferably together to ensure continuity. This training should include information on the questions to ask and the types of questions that should be avoided; information on the protocols that should be followed, the reasons for preferring them, and examples of how not following them causes specific problems; on-the-job training by following and observing trained interviewers during an investigation; and conducting interviews as the primary interviewer (with a trained interviewer on hand). Trainees should have mock interviews recorded (audio and video/digital recordings); these recordings should later be reviewed and critiqued. Personnel involved in child abuse cases should obtain a state license to conduct such interviews. In addition, they should have a background in both developmental and clinical psychology to ensure that they understand both normative and non-normative growth and development. These individuals should also be cognizant of child language barriers and mental disabilities. In locations where an MDT exists, funds should be provided so each member of the team can receive standardized, discipline-specific training. Moreover, specific expert technical assistance should be available for each MDT member as needed (e.g., a professional with an extensive background in the field who can assist in interviewing and investigations).

Training should be provided to all those individuals who are classified as mandatory reporters according to the law. Examples of mandatory reporters include doctors, other healthcare professionals (e.g., nurses), mental health professionals (e.g., psychologists and psychiatrists), schools (e.g., teachers and school counselors), childcare workers, clergy, government agencies, and law enforcement personnel. Currently, many of these individuals—except those specifically tasked with child abuse and neglect—have little to no training on identifying child physical abuse, sexual abuse, and neglect, and on preventing child abuse and neglect. This limit leads to under-reporting and over-reporting, both of which fail the child, albeit in different ways (i.e., by allowing harm to occur, by removing a child when no risk is involved).

Education

Education can help prevent child maltreatment and aid in recovery should child maltreatment occur. The human services discipline in academia should be promoted. Those entering into this discipline—specifically social workers, CPS workers, medical professionals, law enforcement agents, and prosecutors, among others—should be educated on child sexual abuse, child physical abuse, child psychological abuse, and child neglect (hereafter referred to collectively as child maltreatment).

Education on child maltreatment should be extended to children, parents, and the community. For example, sexual education programs at school (e.g., beyond specific programs like "good touch, bad touch") should include age-appropriate information on child sexual abuse and prevention. This will empower youth and enable them to recognize unwanted touching and sexual contact. Such education also provides students with information on how to report such incidents. Moreover, it can help children reduce the self-blame and stigma associated with maltreatment. A public awareness campaign about the nature and extent of child maltreatment should be funded and created as well.

Prevention Programs

The emphasis of professionals in the field of child maltreatment should be more on prevention than on intervention. In 1999, the National Center for Missing and Exploited Children published guidelines for choosing model prevention programs. Three types of prevention programs are explored here: primary, secondary, and tertiary prevention programs.

Primary prevention programs seek to treat problems before they manifest. One type of primary prevention program is education. In addition to the educational programs related to child maltreatment, education can be provided to families to help them improve their parenting styles and functioning as a unit. These programs can help families deal with stress—a particularly important consideration given that stress and other family problems may lead to child maltreatment.

Secondary prevention programs provide treatment when serious risk factors are observed in the family. Examples of such programs include educational programs in schools focusing on teen parents. In particular, students should be taught about child development in school. They need education about infants and children so they will develop proper expectations of age-related growth and abilities. The advantages of such education include that students would have the appropriate child-related expectations needed to effectively deal with children as babysitters or as parents themselves. Through this education, they can evaluate their own home experiences (of being parented) and determine what they can and want to do differently from their own parents or guardians. Such education is also necessary because individuals often do not know how to handle children. Thus, when children are taught this information, they will have the tools they need later on in life to deal with children in nonabusive ways.

Educational programs about substance abuse that are aimed at parents with young children should also be utilized. Providing support and assistance to expecting and new mothers in their home is another recommendation. For example, the Nurse–Family Partnership is a voluntary prevention program that provides low-income, first-time mothers with home visitation services from nurses. These nurses provide education, support, and counseling to mothers to help them have a healthy pregnancy and become responsible parents. In addition, the Maternal, Infant, and Early Childhood Home Visiting (MIECHV) program, which was created under the Patient Protection and Affordable Care Act of 2010 (P.L. 111-148), is designed to meet the needs of children and families in at-risk communities (Children's Bureau, 2012). It specifically seeks to improve the health and development of at-risk children through home visitation programs (Children's Bureau, 2012). Research has shown that home-based programs can effectively stop the physical abuse of children and improve parent–child relationships (MacMillan et al., 2009, cited in Asmussen, 2010). Other secondary prevention efforts may involve programs that provide care to families with special needs children.

Tertiary prevention programs provide treatment and services after child maltreatment has occurred. They seek to increase the quality of life and prevent instances of maltreatment from occurring in the future. For instance, mental health services are provided to those affected by maltreatment—namely, children and families. Tertiary prevention programs are also aimed at preserving the family and improving family communication. Likewise, support groups for families and mentor programs may help mitigate the effects of child maltreatment.

Protocols

Schools and any youth-serving organizations and institutions should develop and maintain up-to-date child maltreatment prevention policies. They should also create protocols to protect children and to identify and respond to suspected child maltreatment. In addition, their protocols should address the problems that may arise if child maltreatment is under-reported or over-reported and if the youth-serving organization or institution does not respond to child maltreatment in an appropriate manner.

Creation of Official Databases on Prosecuted Child Sexual Abuse Cases

Currently, national statistics on the number of child sexual abuse cases that proceed to prosecution do not exist. Accordingly, the authors recommend creating a national database to record child sexual abuse cases that are prosecuted.

Creation of a National Child Victimization Survey

As a supplement to the official statistics on child maltreatment provided by the National Child Abuse and Neglect Data System (NCANDS) and the National Incidence Studies (NIS), the authors recommend creating a National Child Victimization Survey, which collects victimization statistics, akin to those provided by the National Crime Victimization Survey (NCVS), to obtain information on unreported crime. Like the NCVS, the National Child Victimization Survey would ask children (even those younger than the age of 12 years) about their victimization experiences, the crimes committed against them, and the offenders (if known). Children would also be asked if they or their parents reported the incident to the police and, if so, what happened. This survey would provide insights into the dark figure of unreported child maltreatment cases, especially given that it would include information for children younger than 12 years. This aspect is particularly important because currently the NCVS includes information only for children 12 years or older.

Uniform Standards to Substantiate Maltreatment

The actual estimates of physical abuse, sexual abuse, psychological abuse, and neglect depend on the definitions that are used—and these definitions vary across states and districts. What is disconcerting is that currently child maltreatment cases are substantiated differently by all those involved (law enforcement officers, prosecutors, and medical examiners, to name a few). Accordingly, uniform standards on how to identify, investigate, prosecute, and forensically evaluate child maltreatment cases are needed.

According to the authors' research, physical abuse is commonly recorded as "neglect" by CPS workers. This practice skews data and perceptions about the scope of physical abuse and neglect. Accordingly, one recommendation for CPS workers is to separate instances of physical abuse and neglect.

Improving Legislation and Enforcement of Laws Related to Psychological Abuse

At present, there exists a general disagreement on how to define psychological abuse. This lack of a universal definition has hindered the effective prosecution of perpetrators of this crime and obfuscated an understanding of its short-term and long-term consequences. The variations in definitions have also contributed to discrepancies in identification and reporting of psychological abuse across the United States. In turn, this has seriously limited the ability of CPS workers to intervene and protect children from this form of abuse.

Some U.S. states and territories have passed laws focused on emotional and/or psychological abuse (in the literature these terms are often used interchangeably). In Alabama, emotional abuse is defined in § 38-9-2 of the Alabama Code as "The willful or reckless infliction of emotional or mental anguish or the use of a physical or chemical restraint, medication or isolation as punishment or as a substitute for treatment or care of any protected person." In Delaware, under Delaware Code Annotated Title 31, § 3902(2), it consists of "A pattern of emotional abuse, which includes, but is not limited to, ridiculing or demeaning an infirm adult, making derogatory remarks to an infirm adult, or cursing or threatening to inflict physical or emotional harm on an infirm adult." Florida penalizes psychological injury under Florida Statutes Annotated § 415.102. According to this statute, a psychological injury is an "injury to the intellectual functioning or emotional state of a vulnerable adult as evidenced by an observable or measurable reduction in the vulnerable adult's ability to function within that person's customary range of performance and that person's behavior." Likewise, Guam criminalizes mental or emotional abuse. Specifically, under 10 Guam Code Annotated § 2951, such abuse "Includes but is not limited to verbal assaults, insults, threats, intimidation, humiliation, harassment, [and] isolation which provokes fear, agitation, confusion or severe depression."

New Hampshire also includes emotional abuse in its criminal statutes. Pursuant to New Hampshire Revised Statutes Annotated § 161-F:43(a), emotional abuse is defined as "the misuse of power, authority, or both, verbal harassment, or unreasonable confinement which results or could result in the mental anguish or emotional distress of an incapacitated adult." In New York, under Social Services Law § 473, emotional abuse is defined as "the willful infliction of mental or emotional anguish by threat, humiliation, intimidation or other abusive conduct, including but not limited to, frightening or isolating an adult." Additionally, South Carolina defines psychological abuse in the South Carolina Code of Laws Annotated § 43-35-10 as "Deliberately subjecting a vulnerable adult to threats or harassment or other forms of intimidating behavior causing fear, humiliation, degradation, agitation, confusion, or other forms of serious emotional distress." Furthermore, Utah includes emotional and psychological abuse under Utah Code Annotated § 62A-3-301 as the "Intentional or knowing verbal or nonverbal conduct directed at a vulnerable adult including ridiculing, intimidating, yelling, swearing, threatening, isolating, coercing, harassing, or other forms of intimidating behavior that results or could result in the vulnerable adult suffering mental anguish or emotional distress, including fear, humiliation, degradation, agitation, confusion, or isolation."

However, not all states criminalize emotional or psychological abuse. Even in those states that do, practitioners do not pursue prosecution of perpetrators unless this form of abuse is accompanied by other types of abuse or even neglect. Accordingly, the major issue is not legislating against emotional or psychological abuse (although there is a need for improvement in such laws), but rather enforcing the existing statutes. A great example that can be used to guide these changes is found in France. In France, legislators passed a law that makes psychological or mental violence a crime. This "law defines mental violence as 'repeated acts which could be constituted by words or other machinations, to degrade one's quality of life and cause a change to one's mental or physical state'" ("Psychological Violence a Criminal Offence in France," 2010, para. 4). The law further holds that mental violence is to "act or repeatedly say things that could damage the victim's life conditions, affect his/her rights and his/her dignity or damage his/her physical or mental health" (Erlanger, 2010, para. 2). Evidence of psychological violence can take the form of slander, testimony, text messages, and emails (Erlanger, 2010).

Making Decisions in the Best Interests of the Child

The most important recommendation is for CPS workers, social workers, law enforcement officers, prosecutors, and medical examiners to make decisions that are in the best interests of the child. Consider the termination of parental rights. By law, parental rights should be terminated within 15-23 months of the failure of a parent to comply with the family court requirements or the case plan provided by CPS. Presently, this time frame is not always being enforced. Parents often decide (or at the very least inform the family court) at the last minute that they want to comply with the requirements imposed on them. When this occurs, children may be left lingering in the child protection system. To prevent such outcomes, in the authors' view it is in the best interests of the child to terminate parental rights after 15-23 months without any extension, unless extenuating circumstances arise (i.e., medical emergency).

The final decision as to how to proceed should be made in consultation with all those officially involved in the child abuse and/or child neglect cases, especially the members of the MDT. To ensure that the decisions reflect the best interests of the child, what the child wants and how the decision could affect both the child and his or her family should be considered. In practice, this does not always occur—and it sends a message to the child that he or she is not important and deserving of protection.

Consider the case of Rabbi Stanley Z. Levitt, who was accused of child sexual abuse (Lowery, 2012). The victims in this case provided victim impact statements in court. Victim impact statements afford victims the opportunity to describe how the crime has affected them. They invite victims to communicate which financial, physical, psychological, social, or emotional effects a particular offense had on them and/or their family (Zedner, 2004). The purpose of victim impact statements is to take the victim's interests into account (Rock, 2004); thus they are designed to seek and document information about the nature and extent of the effects of a criminal offense upon the victim (Graham, Woodfield, Tibble, & Kitchen, 2004). Furthermore, the victim impact statement is the "principal vehicle for facilitating victim input into sentencing" (Roberts & Erez, 2004, p. 226) and constitutes a public forum through which victims can communicate any harm they may have sustained (Erez, 1994). According to an article in the *Boston Globe*, despite the tearful pleas of victims in court, Levitt received 10 years' probation for sexually abusing three of his students between 1975 and 1976 (Lowery, 2012).

Actions That Need to Be Taken by CPS

It is important that the offending party (i.e., the respondent in the complaint) is held solely responsible for domestic violence. It is also imperative that this individual receive the necessary interventions aimed at treating his or her abusive behavior. In addition, CPS personnel must ensure that they engage batterers directly, develop service plans for them, and monitor the abusers' completion of these plans. Emphasis should be placed on the batterer's actions and on monitoring him or her. CPS workers should warn the abuser that failure to comply with services and protective orders will result in serious adverse consequences.

The nonabusive parent, however, should be provided resources and support to improve his or her situation. Currently, these individuals are considered non-ideal victims and are often denied the services and assistance afforded to victims in general. Moreover, it is vital that CPS and law enforcement agents tasked with investigating and otherwise handling domestic violence and child maltreatment cases do not blame the victim. Doing so may rule out the nonoffending parent's cooperation with these individuals, instead of promoting it. Caseworkers and law enforcement agents should show empathy toward the victims of domestic violence and not threaten these nonabusers with removal of their children if they do not fully participate in the legal process. If it is absolutely necessary to remove children from the care of domestic violence victims, the children should be placed in the care of someone whom the victim trusts. While the child remains with the third party, the victim should be kept informed of the child's well-being and of the progress of the child's case.

Furthermore, CPS needs to improve the process of supervised visitations. There have been cases where parents' visitations of their children are not properly supervised. The case of Felicia and Cody Beemer (who raped their child), along with other cases where parents have abducted children during CPS-supervised visits (e.g., William Burns and Sharon Joyce, who had their child removed due to habitual drug use, abducted their 3-year-old son during a supervised visit; see Juarez, 2011), have brought home the lesson that stricter supervision of such encounters is critical for the protection of children.

Finally, the case loads of CPS workers need to remain low, so as to ensure that each employee gives each case the necessary attention. This strategy would help ensure the efficacious resolution of child maltreatment cases. Nevertheless, the case load should not be measured strictly in terms of the number of cases. The determination of the case load of a CPS worker is not as simple as just limiting the total number of cases; other circumstances must be considered in determining the case load, such as the children per case, the problems the children have, the number of family members, and the family issues, among other factors.

Foster Care and Family Daycare Evaluations

Effective oversight of those persons who provide (and those who seek to provide) foster care is required. Sometimes background checks are not conducted on families seeking to provide foster care. Licenses have also been provided without conducting proper background checks. Even if parents have had one or more of their children removed from the home by CPS, they may still be able to obtain a license to provide foster care.

Accordingly, one recommendation is to ensure that those tasked with vetting potential foster care families conduct thorough background checks to examine the qualifications and credentials of prospective foster care families before they are certified and licensed. In addition, foster care families should be subjected to periodic continuing education and training, thereby ensuring the best care of children in their custody. The same recommendations can be made for family daycare centers. These centers are not appropriately regulated, such that individuals can obtain a license to run such centers even when a family member is a registered sex offender (see, for example, the John Burbine case).

Counseling and Services by Specialists

Specialized (rather than general) services should be provided to children who have been maltreated. These services should be tailored to the type of maltreatment that the child has experienced. Specifically, services and counseling should be provided by professionals with single-specialty backgrounds in physical abuse, sexual abuse, psychological abuse, and neglect. Children who have suffered from these types of abuse or neglect have particular needs that must be met. Currently, counseling and other services are provided by individuals who may not necessarily be specialists in their field, and who may not have expertise with the particular maltreatment suffered by the child. It is recommended that such specialists be hired to provide services to children as needed.

Protecting Prostituted and Trafficked Children

While some laws have been passed to decriminalize prostitution for all youths in the United States, harmonization of laws on the state and federal levels is required. Children should not be charged with prostitution; this runs anathema to other federal statutes (e.g., Trafficking Victims Protection Reauthorization Act of 2013), which clearly state that children of certain ages cannot consent to sexual encounters and that the government's role is to protect rather than criminalize these victims.

Deterring Offenders

In *New York v. Ferber* (458 U.S. 747, 1982), the U.S. Supreme Court recognized that the prosecution of offenders suspected of child abuse is necessary. Specifically, the Court held that "the prevention of sexual exploitation and abuse of children constitutes a government objective of surpassing importance" (p. 757). This objective was reiterated in *Dell'Orfano v. State* (616 So.2d 33 [Fla.], 1993). Specifically, in this case, the court held that the criminal justice system has a "strong interest in eliminating the sexual abuse of children through vigorous enforcement of child-abuse laws" (p. 34). In practice, however, this has not always been observed.

In fact, to eliminate—or at the very least reduce—instances of child abuse and neglect, measures aimed at deterring offenders are required. Deterrence policies are premised on the belief that criminals fear sanctions. If the certainty and severity of punishments increase, then deterrence theory holds that individuals will desist from engaging in crime. For example, deterrence occurs when an individual wants to engage in child sexual abuse; realizes that his or her actions may lead to incarceration; and, as a result, changes his or her mind and decides instead to adhere to the law. There are two types of deterrence: general and specific. General deterrence holds that individuals will engage in unlawful activity if they do not fear that they will be punished or apprehended, whereas specific deterrence holds that punishment should be severe enough to ensure that criminals do not repeat illicit actions. For an offender to be deterred, both certainty and severity of punishment are required. Certainty of punishment means that any offender who commits the crime of child maltreatment will be prosecuted; severity of punishment means that offenders will always receive a significant penalty if they are charged with child maltreatment. Unfortunately, the criminal justice system has often fallen short of achieving these goals in practice.

Prosecutors' unfettered discretion in child maltreatment cases leads to the danger that prosecutors will make decisions based on self-interest, rather than based on the interests of the child and the quest to secure justice for the victim. Because of the difficulties in prosecuting child maltreatment, particularly sexual abuse cases (e.g., young witnesses may be considered unreliable by jurors, the sexual act often occurs with no witnesses other than the victim and the perpetrator), prosecutors often engage in plea bargaining, in which the offender pleads guilty in exchange for a lesser sentence or probation. For example, a 64-year-old man, David Harold Earls, was accused of raping a 4-year-old girl. Usually, the crime of rape carries a minimum 5-year sentence and a maximum sentence of life imprisonment. Despite this, Earls received a 1-year sentence under a plea deal with the prosecutor in which he agreed to plead no contest to first-degree rape and forcible sodomy (Associated Press, 2009). Unfortunately, plea deals and alternative penalties to incarceration are fairly common in child maltreatment cases.

Offenders of child maltreatment should be brought to justice—to help victim recovery, to enable society to understand these crimes and be aware of the situations required to aid victims, and to deter similar conduct in the future. It is imperative that those who commit child maltreatment are punished, whenever necessary and warranted, to the fullest extent of the law; soft penalties or no penalties send the message that individuals may not be punished for the crimes they commit. These outcomes also tell victims that they may not receive justice for the crimes committed against them. Accordingly, this removes the incentives for child victims to report the abuse committed against them. The authors, therefore, recommend that existing legislation be examined to determine if loopholes in the law might allow child maltreatment offenders to escape prosecution and conviction. If any are found, these loopholes should be closed. What's more, the authors recommend better enforcement of existing laws.

Chapter Summary

Young children are at high risk of child maltreatment. Such maltreatment is often the result of the presence of multiple risk factors, which makes preventing child maltreatment particularly challenging. Risk factors in child maltreatment may relate to parents, children, families, social issues, the community, and the system. Even so, the mere presence of risk factors does not necessarily mean that the child will be maltreated. Likewise, an individual with a history of child maltreatment will not necessarily suffer adversity throughout his or her entire lifetime.

The following recommendations are suggested to better protect infants, children, and adolescents from maltreatment: implementing training and education programs; creating protocols for schools and any youth-serving organizations and institutions; creating official databases on prosecuted child sexual abuse cases; developing a National Child Victimization Survey; creating uniform standards to substantiate maltreatment; improving legislation and enforcement of laws related to psychological abuse of children and domestic violence victims; improving evaluations of foster care families and family daycare programs; providing maltreated infants, children, and adolescents with counseling and services by specialists; harmonizing legislation to protect prostituted and trafficked children; and deterring child maltreatment offenders.

Review Questions

1. Compare and contrast the ecological frameworks proposed by Belsky and Bronfenbrenner. In your opinion, which theory explains child maltreatment better?

2. What are the risk factors in child maltreatment?

3. What are the protective factors in child maltreatment?

4. What is currently being done to minimize and prevent infant and early childhood maltreatment?

5. Which recommendations would you make to improve the assessment of the scope of child maltreatment in the United States?

6. What are primary, secondary, and tertiary prevention programs? Provide some examples of these types of programs that deal with child maltreatment.

7. What are your recommendations for improving the processes involved in child protection?

References

Asmussen, K. (2010, April). Key facts about child maltreatment. Institute of Psychiatry, King's College London. http://www.nspcc.org.uk/Inform/research/briefings/Key_facts_child _maltreatment_pdf_wdf76279.pdf

Associated Press. (2009, June 16). Oklahoma residents outraged after child rapist gets 1-year sentence in plea deal. *Fox News*. http://www.foxnews.com/story/0,2933,526763,00.html#ixzz2V5ikMLkz

Azar, S. T., Povilaitis, T. Y., Lauretti, A. F., & Pouquette, C. L. (1998). The current status of etiological theories in intrafamilial child maltreatment. In J. R. Lutzker (Ed.), *Handbook of child abuse research and treatment* (pp. 3–30). New York, NY: Plenum Press.

Balge, K. A., & Milner, J. S. (2000). Emotion recognition ability in mothers at high and low risk for child physical abuse. *Child Abuse & Neglect, 24*(10), 1289–1298.

Belsky, J. (1980). Child maltreatment: An ecological integration. *American Psychologist, 35*(4), 320–335.

Belsky, J. (1993). Etiology of child maltreatment: A developmental–ecological analysis. *Psychological Bulletin, 114*(3), 413–434.

Belsky, J. & Vondra, J. (1989). Lessons from child abuse: The determinants of parenting. In D. Cicchetti & V. Carlson (Eds.), *Child maltreatment: Theory and research on the causes and consequences of child abuse and neglect* (pp. 153–202). New York: Cambridge University Press.

Benard, B. (1991). Fostering resiliency in kids: Protective factors in the family, school, and community. Western Center for Drug-Free Schools and Communities. http://www.eric.ed.gov /ERICWebPortal/search/detailmini.jsp?_nfpb=true&_&ERICExtSearch_SearchValue_0=ED335 781&ERICExtSearch_SearchType_0=no&accno=ED335781

Bronfenbrenner, U. (1977). Toward an experimental ecology of human development. *American Psychologist, 32*, 513–530.

Bronfenbrenner, U. (1986). Ecology of the family as a context for human development: Research perspectives. *Developmental Psychology, 22*(6), 723–742.

Bronfenbrenner, U. (1994). Ecological models of human development. In T. Husen & T. N. Postle-thwaite. (Eds.), *International encyclopedia of education* (Vol. 3, 2nd ed. pp. 1643–1647). Oxford, UK: Elsevier.

Browne, D. H. (1986). The role of stress in the commission of subsequent acts of child abuse and neglect. *Journal of Family Violence, 1*(4), 289–297.

Buchanan, A. (1998). Intergenerational child maltreatment. In Y. Danieli (Ed.), *International handbook of multigenerational legacies of trauma* (pp. 535–552). New York, NY: Plenum Press.

Burgess, R. L. & Draper, P. (1989). The explanation of family violence: The role of biological, behavioral, and cultural selection. In L. Ohlin & M. Tonry (Eds.), *Family Violence* (Vol. 11, pp. 59–116). Chicago, IL: University of Chicago Press.

Byrd, R. (2013, April 9). Adoptive parents sue CSB for $3 mill. *WKBN.* http://wkbn.com/2013/04/09/adoptive-parents-sue-csb-for-3-mill/

Children's Bureau, U.S. Department of Health and Human Services. (2012, December 12). Child maltreatment 2011. http://www.acf.hhs.gov/sites/default/files/cb/cm11.pdf

Christofferen, M. N. (2000). Growing up with unemployment: A study of parental unemployment and children's risk of abuse and neglect based on national longitudinal 1973 birth cohorts in Denmark. *Childhood, 7*(4), 421–438.

Cicchetti, D., & Lynch, M. (1993). Toward an ecological/transactional model of community violence and child maltreatment: Consequences for children's development. *Psychiatry, 56,* 96–118.

Cicchetti, D., & Lynch, M. (1995). Failures in the expectable environment and their impact on individual development: The case of child maltreatment. In D. Cicchetti & D. J. Cohen (Eds.), *Developmental psychopathology* (Vol. 2, pp. 32–71). New York, NY: John Wiley & Sons.

Connors, B. (2013, January 14). Sex offender charged with raping child. *NBC Connecticut.* http://www.nbcconnecticut.com/news/local/Sex-Offender-Charged-with-Raping-Child-186804601.html

Coohey, C. (1996). Child maltreatment: Testing the social isolation hypothesis. *Child Abuse & Neglect, 20*(3), 241–254.

Crittenden, P. M., & Ainsworth, D. S. (1989). Child maltreatment and attachment theory. In D. Cicchetti & V. Carlson (Eds.), *Child maltreatment: Theory and research on the causes and consequences of child abuse and neglect* (pp. 432–463). New York, NY: Cambridge University Press.

Cummings, M. E. (1998). Children exposed to marital conflict and violence: Conceptual and theoretical directions. In G. W. Holden, R. Geffner, & E. N. Jouriles (Eds.), *Children exposed to marital violence: Theory, research, and applied issues* (pp. 55–93). Washington, DC: American Psychological Association.

DePanfilis, D. (2006). Child neglect: A guide for prevention, assessment and intervention. Office on Child Abuse and Neglect, Children's Bureau. https://www.childwelfare.gov/pubs/usermanuals/neglect/chapterfour.cfm

DePanfilis, D., & Zuravin, S. J. (1999). Predicting child maltreatment recurrences during treatment. *Child Abuse and Neglect, 23*(8), 729–743.

Dukewich, T. L., Borkowski, J. G., & Whitman, T. L. (1996). Adolescent mothers and child abuse potential: An evaluation of risk factors. *Child Abuse and Neglect, 20*(11), 1031–1047.

English, D. J., Marshall, D. B., Brummel, S., & Orme, M. (1999). Characteristics of repeated referrals to child protective services in Washington state. *Child Maltreatment, 4*(4), 297–307.

Erez, E. (1994). Victim participation in sentencing: And the debate goes on. *International Review of Victimology, 3,* 17–32.

Erlanger, S. (2010, June 29). France makes "psychological violence" a crime. http://www.nytimes.com/2010/06/30/world/europe/30france.html?_r=0

Ferrise, A. (2012, February 10). Records detail child visitations: CSB admits relaxing standards despite suspect's past. *Tribune Chronicle.* http://www.tribtoday.com/page/content.detail/id/567764/

Finkelhor, D., Araji, S., Baron, L., Browne, A., Peters, S. D., & Wyatt, G. E. (1986). *A sourcebook on child sexual abuse.* Newbury Park, CA: Sage.

Fraser, M. W., Galinsky, M. J., & Richman, J. M. (1999). Risk, protection, and resilience: Towards a conceptual framework for social work practice. *Social Work Research, 23*(3), 131–144.

Fraser, M. W., & Terzian, M. A. (2005). Risk and resilience in child development: Practice principles and strategies. In G. P. Mallony & P. McCartt Hess (Eds.), *Handbook of children, youth, and family services: Practice, policies, and programs* (pp. 55–71). New York, NY: Columbia University Press.

Fryer, G. E., & Miyoshi, T. J. (1994). A survival analysis of the revictimization of children: The case of Colorado. *Child Abuse & Neglect, 12,* 1063–1071.

Fuller, T. L., Wells, S. J., & Cotton, E. E. (2001). Predictors of maltreatment recurrence at two milestones in the life of a case. *Children and Youth Services Review, 23*(1), 49–78.

Garbarino, J. (1976). A preliminary study of some ecological correlates of child abuse: The impact of socioeconomic stress on mothers. *Child Development, 47,* 178–185.

Garbarino, J., & Barry, F. (1997). The community context of child abuse and neglect. In J. Garbarino & J. Eckenrode (Eds.), *Understanding abusive families: An ecological approach to theory and practice* (pp. 56–85). San Francisco, CA: Jossey-Bass.

Garbarino, J., & Crouter, A. (1978). Defining the community context for parent–child relations: The correlates of child maltreatment. *Child Development, 49,* 604–616.

Gillham, B., Tanner, G., Cheyne, B., Freeman, I., Rooney, M., & Lambie, A. (1998). Unemployment rates, single parent density, and indices of child poverty: Their relationship to different categories of child abuse and neglect. *Child Abuse and Neglect, 22*(2), 79–90.

Goldman, J., Salus, M. K., Wolcott, D., & Kennedy, K. Y. (2003). A coordinated response to child abuse and neglect: The foundation for practice. U. S. Department of Health and Human Services, Administration for Children and Families, Administration on Children, Youth and Families, Children's Bureau, Office on Child Abuse and Neglect. https://www.childwelfare.gov/pubs /usermanuals/foundation/foundation.pdf

Graham, J., Woodfield, K., Tibble, M., & Kitchen, S. (2004, May). Testaments of harm: A qualitative evaluation of the victim personal statements scheme. http://www.natcen.ac.uk/natcen/pages /publications/AcrC2101.pdf

Hamilton, C. E., & Browne, K. D. (1999). Recurrent maltreatment during childhood: A survey of referrals to police child protection units in England. *Child Maltreatment, 4*(4), 275–286.

Hanley, R. (2000, August 3). Man and sitter held in rape of baby girl. *New York Times.* http://www .nytimes.com/2000/08/03/nyregion/man-and-sitter-held-in-rape-of-baby-girl.html

Hawkins, W. E., & Duncan, D. F. (1985). Children's illnesses as risk factors for child abuse. *Psychological Reports, 56*(2), 638.

Inkelas, M., & Halfon, N. (1997). Recidivism in child protective services. *Children and Youth Services Review, 19*(3), 139–161.

Jenson, J. M., & Fraser, M. W. (2010). A risk and resilience framework for child, youth, and family policy. In J. M. Jenson & Mark W. Fraser (Eds.), *Social policy for children and families: A risk and resilience perspective* (pp. 5–24). London, UK: Sage.

Jones, D. P. H. (1987). The untreatable family. *Child Abuse & Neglect, 11,* 409–420.

Juarez, L. (2011, May 30). Budget woes take toll on Riverside County child services. *ABC News.* http://abclocal.go.com/kabc/story?section=news/local/inland_empire&id=8161467

Kamerman, S. B., & Kahn, A. J. (1995). *Starting right.* New York, NY: Oxford University Press.

Kotch, J. B., Browne, D. C., Ringwalt, C. L., Dufort, V., Ruina, E., Stewart, P. W., & Jung, J. W. (1997). Stress, social support, and substantiated maltreatment in the second and third year of life. *Child Abuse and Neglect, 21*(11), 1025–1037.

Levy, H. B., Markovic, J., Chaudhry, U., Ahart, S., & Torres, H. (1995). Reabuse rates in a sample of children followed for 5 years after discharge from a child abuse inpatient assessment program. *Child Abuse & Neglect, 19*(11), 1363–1377.

Lohr, D. (2011, June 16). Tennessee woman charged with rape and murder of toddler. *Huffington Post.* http://www.huffingtonpost.com/2011/06/16/tennessee-woman-rape-murder-toddler_n_877698.html

Lowery, W. (2012, August 3). Rabbi Stanley Z. Levitt gets 10 years of probation for abusing three boys. *Boston Globe.* http://www.bostonglobe.com/metro/2012/08/02/rabbi-stanley-levitt-gets-years-probation-for-abusing-three-boys/5iygfQPcpYpvPcJ8SPI0cK/story.html

MacMillan H. L., Wathen C. N., Barlow J., Fergusson D. M., Leventhal J. M., Taussig H. N. (2009). Interventions to prevent child maltreatment and associated impairment. *Lancet 373*(9659), 250–266.

Marshall, D. B., & English, D. J. (1999). Survival analysis of risk factors for recidivism in child abuse and neglect. *Child Maltreatment, 4*(4), 287–296.

McGreal, C. (2001, November 3). AIDS myth drives South African baby-rape crisis "due to AIDS myth." *The Guardian.* http://www.guardian.co.uk/world/2001/nov/03/aids. chrismcgreal

Miller-Perrin, C. L., & Perrin, R. D. (1999). *Child maltreatment: An introduction.* London, UK: Sage.

Murphy, J. M., Bishop, S. J., Jellinek, M. S., Quinn, S. D., & Poitrast, J. F. (1992). What happens after the care and protection petition? Reabuse in a court sample. *Child Abuse & Neglect, 16,* 485–493.

Myers, A. L. (2013, May 1). Steve Smith, Ohio man who raped, killed 6-month-old baby, executed. *Huffington Post.* http://www.huffingtonpost.com/2013/05/01/steve-smith-execution_n_3191783 .html

Nichols, M. (2013, April 17). Africa child rape crisis: Babies as young as 6 months victims of sexual violence in conflict zones. *Huffington Post.* http://www.huffingtonpost.com/2013/04/18 /africa-child-rape-crisis_n_3103558.html

O'Keefe, M. (1995). Predictors of child abuse in martially violent families. *Journal of Interpersonal Violence, 10*(1), 3–25.

Parke, R. D., & Collmer, C. W. (1975). Child abuse: An interdisciplinary analysis. In E. M. Hetherington (Ed.), *Review of child development research* (pp. 509–590). Chicago, IL: University of Chicago Press.

Patterson, G. R., DeBaryshe, B., & Ramsey, E. (1989). A developmental perspective on antisocial behavior. *American Psychologist, 44,* 329–335.

Pears, K. C., & Capaldi, D. M. (2001). Intergenerational transmission of abuse: A two-generational prospective study of an at-risk sample. *Child Abuse & Neglect, 25*(11), 1439–1461.

Pianta, R., Egeland, B., & Erickson, M. F. (1989). The antecedents of maltreatment: Results of the mother–child interaction research project. In D. Cicchetti & V. Carlson (Eds.), *Child maltreatment: Theory and research on the causes and consequences of child abuse and neglect* (pp. 203–253). New York, NY: Cambridge University Press.

Psychological violence a criminal offence in France. (2010, June 30). *BBC News.* http://www.bbc .co.uk/news/10459906

Roberts, J. V., & Erez, E. (2004). Communication in sentencing: Exploring the expressive function of victim impact statements. *International Review of Victimology, 10*(3), 223–244.

Rock, P. (2004). *Constructing victim's rights: The Home Office, New Labour, and victims.* Oxford, UK: Oxford University Press.

Rogosch, F. A., Cicchetti, D., Shields, A., & Toth, S. L. (1995). Parenting dysfunction in child maltreatment. In M. H. Bornstein (Ed.), *Handbook of parenting: Applied and practical parenting* (Vol. 4, pp. 127–159). Mahwah, New Jersey: Lawrence Erlbaum Associates.

Rycus, J. S., & Hughes, R. C. (1998). *Field guide to child welfare: Foundations of child protective services* (Vol. 1). Washington, DC: CWLA Press.

Shaffer, D. R. (2000). *Social and personality development* (4th ed.). Belmont, CA: Wadsworth/Thomson Learning.

Shedlock, J. (2013, June 4). Man indicted for Anchorage double murder, sexual assault. *Alaska Dispatch News.* http://www.adn.com/article/20130604/man-indicted-anchorage-double-murder-sexual-assault

Sidebotham, P., & Golding, J. (2001). Child maltreatment in the "children of the nineties": A longitudinal study of parental risk factors. *Child Abuse & Neglect, 25*(9), 1177–1200.

Steven Deuman convicted of orally raping, murdering his baby daughter. (2012, September 21). *Huffington Post.* http://www.huffingtonpost.com/2012/09/21/steven-deuman-oral-rape-murder-baby-daughter_n_1903283.html

Violence Prevention Alliance. (n.d.). The ecological framework. World Health Organization. http://www.who.int/violenceprevention/approach/ecology/en/

Welsh-Huggins, A. (2013, April 2). Steven Smith, Ohio man who sexually assaulted 6-month-old baby girl to death, seeks mercy. *Huffington Post.* http://www.huffingtonpost.com/2013/04/02/steven-smith-death-sentence_n_2996518.html

Whipple, E. E., & Richey, C. A. (1997). Crossing the line from physical discipline to child abuse: How much is too much? *Child Abuse and Neglect, 21*(5), 431–444.

Wolock, I., & Magura, S. (1996). Parental substance abuse as a predictor of child maltreatment re-reports. *Child Abuse and Neglect, 20*(12), 1183–1193.

Zedner, L. (2004). *Criminal justice.* Oxford, UK: Oxford University Press.

Zero to Three. (n.d.-a). Quality Improvement Center on Early Childhood. http://www.zerotothree.org/about-us/funded-projects/qic/qic.html

Zero to Three. (n.d.-b). Reports highlight impact of maltreatment on the youngest children. http://www.zerotothree.org/maltreatment/child-abuse-neglect/reports-highlight-impact-of.html

Zuravin, S. J., & DiBlasio, F. A. (1996). The correlates of child physical abuse and neglect by adolescent mothers. *Journal of Family Violence, 11*(2), 149–166.

Index